D1738304

THE ART OF
FORGETTING

Studies in the History of Greece and Rome

ROBIN OSBORNE,

P. J. RHODES, AND

RICHARD J. A. TALBERT,

editors

HARRIET I. FLOWER

THE ART OF
Forgetting

Disgrace & Oblivion in Roman Political Culture

The University of North Carolina Press

Chapel Hill

© 2006

The University of North Carolina Press

All rights reserved

Designed and typeset in Minion Pro and Mantinia

by Eric M. Brooks

Manufactured in the United States of America

The paper in this book meets the guidelines for permanence
and durability of the Committee on Production Guidelines for
Book Longevity of the Council on Library Resources.

Library of Congress Cataloging-in-Publication Data

Flower, Harriet I.

The art of forgetting: disgrace and oblivion in Roman
political culture / by Harriet I. Flower.

p. cm. — (Studies in the history of Greece and Rome)

Includes bibliographical references and index.

ISBN-13: 978-0-8078-3063-5 (cloth: alk. paper)

ISBN-10: 0-8078-3063-1 (cloth: alk. paper)

1. Rome — History. 2. Memory — Political aspects —
Rome — History. 3. Memory — Social aspects — Rome —
History. 4. Punishment — Rome — History.

I. Title. II. Series.

DG211.F56   2006

937 — dc22   2006017447

10 09 08 07 06   5 4 3 2 1

For Michael

Once a thing is known it can

never be unknown. It can only be forgotten.

And, in a way that bends time, so long as

it is remembered, it will indicate the future.

It is wiser, in every circumstance,

to forget, to cultivate the art of forgetting.

To remember is to face the enemy.

The truth lies in remembering.

ANITA BROOKNER

Look at Me

One can forgive but one should never forget.

MARJANE SATRAPI

Persepolis

CONTENTS

▾   ▾   ▾

▾   ▾   ▾

MAP & ILLUSTRATIONS

▾ ▾ ▾

MAP

ILLUSTRATIONS

PREFACE

▾   ▾   ▾

The past is a foreign country;
they do things differently there.
L. P. Hartley, *The Go-Between*

Sanctions against memory in Roman culture have been the subject of numerous studies, especially of individual cases or of specific monuments. My study aims to present an overview of the evolution of memory sanctions on the basis of selected examples. In keeping with ancient practice, I have avoided coining a term to describe memory sanctions in Rome. The Latin phrase *damnatio memoriae* is often used for this purpose, and it is undoubtedly useful in its own way, if only as a kind of familiar shorthand to refer to a whole phenomenon. As Friedrich Vittinghoff showed in 1936, however, *damnatio memoriae* is not an ancient term and would not have been used by the Romans themselves to identify their sanctions. Indeed, they did not even have a single equivalent description, since they tended to impose each sanction separately, rather than as a standard package of penalties.

By using the expression *damnatio memoriae*, we have tended to suggest a more formal and static way of behaving than was actually the case in ancient Rome, particularly in the period under discussion here. For example, Dietmar Kienast, in his very useful chronology of Roman imperial history, labels disgraced emperors very much as if they were all treated in the same way and subject to the same standardized penalties.[1] This view represents what many modern historians think about the basic structure of imperial commemoration and political disgrace, even seventy years after Vittinghoff's dissertation was published. There is a danger that we may create and then contemplate not Rome's but our own notions of what disgrace and oblivion should be.

Meanwhile, the following thoughts of Jan Assmann express some of the complexities involved in looking at memory sanctions across time and in different cultures. After speaking of the "structural amnesia" that can sometimes be found in oral societies, he goes on to discuss cultures that use writing.

Its counterpart in literate societies is the willful destruction of commem-orative symbols (documents and monuments), including the burning of books, the destruction of inscriptions (*damnatio memoriae*), and the rewriting of history as described, for example, by Orwell in *1984*. There is (as far as I can see) no comprehensive term to denote these acts of intentional and violent cultural oblivion. They seem to correspond, on the individual level, to repression, whereas structural amnesia corre-sponds rather to forgetting. "Cultural repression" might therefore serve as a term for the various forms of annihilating cultural memory.[2]

Despite this recognition of a phenomenon termed "cultural repression" by Assmann, who has identified it as being shared by many, if not most, com-munities that practice formal commemoration in some way, the discussion that follows does not aim to identify an overarching "category of forgetting" or to create a terminology that would describe such a category. Rather it ex-amines elite memory in Rome as it was constructed, and then deconstructed or reconstructed again, under a variety of circumstances. In addition, the rich memory culture of the plebs in the city of Rome is not treated as a sepa-rate topic here, although it certainly had a history of its own that was not entirely dependent on elite monuments and commemorative rituals.

The text of this book was written between September 2001 and early 2005, with the result that no works published after 2004 have been included in the bibliography. It offers a survey of memory sanctions in Roman culture ar-ranged roughly chronologically from the earliest evidence to the first years of the reign of the emperor Antoninus Pius in the late 130s A.D. This study does not aim to be comprehensive and makes little use of any analysis using statistics, particularly of erased inscriptions or recarved portraits. Rather, my conclusions are based on the examination of traditional memory patterns in Roman culture and of individual examples, whether of disgraced persons or of monuments and texts relating to those persons. Hence the emphasis is on the richness of nuances, in the eye of individual beholders and at the moments when decisions about commemoration were being made, often in settings that were essentially local and parochial. As a result the investigation is more focused on the individual than on the typical. Indeed, at the detailed level, each case reveals its own particular character and impact.

The Greek material, especially from the Hellenistic period, provides the es-sential background to evolving Roman practices. This is particularly the case since evidence about early Rome is scanty and distorted by anachronisms. Consequently, there is no decisive proof that extensive or formal memory

Preface

sanctions were in use in Rome in the fifth or fourth centuries B.C. Meanwhile, there is every reason to think that elite Romans had become thoroughly acquainted with Hellenistic culture in general and memory sanctions in particular during the second century B.C., well before the first punitive sanctions were imposed at Rome on the memory of Gaius Sempronius Gracchus, Marcus Fulvius Flaccus, and others in 121 B.C. Meanwhile, the commemorative practices of the officeholding families (*nobiles*), and the relationship of those families to their peers in the senate and to the community as a whole, form the social context within which republican memory functioned, whether to praise, or to blame, or to pass over in silence.

After some introductory thoughts about the character of remembering and forgetting in chapter 1, the Hellenistic and republican material is treated in chapters 2 to 5, including a detailed discussion of the period from the Gracchi to the Ides of March 44 B.C. in the last two of these chapters. The emergence of punitive memory sanctions and of highly contested representations of recent, and even of ancient, history was a characteristic and defining feature of the late second and first half of the first centuries B.C. In other words, the decline and fall of the Republic ran parallel to the rise of punitive sanctions against the memory of Roman citizens and the use of past history for partisan purposes. Chapters 6 to 9 go on to treat memory sanctions and disgrace in the imperial period from the memory battles over Mark Antony to the aftermath of the death of Hadrian. Special attention is paid to the cases of the "bad" emperors (Gaius, Nero, Domitian) and to the differences in the ways in which each one's memory was treated, both at the time of his death and in the immediately succeeding generations. Meanwhile, women are discussed in detail separately in chapter 7, as their treatment sheds light on the evolution of their public roles during the Julio-Claudian period.

The decision to conclude this study with the case of Hadrian reflects the decisive break in the practice of memory sanctions at the time of their rejection by his successor and adopted heir Antoninus Pius. Hadrian's heir sought a reconciliation with bitter memories of the past and an appeal to his own version of the traditional Roman value of *pietas* (respect, duty, piety, correct behavior), which was reflected in his imperial *cognomen* Pius. By the time memory sanctions were used again in the 190s by L. Septimius Severus, it was in a very different context and in a changed world.

The ancient evidence relevant to this study includes literary texts, inscriptions, art (especially portraiture), archaeological material, and coins. Although I have used all of these various types of evidence, less is said here about the details of recarved or mutilated portraits, which is a very large and complex subject that is essential to an understanding of portraiture, especially of emperors in the first century A.D. However, full notes have been provided for art-historical topics and readers will want to turn first to Eric Varner's very detailed 2004 study *Mutilation and Transformation:* Damnatio Memoriae *and Roman Imperial Portraiture.* As a result, the point of departure here has most often been ancient texts and inscriptions.

The subject of this study is formal commemoration and disgrace that is related to the law, to some degree of commemorative consensus within the community, and ultimately to the question of who had the authority to decide about remembering and forgetting at any particular period in Roman history. At the same time, it is always important to keep in mind that competing memories continued to flourish. Even a clearly attested official disgrace could and did meet with a wide variety of reactions, especially over time, both in the city and in the Empire. In other words, there was rarely a single or simple outcome for a person's posthumous reputation and standing.

In conclusion, the following thoughts of Elizabeth Meyer are especially useful in putting the whole practice of editing, rewriting, and erasing the record of an event or decision into a wider Roman cultural context. In speaking of wax tablets, which were widely used by the Romans and which were supposed to contain a perfect record of what had been written down in an original version of a text (often a law), she points out that no change could be made without the editing process itself being revealed by the wax.

> In short, a tablet's wax serves to reveal change, not to facilitate it. A change is a blemish, a retrospective negative reassessment of a man's *existimatio.* Perhaps from this source spring both the inclusion of erasure as part of the crime of forgery and the special significance always attributed by Romans to what we call *damnatio memoriae,* a visible (even violent) removal of a man's name or a man's image from any public monument on which he might appear. The visible indications of obliteration, the sense of the absent in the present, carried the greatest significance.[3]

This study is about that practice of obliteration, how and when it was undertaken, and what it meant to the Romans at different times in their history.

ACKNOWLEDGMENTS

▾   ▾   ▾

This book has been many years in the making with the result that I owe debts to a large number of people, who have helped me in various ways over more than a decade of thinking and writing about memory and oblivion. Here I would like to make special mention of the following: John Bodel, Glen Bowersock, Corey Brennan, Richard Brilliant, John Graham, Rudolf Haensch, Robert Kaster, John Ma, Maria Mitchell, Robert Palmer, Michael Peachin, David Potter, Brian Rose, Ann Macy Roth, Brent Shaw, Richard Talbert, and Eric Varner.

I have been very lucky to have had the opportunity to work in the very supportive environments of the Classics Departments at Franklin and Marshall College and at Princeton University. For help with editing I owe a great debt to Judith Chien. For assistance with the illustrations I am very grateful to Luca Grillo and Susan Satterfield. The original drawings were made by Leslie Rae Witt. Mary Shelly of the Shadek Fackenthal Library at Franklin and Marshall College and Rebecka Lindau of the Firestone Library at Princeton University provided invaluable assistance with bibliographical issues.

I gave lectures on some of the material in this book in the following places: Franklin and Marshall College, Princeton University, the Institute for Advanced Study in Princeton, Yale University, Brown University, Northwestern University, Columbia University, Cornell University, the University of Pennsylvania, the University of North Carolina at Chapel Hill, Duke University, and as a Loeb lecturer at Harvard University. I am very grateful both for these invitations to speak and for the questions and issues raised by members of the audience in each place.

I received significant financial support from the following institutions: Franklin and Marshall College, the Magie Fund of the Department of Classics at Princeton University, the Princeton University Committee on Research in the Humanities and Social Sciences, the Institute for Advanced Study (Princeton) where I was a member for 2001–2, and the National Endowment for the Humanities, which granted me a summer stipend in 1999 and a year fellowship for 2001–2. Without their support, this research project would not have been possible.

I would like to thank all my family for their encouragement and support over the years, especially Grandmaus, Isabel, and Rosalind. This book is dedicated to my husband Michael, my best friend and most valuable colleague.

Princeton, New Jersey
May 2006

Acknowledgments

Clementis' Hat

The Politics of Memory Sanctions
and the Shape of Forgetting

▾   ▾   ▾

The face of the Lord is set against the doers of evil
To wipe their memory from the earth.
Psalm 34.16

Who controls the past controls the future:
who controls the present controls the past.
George Orwell, *1984*

Any recalling or recording of the past involves selection, both deliberate and unintended. Choosing what to remember must entail also the choice of what to forget, what to pass over in silence, and what to obscure. Consequently, every account of the past is incomplete and partial. It involves a loss, whether for an individual, a family, or a whole community. It is impossible to travel back in time to recover every detail, to relive past experience as if moment by moment. Nor would such a journey even be desirable. Rather, we pay attention to memories of the past in a present that is by definition not the same as the time that is being invoked as "past." Similarly, active recalling itself (re)creates that past from fragmented pieces of evidence, whether in the human brain or on the basis of an archive or at the physical site of some historical action.[1]   ·

The image of the past that is most alive in human memory is seen as a road that leads from that past into the present. A past that is completely disconnected from present experience and circumstances does not remain "memorable." Rather the past, because it comes before the present, is expected to connect in a logical manner to subsequent events and circumstances. Hence our picture of the past shapes both our present identity and our hopes for the future, for what has not yet happened is essentially unknowable. Only the past really stands available — at least apparently — as material in our search for meaning, purpose, and pattern in human experience.

One of the most powerful effects on human memory and perception is the bias created by hindsight.[2] As we look back into the past, we already know what will happen next. The shape of the story is familiar. Therefore, it is natural and inevitable to look for explanations that will accommodate what did happen, rather than what could have happened. Meanwhile, other aspects of the past become easy to forget because they seem irrelevant and become increasingly hard to understand, if they do not lead to results and consequences in our present lives. Our account of the past, whether expressed in terms of history or of memory, is selective and tends to favor information that appears relevant to later events, and especially to present circumstances at the time of recollecting or writing. Hence the perspective of the person or group that guards and (re)produces memory is also vital and may produce a very different narrative from that of another party, even if both are eyewitnesses or have access to similar original sources.

Memory sanctions are deliberately designed strategies that aim to change the picture of the past, whether through erasure or redefinition, or by means of both. Such strategies can be found in most, perhaps even in all, human societies that place distinct value on an account of their past. Conscious manipulation, introduced for a specifically desired effect, must be understood as one vital factor that affects the picture of the past outlined here — in other words, a picture that is by its very nature incomplete and subject to various other distortions. Deliberately imposed modifications resulting from memory sanctions do not impede a perfect view, as if of a landscape on a cloudless and sunny day. Rather they contribute to and interact with many other factors that shape human memory, causing it to produce its own, very particular narrative of the past. An alternate account to the one that has obviously been tampered with would not necessarily represent a "true" and "unbiased" version, but in most cases simply a different version, one that brought out another set of emphases, meanings, and implications. With such considerations in mind, Maurice Baring called his memoirs, which were published in 1922, *The Puppet Show of Memory*.

In Roman thought, memory was not taken for granted as a natural state or product. Rather, oblivion was considered the more normal condition, as

Clementis' Hat

the past receded from the present and was simply no longer connected to it. Hence, as a carefully cultivated and deliberately invoked culture of commemoration, Roman memory (*memoria*) was designed precisely in opposition to the vast oblivion into which most of the past was conceived as having already receded. Such an attitude was the product of a world in which life was often short and unpredictable, with the result that time must have seemed to move quickly, and change to come rapidly with the passing generations.[3] For example, Tacitus ends the biography of his father-in-law with these words: "For oblivion will bury many of the men of old as if they had been without renown or prestige: Agricola will survive for posterity, his story told and handed on."[4]

Naturally, the Romans also drew on similar conceptions of memory in other ancient societies, especially among the Greeks. In Homer the generations of men are likened to the leaves on the trees that so quickly fall and die.[5] Only the fame (*kleos*) of the Homeric warrior, often expressed specifically in terms of the very function of epic poetry itself to immortalize that fame, is seen as a defense against the loss of status brought by oblivion. Similarly, Herodotus sets out to research and to write history so that memorable deeds of both Greeks and barbarians will not pass into oblivion.[6] Roman memory and commemoration were also designed to ward off the constant threat of loss of identity and status within the community, after the death of the individual or of his generation. In a wide variety of settings — for example, in battle or in the writing of literary works — the production of memory was the aim and the reward for effort and achievement.

A vivid picture of the function of Roman memory in a historiographic context is provided by a dream experienced by the elder Pliny, when he was a young man on campaign in Germany. Pliny dreamed that a ghost or image of the elder Drusus, who had died in his prime as a result of a riding accident in his camp in Germany in 9 B.C., came to visit him, with the request that Pliny should undertake to rescue Drusus' memory from oblivion.

Incohavit, cum in Germania militaret, somnio monitus: adstitit ei quiescenti Drusi Neronis effigies, qui Germaniae latissime victor ibi periit; commendabat memoriam suam orabatque, ut se ab iniuria oblivionis adsereret. (Pliny *Ep.* 3.5.4)

▾   ▾   ▾

He began [his history of the German wars] at the time when he was serving in the army in Germany, when he received inspiration from a dream. As he was sleeping the ghost of Drusus Nero, who died in

Germany after winning many victories there, appeared to him. Drusus commended his memory to Pliny and begged him to free him from the assault of oblivion.

Pliny's dream suggests the emotive and very personal urgency attached to active commemoration in Roman elite culture. Drusus himself appears to entrust his memory to Pliny. Past events and the recording of them in narrative form take on meaning through the lives of individual Romans of previous ages, even as later writers like Pliny might come to feel a personal connection with their historical subjects. Pliny's dream also conjures up Roman beliefs about the restlessness of those who die before their time and in unfortunate circumstances, especially through violence. It is tempting to imagine that the ghost of Drusus appeared to Pliny in a camp or other place where Drusus had spent time, or perhaps even where he had died.[7] Despite the fact that his body was returned to Rome for a splendid funeral, Drusus' ghost seems to be haunting the camps and battlefields of Germany, voicing his fears of oblivion in the specific context of conquest and empire, and of the now somewhat faded imperial project of an earlier age.[8] At the same time, these places in Germany should have served to commemorate Drusus, who had received a cenotaph on the banks of the Rhine River.

Drusus was the younger brother of Tiberius, born to Livia soon after her marriage to Octavian, the future emperor Augustus. Subsequently, Drusus was to be the father of Claudius, who was emperor when Pliny had his dream, sometime in the late 40s A.D. By then Drusus had been dead for more than fifty years. This fiftieth anniversary, which closely coincided with the unexpected accession of Drusus' son to imperial power, may have helped "prompt" the dream in Pliny's mind.

Hence, Pliny experienced Germany as a special place of memory for Romans, and notably for Drusus, whose untimely death put an end to his hopes of winning unique personal military honors there. There is, however, an anomaly in the notion that the father of the emperor might be forgotten, particularly in a Roman Empire that his son was expanding with an expedition to Britain. Tacitus, who was more than a generation younger than Pliny, remarks on the vivid popular memory of Drusus.

> *Quippe Drusi magna apud populum Romanum memoria, credebaturque, si rerum potitus foret, libertatem redditurus. Unde in Germanicum favor et spes eadem. (Ann. 1.33.2)*

▾ ▾ ▾

Clementis' Hat

Indeed, the memory of Drusus was vast among the Roman people, and it was believed that, if he had succeeded to power, he would have restored political freedom. This belief also resulted in the same popular favor and hopes being placed in Germanicus [Drusus' oldest son].

If Pliny's history of the Romans in Germany (which eventually extended to twenty papyrus rolls) served as a source for Tacitus, Pliny may have enhanced Drusus' image in the eyes of posterity.[9] It is also likely that Pliny's dream had a more symbolic than a literal meaning: now was the right time to choose Drusus as a subject, because others, including the emperor Claudius, who was himself a historian of distinction, were rediscovering the relevance of this particular ancestor of the Julio-Claudian house. However that may be, Pliny's dream, and the fact that he shared it with others, perhaps in the introduction to his German history (now lost), reveal that the elite Roman memory project was a personally inspired struggle against oblivion in the particular context of the Roman Empire. We know of his dream from a letter of his nephew and adopted son, Pliny the Younger, who includes this episode in a bibliographic list of all his uncle's works. In this secondary context, as narrated by the younger Pliny, the ghost of Drusus speaks also to the literary and political concerns of the early years of Trajan.

Memory sanctions, then, take shape against the background of a natural state of oblivion, as constructed in the Roman imagination of the day. In the sense that they were designed to prevent or remove the commemorative strategies specific to the Roman community, their function is analogous to that of exile, which drove the unworthy citizen outside the territory of the city, into a place that was not Roman. Like the exile, a citizen subject to memory sanctions was denied honorific commemoration within the city's own memory space. In such a rich cultural context, memory sanctions, especially in Rome, did not have a single meaning or purpose but were complex and often contradictory, both in conception and implementation.[10] They corresponded to the evolving memory world of Rome, in all its manifestations. Moreover, any particular sanction or erasure would always have taken on its meaning within its own particular milieu, a historical context that is often lost to us. Memory sanctions often appear to float freely between the extremes of oblivion and disgrace, in a dynamic memory space shaped in part by shame and silence, but in part also by vituperation and ongoing debate about the merits or vices of the deceased.

Ancient societies did not exercise total control over memory, because they generally did not envision a world in which any individual or group could wield the power to excise memory in society. Nor did ancient cultures have a secret police force or other organized mechanisms of surveillance to intrude into the personal and domestic spheres of its citizens. These circumstances should not be labeled as a lack of "efficiency."[11] Because sanctions targeted the formal and symbolic memory spaces of the political elite, not all memory was erased. People who had witnessed the past themselves knew and surely had their own opinions about what had happened. Yet the opinions of most ordinary people (or even the ways in which they might cultivate those memories) counted for little at the various moments when sanctions were imposed by those in power. Rather, sanctions looked ahead to a future that was never too far away in Rome, a future when a new generation would be learning the story of the (not necessarily so distant) past from the collective remembrance and monuments of the city. In addition, those who imposed memory sanctions may have assumed that natural oblivion was on their side. Meanwhile, a few negative examples were always useful, if only as warnings of the dire consequences of delinquent behavior. Despite the occasionally striking similarities, it is anachronistic and often misleading to read Roman memory sanctions simply or primarily in terms of Orwellian erasures and the totalitarian rewriting of history practiced in the twentieth century.

Every culture has its own memory world, within which its chosen sanctions take on their characteristic meaning and significance. The quality of memory is not only personal but also cultural: the memories of the individual mark that person as a member of a particular community. This notion, along with many other thoughts about memory, is brought out by Isabel Allende in her poignant description of her own experience as she sat by the hospital bed of her daughter Paula, who had fallen into a coma from which she would never recover. Like Pliny, Allende was a long way from home (since her daughter had fallen ill in Spain) and was experiencing memory as both powerful and yet at the same time fragile. In a reversal of the pattern found in Pliny, Allende entrusts her own memory to her dying daughter, rather than herself receiving an appeal to keep the past alive.

> In the long, silent hours, I am trampled by memories, all happening in one instant, as if my entire life were a single, unfathomable image. The child and girl I was, the woman I am, the old woman I shall be, are all water in the same rushing torrent. My memory is like a Mexican mural in which all times are simultaneous: the ships of the Conquistadors in one corner and an Inquisitor torturing Indians in another, galloping

Liberators with blood-soaked flags and the Aztecs' Plumed Serpent facing a crucified Christ, all encircled by the billowing smokestacks of the industrial age. So it is with my life, a multilayered and ever-changing fresco that only I can decipher, whose secret is mine alone. The mind selects, embraces, and betrays; happenings fade from memory; people forget one another and, in the end, all that remains is the journey of the soul, those rare moments of spiritual revelation. What actually happened isn't what matters, only the resulting scars and distinguishing marks. My past has little meaning; I can see no order in it, no clarity, purpose, or path, only a blind journey guided by instinct and detours caused by events beyond my control. There was no deliberation on my part, only good intentions and the faint sense of a greater design determining my steps. Until now, I have never shared my past; it is my innermost garden, a place not even my most intimate lover had glimpsed. Take it, Paula, perhaps it will be of some use to you, because I fear that yours no longer exists, lost somewhere during your long sleep — and no one can live without memories.[12]

As Allende suggests, crisis and loss both conjure up the past and change its appearance for us. Trauma can make us feel ready or even compelled to rewrite the past, if only to make a difficult new present more bearable. This effect can be observed in terms both of personal recollection and of the collective experience of a whole society, as it faces political rupture and a transition to a new and uncertain reality.

Memory has a shape, a space, and a cultural meaning. In other words, there is a specific what, where, and how to memory. Just as societies remember differently, so also do they forget differently. Editing and erasure take place within the context of each community's culture of writing, of archives, of images, and of monuments. A forgetting, or lack of commemoration, is defined by the local expectations of what might have happened if memory had been cultivated, either according to or even beyond the accepted norms of the community. Roman erasures can, therefore, only really be read in a Roman context. Cultural memory defines both the individual and the city. In this sense, memory is literally political, for it belongs in the *polis*. The meaning of memory is its effect within its own particular political community. The *polis* or political community, in turn, needs a memory story to explain its identity and past. Whatever the historicity of the details in this memory story, its existence is essential to the functioning of the community in the present.

Like other communities in the Mediterranean, Athens and Rome each had a story of sanctions as part of the narrative of their political emergence. Both Athenian democracy and the Roman Republic were said to have been founded on the expulsion of absolute rulers who were labeled as tyrants. These political cultures, apparently from the start, were designed as "not a monarchy." Such a negative definition had its own impact on political discourse and incorporated the very concept of sanctions into the fabric of the community's political self-definition. Similarly, the Augustan principate was presented, by its founder in his own account of his life (*Res Gestae*), as the restoration of a republic, which had been freed from the tyranny of a faction and from its nameless political leaders, warlords who were represented as a threat to a regular political process.

Whether historical or not, early Roman sanctions appeared essential and integral to the political community (*res publica*). Similarly, the extreme sanctions imposed on King Philip V of Macedonia by the Athenians in 200 B.C. were represented and justified in terms of ancestral custom dating back to the expulsion of the Peisistratids, more than three hundred years before. Meanwhile, the Campus Martius, where Romans met, drew up troops, and on many occasions voted, served to remind them that their public arena had been confiscated from the property of the old royal family of the Tarquins. Sanctions provided one mechanism for activating the political system, even as the government enacted its relationship to the individual citizen (or family) it was now removing from the community of memory.

Memory sanctions are designed to preserve and to protect the special memory space of the community and its political system. Such sanctions are designed to label potential threats, especially the threat of tyranny posed by the individual who becomes too powerful or the menace of war from the traitor who undermines the security of the state by allying with its foreign enemies. The fact that such internal threats can be removed, not only in person but also in memory, serves to assert the power of the community over its own narrative and, therefore, over its present and future direction. The political system is represented as stable partly because of its ability to meet and defeat challenges to its integrity. Sanctions help to rewrite such challenges in order to make them part of an acceptable narrative of continuity and political integrity. In these circumstances either oblivion or shame may serve the community, depending on the perceived needs of the moment. Meanwhile, sanctions represent society's political hindsight. In Roman terms, either the Republic asserts itself in the face of the tyranny of an individual or a faction, or the emperor shows that he can defeat and eliminate a usurper, a disloyal friend or relative, or a revolt in a province.

The function of sanctions within the community, as outlined here, helps to explain the profound shame that memory sanctions represented for members of the Roman elite. The class of officeholders (*nobiles)* was defined in terms of recognition during life and in terms of memory after death. Commemoration was the distinguishing mark of politically elite rank. Hence, if commemoration was limited or banned, the *nobiles* stood to lose their identity and status. Their loss comprised not just the present and future, but also the past, including their connection with their ancestors and with the prestige of their family. The citizen whose memory had been targeted was removed from the collective memory of the *polis.* As the Roman senate put it, when it imposed memory sanctions on Cn. Piso in A.D. 20, by his suicide Piso had tried to remove himself from punishments he feared the senators would impose, punishments that were worse than death. In what follows I argue that we should try to understand this assertion in a Roman context. The price of these additional punishments was considered so high in terms of public status that it became irrelevant to ask who might still hold onto or cherish a personal memory of the affected individual. Such personal recollections would now only reaffirm how far the person had fallen from a previous position of prominence and recognition. This social background explains how and why memory sanctions were the preserve of the elite in Rome, for it was only the political elite who enjoyed the privilege of public commemoration after death. The remembrance of ordinary citizens was in most cases of little concern to those in power and was represented (whether accurately or not) as having no political impact.

At the same time, sanctions must be read as political rhetoric, rather than as mere statements of fact; they reflect a claim on the part of the powerful to impose a narrative and to control the past.[13] Such a claim may or may not be valid or even be put into practice in a consequent way: sometimes it might be little more than an assertion or expression of hope. At this distance in time, the effects of sanctions, especially as measured throughout the Roman Empire, are nearly always hard to gauge. Official sanctions, the subject of this study, were communicated from the top.[14] Audiences for these political statements were varied and included both internal and external groups. Thus reception must always have been a factor, both immediately and in the long term. Did most people understand the messages sent out from Rome and, if so, did they agree with them? The answers varied across time and space. Dialogue could often be dynamic and was not limited to an immediate reaction to the first news of disgrace and political change.

For this reason, ordinary citizens, especially in Rome but also in the provinces, used the language of sanctions to express their own political opinions. Images might be attacked or mutilated. When crowds of angry Romans toppled the statues of Cn. Calpurnius Piso during his trial, the message was clear. They expected the senators to convict Piso and to impose the full range of sanctions on his memory.[15] Their shouts could be heard outside the senate house during the proceedings and certainly had an effect on the atmosphere of the trial. Such outspoken voicing of popular opinion was not unusual in Rome.

In another expression of political opinion, someone attached a sack to a statue of Nero in A.D. 59, after he had ordered the summary execution of his mother Agrippina on a charge of plotting against him.[16] This gesture referred to the traditional punishment for parricide, being sewn up in a sack and drowned. A statue of Agrippina was covered with rags, as if veiled in mourning; graffiti, as well as popular verses, attacked Nero's deed. In this case, the intention was less literal, since everyone surely knew that Nero would not actually suffer a punishment. However, the message was still powerful and direct. The language of sanctions was appropriated by people who had no legal right to free speech. The image of Nero in the sack publicly challenged the official story that the emperor had just escaped an assassination attempt planned by his mother; indeed, it was probably a response to the removal of some of Agrippina's statues in the city. It was clever because it stopped short of actually damaging the emperor's statue, which would have been a crime. Yet a dire punishment was invoked on Nero, perhaps also as a commentary on his delay in returning to Rome after his mother's death. He himself felt guilt, a fact that may have been the subject of gossip in the capital. Above all, the sack let Nero know that ordinary people thought they knew the truth about what he had done — he had ordered his mother to be killed in cold blood — while also demonstrating that everyone could now see that he was well aware of what they were saying about him in his absence from the city. The rhetoric of sanctions could be used to express and explore a political clash, either by imposing or resisting a narrative about recent events presented by those in authority.

The effects of sanctions on the imagination of Roman citizens in the imperial period can also be gauged by the fact that erasures can sometimes be found in private, funerary texts. These erasures attest to the appropriation of the symbols of official sanctions in cases of domestic and family disputes and disappointments. A valuable example is the tombstone of L. Gellius Felix from Rome that features an erasure of the name of his wife, Valeria Onomas<t>e, who had set up the inscription and the tomb for her husband,

FIGURE 1. Epitaph of L. Gellius Felix, Rome, second century A.D.
Erasure of the name of his wife Valeria Onomas < t > e, who set up the inscription.
Department of Classics, New York University, CIL *6.38417a.*

herself, and their descendants (figure 1).[17] In this case, the fact that the individuals involved were freedmen, or descendants of freedmen, shows that this erasure cannot be an official or legally sanctioned penalty of the political kind under consideration here. However, it does suggest that ordinary Romans of the second century A.D. could and did appropriate the language and symbolism of erasure from public and elite contexts.[18] A similar case is presented by a recently published marble cinerary altar, from the environs of Rome, that commemorates C. Vibullius Fidus, procurator of Syria.[19] The name of his wife, who set up the text and altar to her most indulgent husband (*marito indulgentissimo*), has been completely removed. The late first-century text also seems to provide evidence of a family decision rather than the outcome of a public trial. Since the present study is concerned with officially imposed memory sanctions, the topic of private sanctions will not be treated in detail. However, it is certainly a subject worth considering in its own right.

The study of memory sanctions, as a topic in itself, yields certain kinds of results. It is a story that is at least as much about those who designed and imposed sanctions as about their victims, who may or may not have "deserved" them. The inquiry that follows investigates the agency of politicians who imposed erasures on the past or who denigrated their predecessors. Sanctions are always based on a denial of the political rhetoric or landscape of the immediate past, despite or even because of the fact that at the moment of imposition many people are in a position to have personal knowledge about that recent past. The new narrative of the past, constructed by the sanctions, reflects the hopes, fears, and aspirations of those in power at that moment to a much greater extent than it reveals a historical reconstruction of previous events or of the true character of its victims, usually now dead. Hence the chapters that follow are displaced in time from their subjects, for each one investigates what happened afterward, after the fall. This world of "memory" belongs to the "history" of the subsequent age(s). Sanctions illuminate the nature and mechanics of political crisis and violent change; they do not mark the regular transfer of power either in a republic or a monarchy.

The investigation of memory games does not, however, lead inevitably to the re-creation of a detailed alternate narrative, let alone to the definite dis-covery of some core of "truth" obscured by propaganda and vituperation. The analysis of memory sanctions is not, in essence, a project of revisionist history, aimed at the rehabilitation of a series of "stage villains." It tends to reveal how much has been lost or obscured, much of which is beyond recov-ery. Hence the result may be a less "secure" view of the past, a past distorted by shifting images as the disputes of competing narratives resurface. Indeed, memory sanctions pose a fundamental dilemma to research. When truly successful, they presumably remove persons from subsequent record so that we cannot know anything about them. Our study of memory sanctions is necessarily limited to the many that fell short of their apparent goals, or that did not set out to achieve complete erasure.

Nevertheless, some outcomes of such a study can be anticipated. Certainly the nature of various political crises is illuminated by the types of sanctions they produced. Moments of political transition are highlighted and their dy-namics emerge more clearly. Meanwhile, the alternate narratives they created each contains historical information about the past, information that reflects a particular point of view at a given moment. That view may not have been shared by all, or even by a majority, but it does not thereby become irrelevant or simply mendacious. Although details may have been exaggerated to bring out a point, that point may well have more value than the political rhetoric that was spun to support it.

Vivid vignettes of the past (re)emerge, even as they illuminate the fleeting quality of the politics of the moment. Such lively scenes can make the study of memory sanctions and the manipulation of the past compelling, however incomplete the final outcome may be. Such a striking moment is described by Milan Kundera at the beginning of his work entitled *The Book of Laughter and Forgetting.*

> In February 1948, the Communist leader Klement Gottwald stepped out on the balcony of a Baroque palace in Prague to harangue hundreds of thousands of citizens massed in Old Town Square. That was a great turning point in the history of Bohemia. A fateful moment of the kind that occurs only once or twice a millennium.
>
> Gottwald was flanked by his comrades, with Clementis standing close to him. It was snowing and cold, and Gottwald was bareheaded. Bursting with solicitude, Clementis took off his fur hat and set it on Gottwald's head.
>
> The propaganda section made hundreds of thousands of copies of the photograph taken on the balcony where Gottwald, in a fur hat and surrounded by his comrades, spoke to the people. On that balcony the history of Communist Bohemia began. Every child knew that photograph, from seeing it on posters and in schoolbooks and museums.
>
> Four years later, Clementis was charged with treason and hanged. The propaganda section immediately made him vanish from history and, of course, from all photographs. Ever since, Gottwald has been alone on the balcony. Where Clementis stood, there is only the bare palace wall. Nothing remains of Clementis but the fur hat on Gottwald's head.[20]

For subsequent viewers and readers, Clementis' fur hat represents the meager traces that have escaped the ravages of memory sanctions, even as it illustrates the pressing need felt by those who want to change the future, to change the picture of the past at the same time. Even if only Clementis' hat is left, it may still have genuine value as a relic of history and as an evocative symbol of the complexities of a past that has been distorted and effaced.

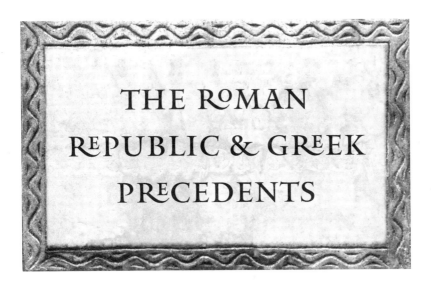

PART I

THE ROMAN REPUBLIC & GREEK PRECEDENTS

Did the Greeks Have
Memory Sanctions?

▼　▼　▼

Οἱ γὰρ ἄνθρωποι πρὸς ἃ ἔπασχον
τὴν μνήμην ἐποιοῦντο.
People shape their memory according
to their present experience.
Thucydides 2.54

In this neatness one perceives a
calculating venom; for to destroy the
context of an erasure might have made it
impossible to tell who was contemned.
Sterling Dow, *Prytaneis*

In an analysis of the function of memory and of punitive sanctions, the
Greeks provide the essential background to later Roman practices, especially
during the Republic, and to the culture of memory that was cultivated under
Hellenistic influence in the wider world of the eastern Mediterranean. One
example can serve to illustrate this point. In 1993 a Greek inscription in honor
of the emperor Claudius and recorded on a marble Doric architrave came to
light at Ilion, the site of ancient Troy. The building in question was named for
Claudius, together with Athena Ilias and the local *demos*, that is, the people
of Ilion.[1] This text contains an erasure of the building's dedicant, who seems
to have been King Mithridates VIII of Pontus, named in the inscription with
his queen.

This Mithridates had attempted to revolt, had been defeated by a Roman army, and had been taken to Rome as a hostage, so the erasure attests to the loyalty of the local people to Rome and especially to the Julio-Claudian family. It is typical of habits in the mid-first century A.D. and of reactions to political crisis under the Julio-Claudians and may also reflect the bitter memories at Ilion of the ravages of an earlier Mithridates, this man's ancestor who had fought Sulla and later been defeated by Pompey. Yet because Ilion itself had a venerable history of erasure, as is attested by its early third century B.C. anti-tyranny law, the practice of political erasure could be part of a regional tradition that was particularly related to the treatment of kings and to local autonomy. Mithridates' role was that of a Hellenistic king, or at least a candidate for that position, who was being dishonored in a city and by a people whom he once patronized. Meanwhile, the Romans played a role similar to that to which the king himself aspired, as they inserted themselves into a milieu that remained essentially Hellenistic in culture, in outlook, and in much of its political rhetoric. The erasure of Mithridates represents a Hellenistic memory sanction that may well have been imposed by the people of Ilion on their own initiative and in accordance with their own political memory space, rather than in imitation of a Roman custom, despite the fact that the emperor Claudius himself made use of a variety of memory sanctions.[2]

Greek Laws and Memory Sanctions

The attitude of the Greek city-states to memory sanctions is primarily revealed in their laws and statutes. The internal stability of the individual cities depended on their being able to deal with threats, whether real or potential, from errant citizens who might disrupt the community or even overturn its government, sometimes seizing power and imposing a tyrannical regime. Such threats could be just as real as the danger of war with neighboring communities, and the two could and often did go together. Political strife (*stasis*) was endemic to Greek politics, and patterns of repeated tyrannies or oligarchies were vivid in the collective memories of many cities.[3] Disaffected citizens might also join foreign enemies, such as the Persians. Even in the earliest times, sanctions against traitors and tyrants are attested in many Greek communities.

A Lokrian law of the late sixth century B.C. demonstrates the regular use of severe sanctions against the worst lawbreakers, such as murderers or violators of other communal civic agreements.[4] Such sanctions included the confiscation of property and the razing of the transgressor's house, which thus spelled the expulsion of the individual and of his family from the community. The razing of the house was a widely attested penalty, which the Greeks themselves dated back to mythical times in the story of the revenge taken on those guilty of the murder of Hesiod.[5] Although not mentioned in the Homeric poems, its place in myth underlines the symbolic significance of such a penalty in the Greek imagination. Greek tragedies often speak of the gods' destruction of the houses of the wicked, and many villains of tragedy were portrayed as tyrannical rulers who misused their power in relation to men or to gods, even as they brought disaster on the cities they were supposed to be leading.

Such destruction was used at Corinth to mark the end of the reign of the Cypselids. At Sparta the houses of individual kings were destroyed, even though the monarchy itself was never in question as an aspect of the traditional system of government.[6] The razing of the house symbolized the ruin of the family and of its position in society. Even in the historical period, the gods were thought to enact their own form of this penalty against particular offenders. Glaukus the Spartan, for example, dared to ask the Delphic oracle whether he could swear a false oath in order to keep a deposit of money that had been left in his care.[7] Although he never actually committed the perjury he was contemplating, Apollo still punished him by making his family and house disappear from Sparta, where he had formerly enjoyed a reputation for justice and fairness.

An archaic sanction that carried distinct religious overtones,[8] the razing of the house went far beyond mere symbolism. It literally destroyed the economic status and social position of the whole family, or at least of the branch that lived in the house in question. The result was that the offending individual would no longer live there, nor would his descendants and relatives. The implication was that this family could no longer coexist with the community at large. In most cities outside Athens, the confiscated land seems simply to have been reused for another purpose, so that all traces of the erasure itself were also removed. Presumably, the whole incident might eventually be forgotten.[9]

Although the razing of a house was not primarily designed as a memory sanction, it could and often did carry this secondary effect. Surely the immediate impact on the surviving family members was initially much more important than the eventual effect on how they were remembered. Moreover, this penalty was not limited to political elites and to a desire to curb their ambitions for power. In the archaic period any murderer could be subject to this punishment, even one whose house was modest and whose memory would have been insignificant. The origins of this sanction seem more probably to lie in the community's desire to rid itself of the pollution associated with crimes such as murder.[10] Meanwhile, the examples in our sources of houses that were destroyed are naturally those of more prominent citizens. It is hard to say how often such a penalty was actually used in any given community, even when the history of a city is well documented.

Additional penalties could be associated with confiscation and destruction of property. Equally severe was the restriction of burial within the territory of the city.[11] Most often this penalty would apply to the offender himself, but it could also involve his descendants (those now going into exile) and even sometimes his ancestors. In the latter case, graves might be dug up and the remains cast out beyond the borders of the community. Cypselus, the founder of the Corinthian tyranny, was thrown over the border unburied, as were the bones of his ancestors. The remains of the Alcmeionids were said to have been cast out twice under the Peisistratid tyranny at Athens, only to be returned subsequently. The Athenians might also institute a trial for treason after death, so that the offender could be exhumed and expelled from Attica.[12]

It seems that the Athenians had at least two locations where bodies were left exposed, probably under guard, so that they would indeed lie unburied rather than simply being deposited just beyond a border and collected by a relative from there.[13] Such exposure of a corpse assimilated the offender to an enemy of the state and made a public display of his new status as noncitizen. The Athenian state still claimed the power to control the ultimate fate of a citizen's body, despite the fact that even the bodies of enemies who had been killed in battle were often returned to their relatives. Individual identity would be lost by exposure in a communal pit, since no grave could be set up elsewhere. How often bodies were exposed is unknown. However, the existence of two recognized pits in Athens suggests again that it was perhaps not as uncommon as the prevailing silence in our sources might lead us to believe.

In this case, it seems fairer to speak of denial of burial as a true memory sanction, especially when a whole family group was affected. The presence of the family in the city was marked by the house of the living and by the graves of the dead. In cases of treason, tyranny, or other egregious violations, a whole family might be removed from the community as if it had never been a part of it. Such a removal could involve an elaborate series of public events, including the razing of the house and the ritual of exposing a corpse, or the digging up of family graves and the casting of old bones over the border. It seems probable that the expulsion of ancestors was more likely to involve prominent families and to represent a much more politicized erasure of family power and influence than the unceremonious casting of a common criminal into a pit reserved for those who had been crucified. The element of civic celebration and the affirmation of political values are well illustrated by the destruction of the tyrants' palace at Syracuse in Sicily in the late fourth century. After his defeat of the tyrants, Timoleon enlisted the help of all willing citizens to come and take part in the demolition work and in the observance of the occasion as a public holiday.[14]

When it comes to the imposition of the death penalty, it seems that many citizens of Athens, especially those of means, were expected to remove themselves from the community by going into voluntary exile and never returning to face execution.[15] This practical solution removed the offender from the city without forcing officials to deal with imposing the death penalty or to decide about burial. By definition, such a man could not be buried inside Attica, so his departure obviated the issue of dealing with his tomb or his body. Meanwhile, his disappearance was convenient for all and might save his family from further consequences.

Athenian law offers the richest source for examples of legislation that mentions the severest penalties, including those that might affect memory,[16] but similar sanctions could be found throughout Greece according to the local customs of each community. At Athens such extreme sanctions are especially associated with measures against tyrants or oligarchs who aimed to subvert the established system of government by the people. Athenian laws developed from the time of Draco and Solon to meet the changing needs of the city as it faced both internal factions and the tyranny of the Peisistratids and to protect Athens' democracy in the fifth and fourth centuries. Athenian penalties were related to the evolving definition of *atimia*, first as a radical loss of rights that made the person an outlaw who could be killed by anyone with impunity, but later as a more constitutional form of loss of certain legally defined civic rights.[17]

Throughout this development there was a consistent stress on achieving the expulsion of the offender (and his family) and enforcing sanctions against his return, rather than on securing his person for execution. Houses might be destroyed to reinforce these laws. Athenian practice grew logically in response to the constant civil strife of the archaic period, when groups of aristocrats battled each other for power and exiles might return with foreign armies or mercenaries to enforce their own political aims. The establishment of the democracy by Cleisthenes was related to the need to control political conflict and violence, as well as to give many more citizens a role in politics.

The democracy of the fifth century moved away from the battles of rival clans to more moderate uses of exile, notably in the typically Athenian form of ostracism.[18] This penalty, which was designed to target especially prominent citizens who might pose a threat to the community, imposed only ten years of exile with no concomitant loss of property or family status. Meanwhile, traitors were fiercely punished with death or exile, confiscation of property, and a ban on burial at home.

What made Athens different from the point of view of memory was its practice of publicly recording the names of traitors and other notorious offenders on *stelai* that were prominently displayed in the city.[19] By providing examples (*paradeigmata*) of individual villains, such inscriptions ensured that their memory would be perpetuated in a negative way that served the purposes of the Athenian democracy. Far from erasure and oblivion, the Athenians' system of memorializing notorious offenders helped to protect the city by describing the individuals who posed the most serious threats to its way of life. These memorials to traitors fit in with the democracy's characteristic emphasis on writing in public and on the teaching of political values through public texts. The earliest to be mentioned was the *stele* on the acropolis that enumerated the names and penalties (*adikeia*) of the Peisistratids in 510 B.C., a monument that could still be read (in its original form?) by Thucydides more than a century later. Other notable inscriptions included one condemning Hipparchus, son of Charmus, which was made by melting down a statue in his honor from the acropolis after his ostracism in 487 B.C., and the markers that labeled the places where the houses of Antiphon and Archeptolemus had been leveled in 410 B.C.

Consequently, Athens redefined the worst offenders as outlaws who had lost not only their citizen status but also their physical place within the community, both in life and after death. The implied, albeit usually silent, consent of the community of citizens as a whole was an important part of this rhetoric of punishment.[20] Oblivion remained the more common lot of the lowly criminal. The notorious elite offender, however, especially the traitor or aspirant to tyranny, was memorialized as such by having his name and deed advertised through special inscription(s). If his house was destroyed, its former location was marked rather than being simply consigned to the vagaries of collective memory. From its earliest days the Athenian democracy arrogated to itself the practice of labeling and controlling public memory in order to preserve its political system, communal values, and way of life. The positive label was initially more significant than any systematic erasures. So the *stele* of the Peisistratids survived together with some of their monuments

FIGURE 2. Peisistratus' dedication of an altar to Apollo Pythios, Athens, c. 521 B.C.
No modifications to this text are visible. *By permission of Oxford University Press,
L. J. Jeffrey, The Local Scripts of Archaic Greece (1991), no. 37 pl. 4.*

and inscriptions, most notably the dedication of the younger Peisistratus to
Apollo Pythios that memorializes his archonship around 521 B.C. (figure 2).[21]
The Athenians apparently felt that the inscription of the decree of outlawry
was authoritative enough to outweigh or to redefine any other honorific text
that might still remain standing.

Amnesty: (Re)Shaping Civic Memory

The Athenians, and other Greeks also, developed another practice that was
a type of deliberate memory sanction, namely an amnesty. According to the
terms of an amnesty, a reconciliation was made between two sides in a conflict, whether within a community or between two rival Greek cities. The
new settlement was based on a pledge to put aside past differences and not to
pursue old grudges. Such a pledge was usually made by both sides in the conflict by means of an oath taken by each person in his own name. Each person
would make a personal pledge to reconcile and to make a new start. This
practice reveals much about the construction of political memory within the
Greek city, as well as between cities. In the Greek view, political relations took
place within the memory space specifically created by the community, and
the role of the past in determining the future was clearly acknowledged. A
new start was made by promising not to use the past as a political weapon.

The standard term used in Greek for the oaths was *ou mnesikakein*, "not
to remember evils from the past" or even "not to misuse memory."[22] In other
words a special verb was created to express the recalling of previous wrongs,
presumably nearly always with a view to seeking some kind of personal vengeance or to provoking political unrest. Rather than using a verb of forgetting
or of reconciling, the Greeks expressed an amnesty in negative terms, literally as a sanction against certain types of or uses of "memory." This was not a
general ban on the act of remembering itself, but rather a specific agreement
about the public use of certain kinds of memories. The agreement relies on
memory and presupposes that people will and must inevitably recall the past

in order to obey the law. The same verb appears outside the actual agreements written on stone, notably in the Attic orators, when speakers accuse
individuals of violating the terms of the famous Athenian amnesty of 403
B.C. An alternative term was a verb of "being angry on the basis of memory"
(*mnasicholesai*). In this case the individual would swear not "to be angry in
remembering the past." The connection of anger with vengeance and strife
is a time-honored Greek concept that goes back to the anger of Achilles
in the *Iliad*. Similarly, the *Odyssey* ends with an exchange of oaths and a
pact between Odysseus and the families of the suitors whom he has killed.
The word "amnesty" was also a Greek term (*amnestia*) but is only attested
later, for example, in the alliance between Miletus and Heracleotis of about
180 B.C.[23]

The practice of banning such memories of evil was current in the fifth
century, as attested in the reconciliation between the Athenians and the Bottiaians in 422 B.C.[24] Other examples include the reconciliation of Athens and
Iulis (362 B.C.) and the amnesty decree from Aliphera in Arcadia (late third
century B.C.). The practice is also celebrated in myth by the reconciliation
of Poseidon and Athena after their contest over who should be the principal
protective deity of Athens.[25] The myth was depicted in sculpture on the monumental west pediment of the Parthenon. According to Plutarch, Poseidon
was happy to share a temple with Athena, and there was an altar dedicated
to Lethe, goddess of Forgetting, at the Erechtheium. Each year the Athenians
apparently omitted the second day of the month Boedromion because that
had been the day of the contest between Poseidon and Athena. By contrast,
the Furies (Erinyes or Eumenides) were characterized as goddesses who kept
alive the memories of evil and whose constant quest for revenge was based
on memory, linked to grief and pollution. In Aeschylus' *Eumenides* the goddesses become the protectors of the city by agreeing to accept legal arbitration
of blood feuds and by taking on an official role as guardians of memory.[26]

Of all the amnesties in Greece, the most famous was the Athenian reconciliation of 403 B.C.; this was the occasion recalled by the emperor Claudius
at the beginning of his reign, when he wanted to enact an amnesty after the
murder of his nephew and predecessor Gaius in A.D. 41.[27] This amnesty en-
abled the Athenians to return to a form of democracy based on the image of
a unified people. All swore to put the past aside and to enjoy reconciliation,
except for the Thirty Tyrants themselves, their closest associates, and those
guilty of shedding citizen blood with their own hands. The importance of this
well-publicized episode lay both in its effectiveness in stopping civil war and
in its function as a paradigm for the future. Despite, and indeed because of,

the disasters Athens had suffered after the huge loss of life in the Peloponnesian War, the humiliating defeat by Sparta, and the strife caused by two oligarchic coups, a new start was decreed. An effective limit was put on revenge
and bloodshed by elevating a law of reconciliation (and consequently also
the legal system in general) as an authoritative tool to put an end to disputes
between citizens.

At the same time, the lawcourts served as venues for exploring and controlling the bitter memories of the past.[28] Athenian legal speeches continually recalled the past rather than keeping silent, but this practice seems to
have served to reinforce rather than to undermine the effectiveness of the
amnesty decree. Open discussion in the courts of its limits and consequences
helped to shape its practical details and to give the community ownership
of the new political order. The price of peace was for all to step aside from
their past roles, whether as defeated oligarchs, victorious democrats, or fearful citizens who had simply tried to stay out of the conflict. At the same time,
the collective guilt and reproaches for what had happened could be virtually transferred to the notorious Thirty, who could serve as scapegoats for
the whole community. Their small and precise number suggested that most
other Athenians had been their victims and that the unity of the community
had essentially remained intact. As a result, the new democracy could be
closely associated with the old, even as the constitutional break of 404 was
isolated and relabeled. Meanwhile, all citizens who remained in the community were to be on an equal footing and hence to emerge as the victors from
the conflict.

The amnesty of 403 B.C. was appropriately celebrated in its own right as an
expression of Athenian civic values and as a basis for shared political life. It
recalled ancient pledges of an end to blood feuds and a respect for laws that
brought to mind Solon and the first establishment of a stable political system.
Yet it also inaugurated a new style of democracy and a renewed appreciation
for the value of the law as the true basis of the political community.[29] The
importance of controlling the memory of the past for the future of the community was acknowledged and brought home to every citizen in his personal
taking of the oath. Control of memory ultimately belonged to each citizen in
his own person, rather than to any representative group or body within the
city. The conception and success of this amnesty became celebrated throughout the fourth century and helped to establish the image of Athens that was
familiar to successive generations.

Erasing Greek Public Inscriptions

The treatment of traitors and political subversives, as well as the public creation of a culture of memory specific to each community, suggests the function of memory sanctions in Greece and especially at Athens. Similarly, erasures can also be found in Greek inscriptions of many kinds and from many centuries that attest to a desire to rewrite history or to remove and to shame the memory of individuals who had fallen from favor.[30] Each Greek city had its own culture of writing, ranging from the rich epigraphical dossier of Athens to the very limited use of writing in Sparta. Most communities may have been somewhere between these two extremes. Consequently erasure would also express different messages in each particular civic and urban context.

Meanwhile, it needs to be kept in mind that a standard Greek practice was to destroy the inscriptions, including the laws and honorific decrees, of one's political opponents by removing the whole *stele* that bore the text.[31] This practice can help to explain why there is not more evidence for erasures in Greek texts. In this way, the Thirty at Athens removed many texts, presumably because public inscriptions were especially associated with the democracy they had overthrown. Their acts can be traced in the extensive restoration program of the new democracy, which reinscribed a whole series of such texts, including proxeny decrees and the sacrificial calendar of the city, which had also become a target. Similarly, the new Athenian democracy of 318 B.C. restored the honors that had been granted to Euphron of Sicyon, who had been given Athenian citizenship in 323 B.C., by inscribing on the same *stele* both the old decree (lines 1–34) and a new one (lines 35–87).[32] These inscriptions may have taken original wording from the archives, but they specifically memorialized the previous destruction and hence also the overthrow of the destroyers and the present restoration in the context of political renewal. Such restored texts communicated a new meaning and recalled a series of events well beyond the inscription of the original decree on the *stele* that they replaced.

The desire to change an inscription is almost as old in Greece as the practice of writing on stone itself. A convenient example is provided by the stone base for the famous bronze statue of the charioteer at Delphi (figure 3).[33] This prominent monument was dedicated by Polyzelus, tyrant of Gela, to recall his victory in an Olympic chariot race around 478 B.C. The inscription was changed later without any damage to the dedication as a whole. While the change did not remove the name of Polyzelus as the victor and dedicant, it served to efface the memory that he had been a tyrant. In other words, the

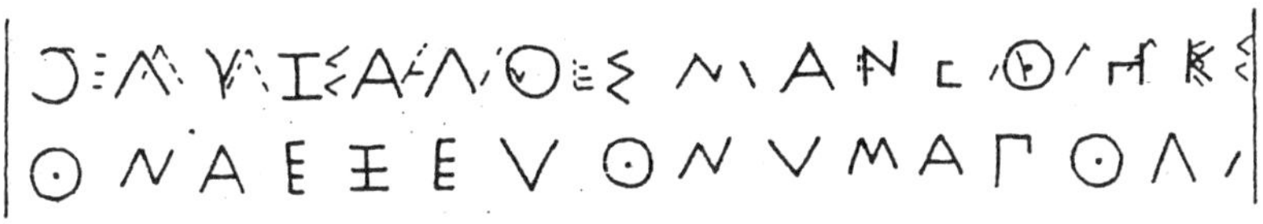

⊃:Λ· Ϋ\Ι:ΑΛΟϵΣ Λ\Α Ν ϲ Θ΄Η Ϟ:
⊙ Ν΄Α Ε Ξ Ε Ϝ ⊙Ν Ϝ ΜΑΓ ⊙Λ /

FIGURE 3. Polyzelus' dedication, base of bronze charioteer, Delphi, c. 478 B.C.
Text emended after 460 B.C. to remove the reference to the Deinomenid tyranny at
Gela in Sicily. *By permission of Oxford University Press, L. J. Jeffrey,* The Local
Scripts of Archaic Greece *(1991), no. 9 pl. 51, Delphi Museum 351.*

Sicilians wanted to keep the memory of the famous victory without memorializing the Deinomenid tyrants, who had fallen from power by 460 but who
had made many lavish dedications at leading Panhellenic shrines in Greece.[34]
The attention given to Polyzelus' dedication illustrates the importance of pilgrimage sites such as Delphi in creating a common memory space shared by
many Greeks from all over the Mediterranean.

Similarly, one of the most famous dedications at Delphi was the tripod set
up by the Greeks as firstfruits of the Persian spoils, whose original dedication
text was erased soon after its inscription. Pausanias the Spartan first wrote a
couplet dedicating the tripod in his own name as leader of the Greeks in the
war against the Persians. According to Thucydides, the Spartans had Pausanias' text erased and inscribed the names of all the cities that had taken part,
and this list is still extant on the tripod (now in Istanbul). When Pausanias
was starved to death by being trapped by the ephors in the Temple of the
Goddess of the Brazen House, it was Delphic Apollo who insisted on honorific burial for Pausanias at the site of his death and on expiation of the curse
the Spartans had incurred through their treatment of him. In the end Pausanias received a tomb marked by a *stele* and two bronze statues in the goddess'
precinct, dedicated as memorials of his death.[35]

Erasures of different kinds that do not target specific individuals can be
found in Greek laws and treaties. For example, the contemporary treaties
between Athens and Rhegion and Athens and Leontini of 433/32 B.C. both
show erasures of the original prescripts and reinscription of new but longer
texts in the spaces.[36] There is a marked difference in the writing style of the
second preamble of the treaty with Leontini. In such a case of elaborate recasting it is not possible to recover the details of the original text. A more easily understandable example is provided by the honors awarded by Athens to
Neapolis in Thrace for loyalty to the Athenians in 409–407 B.C. (figure 4).[37]
Here the references to Thasos as the mother city of Neapolis have been erased
in the first of the two decrees. Such an erasure may reflect a request from

FIGURE 4. Inscription recording a treaty between Athens and Neapolis in Thrace, Athens, 409–407 B.C. Erasures in the opening section removed references to Thasos as the mother city of Neapolis. *Epigraphical Museum, Athens*, EM 6598, IG I³ 101.

Neapolis that constituted an acknowledgment of its image at Athens. The erasure has changed Neapolis' identity in order to express it in a more independent way. A similar erasure of the epithet Eleuthereus for the god Dionysus in a decree of 330 B.C. also represents a political realignment in terms of territorial loyalties.[38]

A complex Greek text might contain multiple erasures made at different times. This is the case with the decree of Aristoteles establishing the Second Athenian Confederacy of 377 B.C., a document that was preserved but adapted to meet the changing political climate (figure 5).[39] This decree from the Athenian *agora* contains an erasure in lines 12–14 that removed about

FIGURE 5.
Treaty of the Second
Athenian Confederacy,
Athens, 377 B.C. Multiple
changes made to the
text at different dates.
*Epigraphical Museum,
Athens,* EM *10397,*
IG *II*^{2} *43.*

half of the rationale for the original alliance. The meaning of the lines in the erasure has been much disputed, but for the present purposes it is clear that as the emphasis of the naval alliance shifted over time, there was an attempt to erase some of the objectives that had been agreed upon at the start. The names of the allies were inscribed in the margins along the sides of the decree. Here also there is a prominent erasure of a name, probably that of Jason of Pherae. The law also contains traditional sanctions against those who break it, including a ban on burial inside Attica or in the territory of any of the allies. In the case of this decree various erasures remained on view in Athens throughout the time that the *stele* itself was visible.

Attitudes to erasures and to the use of the gaps they created in texts were clearly varied and are strikingly illustrated by an anti-tyranny law from Ilion dating to around 280 B.C.[40] Although many Greek cities passed laws to prevent tyrannies, and virtually all of these laws contained clauses outlining sanctions against those who might subvert the city, none is quite as detailed or as fascinating as this particular example from Ilion. A democracy had apparently been set up or renewed recently in Ilion, and this law contains elaborate measures to punish would-be tyrants and to reward those who support and protect the new democracy against them. It seems that a specific recent tyranny had prompted the reissuing of a law that contained traditional elements.

The anti-tyranny law from Ilion contains special measures to remove the name of the tyrant or oligarchic leader from all texts in the city, specifically from lists of priests, votive gifts, and graves. These three enumerated categories are used to describe the types of inscriptions to be found in Ilion, or at least those considered most important as memorials. It is interesting to see that graves and votives given to the gods are included. In each case the offending name is to be chiseled out. In the case of the priestly lists, the space may then be sold; the buyer may insert the name of whomever he chooses, as long as the person is eligible to hold such an office in the city. Clearly no technical problems were envisaged, although it is not specified exactly how the insertions should be made. The provision addresses the desire not to have gaps in the priestly lists that were used for purposes of dating. Erasures in less official texts appear more tolerable. In the case of votives, the people are to decide about the fate of the gift after the erasure, with the proviso that no memory of the original donor can be left. Here also, then, it would be possible to insert another name or to describe the votive as the gift of the people as a whole. In the case of a dedication made by several people, the offending individual's name is to be removed so completely that no traces are left behind. This clause describes the nature of a complete erasure and specifically guards against an incomplete one.

From the Ilion law it seems evident that a Greek city of the early third century might be thoroughly conversant with all the details of erasure and of either displaying or filling the gaps created by removing a name from a variety of texts. It is hard to believe that such detailed provisions existed merely in a vacuum. Rather they must reflect a culture of erasure and memory sanctions that had developed through the use of such sanctions within the individual community, and perhaps also in neighboring cities. Erasure is specifically described as targeting memory and is presented as a tool used by the *demos* to create its own civic space and identity. Some erasures will themselves be removed while others will not. A correctly executed erasure is defined as one that completely removes the name without leaving any legible traces. Memory sanctions seem thoroughly developed by this date, and they present a much more systematic approach than is to be found in archaic anti-tyranny legislation. Moreover, the Ilion law represents the creation of civic identity in the local sphere without reference to the politics of the great Hellenistic kingdoms that surrounded and fought over Asia Minor throughout the third century. The politics of the city still appears or at least claims to function on its own terms in regard to its own civic memory.

Hellenistic Memory Sanctions in Context

The terms of the law from Ilion raise the question of the role of memory sanctions in the political culture of the Hellenistic age, when most Greek cities were no longer as independent as they had been or as they liked to represent themselves as still being. Cities like Ilion and Athens continued to use traditional memory sanctions as tools and deterrents to deal with any of their own citizens who might be planning internal revolution or betrayal. Meanwhile, they now had to deal with a completely new area of foreign policy that involved their relations with the Hellenistic kings, who acted out various roles as successors to Alexander the Great. Skillful handling of international relations might still enable a city to enjoy a degree of internal autonomy and self-determination.

The Greek cities that did not fall victim to the aggression of Hellenistic kings and usurpers tended to use the traditional language and habits of euergetism to describe and control their relationships with the king.[41] The king was thus represented as a benefactor of the community, and his rule was characterized in a euphemistic way. At the same time, he was expected to live up to this positive image as benefactor of the Greek cities, and honors were granted to him in return for gifts, notably for exemption from taxes and for other privileged statuses that could elevate a city in relation to its neighbors and free it from the burdens of empire. A further dimension was added by the ruler cult, which consisted of divine honors offered by communities to Hellenistic kings. The Hellenistic ruler cult began in the time of Alexander the Great, to whom the Greek cities of Asia Minor almost certainly granted divine honors during his lifetime, and it is possible that he requested such honors from the cities of mainland Greece toward the end of his life. After his death, the cult of kings, both living and dead, became a regular feature of political life throughout the Hellenistic world.[42]

In Macedonia, a ruler cult had not traditionally been practiced either for living or for dead kings. From the end of the fourth century onward, however, Greek cities like Athens voted extravagant honors to Hellenistic monarchs — although not to all of them — both in the hope of winning favors for themselves and with a view to influencing the king's policies in a more general way, sometimes to make war on their rivals.[43] Divine honors were a further dimension added to the honors that had been granted to benefactors in earlier ages. They had the advantage of exerting more pressure on the king to live up to his image as a powerful and generous patron of the city. In this way they enhanced what the cities could offer in the elaborate habits of gift exchange that characterized the rhetoric of power relationships between the king and the city.

Dossiers of extant inscriptions attest to the evolving exchange of favors between a king and a community. An illustrative example comes in two lengthy inscriptions from Teos in Asia Minor that record relations between Antiochus III (the Great) and the locals around 203 B.C.[44] Antiochus and his queen Laodike received a divine cult as saviors of the city and were honored with marble cult images that were associated with the god Dionysus and his festivals and were to be kept in his temple. The royal couple were further honored with individual altars. In addition, the king had a priest, a festival, and a bronze cult image in the *bouleuterion* of the city, where the civic leaders paid him homage and he was presented with the firstfruits of the harvest, while Queen Laodike had a special new fountain in the *agora* named for her. The water from this fountain was to be used for the libations in all the various religious ceremonies on behalf of the city and by the brides of the city as they drew water for their wedding ceremonies.

Thus the royal couple received both new cult and honors in their own right, as well as being linked to the most venerable city cults, such as that of

Dionysus, and to civic and family ceremonies such as weddings. The imagery of fertility is especially pronounced throughout the decrees and in the association of Antiochus with the firstfruits of the harvest and Laodike with brides on their wedding day. As a result they were represented as the savior gods who guaranteed the safety and prosperity of the community. The second decree also emphasizes the idea of memory, both as a goddess (Mneme) who receives a sacrifice together with the king in the *bouleuterion*, and as the specified aim of the honors paid to the queen in the *agora*, honors that will last forever and will be seen by all the foreigners who visit the city.[45] The honors voted in the decrees were presented to Antiochus by an embassy and were inscribed on a pilaster at the entrance of the temple of Dionysus at Teos. They have survived in relatively good condition because they were discarded near the west wall of the temple precinct, probably around 190 B.C. or soon after. In the end, the honors proved to be ephemeral, and it is unclear whether such projects as the fountain in the *agora* were ever completed in Laodike's name.

As the inscriptions from Teos show, the granting of such extravagant honors by cities also carried with it the possibility that these grants could be reversed in the same way in which they had originally been enacted.[46] If the city could bestow divine honors, it could also take them away. Such a reversal might come from the city itself, if the king failed to live up to his obligations and the city's expectations, or might be imposed by another king who had now come to control the territory of the city or of the king who had been honored before. After the Romans defeated Antiochus at the battle of Magnesia and subsequently made a treaty with him at Apamaea in 188 B.C., Teos came under the control of the kingdom of Pergamum, and a new ruler cult was established for its king Attalus and his queen Apollonis.

In the fourth century the honors of Philip II (which probably did not include cult) had been canceled at Eresus and Ephesus as a result of a tyrannical coup, which included the overturning of altars and the destruction of Philip's statue in the famous temple of Artemis at Ephesus.[47] Similarly, Demetrius Poliorketes was discredited by his political opponents with the result that elaborate divine honors at Athens were reversed and his rule was labeled a wretched time of servitude.[48] His disgrace in collective memory is starkly illustrated by the erasure of his name from the list of those who had given donations to rebuild the city of Thebes in 304 B.C. Demetrius had contributed 10 percent of the rich booty he had taken from Rhodes, but even this generosity was erased. The history of Hellenistic ruler cults comprises a multitude of grants of honors but also, and equally importantly, of reversals of previous gifts. It seems evident that almost from the beginning, the reversal of these divine honors was envisaged, with the result that many cults dedicated to the eternal memory of a divine ruler were indeed short-lived. Both the cities that offered such honors and the kings who accepted them must have been fully aware of this situation. Consequently, memory sanctions played a regular and important part in Hellenistic diplomacy and power politics, since characteristically shifting spheres of influence and conquests created a changing geopolitical landscape in which kings and dynasties tried to replace their rivals in memory and history, as soon as they had defeated them on the battlefield.

Philip V of Macedon:
The Romans Visit Athens in 200 B.C.

The best-attested example of memory sanctions in a Hellenistic context is offered by the penalties imposed on the memory of Philip V and his ancestors by the Athenians in 200 B.C. as part of the initial stages of the Second Macedonian War.[49] This episode sums up the practice and purpose of Hellenistic sanctions and highlights the Romans in their new role as power brokers in the Greek world of the eastern Mediterranean. As has already been discussed, memory sanctions were very much a part of the rhetoric of Hellenistic power relationships and conflicts, a world that the Romans entered and participated in by observing and often by appropriating for themselves many of the habits and the diplomatic language that they encountered there. The well-worn slogan advocating the "freedom of the Greeks," first used by Antigonus the One-Eyed at the end of the fourth century, was put to great effect by the Roman general T. Quinctius Flamininus.[50] This slogan can be related directly to the relationship of a city like Athens to a king like Philip V. The Athenians used memory sanctions precisely to declare their political independence from Philip and from the whole history of Macedonian hegemony, and there is every reason to believe that their example taught the Romans some valuable lessons in power politics and self-advertisement.

The sanctions against Philip are described in detail by Livy (31.44.4–8), probably drawing on Polybius' narrative, which is no longer extant.

> They immediately passed a resolution, and the people approved it, that the statues and portraits of Philip and all their inscriptions, as well as those of all his ancestors, both male and female, be removed and destroyed. The festival days, rituals, and priesthoods that had been instituted in Philip's honor and to honor his ancestors, were all deconsecrated.

In addition any place where something had been set up or inscribed in his honor should have a curse on it. They decreed that nothing which required a sacred location should be placed or dedicated there in future. On whatever occasion the public priests prayed for the Athenian people and their allies, and their armies and navies, on each such occasion they should pronounce a curse and execration against Philip and his children and his kingdom, his forces on land and sea, and the whole name and people of the Macedonians. A clause was added to the decree that if anyone should later propose a motion with regard to the disgrace and dishonor of Philip, the Athenian people should pass it in its entirety. If anyone should speak or act in opposition to his disgrace or in support of his honor, anyone who killed such a person should be deemed to have killed him justly. Finally a clause was included that all the sanctions that had once been decreed against the Peisistratids should likewise apply to Philip. The Athenians were waging war against Philip with written and spoken words, which are their only strength.[51]

The Athenians thus voted to destroy all the honors for Philip and for the earlier Macedonian kings. What amounted to a completely new political alignment for the Athenians was reinforced by an oath to be taken by all citizens. Anyone who opposed the sanctions (*ignominia*) or tried to reinstate the honors of the king (*honos*) could be killed with impunity. Presumably the ban on any Macedonian's entering Attica was passed at the same time. Erasures in Athenian inscriptions attest to the abolition of the two Athenian tribes named after Antigonus and Demetrius, which were soon replaced by a tribe named in honor of Athens' new Hellenistic royal ally, King Attalus of Pergamum (figures 6, 7).[52]

Livy concludes his section on the sanctions of 200 B.C. by stating that the Athenians specifically imposed on Philip all the same penalties that had been voted against the Peisistratids. This public reference to the paradigm of the Peisistratids demonstrates the symbolic function of such public memory sanctions in Athenian culture. The Athenians thereby declared that memory sanctions were among their most hallowed traditions and were connected to the beginning of the glorious phase of their democracy. At the same time, the historic precedent served to characterize Philip and his ancestors as "tyrants" in the classic sense of the term. The figure of the "tyrant" could be invoked both as the city's most traditional enemy and as the type of the "bad king," who had not been a benefactor but an exploiter and oppressor. The reversal of honors was literal since in 307 B.C. the statues of the Antigonids had been

FIGURE 6. Inscription of 271/70 B.C., with erasure of Antigonid tribe dating to 200 B.C., Athens. *American School of Classical Studies, Athens, Agora Excavations,* ISE 18.

FIGURE 7.
Decree honoring Phaidros,
with erasures dating to 200 B.C.,
Athens. *Epigraphical Museum,
Athens,* EM 10546, IG II² 682.

placed next to those of Harmodius and Aristogeiton, the traditional liberator figures and heroes of the fifth-century democracy.[53] In other words, those who had been the city's liberators were now relabeled as its oppressors. The fierce sanctions against Philip were, in fact, innovative in their wide-reaching effects in Athens, where direct Macedonian rule had ended in 229 B.C. but alliance with Macedonia had continued. The Macedonians, and more than a hundred years of their history, were to be removed from Athens and were to be marked with erasures and curses.

In actual fact, it is both anachronistic and misleading to make a simple equation between the outlawing of the Peisistratids (an Athenian family) and sanctions against Philip (a foreign ruler who was an ally).[54] The Peisistratids were outlawed, but we cannot recover all the provisions recorded on the *stele* put up at the time. It is evident, in any case, that Peisistratid names were not chiseled out everywhere, and prominent monuments were often left standing, such as the Altar of the Twelve Gods. The Athenians seem to have appropriated a number of symbols used by the Peisistratids to characterize the public image of the new democracy, including the famous owl of Athena featured on Athens' coinage.[55] By contrast, the erasures of the year 200 have decisively affected the record of Athenian inscriptions of the third century B.C. (figure 8). A life-sized bronze equestrian statue of Demetrius that had originally been covered with sheets of gold was thrown into a well in the *agora*.[56] These differences can be explained in terms of the looming war with Philip, the weakness of the Athenians and their need for new military allies, and ultimately the character of the Hellenistic ruler cult itself, which had few features in common with the simpler times of the Peisistratids.

It was precisely because the Athenians now carried through a new and drastic erasure of their city's history that they needed to make a historical analogy that would be recognizable, both at home and abroad. They needed to define their own actions, which changed their political alignment, in terms of traditional Athenian norms of political behavior. Drastic action was needed to remove the heavy Macedonian imprint on the city. At the same time, neither the words of the decree against Philip nor the parallels with the Peisistratids were necessarily taken completely at face value, even at the time. Erasures in epigraphic sources were extensive and thorough but certainly not universal. The curses do not appear in the language of Athenian prayers from the 180s and may not have been in use for very long.[57] The penalties themselves, as well as their inscription on a *stele* that Polybius seems to have been familiar with, carried their own symbolism that could allow the Athenians to move on to the next stage in their political lives. We may imagine that the

FIGURE 8.
Honorary decree
for Prytanis of Caristus,
with erasures dating
to 200 B.C., Athens.
*American School of
Classical Studies, Athens,
Agora Excavations,*
ISE 28.

new anti-Macedonian *stele* was probably placed strategically in relation to the *stele* relating to the Peisistratids on the acropolis (whether the original or a restored version). Such a location would have legitimized and advertised the Athenians' ability to shape their own civic image and landscape, even in an age when they relied for the survival of their city on foreign powers, notably the Rhodians, King Attalus of Pergamum, and, to an increasing extent, the Romans.

The chronology of the opening moves in the Second Macedonian War is complex and disputed, and it is important to keep in mind that the Athenians had not been formally allied with Rome before.[58] Their sanctions against Philip came as part of their decision to declare war on him. Rhodes and Attalus were already at war with the Macedonians, and there was every indication that the Romans also had already voted for war or were about to do so. For the present concerns, the chronological details are less significant than the fact that the Athenian resolutions against Philip were adopted immediately before the arrival of a large group of foreigners that included King Attalus himself and official embassies from both Rhodes and Rome. As a result, Athens' sanctions need to be read as partly addressed to this audience and as being both affected by and exerting an influence on those involved in negotiating a coalition that would fight in the upcoming conflict. Attalus and the Rhodians were both part of the traditional world of Hellenistic diplomacy, and Attalus himself benefited immediately from being granted honors in place of those for Philip that were now being erased.

It is impossible to be precise about the role of the Romans in the negotiations. For them the conflict was not new but was represented as the settling of old grudges against Philip that went back fifteen years to his alliance with Hannibal after the disastrous Roman defeat at Cannae.[59] Consequently, they represented the new hostilities as the continuation of a previous war, and later Roman historiography would retroject the alliance with Athens into the third century in order to help justify Rome's aggressive Mediterranean policies. What can be said is that at perhaps the most decisive turning point in their own relations with the Greek world, the Romans ambassadors witnessed one of the most dramatic and extensive erasures of memory ever enacted by a Greek city against a Hellenistic monarch. In their report to their fellow senators after their return, the ambassadors C. Claudius Nero (cos. 207), P. Sempronius Tuditanus (cos. 204), and M. Aemilius Lepidus (cos. 187, 175) would have had no reason not to give a full account of what they had seen. The fact that the city was Athens only made the gesture seem grander and more momentous. The Romans were not yet ready to step into the gap created by the erasures in the way that Attalus was, but they clearly benefited and felt some obligation toward Athens as a result. It was Roman troops who were to save Athens from Philip later that same year. By the time the Romans fought Philip's son Perseus, their commander L. Aemilius Paullus did insert himself in place of his Macedonian royal rival on a well-known victory monument at Delphi.[60]

The Romans saw the effects of memory sanctions in relation to Hellenistic war and diplomacy at the same time as they experienced their ability to sweep away kings like Philip V and Antiochus III and to write new chapters in their own imperial history. Hence most discarded or erased *stelai* from Asia Minor that date to the second century tell part of the story of Roman expansion in terms of the reactions of local Greek cities. An example from Stratonikeia shows that when Caria was freed from Rhodian domination by Rome in 167 B.C., the name of the Rhodian governor who had replaced the Seleucids as the local power broker and honorand was now chiseled off his honorific decree on stone.[61] Rome had become an active player in the Hellenistic world, and it is not surprising that its leading politicians were heavily influenced by its customs, both in their public and private lives. While Rome, like most Mediterranean cities, had its own culture of remembering and forgetting, the vivid and dramatic erasures that Romans witnessed and were the direct cause of throughout the eastern Mediterranean almost certainly affected how contemporary Romans, both at home and abroad, came to think of themselves and of their particular role in creating and destroying the memories of kings and of their empires.[62]

The Origins of Memory Sanctions
in Roman Political Culture

▼   ▼   ▼

Huius supplicio aeternae
memoriae nota inserta est.
Valerius Maximus 6.3.1a

Hi duos illos oculos orae maritimae effodierunt.
Cicero, *De Natura Deorum* 3.91

In twentieth-century studies of Roman history, the beginning of memory sanctions has been primarily associated with the last period of the Roman Republic and especially with the figure of Marcus Antonius, who has often been cited as the first real example of a leading Roman subjected to such treatment. Consequently, memory sanctions in Roman culture have been defined and studied primarily as a phenomenon of the principate, with roots in the triumviral period.[1] Because this particular political context has colored the interpretation of such sanctions, they have been understood largely as legal penalties for treason (*maiestas*) and as evidence of various emperors' efforts to repress aristocratic resistance to one-man rule. Depending on which ancient evidence is chosen as the main focus of analysis, such a reading can appear to be fully justified by the sources.

Certainly, political erasures in inscriptions are almost exclusively documented in the imperial period, with Antonius providing the most prominent early example. Similarly, the recarving of imperial portraits, which offers a particularly powerful example of Roman political memory and its uses, really starts with the images of the emperor Gaius in the mid-first century A.D.[2]

This chapter, however, will argue for a different reading of and context for Roman memory sanctions and their origins by examining them both within the political culture of the Republic and as part of its continuous dialogue with other cultures, most notably in relation to the dynamic political culture of the Greek city-states traced in the previous chapter. Such a reevaluation of the function of memory and oblivion must rely on a broad view of Roman practices as they evolved during the historical period of the Republic, as well as on an interdisciplinary consideration of all types of sources that can inform us about the construction of memory within the Roman political sphere.

The previous chapter presented a variety of evidence for memory sanctions in classical Greek and Hellenistic settings. Within this perspective of longer time, Rome and its politics appear as relative latecomers: the Romans themselves saw their own society as young and relatively unsophisticated, especially when compared with most others in the eastern Mediterranean. As their Republic emerged first to dominate Italy, and then to play an increasingly complex and imperial role within a larger Mediterranean world, the Romans adopted many of the customs and habits, as well as the material culture, of their Greek-speaking neighbors. Waves of Greek influences reflect complex patterns of cultural interactions, from the Etruscanized Rome of the sixth century, to the Greek interests of such early Roman politicians as Appius Claudius Caecus, to the adoption of Greek-style drama and literature in the later third century, to the culture wars of the second century, which were partly expressed through the new medium of historiographic writing in Greek.[3] Within this world of mutual influence, which was in many ways *the* defining pattern of Roman cultural development, many generations of elite Romans became thoroughly conversant with most aspects of Greek life, regardless of whether they themselves as individuals favored the new fashions of their own day or were working to limit them.

Romans may have come to know about the various uses of memory sanctions within Greek city-states and Hellenistic kingdoms and discovered that such sanctions could be used to communicate political messages, particularly between cities and kings. However, memory sanctions had been a part of the political language of the eastern Mediterranean for centuries. Like the Greeks before them, Romans also traveled to the East and especially to Egypt, where the grandeur and antiquity of pharaonic civilization conveyed its own messages about memory and monuments over a much longer time span, messages that could be and are still being reinterpreted by each generation of visitors. Meanwhile, Roman interventions abroad prompted others to react in various ways, including the use of memory sanctions and the rewriting of history, even as communities sought to realign themselves to new political realities.[4]

In this context, it would have been virtually impossible for individual elite Romans not to bring home new ideas about memory and erasure, interpreted within their own frames of reference, just as they imported new deities and Hellenistic cultural capital and material aspirations. Their decision to start writing their own story in Greek for others to read suggests the kind of highly deliberate and conscious choices now faced by those who shaped Rome's political future. The imperial image of their city (and of themselves as its leaders) was now projected in the memory places already occupied by the fabled conquerors of old, by the pharaohs and by Alexander and his successors. At the same time, their own city grew and changed to become *the* Mediterranean capital, even as it (re)defined itself both in relation to other great cities past and present, and to its own humbler origins.[5]

Within this characteristically Roman cultural project, new and antique images of erasure were assimilated in relation to existing Roman concepts of the function of political memory and to the Romans' increasingly reified sense of ancestral customs and life-styles characterized by simplicity and moral rectitude.[6] The results were predictably fascinating and complex. Meanwhile, the nature of the surviving evidence for the early and middle Republic poses very different challenges from those of the principate or of the Hellenistic Greek world, challenges characterized by lack of evidence and by layers of distorting anachronisms in later sources. An examination of the construction and deconstruction of memory in Roman republican politics is nonetheless essential both to a history of memory sanctions in Roman culture in general and also to various characteristic features that survived well into the Empire. Most notable among these features is the role of the aristocratic family as guardian and definer of memory in all spheres.[7]

The Three Early Republican Traitors

The Romans did not have an ancient tradition of historical record keeping of any formal or literary kind. Moreover, even generations after they first encountered historiographic writing in Greek, they did not feel the need to adapt or to imitate such literature within their own community. Rather, it was the decisive defeat of Carthage at the end of the third century that prompted a reevaluation of their own role on the stage of history and a decision, taken by individual senators, that they themselves should start to write their own formal histories, at first in Greek for a Mediterranean audience of which they now saw themselves as a part, and only later in Latin for their own didactic purposes. In other words, until the second century Roman memory had been created and maintained for generations outside the formal genre of written narrative history.[8]

The Romans' memory of their past was not deep and detailed, especially when compared with chronicles such as those found in the temples of Egypt. Although the Roman historical tradition covered the three generations before the first historians with increasing plausibility, it encountered increasing uncertainty in the late fourth century. Appius Claudius Caecus (cens. 312 B.C.) appears to be the first historical figure whose life and policies, despite conflicting traditions, can be reconstructed in detail.[9] The earliest writers of Roman history seem to have given accounts of the founding of the city and then to have jumped ahead to their own time, with scant attention paid to the early history of the Republic.[10] Yet the image of the Republic was founded on the traditions of the exile of the kings: republican history started with a powerful negative example. The *res publica* was by definition not a monarchy. The kings were never forgotten; rather their negative image remained a decisive influence throughout the Republic and beyond.[11] During the following generations, the gaps in Roman history were filled in by using a variety of sources such as the *fasti* and the legends surrounding most memorable events, including those marked by or elaborated from monuments in the city. In addition much was simply filled in by later annalists, partly with a view to commenting on the politics and the personalities of their own day.

The traditions about early Rome contain three examples (which became authoritative and canonical) of Roman citizen traitors who were subjected to various memory sanctions after their deaths: in chronological order they are Spurius Cassius (485 B.C.), Spurius Maelius (439 B.C.), and Marcus Manlius Capitolinus (384 B.C.). By the late Republic, these men and their punishments seem to have been as well known as any episodes in early Roman history. As a consequence they feature in Livy's history, in a pattern of three culminating with the fall of Manlius, an episode that is carefully placed and thoughtfully elaborated by Livy to reflect upon the character of memory in the city and on the tensions surrounding the fall of a leader whose own greatness has become a threat to the community he had once saved.[12] By the 20s B.C. Livy clearly felt that Manlius was worth writing about in detail, and he was confident that his readers would want to read such an extended treatment of the ruin of one of Rome's saviors. The traitors command similar interest from Dionysus of Halicarnassus, who was also writing during the time of Augustus. Fragments of earlier historical writers show that Sp. Maelius was discussed by Cincius Alimentus and by Calpurnius Piso.[13] There is no real reason to doubt that some version of these stories could be found in the traditions recorded by the very earliest Roman historians.

However, it is also clear that the final versions produced in the late Republic, which are the only ones now extant, had been substantially recast to reflect the political conflicts and the violence of contemporary Rome. While this observation affects much of the account of the early Republic, it applies in a very special way to these three incidents, which had also come to be associated with each other in an ahistorical manner.[14] It was precisely the stories of the disgraced traitors that took on a completely new relevance with the death of the Gracchi and throughout the series of conflicts that marked the most prominent stages of the Republic's decay, from the introduction of the *senatus consultum ultimum* to justify the attack on Gaius Gracchus and his associates, to the civil carnage under Marius and Sulla, to the outlawing of Catiline and the summary execution of his supporters. Assassination and judicial murder became commonplace in a development that could only be made sense of with reference to ancestral precedents.

There can be no doubt that whatever one's view of the early traditions in general, these particular ones were intensely used and reused for partisan political purposes over several generations and by a variety of different groups.[15] Moreover, many of our principal informants, including Cicero, themselves had a vested interest in the elaboration of historical *exempla* that would support the courses of action they had already taken or were advocating for the future. Because these episodes were recast in a variety of mutually exclusive versions, it has become virtually impossible even to disentangle the way in which the traditions developed over time, let alone to establish any objective criteria for distinguishing "fact" from "fiction."

At the same time, the traitors themselves cannot be dismissed out of hand, and their stories became powerful paradigms in the civil conflicts of the late Republic. Their legends exemplify the rhetoric of the time of the Gracchi and immediately thereafter. Yet reading them simply in terms of later times can ultimately only offer a partial solution to the challenge they pose.[16] These traitors were not invented out of whole cloth; rather they provided persuasive models for later debates precisely because they had been well known, at least in name and outline, in the historiography and shared perception of the past before the Gracchi. `It is surely revealing that more such episodes were apparently never invented, in order to assimilate earlier times more closely to the extensive and punitive memory sanctions of the late Republic. The paradigm of disgrace and sanctions against memory hangs over the early Republic, and it is associated with special moments of crisis, such as times of famine and the aftermath of the sack of Rome by the Gauls in the early fourth century B.C. While these crises have been recast to reflect later social and economic problems, basic issues of food shortages, debt, and land distribution and the question of who would represent the political concerns of ordinary citizens were in fact perennial throughout antiquity.[17]

For the purposes of the present discussion, it suffices to focus on the nature of the disgrace and punishment inflicted on these men, which is an issue somewhat independent of the details of their programs or of the nexus of political rivalries in which they were entangled. Their cases were essentially distinct from each other both in terms of the issues and of the historical context. What they apparently have in common is the charge of *adfectatio regni*, a charge that must have arisen from the fear of a return to a monarchical system of government at a moment of crisis, when the republican government appeared unequal to the task of keeping order or assuring the food supply.[18] At these moments Rome seemed to be behaving more like a Greek city, many of which also feared or suffered the rise of tyrants in moments of crisis and popular unrest.

Finding an example of such a charge in the earliest time of the Republic in the story of Sp. Cassius is not surprising, although his apparently plebeian background continues to pose problems of interpretation.[19] The *fasti* and other sources suggest that Cassius was remembered as the most prominent politician of his day and that his fall was followed by a marked period of dominance by the Fabii, a pattern that might indicate a kind of internal coup. The oldest versions of his punishment seem to ascribe responsibility to his father and to make the whole story an example of the powers of a father and how he could exercise them to preserve the status quo.

There is, however, little erasure of memory here, especially if one accepts that a statue of this same Cassius was removed by the censors as late as 158 B.C. The third-century temple of Tellus where this statue had been set up was said to have been built on the spot where Cassius' house had stood, although this really makes no sense at all if Cassius was still in his father's power and his *peculium* had been used for a religious dedication by his family at the time of his death.[20] The destruction of his house appears as an element that may have been introduced to assimilate him to later traitors. Similarly, it seems that both the inscription of the Cassii on an ancient bronze statue of Ceres and the (much later?) statue of Cassius himself in front of the temple of Tellus cannot be clearly related to any version of his death that has come down to us.[21] As a result, there is little in his story to support a very early republican tradition of "erasure of memory," especially since Cassius' death seems to have been commemorated primarily by a religious dedication made by his family, with overtones of expiation.

Unlike Cassius and Manlius, Sp. Maelius appears a much less historical figure, with nothing to his credit beyond the legends surrounding his fall.[22] He himself does not have any family relationships with the political elite and may even be a figure invented out of whole cloth to explain the topography of the Aequimelium, an open area to the south of the Capitol, allegedly on the spot where his house had been destroyed, that was used as a market for sacrificial animals. His legend is part of the family history of the Servilii, explaining their *cognomen* Ahala (which refers to the dagger concealed under the armpit of the assassin), and of the Minucii, accounting for their connection with distributions of grain. These family traditions also seem to present etymological glosses that were invented later, especially in the case of the name Ahala, an Oscan name of great antiquity. Moreover, the fact that Ahala's story provided such a convenient justification for political assassination from the death of Tiberius Gracchus onward meant that this legend became seriously distorted. Maelius did appear in the history of Cincius Alimentus in the first generation of Roman historiography, but the details were probably simple, recording no more than the fact that Maelius had been killed by Ahala under suspicion of tyranny. Maelius' story can provide no secure confirmation of formal postmortem sanctions in Rome in the fifth century B.C.

By contrast, M. Manlius Capitolinus, a hero of Roman resistance to the Gauls in 390 or 387 B.C., is a historical figure whose fall is much more reliably attested than those of his fifth-century predecessors.[23] Moreover, Livy is surely right in recording a ban on the private houses of patricians on the Capitol at around the same time, although the connection with Manlius' disgrace is tenuous. The *cognomen* Capitolinus was associated with a number of patrician families, notably the Quinctii and Manlii, all of whom stopped using it by the middle of the fourth century.[24] It was a hereditary name connected with families who had private houses on the Capitol; since such families were all patricians, we may conclude that the ban was specifically passed against patricians. This change makes sense in the context of urban renewal and a decision to reserve the Capitol as a sacred space after the departure of the Gauls.

Meanwhile, the tradition about the destruction of the house of Manlius himself, and its subsequent replacement by the temple of Juno Moneta in 344 B.C., cannot be archaeologically confirmed despite recent studies of the area.[25] Rather it seems that the fourth-century temple of Juno was built on

THE ROMAN REPUBLIC

top of a sixth-century temple (also of Juno?). Because there is no identifiable trace of a domestic structure here or of the violent destruction of any building, suggestions that Manlius lived in the temple or in part of it, either during the siege or afterward, remain purely hypothetical. Meanwhile, the *cognomen* Capitolinus suggests the existence on the Capitol of a hereditary *domus* of the Manlii, which should have been a recognizably domestic structure.

On the other hand, the ban on the *praenomen* Marcus in the family of the Manlii is a much better attested memory sanction.[26] It can be shown to have been observed by the patrician Manlii, who had used the *praenomen* Marcus before that time. Such a tradition was typical of the practices of patrician *gentes* and of their family memories, as the patrician Claudii did not use the *praenomen* Lucius after two Claudii of that name had been found guilty of crimes. Perhaps significantly, Marcus was also the name of Manlius' opponent, Camillus. It is unclear whether the Manlii set the precedent for such a treatment of a *praenomen* in the 380s or whether it was already a traditional practice at that date.

What does seem clear is that Manlius' fall was a major event within the Roman community and that at least one type of sanction was imposed on his name by his family, who apparently advertised its decision.[27] In doing so, the family would have endorsed his execution, whatever exact form it had taken. It appears highly unlikely that the community intervened to destroy the family home of the Manlii at the same time. Rather, the fact that this was a moment when private houses in general were removed from the Capitol to make more space for old and new religious cults has become associated in a special way with the pretensions of Manlius and with his spectacular fall. The Manlii certainly survived Capitolinus' disgrace and remained a prominent and powerful family.

The very little evidence of memory sanctions in early Rome supports the notion that memory was conceived of as primarily the sphere of the family rather than of the state. The fact that two of the most prominent patrician *gentes*, the Claudii and the Manlii, did practice a ban on a *praenomen* for convicted criminals is notable and suggests an origin of such memory sanctions within the characteristic Roman naming pattern that linked the generations closely together. Meanwhile, it is significant that such a ban was not exclusively associated with a single political charge of treason in the way that memory sanctions came to be used in later Roman practice. Nor is it even explicitly connected with death or with exile as formal legal penalties. Rather, the family decided whom to celebrate and how, and whom to shun. Around the same time, the patrician families who had lived on the Capitol all seem to have decided to stop using the *cognomen* Capitolinus, perhaps of their own accord but possibly also under some pressure from the senate or perhaps under the shadow cast by Manlius' pretensions and disgrace in the eyes of the community.

Although the tradition about the destruction of houses in Rome rests on very shaky foundations, it was persistent for these and other early Roman figures.[28] It makes best sense in the case of Vitruvius Vaccus, not himself born a Roman citizen but an outsider who had acquired an unusual standing within the community. Vitruvius was executed in 329 B.C. after leading the resistance of the Volscian town of Privernum against Rome. Many early republican families, and especially the politically powerful aristocrats, owned inherited family houses, usually in strategic locations in the city. It is hard to imagine that many of these inherited *domus* were destroyed by order of the senate or of a magistrate as a result of a crime committed by a single family member. Such a penalty would have been a serious blow to the financial and social position of the whole *gens* and would have been strikingly at odds with the rest of early republican political culture. Clearly the Claudii and Manlii were not subjected to such a dramatic loss of status or resources in their early history.

Rather, the legends of such destruction grew as a result of etymological elaborations of traditional place-names and by analogy with Greek practices, since the houses of tyrants and aspirants to tyranny were regularly razed in Greek cities, even as whole families might be targeted for penalties and for exile from the community.[29] Such customs could be adduced to create a similar topography that warned against tyranny in Rome. In fact, the Roman Republic had been more successful in avoiding episodes of tyranny than the Greek cities, perhaps precisely by building an aristocratic consensus that limited excessive competition or fierce reprisals and that forged links between the powerful families and the community as a whole. Economic crises might create a situation where tyranny was feared, but Roman politics did not degenerate into civil conflict between rival warlords and their families during the early or middle Republic.

The well-known stories of the destruction of various early houses provide powerful evidence for anachronistic and Hellenizing distortions of early traditions. In particular, they suggest that there was a concerted attempt to build up an image of the man who wanted to seize power (*adfectator regni*), whose political ambitions could be retrospectively characterized and censored by means of the time-honored Greek penalty for tyrants, the razing of the house. Over time the accretions to these early episodes in Roman history in turn created an artificial topography of disgrace within the city itself that could serve as a rhetorical support for republican political values and could also stigmatize popular politics or the excessive power of the individual, who was construed as posing a threat to the whole community.[30]

Memory and the Political Culture of the Nobiles

Roman political culture changed decisively in the late fourth century B.C. with the rise of the nobility of office that replaced the traditional monopoly of the patrician families, whose members had previously been the only ones eligible for magisterial office or for priesthoods, and consequently for membership in the senate.[31] The new elite (*nobiles*) based its political status on the holding of high office and on wealth, while its members were drawn from the leading families of both the patricians and the plebeians. Their emergence in the late fourth and early third centuries was associated with the development of the culture of the classic Roman Republic and with its striking success as a Mediterranean power.[32] The internal strength of the Roman community, which allowed it first to resist the Carthaginians and then to build an overseas empire, was based on a balance of competition and cooperation, as individual *nobiles* took turns in office and debated policies in the senate. An increasingly elaborate and formalized set of rules and conventions allowed for controlled competition at elections and in achieving other prestigious awards, such as the right to celebrate a triumph after a military victory.

Within this republican political system, individuals and their families could achieve status and rank through a series of successes in election to high office, as well as through the subsequent public recognition of their achievements in these various civic functions. In a society where politics was generally agreed to be the most prestigious sphere of achievement, a family's profile was created through the sum of its individual members. The greater competition resulting from the introduction of plebeian magistrates created a dynamic atmosphere of emulation, accompanied by an ever increasingly creative display of personal valor and virtues.

Various mechanisms were developed to channel and to control this aristocratic competition, always with a view to keeping a single individual or family from gaining supreme power within the state, while at the same time designing the competition so that it would preserve a sizable number of established families within the system. Such habits of self-preservation have been especially recognized in repeated sumptuary legislation and in laws that prescribed acceptable senatorial life-styles.[33] These laws were primarily designed to protect senators from the need to expend their patrimony on wasteful competition for clients or votes. Maximum expenditures for all manner of items, as well as discouragement of luxuries, were crafted to limit conspicuous consumption and to conceal the widening gap between rich and poor. The ban on senatorial involvement in commerce, especially at sea, protected senators from the devastating losses that such speculative business ventures often brought with them. The Romans struggled for generations to try to ensure that rank and influence would never be ultimately or too publicly defined by money.

The suggestion that Roman society both should and did operate principally on the basis of traditional norms of behavior (which effectively limited competition to certain areas and which defined the rules of the game within those designated areas) was reinforced by the role of the censors as the most senior Roman magistrates.[34] From officials who merely recorded a list of citizens for census purposes, mainly connected with military needs, the censors developed in the late fourth century into magistrates with sweeping powers to criticize and to demote citizens from their rank in society, even as they also addressed general exhortations about correct conduct to their fellow Romans. The census itself took on an increasingly symbolic function, and the disapproval of the censor came to signify ruin and shame. This shame was intimately connected with the recording of the name and status of the citizen on the censors' list. A disgraced or demoted person would be marked with the *nota* of the censor, a mark of shame that could be accompanied by a written explanation of the reason why the man was judged unworthy of his previous position in society.[35]

At the same time, a man's name would be removed from the list of those in his class, a list that was solemnly read aloud at the conclusion of the census. For a senator, a demotion would result in his name being removed from the list of those enrolled in the senate. Reasons for such demotions included dereliction of duty, issues of inappropriate life-style, moral turpitude, loss of wealth, and conviction on a criminal charge. The actions of the censors nearly always applied to elite males, and thus the censors functioned as a kind of further guarantee of senatorial behavior and life-style. It is characteristic of the rhetoric of Roman disgrace that demotion by the censors involved both an erasure from a previous position of prominence and a simultaneous mark of shame that recorded the individual's ruin.

Meanwhile, accepted aristocratic norms protected most defeated generals from suffering consequences even after serious military losses.[36] Defeats could be conveniently explained in terms of the behavior of the troops or the will of the gods, leaving the general to continue with his career in all but the most egregious cases of incompetence or willful negligence. His peers in the senate effectively accommodated his losses on the understanding that he might do or had done the same for them. The treatment of defeated generals operated in a way very similar to sumptuary legislation, serving to preserve the sphere of the *nobiles* and to protect against careers' being ruined either by risky financial speculations or by bad luck on the battlefield.

In this context memory played a decisive and central role, for both patricians and plebeians. Whereas each politician needed to keep his achievements in the public eye in order to advance his career during his own lifetime, a related goal of equal importance was to leave behind a favorable memory of his life that would enhance his family's standing and help his relatives gain access to similar or to even greater honors.[37] It is striking that many families were successful in producing magistrates, especially consuls, over numerous generations, in patterns that attested not only to their own resourcefulness but also to the stability and efficiency of the system as a whole.

The term *nobilis*, used to describe the aristocrat defined by political office, originally meant no more than "well known" or "notable."[38] In other words, the Roman political elite defined themselves semantically in terms of publicity, rather than of public service or wealth or birth. Status was defined by public face — in other words, by dress, status symbols, and customs that set senators apart from other Romans, regardless of how rich or wellborn the others might be. At the same time as this political culture was developing, there came into being the monuments, public spectacles, and habits that distinguished a Roman politician during his lifetime and that aimed to preserve his memory after death. Such memory devices were not separable from the political system and were owned by the *nobiles* as a social caste. In other words, Roman memory was political memory: Roman republican history was synonymous with the gentilitial traditions and pretensions of the office-holding families. Significantly, once narrative historiography came into being in the early second century, it was written by senators.

The types of cultural artifacts that (re)produced Roman political memory included the texts of inscriptions, public buildings that were mostly erected by victorious generals (temples, basilica), victory monuments, family tombs, historical paintings (often kept in temples), honorific statues, and public processions such as those at games and at triumphs.[39] Nearly all of these had to be approved by the senate and were consequently limited to officeholders. Competition was fierce but was limited to a restricted circle of elite senators. At an early stage of this process, the status of the holder of curule office seems to have become associated with his right to an *imago*, a wax mask portraying him in a recognizable manner. This mask, although probably made during his lifetime, was first seen at a magistrate's own funeral, worn by an actor who was marked out with the symbols of the highest political office the politician had held, and subsequently at the funerals of all his officeholding relatives. When not in use at a funeral, the mask was stored in a cupboard (*aediculum*) in the *atrium* of the family home, where it was often put on display and was identified with a label (*titulus*) that also recorded a summary of the decedent's career. Polybius was especially struck by the funeral rights of Roman politicians, which allowed them to honor the dead man in the context of a vivid and spectacular recreation of family history and to bring their history to life in a way that reaffirmed the shared values and aims of the community as a whole.

The Roman nobility of office was perhaps unique in having its ultimate symbol of status be a type of portrait (*imago*) that was purely commemorative and that only appeared after death. In other words, being a *nobilis* meant more than being "known" in one's own lifetime: it entailed being "remembered" in a specific way after death. All citizens were traditionally invited to such a man's funeral, and thus the full value of this "fame" could only really be realized after death. Just as a man's identity was thought of in terms of his face and its recognition by his fellow citizens, that identity and recognition were then immortalized by his mask and its public display.[40] Polybius saw such postmortem tributes as essential to the Roman spirit of public service and sacrifice. The special mask-portrait enjoyed pride of place in the family home to impress visitors and future generations of family members. Such cultivation of memory created a "living" tradition that would be known to many of all ages and backgrounds within the city. Only the elected politician could enjoy this special *memoria* that defined the story of the community as a whole at the same time as it described his personal identity. Initially only memory, rather than what we would call history, founded the political community of the *nobiles*, and that memory was the ultimate goal of the individual both for himself and for his extended family.

The *memoria* of the *nobiles* was pervasive in Rome, both in public and in domestic settings. It functioned as a means of both competition and cooperation. The example of the individual allowed him to be compared with others in his own family and in other families, from all ages of the city's past. In this sense elite memory was essentially ahistorical, even as it created and recreated parades of "ancestors" from every age, who reappeared within the city in the ever-timeless present of each funeral procession.[41] Yet, such spectacles went well beyond the mere calculation of individual merit to reaffirm the strength of each family and of the political system as a whole. All could share in the celebration of memory and in the sense of the community. Death served to reaffirm life and continuity, perhaps most poignantly in the funeral eulogy that was often delivered by a young family member making his first public appearance.

The creation and maintenance of this memory culture was primarily the responsibility of each family, in consultation with sympathetic peers in the senate. No firm delineation existed between public and private spheres, and the family arranged the funerals and worked to preserve buildings and monuments put up by earlier generations. While the senate had to agree in each case to the initial grant of a statue in a public place, or of a temple, or of a triumph, the memory of each would be cultivated and celebrated by the family. Eventually the censors might also reprimand families that did not maintain their traditional cults and buildings, but we have very little information about how often this actually happened. Most likely, the family, and especially the *paterfamilias* and his *consilium*, shaped the family's memorial traditions in each generation.

Memoria *and* Oblivio

In Rome, memory sanctions developed slowly and within the sphere of family influence. They were related above all to the image the family wanted to convey within the city and, to a lesser extent, within the Roman sphere of influence as a whole. Most citizens simply did not have access to commemoration of any formal or honorific sort, since the creation of *memoria* within the city was the purview of the *nobiles*, those who were known in public. Initially, sanctions related to the creation of memory were also needed, as the choice of what to remember inevitably also included a proportionate choice about what was not worth commemorating. Because each family and the senators as a caste were highly motivated to present the best possible image of their past glory, the kinds of traditions to be found in published eulogies were often embellished.[42] Conversely, families might also decide to edit failures, sometimes by choosing not to recall a family member who had been disgraced or who had simply not achieved high office. By definition, *memoria* recalled the successful and famous rather than the obscure and unsuccessful. In practice, every gentilitial tradition focused on officeholders to the exclusion of those who died young or who failed to be elected — in other words, those who had not earned the right to be represented by an *imago* after death.[43]

Relatively few attested examples of such family editing have come down to us, but those that have survived are suggestive of norms of behavior that were largely hidden from public view and from posterity. The family of the patrician Cornelii offers several examples. The most striking is the erasure on the third-century sarcophagus of L. Cornelius Scipio Barbatus from the tomb of the Scipios near the Via Appia (figure 9).[44] Despite the fact that this sarcophagus was the most splendid in the tomb and memorialized the founder of this family group in a central location of the burial chamber, the first two verses of Barbatus' epitaph had been carefully erased some time later. The erasure is obvious, and the partial survival of a horizontal line at the end of the erasure proves that the section that was removed formed part of the same verse text. Moreover, the erased part of the stone shows signs of small flecks of red paint like that used to highlight the surviving letters. Because the family had exclusive access to the tomb, which would usually have been closed and which went out of use before the last generations of the Republic, the erasure can only have been carried out during the middle Republic on the instructions of the family. The erasure in Barbatus' epitaph poses an as yet unsolved problem, especially since the extant text contains his full name and his career; no expected elements are obviously missing, a fact that may suggest that an unusual claim has been removed.

It is hard to believe that a formulaic opening of some kind, containing a general claim to excellence, was erased merely because it was used by others. In fact, such a formula would have been more likely to have been preserved. At the same time, the whole text would have been eulogistic, as are all the inscriptions from the tomb: nothing negative could have been recorded in this funerary context. Rather, the family must have decided that the opening of the epitaph no longer fit in with its current version of Barbatus' life and of its general picture of family history in the early third century. The erasure must have removed a specific claim, perhaps to be the first in some field. If the claim was removed here, in a private family context, it was presumably also removed in more public places, by the rewriting of other inscriptions or of the *titulus* for Barbatus' *imago*. In any case, it is striking that one of the very earliest Latin texts we have should contain an erasure, thereby suggesting that the habit of editing was perhaps as old as that of writing on stone itself. Moreover, the erasure did not target a man who had been disgraced, but rather someone whose story needed to be "updated" in some way. At the same time the reason must have been pressing, since it caused such a blatant marring of the earliest, longest, and most prominently displayed of the family eulogies in the tomb.

FIGURE 9. Sarcophagus and epitaph of L. Cornelius Scipio Barbatus,
Tomb of the Scipios, Via Appia, Rome. Erasure of the first two lines of verse,
leaving six more verses intact. *Musei Vaticani, archivio fotografico
neg. no. XVIII.19.12,* CIL *6.31587 =* ILS *1 =* ILLRP *309.*

A related phenomenon can be seen in the same tomb on the epitaph of a
Publius Scipio who was *flamen Dialis* (figure 10).[45] This individual was originally commemorated as if he had died young and had held no offices or honors at all. He was simply labeled as someone who would have surpassed the
glorious tradition of the ancestors if he had lived. At a later point a first line
was squeezed into the limited available space in smaller letters that are not
aligned with the main text, which recalled that he had held the office of *flamen Dialis*. This addition, which was written by a different hand, effectively
changes the whole tone of the commemoration and suggests that his rank as
a priest and senator had simply been passed over in silence before. It is possible that this Publius was a son of Scipio Africanus, and that his state of health
precluded a political career. In that case, Publius' adopted son Aemilianus
may have been the one to add the additional line to dignify the memory of
his father. Africanus' son Publius, however, was augur and the holding of two
such priesthoods would be very unusual.[46] Alternatively, and perhaps more
plausibly, this Publius may be a Scipio who is otherwise undocumented.

Africanus himself had insisted on the promotion of his much less gifted
brother Lucius and demanded that Lucius be given the command against
Antiochus III in Asia Minor (with himself as deputy). In a famous scene in
the senate, Africanus apparently tore up Lucius' account books from the war

FIGURE 10. Epitaph of P. Cornelius Scipio, *flamen Dialis*, Tomb of the Scipios, Via Appia, Rome. First line added later to an original text of only six lines. *Musei Vaticani, archivio fotografico neg. no. III.18.23,* CIL 6.37039 = ILS 4 = ILLRP 311.

in Asia rather than render an account to his fellow senators.[47] Meanwhile, Africanus' own possible disgrace and withdrawal from Rome at the end of his life remain essentially unexplained.[48] It seems, however, that the prominence of the family following Africanus' defeat of Hannibal caused some internal tensions over how the family should present itself in public. This included limits placed by the family on Africanus' sons, who were perceived as not living up to their father's heritage, perhaps simply because of poor health but possibly also for other reasons. In any case, it was recorded that the family deprived a son of Africanus (probably Lucius, pr. 174 B.C.) of the right to wear and use a signet ring with a portrait of his father on it.[49] The same incident is related to the family's interference with this Scipio's exercise of his magisterial office. The principle of taking turns in office depended on an adequate pool of qualified candidates from elite families. As a result, the system worked best for everyone if the political families discouraged weaker members from seeking high office and public recognition. Their own control of family memory also meant that they did not need to advertise how many had fallen short, but could focus on creating an image of unbroken successes or of promising youths who had died tragically young.

The family traditions of the Claudii, already referred to, should also be recalled here.[50] The family's decision to stop using the name Lucius after two men of this name had been criminals proved that a family might adopt strategies that were essentially independent of specific legal penalties. The ban on a *praenomen* suggests the exemplary function of Roman naming patterns, as each generation was encouraged and expected to imitate those of the same name. Equally, banning a name could help to remove the memory of previous generations that would no longer be recalled in this way. The effectiveness of such a ban depended on a family consensus about naming patterns across many generations. Like the examples mentioned previously, the decisions taken by the family presuppose a mechanism for shaping policies, presumably within a family *consilium*. The creation and cultivation of memory and identity were group exercises, whether to promote or to obscure certain individuals or episodes from the past.

None of the narrative histories we have seem to be purely gentilitial products; rather they were shaped by a variety of historiographic influences and conventions. Similarly, we do not have access to detailed information about any specific funerals, and the surviving fragments of funeral speeches are meager. However, it seems clear that leading figures of the past could be subject to increasingly complex traditions that might be both positive and negative, as their descendants struggled for power, sometimes in direct opposition to rival families, which would want to promote their own ancestors.

A convenient example is provided by the traditions about M. Claudius Marcellus, the conqueror of Syracuse.[51] A controversial figure in his own lifetime, Marcellus became a subject of tremendous debate during the second century, as Romans struggled to assimilate or to resist the influence of Greek culture. Marcellus was especially remembered for the booty he had brought back from Syracuse and for his display of it within the city. On the other hand, his unexpected and disastrous death in an ambush also created heated debate over whether he had offended the gods and should be seen as an example of impiety and incompetence. Eulogy competed directly with vituperation, and both sides produced accounts that were distorted and increasingly removed from the historical and cultural context of the later third century. The traditions about Marcellus' life and career reveal a number of tendencies that developed over the two centuries between the ambush that ended his life and the time when Livy felt overwhelmed by the intricate and contradictory narratives about his end.[52] Marcellus' deeds were subject both to denigration and to erasure or omission, most notably in the account of Polybius, who is particularly negative about Marcellus. At the same time, the continued prominence of the Marcelli fostered elaboration of a hagiographic tradition about him and even about his death, which culminated with the funeral eulogy delivered by Augustus for his nephew Marcellus, in which the *princeps* suggested that Marcellus' ashes had been returned to the family by Hannibal in a silver urn.

In this way, the past and memory itself were increasingly a battleground in the struggles over contemporary issues. Rather than speaking about innovation or about the future as a context for present action, Roman rhetoric expressed its debates in terms of the past and within culturally determined frameworks of praise or blame of past individuals. Historiography was a particular venue for these debates, but it was not isolated from the same issues as explored in oratory, family spectacle and iconography, and in the monuments and visual culture of the city. Such typically Roman "memories" of Marcellus as an exemplary figure, either of excellence or of dishonor, became increasingly anachronistic and distorted by the political debates of later generations. Marcellus' booty was not exceptional, even in his own day, nor was he the only Roman general killed by Hannibal in an ambush: yet he became the example of each of these things in a way that would not necessarily have been predicted during his own lifetime.[53] Like the sarcophagus of Barbatus, the traditions surrounding Marcellus took on new controversial meanings that led to a rewriting of the past, completely outside the context of a formal disgrace.

Influences on Roman Memory Sanctions

Memory sanctions within Roman culture had arisen under the influence of a variety of very different needs and pressures. Of these, five forces seem to have been most powerful in the shaping of Roman memory and disgrace during the middle Republic: the family practices of the *nobiles* in their efforts to maintain and to enhance their family's standing in politics; the public scrutiny and disgrace imposed by society (the senate) on the political elite (especially through the agency of the censors); the development of public vituperation in oratory and historiography; the encounter with Greek and Hellenistic examples of memory sanctions outside Italy; and the rhetoric of empire, as Rome came to play an increasingly dominant role in the Mediterranean. Rome itself, through the agency of its generals, was engaged in rewriting the history and political geography of its world, which included an account of Rome's own place in it and the meaning of its actions in relation to what had come before.

The first three sources of influence are closely interrelated in a system of time-honored practices. The role of the family was traditional but surely changed significantly with the introduction of the new elite of the *nobiles*. It was now possible for a family to rise into the political class through merit and achievement. However, the accompanying conditions also meant that families could lose their position in ways that had been rare in a closed hereditary system of power. Increased competition meant that prestige had to be emphasized and displayed in as many new ways as possible; failures could be more serious than in the past, for the system as a whole and even for established families. As noted previously, limits on competition soon evolved and continued to be a perennial concern of the senate throughout the Republic. Meanwhile, the new role of the censors in determining who was and who was not to be in the senate encouraged and reinforced a family's own processes of self-selection. At the same time, rhetoric and historiography developed to express political competition but remained in the hands of the political families. The power to speak in public, or to commission public performances, was a carefully guarded monopoly of the elected magistrates during their year in office.[54]

By contrast, the last two of the five factors relate to the role of Romans outside their own home territory and culture. Here again modes of thought were initially absorbed and reinterpreted primarily by senators, and especially by the most prominent among them, who were the ones to travel outside Italy and to shape Roman diplomatic discourse overseas. Roman politicians came into regular contact with examples of Greek memory sanctions, especially during the second century B.C. Roman intervention led directly to erasures of past patrons so that the new political balance of power could be inscribed. The Romans may or may not have overtly encouraged such sanctions; in either case, they benefited from them.

Roman senators changed their way of living as a result of Rome's expansion in the East, in terms of life-style, literary culture, religious practices, domestic architecture, and material culture in general. New uses of memory, erasure, and history fit into this overall pattern of cultural development, as Romans adopted and adapted Greek customs to accommodate them within their own traditional practices. It is said that in the early third century B.C. Kineas, the envoy of King Pyrrhus of Epirus, had already called the Roman senate an assembly of kings.[55] Certainly, a century later the image and life-style of leading senators and their families was increasingly assimilated to the splendor of Hellenistic court life. These were the men who defeated and dictated terms to the Hellenistic monarchs, whose inherited wealth became their personal booty.

In this context, the monument of L. Aemilius Paullus at Delphi can illustrate the evolving attitude of the Romans and their decision to insert themselves into the political space previously occupied by a Hellenistic monarch (figures 11, 12).[56] The monument apparently consisted of a single large rectangular column with a detailed frieze of Romans fighting Macedonians. On top it carried a bronze equestrian statue depicting Paullus as the victorious general. The simple inscription (found in front of the temple of Apollo at Delphi) labels it as a booty monument, and indeed as booty itself. Aemilius Paullus is described as the agent, and he takes full credit, without any mention of Rome. As *imperator* he puts himself on an equal if not a superior footing to Perseus, who is named as king. Originally the column had been designed and started by Perseus, king of Macedon. Its position at Delphi, however, served to advertise the glory of the final victor, in this case Paullus rather than Perseus. The symbolic importance of the monument is further revealed by the magnificent frieze, which illustrates known details of the battle of Pydna in 168 B.C., which marked Paullus' decisive defeat of the Macedonians. Paullus must himself have commissioned the frieze, and he must have been involved in redesigning the monument to place himself and Rome's conquest in this Panhellenic context. The monument would have gained its full meaning from its prominent context in the sanctuary and near many other victory monuments from every age of Greek history. At the same time, Paullus was doing much more than saving money by appropriating the monument of Perseus. He was erasing the previous image of Perseus and replacing it with an image of his defeat, reshaped in terms of Roman victory. Yet this victory monument also memorialized Paullus himself, in place of Perseus and as if he were his successor. It was this same Paullus who remarked on the need to use spectacle and publicity as much as armies in defeating one's enemies.

A generation later, the year 146 B.C. saw the ultimate use of erasure by the Romans in their bid for a Mediterranean empire. That year witnessed the virtually simultaneous destruction of two of the oldest and most famous cities of the Mediterranean, Corinth and Carthage.[57] In both cases the looting and subsequent destruction were deliberate and planned, not a result of accidental fire or a by-product of the final stages of a siege. Rather both cities were captured first and then destroyed, with the deliberate intention of creating an erasure that would memorialize Roman military and political might. The position of both cities, with great harbors and inherited trade networks, balanced the expanding spheres of Roman might in Africa and in Greece. The timing was calculated to inaugurate a new era, even as older eras of counting by the age of these other cities (both by tradition older than Rome) were brought to an end. The Romans imitated and outdid the legendary Greek destruction of Troy immortalized by Homer, as well as the conquests of an Alexander or a Demetrius who could be engaged in only one such siege at a time. They were memorializing their very ability to wage a successful war on two fronts against very different enemies.

FIGURE 11. L. Aemilius Paullus' monument at Delphi: inscription, c. 168 B.C.
Drawing by Leslie Rae Witt, CIL *1.622 =* ILS *8884 =* ILLRP *323.*

Meanwhile, the Romans wrote their own ending to their long struggle
with Carthage, an ending that was then reflected back on the very different
story of the third-century conflicts. They also recast their cultural borrow-
ings, whether in the form of Corinthian art or of Carthaginian technical and
agricultural knowledge, once those places of origin no longer existed to recall
earlier contexts and meanings. Their own city had grown during the second
century, but its size and splendor were reinterpreted by the destruction of the
two other great cities, cast as rivals in the rhetoric of empire. Whereas Paullus
was imitating Perseus by stepping into his shoes, Mummius and Scipio Aemilianus went several steps further by wiping whole cities and their political
cultures off the map. The impact and message of erasure had been thoroughly
debated and embraced in the Roman senate by the 140s B.C. Its destructive
force would soon be felt within the sphere of Rome's own domestic politics.

Disgrace and the Manlii

This investigation of memory sanctions in the middle Republic concludes
with a consideration of the sanctions imposed in a single memorable instance. A sense of continuity within families and within the community as a
whole could be especially expressed by the removal of those who were judged
not fit to carry on the traditions of the past. General trends and cultural habits were usually experienced one case at a time. The patrician Manlii provide

FIGURE 12. L. Aemilius Paullus' monument at Delphi: reliefs, c. 168 B.C.
Drawing by Leslie Rae Witt, CIL 1.622 = ILS 8884 = ILLRP 323.

the most compelling example, since their practices of disgrace stand both at the beginning and at the end of the classic Republic.[58] The ruin of M. Manlius Capitolinus in the early fourth century marks the very beginning of any historical account of Roman disgrace: it became synonymous with the refounding of the city after the Gallic sack. Yet his disgrace contained a glorious element: because it had resulted from his greatness and his influence, qualities that made him a threat to the community, his memory surely continued to be cultivated by his family, and Cicero suggests that at the end of the Republic the family did indeed display a mask representing him in its *atria*.[59]

The proud traditions of this family were reenacted in 140 B.C. in the disgrace of D. Junius Silanus (who had been born a Manlius).[60] Junius was found guilty of extortion in Macedonia, where he had served as praetor in 141. Upon his return to Rome, he was convicted and committed suicide after being censured by his father, T. Manlius Torquatus (cos. 165 B.C.). Torquatus subsequently did not attend the son's funeral but held his own *salutatio* that morning in his house, as if it were a day no different from any other. On this occasion, the father was said to have been inspired by the sight of the *imagines* of his ancestors to feel that he had behaved correctly and that the system of family memory provided him with the examples he needed to make appropriate choices in times of need. The scene of the censorious father in his *atrium*, contemplating the masks of the ancestors and their function in his house, has much to tell us about Roman political culture.

Torquatus had imposed the most extreme disgrace on his son, whose funeral did not reflect his status as a senator of praetorian rank. The son was not represented by a mask himself, and his funeral was not accompanied by the masks of his ancestors, indicating that he was no longer a family member and would not be recalled in any of the usual ways in the future. Moreover, his death was not mourned in his family home, and his body had not been laid out there. Rather the cupboard doors stood open in the *atrium* so that

THE ROMAN REPUBLIC

anyone could see that the ancestors were neither in mourning nor present at his funeral. The implication is that Junius was not buried in a family tomb and his status was that of a person who had been disinherited. It seems most likely that none of his relatives attended his funeral.[61]

Consequently, it emerges that the family was still in a position, and perhaps even expected, to impose disgrace on a member who had proved unworthy. Suicide offered no reprieve. Once the family had banished Junius from its gentilitial memory, he effectively also lost all posthumous recognition of the status he had had as a citizen and a magistrate. It was as if he had never been born, or had been born into an obscure family of paupers. This extreme form of erasure contrasts rather starkly with the self-satisfaction of his father Manlius Torquatus, whose own behavior now offered an example of revived family tradition. In other words, the erasure of one member could be seen to leave the family intact — or possibly even in a better position — for having lived up to the stern example of earlier ancestors. Memory sanctions were presented as part of the traditions of Rome's oldest families, the patricians. At the same time, the interests of the family and of the community were represented as coinciding perfectly, so that the one supported the other — even as the old families were recognized as repositories of Rome's finest and most upright ways of behaving. Meanwhile, the outcome of this story was not expressed in terms of legal penalties, and the senate apparently did not communicate with the family or comment on its actions. No role was left for the censors in this case. One can read Junius' disgrace as a statement by the family that its own time-honored ways of dealing with an offender were much more effective than any conviction in the new public extortion court.[62]

The family traditions of the Manlii reveal the complex position of memory sanctions by the late second century B.C. Such sanctions still essentially belonged to the families: because the families created memory, they also were the ones to destroy it. The more ancient the family, the greater the loss for the outcast, as the spectacle of memory would have been so much grander. Yet, arguably the Manlii themselves could more easily afford to sacrifice any one member, even a praetor, precisely because of their established position. Office and rank in society were not created within the family but in the public sphere of politics and elections. However, the commemoration of that rank, which actually comprised its ultimate expression, belonged to the family. Meanwhile, society as a whole could be said to benefit by the removal of the offender. Memory sanctions after public conviction expressed a powerful consensus between the family and the senate or the courts, as all had come to an agreement about the egregious nature of the offense.

The father Manlius maintained his rank and *auctoritas* as an ex-consul, by sacrificing his relationship with his son to a standard that could be expressed equally well either in terms of gentilitial tradition or of the expectations and values (*mores*) of the community. Such disgrace demonstrated that ultimately there was no difference between family identity and a man's identity within the community of citizens. Roman history could be envisioned and represented as synonymous with gentilitial tradition. There was no distinction between public memory and private memory in the cultural world of republican senators. While the republican oligarchy was fully functional, memory sanctions offered an invaluable and characteristically Roman safety valve to preserve both the family and the political status quo, expressed above all by the aristocratic consensus in a senate composed of peers. The use of memory sanctions was not necessarily related to a specific charge or to the death penalty, which was not frequently used during the Republic, especially against elites. Yet nothing could be more striking than the contrast between the treatment of D. Junius Silanus in 140 by his family and the punitive sanctions imposed on Gaius Gracchus, Fulvius Flaccus, and others barely twenty years later. Those new sanctions expressed and exacerbated the profound political rift that had opened in Roman society, a rift that was marked by brutal violence and by the suspension of laws and norms of consensus that for so many generations had provided the framework for memory and disgrace.

Punitive Memory Sanctions I
The Breakdown of the Republican Consensus

▾   ▾   ▾

Et Sextus Titius, quod habuit imaginem
Lucii Saturnini domi suae, condemnatus est.
Cicero, *Pro Rabirio Perduellionis Reo* 24

Et M. Flacci et L. Saturnini seditiosissimorum
civium corporibus trucidatis penates ab
imis fundamentis eruti sunt.
Valerius Maximus 6.3.1c

The study of memory, habits of commemoration, and sanctions against memory offers a revealing perspective from which to view the increasing chaos and breakdown that characterized Roman political life in the period from 133 to 43 B.C. Traditionally the so-called crisis of the Republic is described as starting with the tribunate and violent death of Tiberius Sempronius Gracchus in 133 B.C.[1] In a history of memory, however, the decisive break comes after the suicide of Tiberius' brother Gaius Gracchus in 121 B.C., when punitive memory sanctions were first deployed by the senate. The sanctions, when combined with simultaneous summary executions and confiscations of property, represented an attack on the social, political, and economic status of the targeted individuals and their whole families and effected a dramatic rupture with previous practices. In this new climate, members of the political elite in the senate now attempted to eliminate their rivals through disgrace and/or erasure after death. The character of Roman politics was permanently transformed by these aggressive memory wars within domestic partisan conflicts, which led to the increasingly frequent practice of erasing or damning the memory and achievements of Roman citizens of the highest social class. The punitive sanctions forged in the struggles of the late Republic would go on to be used both by and against the emperor, once a system of one-man rule had been established.

The close connection between the development of such punitive sanctions and the deterioration of the characteristic republican system of government based on political consensus is especially noteworthy. The senate now dictated memory sanctions to elite families through new kinds of resolutions and laws: both the family and the individual found themselves in a different relationship with the senate and with the other leading political families in a shifting landscape of power politics. Yet this shift occurred without the Roman *paterfamilias* losing any of his traditional wide-ranging powers to enforce his will on the members of his family and his household.[2] Punitive sanctions did not emerge suddenly in a single moment of crisis or as the weapon of one particular faction or social group. Rather these penalties developed slowly and piecemeal in response to a series of violent conflicts and to increasing general civil instability. Sanctions were used to try to restore order and control in a community that had lost its sense of balance and cohesion, and which was unable to find mechanisms for mediating civil discord. Such mechanisms, whether traditional or new, were designed to avoid the deployment of illegal violence or the arbitrary use of force in a state of emergency — in other words, the recourse to political action outside traditional constitutional norms.

Punitive memory sanctions designed to control contemporary civil strife defined it in terms of a conflict between right and wrong, or rather between legitimate leaders and discredited outlaws. The removal of the outlaw(s) (former citizens) from communal memory served to (re)affirm the final political solution of the day and to defuse recent partisan conflicts, while justifying whatever actions had been taken to restore order. Meanwhile, such punitive measures rarely seem to have had the desired effect either of (re)creating political unity or of prompting people to move on from partisan strife. Rather, memories of the disgraced haunted generations of their successors, even as they in turn continued to use the same or even more elaborate memory sanctions against their own political opponents.

The Invention of Punitive Memory Sanctions in 121 B.C.

Many writers, both ancient and modern, treat the Gracchi brothers together, and hence give their name to a single program of reform or to an identifiable era.[3] This approach is compounded by the pronounced use of hindsight in viewing these second-century tribunes in light of subsequent developments over the next seventy years or so. By contrast, an investigation focused on memory and commemoration immediately and decisively brings out the difference between the brothers, their programs, and how they were treated by their contemporaries, most notably their opponents. Gaius committed suicide when a state of emergency was declared after he and his followers had seized the Aventine section of Rome.[4] Many have interpreted his final actions as open revolt, which caused the consul Lucius Opimius to pass the first *senatus consultum ultimum*, thereby calling citizens and soldiers to arms against the Gracchan insurgents. The final clash was not caused by a specific piece of legislation or by a disputed election. Rather Gaius was a private citizen whose use of massed supporters, violent rhetoric and actions, and apparent secession called forth a response, albeit an unprecedented and harsh one, from the consul who was the chief executive officer and most senior army commander. Although not officially an outlaw, Gaius apparently did have a price on his head (under what legal circumstances remains unclear), a price that was then paid to the person who actually did present Gaius' head to Opimius.[5]

Gaius was not designated, either formally or informally, as an "enemy" of Rome. However, he was the first aristocratic citizen to be treated as such, initially in the use of the formal emergency decree of the senate and the mobilization of special forces troops (Cretan archers) against him, and subsequently in the extensive postmortem penalties imposed on his social status, his political legacy, and his memory. The clash between Gaius Gracchus and Lucius Opimius had had every appearance of a civil war, with opposing sides holding different parts of the city and some heavy fighting in the streets involving weapons. For the first time, the senior magistrates in office had attacked a group of Roman citizens in their own native city. These citizens were then judged to have effectively forfeited their status as Romans and to merit being removed from the collective memory and record of the city.

The difference between the treatment of Gaius and what had happened to Tiberius could hardly be more striking and suggestive. In other words, if we fail to distinguish between the fates of the two brothers, we miss the whole impact of their violent deaths. Tiberius was not killed by a consul, or in connection with any senatorial resolution, or even with weapons. Ancient sources stress that no weapon was used but that his attackers broke up furniture in order to make use of chair legs as cudgels.[6] Nor were any formal memory sanctions imposed on Tiberius after his death. Indeed, the consul P. Mucius Scaevola had refused to move against Tiberius, despite the likelihood that the latter would be elected to an illegal consecutive term as tribune of the plebs. The consul, a legal expert, asserted his own confidence that any contravention of the law or of constitutional practice could be invalidated through due procedure, if and when it occurred. If he later justified the killings, as Cicero claims that he did, these second thoughts reflected his desire to put an end to strife rather than a reasoned repudiation of his earlier legal opinion.[7]

On his own initiative and purely on the basis of his religious office, the *pontifex maximus* P. Cornelius Scipio Nasica, who was a private citizen, led a group of senators to attack Gracchus and his followers. He caused one of the other tribunes of the plebs, Publius Satureius, to be the first to strike Tiberius down, although Tiberius was a sacrosanct tribune still in office, and perhaps in the very act of praying or having just prayed to inaugurate an assembly of the people in front of the temple of Jupiter Optimus Maximus on the Capitol. The main responsibility for what happened is ascribed in the ancient sources to the *pontifex maximus* Nasica, who led the killers of Tiberius.[8] He was aided by at least one, perhaps several, of Tiberius' fellow tribunes, as well as by the aedile of the plebs Lucretius, who was responsible for throwing the corpses into the Tiber, thus denying burial to those who had been murdered.[9] Because this violence decisively contravened Roman religious and cultural norms, it was recognized as marking a decisive rift in the life of the Roman community.

Scaevola was right: whereas an illegal election assembly and its result could have been declared invalid, the killing of a sacred tribune of the plebs on consecrated ground during an inaugurated assembly of the people caused a scandal and breach of civic life that could not be undone. The fact that the man responsible for the deaths, whether he took an active role himself or not, was Tiberius' first cousin merely added another dimension of pollution, for the sacrosanct blood that had been shed was also kindred blood. It was surely Nasica himself who refused the family's request for the body of Tiberius, despite the fact that they had apparently offered to bury the body quietly that same night, thus forgoing the usual aristocratic funeral with its political overtones and elaborate public spectacle.[10]

It is implausible that the attack on Tiberius' assembly was unplanned or that Tiberius was killed by accident in a chaotic scene of rioting.[11] No ancient source suggests this, nor did discussion of the events after they had happened ever indicate that anyone even tried to make such an argument. Rather these deaths were deliberately caused by Nasica, who went to the senate that day with a plan he intended to put into action, and surely also with some accomplices who were fully aware of that plan. Should Scaevola fail to take the lead against Tiberius — an event that cannot itself have been completely unexpected in senatorial circles — Nasica had every intention of intervening. The other consul, L. Calpurnius Piso Frugi, was in Sicily dealing with the ongoing slave war, which culminated in the siege of Henna.[12] As a result, Scaevola was the leading magistrate in Rome at the time of Tiberius' death. He represented the chief executive authority in the city and had, in addition, considerable personal standing (*auctoritas*) as a legal expert. Nasica could not have expected anyone to follow him if he, a private citizen, had simply made a political claim to power that supplanted the authority of the consul Scaevola. Such an action would have been even more egregious than Tiberius' election to a second, continuous tribunate, for it would have been a completely illegal seizure of supreme power. Instead, Nasica had to take the lead based on his position as *pontifex maximus*, making a claim to religious authority, insofar as such authority could be perceived as independent of political power in Rome. Nasica was certainly fully aware of the religious taboos he was breaking: he needed a religious justification in order to undertake such a bold action in the first place.

Accounts of Tiberius' last day are not as detailed or as reliable as could be wished, but the reaction to his death can help explain it in its contemporary context. The very horror of what happened forced the senate, and perhaps even Scaevola himself, to close ranks and try to justify events. This reaction led to senatorial support for Nasica and prosecution of more adherents of Tiberius Gracchus, including his Greek teachers who were probably not Roman citizens.[13] It is suggestive that at least one follower of Gracchus, P. Villius, a Roman citizen, was apparently executed in an unusual ritual that involved being shut in with poisonous snakes. These trials have the appearance of events staged for high publicity in the city. In other words, the senate approved, or at least permitted, a series of measures designed to inspire fear in any who might sympathize with Tiberius and to preclude open debate. At the show trials Tiberius Gracchus was characterized by Nasica and others as a man who was dangerous and who had been on the point of seizing power in the state at the time of his death. Such trials served to recall earlier moments of crisis in Rome — for example, the special measures taken by the consuls and senate in 186 B.C. against followers of a Bacchic initiation cult, which was also presented as a type of conspiracy.[14] At the same time, there is no reason to think that very many people were executed or exiled as a result of these legal proceedings. Most of the casualties occurred on the same day of Tiberius' own death.

The political rhetoric of the show trials and of senatorial endorsement of Nasica can be taken as a measure of the strength of elite support for Tiberius' suppression, or at least of fear of its consequences. In fact, it is essential not to allow this rhetoric to obscure the profound and wide-ranging negative reaction among Roman citizens against the murder of a tribune, and the attendant loss of control of the situation by those officially in power. Nasica himself was forced to leave the city because of the outcry and sense of revulsion against him.[15] He went on an embassy to Pergamum, where he died, probably in the following year. No statue of Nasica was to be seen in Rome until the 50s B.C. His death abroad was just one of many events that were seen at the time as portents and omens of the serious religious rupture that had been caused within the Roman community. Popular unrest can be related not only to Nasica's departure but also to a whole series of prodigies, as well as to emotional statements and appeals at public meetings (*contiones*) representing a variety of political reactions.[16] The pressure on the senatorial elite was both political and religious. Although Scipio Aemilianus returned from Spain covered with glory after capturing Numantia, he quickly lost popularity in Rome when he appeared to condemn Tiberius in a public meeting, after being questioned by a tribune about the murder of his brother-in-law (and cousin) by another cousin.[17]

The senate decided to consult the Sybilline Books, which were kept in the temple of Jupiter Optimus Maximus on the Capitol, very near where Tiberius had died, about the number of disturbing prodigies. The senators now hoped to restore order through traditional methods of expiation rather than through repression and executions. Their interpretation of the message given by the oracular books provides a vital key to their reading of Tiberius' death. The oracular books suggested that the Romans must placate the "oldest" Ceres in order to restore their good relationship with the goddess, who was important for their very survival, as well as being a central figure in the traditional politics of the urban plebs.[18] As a result a commission was sent, at considerable expense and effort, to make offerings to the ancient and venerable cult of Ceres at Henna in Sicily, since the plain of Henna was said to be the site of the rape of Proserpina and therefore the birthplace of the original cult of Ceres. These offerings are important as indications both of the seriousness of the crisis after Tiberius' death and also of the way in which the senate tried to define and deal with that crisis, once its initial strong-arm tactics had apparently fallen short. Henna was a highly significant choice of venue not simply because this cult center was far from Rome and considered by the western Greeks to be older than the renowned cult at Eleusis, but because the Romans had just recaptured Henna after a long and bloody siege. Henna had been the headquarters of the slaves who had revolted in Sicily, and especially of their Syrian leader Eunous, who styled himself "King Antiochus" and was a follower of the Syrian goddess.

The decision to send ambassadors to Henna must have been made in 132 B.C., following the capture of the city by the Romans, and in the specific context of a ceremonial Roman restoration of the ancient honors of Ceres at Henna.[19] At about the same time, also on the advice of the Sybilline Books, ambassadors from Rome visited all the altars of Aetnean Zeus in Sicily, offered sacrifices at each, and erected fences that made them accessible only to people with traditional privileges connected to the cult. By now some time had passed since Tiberius' death (late summer–autumn of 133), and Nasica had probably already left for Pergamum, so a conscious choice was made to associate the death of Tiberius and the events surrounding it with the more recent Roman victory in Sicily.[20] Tiberius had himself made an issue of the slave revolt, and of its causes and implications for Roman politics.[21] But was Ceres angry with Gracchus, perhaps over some aspect of his agrarian legislation or over his alleged attempt to seize power? Or was her wrath directed at those who had killed a sacrosanct tribune?[22]

Because several points of view could be appeased by this solemn offering, perhaps the interpretation was deliberately left open, in an effort to achieve at least the impression of renewed consensus. In addition, the restoration of the dignity of Ceres at Henna might be expected to divert attention and blame from events in Rome. It could be argued that Ceres was angry because her most ancient cult site had been desecrated by the slave army and its Syrian leader. Prodigies and terrible events, including those surrounding the death of Gracchus himself, could all be interpreted as a consequence of the goddess's anger. Such a reading would not only focus attention on positive Roman achievements in Sicily but also suggest that no individual Roman was primarily at fault. Rather divine wrath had struck Rome because of sacrilege in Sicily, and recent misfortunes were all symptoms and results of Ceres' formidable anger.

The interpretation suggested here for the propitiation of Ceres at Henna is congruent with traditional Roman reactions to major crises, especially military ones. Defeats were often blamed on the gods, whose wrath could be caused by many factors, including religious faults that were unknowingly committed by commanders in the field or by other Roman leaders.[23] In this way the community could face major losses and defeats without blaming its leaders, while at the same time soon regaining confidence that the same pattern of disaster would not repeat itself once the religious issues had been correctly resolved through the appropriate sacrifices or other rituals. Such mechanisms of explanation/expiation had worked to build consensus within the Roman community throughout the middle Republic and probably even earlier. It is significant that the senate's final reaction to the death of Tiberius and its aftermath was to step away from the partisan politics that had marked immediate responses from all parties and to seek a new start, while simultaneously trying to defuse the whole issue of right and wrong, blame and fault, pollution and religious transgression.

There are many indications that Nasica's own attempt to justify the killing of Tiberius failed in the days and months after the murder. Meanwhile, the death itself was immediately and bitterly divisive within the community. No actions were taken against the family of the Sempronii or against Tiberius' property. His legislation remained untouched; the agrarian commission he established seems to have started work with speed and energy, with P. Licinius Crassus, who would be consul in 131 and *pontifex maximus* to succeed Nasica, elected to replace Tiberius on the board of three.[24] Reelection to the office of tribune was soon also legalized. To many, Tiberius' legacy could have seemed assured by his death, which appeared in Rome as the death of a martyr for a popular cause.

Yet how *had* Nasica explained his murder of Tiberius? The failure of that justification does not make it any less significant, for it is evident that events unfolded very differently in 121 precisely because Nasica had been forced to leave Rome. The clues lie in the figure of the *pontifex maximus*, with his head covered by the hem of his toga and thus showing the purple border. The crowds that had just been eagerly defending Tiberius now turned and fled in panic before Nasica, despite the fact that he and his entourage carried no weapons. It has been plausibly argued that this terrifying high priest used the ancient formula of *consecratio* to consecrate Tiberius to Jupiter, on the grounds that the tribune was about to seize power as a tyrant.[25] What we have here is a calculated attack, based on the religious authority of the attacker and on archaic Roman ritual. The whole drama was carefully staged, from the curse of the *pontifex* that made Tiberius subject to immediate death, to the first blow struck by his fellow tribune, to the aedile who disposed of his body in the river on the same day. Only a scenario based on specific religious norms could have made Nasica and his followers so bold in their attack and so confident that Gracchus' followers would yield before them. In this way, the *pontifex* also avoided the risk of facing the veto of a tribune. The shock of the new, and of the spilling of sacrosanct blood at the electoral assembly, was balanced by the shock of the old, as a fearful archaic ritual of bloodletting apparently returned for the first time in many generations.

Nevertheless, Nasica's plan failed, despite — and because of — the fact that Tiberius and many others lay dead on the Capitol. The impact can be gauged by the *cognomen* that was now imposed on the aedile Lucretius, who was called Vespillo.[26] This name suggests the public degradation of status and the religious pollution popularly associated with the man who had thrown Tiberius' body into the river. Similarly, accusations of tyranny were bandied about in public meetings and became attached to other leading figures identified as possible opponents of Tiberius — even Aemilianus, who had been in Spain at the time of the violence. On a political level, the charge of tyranny against Tiberius Gracchus might be debated backward and forward for years to come, but it had shown itself to be incapable of resulting in anything that remotely resembled political consensus. Furthermore, the religious act of consecration, however carefully and correctly he may have performed it, did not save Scipio Nasica from the full consequences of shedding sacred blood. As a result, Nasica, not Tiberius, was driven from Rome and was treated as an exile with the curse of impiety on him.

In this context, Ceres was called upon by the senate to rescue Rome from partisan strife and failed leadership.[27] The decision to turn to the goddess was a sign that the explanations and actions of both sides in the political clash had failed to restore a sense of order. Tiberius had acted rashly and illegally, especially in his treatment of the office of tribune, in its relation to collegiality within a board of ten, and in its limit to the single year of office assigned to each board of ten men. Although his methods could reasonably be interpreted as a threat to traditional Roman political culture,[28] Nasica's intervention had broken even more rules and norms and resulted in a religious pollution that also threatened the community. Why and how could such terrible events have happened? How could the senate and the Roman people be so betrayed by both their tribune and their chief pontiff? How could Roman armies be stalling in prolonged and costly conflicts in Spain and Sicily, at the same time they were facing a new revolt in Asia? Only a deity could provide both explanation and healing, preferably a goddess who could address issues of consecration, community, and the future survival of Rome and the Roman way of life.

Tiberius' death appears as an aberration, a kind of unique horror that took the form of an anachronistic and ultimately clumsy recalling, in the later second century B.C., of early Roman legends about tyrants and especially about the role of ritual killings in Roman society.[29] No one ever wanted to repeat any part of what happened in 133, least of all the senators who had lost control in their misguided attempt to justify Nasica's extreme actions. The situation of 121 was completely different, as each side in the evolving climate of political conflict looked to new policies and strategies for approaching the violent confrontation that seemed to be looming.

Gaius Gracchus and his followers were much better organized and prepared than Tiberius had been, but they seem to have been too quick to resort to the kind of random violence that led to the first casualties. Their seizure of the Aventine section of the city and their refusal to negotiate with the senate gives the impression that they had taken a leaf from Nasica's book, thereby recalling early political strife and the solutions of another age and time, a time that predated the full development of the republican form of government based on consensus and compromise. The consul L. Opimius was also well prepared with weapons, special Cretan archers, and the precaution of a novel type of mandate in the form of an extraordinary decree of the senate that formally recognized an unspecified threat to the community and encouraged the consul to use his full authority and powers to defend Rome and its political status quo. His full-scale attack on the Gracchan forces and the price he put on the heads of their leaders suggest a situation of (civil) war, very different from the events on the Capitol in 133.

Just as the preparations and the rhetoric before the attack were different, so also the imposition of punitive sanctions on Gaius Gracchus, Fulvius Flaccus, and other members of the political elite was a quite novel and carefully conceived feature of the emerging political climate.[30] Their bodies were also thrown into the Tiber, and mourning in the family was additionally banned. Property was confiscated and the house of M. Fulvius Flaccus was destroyed. Some children also died in the violence, most notably the young son of Fulvius Flaccus. Gracchus' laws were annulled. There was even an apparently unsuccessful attempt to deprive Licinia, the wife of Gaius Gracchus, of her dowry, which would certainly have involved a considerable sum and would have affected the property of her father's family, the Licinii Crassi.[31] In other words, punitive sanctions were extremely wide-ranging and included reprisals against the family, even against some children who were under age, and women: mothers and sisters were forbidden to mourn, and new widows were threatened with the loss of their own social and economic status. Individual leaders were shamed and branded as traitors, even as their families lost property. The political future of these families must have seemed in doubt, at least at the moment. Similarly, large numbers of Gracchus' followers of lower social status were executed afterward, although memory sanctions were apparently reserved exclusively for the political elite.

The break with the past was stark and was symbolized in a visual way by the kind of scars left on the urban landscape where a house had been destroyed. The site of Fulvius Flaccus' house still stood empty some twenty years later when Q. Lutatius Catulus built a portico there.[32] Other sites on the Palatine may also have been affected. Once again the implied comparison with early Roman traitors was evident. For whatever the actual historicity of these early stories was, Romans of the 120s B.C. apparently believed that there had been earlier aspirants to tyranny and that their most typical and obvious punishment had been the destruction of their houses, continually recalled in the legendary topography of the city.[33] In a typically Roman way, striking innovation was presented as a revival of venerable tradition. Yet the impressive distance in time from these early "precedents" in itself would have stressed the present break with the much longer and more recent tradition of consensus-based politics. Interestingly, there was apparently no mention of any consecration to either Jupiter or Ceres, whether of persons or property.

Where Gaius was living just before his death is unclear, although he is reputed to have moved to the Forum from the Palatine toward the end of his life.[34] While numerous ancient sources attest the destruction of Fulvius' house, despite or perhaps because of his rank as a former consul, the fate of Gaius' house is not made explicit. Gaius' property was confiscated, but what did it consist of?[35] It would have been anomalous if Gaius' house had been spared while Fulvius' was destroyed. Rather the absence of a site commemorating Gaius' former residence suggests that he did not own a house of his own, perhaps not an unusual situation for a younger son. His mother Cornelia, or an older sibling (if one was alive), may have owned the family house on the Palatine where his father had lived. Gaius may have lived on the Palatine in a house that belonged to his wife Licinia. His move to what was probably rented accommodation in the Forum area was perhaps designed partly to protect Licinia, her assets, and their children, in the event of his violent death.

Plutarch seems mistaken in claiming that Licinia was deprived of her dowry. The *Digest* records a decision of Scaevola granting the restoration to Licinia of dotal property that was destroyed in the civil unrest (*seditio*) caused by Gaius.[36] This damage could well have been the result of mobs attacking her house, as is suggested by Appian's narrative. The failed attempt to deprive Licinia of her dowry may have been aimed at seizing and destroying the house she and Gaius had lived in, although that house belonged to her and was part of her dowry. As a result, it seems that Licinia's house and its contents, far from being confiscated by the state in 121, were restored at public expense.

The economic impact on the Sempronii of the sanctions against Gaius Gracchus is hard to measure. Certainly, Cornelia, the mother of the Gracchi, continued to live for some time longer at her villa at Misenum, where she still entertained in grand style to the end of her life.[37] Nor is it evident that any sanctions affected the inheritance or dowry of Sempronia, sister of the Gracchi and wife of Scipio Aemilianus. As already noted, Licinia, the widow of Gaius, also maintained her social and economic status. There were limits to which the leading senators were willing to tolerate the new punitive sanctions that might conceivably cut a wide swathe through the fortunes and social standing of in-laws and relatives of the disgraced. The power of those imposing these first punitive sanctions should not be overestimated. They were testing and encountering the extent of aristocratic acceptance of punitive sanctions, both in terms of memory and of property rights.

At the same time, it would be inaccurate to characterize Opimius' solution to the Gracchan problem as a purely political one, in contrast with Nasica's religious actions. His ultimate gesture was also religious, for he conducted a ritual purification (*lustrum*) of the city, a formal acknowledgment of the pollution caused by the blood that had been shed, and he built a large, new temple to the goddess of Concord (Concordia) near the Forum.[38] This last gesture was particularly striking, as this was the first temple that could be associated with an armed victory over fellow citizens within the city. Opimius' temple must be viewed in its own context, not merely with the hindsight provided by the subsequent use of concord as a political slogan of the "*optimates*." Temples had for several generations been built mainly with booty money and had celebrated Roman victories over foreign enemies. Statues and cults had sometimes been set up after the resolution of a crisis of another kind, but this had become rarer in the middle Republic.[39] Opimius' deity may have suggested the pious hope of a return to peace and societal consensus, but the temple itself, like other Roman temples, inevitably seemed a claim to absolute personal victory corresponding to humiliating enemy defeat. Graffiti soon mocked the temple of Concord as a monument to discord.[40]

By suggesting that consensus and harmony had been restored, the temple itself paradoxically raised the very question of what such a consensus would or could now look like after the bloody events of 121. Gaius and his associates had been removed from the community after their deaths and had been treated as enemies, even if never formally designated as such. The temple of Concord, and its neighboring *basilica Opimia*, would continue to remind Romans of Opimius and of his new politics of party victory at the expense of the very consensus he claimed to espouse and to restore. It would be very interesting to know how this ambitious building project was financed and whether any goods confiscated from the disgraced were used. It would also be revealing to discover how the site of the temple was related to the statue of Gaius' father or any other monuments that recalled the Gracchi in the general area of the Forum.

Meanwhile, other Romans felt able to honor the memory of the Gracchi in their own particular ways and showed openly that they were in disagreement with Opimius' reading of recent events. Plutarch attests to a spontaneous popular cult of the Gracchi that he dates to soon after the death of Gaius Gracchus.[41] His notice, though very compressed, contains useful information.

> The people were intimidated and humiliated by what had happened, but a little later they showed their longing and grief for the Gracchi. For they displayed and set up their images in public and they consecrated the places where they had been killed. They offered to them all their firstfruits, but many offered sacrifice daily and prostrated themselves, as if they were visiting the shrines of the gods. (Plutarch *C. Gracch.* 18.3)

The Gracchi, not surprisingly, were closely associated with the places where they had died; in both cases the area had already been consecrated, because they died within sacred precincts. Offerings were made at these places. Portrait-like images of the Gracchi, perhaps small statues or busts, were also "displayed" or "shown" (*anadeiknumi, protithemi*), and altars received seasonal firstfruits in their honor. Some people offered them daily divine honors, including prostrations. Plutarch's language makes clear that these were special divine honors that were equivalent to a new cult, not the usual honors that Romans paid to the deceased, especially at the tomb. Moreover, not all these activities took place at the locations where the brothers had died, although these spots certainly did become places of popular pilgrimage. The daily honors and the associated altars seem to be numerous and in many locations. It is logical to imagine such honors at least partly associated with compital shrines in the local neighborhoods of Rome (*vici*) and perhaps sometimes also within individual homes, as is attested for later popular leaders.

By this date many Gracchan boundary stones had been erected to mark the intersection of property lines in the countryside, the equivalent of urban *compita*.[42] These stones were all inscribed with the names of the three commissioners, most notably Gaius himself. Like the popular cult of the Gracchi, these boundary markers were most important in demonstrating the meeting of public and private spheres of interaction. A small but significant number of these stones are still extant, mostly in a very weathered condition and some found *in situ*. None show signs of erasure, and one was even restored in the 70s B.C. The erasure of names from inscriptions was apparently not a practice introduced in 121. Ordinary people may have associated the Gracchi with property rights and the sacred places on property lines, whose local gods, the *lares compitales*, were seen as protectors of all who lived in the neighborhood. The cult of the Gracchi could also have expressed the Roman people's appeal for the preservation of their property rights, which had been (re)established since 133, as well as a warning of the severe penalties that were traditionally imposed on any who moved or destroyed boundary stones.

The popular cult of the Gracchi demonstrates the limits of punitive memory sanctions and the character of popular reaction to their first use within the city of Rome. The precise date of this cult's origin remains unclear, as does its duration. Probably it was relatively short-lived, although Plutarch seems to refer to several seasons of firstfruits. Official suppression or reaction is not recorded. The appearance of these honors suggests that images and portraits of the Gracchi had not been officially banned. Meanwhile, this popular cult, however ephemeral, shows the nature of plebeian culture, a culture that had its own rituals, images, and venues of commemoration[43] and would emerge to challenge the culture of the *nobiles*, especially in the realm of collective memory. A separate political sphere of the plebs, and its reassertion in the face of aristocratic politics, also brought to mind the early struggles of the emerging Republic.

There was an action and a reaction: dishonor and erasure were answered by divine honors and popular images. The first punitive memory sanctions prompted the plebs to move outside the targeted memory space of the *nobiles*, in order to reveal that they still had their own memory world, and that it might be just as political as that sanctioned by the senate or the noble families, while being more ubiquitous and much harder to control or even to define. The plebs effectively claimed the Gracchi as their own and, in so doing, revealed their own political voice and their claim to a political memory.

There is no reason to imagine that this popular homage to the Gracchi was a reaction to the dedication of Opimius' temple of Concord.[44] Rather these cult rituals surely constituted a swift answer to the dishonor done to Gaius' body, the ban on mourning, and the immediate attack on his memory. In that context Opimius' temple may be read as a response to the new cult of benefactors or local heroes addressed to the Gracchi. Although Opimius was acquitted at a trial in front of the people in 120, he was condemned and exiled ten years later, at a time when more internal unrest, religious anxiety, and military failures had created the right conditions for popular revenge.[45] Hence Opimius provides the prime example of a consul who was eventually indicted and ejected from the community, even as his actions, when put together with the failures of others, invited a more general questioning of the competence and honesty of leaders from the traditional political families. In the end, the victory of Opimius and other senators in 121 was relatively short-lived, whereas the backlash against them was fierce and enduring.

Sextus Titius' Portrait of L. Appuleius Saturninus

After the disgrace of Gaius Gracchus, the senators who had opposed him were caught off guard by the portraits of the two brothers, openly displayed and deployed as symbols of political allegiance, and by the exceptional honors paid to the brothers' memory. The next time a tribune died violently after the implementation of a *senatus consultum ultimum*, a new generation of senators tried to ensure a different outcome. In this sense the events of the years 100–98 offer a kind of commentary on or reading of what happened in 121, as well as evidence of how the memory of the Gracchi and their opponents had been debated in the twenty years that had passed. An escalation in the punitive use of memory sanctions, which is quite evident around 100, formed part of that reaction and expressed the very real fear that violence would lead to the creation of yet more martyr tribunes, whose memories could be used to inspire new programs of reform and resistance.

Lucius Appuleius Saturninus had been tribune in 103 and held the office again in the year 100.[46] Although initially a political ally of Marius, Saturninus' association with C. Servilius Glaucia and his attempt to pack several of the following year's political offices with his friends caused an increasingly violent and unstable situation to develop. After the murder of C. Memmius, who had been a candidate for the consular elections, the senate passed the decree of emergency for only the second time and turned to the consul Marius to save the state from Saturninus and his associates. Marius besieged Saturninus and Glaucia on the Capitol and apparently granted them a promise of safe conduct at the time of their surrender. However, they were lynched by a mob after Marius had imprisoned them in the senate house (*curia Hostilia*). Like Nasica and Opimius before him, Marius faced political ruin over his handling of the crisis and its aftermath.

The events of 100, however, did not represent the simple repetition of earlier patterns of behavior. Indeed, a number of new strategies emerged. For the first time a consul led an attack, sanctioned in a general way by the senate's emergency decree, against a tribune (Saturninus) and a praetor (Glaucia), both of whom were still in office. In this sense a significant step had been taken toward a state of total civil war, in which different magistrates elected to serve in the same year each claimed to uphold or represent the community and its constitution. This year had seen the political assassination of a candidate for high office (C. Memmius). The attempt to install members of a political faction in a number of offices for the following year involved much violence, disregard for electoral laws, and the vision of a kind of control over who was elected that would not be fully realized until the political arrangement of the "first triumvirate" in 60 B.C. Saturninus is also apparently the first man to use formally organized and armed groups of followers (what we would now call "gangs") in the streets and in the assemblies.[47]

Saturninus had himself recalled and used the memory of the Gracchi for his own purposes. His program of reforms had stressed Gracchan themes since 103 and he had sponsored the political candidacy of L. Equitius, who falsely claimed to be a relative of the Gracchi.[48] Despite the fact that Equitius had been denounced as an imposter at a public meeting (*contio*) in 101 by Sempronia, sister of the Gracchi, popular hopes ran high, and Equitius was elected to the tribunate for 99, together with Saturninus himself and Sextus Titius. Although there is no ancient evidence to suggest that the cult of the Gracchi still existed, at least in any extensive and publicly visible form, other statues in the city recalled the Gracchan past in various ways. The statue of Tiberius Sempronius Gracchus (cos. 177) is attested in the Forum in 121, where it was visited by Gaius Gracchus shortly before his death, and it was probably still there in Saturninus' time.[49] A statue of Cornelia, daughter of Scipio Africanus and mother of the Gracchi, was erected in the *porticus Metelli* at an unspecified time, whether near the end of her life or soon after her death.[50] This statue also has been directly connected with the events of 100; however, it is more likely that it had been erected earlier, in order to honor her at the time of her death, which seems to have come before 101. In other words, we may imagine that the parents of the Gracchi were both represented by honorific statues in public places in Rome in 100. Moreover, Q. Lutatius Catulus had recently built (or was in the process of building) his portico on the Palatine, which either covered or at least redefined the area of the house of his kinsman Fulvius Flaccus. Catulus' portico itself drew renewed attention to the punishment imposed on Flaccus, just as honors for the parents of the Gracchi must have recalled their sons.[51]

Like Gaius Gracchus, Saturninus was soon subject to a variety of post-mortem penalties, proposed by the tribune P. Furius. Despite the fact that Saturninus came from an old and distinguished family and had been killed completely illegally by a mob, his property was confiscated and his house was destroyed.[52] His legislation of 100 was revoked, although earlier laws of 103 seem to have remained untouched. As to the fate of his body, he can hardly have received more than a hurried and secret burial at night. Alternatively, his killers may have thrown his body into the Tiber without any official sanction. In addition to these penalties, his portrait was also banned in all media and all locations.[53] Although attested only later, it makes sense to include this ban with the other penalties proposed by Furius in 99. Saturninus seems to be the first Roman citizen to have had his portrait officially banned at the time of his death.

The ban on Saturninus' portrait is mainly attested by Cicero in his speech in defense of C. Rabirius, delivered in 63 B.C. In this speech, Cicero refers to the trial of Sextus Titius in 98 B.C., as a result of which Titius was exiled specifically because he possessed a portrait of Saturninus in his house.[54] Cicero's words show that this ban had never been lifted, as he points out to his opponent of 63, Labienus, who was parading a portrait of Saturninus in front of the consul Cicero during Rabirius' trial. Similarly, Titius was never recalled from exile. In the following year, a certain Gaius Appuleius Decianus, tribune of the plebs in 98, was also exiled because he had publicly mourned Saturninus at the trial of P. Furius, a trial that took place in public before the people during Decianus' tribunate. In both cases political allegiance had been declared, either in words or through the possession of a portrait that was seen as politically subversive. In 98 and 97 equestrian juries convicted both men on a charge of treason (*maiestas*). The case of Sextus Titius attests the first ban on a portrait and shows that this ban was enforced under a law *de maiestate*, the first regular treason court in Rome, which had been established by Saturninus himself some five years before in 103.

In his tribunate, Sextus Titius had attempted to pass another agrarian law, in the tradition of Saturninus and the Gracchi, although he had been prevented by bad omens and by the veto of several of his fellow tribunes.[55] Yet his conviction was linked with Saturninus' portrait, rather than with any seditious actions or plans of his own. This fact can be taken as another indication of how stringent the ban on Saturninus' portrait must have been. It must have covered all portraits, whether in public or private places. On the other hand, Decianus, who was a relative of Saturninus, was convicted not for owning a portrait of a traitor but for mourning him in public. A ban on mourning in the family may also have been passed. The point of the portrait in Titius' house, however, was precisely that it was being kept not by a relative in a traditional setting but rather by a political disciple to preserve and continue a legacy, which also claimed a Gracchan inheritance. Because it must have seemed a sure thing to Titius' opponents — at least surer than an elaborate indictment of his failed agrarian law, or of any of his other political initiatives — his conviction with regard to the portrait is evidence both of the power of political portraits in Rome at the beginning of the first century B.C. and of the fierce memory sanctions that had now emerged as a result of a generation of political conflicts.

Like the Gracchi, Saturninus came from a politically established family of *nobiles*. Yet, like them, he had failed in his lifetime to earn honorable commemoration in the public places of the city. He had not been a general, and so he had no trophies or temples built with booty money. Nor had he managed to reach high office in the senate, which would have made him eligible for the grant of a public, honorific statue. Moreover, since he had not been elected aedile (or to any higher office), he had not earned the right to be represented by a wax ancestor mask (*imago*) after his death.[56] In this cultural context, the ban on any and every image of Saturninus is striking and must surely relate to the posthumous popular cult of the Gracchi around 120. In the case of Gaius Gracchus, it is understandable that his portraits and statues were *not* banned in the first instance, because there were none in public places at the time of his death, and he was not entitled to a wax mask. Who could have imagined that images of the Gracchi would soon appear, in whatever format(s), in a number of places in the city?

Yet, by 99 the political scene had changed, and the politics of portraiture had also evolved, partly as a result of the prominence of Marius, six times consul since 107, who was surely represented by several statues in Rome.[57] It is impossible to say whether Saturninus distributed his own portrait in small formats to his followers during his lifetime. Evidence from signet seals suggests that glass-paste portraits of political leaders were in circulation in significant numbers during the second century B.C.[58] The nature of the image owned by Sextus Titius remains elusive, however. Was it a special portrait made after Saturninus' death, perhaps even one that portrayed him in some way as a martyr, or one that Titius had owned for some time and may have received from Saturninus himself?

This first ban on political portraits did not target any of the traditional portrait types of the political elite, such as honorific statues approved by the senate or traditional wax ancestor masks kept and displayed by the family. Nor did it perhaps address any images existing at the time of death. Rather it was directed at posthumous portraits that were overtly political in nature. As Cicero attests, such portraits declared political allegiance, honored the dead man himself, and invoked his memory, a memory that could lead to sympathy and regret. Memory linked to portraiture was seen as subversive and powerful, especially in its appeal to the emotions of ordinary citizens, most of whom probably could not read.

It is a fine irony, which cannot have escaped the notice of contemporaries, that Saturninus' portrait was punished under the terms of his own law, the *lex Appuleia de maiestate* of 103.[59] Saturninus' law had originally been designed as a *popularis* tool, to create a venue for the prosecution of senators, especially Saturninus' more conservative opponents, before an equestrian jury. The initial focus of the law was the arbitrary use of force by magistrates in putting down sedition within the city of Rome. The law was designed to complement Gaius Gracchus' law forbidding the execution of a Roman citizen without a trial. Hence the first *maiestas* law was passed in a Gracchan tradition of popular legislation and of the protection of basic citizen rights by tribunes operating within the city's limits. However, the wording of the law must have been so vague that it was easy to use even against Titius, the owner of a portrait of a "traitor," albeit a traitor who had never himself been accused or convicted of *maiestas*. In this way Titius' trial provided the first association between *maiestas* and sanctions against memory. Titius was convicted of *maiestas* because he had openly kept a portrait of a man whose images had been banned by law. Ten years before Sulla's first march on Rome, portraits of "traitors" were subject to destruction, and the penalty for their possession was exile. However, it was Sulla himself who first openly designated Roman citizens as "enemies" (*hostes*). The senators who devised the ban on Saturninus' portrait were thinking of the unofficial, popular portraits of the Gracchi, not of their own honorific and traditional iconography. They did not foresee that the weapon they had forged would very soon be turned against them and the range of their own commemorative practices.

Punitive Memory Sanctions II
The Republic of Sulla

▾　▾　▾

Eidem consules, si appellandi sunt consules,
quos nemo est quin non modo ex memoria,
sed etiam ex fastis evellendos putet . . .
Cicero, *Pro Sestio* 33

Sulla's New Republic

Sulla was a deeply ambiguous figure during his lifetime, and he is no less so today.[1] Of particular import is the question of how large a caesura his career and reforms made in Roman political life. It has become a truism that Sulla was able to reform and reestablish the Republic but could not make either his friends or his enemies forget the example of his own extraordinary ambitions and powers. For the purposes of the present study, it would be hard to overestimate the effect of Sulla on the way political memory was treated and conceived of in Rome. His actions show the full potential impact of memory sanctions on a traditional political culture. Sulla marched on Rome in 88 B.C. in order to stake his claim to the command against Mithridates in the East. Sulla was the first Roman to march on his home city, and he took it by force. Virtually his first act as master of Rome was to declare twelve of his leading opponents, including P. Sulpicius the tribune and C. Marius his former commanding officer, to be "enemies" (*hostes*).[2] This declaration carried with it the loss of all citizen rights: the affected person could be killed with impunity, all property was forfeit, and memory sanctions were the logical conclusion. Only Sulpicius was caught and killed, but the others, including the great general Marius, had to flee for their lives.

Sulla's declaration of a living political rival as a *hostis* in 88 B.C. came as the result of developments in political conflict and punitive memory sanctions that had been imposed after the death of Tiberius Gracchus in 133. Some forty-five years of divisive debates and bitter tactics of revenge taken on fellow citizens produced a vision of total annihilation that would be visited on political rivals in partisan disputes, with virtually no regard for traditional republican politics, for the position of magistrates, or for the rights of citizens. The time for debate and compromise was now past; it was a fight to the death to shape the memories of future Romans, a fight that extended even beyond the grave. Sulla's extreme measures can be read in various contexts, perhaps most notably in light of the unparalleled prominence of Marius, already six times consul, who now seemed poised to attempt a political comeback.[3] The rise of Marius had been closely associated with increasingly shrill attacks on the *nobiles*, both as individuals and as a class. These attacks combined internal political bitterness, and what Sallust characterized as class warfare, with mounting pressure from abroad, especially in the serious wars against Jugurtha in Numidia and against the Gallic and German tribes in southern Gaul and northern Italy.[4] Mithridates VI of Pontus, the Romans' new enemy in the East, also saw the growing instability of Rome as an opportunity for his own imperial projects.

There can be no doubt that the tribune P. Sulpicius acted unconstitutionally when he deprived Sulla of his command in the East. It was Sulla, however, who first attacked the city with a Roman army and who was the first to deny a Roman his status of citizen by specifically designating him as the equivalent of a foreign enemy. The consequences of Sulla's actions were soon revealed. As soon as he left with his army to fight Mithridates, Sulla was himself declared a *hostis*, with the result that he stood to lose not only his command but also his own position as a citizen.[5] His property was confiscated, and his house on the Palatine was demolished. His wife Metella and their children fled as refugees to Greece in search of him. Although no ancient source directly describes it, statues and monuments that recalled Sulla were certainly also destroyed at the same time. All memory of him was eradicated in the city.

The situation in Roman politics can be described as one of complete *stasis* or division between Sulla and his rivals, soon led by L. Cornelius Cinna, who repeatedly held the consulship in Sulla's absence. This division seems the more striking because it was enforced by two opposing members of the extended patrician family of the Cornelii. The conflict was even more destructive than the clash between Tiberius Gracchus and his first cousin Cornelius Scipio Nasica. Yet many Romans were essentially undecided and were watching from the sidelines: they were also an important part of the intended audience for both the self-aggrandizement and the punitive sanctions employed by each side to create its own version of the present, based on its particular and selective picture of the past. Punitive sanctions now moved into the sphere of the living and were no longer just a weapon to be used against a rival who was already dead. Such sanctions were increasingly frequent and were employed by each side in the conflict. As a result, the politics of the 80s B.C. were dominated by intense confusion and uncertainty. Who represented the legitimate government in Rome? Who represented Rome in the war against Mithridates? Who was a citizen and who an enemy? To whom did soldiers owe their allegiance? What was the relationship of contemporary politics to the traditional political system of the Republic?

Even before 88 there were signs that Sulla in particular was advertising himself at the expense of others, whether they were already his "rivals" or not. In this sense his use of punitive sanctions reflected years of careful thought and jockeying for position; they were not simply an angry reaction to the politics of the moment. Not surprisingly, given the prominence of Marius between 107 and 100, some felt the need to exert themselves in new ways, in order to gain some recognition and political capital for themselves. One of those was Q. Lutatius Catulus, Marius' fellow consul in 102 and also a general who had fought against and had triumphed over the Cimbri.[6] The portico he built commemorating his victory challenged the memory of Marius as the ultimate victor at Vercellae. His temple of Fortuna Huiusce Diei in the Campus Martius recalled his family traditions and answered Marius' stress on personal achievement and courage by attributing the victory over the Gauls to the special favor of the gods, in particular a goddess of fortune. Catulus also wrote a memoir of his consulship, stressing his own role at the expense of Marius. In his consulship of 102, Catulus was the first to honor a woman, his mother Popilia, with a traditional aristocratic funeral procession of ancestors and a eulogy from the *rostra* in the Forum. Sulla had served with Catulus against the Cimbri and had surely learned several lessons from his commander's ambitions and his self-presentation.

Meanwhile, libations had been poured for Marius at the evening meal by Romans after the final Roman victory over the Celts at Vercellae in 101, in a spontaneous expression of the popular belief that he had indeed saved Rome from the Gauls.[7] Unlike the Gracchi, who received posthumous images, first-fruits, and sacrifices after death, Marius was venerated with libations in his own lifetime. In addition, he triumphed; although offered two such celebrations, he accepted only one. He was also, of course, reelected yet again as consul for 100. For both his victory over Jugurtha and for his Gallic victories, Marius had erected trophies in the form of splendid gilded statue groups, one of which stood on the Capitol. He was himself represented by statues in these groups, and probably also elsewhere in Rome. In addition he had erected a new temple to Honos and Virtus, thus recalling the achievements and temple of Marcus Claudius Marcellus, the third-century Roman leader who had held the largest number of consulships before Marius himself. On 1 January 104, the day of his triumph over Jugurtha, Marius had even tried to enter the senate dressed in triumphal garb, although the scandal this caused forced him to leave in order to change his clothes.[8] It is no wonder that Catulus felt the need to assert himself and that Sulla might form the idea that remarkable new honors could be won by someone who appeared as Rome's savior.

The date of Sulla's first real break with his former patron and commanding officer Marius is hard to establish with any certainty.[9] Ancient sources like Plutarch seem to imagine an enmity that developed as early as Sulla's capture of Jugurtha in 105. This view has been attributed to the memoirs of Sulla himself and has consequently been called into question as essentially propagandistic. Alternatively, it has been argued that Sulla's break with Marius should be dated after 100, when Marius was weakened by the fiasco of the rise and fall of his political ally Saturninus. According to this argument Sulla would not have challenged Marius while the latter was still at the height of his power.

Plutarch tells us of Sulla's signet ring that showed the moment when King Bocchus of Mauretania handed Jugurtha over to Sulla, and he implies that the ring was made soon after the event it portrayed.[10] Sulla may have used this ring by the time of his praetorship in 97, and most probably even earlier, as part of his campaign to be elected to high office and to his own army command. The scene on the ring can be reconstructed from a coin minted in 56 by Faustus, Sulla's son (figure 13). It was also rendered as a gilded monumental statue group, surrounded by victories, that was set up on the Capitol by Bocchus of Mauretania in 91 B.C., as a gift to the Roman people. According to Plutarch, the ring predated the statue group by some time, and there is no real reason to doubt his testimony. It may be that the ring was conceived and even manufactured not long after Marius' spectacular triumph over Jugurtha on 1 January 104. Sulla could then have decided how and when to use it in the years that followed. Or he may have been inspired by the independence of Catulus to rethink the matter of his own self-representation, especially in relation to Marius. Regardless of which chronology seems most plausible, a general picture of Sulla emerges as a man whose self-image had consistently

FIGURE 13.
Denarius of Faustus Sulla, 56 B.C., showing Jugurtha being handed over to Sulla by Bocchus. The image on the coin reflects the iconography of the gilded statue group set up by Bocchus in Rome in 91 B.C. and the signet ring used by Sulla even before that date. *Ashmolean Museum, Oxford,* RRC *426/1.*

been built around the erasure of the achievements of others, including, most notably, his first commanding officer. On the other hand, Marius himself had won his first consulship as a critic of his own former commander, Metellus Numidicus.[11]

After 87 Sulla's self-presentation and image were naturally decisively shaped in reaction to his new status as an enemy (*hostis*) in Rome. As a matter of fact, he had to live with this label for a rather long time and on campaign as a general, in comparison to Marius and others who returned to rehabilitation in Rome soon after the *hostis* declarations of 88. Most notably his reliance on divine help and his presentation of himself as a charismatic leader, inspired and sent by the gods, makes good sense in this particular context. His expulsion from the Roman political community only encouraged his tendency to move into the sphere of the gods. Sulla was fighting in the East against Mithridates, who presented himself as the New Dionysus; no doubt his own ambiguous situation led to Sulla's rather premature truce and settlement with Mithridates, whose challenge to the Romans would continue for many more years. He signed a peace with Mithridates so that he could return to Rome and reestablish himself. Sulla, however, was never really open to any kind of compromise or negotiation with Cinna and his followers who remained in Rome. Sulla himself appears to have felt that he faced either annihilation or — if he managed to seize Rome a second time with his army — supreme power. When he did return to the city in 82, he returned to live again on the Palatine, although it is unclear whether he lived on the site of his previous house. There can also be little doubt that he reconstructed Bocchus' Jugurtha monument on the Capitol, which had surely been dismantled by Marius and Cinna[12] (figure 14).

The ultimate caesura in Roman memory was caused by Sulla's proscriptions, which followed very shortly upon his recapture of the city on 1 No-

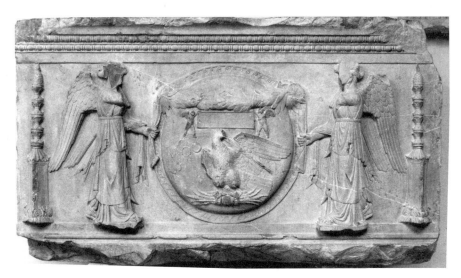

FIGURE 14. Base found at San Omobono in Rome, probably from Bocchus'
monument for Sulla as restored after Sulla's return to Rome in 82 B.C. *Musei Capitolini,
Rome, archivio fotografico dei Musei Capitolini, photo Maria Teresa Natale.*

vember 82, and officially lasted until 1 June 81.[13] These lists of citizens marked
for death and confiscation of property were all the more sinister in that they
supposedly represented Sulla's limit on the indiscriminate carnage that had
immediately followed his victory at the battle of the Colline Gate. Whereas
the formal declaration of citizens as *hostes* may be interpreted as the full development of ideas and policies that were already implicit in the events of 121
and 100, the posting of lists of names and the whole concept of "proscribing"
were certainly new in Roman political culture.

Whitened boards were displayed that listed the names of the victims
painted in red letters, and Sulla's special ideology of revenge was characterized by the paradox of publicly displaying the names of those who were about
to be erased. It is unclear whether Sulla's law (*lex Cornelia*), which gave formal legal justification to the killings and confiscations, was officially labeled
as a law about "enemies" or about "proscriptions."[14] These lists inspired fear
even among people who could not read, or could only read at a very basic
level. Their stark symbolism, as if of names written in blood, was surely reinforced by the spectacle of torture and ritual executions in the public spaces
of the city. The removal of the lists, presumably on 1 June 81, would in itself
have marked a new era that claimed to put an end to the past even as the
names of these enemies of Sulla disappeared. In each case, Sulla revealed his
own power over life, death, family status, property, and memory. He had not

only the power to destroy his enemies, whether foreigners or Roman citizens, but also the power to put an end to destruction and to proclaim a new era of peace and stability.

Those on the proscription lists were immediately subject to execution and to the confiscation and public sale of all their property. In addition, their descendants were excluded from public life for two generations.[15] The format of the proscription lists imitated lists that were posted to advertise public auctions of property that was to be disposed of by the state. In this sense it was as if the people themselves disappeared before their deaths even as their names were posted for all to read. These were people who had lost their status even as people, let alone as citizens. They were effectively already dead as their names were being read, and even their relatives had lost their economic and social status. Their appearance on a list now advertised the price to be paid to anyone who wanted to kill them. The rhetoric of the lists was a rhetoric of public sales, auctions, and money to be made, whether directly as blood money paid for the victim's heads or in the form of profits to be made from their property and estates, including the inherited houses and lands of their families.

The names on the lists were often paralleled by the display of heads at the *rostra*, another new practice designed to impose shame as well as fear.[16] Some even believed that heads were kept in Sulla's own *atrium* at home, the room that would have housed the cupboards storing the ancestor masks of the patrician Cornelii. Whether at the *rostra* or in an *atrium*, severed heads represented a striking and dramatic reversal of the commemoration bestowed by the wax ancestor masks that Roman politicians earned with high political office. And the reversal was evident in the very same spaces where honor would have been paid through the use of this special medium of portraiture, either in the home or at the funeral. Indeed, most of the heads displayed may have belonged to the very Romans who would normally have been honored with a wax mask and would have been eulogized in the Forum from the same *rostra*. Meanwhile, Sulla specifically banned the wax masks of his enemies. The precise reversal of the usual modes of political recognition would have been evident to all, even as the heads were left on the *rostra* to decay.

Thousands of elite Romans were killed, from men of consular rank to those of equestrian status. The largest number were equestrians, and it is striking how few names can now be recovered. Sulla's methods were extremely effective: the memory of most of his victims has been irretrievably lost. By appropriating the slaves of the proscribed and freeing them in his own name, Sulla literally replaced the names of their former masters with his name. Ten thousand such Cornelii were said to live in Rome.[17] At the same time, some measures were aimed specifically at the memory of the most prominent, notably Marius himself and his relatives and closest associates. Marius had died in 86, but his body was exhumed from the grave beside the Anio River and his ashes scattered.[18] In Rome all memory of him was removed and his trophies were taken down. Because they were dedicated as religious offerings, they seem to have been ritually buried rather than destroyed. Thus Marius' memory was buried in Rome, while his remains were exhumed outside the city. No ancient source speaks about his inscriptions, most notably the dedicatory text on the temple of Honos and Virtus. The text may have been erased, or perhaps even replaced by another. However, the temple was certainly still associated with Marius in later times.

No matter how the evidence is interpreted, Sulla's actions went well beyond the bloodshed that had undoubtedly taken place in his absence under Cinna's regime. As already noted, Sulla was a highly successful innovator in the field of memory sanctions, partly because he was the first to use such sanctions punitively from a position of supreme power in the state. Marius, who had been consul seven times and who had in his own lifetime received libations from his fellow citizens, was not recalled by a single image or monument in the city from 82 until the restoration of some of his honors in the 60s by his relative Julius Caesar.

At the same time, these individual erasures must be read in terms of much larger erasures in the topography of the city. Sulla did not destroy private houses; instead he sold them for profit and to reward his faithful supporters. But he did replace the whole area of the senate house (*curia Hostilia*), *comitium*, and the old *rostra* with new and larger structures to accommodate his expanded senate.[19] It is suggestive that the old *rostra*, where the heads of the proscribed had been displayed, was very soon itself dismantled. The whole end of the Forum was now marked by its designer Sulla; the new senate house was now probably called the *curia Cornelia*, and the whole design was enhanced by the gilded equestrian statue of Sulla himself, which had been voted for him immediately after his return to Rome (figure 15).[20] The statue's importance as a central icon of Sulla's New Republic is revealed by its appearance on a coin of 80. This was the first coin minted in Rome that portrayed the statue of a living man. Of course, depicting Sulla's statue on the coin is not quite the same as simply putting Sulla's head on the coin (which never happened), but the difference is not great, and it may not have been evident to ordinary Roman viewers. At the height of his power Sulla used a signet ring with three trophies on it.[21] Whether this image, reflected in a later

coin of Faustus, also refers to a monument in Rome is uncertain. Neverthe-less, Sulla's three trophies clearly outdid Marius' two, just as Sulla's equestrian statue was designed to take on its full meaning in a context where Marius had once been but was no longer commemorated. The parallel development of new images and of memory sanctions is suggestive.

The most (in)famous of Sulla's victims was Marius' own nephew, M. Marius Gratidianus.[22] He was the highest ranking of the Marians to be captured alive by Sulla, since Cinna had been killed by mutinous troops in 84. His death became the most notorious example of the horrors of the proscrip-tions, as it seems Gratidianus was slowly tortured to death by Catiline on the tomb of Catulus as a kind of human sacrifice. The episode ended with Gra-tidianus' head being presented to Sulla while Catiline washed the blood from his hands in the basin in front of the temple of Apollo Medicus. As praetor in 85 Gratidianus had taken credit for the revaluation of the coinage and the elimination of debased coins. As a result he had received statues, as well as offerings of incense, candles, and wine in all the neighborhood shrines to the *lares compitales* at the crossroads.[23]

These honors were connected with the tribes but were situated in the local neighborhoods (*vici*). They reflect Gratidianus' popularity in the city and his close connection with the politics of the plebs. While these offerings pro-vide an obvious precedent for the honors paid to the *genius* of Augustus at these same local shrines, the cult may well have been traditional and quite old. It is important to make the connections between cult offerings made to the Gracchi, to Marius, and to Marius Gratidianus at various times between 120 and 82. The latter two received such offerings in their own lifetimes. The gifts and libations involved were very simple and reflect the most basic level of everyday religious ritual in the Roman home or neighborhood. All these rituals may have some link with the homage paid to the *genius* of each male who was a head of household, and also to various *lares*, whether they were protectors of the individual home and family as in the case of Marius himself, or the protectors of the local area like Gratidianus.

Gratidianus' death seems connected to the special honors he had received during his lifetime. As Sulla approached the city, the regular offerings, along with any images associated with them, were quickly destroyed. Yet it is hard to believe that their existence was not well known to all, especially to Sulla, whose self-presentation in terms of a divine mission must have seemed the logical response to the popularity of the Marians. Honors for Sulla are also attested in a neighborhood context. At the same time, some of the elaborate details of Gratidianus' gruesome death may have been embellished because he had been killed by Catiline.[24] Cicero and others demonized Catiline, who was to be declared a *hostis* in 63, and who fell in battle as he led an army against his own country. Consequently, great care is needed if the stories of Gratidianus and Catiline are to emerge with any accuracy, and if the politics of the late 60s and 50s are not to distort our picture of Rome under Sulla. Nonetheless, Gratidianus' death cannot be completely explained away; it had been spectacular and bloody. The reversal of his honors and the degradation of his extraordinary status make sense in the context of the shame imposed on other senatorial victims. The role of Catulus' son as the avenger of his father's enforced suicide must also be taken into consideration. It is possible that Catiline has (at least partially) eclipsed Catulus in the accounts of Gratidianus' death that have come down to us.

The senate had struggled for more than fifty years before Sulla's dictatorship to control the memory of tribunes (and others) who had been killed in questionable and violent circumstances. Yet in all this struggle over politics and memory before Sulla, the traditional culture of the *nobiles* had remained largely untouched. In that sense, the senators had probably felt relatively safe. After all, a previous clearing of unauthorized statues from public places in 158 B.C. had only served to protect the special kudos of a statue approved by the senate.[25] Similarly, no elite families had been demoted, and the Sempronii Gracchi continued to be prominent even into the age of Augustus. Sulla, by contrast, targeted the whole range of images and honors in all media, even as he himself had been subject to similar erasure in Rome in 87. Despite superficial similarities, his proscriptions were of a completely different nature and purpose than previous memory sanctions. Sulla's actions represented a decisive rift in the aristocratic culture of political memory in particular and of consensus-based power sharing in general. One might argue that only a patrician whose family status was not specifically connected to the concept of a republic and its officeholding elite could be so ruthless and sweeping in his attack on the culture of the *nobiles*. Moreover, Sulla's laws imposing memory sanctions on his opponents remained in force until the dictatorship of Caesar.

The formal declaration of a citizen as a *hostis* broke not only with traditional models of consensus politics but also with the very conception of what political competition in Rome entailed. Continuity with the past had been broken, both with the more distant past of the Punic wars and the Rome of Cato the censor, and also with the more recent troubles and debates over reforms and over the evolution of Roman politics to meet the challenges of a huge empire. Sulla's sanctions broke the continuities within families, between families, and in the community at large.

Memory had been interrupted and history rewritten. Sulla rewrote much of the story himself, with careful attention to detail and to the consistency of his message. It was his texts and monuments that now characterized the city, whose sacred boundary (*pomerium*) he had enlarged. The topography of the Forum and of the new temple of Jupiter Optimus Maximus on the Capitol represented his vision of a New Republic, the capital of a world empire directed by a strong senate and regulated by a revised and more comprehensive system of laws and lawcourts.[26] Within this new Rome, Sulla appeared as a founder figure. His position and achievements were celebrated in a special way by his great triumph over Mithridates in late January 81, and by the annual victory games he instituted to recall his success at the Colline Gate on 1 November.[27] Sulla also devoted the last two years of his life, after his retirement from Rome to the area of Puteoli, to the writing of his own account of his life in twenty-two books.

Although only meager fragments survive, the scale of these memoirs was quite unprecedented, and their expansiveness is all the more striking since little space seems to have been given to the time of the dictatorship itself or to a detailed exposition of his new constitution.[28] This account was not a vision for his New Republic and for the future, but rather a very detailed and partisan version of the past, much of which must have concerned the actions of his enemies as much as his own deeds and thoughts. His aim was to justify his own actions, especially his two marches on Rome, and to assert that he had not lost his citizen status between 87 and 82, in light of the kind of memory attacks he had both pioneered and been subject to himself. The writing of highly personalized memoirs, which in most cases both denigrated and erased political opponents, had become something of a fashion at the end of the second century. Sulla, however, exploited this genre in a monumental way quite unlike earlier writers. His version seems to have had a real effect on how the 80s were recalled, both by contemporaries and by later writers, most notably Plutarch. Plutarch's narrative also reveals the great emphasis Sulla placed on divine signs, dreams, and omens that had guided his choices and confirmed that his actions had divine approval. The removal of traditional societal and cultural constraints and patterns of behavior, combined with the instability and violence of the times, encouraged Sulla to retreat to a higher ground and to remove himself from the politics of Rome into a world dominated by divine fortune that could validate both the means and the end of his political career.

A prime example of the effects of Sulla's own account of his times can be found in the memory of Lucius Cornelius Cinna.[29] Cinna was not killed by Sulla, for he was already dead when Sulla returned from the East, nor could his name appear on any proscription list. However, Sulla did order Julius Caesar to divorce Cinna's daughter and threatened him with proscription when he refused. Caesar was deprived of the office of *flamen Dialis*, to which he had been appointed by Cinna, in succession to L. Cornelius Merula.[30] It is apparent, then, that Cinna's relatives were targets of Sulla. In addition, Cinna has effectively been erased from history by Sulla and replaced with a mere cipher by the same name. It is now impossible to write a history of Cinna in any detail. Not only is his political program vague; we do not even know whether he had a program of any complexity at all. His time in Rome has become a virtual blank, as everyone was apparently simply "waiting for Sulla." To assume that there was no more to Cinna than what we now have is to accept Sulla's version of events in Rome in the years 87–82. Sulla effectively identified himself with the Roman state, which he could naturally do more easily in retrospect, once he had seized absolute power and reformed the Republic. Erasure of his enemies from history was essential to the vision of his New Republic as the only legitimate government.

Caesar never rehabilitated the memory of his father-in-law Cinna as he had that of Marius, despite the fact that he remained married to Cinna's daughter until her death in 69 B.C. Caesar may have learned political lessons from Cinna, although this process has been obscured for us. Meanwhile, Sulla was honored with the first funeral at public expense, a funeral fit for the foremost man in Rome.[31] It is notable that his followers did not respect his wish to be interred according to the family custom of the patrician Cornelii, but chose to cremate him so that his body could not later be desecrated. He was buried on the Campus Martius, a very rare honor at the time and an enduring memorial to his position at the end of his life.

The Republic of Sulla was built on the erasure of the recent past and the recasting of history in his own lifetime, which is to say after the year of his birth, 138 B.C. That erasure also affected the way Romans remembered, and apparently had increasing difficulty remembering, their traditional republican culture, which had been characterized by an emphasis on consensus and on working toward compromise and balance within an aristocratic society based heavily on the recognition of merit and on the sharing of power. Sulla's world was very different: it was a world characterized by a cosmic struggle between good and evil, as Sulla himself, warrior of the gods and executor of divine retribution, annihilated his evil enemies completely and erased their memories in order to usher in a new era of peace and harmony. This new "consensus" of Sulla was based on force and on the necessity of agreeing with Sulla himself, and subsequently with his new, mighty senate that was expected to wield unprecedented power and absolute authority. Hence the New Republic depended precisely on the elimination of opposition, and even of much political debate. This highly problematic relationship to a suppressed and traumatic past proved to be a central factor in the inherent instability of Sulla's new political system.

Playing with Fire: Cicero, Catiline, and Clodius

Sulla's shadow hung heavily over the "last generation of the Roman Republic."[32] Romans did not and could not immediately forget the proscriptions, or those who had been proscribed, or society's enormous losses. Signs of Sulla's new order were to be found not only in Rome but throughout Italy. Both Sulla's veterans and those whom he had dispossessed lived with his legacy on a daily basis. Political struggles continued, as well as some military conflicts among Romans. The revolt of Lepidus in Etruria presented a direct challenge to Sulla soon after his death. Sertorius continued his own opposition and quest for personal power in Spain until his death in 73. Tensions over constitutional issues led to the restoration of the powers of the tribunes in 70, and thus to significant revisions of Sulla's vision of the Republic. Meanwhile, the figure of Pompey, a man of extraordinary power whose career was based on the use of force and of armed dependents, vividly recalled his former patron Sulla and suggested the possibility of another dictatorship. Whatever one's opinion of Sulla's Republic, it was evident to all that right from the start several prominent Romans were operating outside its rules.

Marcus Tullius Cicero was a witness to the age of Cinna and Sulla at a formative stage of his own development, and he is our most important contemporary source for the years from 80 to 43.[33] Cicero's reaction to Sulla remained complex and was continually affected by the political issues of his own day. On the one hand Cicero had dared to criticize Sulla's *domestica crudelitas* openly, even in his own lifetime. He also represents one of the very few republican voices to speak favorably of Marius and of the Italian equestrian milieu he came from in Arpinum. Cicero was in fact a relative of Marius Gratidianus and, as such, of Marius himself. Yet many of Cicero's mentors and early teachers had been killed by Cinna and the Marians in the 80s. Because he was connected in various ways to both sides in the civil conflicts of the 80s, Cicero had started his political life in a situation of extreme stress and ambiguity. Moreover, he had stayed in Rome and had been an eyewitness to the repeated, violent political changes that occurred. The circumstances of this beginning surely help to explain some of his later policies and ambivalences.

As consul in 63 Cicero advocated a policy that he himself described as *concordia ordinum*, a policy of cooperation between social groups, particularly between the senators and the equestrians.[34] Yet Cicero the consul was one who fought to maintain Sulla's penalties on the families of the proscribed, even twenty years after they had been imposed and at a time when there were many calls for reconciliation. Despite his incisive criticisms of Sulla, at least on some occasions, Cicero was a staunch upholder of the constitution as designed by Sulla, and especially of the new, extensive powers of Sulla's expanded senate. It was this new Sullan senate that could and did offer the opportunity of an illustrious political career to an Italian like Cicero.

More importantly, during his career Cicero himself emerged as a leading advocate of punitive memory sanctions, adopting tactics that could be and perhaps sometimes were described as "Sullan." Yet it was Catiline who remained primarily associated with Sulla's name, even after he deployed an eagle of Marius at the head of his rebel army.[35] Cicero's interactions with his two principal political rivals of the 60s and 50s, Catiline and Clodius, illustrate the harsh climate of political discourse, the use of punitive sanctions even against the living, and the characterization of political divisions as absolute struggles ending either in victory with glory or in death with disgrace. Strikingly, Cicero cast Catiline as one who would overthrow the constitution, causing indiscriminate massacres, disregard for property rights, and even the deliberate burning of the city.[36] In other words, Cicero's own role as Rome's savior and as a father figure to the Republic (*parens patriae*) was directly dependent on the demonization of Catiline and on his eventual death as an enemy of the state.

Cicero's extreme stance was also shaped by the fact that many in the senate continued to sympathize with Catiline, well into the autumn of 63. It was Cicero who brought back both the *senatus consultum ultimum* and the declaration of Roman citizens as *hostes*.[37] Moreover, it was Cicero who executed the associates of Catiline, including a praetor in office who was a member of a patrician family, without a trial and without giving them a chance to defend themselves. These actions significantly extended the definition of a *hostis*, ostensibly to include any man who could be accused of plotting against the state, even if no plans had actually been carried out and the individual was now in custody; whatever threat he might have posed to the state had presumably been averted.

Echoes of earlier struggles were evident, and the memory of Sulla must have been vivid in the minds of many Romans. Cicero's subsequent exile, as well as the accusations that he had behaved like a tyrant, make clear that his particular version of the events of 63 was far from being universally acceptable to his contemporaries.[38] At the same time, it may seem implausible that he modeled himself directly on Sulla, despite the use of tactics that had been perfected by the dictator. Rather, Cicero probably looked more to Catulus and to his rather successful use of the *senatus consultum ultimum* and a *hostis* declaration against Lepidus in 78.[39] Events, however, were less predictable than Cicero's selective use of carefully crafted historical *exempla* in his various speeches might suggest. Despite, or perhaps because of, his very closeness to Roman politics over the twenty years before his consulship, Cicero seemed unable to develop a plan of action that would avoid the political consequences of yet more illegal bloodshed, of the clash of two Roman armies, and of the further erosion of citizen rights, a development that inevitably affected the stability of the very Republic Cicero claimed to be defending. The casting of Pompey as a possible "second Sulla," who might invade Italy from the East on the pretext of putting down Catiline, also carried with it the distinct danger of the self-fulfilling prophecy. Ultimately Cicero himself had to leave Rome, even as Nasica, Opimius, and even Marius had been forced to do, after each of them "saved" the state.

Cicero's actions taken against Catiline were particularly resonant in the later 60s, after Caesar had brought back the memory and monuments of Marius and the continued unrest, debt, and misery caused by Sulla's settlements created a constituency for Catiline. Competing versions of the past were on view in Rome even as old grievances were still festering, and the possibility of new agrarian legislation recalled the reforming tribunes of the late second century. In 63 Cicero himself agreed to defend C. Rabirius in a trial that revisited the contested events surrounding the lynching of Saturninus almost forty years before, while the trial also questioned the legal implications of the *senatus consultum ultimum*.[40] Was Rabirius guilty of the murder of Saturninus or not? No official verdict was ever reached. Meanwhile, Pompey's success in a series of special multiyear commands, commands that Cicero had actively supported, was itself a kind of challenge to the community whose interest he was supposedly representing.

Modern scholars have rightly become dismissive of the historicity of the so-called First Catilinarian Conspiracy that had allegedly been planned for 66/65.[41] However, its very lack of substance should sound a warning about the increasingly bitter political climate. The rumor was that Catiline had planned the murder of the consuls of 65 on the day they took office, in preparation for his own seizure of power. Cicero seems responsible for effectively fabricating this attempted coup by Catiline in order to enhance his own image, as he was preparing for the consular elections in 64. This tactic in itself is hardly excused by Catiline's later actions. The autumn of 63 was also characterized by Cicero's repeated attempts to provoke Catiline into leaving the city and joining the army of the disaffected led by C. Manlius in Etruria. In his first speech against Catiline, Cicero represented Rome itself as urging Catiline to leave the city.[42] In a fundamental way, the threat of Catiline was both exacerbated and even partly created by Cicero, in rhetoric and in actual fact, first in order to win election to the consulate as a new man who faced fiercesome odds, and then to appear during that very same consulate as the savior of Rome in an hour of extreme crisis.

In other words, the illegal execution of the Catilinarians in December 63 was the not altogether unexpected climax of several years of Cicero's emotional and dramatic pronouncements about internal enemies of the Roman state. Moreover, the fact that Cicero only had a little time left as consul was evidently a factor in his own personal motivation to execute these men, since others would be responsible for the defeat of Catiline and his army in the following year. Cicero's moment of glory, short-lived though it was, came with his popular acclamation as savior of Rome from imminent threat, a threat of massacre, arson, and tyranny. It was precisely the harsh and degrading execution of the Catilinarians that made that threat seem credible, at least at the time. Cicero was the first consul to execute a praetor in office without a trial, a step beyond the actions of previous Roman leaders in crisis situations. In doing this, he also revealed his own insecurity, both as regards his ability to keep the conspirators securely in prison and in his belief that the court system would fail to bring them to justice once he was no longer consul. Cicero's fears speak to the limits of his own political powers but also to the state of the republican governmental structures by the late 60s.

Afterward, particularly after his return from exile, Cicero worked hard to dispel his own image as a tyrant by rewriting history, both recent and more distant.[43] What he says about earlier events, especially those involving emergencies declared by the senate, is nearly always highly colored by his personal interests and concerns. His own version of his suppression of Catiline needed to be elaborated and fitted into a suitable frame of edifying historical precedents. At the same time, Cicero could cast himself as a Roman politician in a tradition upheld by such distinguished earlier leaders as the patrician Scipio Nasica and even the great popular general Marius himself. Needless to say, Cicero never cited Sulla as a model for his own behavior. Meanwhile, the facts about Catiline have been largely obscured by Cicero, replaced by his own elaborate version of events, although in 59 B.C. there were still some who left flowers on Catiline's grave.[44]

Despite his extensive rhetoric about Catiline, Cicero's career was perhaps even more decisively shaped by his subsequent clash with Clodius the tribune, a clash that was a distinctive feature of the politics of the 50s. Clodius was known for his unparalleled use of gang violence in Rome: much of that violence was directed against Cicero, whose actions in 63 and 62 gave Clodius the perfect excuse to launch his own career as defender of the plebs and their traditional civil liberties and interests.[45] Each of the two politicians, one a patrician although adopted as a plebeian, the other a "new man" from Arpinum, used punitive sanctions against the other. The vituperative politics of their words and their actions was remarkable, and yet neither man seems to have paused even to consider how the continual use and consequent normalization of terror tactics and of memory wars would affect Roman civic life. If this was the character of republican politics, then what constituted the Republic of the 50s?

Clodius attacked Cicero for executing Roman citizens without a trial. After Cicero withdrew into a voluntary exile, mobs sacked his house on the Palatine, and his property was subsequently confiscated.[46] The house was at least partially destroyed and then sold at public auction. Clodius himself, whose own house was very nearby, acquired the property through a middleman and erected a shrine to Liberty (Libertas), which occupied some of Cicero's property, and impinged on Catulus' portico that commemorated his victory over the Cimbri. Cicero's villas at Tusculum and Formiae were also damaged and his family was harassed. Clodius depicted Cicero as one of the early aspirants to tyranny in Rome, at the same time seeking to benefit both politically and materially from his rival's disgrace. Clodius' gangs (and others?) were probably visible from the Forum as they ransacked the property. The shrine and portico Clodius built were both a kind of personal victory monument and the manifesto of a popular political program. The space could be used for larger meetings of Clodius' followers.

After Cicero's return from exile, the issue of his house continued to be paramount and the state-funded rebuilding was not completed until the mid-40s. It had originally belonged to M. Livius Drusus, and Cicero had acquired it in 62, through much borrowing, as a symbol of his position as a man of consular rank in Roman society. Even after the senate and pontiffs had approved the removal of Clodius' shrine and the rebuilding, at public cost, of Cicero's house and Catulus' portico, Clodius and his gangs made repeated assaults both on Cicero himself and on the workmen who were doing the rebuilding. Cicero, in turn, made use of Milo and his gangs in several attacks on the tablets inscribed with the various laws of Clodius. Not only the measure outlawing Cicero after he had left Rome but all Clodius' laws, the monuments to his tribunate, were affected. These violent episodes destroyed the official copies of various laws on the Capitol, as well as others that Clodius posted on his own house. In response Clodius posted more inscriptions, some of which represented new attacks on Cicero. When Clodius was killed in gang violence a short distance from Rome in January 52, Cicero defended Milo on a murder charge, claiming that he should rather be rewarded for ridding Rome of Clodius. Cicero even suggested that Clodius' assassination should be recognized as the beginning of a new era for Rome.[47]

After the Ides of March 44, Cicero played a similarly central role in the political developments that led to the formation of the Second Triumvirate, which would rule the Empire for the next ten years. It was Cicero who urged the Liberators to call the senate to a meeting on the Capitol after the assassination and to condemn the memory of Caesar.[48] Brutus consistently saw things differently and sought a compromise, both as regards Caesar's memory and in his relationship with the consul Antony.[49] In the complex politics of the next eighteen months, Cicero repeatedly called for a *hostis* declaration against Antony and treated him as an "enemy" even in the absence of an official measure outlawing him. His series of speeches against Antony, which he called *Philippics*, fostered division and partisan strife. Not surprisingly, Cicero's name featured prominently on the proscription list drawn up by the new triumvirate late in 43, after Cicero's protégé Octavian had decided to make common cause with Antony and Lepidus against Caesar's assassins.

Both Clodius and Cicero met violent ends, and neither man received a traditional funeral; their deaths marked distinct stages in the disintegration of republican politics and the emergence of a system of one-man rule. Clodius, the supreme leader of gangs, was killed by a rival gang, and the flames of his funeral pyre destroyed the senate house that Sulla had built. The violence was so great that Pompey was called upon to restore order by becoming sole consul. Not dissimilarly, Cicero was proscribed, summarily executed, and had his severed head and hands displayed on the *rostra*. Even as he had experienced exile like Nasica and Opimius, he was proscribed, murdered, and mutilated like Marius Gratidianus. It is notable, however, that Cicero was not subjected to any punitive sanctions after death, and his reputation was not attacked.[50] His son Marcus went on to share a consulship with Octavian in the year after the battle of Actium and announced the death of Antony in Rome. Most importantly, many of Cicero's writings have survived, and his copious correspondence was published after his death. Our picture of the period would be radically different if his books had been burned; conversely, if he had been more ready to compromise, he would surely have survived to comment on and perhaps even to play a role in the new age created by Caesar's heir.

Clementia Caesaris:
Divus Iulius and the Memory of the Liberators

The memory of Julius Caesar was linked to the memory of Marius and to Caesar's own stance toward the past and toward the politics of memory. Caesar had faced very real danger, as well as social and economic demotion, under Sulla, whom he had defied in refusing to divorce Cornelia, the daughter of Cinna.[51] Later, Julius Caesar gained his first real political recognition in Rome by openly challenging Sulla's memory and his memory sanctions. In his first political steps, Caesar prosecuted two allies of Sulla, Dolabella and Antonius, albeit unsuccessfully.[52] Then in 69, the year after some elements of Sulla's constitution had for the first time been modified by new laws, Caesar was quaestor. During his quaestorship, Caesar paraded the wax ancestor masks of Marius and of his relatives, presumably also including Gratidianus, at the funeral of Marius' widow Julia, who was Caesar's aunt.[53] Without any warning Marius suddenly appeared again in the city in triumphal dress and, accompanied by the masks of his relatives, paraded to the Forum from his house to be eulogized from the *rostra*. Unfortunately, the tiny surviving fragment from Caesar's funeral oration for his aunt does not reveal how he described any of the Marians or whether he justified himself through a direct critique of Sulla's memory sanctions. The general impression is that Caesar simply behaved as if Sulla had never existed, displaying an attitude that was itself a powerful kind of erasure; he gave Marius and his other relatives the customary honors associated with aristocratic funeral ritual.

The result was a sensation in the city, and an enthusiastic response from the crowd, who recognized and greeted "Marius" for the first time since his own funeral in 86. Caesar probably also included references to Marius' victories, both in props paraded in the procession of the ancestors and in his funeral speech. Thus Caesar consciously launched his political career on a Marian platform, and he did so with considerable success, no doubt partly due to his formidable oratorical skills. It remains unclear whether the Marians were now to be seen regularly at family funerals, and whether Caesar kept their *imagines* in his own *atrium*. It would be the logical next step to restore the memory of Marius in the everyday lives of the family. It also made sense for Caesar to issue his first challenge to Sulla's sanctions precisely in the area of family traditions, an area normally covered by custom rather than by law.

Caesar repeated his popular success at the funeral of his wife Cornelia later that same year.[54] Cornelia, the daughter of Cinna, was the first younger Roman woman to be publicly eulogized from the *rostra*. It is hard to see how references to Cinna himself could have been completely avoided, although no ancient source alludes to the *imago* of Cinna or to any public praise of him by his son-in-law Caesar. If Caesar honored Cinna as he had Marius, it did not, apparently, have the same lasting impact on the Roman imagination. Meanwhile, Caesar had also supported an amnesty for the associates of Lepidus, who had revolted against the Sullan constitution in 78/77, most notably his own brother-in-law, L. Cornelius Cinna.[55] Yet soon after Cornelia's death, Caesar proceeded to marry Pompeia, the granddaughter of Sulla.

In 65, the year he was aedile, Caesar went a step further and suddenly restored Marius' statues and trophies, overnight according to Plutarch.[56] This must also have involved careful planning, and it caused another major public reaction in the city. Once again the challenge to Sulla was simple and direct. Moreover, this time Caesar effectively created permanent public memorials to the clash between the two men, as Marius' monuments could now be seen at the same time as Sulla's and sometimes in the same place, such as the Capitol. A heated debate in the senate followed, as Caesar had, on his own initiative, stepped beyond the sphere of family memory to restore Marius in public and sacred spaces in the city, in violation of Sulla's existing laws. Yet a decision was made to tolerate the restoration, thus further undermining the legality of what Sulla had done to his victims. Caesar, then, evoked vivid popular memories of Marius, but at the same time recalled the violent suppression that had followed. In this sense, his actions may have done more to stir up old quarrels than to restore a sense of balance. In 64, in his role as supervisor of murder trials, Caesar accepted accusations against men who had acted as informers and had killed citizens during Sulla's reign of terror.[57] When Labienus displayed his "illegal" portrait of Saturninus in 63, he was surely inspired to such boldness partly by Caesar's example.

It was also in the late 60s that Caesar as praetor challenged the role and prestige of Q. Lutatius Catulus (cos. 78), who had been a principal ally of Sulla and defender of his constitution. He accused Catulus of mismanaging the funds for the rebuilding of Jupiter's temple on the Capitol and hence demanded that Catulus' name be removed from the dedicatory inscription that marked the completion of the temple's lengthy restoration in 69.[58] Catulus, therefore, appears as a rare example of a man whose achievements Caesar wanted to erase. In 46 the senate did in fact vote for the erasure and for the substitution of Caesar's own name on Jupiter's great temple, although this measure was never carried out. Such an appropriation of a specific building from Catulus, and ultimately from Sulla himself, whose role had been taken over by Catulus, illustrates a maneuver that would become characteristic of later, imperial efforts to appropriate the policies and projects of a predecessor. Perhaps Caesar felt that Catulus' name should not have been in the dedication in the first place. It may also be that Caesar's action imitated Marius in his conflict with Catulus' father (Q. Lutatius Catulus, cos. 102) and with Sulla over who should receive the ultimate credit for victories in Numidia and against the Gauls. Catulus was surely also closely connected with, if not ultimately responsible for, the violent death of Marius Gratidianus.

At the beginning of his career, then, Caesar had challenged Sulla's memory sanctions, and he went on to avoid his example in many ways. In 49, in his first dictatorship, Caesar restored political rights to the sons and other relatives of the proscribed.[59] He did not uphold earlier memory sanctions, nor did he kill and erase his own political rivals. Caesar did not want to kill Pompey and gave him an honorable burial. His policy of clemency was deliberately designed as a contrast with the memory of Sulla. He did not restore a republic and the power of the senate, nor did he resign from his dictatorship after he had defeated all his enemies and become master of the Roman Empire. He did not wait until retirement to publish his own version of events, his justification of his leadership, and his relationship to the Roman state.[60] When news reached Rome of Caesar's victory at Pharsalus, Sulla's equestrian statue at the *rostra* was toppled, along with the statues of Pompey.[61] But Caesar restored them all when he returned to Rome. When he eventually fell to the assassins' daggers on the Ides of March 44 B.C., his killers were those whom he had not erased, and he lay dead at the feet of Pompey's statue, which he had restored and which was now marked with his own blood.[62] Ultimately he missed both the chance at conquests in the East and the retirement at the height of his power. Meanwhile, neither the killers nor those who mourned Caesar could easily agree what to do with his memory.

Caesar was an exceptional figure, who had built his career in Rome on the popular traditions developed by the reforming tribunes starting with Tiberius Gracchus, by Clodius, and especially by Marius. In the last years of his life he had received what amounted to divine honors, and he may have been formally deified shortly before his death.[63] Rome was full of his statues and of the image of his supreme power, on coins and buildings, as well as in laws and especially in his new calendar. He had also considered whether to take the title *rex* and to (re)create a monarchy in Rome.[64] The ordinary people of Rome, however, did not appear receptive, at least in 44, and so Caesar ostentatiously refused the diadem offered to him by Antony at the feast of the Lupercalia, a month before his death. However, the people were also unenthusiastic about the restoration of a republic, as Caesar's assassins learned to their own cost. Brutus and Cassius had assumed they would be greeted as heroes and saviors who had killed an oppressive tyrant and that the day would end with celebration as Caesar's body was being thrown in the Tiber.[65] But the murderers received only limited acclaim from other senators and from Roman citizens, and the amnesty proposed by Antony proved short-lived. The Liberators lost any hope of political control, or even of safety in Rome, after Antony gave Caesar a martyr's funeral that incited intense popular sympathy for the people's great benefactor who had been killed by his friends.[66] In fact, neither Caesar nor his killers were about to restore a republic in 44.

In the aftermath of the high drama provided by Caesar's funeral, a popular cult arose in the Forum at the site where his body had been cremated. These divine honors for Caesar were especially cultivated by a certain Amatius (or Herophilus), who called himself Gaius Marius and claimed descent from Rome's great general.[67] This "Marius" set up an altar and a column to honor the new divinity and called for the death of the Liberators. Once again, a popular cult in honor of a benefactor challenged the senate, and especially the consul Antony, who had been named but never actually inaugurated as *flamen* to Caesar in his lifetime. At first the cult was tolerated, but in mid-April "Marius" was executed without a trial, and by the end of the month Dolabella, who had initially joined the Liberators on the Capitol, destroyed all traces of the cult in honor of Caesar in the Forum. At the same time the Liberators left the city. In the immediate aftermath of his death, Caesar alternated between tyrant, martyred popular politician, and god, but a solution was not quickly found. By late July Caesar's heir Octavian was celebrating lavish games, the *ludi Victoriae Caesaris*, in honor of Caesar's memory, effectively following in the footsteps of "Marius."

The memory of Caesar was ultimately defined by the political needs and ambitions of those who survived him: no one could remain neutral in this political climate. The inevitable result was that each party claimed to represent the Republic, and each party called its rivals *hostes*.[68] The new triumvirate of Antony, Octavian, and Lepidus, formed in late 43, soon promoted Caesar to be Divus Iulius, while banning the use of his mask in any context.[69] Making him a god turned out to be the most convenient outcome for those who followed in his footsteps, since it also removed him from the crowd of martyred popular politicians, as well as from the usual realms of Roman memory. Octavian may have started his career as Caesar's heir and avenger, but this role did not last into the new age of the more stable principate, with its stress on reconciliation and restoration, rather than on political assassination and revenge. The memory of the divine Julius could, in time, become something of a liability.

The difficulty in dealing with Caesar's memory is matched by the deep ambivalence many Romans felt for the Liberators, and especially for their leaders, Cassius and Marcus Brutus.[70] As senators and close associates who became the killers of the first Caesar, they were especially controversial during the age of the Julio-Claudian emperors, but the debate did not end with the death of Nero. Like the suicide of Cato, the deaths of Brutus and Cassius represented a heroic tradition of "republican" resistance that could inspire a range of opposition to individual emperors or to a system of one-man rule as such. Yet their very failure to restore a republic and their own part in unleashing a long and bitter period of civil conflict also affected the way people remembered them. In his final clash with Octavian and Antony, Brutus appeared as another Roman warlord, who had seized and exploited a large part of the Empire for his own political purposes, and whose final struggle resulted in huge numbers of Roman casualties.

After Philippi, Brutus' writings continued to circulate freely, but his memory was attacked and suppressed by Octavian. When Brutus' sister Junia, who was the widow of Cassius, was buried in fine style in A.D. 22, Brutus and Cassius were said by Tacitus to be the more conspicuous by their absence from the grand procession of the ancestors, over sixty years after Philippi.[71] Similarly, a relative of Cassius, C. Cassius Longinus, met his death under Nero for keeping a bust or ancestor mask of the Liberator Cassius in his house. By the time of Pliny and Trajan, however, it was possible to keep portraits of the Liberators and of Cato in private houses.[72]

By contrast, Tacitus' account of the treason trial of the historian A. Cremutius Cordus in A.D. 25 paints a vivid picture of the competing traditions of the first century A.D.[73] Cordus was accused and his history books burned after his suicide because he had praised the Liberators and had particularly called Cassius the "last of the Romans." Cordus' speech in Tacitus is an eloquent plea for freedom of speech and an appeal to the victors in political conflicts not to erase the voices and views of their defeated opponents from the record of the past. Evidently, historiographic authors writing before Cordus had praised the Liberators, notably Asinius Pollio, Messalla Corvinus, and Livy. Negative views of them were propagated by Augustus himself and can be found in Josephus, Valerius Maximus, and the anonymous *De viris illustribus*. Both negative and positive can be found in the major extant narratives, especially the biography of Brutus by Plutarch and the account of the civil wars by Appian. When another Gaius Julius Caesar (the emperor Caligula) was assassinated in A.D. 41, the memory of the Liberators could serve as much as a warning that the murder of a tyrant could lead to civil war as an inspiration or a call to action.[74]

Punitive Sanctions in the Politics of the Late Republic

At some time during the period of the late Republic, statues of the sixth-century Athenian tyrant slayers Harmodius and Aristogeiton, copies of those to be seen in Athens, were erected on the Capitol in Rome.[75] It is characteristic of the politics of the period after the Gracchi that there is no one historical context to which such a statue group can definitely be attributed. It could perhaps have been put up already by Scipio Nasica as a representation of his role in the death of Tiberius Gracchus, although he had little time before leaving for Pergamum. Alternatively, it could be a bit later and may have been designed to suggest that both Gracchi brothers were tyrants, like the Peisistratid brothers Hippias and Hipparchus whom these Greek freedom fighters aimed to kill. Equally, and perhaps most plausibly, it may have been erected by Sulla, the conqueror of Athens, after his triumphant return from the East and his defeat of the Marians. The Greek heroes took on a completely new and contemporary meaning in a Roman setting, whatever the precise context may have been. At the same time, the statues attest to the renewed search for continuity with a distant and even foreign past, in order to give an acceptable and reassuring meaning to a rapidly changing and unstable present.

Because the break with the traditional Republic and its politics of consensus was violent, traumatic, and not easy to negotiate, Romans sought to escape from this present into the "simpler" times of that imagined past, away from the complex strife of the contemporary scene.[76] Meanwhile, it was equally problematic to find a reliable version of past events that would be widely accepted. The history of the early Republic was becoming increasingly distorted as it was being elaborated in multiple versions to accommodate different political outlooks. Yet the very habit of casting the present in terms of previous episodes of republican history suggested the false notion that a stable republic was destined to emerge from contemporary conflicts by analogy with what appeared to have been the earlier pattern. Violence and punitive sanctions were justified as the defense of an idealized "traditional" republic, now identified with each leader's own political stance; thus the very characteristics and qualities of earlier republican politics were effectively obscured.

The consensus politics of the "classic" Republic had been based on compromise and on the absence of ongoing partisan divisions or bloody vendettas, whether against individuals or families. The new politics of the late second and early first centuries B.C. did not represent an escalation of the competition inherent in traditional Roman republican politics, but rather composed a completely different pattern of political behavior. This new political climate changed the basic definition of both cooperation and competition, at least as these had been understood before in Roman republican terms. The new political game was a zero-sum game in which one side aimed to prevail by the complete erasure and defeat of its political opponents. Consequently, this game was also played in a different and new memory space that was characterized by competing and partisan "histories," which tended themselves to obscure and to devalue the traditional memory world of the *nobiles*. All factions were employing similar tactics, and rivalries were absolute. There were many Romans who were deliberately and successfully erased from the community's shared picture of the past.[77]

The history of punitive memory sanctions in the late Republic can be represented by the two figures that mark its beginning and its end, Gaius Sempronius Gracchus and Gaius Julius Caesar. Both men faced either erasure or divine honors after death. Each of these options was outside the traditional memory practices of republican politics; neither type of remembrance could be represented by an *imago* mask. In other words, political leaders, especially those who appealed to ordinary citizens, now used methods and gained power and rewards that were essentially outside the republican system. The memory of such men was highly problematic, both for their supporters, who made them the equivalent of gods or heroes, and for their opponents, who represented them as tyrants or traitors. As a result, the memory space of the years 121–43 B.C. was unstable and did not reflect earlier patterns. Its stark choice between honor and disgrace echoed Hellenistic themes and recalled the shifting relations of kings with Greek cities, in an increasingly Hellenized Rome that was moving toward monarchy. Meanwhile, the new and elaborate funeral honors paid to the women from the political families, whether Catulus' mother Popilia or Cinna's daughter Cornelia and Cornelia's own daughter Julia, also represented a decisive step outside the republican tradition, with its focus on the community of male citizens celebrating the memory of their duly elected officeholders after death.[78] The form and content of Roman memory both represented and influenced the evolving patterns of Roman politics. However, the developments of these years were not simple or incremental or linear. They were marked by cycles and by a strong caesura during the dictatorship of Sulla.

PART·II

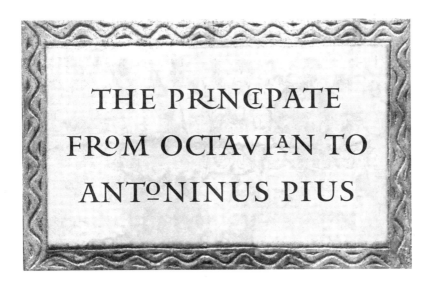

THE PRINCIPATE FROM OCTAVIAN TO ANTONINUS PIUS

Memory Games

Disgrace and Rehabilitation in the Early Principate

▾   ▾   ▾

Quo magis socordiam eorum inridere libet,
qui praesenti potentia credunt extingui posse
etiam sequentis aevi memoriam
Tacitus, *Annales* 4.35.6

The beginning of the principate marked the introduction of changes to virtually every area of the political and social life of Rome's leading citizens and of their families. The figure of the *princeps*, the leading man in Rome, now overshadowed the achievements and ambitions of others. Similarly, his family evolved from being a branch of the Iulii Caesares to being the *domus Augusta*, eventually even described as the *domus divina*.[1] Its prominence increased steadily over time with the (re)creation of the topography of the city through imperial buildings and inscriptions, the appearance of the ruling family in art and on coins, and the extension and multiplication of its dwellings. It came to monopolize the traditional aristocratic rituals of power, such as the triumph, the display of booty, and the erection of new public buildings within the city. By the time of Nero's death, the emperor had appropriated the Palatine district where the aristocrats of the Republic had lived. At the same time, the picture of the past was reshaped in a teleological way to suggest that all previous ages had been tending toward the Augustan age, this new golden age that was inaugurated in a special way by the celebration of the secular games in 17 B.C. Augustus created his own particularly Roman version of "modernity" and of the "end of history." His age had profound effects both on the way Romans spoke about their past and on the way they assessed their own times in relation to that past.

The Augustan age has been the subject of extensive studies, mostly from a positive perspective: Augustus can be appreciated both as an innovator and as a renewer of traditional Roman customs and society. Yet his reforms and his image inevitably displaced competing versions of the past, even as they displaced prominent individuals who were in competition for glory and for their own position in Rome's history. At the same time, his regime fostered a renewed sense of *memoria* and of its uses. The distant past became fashionable and was recalled and re-created in a wide variety of monuments and rituals. New "memories" were also fashioned, memories that revolved around the central role of the *princeps* as leading citizen and savior of Rome. Caesar's heir created a unique persona for himself, starting with his new name of Augustus in 27 B.C. and culminating, some twenty-five years later, with his acclamation as *pater patriae* in 2 B.C. The image of the benign elder statesman and of his golden age of prosperity displaced the violence and lawlessness of Octavian, the teenage warlord who once had played a decisive role in reintroducing proscriptions to exterminate his political rivals. Along with this fundamental shift in political culture came a different and much more nuanced use of memory sanctions. Augustus' actions reveal his desire to distance himself from the kinds of punitive sanctions that had become a norm, especially in the 50s and 40s B.C. He preferred to appropriate and to reshape the past and its image slowly and in more "constructive" ways.

Marcus Antonius

The Augustan change is exemplified in the treatment of the memory of Antony by Octavian, immediately after his return from the East as the victor of Actium. It should come as no surprise that the senate had attacked the public image of Antony after it learned of his decisive defeat.[2] Its decision reflects the expectations created by the power struggles between the republican dynasts starting with Marius and Sulla, as well as the previous record of Octavian himself. Dio's account seems preferable to that of Plutarch, who presents what appear to be standard postmortem sanctions that follow a later imperial model, under the auspices of Marcus Cicero, son of the orator who had been a victim of Antony in the proscriptions. While it is true that Cicero was consul when the news of Antony's death reached Rome, actions against his statues and inscriptions (both destruction and erasure), the declaration of his birthday as a day of ill-omen, and a ban on the use of the *praenomen*

Marcus by the family of the Antonii seem to predate his death. They reflect his status as a (defeated) *hostis*. After the capture of Alexandria and the death of Antony, however, the reaction seems to have been one of silence about the defeated, accompanied by honors for the victor and a holiday to mark the victory.

Meanwhile, it is unclear whether the senators went a step further in their enthusiastic expectation of the news that one man now controlled the Empire by formally extending the sanctions to include Antony's ancestors.[3] Erasures of Antony's ancestors from the official records of Rome's magistrates (*fasti*) would have constituted a radical reshaping of the past, and they may or may not reflect the precise injunctions of the senate: they could equally have been the result of individual enthusiasm or of simple error caused by confusion or haste. A whole family was apparently to suffer oblivion, even as the holiday for the great victory at Actium would recall and celebrate Antony's defeat every year.

It was a decisive turning point when Octavian chose not to accept the senate's solution. He did not restore all the individual honors for Antony, but the symbolism of the *fasti* themselves, with their seamless record of officeholders stretching from the earliest times to his own day, was too important and monumental to be defaced by the scars of erasure. Rather, the reinsertion of Antony's name reveals the extent of Octavian's control over commemoration, at least within the city of Rome.[4] It also reminds us that a text like the *Fasti Capitolini* or the *Fasti Triumphales* belonged to Augustus no less than the *Res Gestae* and represented inscriptions put up by an individual Roman rather than by the senate (figure 16). At the same time, the clemency of Rome's ruler could serve to obscure the bitterness of the previous conflict and the challenge presented to Caesar's heir. The emphasis on the consensus of all well-intentioned citizens in Italy could not easily coexist with punitive sanctions of the kind imposed by political leaders in the context of earlier civil wars. Augustus had no desire to commemorate civil strife. In his own account of his life in his *Res Gestae*, he characterized each of his nameless political opponents as the leaders of a minority faction.[5] He consistently ascribed to himself motives and methods that were fundamentally different from theirs, seeking to recast the way silence and sanctions were used against Roman citizens within the sphere of political discourse.

The partial rehabilitation of the memory and status of Antony was also inevitably shaped by his close family relationship to Octavian. Antony had been the young Octavian's ally and had been married to his sister, Octavia, by whom he had two daughters.[6] Octavian had used the gradual breakup of

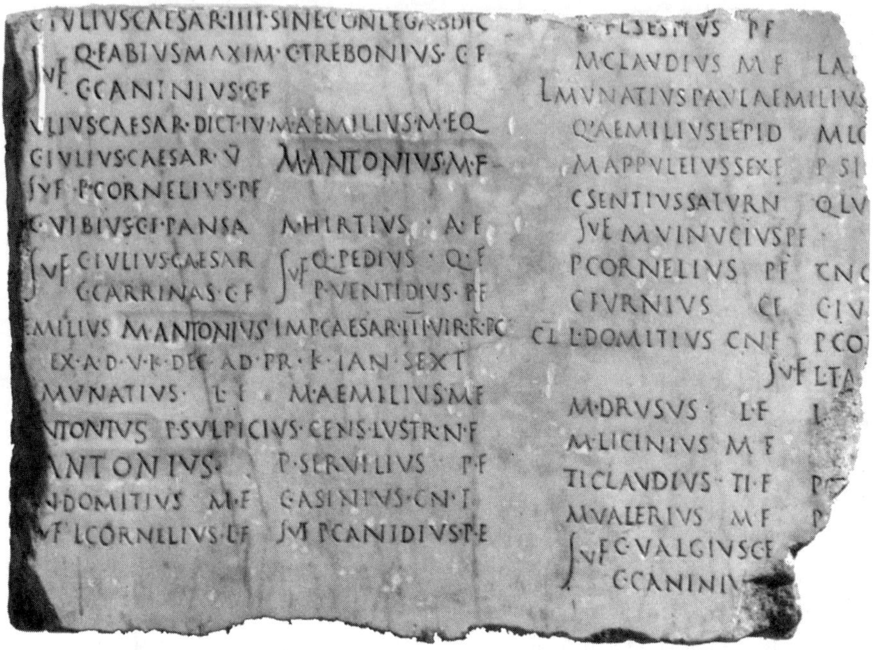

```
CIVLIVSCAESAR IIII SIN EC ON LEG…SDIC        …FLSESMVS PF
 Q FABIVSMAXIM CTREBONIVS C F              MCLAVDIVS M F  LA
 CCANINIVS CF                             LMVNATIVS PAVL AEMILIVS
 LIVSCAESAR DICTIVM AEMILIVSM EQ          Q AEMILIVS LEPID  MLC
 CIVLIVSCAESAR V   MANTONIVS MF           MAPPVLEIVS SEXE  P SI
 VF PCORNELIVS PF                         C SENTIVS SATVRN  Q LV
 VIBIVS CF PANSA  A HIRTIVS A F           VE MVINVCIVS PF
 VF CIVLIVSCAESAR   Q PEDIVS Q F          PCORNELIVS PF  CN C
    CCARRINAS CF     P VENTIDIVS PF        CIVRNIVS  CE  CIV
 AILIVS M ANTONIVS IMPCAESARITIVIR RPC   CL LDOMITIVS CNE  PCO
 EX A D V E DEC AD PR E IAN SEXT                           VF LTA
 MVNATIVS LE  M AEMILIVSM E
 TONIVS PSVLPICIVS CENS LVSTR NF         M DRVSVS  LF   L
 NT ONIVS   P SERVILIVS PF               M LICINIVS M F
 DOMITIVS M F  C ASINIVS CN I            TI CLAVDIVS TI F  PE
 F LCORNELIVS CF  M PCANIDIVS PE         M VALERIVS M F   P
                                           VF C VALGIVS CE
                                             CCANINI
```

FIGURE 16. Restoration of Antony's name in the *Fasti Colotani*, Rome. *Musei Capitolini, Rome, archivio fotografico dei Musei Capitolini*, photo Maria Teresa Natale, II 13.1.18.

their marriage to enhance his picture of Antony as a traitor, who had deserted his Roman wife and children for the embrace of a foreign queen. At the same time, he had honored his sister with public statues and with the sacrosanctity usually reserved for Roman magistrates, particularly tribunes of the plebs. It seems that Octavia lived in Antony's house in Rome, and she continued to care for at least one of his children by Fulvia along with her own, until he divorced her and she was forcibly removed on his instructions. Antony's eldest son Antyllus met his death in Egypt, while Iullus Antonius (his other son by Fulvia) and Cleopatra Selene (his daughter by Cleopatra) were brought up by Octavia in Rome. The fate of Alexander Helios and Ptolemy Philadelphus, Antony's sons by Cleopatra, is unknown: there is no evidence for their lives as adults.[7]

It seems likely that Octavia also had a hand in shaping family policy and practice since it is recorded that Augustus was especially fond of his sister. Augustus' initial plan was for the future of his dynasty to rest on the marriage of his daughter Julia to his sister's son Marcellus. Octavia did not remarry but presided over her own *domus*, probably in the house of her brother the

THE PRINCIPATE

princeps, while bringing up Antony's descendants as part of the new *domus Augusta*. This policy conveniently also meant that the new leading family naturally included the heirs both to Antony's own inherited patrimony and to the vast wealth he had acquired in the East.

Octavian's decision to include the Antonii within his own family and to limit sanctions against Antony himself can be understood in a number of different ways. On one level, it represents a return to the traditional sanctions of the middle Republic, which had tended to keep scandals within the family circle in order to preserve the expectations of the next generation. At the same time, this policy was an overt rejection of the punitive political sanctions of the late Republic. Yet it may also have been partly dictated by the public image that had been created for Octavia as the rightful wife of Antony and as a symbol of Roman family values. Despite the devastating propaganda against Antony as a renegade who had deserted his family and his country, the ultimate victory at Actium and the subsequent triumph were celebrated over Egypt and its queen Cleopatra VII. Meanwhile, a golden statue of Cleopatra dedicated by the divine Caesar himself continued to stand in the temple of Venus Genetrix, even after Antony's images in Rome had been destroyed.[8]

Widespread erasure of Antony's name outside Rome is not easy to document.[9] His name seems to have remained intact in a letter to the *koinon* of Asia but has been lost from the beginning of a similar letter found in Aphrodisias. He appears in some of the documents later inscribed on the archive wall at the theater in Aphrodisias. His name can also be read, with the epithet "divine new Dionysos," on an ephebic monument at Athens. Even in Alexandria a statue base has survived dedicated to "Antony the Great, unrivaled among lovers." Colossal statues of Antony in Egypt had been recarved from earlier ones of Eumenes and Attalus.[10] Yet an inscription at Corinth has an erasure of the name of his grandfather. At Sardis Antony is recorded on several texts, one of which bears a striking erasure of twenty lines, apparently removing a whole letter written by Antony (figure 17).[11] This fascinating *stele* records a decision of Caesar about the asylum rights of local temples dated to 4 March 44 B.C., only eleven days before Caesar's murder. The inscribed decree, which was probably among the unfinished business of Caesar that Antony enacted, seems to have been prominently displayed at the entrance of the temple precinct of Artemis at Sardis.

The future plans of the new *princeps* seemed to be better served by recourse to the old Roman way of dealing with a traitor within the family. Yet the legacy and memory of Antony continued to be invoked by various family

FIGURE 17.
Decree of Julius Caesar
about asylum rights of
local temples with erasure
of a letter of Mark Antony,
4 March 44 B.C., Sardis.
IG *Archiv, Berlin. Volkmar
von Graeve.*

members until the very end of the Julio-Claudian dynasty. In that sense, the ultimate outcome was not what Augustus had envisioned during his lifetime. He was forced to deal with adultery or outright treason on the part of Iullus Antonius, Antony's oldest surviving son, who had been named after Julius Caesar, and to recall Antony's close relationship with the Julian family.[12] Iullus' son Lucius (rather than Marcus) Antonius then spent the rest of his life in exile in Massilia (Marseille), but he was buried in the tomb of the Octavii, by special permission of Tiberius.

The memory of Antony was especially recalled in the names of his daughters, the two Antonias, the younger of whom became one of the most prominent and influential women in Rome.[13] Her grandson Gaius abolished the celebration of the Actium holiday and thus openly dignified his descent from Antony through Antonia, whom he honored with the name Augusta.[14] Claudius also recalled the Antonii, not least by naming one of his daughters Claudia Antonia. The memory of Antony was thus both preserved and cultivated by his relatives over several generations after his death, although his daughters by Octavia can hardly have known him personally. His relationship to the Julii continued to be complex and powerful, as his descendants emerged to inherit the Empire created by Augustus. Antonia Augusta, wife of Drusus and mother of Germanicus and Claudius, appears to have exercised a decisive influence, although she was born at the very moment when Antony left Octavia for Cleopatra.

The legacy of Antony represented a form of competition with Augustus from a rival noble family and from a luxurious life-style with pretensions to Hellenistic kingship that seems to have held a special appeal to younger generations of "Julio-Claudians." Yet it could not be separated from Augustus' own bloodline. Nero, the last Julio-Claudian emperor, was directly descended from Antony both on his mother's and on his father's side. His mother's marriage to her uncle Claudius (also a grandson of Antony), and his adoption as Claudius' son, only compounded this relationship.

Senatorial Self-Representation under Augustus: L. Munatius Plancus and M. Licinius Crassus

Hindsight inevitably draws our attention to the monuments of the *princeps* and his family, which were to dominate the new imperial topography of Rome. However, the process of transforming the city was gradual, and Augustus had initially encouraged fellow aristocrats to help in refurbishing buildings traditionally connected with their own families.[15] The extent of the monopoly he would later come to exercise over honorific texts and artistic expression could not have been anticipated from the start. The last triumph and manubial buildings outside the circle of the imperial family date to 19 B.C., more than a decade after Actium.

Leading men were still honored with new monuments, such as the extensive dedications in the Campus Martius near Pompey's theater (in what is now the Largo Argentina), especially in the early years of Augustus.[16] Here, a large building known as the Porticus ad Nationes seems to have served as a typical venue for the honoring of provincial governors with statues and texts. The original trend may have started with the depiction of Pompey, surrounded by fourteen peoples, in the vicinity of his theater. Eventually, only members of the imperial family and their closest associates were honored here. Yet there is significant epigraphical evidence that attests to the numerous and sometimes large dedications to senators who were governors of provinces in the early Augustan age.

L. Aelius Lamia seems to have been especially prominent, with an extensive set of texts put up by the communities of Hispania Citerior, probably soon after his return from being governor in 22 B.C.[17] Fragments of eight texts could have been part of a single monument about five meters long, possibly associated with statues or busts. The same area has yielded fragments of a large base, perhaps for an equestrian statue, labeled with a bilingual text in honor of M. Licinius Crassus Frugi around the time of his consulate in 14 B.C.[18] Even more impressive were the monuments for an unidentified proconsul surnamed Rufus put up in the area later occupied by Augustus' great sundial with its Egyptian obelisk by eight or nine cities in Bithynia and Pontus.[19] Rufus' base (for a statue group?) looks as if it might have been as long as nine meters; it would have dwarfed many famous republican dedications, such as Bocchus' statue group in honor of Sulla's capture of the Numidian leader Jugurtha. It comes as no surprise that Rufus' monument seems to have been dismantled within a decade or two so that it could be replaced by Augustus' new urban scheme.

Enough evidence, especially from the fragments of inscriptions, suggests that leading senators continued receiving honors in art and text that rivaled those accorded Augustus during the early years of his principate. Indeed, it is not easy to say exactly when and how this type of "open competition" came to an end, even in the city of Rome.[20] Moreover, some individuals may not even have seen themselves as overtly "competing" with Augustus, but believed rather that they were simply receiving the customary recognition of their role in public life. In this context, two examples can serve to illustrate

FIGURE 18. Epitaph from the Tomb of L. Munatius Plancus, Tibur, after 22 B.C.
Drawing by Leslie Rae Witt, CIL 10.6087 = ILS 886.

various strategies employed by the *princeps* to negotiate his own position in relation to his most prominent fellow Romans.

The epitaph of L. Munatius Plancus from his monumental tomb at Gaeta is particularly revealing (figure 18).[21] Plancus, the first in his family to rise to prominence in Rome, had enjoyed a brilliant political career, as well as a fine reputation as a man of letters, orator, pupil of Cicero, and friend of Horace. Once a legate of Caesar in Gaul, he had celebrated a triumph and had twice been acclaimed as *imperator* by his troops. Despite his friendship with Antony (whose marriage to Cleopatra he had witnessed) and the proscription of his brother (L. Plotius Plancus), he managed to join Octavian in 32 and apparently revealed to him the contents of Antony's will. He was consul (with Lepidus the triumvir) in 42 B.C. and censor in 22 B.C., and he built a temple of Saturn near the Forum in Rome with his own booty money. He had been a key figure in the senate, having proposed an amnesty for Brutus and Cassius after Caesar's assassination in 44 B.C. and again when he put forward the name of "Augustus" for Octavian on 16 January 27 B.C. The inscription on his tomb is simple but powerful and communicates — within a traditional republican epigraphical format — his preeminence in Rome. Yet its position on a monumental tomb decorated with a frieze of weapons, with a special focus on trophies and awards for military valor, reflects the heightened competition of the civil war era.

Plancus aspired to the same kinds of achievements and public recognition as Augustus, as statesman, priest, successful general, builder, patron, and founder of colonies. In 44/43 B.C. he was the founder of two colonies for Roman veterans within Caesar's Gallic sphere of operations, at Raurica (Augst) and at Lugdunum (Lyon).[22] His epitaph and tomb survived to commemorate his life, but his veteran colonies were renamed, so that Raurica became Augusta Raurica in honor of the new *princeps*, who had first been called Augustus by Plancus himself. In this way, the expansion of Augustus' role as supreme leader and patron impinged progressively upon the status and memory not only of his rivals but also of his allies.

A more serious challenge to Augustus' prestige came from M. Licinius Crassus, grandson of the triumvir.[23] Shortly after Augustus' splendid triple triumph in August of 29 B.C., Crassus, who had been Octavian's consular colleague the previous year, killed Deldo, chief of the Bastarnae, with his own hand. If Crassus had managed to dedicate *spolia opima* in 27, it would have put him in a strong position to be seen as an emulator of and successor to Romulus.[24] There can be no doubt that such a dedication would have been an embarrassment for Augustus, regardless of how friendly he may have been with Crassus by this date.[25] We know that Crassus did celebrate a triumph on 4 July of 27 and was entitled to be hailed as *imperator*.[26] He disappears from our record after this, although his adoptive son M. Licinius Crassus Frugi, the consul of 14 B.C., was honored by an equestrian statue at the Largo Argentina.[27]

In order to understand Crassus' position in 27 B.C., it is essential to consider the magnitude of his achievement, both as a general and as a warrior. In an age when single combats had become largely a thing of the past, he personally killed the enemy leader, although it does not seem to have been in a formal pitched battle. He was the first and apparently the only Roman general ever to come close to repeating Marcellus' feat at Clastidium in 222 B.C. Crassus' extensive campaigns figured largely in Livy's and later in Dio's account of these years.[28] From Dio we also learn that he recaptured Roman standards, which C. Antonius (cos. 63) had lost in 59 to the Getae, who kept them at their fortified stronghold of Genucla.[29] His influence is revealed by inscriptions hailing him as *imperator* at Athens and at Thespiae.[30] There can be little doubt that he aimed to excel and to attain a reputation equal to that of the leading Roman heroes of the Republic and of his grandfather, the triumvir. The recaptured standards must have been features of his triumphal procession, and it would be interesting to know where they were then stored or dedicated. The silence in our sources (including the *Res Gestae*) on this last point is striking, especially in light of Augustus' own emphasis on recaptured standards, notably those regained from the Parthians ten years later.[31]

Given Crassus' family pedigree and his own personal merits, it is hard to imagine that he would not have aspired to the *spolia opima*, yet he clearly did not dedicate them. There is no record of what he did with Deldo's armor.[32] Crassus, as proconsular governor of Macedonia, was fighting under his own auspices and had *imperium*.[33] This state of affairs is confirmed by the fact that he was subsequently hailed as *imperator* and celebrated a triumph. There could be no doubt, either then or now, that Crassus met all the traditional criteria for dedicating *spolia opima*. Why then did he not dedicate them? It seems probable that Augustus played a decisive role.[34] Augustus may have argued, basing his opinion that only a consul in office could dedicate *spolia opima* on the inscription on the linen corselet of Cornelius Cossus, which he had "discovered" during the restoration of the temple of Jupiter Feretrius.[35] Where and how did Augustus present his case? A likely venue is a meeting of the *pontifices*, whom Crassus would have consulted about the correct procedure for making so special a dedication.[36] Such a meeting would have been an essentially private forum. Meanwhile, we are noticeably ill-informed about Crassus despite the accounts of his campaigns in 29/28. There is a silence in our sources about his *spolia opima* and especially about his life after 4 July 27. That silence could have been caused by his death soon after his triumph, but we simply do not know.

C. Cornelius Gallus, the Poet

Augustus' intervention is more visible in the case of the poet C. Cornelius Gallus, friend of Virgil, Asinius Pollio, and the *princeps* and also his first prefect of the new province of Egypt.[37] Gallus was an influential figure in the literary circles of Rome, as has been confirmed by the discovery of fragments of his elegiac verses on papyrus from Egypt. He is generally recognized as the founder of the genre of Latin love elegy. He was also the first to be entrusted with control of Egypt, Octavian's personal province that no senator could enter without special permission. Gallus, an equestrian from Forum Julii (Fréjus), had won Octavian's trust during the Actium campaign, when he was serving as *praefectus fabrum*, and in 30 B.C. assumed military command over the newly subdued territories, becoming the first Roman to have an official post there.

Dio connects his fall with the way in which he exercised and advertised his power in Egypt; additional evidence points to problems with his behavior in Rome.[38] The scanty literary tradition about him has been decisively supported by the discovery of his boastful trilingual inscription from Philae. Augustus apparently recalled him and renounced their friendship, banning Gallus from his house and from any of his provinces throughout the Empire. Gallus seems to have been directly threatened by legal action and by censorship in the senate. He took his own life in 27 or 26 B.C., apparently when faced with the confiscation of his estates, which he probably owed to Augustus.[39] His situation was completely different from that of a senator, since he owed his entire career and his social standing in Rome to Octavian, whose personal deputy he was. The renunciation of the *princeps'* friendship meant the ruin of Gallus. Voluntary exile to his hometown apparently did not appeal to the ambitious prefect. The renunciation of friendship was a way of reminding Gallus of his relationship to his patron. Yet Gallus, not unlike Licinius Crassus, did not fit into the new scheme of a restored Rome under the leadership of one man.

The destruction of Gallus' monuments, surely soon after his death, must be linked to the extraordinary position of Augustus in Egypt, as pharaoh in succession to the Ptolemies. Gallus' memory was erased and has left little trace behind. The inscription from Philae provides the evidence both for Gallus' pretensions and for the way in which his texts were removed.[40] The stele, which bears the date of 17 April 29 in its hieroglyphic text, was thrown down and broken. It was then incorporated in the foundations of an altar in front of the temple of Augustus at Philae, which was built in 13/12 B.C. There is no erasure of Gallus' name here because the whole stone was removed from view. Its trilingual texts have a more boastful Latin version in larger letters at the top of the *stele*. Though glorifying Roman imperial power in a new sphere, it is expressed in terms of the celebration of Gallus himself as the representative of Rome on the spot — a view hardly in accord with Augustus' new position. Nor is it evident that a senatorial decree would have been needed to remove Gallus' texts in Augustus' own province; that could have been effected at the discretion of the *princeps*.

The removal of another text of Gallus, one that had been put up before he was named prefect of Egypt, is especially telling. In this case the text does not seem at all offensive in itself. The red granite obelisk, which now stands in front of St. Peter's basilica, was brought to Rome from Egypt and set up in his private racetrack in the area of the Vatican by the emperor Gaius (figures 19–21).[41] At that time it was already inscribed with a dedication to the deified Augustus and to the emperor Tiberius. The same inscription was carved on both the east and west sides of the shaft, probably by a prefect of Egypt, soon after the death of Augustus and the succession of Tiberius. There seems to have been a halfhearted attempt to remove this inscription at the time when the shaft of the obelisk was cut back in order to mount it in its new setting in Rome.[42]

A close examination of the stone has revealed that there was a different duplex inscription, which was originally underneath the present one.[43] This

THE PRINCIPATE

FIGURE 19. Vatican Obelisk, St. Peter's Square, Rome, brought to Rome by
Gaius (Caligula). *American Academy in Rome, Fototeca Unione 905.*

earlier inscription was not carved but composed of bronze letters (probably
gilded) which were attached to the stone by means of spikes on the back of
the letters. Examination of the spike holes that remain in the stone has made
it possible to reconstruct the earlier text. It records the establishment of a
location in Egypt called Forum Iulium by Gallus, *praefectus fabrum* or staff
officer, acting on the instructions of Octavian.[44] The inscription must date to

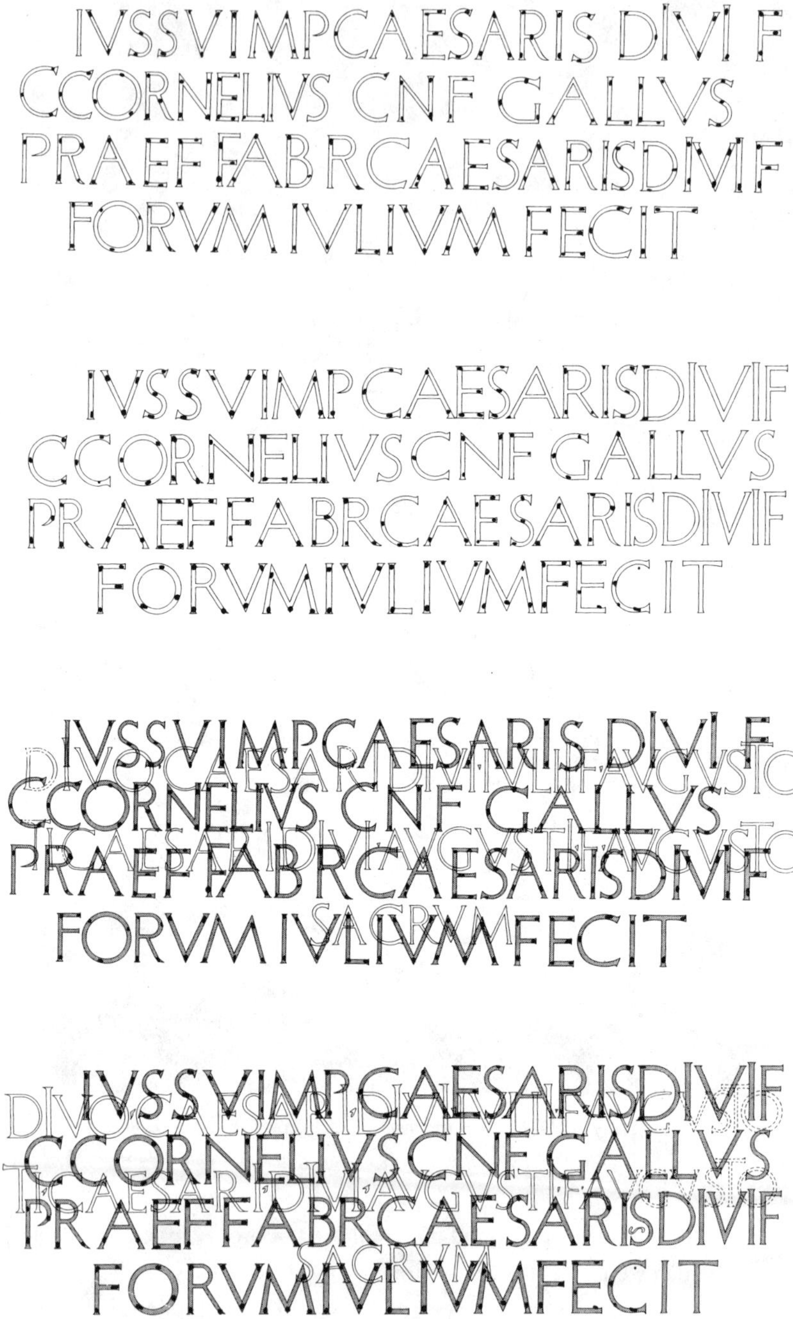

IVSSV IMP CAESARIS DIVI F
C CORNELIVS CN F GALLVS
PRAEF FABR CAESARIS DIVI F
FORVM IVLIVM FECIT
IVSSV IMP CAESARIS DIVI F
C CORNELIVS CN F GALLVS
PRAEF FABR CAESARIS DIVI F
FORVM IVLIVM FECIT
IVSSV IMP CAESARIS DIVI F
DIVO CAESARI DIVI IVLII F AVGVSTO
C CORNELIVS CN F GALLVS
TI CAESARI DIVI AVGVSTI F AVGVSTO
PRAEF FABR CAESARIS DIVI F
SACRVM
FORVM IVLIVM FECIT
IVSSV IMP CAESARIS DIVI F
DIVO CAESARI DIVI IVLII F AVGVSTO
C CORNELIVS CN F GALLVS
TI CAESARI DIVI AVGVSTI F AVGVSTO
PRAEF FABR CAESARIS DIVI F
SACRVM
FORVM IVLIVM FECIT

FIGURE 20. Inscriptions on the Vatican Obelisk. Earlier text of bronze letters put up by C. Cornelius Gallus as *praefectus fabrum* in 30 B.C. to mark the establishment of Forum Iulium. *Courtesy of Géza Alföldy, drawing by Thomas Merz,* CIL *6.31191* = ILS *115.*

DIVO·CAESARI DIVI·IVLI·F·AVGVSTO

TI·CAESARI DIVI·AVGVSTI·F·AVGVSTO

SACRVM

DIVO·CAESARI DIVI·IVLI·F·AVGVSTO

TI·CAESARI DIVI·AVGVSTI·F·AVGVSTO

SACRVM

FIGURE 21. Inscriptions on the Vatican Obelisk. Later carved text dedicated to Divus Augustus and to the emperor Tiberius, dating to soon after the death of Augustus in A.D. 14. *Courtesy of Géza Alföldy, drawing by Thomas Merz.*

the time when Gallus was active in Octavian's military campaign in Egypt in 30 B.C.

Gallus, as a parvenu who had made a career in times of civil war, probably did not have many monuments to speak of outside Egypt. Therefore, the very possibility of leaving a permanent record of his name in ways usually reserved for senators, not to mention the new medium of the obelisk, may have proved a special temptation for Gallus. No inscriptions have survived to attest to his position in his hometown of Forum Julii. It is possible that he did appear in some texts in Rome: an example of a fragmentary early Augustan text that has the name of the dedicator erased provides a tantalizing possibility.[45] The text seems to commemorate the construction or restoration of a temple; however, the individuals and their context have been lost. Similarly, whether Augustus took action to destroy any of Gallus' writings is unclear. The exiguous and rather vague evidence about Gallus' death and disgrace suggests the power of the *princeps* to eliminate a former friend quickly and quietly, especially if that person did not come from the traditional political elite.

"Opposition" to Augustus?

The issue of "opposition" to Augustus is essentially separate from the competition inherent in the traditional displays of status and prestige that had defined the careers of officeholders in the eyes of the Roman public for centuries.[46] Augustus' position as the most powerful man in Rome, and in its Empire, was bound to make him a potential target for anyone who would have preferred a different political order. In each generation some might naturally aspire to such preeminence themselves, while others might look back with longing or frustration at the image(s) of a republican past that had characterized Roman political and cultural identity for so long. In addition, traditional Roman antipathy to monarchy, which had only been confirmed by generations of interaction with Hellenistic kings and tribal princelings, was bound to pose a challenge to Augustus, no matter how skillfully he (re)created a republican facade for his power. Danger might also come from Greek notions of the tyrant as a corruption of the good ruler. Meanwhile, the ghosts of Caesar and his assassins could not easily be exorcised, even with the passage of time and the creation of an official cult for Divus Iulius.

Yet the evidence for any serious opposition to Augustus, especially outside the struggles for succession that plagued his own extended family, is surprisingly scanty and has led to sharply differing reconstructions of the political climate under the first *princeps*.[47] The Augustan age was a time of transition and many in the senate found it hard, even over more than a generation, to become accustomed to the permanent presence of a *princeps*. Generalized resistance, notably to his program of moral and social reforms, was sometimes vocal and public.[48] A case can be made for a significant degree of long-term friction, especially with senators from prominent republican families and with the descendants of the great warlords of the late Republic.

Nevertheless, evidence for conspiracies to remove Augustus is very sparse: Tacitus could see no serious rivals, presumably because so many had died in the civil wars and the proscriptions. The loss of Augustan historiography is also a decisive factor in shaping our picture. The list of conspirators to be found in later writers is peopled by shadowy figures, many of whom were in fact close associates of Augustus who had had a falling out with him, especially in the initial period when his role and public powers were still being defined.[49] Individuals like Fannius Caepio, Murena, or Egnatius Rufus remain open to a variety of interpretations. Cn. Cornelius Cinna Magnus seems a plausible character in an opposing role, but he is only exiguously attested by Seneca and Dio. A number of others are nameless. That Augustus developed his position in the Roman state in reaction to a series of threats from opponents has been decisively refuted in contemporary scholarly opinion; nevertheless, debates about the balance of power in the state, within the circle of the imperial family, in the senate and the lawcourts, and no doubt elsewhere continued. Augustus himself appears to have been more tolerant of such criticism at some stages of his long life than at others.

If writing a history of opposition to Augustus is difficult, assessing the use of memory sanctions during his reign is even more challenging.[50] This situation stands in stark contrast to the years under Tiberius, when sanctions against the memory of prominent individuals were regularly put into effect and enforced, especially through the use of treason trials, but also in cases of individuals like Sejanus, who was never subject to any judicial procedure. In his use of disgrace and dishonor, Tiberius does not appear to be following Augustan precedents closely, at least according to the picture given by the surviving sources.

At the same time, Augustus was clearly engaged in a dynamic long-term project involving the construction of memory in every public sphere of Roman life.[51] He had managed to eliminate Antony, one of the greatest generals of the Republic, without resorting to a full range of punitive postmortem sanctions, mostly by absorbing Antony's household within his own extended family. He had no desire to be seen as an imitator of the memory sanctions of the late Republic: his position of power was based on concepts of consensus and harmony, especially in Italy. Public recognition of dissent, especially through hostile sanctions, could actually undermine the carefully crafted image of his preeminent *auctoritas*.

His silence about Brutus and Cassius is telling: it matches his revival of the memory of the great Pompey, who was also a relative of his.[52] By the time of its completion, his temple of Mars Ultor and its new forum complex had become a memorial to Roman heroes and to Rome's imperial successes, rather than to any single victory over political rivals or to revenge exacted in a blood feud. Augustus was skillful in displacing public memory and the status displays of the traditional political families with new constructions of the past, which logically also reinforced the new politics of the present. At the same time, he tended to remove the gaps and scars of these erasures by celebrating his own magnificent constructions and status rituals.

Stories of his opponents are not much in evidence, suggesting that they may have been obscured or "lost." Modern debates about how to interpret our sources have tended, through the very compelling details of their competing reconstructions, to obscure how little we can actually claim to know.[53]

Later historiographic traditions may not recall some episodes or individuals, and crucial details often seem to be missing. Whether this is the result of chance survivals in our sources or of the effectiveness of Augustus' deliberate control over information is difficult to say.

The exile of Ovid, perhaps never much noticed outside his immediate circle of family and friends, can serve as a case in point. His biographical writings provide us with the fullest information about any individual who was punished by Augustus in what has been interpreted as a political context.[54] Yet his fault, beyond the publication of erotic poetry that could be seen as morally objectionable but that had been tolerated for years, remains shrouded in mystery. Though on the tip of his tongue, the truth seemingly cannot be spoken. Very few people in Rome knew what the offense was, and none of them left a record behind. Theories have proliferated, but the silence itself is more telling, especially with regard to the powers of the *princeps* to impose his own version of events, at least for those outside his inner circle. It is equally remarkable that Augustus did not trouble to impose any sanctions on the memory of Ovid, nor did he stop Ovid from publishing more poetry; he continued to send new poems to Rome from the Black Sea. Perhaps Augustus' political objectives were achieved without using the kinds of sanctions that in themselves drew attention to dissenters or rivals; perhaps, as Ovid might attest, Augustus' private sanctions were in truth more potent than legal penalties.

Maiestas *under Tiberius:* *The Case of Cn. Calpurnius Piso*

The reign of Tiberius stands in stark contrast to that of Augustus in that we have a wealth of information about tensions between the emperor and various senators, about the use of treason trials as weapons against political rivals, and about a wide array of memory sanctions.[55] Tiberius did not manage to maintain the appearance, or even the expectation, of civil discourse with his fellow aristocrats. At the same time, his plans for the succession came to a sad end with the deaths of his heirs Germanicus (A.D. 19) and Drusus (A.D. 23). His withdrawal from Rome to Capri (A.D. 26) created an unusually strained atmosphere, shaped by mutual suspicions and disappointments that could produce violent results, such as the purges that followed the fall of Sejanus. The negative picture of Tiberius in surviving literary sources, especially in Tacitus, has been heavily influenced by this last stage of his life.

Meanwhile, the senate emerged as the forum both for judicial procedures involving prominent Romans and for debates about elaborate "additional" penalties targeting the posthumous reputations of those convicted.[56] Suicide became a popular option, but treason trials continued in the severest cases even after the death of the accused. In this context, Tiberius came to be remembered as one who favored archaic penalties and legal norms.[57] Yet the senators themselves must bear at least some of the responsibility for proposing memory sanctions against members of their own circle. Tacitus' use of the daily records of senatorial debates (*acta senatus*) provides a rich source not only for the penalties imposed but for a range of novelties, rejected by Tiberius but clearly meant to gain their proposers some political advantage from the *princeps*. The interest in sanctions against memory can be understood as a kind of negative equivalent to the development of ever more elaborate posthumous honors, rituals, and memorials, especially for Germanicus and Drusus.

At the same time, the memory of members of the elite seems to have been increasingly cast in terms of the memories of the *domus Augusta*. Of special note is the funeral of Junia, sister of Brutus and wife of Cassius, which included the ancestor masks of twenty leading families (A.D. 22).[58] Junia (and her relatives) staged a spectacle to rival the grand funerals of the imperial family, and especially the funeral of Augustus, which had appropriated the masks of other leading families of the Republic. She was unable to include Brutus and Cassius in the procession, although Tacitus claims that they were the more conspicuous for their absence. Her answer to the imperial family was to take no notice of Tiberius in her will, although a mention of the emperor had become customary by this time. Her actions, and the publicity accorded them, demonstrate the role that senatorial families still aspired to in shaping memory in the public life of the city. Junia could use both displays of status and prestige, and targeted silences, even as the Julio-Claudians had done.

Remarkable light has been shed on memory sanctions under Tiberius by the discovery in Spain of a document circulated to all the provinces in A.D. 20. Under the title of *Senatus Consultum de Cn. Pisone patre*, the document gives an official account of the punishments imposed on Cn. Calpurnius Piso, who was posthumously convicted of treason in connection with the events surrounding the death of Germanicus in Syria (figure 22). The document provides us with the only example of the full official details of such posthumous memory sanctions and affords a comparison with the descrip-

FIGURE 22. *Senatus consultum de Cn. Pisone patre*, copy A,
Roman province of Baetica, Spain, A.D. 20. *Museo Arqueológico de Sevilla,
Junta de Andalucia, Consejería de Cultura*, CIL 2.5.900.

tion of Piso's trial in Tacitus, the fullest account of any treason trial in his
Annales.[59] Yet, at the same time, caution is called for: Piso's trial was a truly
exceptional event, still vivid in the memories of those who had witnessed
it and who passed on their own oral versions to Tacitus and to his generation. Tiberius and the senate faced a genuine political crisis, both in Rome,
where ordinary people held Piso responsible for Germanicus' death, and in
the provinces, where the clash of Roman troops over Piso's attempt to return
to Syria after Germanicus' death had raised the renewed specter of civil war.
Their response was a mixture of traditional remedies and innovation.

It was decided to try Piso for treason because a conviction under the traditional *maiestas* law, which addressed abuse of power by provincial governors, seemed assured and carried with it the severest penalties available for
a senator under Roman law. A murder trial could have been a political disaster, particularly since Piso was almost certainly innocent.[60] The penalties
imposed, especially upon his memory, were as traditional as the use of the
republican definition of treason — in this case, Piso's deserting his province
while he was still in office and then returning to retake it, after having tampered with the loyalty of the troops. The result had been a battle between opposing Roman forces, each supporting their own man for governor. Among
the sanctions, one may particularly note the demolition of parts of the house
(those built by Piso himself), a penalty that was traditionally associated in
the Roman imagination with aspirants to tyranny. Similarly, the ban on the
praenomen Cnaeus could recall such a ban in the cases of M. Manlius Capitolinus, who had surely provided the precedent in the case of Antony.[61] The
use of such venerable penalties and the decision *not* to impose novel ones,

such as a golden statue in the temple of Mars Ultor or an altar of Vengeance (probably in the same place), served not only to label Piso as an archetypal traitor, one in a series of exemplary villains, but also to justify the whole way in which he had been treated.[62] At the same time, the publication of the outcome of the trial in every major provincial city and in the winter quarters of all the legions was surely unparalleled and resulted in the memorializing of Piso, even as his memory was ceremonially removed from an array of more traditional contexts.[63] The political needs of the moment were in conflict with the more usual sanctions against Piso's memory.

Piso's punishments stress the continuity and dignity of his aristocratic extended family, who are invited to join their peers in the senate in shunning his memory by not mourning him publicly, by not displaying a wax mask representing him either in their homes or in their funeral processions, and by supporting the decision to remove all his portraits (with their inscriptions) from public and private places.[64] Despite the overarching importance of the *domus Augusta*, the family of the Calpurnii was accorded full public recognition for its role in creating and maintaining the memory of deceased family members, both for itself and for the Roman public at large. The senate's decree concerning Piso suggests the status and dignity accorded to Roman aristocratic family units, as long as they were seen to be in harmony with the *domus Augusta*. In other words, they were required to show full and public support for the political status quo.

The return of their property, their traditional patrimony, made perfect sense in this context and was due not to unusual influence with the *princeps*, but rather to the Roman conception of the family as a unified social entity across the generations and as the basis for society as a whole. The insertion of the person of the *princeps* into the process of handing on this patrimony from one generation of Calpurnii to the next is another example of how the *domus Augusta* had managed to encroach upon the space of other noble families and of their traditional common forum in the senate. Piso's estate in Illyricum, which had been given to him by Augustus as a gift, was an entirely different matter; it was naturally confiscated and returned to the imperial patrimony.[65]

The erasure of Piso's name was ordered on only one text, namely the inscription on the statue of Germanicus dedicated by the *sodales Augustales* on the Campus Martius, near the altar of Providentia.[66] The erasure here reflects the need to preserve this particular inscription, dedicated by a group of aristocrats to Germanicus in a strategic spot in Rome, while all the honorific inscriptions associated with Piso's own statue bases were removed. The fact that Germanicus had renounced his friendship with Piso, and had then held him responsible for his death, made Piso's name on this particular statue base intolerable, as it impinged upon the memory of Germanicus himself.[67] This example demonstrates how carefully Roman memory sanctions were tailored to the individual case. Other inscriptions mentioning Piso have survived; some of these have erasures in them that can now be attributed to individual and local initiatives rather than to an explicit senatorial directive.

Particularly notable is the erasure of Piso's name in the record of votive games to celebrate Augustus' return to Rome, given in 7 B.C. by Tiberius as consul along with his colleague Piso.[68] Whether the initiative for the erasure of his old friend came from Tiberius himself or from someone trying to please him remains unclear. Either reconstruction is problematic. Piso's name has been restored in an erasure in the Arval record created by the removal of the name of the person who replaced Augustus in A.D. 14, yet Piso's age makes him an unlikely candidate for this spot.[69] Piso's removal from an altar dedicated to Augustus in Spain has long been seen as a local issue.[70] Similarly, the removal of the name of his brother, Lucius Piso the augur, from a base dedicated to the brother's wife Statilia in the famous temple complex of Hera on Samos seems to have involved a case of mistaken identity coupled with (misplaced) local enthusiasm.[71] The erasures in these texts appear to parallel the multiplication of copies of the senate's decree condemning Piso that have been found in the province of Baetica, in southern Spain. Local initiative interpreted the senate's injunctions, often for its own political reasons.

The reverse can be seen in the case of a monumental inscription in bronze letters from the old forum at Leptis Magna (figure 23).[72] This text may originally have been on the front of a nearby temple, but it was displaced to the pavement of the forum and then preserved a second time when the forum was repaved in the time of Claudius. The simple text in the nominative recalls that Piso was proconsul of the province of Africa (in A.D. 5/6?), to which Leptis was an independent neighbor, still organized as a Punic city. Piso seems to have been the first Roman proconsul who was active in this area, and he left a distinct memory, which was presumably reinforced when his son and grandson, both called Lucius, were also proconsuls of Africa. Far from erasing Piso's rather showy text, the local government decided to preserve it, even when this involved considerable effort. In effect Piso's inscription was recreated so that his memory could be recalled, regardless of his disgrace in Rome.

Piso is portrayed in the senate's decree as one who no longer behaved in any of the appropriate ways toward the imperial family, especially toward

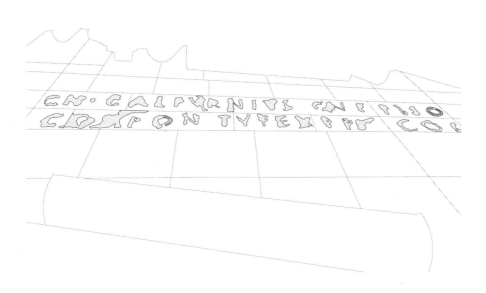

FIGURE 23. Inscription of Cn. Calpurnius Piso in the Forum
at Leptis Magna, North Africa, A.D. 5/6? *Drawing by Leslie Rae Witt
after Africa Italiana 8 (1940), 20 fig. 11, IRT 520.*

Germanicus and Tiberius.[73] The senate's wording illustrates the role of exemplarity in Roman imperial culture: Germanicus is the model prince, while Piso is his opposite, the evil villain. Meanwhile, Tiberius is the model emperor, and the excellence of the *domus Augusta* motivates lengthy commendation of its individual members. The rhetoric of exemplarity links the individual with the family and with society in general, as each person wins praise for fulfilling his or her appropriate role. In this ideal, hierarchical community constructed by imperial rhetoric, the sanctions against Piso's memory must necessarily also appear both ideal and normative. They illustrate the way in which Piso had forfeited his role in society, his elite status, and also his individual identity, all of which are specifically understood, at least in this context, as constructs of that same society and of his family as agents within it and of it. Consequently, if we want to understand the mentality of the Roman senators, as expressed in terms of their own value system, we must take seriously their assertion that these memory sanctions, many of them strictly honorific, could be construed as being worse than death, at least for a man like Piso. Memory sanctions deprived him of public recognition and of his place within the family, recalled in the most traditional ways by his mask in the family *atrium* and by his eldest son's name and filiation. The need to advertise the outcome of the trial was essentially a separate issue, having to do with the continued political unrest in the Empire, and it may or may not have corresponded in time to the end of the legal procedure.[74]

Memoriae Agrippinae

Soon after the death of Livia in A.D. 29, Agrippina, daughter of the elder Julia and Agrippa and widow of Germanicus, was exiled to the island of Pandateria in conjunction with the disgrace of her eldest son (Nero Caesar). She died there, either by suicide or starvation, in A.D. 33.[75] Yet her disgrace has been almost completely obscured by her official and extensive rehabilitation, less than four years later, when her son Gaius succeeded Tiberius as the next emperor. Her case provides the only example of a Julio-Claudian whose memory was rehabilitated in a formal way. As a result, she was accorded an honorific status that was probably more elevated and visible than the one she had enjoyed during her lifetime. Because the image of her that has come down to us reflects the influence and the ingenuity of her children and grandchildren, it is hard to fit her into a discussion of disgrace. Just as sanctions against memory had developed under the Julio-Claudians, so also the memory game of enhancing the image and status of individual ancestors was essential to a ruling family that reconfigured itself several times in succession.

It is hard to be precise about what, if any, sanctions were imposed on the memory of Agrippina, who died the year after Livi(ll)a's memory had been officially erased. Tacitus does not speak of extensive official measures.[76] Tiberius seems to have issued a communication of some kind in which he attacked Agrippina's memory, accused her of adultery with Asinius Gallus (who had also recently died in prison), and pointed out that she had not been shamed as a criminal by having her body exposed on the Gemonian stairs. His remarks need to be understood in their historical context, in a year when further associates of Sejanus had their bodies exposed. Yet in the case of Agrippina, Tiberius seems to have impugned her memory without actually taking any formal steps against her. He contented himself with exploiting the fact that she had died, perhaps coincidentally, on the same day as the execution of Sejanus two years before (18 October), so that the memory of her demise could be observed on the same occasion without adding to the official calendar. The day was to be marked by an annual sacrifice to Jupiter. Suetonius also records a sacrifice to Jupiter on the Capitol, accompanied by a gold dedication that was curiously designed to recall Tiberius' *clementia* toward Agrippina, a virtual memorial to the fact that she had *not* been subject to public sanctions. He adds that her birthday was to be observed as a day of ill omen. She was excluded from the Mausoleum of Augustus, presumably as a sign of disinheritance from the family.

There is no word of any official action against her inscriptions or her statues. Only a few texts and one statue have survived from the period of her lifetime, while there is no extant example of an erasure of her name. In accordance with the restrained practices in honoring imperial women current under Tiberius, she had not appeared on any coins in the capital and her birthday had not been publicly recognized. Yet individuals clearly owned small portraits of her, perhaps including paintings that they used during public protests in support of her in Rome.[77] In the East, she had been commemorated both as a child, as daughter of Julia and Agrippa (at Thespiae and possibly also at Samos), and then as wife of Germanicus (at Samos and Andriaca, and possibly also at Lindos and Aesernia). She is well attested in the posthumous honors for her husband, both in Rome and elsewhere.[78] Her statue and name remained intact throughout antiquity in the old forum at Leptis Magna, in an extensive group from which first Livi(ll)a and then Messalina were removed. The Leptis group seems to demonstrate that no senatorial decree targeting her memory was circulated. Yet it remains surprising that there is not more surviving evidence for honors from the East dating to the time of Germanicus' special command in Syria. Surely many cities would have honored the popular and charismatic couple Germanicus and Agrippina, just as they had Julia and Agrippa a generation earlier. The couple had traveled widely in the eastern Mediterranean and had often met with an enthusiastic reception. It is possible that local initiatives were sometimes taken to remove Agrippina's honors, although such decisions might also have impinged on the posthumous honors for Germanicus himself. Such initiatives would in turn have been completely out of place as soon as Tiberius died, less than four years later.

The elaborate and highly publicized restoration of his mother (and brothers Nero Caesar and Drusus Caesar) was one of the very first acts undertaken by the new emperor Gaius, after he had buried Tiberius with great ceremony.[79] Whatever the precise legal situation may have been, Tiberius' will, which had named Gaius joint heir with Tiberius Gemellus, was set aside. Gaius had no wish to denigrate the memory of Tiberius and seems even to have proposed divine honors that were vigorously opposed by the senate.[80] He simply juxtaposed the grand public funeral and eulogy for Tiberius with a complete reversal of Tiberius' family strategy. Gaius himself fetched the remains of Agrippina and carried them in solemn procession to the Mausoleum of Augustus, where they were laid to rest. His mother was commemorated in inscriptions both inside and outside the building (figure 24).[81] Magnificent games recalled Agrippina, and the *carpentum* used in the circus procession on that occasion was immortalized on a series of *sestertii* struck throughout the reign of Gaius (figure 25). These coins were the first to be dedicated to a royal woman without any reference to the reigning emperor. Moreover, their message overtly recalling Agrippina's memory (MEMORIAE AGRIPPINAE) also represented a new approach to the act of commemoration, both as spectacle and as monument, through the symbolic imagery of the *carpentum*. Her birthday was now observed every year by the Arval brothers, and probably by other public priests as well.

The procession that brought Agrippina's remains home drew on images of a triumph, but it also recalled her own journey home from Syria with the ashes of Germanicus. The complexity of the message, and of the multiple media employed to make it effective throughout the Empire, suggests Gaius' subtlety and skill, as well as his sense of drama and of artistic possibilities. Agrippina was his own direct link to Augustus, and so her memory served to bolster his political position. The restoration of Agrippina's memory must also be seen in the context of the dedication of the temple of Divus Augustus by Gaius in the same year. The ancient sources are virtually unanimous in attesting Gaius' popularity at the time of his succession, as the promising son of the great Germanicus who was destined to offer Rome a new start after the grim final years of Tiberius.[82] He did not need to honor his mother in the way that he did, and to a greater degree even than his father Germanicus. His program of restoration, therefore, reflects both his own personal feelings about Agrippina and his reaction to Tiberius' denigration of her since her death. His sisters may well have helped him to design his new memory project: his sister Agrippina certainly continued with a similar commemorative strategy as soon as she came to prominence as the wife of Claudius.[83]

A rich body of evidence attests the celebration of the elder Agrippina under Gaius, in statue groups, texts, and on provincial coins from a number of cities. Glass phalerae provide examples of her image that could be owned by ordinary people. Inscriptions from Aphrodisias and Messenia echo the carefully designed wording of her epitaph in the Mausoleum in Rome, suggesting that its text was officially circulated, just as the various honors for her

FIGURE 24. Epitaph of Agrippina, wife of Germanicus, from the
Mausoleum of Augustus, Rome, A.D. 37. *DAIR 41.2310, photo Faraglia,*
CIL *6.40372* = ILS *180, Capitoline Museum no. 2094.*

daughters were.[84] She was similarly recalled, although less widely, in the last
years of Claudius' reign once he was married to her daughter Agrippina. The
latest evidence is for a gold shield portrait at Gabii from the early 50s, which
names her as grandmother of Nero.[85]

So it seems that the bulk of the epigraphic and artistic evidence connected
with Agrippina is commemorative and represents a reconstructed image of
her role and importance as an ancestor of individuals who were not them-

FIGURE 25.
Obverse and reverse
of a *sestertius* of Gaius
honoring his mother
Agrippina's memory,
A.D. 37–41. The reverse
shows the *carpentum*
carriage awarded as a
special honor in her
memory. *Ashmolean
Museum, Oxford.*

selves born to be heirs to imperial power. The same is true, in a somewhat different way, for the portrait of her in Tacitus, which was recorded in the early second century.[86] Tacitus' portrayal is remarkably positive, even idealized, and allows her to emerge as a dynamic and inspirational woman in complete contrast both with her family members (her disgraced mother and sister, her wicked step-grandmother Livia, and the adulterous Livi(ll)a, who was the other daughter-in-law of Tiberius) and with the general tenor of Roman society at the time. Like her husband Germanicus, Agrippina is a romanticized figure who epitomizes the values and aspirations of an earlier time. Yet she also plays an active role in giving advice and, on one memorable occasion, even saves the Roman army by preventing the blockage of its escape route from Germany. She is the focus of the soldiers' loyalty and represents the hope for the continuation of the dynasty. The grandeur and tragedy of her life is overshadowed by a dark fate even while her story encapsulates all the noblest hopes of Romans in her age. This Tacitean picture surely owes much to her rehabilitation by Gaius and to the memoirs of the younger Agrippina, at whatever time the latter text may have been written.

The Erasure of C. Asinius Gallus

Agrippina's fate is linked with that of C. Asinius Gallus, who also died in confinement at about the same time. The case of Asinius remains one of the most fascinating and yet perhaps least appreciated in the history of erasures in Latin inscriptions.[87] Asinius was an exceptionally prominent man, a long-standing member of Augustus' inner circle of advisers, and son of the great historian Gaius Asinius Pollio. Gallus' brilliant career was matched by his high profile as a man with an independent voice in the senate. He emerges, especially in Tacitus' narrative, as an outspoken critic, who repeatedly engaged the emperor Tiberius in debate on a variety of topics. His many speeches make him the most prominent of Tiberius' senatorial victims in Tacitus' account. The awkwardness in his political relationship with Tiberius was exacerbated by the fact that, until her death in A.D. 20, Gallus was married to Vipsania Agrippina, the deeply beloved first wife of Tiberius and mother of his only son Drusus. Tiberius had been forced to divorce Vipsania in order to marry Augustus' daughter Julia, with whom he was to have a deeply troubled relationship. By contrast, Vipsania and Gallus had a large family, including a number of sons who went on to political careers.

Tensions between Tiberius and Asinius came to a head in A.D. 30, at a time when Asinius seems to have been a supporter of Sejanus. The senate was ready to turn on Asinius, and the senators were apparently prepared to condemn him even without a hearing, but Tiberius ordered him to be kept under arrest in close confinement, presumably in the custody of a senior magistrate.[88] Asinius died after three years of such domestic imprisonment, either by suicide or starvation, shortly before the death of Agrippina, whom Tiberius posthumously accused of adultery with him. Such a long time in custody, especially for a senator, was highly unusual. Although he had evidently been charged, his case never came to trial, mainly because the emperor seems to have envisioned hearing it himself. Tiberius, however, did not return to Rome, and Asinius was never taken to the emperor on the island of Capri for trial. The nature of the charge seems to have involved Sejanus, and despite the deaths of many other associates of Sejanus, several of whom had their bodies exposed on the Gemonian stairs in 33, Asinius died in private. His body was released to his family, who presumably buried him in the family grave of the Asinii at the Vatican, where his wife Vipsania was buried.

Of the more than forty inscriptions that bear Asinius Gallus' name, a significant number have been erased, and of these some have then had his name restored in the same place in the text. The evidence shows that, although Asinius was never convicted or even brought to trial, his memory was subject to attack throughout the Empire, presumably soon after his death in 33, but then restored. His rehabilitation can surely be connected with the continued prominence of his sons and with the death of Tiberius himself in 37. It is tempting to situate the restoration of his name in the very early part of Gaius' reign, at the time when Agrippina's ashes were returned to Rome. Agrippina's and Asinius' disgrace had been interconnected by Tiberius' accusation of adultery, although this may never have been a formal charge against either of them. The restoration and celebration of Agrippina's memory by the new *princeps* could have provided a suitable opportunity for other families to pay respects to the memory of their own deceased members who had been victims of Tiberius. Of Asinius' sons, one held the consulship and another was proconsul of Asia under Gaius, so that both would have had the emperor's ear.[89] The numerous erasures of Asinius' name suggest a decree of the senate condemning his memory that was widely circulated. The reinscribing of his name is mainly attested in Rome itself. The rehabilitation may have been the result of a family initiative: whether the senate would have been involved remains unclear, but Gaius would surely have given his permission. Indeed, the restoration of Asinius' honorific status could have represented another way to rehabilitate the memory of Agrippina.

Asinius Gallus' texts in Rome are especially numerous, since his name appears on a series of boundary stones set up to mark the banks of the Tiber River (figure 26).[90] Of twenty-two extant boundary markers with Asinius' name erased, ten have had his name reinscribed. Similarly, his name has been reinserted in a fragmentary inscription that was found in the area of the Flavian amphitheater; the text commemorated the votive games celebrated to mark the return of Augustus to the city in 8 B.C., during the consulate of Asinius and his colleague C. Marcius Censorinus.[91] These texts show that Gallus' name has been restored in Rome in inscriptions that were set up in connection with his official duties as consul in 8 B.C. Asinius' name appears

FIGURE 26. Boundary marker from the Tiber set up by the consuls C. Asinius Gallus and C. Marcius Censorinus, 8 B.C. Gallus' name was erased in A.D. 33 and restored in A.D. 37–38. *Ministero per i Beni e le Attività Culturali, Soprintendenza Archeologica di Roma, Museo Nazionale Romano,* CIL 6.31541c.

in three places in the officially inscribed commentary on the *ludi saeculares* of Augustus celebrated in 17 B.C. One of these entries has been erased.[92] The erasure of the name of his father Pollio (as consul for 40 B.C.) in the *fasti* of a local neighborhood in Rome surely represents a case of mistaking the father for the son, despite the chronological muddle that the error involved (figure 27).[93] It remains unclear whether Asinius' name was regularly removed from more private contexts, such as the epitaph of his wife Vipsania. At Laude Pompeia (Lodi), his name was erased in a dedication to Vipsania, who is identified as the mother of Drusus Caesar.[94]

Erasures in the provinces are equally revealing. A set of four monumental bilingual inscriptions from Ephesus were set up in 5 B.C. to mark the restoration of the precinct of the famous temple of Artemis, as well as the building of a wall around a shrine of the imperial cult (figure 28).[95] Asinius was the governor of Asia and was in charge of the project. His name has been removed, both from the Latin and from the Greek versions of the text, but it is still legible in two places. By contrast, Asinius' name was removed from an epitaph of a prominent local family from Geneva, in this case a Roman citizen whose father still bore a Celtic name.[96] Asinius' name had been used in a dating formula, together with that of his fellow consul. It is possible that this family, who had recently acquired Roman citizenship, wanted to appear more "Roman" by using this official dating formula, which is only rarely found on tombs. This text is one of the oldest datable Roman inscriptions from Switzerland. Asinius' name was not erased in similar dating formulae in Italy.

It is not surprising to see Asinius Gallus' name on a dedication to the *domus Augusta* from Teate Marrucinorum, the native town of his family.[97] This text seems to date to some time after the death of Tiberius. From this inscription we learn that Gallus had built an aqueduct for the local community and that he was warmly remembered there. His name also appears intact in Augustus' letter to the people of Cnidos, written in the second half of 6 B.C. and set up on a stele at Astypalaea.[98] By the time of Gallus' disgrace, few locals may have remembered that his name was to be found in this lengthy inscription about a local legal case, which would itself have dated to a generation earlier. The stone must have remained intact, as it was later used for a letter of Hadrian. It provides a fascinating glimpse of Asinius, here styled in Greek as "my friend" by Augustus, helping the emperor collect testimony in a provincial murder case that had been referred to Rome.

The sanctions passed against Asinius Gallus' memory seem, then, to have been short-lived and to have been attributable, even by people at the time, to the personal hatred that Tiberius felt for his old rival. Asinius, who would

FIGURE 27. *Fasti* of some *Vicomagistri*, Rome, late 2 B.C.
(with some later additions to the text). Erasure of C. Asinius Pollio
(cos. 40 B.C.), father of C. Asinius Gallus, presumably at the time of his son's
death in A.D. 33. *Ministero per i Beni e le Attività Culturali, Soprintendenza
Archeologica di Roma, Museo Nazionale Romano, MNR 121558.*

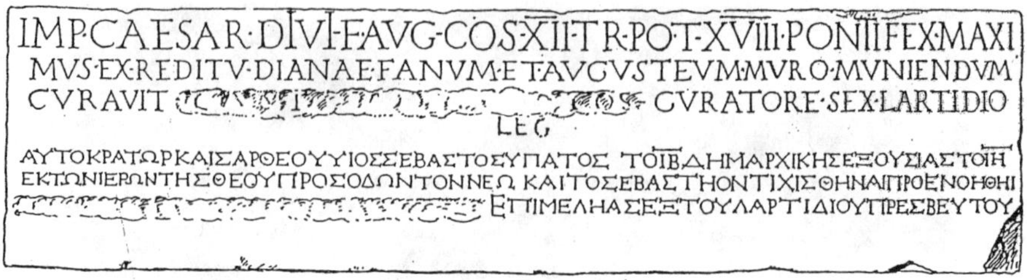

FIGURE 28. Inscription recording the restoration by Augustus of the
temple and precinct wall of Artemis, Ephesus, 5 B.C. Erasure of C. Asinius Gallus'
name both in the Latin and in the Greek versions of the text, c. A.D. 33.
From Hicks (1886–90) 522–4, CIL 3.7118 = ILS 97, British Museum.

have been in his mid-seventies when he died, might well have appeared as a
particularly pathetic victim of the malice of his close contemporary Tiberius.
The widespread erasures of his name can be used as evidence for the repres-
sive political climate following the purges of Sejanus, his followers, and various members of the imperial family. Similarly, the rehabilitation of Asinius
reflects the new political culture under Gaius and a degree of denigration, albeit indirect and sometimes subtle, of his predecessor. The restoration of the
memory of Gallus helps to explain the view of Tiberius held by a senatorial
historian like Tacitus, especially during his later years. Gaius also restored the
writings of T. Labienus, Cremutius Cordus, and Cassius Severus, thus revealing that these had not really been destroyed.[99]

Gaius' Ghost and the Memory of the Caesars

Gaius is surely the most difficult of the Julio-Claudians to assess, and perhaps
the most elusive of any of the emperors about whom we have a viable literary tradition.[100] It is evident that the traditions of senatorial historiography
were exceedingly hostile to him. Their accounts do isolate certain apparently
typical characteristics — cruelty, despotism, sexual deviancy, phobias, and ir-
rational behavior that could plausibly be labeled insanity. Yet the reconstruction of a Gaius who eventually came to reject the principate as constructed by
Augustus in favor of a Hellenistic-style monarchy presents a more compelling
picture, albeit of a cynical and calculating ruler.[101] It would be impossible to
claim that Gaius had had a stable family background or that he had been appropriately prepared to succeed in government. His rapid assassination only
served to confirm the assumption that there must have been something seriously wrong with him or at least with his relationship with the Roman elite.

At the same time, the negative traditions concerning Gaius — who was by no means the only emperor to face early challenges — seem exaggerated and based on hearsay and malice. A change of ruler inevitably produced tensions, even for Tiberius, who had succeeded in a highly regular way and who had two adult male heirs, both popular and well qualified to succeed. Although ultimately drawing on the experiences of those who had known Gaius personally, many narrative sources were written from hindsight and after the fall of Nero, in the changed climate of the new Flavian regime.[102] The struggle to paint a historical, or even credible, picture of Gaius, especially within the context of his own times, has made his memory particularly problematic, even though it was never officially condemned.

Despite the loss of Tacitus and Dio, the circumstances surrounding Gaius' death can be reconstructed with some accuracy: Gaius was murdered by members of his own Praetorian Guard in the middle of the last day of the Palatine Games in A.D. 41.[103] The involvement of some members of Gaius' household should also not be underestimated, especially the freedman Callistus who remained influential under Claudius.[104] Soon after, his wife and young daughter were also killed. The ensuing shock was widespread. Gaius was the first emperor to be assassinated; he met the same fate as his namesake Gaius Julius Caesar, exactly a century after Caesar's first consulate and some eighty-five years after the Ides of March. It should come as no surprise that on the day of the assassination the crowd in the theater, which was well aware of how heavily guarded the emperor was and of the known loyalty of both the Praetorians and the German bodyguards to the whole Julio-Claudian family, initially reacted with sheer disbelief. Some chaos ensued and there was a brief power struggle between the Praetorians, who favored Claudius as the next emperor, and the senators, who seem to have wavered between a restoration of the Republic and exercising the right to choose the next *princeps* from among their own number. The result was inevitable once all the soldiers in Rome had sworn their allegiance to Claudius. A month passed before the new emperor entered a meeting of the senate and then he came with an armed escort.[105] The following year saw a major revolt against Claudius led by a group of senators and briefly supported by the legions in Dalmatia; the aftermath of that revolt was a bloody purge.[106]

The remembrance of Gaius posed a continuing challenge to the inhabitants of Rome and especially to his uncle and successor Claudius. It seems that Gaius was unpopular with many sections of the city's population at the time of his death.[107] Josephus claims that the common people honored the memory of his assassin Cassius Chaerea during the festival of the Parentalia in

February, when families paid their respects at the graves of their relatives.[108] Chaerea's grave may have become the focus, at least in 41, of a popular cult, which would have cast him as a liberator and Gaius as a tyrant. Meanwhile, it is notable that Gaius' ghost was said to have haunted both the Horti Lamiani, where his hastily cremated body had been buried in a shallow grave, and the area of the Palatine where he had been killed.[109]

The persistence of these rumors led to the exhumation of his body and to completely new funeral rites carried out by his sisters as representatives of the family. It seems likely that his ashes were then placed in the Mausoleum of Augustus, perhaps in an unmarked location.[110] This solution would have provided due respect to religious scruples and had the advantage of removing the separate "tomb of Gaius," which had apparently become the focus of unwanted attention and notoriety. Burial within the family tomb also allowed him to be reabsorbed into the group in a way that could help to erase his individual identity. The ongoing need to deal with his corpse parallels the need to deal with his memory.

Gaius' presence on the Palatine apparently continued until the building where he had died burned down in 80, to be replaced by the extensive new palace of Domitian.[111] The persistent tradition about Gaius' ghost is striking in a Flavian context and recalls the prominence of certain Flavian family members in his day, as well as a fragmentary inscription from Spoletium that recorded a dedication in honor of Gaius by a certain Polla, perhaps the mother of Vespasian.[112] The ghost stories seem to conjure up a vivid memory both of Gaius himself as a character and of the violent nature of his unexpected death.

A strategy for dealing with Gaius' memory was slowly developed by Claudius over a number of years. The decision not to impose formal sanctions on his memory makes sense, both as a gesture of family solidarity and in light of Gaius' own very public policy of restoring full honors to the family of Germanicus, Claudius' brother. The invalidation of his legal acts merely put Gaius in the same category as Tiberius, a man who was not fondly recalled but who had not been formally dishonored. Neither Gaius' birthday nor the day of his death was marked by any special observances. Rather, silence prevailed on both occasions.

Gaius' statues, which had been put under guard at the end of his life because they were apparently becoming the target of attacks, were simply removed quietly during the night (figure 29).[113] This convenient solution also reflects Claudius' strained relationship with the senate at the beginning of his reign. He needed to deal with Gaius' public portraits quickly, but he surely

FIGURE 29. Portrait of Gaius Caligula, marble (probably Luna) recovered from the Tiber River near the Milvian Bridge in Rome. *Yale University Art Gallery, photo Joseph Szaszfai, 1987.70.1, Peggy and Richard Danziger, LL.B. 1963, George Hopper Fitch, B.A. 1932, Allen Grover, B.A. 1922, Leonard C. Hanna Jr., B.A. 1913 Fund, John Heinz III Charitable Trust, and the H. J. Heinz Family Fund.*

did not want to defer the matter to the senate. Several images of Gaius recovered from the Tiber suggest a rapid effort to get rid of them, as well as to dishonor his memory by evoking the treatment of corpses of criminals or of victims from the arena. A significant number of statues were also put in warehouses and recarved to represent either Claudius or even Augustus and later Titus.[114] Gaius' case provides the first example of this practice, which was subsequently applied especially to portraits of Nero and of Domitian.

Tiberius had tended to eschew elaborate public self-representation at the end of his life, but there is every indication that Gaius was eager to make a new beginning and to create an image of himself to reflect his imitation of Augustus (figure 30). It is notable that more portraits of him in a small format, designed for private possession and veneration, have survived than for any other emperor.[115] Such portraits reveal the initial enthusiasm felt for the young ruler but may also mirror a policy fostered by the emperor himself. At least one of these was mutilated before being thrown in the Tiber. Similarly, Josephus records that when the consul Cn. Sentius Saturninus delivered his rousing speech about the restoration of freedom after tyranny, he forgot to remove the ring he usually wore, which bore an image of Gaius engraved on a gem.[116] Another senator, a certain Trebellius Maximus, snatched the ring from Sentius' finger and the image was broken, perhaps by being thrown to the ground in the ensuing scuffle. The anecdote about Sentius' ring suggests that images of Gaius were ubiquitous and were put to highly political use. Indeed, many private portraits surely also indicate numerous public ones. Gaius' obsessive concern with his own public image, especially in a monumental format, is well attested in the sources.[117]

Moreover, the whole subject of memory sanctions had apparently already arisen in the senate, on the very day of Gaius' death (24 January 41). Suetonius is the only source to record a different debate in addition to the more famous one about the restoration of a free republic.[118] This related motion apparently proposed memory sanctions against the whole family of the Caesars and the demolition of their temples. Although not well attested in any detail, such a debate is not in itself incredible. The restoration of any kind of republican constitution would have entailed difficulties in a city that was now dominated by the statues, texts, and memorials of the *domus Augusta*. Suetonius' wording suggests a sweeping twofold proposal. First, memory sanctions of a traditional kind would be imposed against the "Caesars" (presumably like those in fashion under Tiberius): statues and texts would be removed and the area around the Mausoleum of Augustus might even be modified. A second, more radical plan envisaged the destruction of the Caesars' temples,

FIGURE 30.
Small portrait of
Gaius Caligula on globe,
bronze. *Brooklyn Museum
of Art, 21.479.12, Bequest of
William H. Herriman.*

which would have meant the official dismantling of the imperial cult with all its public trappings and buildings. A list of their temples would have included the temples of Divus Iulius and Clementia Caesaris, and especially the new temple of Divus Augustus, inaugurated by Gaius himself at the beginning of his reign.[119] It is also possible that these temples could have been renamed for other deities.

If such a decree had been passed, the effort and cost required would have been enormous. The proposals recall both the general impact of Augustus and his successors on the topography of Rome, as well as the particular policies of Gaius. It was Gaius who had finally chosen to destroy the statues of republican statesmen, which Augustus had removed from the Capitol to the Campus Martius. It was also Gaius who had forbidden the remaining families of the republican aristocracy to use traditional symbols of family pride, such as the torque of the Manlii Torquati and the *cognomen* of Magnus revived by the descendants of Pompey. Gaius had deployed his own image in a political space created by the undisguised destruction of republican commemoration; a reverse policy apparently sprang naturally to mind as soon as he died.[120]

In this context, it is understandable that Claudius proceeded with caution and against a background of honors for other family members, including the deification of his grandmother Livia Drusilla. Claudius needed to strengthen his own tenuous position while dissociating himself both from Gaius' reign and from his death. Because the senate was not called upon to issue a decree, it is not known what kind of official message was sent out from Rome. News of the assassination of Gaius could certainly also have provoked a range of local reactions throughout the Empire. The evidence from surviving inscriptions is not easy to interpret.

The number of inscriptions which attest to an erasure of Gaius' name, often characteristically targeting his *praenomen,* is not large and appears somewhat random. Of a dozen surviving erasures four involve removing his name from bases in honor of his deified sister Drusilla, whose cult does not seem to have been formally abolished (figure 31).[121] Only a single dedication, from Halasarnae (Kos), has an erasure of Drusilla's own name (in a text that does not mention Gaius). Multiple erasures of Gaius in one town come only from Pompeii, in the inscriptions of a local form of imperial cult, which may have come to an end with the death of Gaius.[122] The cult, which was administered by annual officials, may have been specifically associated with the Julian family, of which Claudius was not a member. Even here Gaius' name is erased in only two of three texts from his reign. Similarly Gaius is removed from one document from Alexandria but remains in another identical one of the same

FIGURE 31. Base honoring Drusilla as sister of Gaius, from the precinct of the temple of Hera, Samos. Erasure of Gaius' name and titles. *DAIA 1973/1937 Wagner, IG 12.6.1 no. 411.*

FIGURE 32. Lead weight found in the sea near Corsica, showing erasure of Gaius' initial C. *Drawing by Leslie Rae Witt, AE 1992.913.*

date. Yet individual erasures can be found as widely scattered as Cyzicus, Samos, Attica, and Bologna. Gaius' *praenomen* has been erased even from a lead weight recovered off the coast of Corsica (figure 32).[123] On an arch at the entrance of the forum at Thugga in North Africa, the dedicatory inscription has been erased and reinscribed for Claudius, apparently in the same hand (figure 33).[124]

At the same time, relatively few inscriptions containing the whole name of Gaius have survived intact, and because so many texts that can be attributed to him are fragmentary, it is hard to say how often his name was actually erased. Based on the remains of more than sixty inscriptions, however, a number of reconstructions are possible.[125] This is especially true if inscriptions such as labels on water pipes, epitaphs, or receipts for goods are discounted: such texts were rarely erased in any case. Yet, it seems probable that many honorific inscriptions were simply removed, especially if Gaius was the main or only honoree. It is simply impossible to be sure what happened

FIGURE 33. Arch with inscription of Gaius Caligula recarved for his successor
Claudius, Thugga, North Africa. *Drawing by Leslie Rae Witt*, CIL *8.1478*.

in many cases, such as at the new temple for Gaius at Miletus, which was to
serve as a focal point of his cult in the province of Asia.[126] At the same time,
his disgrace did not include other family members and their honors needed
to be maintained, since the dynasty was to be strengthened rather than being
removed.

The surviving complete texts do provide a revealing picture of his activities, which is especially valuable because his reign was so short. Honors for
his parents were very important to him, and in one case statues commemorating Germanicus and Agrippina as the parents of the emperor Gaius were
preserved in the theater at Thera, where they were eventually flanked by a
new statue of Vespasian, presumably in place of a previous one of Gaius.[127]
Dedications to or for Gaius survived at Syene (Egypt) and from Vienne (Nar-
bonnensis), Mytilene (Lesbos), and Spain. Near Lago Maggiore a dedication
was put up by a certain Narcissus, who may well be the freedman later so
powerful under Claudius. Three texts, two of which are in very good condition, preserve details of the oath of allegiance sworn to Gaius in 37. A dossier
of inscriptions from Akraiphia in Boeotia attests to details of the imperial
cult under Gaius, who presented himself in a very different way and accepted
many more honors than Tiberius had. At Cyzicus Gaius is erased in one local
decree but preserved in another. The richness of the combined evidence is
remarkable and suggests something of the impact he made during his short
reign.[128]

Claudius' policy of actively fostering statue groups of the imperial family
was a logical move at the beginning of a new reign but also corresponded to
the numerous groups that had been set up under Gaius, especially initially
and then again after the death and deification of Gaius' favorite sister Drusilla.
At least eighteen statue groups are attested and many more surely existed.[129]
Several of these groups show signs of having been reorganized in order to
remove Gaius and to insert, or to give new prominence to, Claudius. These
include the large groups at Ocriculum, Rusellae, and Velleia, all of which

THE PRINCIPATE

have portraits of Caligula recut as Claudius.[130] At Velleia the inscription of Drusilla seems to have been replaced in order to remove Gaius. Yet three portraits of Caligula from statue groups have survived intact and in their original contexts, at Gortyn (Crete), Aesis (Umbria), and Luna (Etruria).[131] In all about forty unaltered portraits in the round are still extant, as well as other images on cameos and glass phalerae. Consequently, we can see that Gaius' encouragement of imperial statue groups must have been effective and that it took time and local willingness to rework these ensembles.

The diffusion of Gaius' images similarly reflects what must have been a rich iconography in various media to be seen in Rome itself. Fragments of dedications for his well-being have also survived from Rome. Gaius' name has remained intact on the epitaph he put up for his mother Agrippina in the Mausoleum of Augustus.[132] His name must have been prominently recorded in the dedicatory inscription of the important new temple of Divus Augustus that he inaugurated near the beginning of his reign (figure 34). His commemoration of the dedication on a coin conjures up the image of the day, which was Gaius' birthday in his accession year, and of his close association with Augustus. It remains unclear whether the inscription would have been replaced and, if so, how soon; such an operation could not happen quietly or overnight. The same argument must also apply to his restoration of the theater of Pompey, where he apparently advertised his own name even as he removed those both of Pompey and of Tiberius.

The question of what happened to Gaius' coins has caused much debate.[133] They are rare in coin hoards and several show signs of damage, including the telltale erasure of the initial C for Gaius (often spelled Caius). Yet many have survived, notably the fine series of *sestertii*, which included scenes of the dedication of Augustus' new temple, the memorial *carpentum* of Agrippina, Gaius addressing his troops, and his three sisters in a pose recalling the three graces. Like the inscriptions, the coins provide invaluable evidence to supplement the historiographic sources. Yet according to Dio, his *aes* coinage was recalled and melted down two years after his death, which is to say around the time of Claudius' expedition to Britain. Even if an official recall was issued, we cannot know how many complied or how widely the operation of collecting old coins was carried out.

In the *Fasti Ostienses* a different and entirely local solution to the problem of Gaius' memory was adopted.[134] His name was recorded but in a simplified form as C. Caesar, with the result that it could be used to retain the chronological framework for events without dignifying Gaius with any imperial nomenclature or titles. The delay regularly involved in inscribing these annual

FIGURE 34.
Sestertius celebrating the dedication of the temple of Divus Augustus in Rome by Gaius, A.D. 37. *Ashmolean Museum, Oxford,* RIC 12 p. 111 no. 36.

records at Ostia apparently allowed local officials time to react to the rapid changes brought by the deaths of Tiberius and Gaius within a period of four years. This recasting of Gaius as a kind of marginal figure stands in stark contrast to the acts of the Arvals that were regularly inscribed at the end of each year. Their records are especially well preserved for the year 38.[135] They show the elaborate details of imperial cult observances and of the figure of Gaius as a fellow Arval. The context of the sacred grove protected the Arval texts from most erasures, and thus they can provide a unique insight into the mood and tone of a particular moment.

In addition, Claudius' own voice has come down to us in two remarkable texts that allude to Gaius after his death, but in differing ways. The record of Claudius' expansive rebuilding of the *aqua Virgo* in 45/46 recalls, in a rather disobliging way, damage done to this aqueduct by Gaius.[136] In fact it seems evident that Gaius himself had initiated the very same project of refurbishment. Apparently Claudius felt the need to denigrate Gaius, rather than simply passing over him in silence. A degree of continuing insecurity is suggested by this response. Similarly, an edict of 46 dealing with a local boundary dispute in northern Italy also mentions Gaius, simply by his first name.[137] The text seems to reproduce Claudius' own turn of phrase as he blames Tiberius for his lengthy absence from Rome in the same breath as he casts another aspersion on Gaius, whose name he does not hesitate to introduce, once again in a context where he could have avoided mentioning him. On this occasion we catch a glimpse of Claudius in a pensive mood but apparently not feeling benevolent toward the memory of his nephew Gaius.[138]

The first eighty years after Julius Caesar's assassination were very much overshadowed by the image and memory of his close associate Mark Antony, whose descendants became the rulers of the Roman Empire over three generations. The period from the rise of Octavian to the reign of Claudius saw a broad variety of memory sanctions developed parallel to the general recasting of the past to accommodate a new political system and a particular ruling family. Augustus' new use of modified sanctions offers an instructive commentary, by one in a position to know, on the destructiveness and bitter consequences of the punitive sanctions of the late Republic, from the time of the Gracchi onward. A new vision of Rome's future prompted reevaluation of the discourse about the past. The new *princeps* tried other ways of (re)writing Rome's story. Yet the Augustan vision of a unified Rome and Italy did not endure and formal memory sanctions reemerged soon after his death both in the hands of his successor Tiberius and of the senate. The murder of Gaius recalled that of his ancestor (now Divus Iulius) and the dilemmas associated with an assassination of Caesar. Claudius' historical knowledge and his own weakness prompted his extreme caution with the memory of his nephew Gaius, a policy he would not follow after the execution of his wife Messalina. The material in this chapter must be closely related to the treatment of Julio-Claudian women in the next one.

Public Sanctions against Women

A Julio-Claudian Innovation

▾ ▾ ▾

Iuvit oblivionem eius censendo nomen et
effigies privatis ac publicis locis demovendas
Tacitus, *Annales* 11.38.3

Official sanctions against the memory of women did not exist in the public sphere of Roman life during the Republic. The single exception is provided by the Vestal Virgins; they were the only college of public priestesses in Rome, and infractions against their religious duties, particularly loss of virginity, affected the whole community.[1] The Vestals were subject to the authority of the *pontifex maximus*, who acted as *pater familias* in their case and had the power to punish or execute them. An unchaste Vestal would be buried alive in an underground chamber set up to look like a bedroom in a house, with a small amount of food provided, so that she was not actually put to death directly by the *pontifex*. Such a Vestal's death reflected not only her sacred and liminal status but also a pattern that was traditional within the Roman household from a very early period. The members of the family, under the direction of the oldest male relative, would themselves deal with errant women, and especially with cases involving chastity and the integrity of the family.[2]

Women were not subject to accusations of treason (*maiestas*) during the Republic. Only holders of high office could be charged under this law, and they were all men of the senatorial class. Women might be accused of murder, and especially of poisoning, and could then face the death penalty. However, as is illustrated by the famous case of the so-called Bacchanalian conspiracy in 186 B.C., women who came to the attention of the magistrates were traditionally handed back to their families for the imposition of the death sentence.[3] In this way, women were subject to their families both initially and ultimately. Only women without any living relatives needed to be dealt with by the magistrates. Such norms were evidently still in operation under the emperor Tiberius, as is revealed by the case of Appuleia Varilla in A.D. 17. She was consigned to her family, which was expected to exile her from the city, in accordance with the sentence of the court.[4]

The traditional result of the situation of women in Roman law and society during the Republic was that the senate did not impose official sanctions against their memories, nor were they ever declared enemies of the state (*hostes*). The family decided how to recall each woman who died, and this was usually done within a restricted circle of relatives and friends. The first public funeral for an older woman of senatorial rank was celebrated at the very end of the second century B.C., but this custom was not extended to younger women until Caesar honored his first wife Cornelia, the daughter of Cinna, in 69 B.C.

The multiplication of public honors for the female relatives of prominent Romans in the East is a separate phenomenon, which was inspired by Hellenistic models rather than being influenced by the senate in Rome. The first married woman to receive a statue in a public place in Rome seems to have been either Quinta Claudia (*matrona* or Vestal?), or Cornelia, mother of the Gracchi, whose statue was erected in the *porticus Metelli* near the end of the second century B.C. Although some women received statues in public places during the last two generations of the Republic, perhaps not many of the statues were in Rome itself. Despite the very active deployment of different coin types to advertise ancestry and political status during the first century B.C., very few issues portrayed mortal female ancestors, whether historical or mythical. Fulvia, the wife of Antony, was the first living Roman woman to have her image on a Roman coin, but by then the Roman Republic no longer existed.[5] Fulvia herself was also the target of much vituperative and hostile propaganda, some of which portrayed her or treated her like an elite Roman man, a politician or general.[6]

Public and collectively shared memory was created by images, texts, public rituals, and monuments in the city. Since most republican women, even those of the highest status, were not accorded any such recognition, they were also not subject to sanctions that removed any commemoration of them from public spaces. Indeed, the characteristic naming pattern of female Roman citizens, which designated them by a single name shared by all women in the same male line of descent, demonstrates the traditional custom, which did not afford women individual identities outside the household.[7] Things started to change during the triumviral period, with the prominence of women such as Fulvia, and especially with the new public honors granted by Octavian in 35 B.C. to his sister Octavia and to his wife Livia Drusilla. Octavian made the revolutionary decision to accord the women of his family a public face and recognition of the kind previously reserved for magistrates and priests.[8] Less than ten years after the death of Julius Caesar, his political heir set a course for the increasing prominence of the women of the new ruling family in a wide variety of spheres and venues.

The eventual creation of a *domus Augusta* need not in itself have entailed such a public role for the women of the family. Rather, it was Augustus' policy to promote the image of his female relatives, and especially his wife and sister, who dedicated public buildings in their own names and behaved like patrons in a range of contexts. Augustus' stress on women fitted with his moral and social renewal of Roman society, as well as with his dynastic ambitions to hand on the political system he had created to a blood relative. The repeated failure, over successive generations, to produce a surviving male heir in a direct paternal line made relationships through women vital to the future of the Julio-Claudians. The women of the *domus Augusta* were expected to play a role in politics, as supportive daughters, wives, and mothers of Rome's rulers, but also as examples of the family life and of particular virtues that were claimed to be the hallmark of Augustus' new golden age.

Even as Julio-Claudian women took part in struggles over dynastic politics and moral norms, other women also became increasingly involved in the new political culture created by the imperial system. Augustus had criminalized adultery and thus introduced an unprecedented and politicized charge that could be deployed for a variety of reasons to ruin a prominent woman or man. After treason (*maiestas*) was extended, especially under Tiberius, to include actions and words that criticized the emperor, his deified parent, or his family, women also became defendants in such cases. Similarly, by accompanying their husbands on official business in the provinces, wives could now be subject to charges of supporting any treasonable failure in the duties of a Roman commander or provincial governor. Plancina, the wife of Cn. Calpurnius Piso, was accused of virtually the same crimes as her husband during his treason trial of A.D. 20,[9] an accusation that would have been unthinkable in the Republic. The subsequent senate debate about the role of high-ranking women in the provinces of the Empire, and the ban on wives accompanying their husbands abroad, revealed some of the unintended results of the public role that had emerged for elite women during the reign of Augustus.

Julia, Augusti f.

The year 2 B.C. was a watershed for Augustus: he dedicated his new forum with its temple of Mars Ultor, he held his thirteenth and last consulship, he sent his adopted son Gaius Caesar to the East to fight the Parthians, he took the name of *pater patriae* (the ultimate definition of his role in the Roman state), and he banished his daughter Julia on grounds of adultery. It would be difficult to overestimate the sense of public scandal and personal disappointment that were involved with the ruin of Augustus' only child.[10] Throughout her life, Julia had been at the center of his dynastic policy, and she was the vital link in his direct line of descent. He had prided himself on her strict upbringing. While her marriage to Tiberius had not been a success, it was he rather than she who had withdrawn from Rome into exile. Julia should have been at the height of her influence once her two eldest sons had been adopted as the heirs of Augustus. Her disgrace does not fit with anything else in Augustus' policies or with the pattern of Augustus' plans over the previous two decades.

Julia's fall, an event that contrasts sharply with the apex of Augustus' power in 2 B.C., may not have been merely coincidental. Indeed, Julia might have become expendable precisely because her oldest son had assumed his *toga virilis*, even as her/his father's position in the state had reached its final definition. In other words, the setting and timing of her fall may fit into the other events orchestrated for this pivotal year. The timing may also suggest that Julia was now seeking a divorce from Tiberius and remarriage, or perhaps that she wanted no more than a life of her own. However that may be, Augustus seems to have been taking care of old business in sending his only child away from Rome forever.

Julia was accused of adultery, a charge many scholars have seen as a cover or substitution for a more political one.[11] The details of her political aims and aspirations have naturally been lost. The death of Julia's cousin, alleged lover, and fellow conspirator, Iullus Antonius, is reported in various conflicting versions in surviving sources.[12] Whether he was executed or whether he committed suicide, perhaps even before any formal charge could be brought against him, remains unclear. Tacitus has Tiberius remark on the fact that Iullus' name was not removed from the *fasti*, although that decision seems to follow what had become an accepted pattern. The details of any punishments imposed on him have been lost: sanctions against his memory are not attested. Yet the banishment of his son, who was still very young at the time, seems unusually harsh. It may have been meant to serve a symbolic purpose, rather than to reflect any fear of a real threat from Antony's male line. Sempronius Gracchus, another alleged lover of Julia, was exiled and was not executed until after her death.

Augustus punished Julia inside the family, without recourse to a public trial. At the same time, his actions resonate with his new position as "father of the country," a definition of his role in Roman society that he had been working toward for many years. She was exiled and initially kept in close confinement on the island of Pandateria. After a few years, she was allowed to return to the mainland and to live more comfortably in Rhegium. It is notable that her mother Scribonia chose to be her companion during her long exile. Throughout the reign of Augustus, Julia had the use of her personal property (*peculium*) and an allowance from her father. Yet, she was not accorded any privileges, under Augustus' marriage legislation, for having borne three children. In a sense, her disgrace was very public, and Augustus informed the senate in a letter of the actions he had taken. But his decisions reflected his authority within his household and were largely traditional, such as Julia's exclusion from the family burial site at the Mausoleum of Augustus on the Campus Martius. Her death very soon after Augustus' own can hardly be coincidental, but was very probably a consequence of the policy of Tiberius, just as her remaining son, Agrippa Postumus, had also been rapidly disposed of.[13]

Julia's memory was never officially banned, either at the time of her initial disgrace or when she died, probably of starvation, some sixteen years later. Augustus did not impose such punishments on members of his own family. Yet some message about Julia's fall seems to have been sent out from Rome, since no statues or inscriptions were put up in her honor after 2 B.C. It appears likely that her status as a member of the *domus Augusta* was simply withdrawn, through a traditional form of disinheritance. Some local communities may have made their own decisions to remove her images quietly. Her portraits have been lost, although she must appear somewhere on the reliefs of the Ara Pacis and perhaps elsewhere. The first dynastic statue groups of Julio-Claudian family members date from about 17 B.C., when Julia was very visible. Evidence survives for at least twenty-eight Augustan statue groups erected before 2 B.C., and Julia is directly attested in eleven of these. There were surely many more.[14]

An impressive series of inscriptions in Julia's honor from the East, many originally accompanied by statues, is still extant.[15] Most of these texts originated between 16 and 13 B.C., when her husband Agrippa was active in the eastern Mediterranean and Julia accompanied him there, visiting numerous

FIGURE 35. Inscriptions on the gate of Mazaeus, freedman of Augustus, and Mithridates, freedman of Agrippa, south entrance of the *agora*, Ephesus, 4–3 B.C. *Photo courtesy of C. Brian Rose,* ILS *8897.*

cities herself and staying with him in his winter quarters. More than twenty communities in the Greek-speaking East are attested as recognizing her, often with divine honors. Her statues stood in the most famous Greek cities and sanctuaries, for example, at Delphi in front of the temple of Apollo, near the great temple of Hera at Samos, and on Delos. Some of these texts remained very prominent, such as the inscriptions for Julia and Agrippa on the triple arch, which would have had statues on top of it, at the southern entrance to the *agora* at Ephesus (figure 35). Similarly, Lollia Antiochis, a leading citizen of Assos, dedicated a bath complex to "Aphrodite Julia" and to the local *demos*. At Priene and Euromos, Julia was celebrated specifically as the bearer of beautiful children.

It is especially striking to come across a few inscriptions, which were set up to her as the wife of Tiberius, after the death of Agrippa in 12 B.C. Notable examples come from Lindos, Palaepaphos on Cyprus, and Noricum.[16] An imperial statue group from Egypt and the *agora* gate at Ephesos were also set up shortly before Julia's disgrace. The dedication in the sanctuary of Aphrodite at Palaepaphos is very fragmentary and the location is uncertain. However, the well-preserved inscriptions from the area in front of the temple of Athena

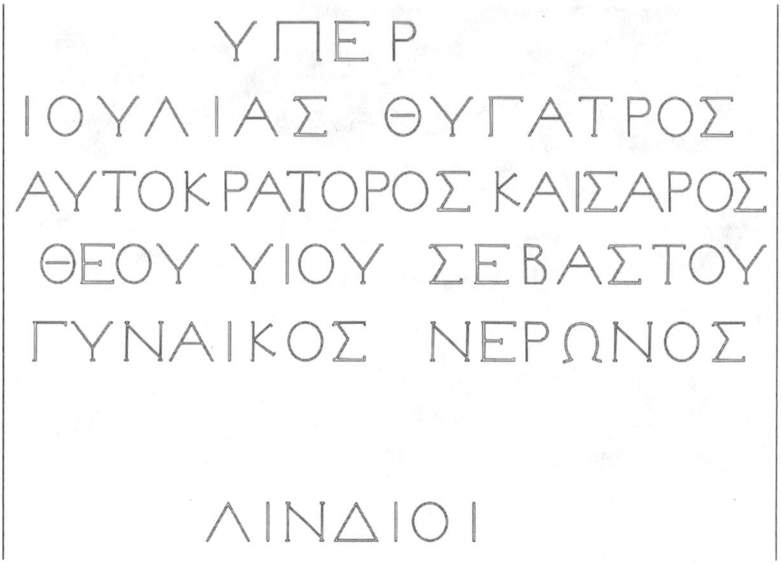

ΥΠΕΡ

ΙΟΥΛΙΑΣ ΘΥΓΑΤΡΟΣ
ΑΥΤΟΚΡΑΤΟΡΟΣ ΚΑΙΣΑΡΟΣ
ΘΕΟΥ ΥΙΟΥ ΣΕΒΑΣΤΟΥ
ΓΥΝΑΙΚΟΣ ΝΕΡΩΝΟΣ

ΛΙΝΔΙΟΙ

FIGURE 36. Inscription from a statue base of the elder Julia as wife of Tiberius, next to statues of Tiberius and his brother Drusus, acropolis of Lindos, Rhodes, 6–2 B.C. *Drawing by Leslie Rae Witt*, ILindos *2.385c.*

on the acropolis of Lindos on Rhodes offer a typical example of a prestigious location in a famous sanctuary, where later imperial statue groups came to be added over time to the initial group of Tiberius, his brother Drusus, and his wife Julia (figure 36). Tiberius himself was surely familiar with this group, which was probably erected primarily to honor him when he came to live on the island in 6 B.C. Yet, even such texts, which could recall especially painful memories of a failed marriage and an unwelcome period of exile, were not removed or altered.[17] Julia's image in the East seems to have remained essentially unchanged, as if frozen in time.

Julia was recalled on an inscription of members of her own household in Rhegium, where some of them continued to live for decades after her death.[18] A text from Rhegium also attests to the presence of Scribonia, Julia's mother, who chose to share her daughter's long exile (figure 37, 38). Even her disinheritance would not necessarily affect her slaves and freedmen. What happened to any monuments in Rome itself is harder to say. The Ara Pacis remained unaltered, but it does not have labels to identify the figures. At certain moments, Julia played a prominent role in the public life of the city. She and Livia provided a banquet for the people in 9 B.C. to celebrate Tiberius' *ovatio.*[19] She may also have been involved in the restoration of shrines or in

FIGURE 37. Epitaph of C. Iulius Gelos together with his father
C. Iulius Thiasus (freedman of the elder Julia) and his mother Iulia
(freedwoman of Livia, called Diva Iulia Augusta), Rhegium, Claudian.
Su concessione n. 52 dell' 01/12/2004 del Ministero per i Beni e le Attività Culturali,
Museo Nazionale Archeologico di Reggio Calabria, AE 1975.289.

other public building projects, just as Livia and Octavia had been in the early
part of Augustus' reign. If there was an erasure of her activities and her image
in Rome, it has been successful. A rehabilitation is not well attested, but there
may well have been a gradual thaw, starting under Caligula.[20]

Disgrace in A.D. 8

Julia and Agrippa's daughter Julia, the granddaughter of Augustus, lived in
exile between A.D. 8 and her death in A.D. 28. She is a more shadowy figure, a woman who had been much less prominent than her mother and who
was only in her mid-twenties at the time of her disgrace.[21] The child she was
pregnant with at the time was exposed, perhaps to help support the charge of
adultery. Yet somewhat surprisingly, her exile to Trimerum did not seem to
affect the status of her mother. Unlike her mother, the younger Julia was not
obviously the focus of continued political demonstrations and agitation. Her

FIGURE 38. Epitaph of L. Scribonius, freedman of Scribonia, first wife of Augustus and mother of his daughter Julia, Rhegium. *Su concessione n. 52 dell' 01/12/2004 del Ministero per i Beni e le Attività Culturali, Museo Nazionale Archeologico di Reggio Calabria.*

survival for many years under Tiberius suggests that Augustus' successor did not see her as a threat. Like her mother, she was banned from burial in the Mausoleum of Augustus. She was recalled only on one rather mysterious inscription, now lost, from Thasos, where her name apparently appeared under that of Livia and next to her mother Julia.[22] It was Livia who supported her step-granddaughter with an allowance throughout her long exile.

Her husband and cousin, L. Aemilius Paullus, a grandson of Lepidus the triumvir, was apparently exiled and his name was erased in at least one private text.[23] Clearly the charge against him was political. An alternate tradition that has Aemilius Paullus being executed for treason is unreliable. Yet it is interesting to note that Julia's husband died in exile shortly before Augustus in A.D. 14, while her alleged lover, D. Junius Silanus, was excluded from the circle of Augustus' friends and went into voluntary exile. Augustus' adultery laws did not impose exile on a husband whose wife had been unfaithful to him, let alone suggest that adulterous lovers should be treated with more leniency than wronged husbands. Silanus returned to Rome in A.D. 20, with Tiberius' permission, and then lived in the city as a private citizen. The case of the younger Julia illustrates a patently political use of the charge of adultery and a strikingly different treatment of men and women who were involved in the same set of circumstances in A.D. 8. The poet Ovid was another who suffered a more permanent and harsh exile that seems to have been connected with these same political circumstances.[24] The fates of the two Julias, under Augustus and Tiberius, provide the vital context for the first official sanctions against a woman, imposed on Livi(ll)a in January 32, only a few years after the death in exile of the younger Julia.

Livi(ll)a and the Fall of Sejanus

Livilla was no more than a diminutive form of the name Livia, although it was used by Suetonius and Dio in writing historical accounts. Her full name can only be recovered with the help of inscriptions put up by her freedmen, of which we have ten: it was Claudia Livia Julia.[25] This pattern is not untypical for victims of erasure: their own names disappear from public texts, but the names and inscriptions of their slaves and freedmen remain unaffected, especially in a funerary context. Thus Livi(ll)a's case reconfirms that sanctions against memory in Roman culture were particularly targeted at the high and mighty, within their own specially defined sphere of *memoria*. Elsewhere, her name has not survived in any inscriptions from Rome.[26]

Livi(ll)a was the daughter of Drusus, younger brother of the emperor Tiberius, and of Antonia the younger, daughter of Octavia and Mark Antony. She was probably born in or soon after 14 B.C., between her two brothers, Germanicus and Claudius. The importance of her brothers serves as an indication of her own rank and expectations. She was a granddaughter of Livia, a great-niece of Augustus, a niece of Tiberius, and also a granddaughter of Mark Antony. Her aspirations are revealed by her marriage to Augustus' adopted heir Gaius Caesar in 2 B.C., on the eve of his departure for the East. Subsequent events have obscured what must at the time have been a very splendid royal wedding.

Livi(ll)a was destined by Augustus to be the wife of his eldest son and heir. After the deaths of Gaius and Lucius, new arrangements were made for the succession in A.D. 4, when Augustus adopted Tiberius, and Tiberius in turn adopted Germanicus (Livi(ll)a's brother). Because her marriage to her first cousin Drusus, the son of Tiberius, also took place in this dynastic context, she had an important role to play in Augustus' plans for the succession as they developed. It is unclear how many children Livi(ll)a bore Drusus: we know of the death of one son in A.D. 15, and of three surviving children.

Her strategic position in the ruling family has been strikingly confirmed by the new *Senatus Consultum de Cn. Pisone patre*. On the occasion of the punishment of Cn. Calpurnius Piso in A.D. 20, Livi(ll)a is thanked among the other members of the ruling house immediately after Agrippina, wife of Germanicus, and Antonia, mother of Germanicus and Livi(ll)a.[27] At this point the senate and citizens throughout the Empire were reminded of her special family relationship and of the high opinion that Livia and Tiberius had of her. Thus Livi(ll)a's public image was related not only to her formal position, based on birth and marriage, but also to her personal qualities. Nothing could provide a more striking contrast with her precipitous fall and her public disgrace some eleven years later. The quality of the senate's commendation of her can be directly connected with the birth of her twin sons, Germanicus and Tiberius Gemellus, in A.D. 19 soon after the death of Germanicus. In this case also the new senate's decree provides additional information to confirm Tacitus, who takes special note of how pleased Tiberius was at the birth of the twins.

Livi(ll)a's life, then, was marked by a number of reversals of fortune. Although Gaius Caesar's early death had deprived her of her position as the wife of the heir, her brother Germanicus' equally untimely death meant that she regained that lofty situation, even as she gave birth to twin sons. This event was much celebrated and she enjoyed a very special position between A.D. 19 and 23, after which her husband Drusus' death, coupled with the death of one of their twins, created enormous uncertainty about the succession. Yet Livi(ll)a did not lose her importance when her husband died. Rather, she was now a very attractive match herself, as is made abundantly clear by Sejanus' attempt to persuade Tiberius to let him marry her in 25, as soon as the customary period of mourning for her previous husband was over. A marriage with her offered Sejanus the prospect of recreating for himself the position of Agrippa, who had been married to Augustus' daughter Julia and had served as guardian of the emperor's heirs in the next generation.

Tiberius, however, chose not to make a new arrangement for the future. When the *princeps* withdrew from Rome to Capri in 26, he left both Germanicus' and Drusus' widows unmarried. The resulting situation of tension and competition within the imperial household led to disaster for the family of Germanicus and to the rise of Sejanus to extraordinary power, without himself becoming either Tiberius' officially designated heir or an actual member of the *princeps'* family. Yet the peak of Sejanus' power in 31 also saw his summary execution and the ruin of many who had been close to him, including Livi(ll)a, who paid the heavy price of her life and her posthumous reputation.[28]

Livi(ll)a comes alive for us primarily in the account of Tacitus, our fullest single source for this period. Though not much concerned with Livi(ll)a in her own right,[29] Tacitus uses her as a foil in his narrative, initially for Agrippina, the virtuous wife of Germanicus, and then for Sejanus, the cunning schemer. Because Tacitus wants to create a series of contrasts between Germanicus and Drusus and to stress the tensions between their families after their deaths, competition between their wives becomes an important part of this pattern. Livi(ll)a is always less favored in Tacitus' narrative, for she is the wife of the less brilliant prince and cannot match the fertility and grandeur of Agrippina, the granddaughter of Augustus. She is also less favored by public opinion (*fama*) in the dynamics of Tacitus' narrative. Even the birth of her twins is presented as an ominous sign for the future of Germanicus' house.

For Tacitus the year 23 and the death of Drusus is the decisive turning point in Tiberius' reign. He places Livi(ll)a's shameful adultery very early in *Annals* 4, at the very start of the second part of Tiberius' reign. Tacitus realizes that many fanciful stories have grown up around the death of Drusus. He is at pains to insist that Tiberius could have played no active part in his son's death. Yet Tacitus never questions the role assigned to Livi(ll)a, apparently only revealed many years later by information in a letter sent by Sejanus' former wife, Apicata, to Tiberius. Sejanus' sudden ruin in 31 cast a long shadow back over previous events, including the death of Drusus, which had apparently aroused no suspicions at the time. Similarly, Livi(ll)a's involvement with Sejanus just before his fall, whatever its exact nature, has also been projected backward to suggest that she was unfaithful to her husband even within his own lifetime and that she actively conspired to bring about his death.

The improbability of a scenario in which Livi(ll)a would be tempted to enhance her political situation by becoming involved with Sejanus, at the very moment when she was the wife of the heir and the mother of his twin sons, is outweighed in Tacitus by conventional moralizing about the wickedness of the adulteress. Tacitus asserts that his version of events is the most reliable, the one best supported by the available evidence (such as the torture of Drusus' slaves Eudemus and Lygdus), and the most widely accepted. This assessment may well be true, but it also reveals the extent to which the stereotypes of the wicked adulteress were current and accepted. At 4.3.4, Tacitus calls Livi(ll)a *paelex* (mistress/concubine):

atque illa, cui auunculus Augustus, socer Tiberius, ex Druso liberi, seque
ac maiores, et posteros municipali adultero foedabat, ut pro honestis et
praesentibus flagitiosa et incerta exspectaret.

▾   ▾   ▾

And she, whose (great) uncle was Augustus, her father-in-law Tiberius,
and who had had children by Drusus, brought disgrace upon herself,
as well as upon her ancestors and her descendants, with a small-town
adulterer, in order to stake her future hopes on uncertain and shameful
prospects instead of her present, respectable situation.

So we can see that Tacitus' account has been heavily influenced by Livi(ll)a's
subsequent disgrace, with the result that he does not reassess her motives and
actions according to probability and logic in the way that he does for Tiberius, at least on the occasion of Drusus' death. Her shame is in proportion
to her previous exalted situation, as Tacitus himself takes pains to explain to
his readers. His words invite further investigation of the sanctions against
Livi(ll)a's memory, which had been in place for more than seventy years by
the time that Tacitus was writing.

Livi(ll)a was ruined by her association with Sejanus, yet her disgrace was
very different from his.[30] Sejanus' ruin was a very public affair, and inevitably
so, given his elevated status at the time of his death, and the many honors
that he had been accorded.[31] Fierce sanctions may also reflect a feeling that
Sejanus had risen above his station, so that he was being deprived of honors
that he had no right to in the first place.[32] Mourning for him was banned, his
property was confiscated, a statue to Libertas was voted in the Forum, and
the day of his death was to be celebrated by an annual festival, even as his
birthday had been celebrated before. In an unprecedented and illegal procedure, even his young children were executed and their bodies exposed on
the Gemonian staircase. The publicity accorded these unfortunate events is
indicated by the record preserved in the *Fasti Ostienses*, both for 31 and for
32, when more of his followers were executed and had their bodies exposed
(figure 39). Sejanus' case differs markedly from those of others who had previously suffered sanctions against their memory under Tiberius (notably
Scribonius Libo Drusus, Cn. Piso, and C. Silius), because he was executed
without a trial, and perhaps even without a formal charge of any kind.

Sejanus' name as ordinary consul for 31 is omitted from most *fasti* of Tiberian date, and his images were destroyed.[33] Quite a spectacle must have been
provided, as Sejanus had been honored with many statues, some of which
had received cult offerings, with altars of Amicitia and Clementia, where his

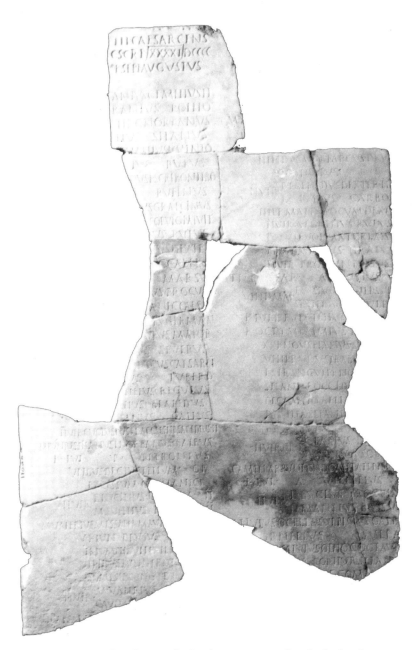

FIGURE 39. *Fasti Ostienses* for October A.D. 31 recording the deaths of Sejanus and his children, as well as the suicide of his former wife. *Archivio fotografico della Soprintendenza per i Beni Archaeologici di Ostia, Ce.*

image stood next to those of Tiberius, and with portraits associated with the standards of the legions in the provinces. Private individuals no doubt also owned portraits of him. In all these places his portraits were now destroyed, and no image of him has survived to be securely identified.

Oaths had also been taken by Sejanus' Tyche and prayers offered for his safety, apparently in the context of similar oaths and prayers for Tiberius at the beginning of each year (perhaps starting in the year 30). Consequently, special emphasis was placed at the beginning of the year 32 on the new oath of allegiance and the prayers for the emperor alone, without his faithful partner. It was precisely in January 32, in the context of continuing tensions and of the senate's desire to affirm its loyalty to Tiberius, that sanctions were imposed on the memory of Livi(ll)a, who by now had apparently been dead for some time.

At Romae principio anni, quasi recens cognitis Liuiae flagitiis ac non pridem etiam punitis, atroces sententiae dicebantur in <ef>figies quoque ac memoriam eius, et bona Seiani ablata aerario ut in fiscum cogerentur, tam<quam> referret. (Ann. 6.2.1)

▾   ▾   ▾

But in Rome at the beginning of the year, as if the shameful deeds of Livia had only recently become known, rather than having been punished already before, harsh measures were passed against her images and also against her memory, and the estate of Sejanus was taken away from the treasury, to be transferred to the imperial exchequer, as if it made a difference.

This brief sentence has much to tell us about the sanctions against Livi(ll)a. The wording surely indicates that she did not commit suicide. Rather she was "punished," but not in a public trial. Dio indicates that she disappeared inside the imperial *domus*,[34] suggesting that Tiberius dealt with her himself. Rumor had it that she had been starved to death by her mother Antonia, the person identified by Josephus as a key player in turning Tiberius against Sejanus. Tiberius had also decided to deal with Agrippina and her sons himself. However, in Livi(ll)a's case, a harsher penalty than exile or imprisonment was chosen.

In fact, Tiberius was employing the traditional, republican way of dealing with an errant woman, especially an adulteress, inside the household. Similarly, the use of starvation as a method of execution recalls the established method of punishing an unchaste Vestal Virgin. All citizens would be silent and avert their gaze as the condemned Vestal walked through the streets to

THE PRINCIPATE

be buried alive. That Tiberius behaved as a traditionalist should come as no surprise. The result was that Livi(ll)a literally "disappeared" — Dio is not sure exactly how or when she died. Tiberius favored older legal precedents concerning the status of women within his household, at the expense of Augustan innovations favoring mothers of three children.

There was no public funeral for Livi(ll)a, or any outward acknowledgment of her death. The family did not mourn her, and she was not buried in the Mausoleum of Augustus with her husband, father, brother, and other relatives.[35] On the other hand, and in contrast to the treatment of Sejanus and his relatives and associates, her body was not exposed to public shame and ridicule in the city. Indeed, we may imagine that no public notice at all was taken of her death. The desire to remove her quietly contrasts strikingly with the public sanctions against her memory of January 32, the first such sanctions imposed by the senate on a Julio-Claudian, and probably the first on any Roman woman. Tacitus speaks of forty-four speeches delivered in the senate against Livi(ll)a's memory (*Ann.* 5.1.1), which leads us to question why Livi(ll)a suffered mandatory erasure, an act that would itself have been of public record in the *acta senatus*, which is presumably where Tacitus read about it.

The real reason must be connected to Livi(ll)a's prominence and to her existing public image, aspects that have tended to go largely unnoticed because of the very negative picture of her in our surviving sources. There is more to her story than the stereotyped contrasts with Agrippina or Sejanus reveal. She had been highly favored at various points in her life, and, as was the case with Sejanus, her fall was sudden and unexpected. Whereas families had dealt with errant female members in private during the Republic, this traditional solution no longer had the same efficacy in the case of a woman like Livi(ll)a, because it did not remove her statues and inscriptions, nor did it obliterate her public image in Rome and throughout the Empire. The fierce sanctions against her memory reveal the degree to which she had been publicly celebrated before, as wife of Drusus, as mother of the twins, and as a member of the *domus Augusta*.

Inscriptions in various languages, some of them recently discovered, as well as evidence for imperial statue groups, can help to give some indication of the nature of Livi(ll)a's public honors, and of the types of erasure and destruction that were carried out. They provide the essential background to the notice in Tacitus. Livi(ll)a's portraits were destroyed by order of the senate, with the result that none can now be securely identified.[36] Some cameos have been assigned to her, but we cannot be sure that they represent Livi(ll)a, since her image does not appear on any surviving coins. Yet there is evidence to suggest that she did appear regularly in imperial statue groups, of which at least fourteen are attested for the earlier part of Tiberius' reign.

That she received quasi-divine honors in the East, just as other Julio-Claudian women had, is directly attested in the inscription for a statue of her mother Antonia. The statue, erected at Ilion by Philon, son of Apollonios, at his own expense, honors Antonia as his patroness and goddess, in her own family context as sister-in-law of the emperor Tiberius.[37] She is described as mother of Germanicus, who is apparently still alive, and of Claudius, and also of Livia, who is called "divine Aphrodite of Anchises." Presumably the statue was originally in a public place in Ilion, the ancestral home of the Julian family. Even so, it is not so surprising that Livi(ll)a's name has not been erased on a dedication that actually honors her mother and was not new at the time of her disgrace. Similarly, a day of the Kaisareia festival held at Gytheum near Sparta early in the reign of Tiberius was dedicated to the "Aphrodite of Drusus," while other days were dedicated to the "Tyche of Livia" and to the "Nike of Germanicus."

However, evidence of the widespread erasure of Livi(ll)a's name is available elsewhere. Her name was erased in a long Neo-Punic text in honor of the imperial family, which was inscribed on the lintel of the temple of Roma and Augustus in the old forum at Leptis Magna (figures 40, 41).[38] The text was put up by some local magistrates, who bear the title of *suffetes*. It describes the statues of the imperial family that were erected in and around the temple. Remains of the statues, and of some bases, have been discovered in the immediate vicinity, and it is noticeable that Livi(ll)a's is the only image of which no trace has been found. The overall composition of the group can be reconstructed with some confidence. Monumental statues of Augustus and Roma could be found inside the temple *cella*, while Tiberius and Livia were placed on either side of the door. In front could be found a long base with a central *quadriga* that contained images of Germanicus and Drusus. They were surrounded by the women of their families, so that the statue of Livi(ll)a was placed near her husband Drusus, accompanied by an image of his mother, Vipsania Agrippina. The whole ensemble must have been very impressive, with Germanicus and Drusus almost twice life-size, and the women represented slightly over life-size. The group clearly stayed in place throughout antiquity.

In this case, the statue group seems to have been put up in response to the parallel honors granted to Germanicus and Drusus after their deaths. In other words, it is a commemorative group, erected after the death of Drusus

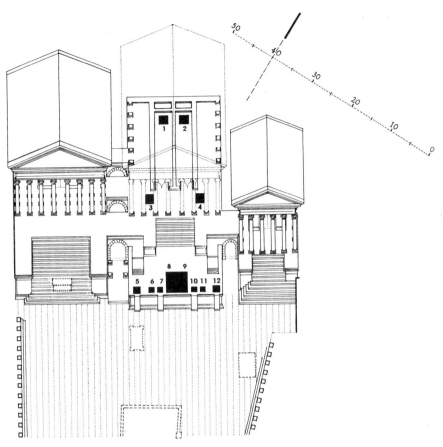

FIGURE 40. Leptis Magna: Old Forum and statue group honoring Germanicus and his brother Drusus in front of the temple of Augustus and Rome, A.D. 23–31. 1. Augustus; 2. Rome; 3. Tiberius; 4. Livia; 5. Augustus; 6. Agrippina, wife of Germanicus; 7. Livi(ll)a, wife of Drusus; 8. Germanicus; 9. Drusus; 10. Antonia, mother of Germanicus; 11. Vipsania Agrippina; 12. Claudius. *Drawing by Eric Fulford.*

in 23. It amalgamates the honors for the two princes, while it imitates the statue groups put up in Rome on the triumphal arches voted to each prince. It must have been completed before the beginning of 32, when sanctions were imposed on Livi(ll)a's memory. It suggests the reactions of inhabitants of the provinces, both in Roman and in local urban communities, to the honors described in the senate's decrees for Germanicus and Drusus. It also reflects a similar sensitivity to the senatorial decree censuring Livi(ll)a, which must have been widely published as a separate document. It is especially striking to see Livi(ll)a's name erased in a Neo-Punic text in a town that did not at that date have a Roman municipal structure.

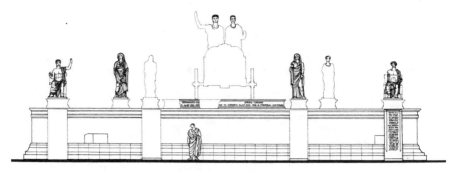

FIGURE 41. Leptis Magna: reconstruction of the statues on the podium in front of the temple of Augustus and Rome, A.D. 23–31. From left to right: Augustus, Agrippina, Livi(ll)a, Germanicus and Drusus in the chariot, Antonia, Vipsania Agrippina, and Claudius. *Drawing by Eric Fulford.*

Inscriptions on bronze from Spain have confirmed the details of the elaborate honors voted by the senate for Germanicus in 19, which were then also repeated in an even more effusive manner for Drusus four years later. The *Tabula Siarensis* describes for us, among other things, the arch for Germanicus in the Circus Flaminius in Rome, which featured statues of twelve members of the imperial family, with Germanicus in the middle in a *quadriga*. Livi(ll)a was included on this arch, and surely also on the arch in honor of her husband Drusus, which we know was finally dedicated in March 30.[39]

The senate chose to place Germanicus' arch near another group of imperial statues, put up by C. Norbanus Flaccus, fellow consul with Drusus in A.D. 15, at the very beginning of the new reign.[40] Norbanus' group was an important and well-known display of the *domus Augusta* in its own right, although we do not know exactly who was included. I would argue that his group was more rather than less extensive, representing the wives of Germanicus and Drusus and perhaps even some children. It seems illogical to posit that a restricted statue group would have been acceptable in Rome in 15 to celebrate the new dynastic situation under Tiberius, since such groups were extensive by 19. Similarly, the language of praise and the individual commendation of so many family members by the senate at the end of Piso's trial strongly suggest that the concept of an extensive *domus Augusta*, stretching over several generations and including both sexes, was well developed by the year A.D. 20. The same picture can be extrapolated from the exile poetry of Ovid.[41]

Further confirmation comes from a newly reassembled inscription from Messenia, which records local reactions to the news that Augustus had died and that Tiberius was now the new emperor (figure 42).[42] The text, originally

THE PRINCIPATE

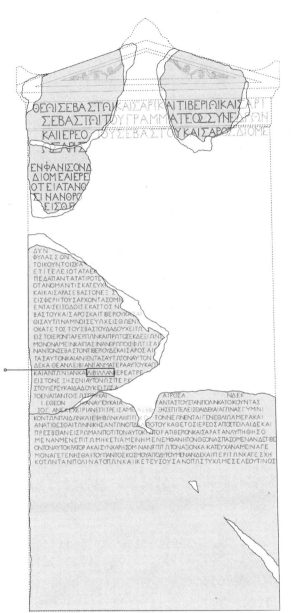

FIGURE 42.
Inscription celebrating the accession of Tiberius as emperor, Messenia, A.D. 14. Livi(ll)a's name is intact here. *Drawing by Leslie Rae Witt,* AE *1993.1414 = SEG 41.328.*

very extensive, can be associated with the local Sebasteion, a building connected with the imperial cult. The inscription is now rather fragmentary, but it does reveal something of what was going on in the Peloponnese in A.D. 14/15. A festival of several days was held, and an annual priesthood of the divine Augustus was instituted. It is notable that Divus Augustus' wife, also referred to with a divine title, is still called Livia in this text, rather than Julia

Augusta. It was decided that an embassy should be sent to Rome to present condolences while also congratulating Tiberius on his new position as "*hegemon . . . of the whole cosmos.*" At the same time, matters of local concern were to be presented to the new emperor. Again, there seems to have been a long introductory section in which various imperial family members were mentioned, including the name Livilla (LIBILLA). Once again, she appears next to her mother Antonia.

Evidently, Livi(ll)a was honored by many portraits and inscriptions, some from the very beginning of Tiberius' reign, others set up to mark the birth of the twins in 19, still more to honor the memory of Germanicus, and then of Drusus, on the occasion of their deaths. The reconstruction of her public image presented here involves the wider dissemination of portraits of Julio-Claudian women at an earlier date than many have supposed. Whether her portraits had been associated in any context with those of Sejanus, most of which were presumably erected between 29 and 31, we will probably never know.

Livi(ll)a's exact relationship to Sejanus in 31 has been deliberately obscured. Evidence suggests that Sejanus was engaged to be married to a Julio-Claudian woman at the time of his death. Dio, as preserved by Zonaras, says that his betrothed was named "Julia."[43] Many have assumed that she was the daughter of Livi(ll)a and Drusus, who would have been in her early twenties at that time. But some have suspected that Livi(ll)a herself (who would have been about forty-five) was actually his intended wife. Zonaras is confused about Livi(ll)a's name: elsewhere he says that she could be called either Julia or Livia. Livi(ll)a died close to the time of Sejanus' death, while her daughter Julia did not. In his notice of Julia's subsequent marriage to C. Rubellius Blandus in 33, Tacitus does not refer to a previous betrothal with Sejanus (*Ann.* 6.27.1). His silence here seems to be decisive.

If Tiberius had agreed to entrust Sejanus with a role as guardian and possible future regent for Tiberius Gemellus, or indeed for Gaius (Caligula), it would seem undesirable to marry him to Julia, who could be expected to bear him children who would also be Julio-Claudians. At this moment a marriage to Livi(ll)a, an alliance already discussed in 25, would seem much more advantageous, for both Tiberius and Sejanus. Suetonius (*Tib.* 65.1) claims that Tiberius "deceived" Sejanus with promises of a marriage alliance and of the tribunician power. It is notable that the official tradition attributes Livi(ll)a's fall to her part in Drusus' death eight years earlier, with hardly a word of her relationship to Sejanus in 31.

It has recently been suggested that Livi(ll)a's name should be restored in the *Fasti Ostienses* as the wife of Sejanus who committed suicide on 26 October 31.[44] This interpretation posits a secret marriage between Livi(ll)a and Sejanus, a marriage that, it has been argued, led directly to Sejanus' own fall once Antonia informed Tiberius about it. In fact, there is not enough epigraphical evidence to support this new reconstruction, nor does it fit in with the silence in our other sources about Livi(ll)a's death.

The *Fasti Ostienses* provide valuable evidence for the public recording of the disgrace of Sejanus' entire family, and for the full names of his children. It is most reasonable to restore a wife, whose name has been lost, under the notice for 26 October 31. Consequently, previous editors have inserted the name APICATA in the space, to designate the woman whom Sejanus had divorced in 23. Tacitus also refers to her in this way, as "Apicata Seiani," although obviously she was no longer married to Sejanus in 31. Sejanus' name is used to label her because her own name would not otherwise be readily recognizable to Tacitus' readers. Dio tells us that she committed suicide, although he dates her death after that of her children. According to the *Fasti Ostienses*, she killed herself two days after the execution of her oldest son, but before her younger two children died. Our sources, then, seem largely in accord with each other.

Yet there does not seem to be room for her name in the lacuna on the stone in Ostia. A short name, like Livia, is the most that would fit in the available space. In fact there is a very simple solution to this apparent problem. Apicata is not the *nomen*, but rather the *cognomen* of this woman. We do not know what her *nomen* was, although one suggestion has been Gavia. Be that as it may, the name in the space was a short family name and it belonged to the woman commonly referred to as Apicata, who was the mother of Sejanus' children. By contrast, the date of Livi(ll)a's death was not advertised anywhere in public, and she was not officially referred to as the wife of Sejanus.

Sufficient evidence shows that Livi(ll)a was a prominent and publicly recognized member of the *domus Augusta*, beginning in the reign of Augustus, and especially during the reign of Tiberius, right up to the time of her death in the last few months of 31. Because her death was sudden and secretive — it was apparently not preceded by any public accusations or disgrace — there were probably no demonstrations by the populace either for or against her. She did not suffer the exile that had become the customary punishment for adultery by this date. What evidence we do have suggests that she was put to death within the household, in a manner that had been traditional during the Republic. In keeping with her fate, her family did not allude to her death in public, and she simply disappeared. However, the prominence of her public image, not least upon the arch recently erected to commemorate her husband Drusus, led to a subsequent change of approach.

In January 32 her death was first publicly acknowledged, and leading senators now proposed an official ban on her name and image, presumably with some reasons given. This ban, contained in a *senatus consultum*, was circulated and put into effect throughout the Empire in the following months. It would be interesting to know whether the senate's text made any reference to a trial conducted by the emperor within his own household. Livi(ll)a's case illustrates the emergence of official sanctions against the memory of members of the ruling house, and particularly against women, as well as the tensions between disgrace and oblivion within Roman society. It was the suddenness of her fall and the importance of her public images and honors that made an official disgrace desirable. These sanctions seem to have been largely effective, and they provided the precedent for the treatment of Messalina in A.D. 48.

The Memory of Messalina

The sanctions against the memory of Valeria Messalina were probably the fiercest against any Julio-Claudian woman, and they were the first to target the wife of a reigning emperor.[45] Again, they suggest the previous political importance of Messalina and the prominence of her image in public places. These sanctions were also especially related to the situation and to the ambitions of her successor, Julia Agrippina, who married her uncle, the emperor Claudius, only a few months after Messalina's death. It was, however, not simply a case of one imperial wife taking the place of another. Agrippina also managed, almost immediately, to replace Messalina's son Britannicus as Claudius' principal heir with her own son L. Domitius Ahenobarbus, adopted early in A.D. 50 with the name of Nero Claudius Drusus Germanicus Caesar.[46] Agrippina aspired to be the wife of the *princeps*, confirmed by the title Augusta (which no previous wife of a reigning emperor had enjoyed), together with a formidable role in political life.

It suited Tacitus' narrative purposes to make a complete contrast between Agrippina and Messalina, between the consummate politician and the degenerate harlot.[47] However, his interpretation does not necessarily follow from the events as he has recorded them. Moreover, the loss of his account of Claudius' reign before A.D. 47 especially affects our ability to understand and assess his overall portrayal of Messalina.[48]

Claudius did rely heavily on his wives, partly because of his physical handicaps, and this had been the case from the very beginning of his reign. Messalina's victims, supposedly sacrificed to her greed and lust, nearly all represented possible political threats to Claudius himself, or to the succession of Messalina's children. Nothing Messalina did before her marriage to Silius just before her death seems obviously misguided or illogical, according to the patterns of behavior dictated by the need for political survival,[49] and her example surely set the stage for Agrippina, who seems not to have stopped at the murder of an emperor in order to put her son Nero on the throne. The very need to eclipse the recently deceased Messalina must have been a decisive factor in Agrippina's presentation of herself in public. Agrippina's higher profile, especially on state occasions, can be seen as the logical consequence of her sudden elevation but also of Messalina's previous position.

Claudius was put in power by the Praetorian Guard, against the wishes of a large number of senators.[50] His debt to the Praetorians was openly acknowledged in his generosity to them and on his early coinage, which he minted to pay them. He was the first emperor to be in this relatively precarious position, in complete contrast with the orderly succession of Tiberius and the popular enthusiasm that had greeted Gaius. Regardless of the role he may have played in the murder of Gaius and in his own subsequent preferment, Claudius faced a more challenging task in keeping his position and in passing it on to his young son, who was born soon after his accession. Many of his policies, including his desire to win the right to celebrate a triumph and to expand the Empire (against the wishes of Augustus), can be connected with his need for wider public recognition.

Claudius married Valeria Messalina during the reign of his nephew Gaius Caligula, at a time when he himself had just emerged into public life for the first time. Messalina was closely related to the *domus Augusta*, and her parents were cousins.[51] She was a great-granddaughter of Octavia both on her father's and on her mother's side. She was also a great-granddaughter of Antony. That made her a cousin of Claudius, but also a first cousin of Ahenobarbus, the future Nero, who had been brought up partly in the house of Messalina's mother, Domitia Lepida. Messalina was chosen to be Claudius' wife with his new public role in mind. She and her husband must have shared the objective of maintaining his power so that it could be passed on to their son, renamed Britannicus to celebrate Claudius' British conquests. Yet Messalina was displaced by a wife who was the only available woman directly descended from Augustus himself, despite the incest that this marriage involved. This outcome may well reflect on Messalina's shortcomings or miscalculations, but it surely also suggests a great deal about the evolving political needs and weaknesses of Claudius himself. Agrippina's ambitions must also have played a role.

The result was that Messalina was the victim of a kind of coup; she suffered a fate not unlike that of an emperor who has been overthrown and is replaced by another ruler. She was apparently not subject to a traditional charge of adultery or to a trial, even within the household. She was summarily executed very soon after she had apparently married Silius. Her marriage with C. Silius remains a surprising if well-attested event, which could just as easily have been a reaction to her impending fall rather than being its cause.[52] Tacitus' claim that she, in some sense, craved infamy (*infamia*) functions as a self-fulfilling prophecy and begs the question of his sources for Messalina's unfulfilled plans and her motives. Tacitus' picture of the helpless and unresponsive Claudius, caught off guard by domestic events even as he was carrying out his duties as censor, forms a plausible and satisfying pendant to the earlier scene (now lost in Tacitus' version) of the terrified Claudius hiding behind a curtain in the imperial palace, only to be elevated to supreme power through a chance encounter with a scavenging Praetorian. An alternative reconstruction might see a more logical and direct connection between Messalina's fall and Claudius' position as censor, which saw him celebrate the secular games and plan his extension of the boundaries of the city. Like Augustus, Claudius seems to have been, at least formally, at the height of his powers at the moment when he acted against a close female relative.

Tacitus records the formal measures enacted against the memory of Messalina, which constituted only the second senatorial censure of a woman. Her name and portraits were to be removed from all public and private places.[53] Claudius is said to have behaved as if she had simply disappeared: he put her out of his mind, at least in the way he behaved in public. The surviving evidence suggests that the instructions regarding Messalina's memory were carried out with great thoroughness. The identification of her portraits remains highly controversial, although her image may survive on some cameos. Claudius followed the example of Gaius in putting emphasis on his family, both living and dead, and many statue groups were set up beginning in the early days of his reign. Messalina's surviving image on coins from Bithynia and Egypt is not individualized enough to reveal anything about her portrait types. Her name is attested in the inscriptions of her freedmen, especially from within the family burial complex established by her grandmother Marcella, where it is possible that she herself was also buried, after her body had been given to her mother. An unusual epitaph bears her name as the dedicant on a stone she set up in memory of a family freedman, L. Valerius Threptus, who died at the age of sixteen. Presumably the funerary context helped to preserve her name in this case.[54]

Very few public texts remain with Messalina's name and several striking erasures attest to strong reactions to her fall. The most obvious example from Rome is an ex-voto dedication of C. Julius Postumus, prefect of Egypt, to Claudius and his family in A.D. 47/48, which was found in the Forum of Augustus some time before 1550 (figure 43).[55] The fine marble base supported a dedication, perhaps a small statue, which is described in the text as being made of sixteen pounds of gold. The costly gift commemorated a vow for the safety of the emperor and his family by a loyal official, who had served as governor of Egypt, the emperor's own personal possession. Claudius' name appears in noticeably larger letters both in the second and again in the last line of the text. Egypt is written with one of the new letters Claudius added to the Latin alphabet, which were only used during his reign.

Messalina's name, as well as the pronoun that designated them both as parents of the children, has been erased by an exceptionally deep gouge. The resulting text makes grammatical sense, at the expense of considerable disfigurement of the stone. Postumus' dedication was virtually new when the honor accorded to Messalina became inappropriate to the changing political situation. Whether Postumus was himself responsible for the erasure or whether it would have been carried out at the order of a magistrate in the city is unknown, and his personal reactions are beyond recovery. Did he view it as the defacement of his costly monument or as an opportunity to gain even more political capital than he already had through the initial dedication? This text is in any case emblematic of a type of inscription of which there must have been many, put up to express a general feeling of loyalty to the emperor or to mark vows made on a specific occasion, such as for the success of the British expedition. It would not have been unusual to include Messalina in these vows, as seems to have been the case in a more fragmentary inscription from the Palatine.

A dedication from the city gate of Verona inscribed in A.D. 44 would have been just as prominent (figure 44).[56] In this case the erasure follows the shape of the letters so closely that it actually highlights Messalina's name rather than removing it. It certainly does not render it significantly less legible. Found re-used in a medieval gatehouse, this text was probably on display throughout most of antiquity. Similarly, the base for a statue of Messalina was completely erased in the old forum of Leptis, where it was discovered *in situ* in the 1920s. In this urban context it could be read as a pendant to the nearby erasure of Livi(ll)a. A further erased base at Arnae in Lycia also previously honored

FIGURE 43. Ex-voto dedication by C. Julius Postumus, prefect of Egypt, of an object made of sixteen pounds of gold on behalf of the health and well-being of Claudius and his family, Forum of Augustus, Rome, A.D. 47/48. Messalina's name has been erased after her death in 48, as well as the pronoun EORUM to denote the fact that the children were hers by Claudius. *Musei Capitolini, Rome, archivio fotografico dei Musei Capitolini, photo Maria Teresa Natale*, CIL 6.918 (31202) = ILS 210.

Messalina. It is telling that no further inscriptions have been found, especially in the East, although there must have been many. The senate's decree enjoining the removal of Messalina must have been followed very shortly by the announcement of Claudius' new marriage to Agrippina, and then by the new imperial adoption of Nero. It was logical, although not a universal practice, that Agrippina's image and name should replace that of Messalina, in a way that had not happened with Livi(ll)a some seventeen years earlier.

We may suspect that Messalina was replaced by Agrippina on the monument in honor of the Claudian family (*ara domus Claudiae?*) near the Ara Pacis, which was restored by Claudius in A.D. 41–43.[57] This monument seems originally to have been erected by Tiberius in 22, and featured a series of inscriptions (now very fragmentary) naming members of the imperial family in the nominative, in the style of *elogia*. These could also have labeled a series of statues near the altar. In this context, Nero, with the new name of his adoption, appears on the same slab next to Drusus, brother of Claudius. The texts were inscribed by the same hand, which suggests that Drusus' text had been recarved from an earlier version in order to accommodate Nero next to him. In other words, the whole monument was probably reconfigured after 25 February 50 but before the death of Claudius on 13 October 54. It can be taken as an indication of the efforts that were expended on the new image of the imperial family in the early 50s.

Other monuments must have existed in the city of Rome, but they are hard to identify from extant evidence. Two further possible examples seem worth taking into account, namely an arch put up to celebrate victory over Britain and a newly excavated dedication found next to the Arch of Constantine. Much was made of Claudius' British triumph in 43, and Messalina also

THE PRINCIPATE

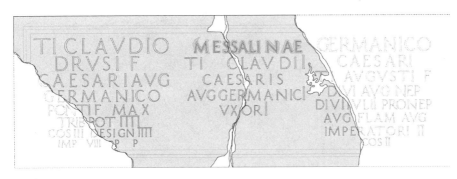

FIGURE 44. Inscription honoring Claudius, with his brother Germanicus, and his wife Messalina, city gate, Verona, A.D. 44/45. Messalina's name was erased in A.D. 48. *Drawing by Leslie Rae Witt, AE 1992.739b.*

rode in the procession in a *carpentum*. The senate voted Claudius a triumphal arch, which was advertised on various coins starting in A.D. 46/47.[58] Yet the remains of an arch on the Via Lata, which was part of the Aqua Virgo at an important point on Claudius' new city limit, can be securely dated to A.D. 51 (figure 45). The time lag between the dedication of the latter arch and the British triumph is striking. This arch can be associated with a series of texts (and statues?) of the imperial family, including Germanicus, Antonia, Agrippina, Nero, Octavia, Britannicus, and Claudius himself. The dedicatory text clearly associates the arch with the celebrations for the capture of the British chieftains, including Caratacus, in 51. While it marks the end of hostilities in Britain, it does not refer to the triumph or to the initial conquest. Extensive discussions of the text have failed to produce a satisfactory explanation for the timing or for the tenor of the arch's dedication.

Messalina's disgrace itself suggests a possible solution. What we have in the Via Lata arch is a second arch to celebrate the conquest of Britain, in a context that would allow Agrippina and Nero to be associated with Claudius' military achievements. Just as Agrippina was given a key role to play in the ceremonial handing over of the defeated chiefs, so she was also prominent on and near the arch commemorating that event. Time and money were saved by incorporating the arch into the Aqua Virgo at a strategic location. What happened to the first arch, the one actually voted to mark the triumph, is unclear. It may have been reworked in some way.

At another frequented location in the city, a group of musicians who played wind instruments put up a statue group to the imperial family, which was extended near the beginning of Claudius' reign to include a group of three statues in an *aediculum* (figure 46).[59] Claudius stood in the middle of

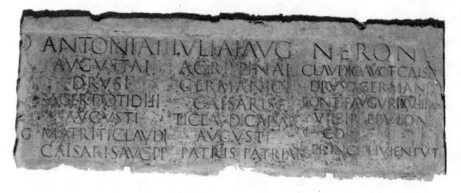

FIGURE 45. Inscription for statues (dedicated by the senate and Roman people?) from near an arch of Claudius, Via Lata, Rome, A.D. 51–54. Antonia, mother of Claudius, Agrippina, wife of Claudius, and Nero, adopted son of Claudius.

DAIR 71.1958, CIL 6.921 = ILS 222.

the three with Divus Augustus on his right. To his left stood another person, but no trace of the text identifying this third figure survived the reconfiguration of the base to include Nero and Agrippina (with Claudius and Augustus) in 55/56. Suggestions for the missing person have so far been Drusus, Antonia, Germanicus, and Messalina. In fact, Messalina seems the obvious choice here, in harmony with her importance around the time of the dedication in A.D. 42. Her disappearance from the group also makes perfect sense, whereas the elimination of a figure such as Germanicus would seem unprecedented and improbable.[60]

Similarly, the image of Messalina in the literary sources has been heavily influenced, and probably distorted, by a negative picture of her created after her disgrace.[61] There is little that is positive in the surviving accounts of Tacitus, Suetonius, or Dio. Juvenal, writing in the later years of Trajan's reign, paints a caricature of Messalina in one of his most famous satires. He presents her as a whore, using language that parodies the medical writers who described sexual addiction as a physical disease. A similar picture of sexual excess can be found in Pliny the Elder, writing in the mid-70s. Yet it is not in evidence in the *Apocolocyntosis*, written shortly after Claudius' death, or in the *Octavia*, dating to immediately after the fall of Nero. In the mid-50s Seneca's Messalina appears as a victim of Claudius, shamefully put to death without a trial. She leads the throng of ghosts who accuse Claudius of their wrongful deaths. By 68 the *Octavia* presents her as a different kind of victim, a tragic victim of Venus, who is subject to divine madness. However, these few pieces of evidence do not allow any detailed reconstruction of an alter-

FIGURE 46. Dedication of a guild of musicians honoring the imperial family,
found near the Meta Sudans, Rome, A.D. 55/56, after the erasure of Messalina in 48.
There are signs that Agrippina's name has been plastered over after 59.
*Ministero per i Beni e le Attività Culturali, Soprintendenza Archeologica di Roma,
Museo Nazionale Romano,* CIL 6.40307.

native, more positive tradition, while other texts from the 50s and 60s have
their own very special biases since their purpose was to attack the memory of
Claudius and of Nero. By contrast, the evidence from art and inscriptions attests to the remarkably widespread and systematic destruction of Messalina's
memory in 48.

Agrippina, Mother of Nero

The murder of Agrippina by her son Nero was one of the most notorious
episodes in the violent history of the Julio-Claudian house.[62] Her influence,
especially with the Praetorian Guard, meant that Nero initially tried to stage
an accident involving a collapsible ship in order to remove his mother. When
that plan failed, she was murdered by a detachment of the Misenum fleet in
her villa on the Bay of Naples. Her body was immediately cremated and was
buried on the grounds of her property on the night of her death. It is notable
that Nero did not appropriate or destroy her house, as Augustus had done
with the villa of his granddaughter Julia, but rather simply avoided the whole
place during the remaining nine years of his life. After his death, members of
her household put up a tomb in her memory on the Misenum road. Agrippina was an exceptionally powerful woman whose freedmen are attested well
into the second century and even as far away as Jericho.[63]

Although he probably convinced few people, Nero resorted to the strategy
of labeling his mother as a traitor, who had been executed after making a
failed attempt on his own life.[64] Agrippina had died in March, but the em-

peror did not return to Rome until late June. Meanwhile, Nero sent a letter of condemnation about Agrippina, apparently written by Seneca, to the senate. The accusations against her in the letter included charges relating to the reign of Claudius. In Rome elaborate sacrifices of thanksgiving for Nero's safety were held, and Agrippina's birthday (6 November) was declared a day of ill omen. Her death was to be recalled by annual games, during the festival of Minerva when her "conspiracy" had come to light, with thanksgiving for Nero's safety in all the temples of Rome. A golden statue of Minerva, accompanied by Nero, was to be set up in the senate house. Tacitus' account of the sanctions against Agrippina are detailed, and yet he says nothing specific about a senatorial injunction removing her statues. He also sees Nero's restoration of several people formerly banished by Agrippina as a posthumous criticism of her. The return of the ashes of Lollia Paulina to a new tomb specially built for her was typical of the kind of memory game that had been initiated by Caligula. Nero's final return to Rome was celebrated by general festivities, by the senators and populace coming out to meet him with their families in holiday clothes, and by his own thanksgiving in Rome's principal temple on the Capitol.

There can be no doubt that Agrippina's openly acknowledged position of power was unlike that of any other Roman woman before the Severan period.[65] Her influence reached its peak in the first year of Nero's reign, when she had her own detachment of German bodyguards, her own Praetorians, and two lictors to accompany her in public. Even the chief Vestal Virgin was escorted by only a single lictor, as was Augustus' wife Livia (Iulia Augusta) toward the end of her life. The official nature of Agrippina's position had been publicly demonstrated by her being seated next to Claudius on official state occasions like the presentation of the captured British chieftains. It was even more striking under Nero, when a valuable inscription from Corinth records that C. Iulius Spartiaticus held the office of *procurator Caesaris et Augustae Agrippinae*.[66] In this case, an official was apparently jointly appointed by Nero and Agrippina (probably soon after the death of Claudius), as if she were indeed openly recognized as the co-ruler of the Empire. It seems unlikely that Spartiaticus was the only one. This revelation of her power is equally reflected on coins and in the iconography of the reliefs from the Sebasteion at Aphrodisias, where Agrippina appears first as an apparently equal partner with Claudius and then crowning Nero as emperor, a scene also shown on a cameo in Cologne (figure 47).[67]

Agrippina's case presents a rare example of a woman whose well-attested fall (and apparent disgrace) did not prevent the survival of many images and

FIGURE 47. Relief showing Agrippina with a cornucopia crowning
her son Nero as emperor, Sebasteion, Aphrodisias, A.D. 54–59.
Aphrodisias Excavations, New York University.

texts honoring her. Her portraits are securely identified and have been classified into four (possibly five) types: she appears on coins from Rome and the
provinces, on cameos, on inscribed gems, in statue groups, and on reliefs.
Her inscriptions survive in more than twenty cities, both in the East and in
the West of the Empire. The material evidence reveals very few sanctions,
especially in light of the fact that she was only really prominent for a period

of ten years. A single Latin epigraphic text from Puteoli shows an erasure of her name, but her inscriptions appear intact elsewhere in the cities around the Bay of Naples.[68] A base from Epidaurus also had her name erased from a Greek text that honors her with Claudius. Another statue base in Epidaurus has a partial erasure below her name and has been reused for Statilia Messalina, wife of Nero. A single gold coin of Claudius has a mark across Agrippina's face that seems to be deliberate. In some texts, however, Nero's name has been erased while hers has remained intact.

Particularly striking is the appearance of Agrippina's ghost in the *Octavia*, an avenging fury on stage who accuses Nero of having destroyed her statues and inscriptions throughout the world, on pain of death.[69] However, this is not necessarily an assertion that should be taken at face value. Outside the capital there was apparently no systematic effort to attack her memory, even in Italy. The extant material evidence fits Dio's account, which speaks of people toppling statues hurriedly in anticipation of Nero's return. Yet, as the Arval records reveal, he did not enter the city until late June. If a decree with sanctions had been passed immediately after her death, it would surely already have been implemented. The *Octavia* may have seemed plausible when it was performed in Rome soon after Nero's death, but it has little to tell us about the situation in the rest of the Empire. The contrast with Messalina is especially revealing. Nero's own ambivalence about his mother's death, and his anticipation of public reaction, must have played a role here. There is evidence that he had planned divine honors for her, if her death could have been made to appear accidental. If a decree was passed against her in 59, it was simply not circulated as widely as other such decrees had been.

In Rome itself her name survived next to Nero's on the inscriptions from the Claudian arch at the Via Lata (see figure 45).[70] These texts were found close to the arch and cannot, therefore, have been removed to a warehouse, but seem to have remained on display after the end of the Julio-Claudian dynasty. The same may have been the case for the Claudian family monument near the Ara Pacis. By contrast, the excavation of the area of the Meta Sudans has revealed the blotting out of Agrippina's memory in a busy area of Rome's center.

In 55/56 the players of wind instruments, who had been honoring members of the imperial family in the same location since 12 B.C., decided to expand their shrine to include four labeled statues on a long base faced in marble (see figure 46). They recopied their previous dedications to Augustus (from 12 B.C.) and Claudius (from A.D. 42) and added Nero and Agrippina.[71] Nero stood between Augustus and Claudius, while Agrippina stood at the end, next to her husband Claudius and balancing the figure of her great-grandfather Augustus. The shrine was ultimately destroyed in the great fire of A.D. 64 and was covered over with the rubble and fill that formed part of the foundations for the Domus Aurea. Agrippina's name is clearly visible and yet there seems to be a sort of halo around the letters. In addition, it is notable that the word ROMANI appears twice, both under Agrippina's name and under Claudius' name.

Such a base posed a problem since it was not easy to remove any one individual without dismantling the entire shrine. What seems to have happened here is that Agrippina's whole slab was either plastered over or turned, with the result that the word ROMANI needed to be reinscribed on the adjacent slab. Thus the *aediculum* once again had only three statues in it, as had been the configuration in the design implemented in A.D. 42. This is the only material evidence for the possible use of plaster to cover a name. It is all the more revealing since the guild of musicians in question would surely have served the imperial family regularly and would have been familiar with its members, especially in their public roles.

Agrippina's erasure in the Puteoli text is especially notable.[72] The text was set up to commemorate games held over two days in February A.D. 56 in honor of Nero, Agrippina, Jupiter Optimus Maximus, and the Genius of the colony of Puteoli. The dedicators are the Augustales, a group of freedmen who served in the imperial cult. Parts of both Agrippina's and Nero's names have been erased, presumably at different times. The local officials had tried, over a turbulent decade, to preserve the commemoration of their games. Their partial erasure of the names resulted in an emperor who is simply styled "Claudius Caesar Augustus" and an unnamed woman now simply called "Augusta." Their compromises preserved their allegiance to the ruling house both after Agrippina's murder and after Nero's suicide. Puteoli was quick to declare for the Flavians and received the new name of *colonia Flavia*, and so it comes as no surprise that Nero's name was erased here. By contrast, Agrippina's inscription remained intact in an extensive statue group at nearby Herculaneum, set up by L. Mammius Maximus, a soldier of the urban cohorts who was also an Augustalis. It is apparent that local reaction to Agrippina's death varied even among people who were close to the events.

A possible rehabilitation of Agrippina has been posited but remains highly controversial.[73] Two portraits have been identified as posthumous images of Agrippina, one found in the market of Trajan and the other from Cologne, the city of her birth. Inscriptions seem to attest to the preservation of her memory among former members of her household during the second century; however, the authenticity of a small marble base erected specifically to her memory by her former slave, who was apparently later part of Trajan's household, has been questioned. Fragments (now lost) of an imperial inscription found at the Via Nazionale seemed to show that she was once honored next to Flavia Domitilla, the wife of Vespasian. It is evident that Vespasian cultivated the memory of Claudius, his former patron, partly to balance his systematic erasure of Nero. This veneration of Divus Claudius did not include any rehabilitation of Messalina, and a thorough rehabilitation of Agrippina may seem odd, since she was always so strongly identified as the mother of Nero. However, it is also possible that she (re)gained some continuing posthumous sympathy as one of Nero's victims. Her memory could also have been associated with the temple of Divus Claudius on the Caelian, which she had started. Vespasian, who dismantled the nymphaeum Nero had built on the same site, completed this temple. A remarkable life-size statue of Agrippina, made of Egyptian basanite, came from this area and was probably kept in Vespasian's temple in honor of Claudius (figure 48).[74] On the other hand, because the disgrace of Agrippina was somewhat superficially carried out, it may, in fact, be misleading to speak of her rehabilitation; her texts and images could still be seen, albeit in diminished numbers in Rome.

Tacitus' Julio-Claudian Women

Any picture of the lives of the Julio-Claudians is inevitably dominated by Tacitus' narrative, especially for the women of the family. His account contains a number of marked biases, such as his focus on the noble wife of Germanicus, as well as the rhetorical and literary patterns that give a dynamic shape to his work. Because he was writing in an age when imperial women appear to have been a great deal less prominent in public, and certainly less in evidence in dynastic politics, he tends to be highly critical of the ambitious women of the Julio-Claudian family from an earlier era. His habit of setting up contrasts between characters is memorable but gives an artificial shape to his narrative. The central contrast between Germanicus and Tiberius, which shapes the opening books of the *Annales*, is enhanced by contrasts between various of their female relatives.

It is notable how much attention Tacitus gives (at least in the surviving narrative) to the two Agrippinas, at the expense of other female characters.[75] They are particularly interesting for him and provide a striking example of a good mother and a bad daughter. In addition, the life and career of the younger Agrippina illustrate the most dramatic reversals of fortune, and her

FIGURE 48. Basanite statue of Agrippina, wife of Claudius, from the temple of
Divus Claudius on the Caelian, Rome, 70s A.D. *Musei Capitolini, Rome,
archivio fotografico dei Musei Capitolini, photo Maria Teresa Natale.*

memoirs seem also to have influenced the narrative. Certainly, the very positive picture of the elder Agrippina, especially in the depiction of her private conversations and aspirations, owes something to the daughter's account. Yet the older Agrippina, like her daughter, also had a very public role and was often active in spheres that had been previously reserved for men. The contrast between Agrippina, wife of Germanicus, and Plancina, the wife of Piso, who is said to have overstepped all boundaries in her public appearances in Syria at banquets and before the troops, seems, nevertheless, largely a dramatic creation. The two women frequently appear to behave in essentially similar ways, just as Messalina and the younger Agrippina both pursued parallel political goals using many of the same means.

Tacitus wrote according to his own social and political biases and in order to tell a dramatic story. However, he was also dependent on his sources. A combination of the tendencies in his narrative and the patterns of disgrace and rehabilitation reflected in his sources, which had been replayed with complex variations throughout the first century A.D., results in an account that has been filtered and shaped in a highly political and dynastic way. Consequently, the favorable picture of the older Agrippina is probably the creation of a combination of posthumous sources; it was no doubt inspired by the apologetic memoirs of her daughter and by the extensive and successive rehabilitations of her memory, especially under Gaius, but also in the last years of Claudius' reign. The house of Germanicus and Agrippina produced the Julio-Claudian emperors who succeeded Tiberius, and it was only natural that their family traditions should flourish, especially at the expense of highborn women like Livi(ll)a or Messalina who were not recalled by influential descendants. The enactment of formal sanctions against the memories of Livi(ll)a and Messalina reflects the high stakes involved in the Julio-Claudian memory game after the death of Augustus, even as it shows the role accorded to women in shaping and perpetuating memory and status. Yet any attempt at an archaeology of the various layers of information and interpretation faces formidable challenges, as well as gaps and erasures that were concealed, perhaps even from Tacitus himself.

The Memory of Nero,
imperator scaenicus

▾　▾　▾

Detur hoc inlustrium virorum posteritati, ut quo
modo exsequiis a promisca sepultura separabantur,
ita in traditione supremorum accipiant
habeantque propriam memoriam.
Tacitus, *Annales* 16.16

The previous two chapters have elucidated memory sanctions under the Julio-Claudians, both male and female, by exploring particular examples in some detail. As the first imperial dynasty, the Julio-Claudians inevitably formed a transition between the violent and highly competitive political climate of the late Republic and the very different world of prosperity and peace that came to characterize the high Empire. The principate was being defined and redefined throughout the Julio-Claudian period, even as the expectation of a hereditary system of succession was repeatedly evoked, only to be defeated in each generation. Consequently, each Julio-Claudian ruler needed to (re)position himself strategically in relation to his predecessors as well as to possible competitors, many of whom were in any case relatives in his extended family. Memory was consistently and variously recreated to suit the political needs of the moment: memory sanctions in many forms were often in use, most publicly within the leading family itself. Even as the imperial cult came into being, the *divi* remained a somewhat ambiguous and problematic group, whose temples were slow to be built in Rome itself.[1] Each new ruler effectively faced the challenge of how to shape the memory of his predecessor(s) in order to define and strengthen his own position, especially at the beginning of his reign.

Both this chapter and the one that follows are concerned with a closely related phenomenon, namely the use of memory sanctions at moments of transition between dynasties, when a ruling family was replaced by a different individual or family. Needless to say, such transitions tended to be violent and illegal; they happened unexpectedly and had to be (re)presented in public after the fact. The violent death of an emperor and the simultaneous seizure of power by a usurper whose claim was not based on a family relationship posed its own memory challenge.[2] Inevitably the dead emperor now became subject to memory sanctions of various kinds even as the message was sent out around the whole Empire that a new ruler was in place.

At the same time, that new ruler took over as head of the *domus Caesaris*, so that his usurpation was really twofold. The names "Caesar" and "Augustus" remained hereditary within the household set up by the Julio-Claudians, but they came to function more as imperial titles than as personal or family names. In 68 Galba quickly discovered that his initial decision not to use these names needed to be reversed before he entered Rome as the new *princeps*.[3] Similarly, the conception of the principate as a unified system (rather than as a succession of discrete dynasties) was revealed by the way in which a new emperor would invariably appeal to the example of Augustus, thus presenting himself as a true successor who offered both a welcome new start and a return to hallowed "Augustan" norms and practices. Meanwhile, no one wanted to perpetuate the memory and example of the act of usurpation, most especially when successful, which might inspire another to threaten even the best-established emperor.

Even as power was asserted at moments of extreme uncertainty and instability, memory sanctions were integral to the establishment of a new dynasty. The image of the previous emperor needed to be both removed and denigrated, in a wide variety of contexts. At the same time, the act of seizing power itself needed to be dealt with, often through distortion or erasure. In addition, others involved in the change of regime, whether on the victorious or on the defeated side, usually had their own vested interest in "forgetting" the precise sequence of events and their own role in them. In this way, memory sanctions might be especially useful in allowing a new political regime to function, using many if not most of the same people who had experience in government before, while putting the blame firmly on the dead "tyrant" and a few of his closest allies.

Nevertheless, the new emperor needed to be seen to be an effective replacement, especially in areas in which his predecessor had been particularly active. The erasure and/or denigration of the previous ruler was accompanied by policies and actions that contrasted or competed with what was, in fact, most "memorable" from the immediately previous years. In this way the new ruler inevitably played to the (albeit often unacknowledged) collective memory of the past while asserting his own role and right to shape the public image of that same past. Various shadows of the previous regime remained, either in the foreground or in the background of the new emperor's actions. The examples considered in these two chapters are the disgrace of Nero and of Domitian, who had both succeeded as legitimate and designated heirs of their predecessors according to a hereditary pattern and who had each reigned for about fifteen years. However, the patterns to be found after 68 and 96 are also relevant to later changes of dynasty, most notably the rise of the Severans in the 190s.

Nero the Enemy

Nero was the first emperor to be officially declared a *hostis* (public enemy) by the senate during his own lifetime, as the culmination of his increasingly tense standoff with the political elite, a clash that dominated the last four years of his life, at least according to the picture painted by hostile senatorial sources.[4] The senate effectively staged a kind of coup against Nero without at that same moment actually recognizing any rival claimant to power. The Praetorians, and then also Nero's personal German bodyguards, were persuaded to desert Nero, first by being told that he had already deserted them (allegedly by fleeing to Egypt) and then by the promise of a huge donative (which Galba refused to pay when he heard about it). Due to the illness of his fellow Praetorian prefect Tigellinus, Nymphidius Sabinus was able to deceive the guard, which seems still to have been essentially loyal to Nero.[5] Nero himself lost hope in a situation in which a variety of possible options still lay open to him. Nero's own gradual withdrawal from the role of ruler, subsequent revolts partly caused by that withdrawal, and ultimately his sudden and intensely personal despair led to Nero's death. No single individual or group removed Nero from power, and there was no clear successor in Rome at the time of his suicide. The senate had claimed the legal right to put Nero to death as a *hostis* but had no real power to enforce that order or even to choose a successor once Nero was dead. The Praetorians were in

search of another *princeps*, one who would pay them the promised donative.
Meanwhile, in the eighteen months following Nero's death, various leading
Romans would consider making a bid to succeed him.

The legally sanctioned label *hostis* had profound consequences for Nero's
memory but was starkly at variance with the general feeling of many ordinary people, especially in Rome and in the Greek East. The arrangements
made for Nero's funeral speak to the situation immediately after his suicide.[6]
Despite the fact that Galba had paraded the portraits of Nero's prominent
victims when he first made his own bid at New Carthage in Spain, he saw to it
that his own freedman Icelus arranged for a dignified and proper funeral for
Nero in keeping with his status as a member of Rome's political class. Nero
was buried in the robes embroidered with gold that he had worn for the New
Year's celebration, in a sarcophagus of porphyry with an altar of Luna marble
above and an enclosure of white marble from Thasos around his grave. His
burial in the family tomb of the Domitii on the Pinician Hill facing the Campus Martius (re)placed him firmly within the context of his biological father's
family and severed his connection to the Julio-Claudians, who were buried in
the Mausoleum of Augustus.

The trouble taken to give Nero a proper funeral and tomb does not accord with his status as a *hostis*. Indeed, Galba's plan, actually carried out by
women of Nero's own household, suggests an honorable memory of Nero, as
a Domitius Ahenobarbus, while at the same time asserting and confirming
Galba's claim to be the new and legitimate head of the house of the Caesars.
It could also be read as an implied criticism of the senate, whose designation
of Nero as a *hostis* seems to have become largely irrelevant. The altar of Luna
marble attests to the intention of cultivating Nero's memory in a traditional
and honorific family setting. It does not indicate disgrace but rather redefinition, and it symbolizes the earliest attempt to control the memory of Nero.[7]
Galba was a true prophet: he had foreseen that people would come, regularly
and consistently, with flowers to decorate Nero's tomb, even as they cultivated his memory in a variety of other ways. Suetonius' detailed knowledge
of the tomb suggests that it continued to be a well-known location in Rome.[8]
Clearly Galba preferred to deal with a proper "tomb of Domitius" rather than
with the consequences of a hasty burial or of a Nero not properly disposed of,
perhaps even thrown into the Tiber.

However, Galba survived Nero by barely eight months, with the result that
his intentions and plans also came to nothing. Nero should have been irrelevant to the bloody power struggles of the long year 69, as Galba was be-

trayed by Otho shortly after Vitellius revolted from Galba with the backing of the legions on the Rhine. Otho's suicide did nothing to bring peace; Vitellius was soon challenged by Vespasian, and the consequences of civil war were enacted both on the battlefield in Italy and in Rome itself, where even the Capitol with its great temple of Jupiter was burned to the ground as Romans fought each other in the streets. Yet the memory of Nero continued to overshadow political discourse and to affect his successors' claims to legitimacy in a chaotic and violent post-Julio-Claudian political landscape.[9]

As we have noted, Galba had acted more cautiously than is often realized with regard to Nero's memory, despite the fact that he had openly challenged Nero during his lifetime. Both Otho and Vitellius tried to support their respective political positions by representing themselves as true heirs to Nero. Otho restored the statues of Nero and of his second wife Poppaea Sabina (to whom Otho had himself been married), set aside funds to complete the Domus Aurea, and courted Nero's widow Statilia Messalina. He even called himself Nero Otho, at least for a while.[10] Vitellius also worked on and lived in part of the Domus Aurea and staged elaborate public sacrifices to honor Nero's memory in the summer after his death.[11] Both Otho's and Vitellius' coins recalled Nero's portrait and politics. Indeed, the clash between Otho and Vitellius early in 69 appeared essentially as a conflict between two deutero-Neros, either of whom would presumably have honored Nero's memory (in his own way) and have continued at least some of Nero's initiatives if he had been successful in holding onto power in the long run.

These various invocations of Nero's image and legacy must reflect some popular feelings, both in Rome itself (among the people and the Praetorians) and with the various legions involved in trying to win the Empire. There would have been no point in all of this rhetoric and spectacle if Nero really had been by now a discredited figure. Similarly, the Flavian decision to present a public stance and tone completely at variance with Nero also serves to confirm the continuing power of Nero's image in the 70s and even beyond.[12] As a result, Nero's memory is not easy to define. People living outside Italy would have heard a bewildering succession of messages, both about who was in charge at Rome and about the official attitude toward Nero's memory. Consequently, it is hardly ever possible to date or to interpret the exact historical and political context of any individual posthumous attack on Nero's memory.

Nero on Stage in A.D. 68

The most unusual critique of Nero's memory is in the form of a historical drama, in the genre commonly known as the *fabula praetexta*, that presents a thoroughgoing indictment of Nero both as a ruler and as a person. This play has been controversial and has generated extensive discussion as regards its historical and its literary interpretation.[13] Meanwhile, it is a central text for the study of Roman memory sanctions, since it deals not only with Nero's memory but also discusses such sanctions at some length during the drama itself. In this sense it is a very rare text, offering a first-century Roman commentary on memory sanctions, rather than simply recording their effects. It should be considered as analogous and complementary to the *Senatus Consultum de Cn. Pisone patre* of some fifty years earlier for the light that it sheds on the culture of memory and disgrace in first-century Rome. Yet its full meaning can only be understood within its original historical context.

Although the author and date of the play are not directly attested by any ancient evidence, a likely context can be deduced from the text itself. The play is set in the year 62 and deals with Nero's divorce of Octavia and marriage to Poppaea Sabina. However, the prophecies both about a great fire and about Nero's ultimate ruin show that the author is writing after the death of Nero. This fact, as well as many characteristics of the play's style and vocabulary, indicate that Seneca, who died in 65, cannot be the author. Rather the author is an admirer of Seneca, who has read many of his writings, including the *Ad Helviam* and *De Clementia*, and is also familiar with Senecan tragedy.[14]

It is hard to place the play much after Nero's death, especially in a Flavian context. The play is heavily focused on impending doom and on the fall of the Julio-Claudian house, which is vividly evoked in the manner of Greek tragedy. Its dramatic setting in 62 is somewhat artificial, since it looks both backward and forward in time. It is an intensely political (rather than a psychological or sentimental) play that mirrors the concerns of the author and his audience in their own day. It is notable that there is no hint of any civil war or violence to come after Nero's fall, nor of the new political and cultural tone of the Flavian regime, the saviors and restorers of the city of Rome and of the whole Roman world.

Although the play can most plausibly be dated soon after Nero's death, it cannot have been written under either Otho or Vitellius, both of whom cultivated a positive image of Nero. In other words, a Galban context is by far the most logical, based on the evidence of the text itself.[15] This historical moment also makes best sense of the anonymous Praetorian prefect and of the general effort to portray the Praetorian Guard in a favorable light, in the aftermath of its role under Nero. Tigellinus, Nero's prefect, was still alive under Galba and had become a supporter of the new regime, albeit an unpopular one. Otho himself, also now a close ally of Galba, does not appear as a former husband of Poppaea or as the drinking companion of Nero. Similarly, the repeated references to republican history, made mostly by the first Chorus but also by Octavia, make sense under Galba who was trying to recreate a much more "republican" tone in government and public life. There is no internal reason to argue that this play was never performed: on stage it would have been most effective under Galba late in 68, with the emperor himself in the audience after his return to Rome in October.

The staging of the play was surely a high political drama, perhaps of a unique kind.[16] The choice of Octavia's name (rather than Nero's) as the play's title suggests that the play may have been performed specifically to mark the return of her ashes to the Mausoleum of Augustus.[17] Alternatively, the *ludi plebei* of early November 68 would also have offered a prominent and splendid venue.[18] The theater of Marcellus could have afforded proximity to the portico named for another popular Octavia (sister of Augustus), as well as to its own shrine of Pietas. On the other hand, the theater of Pompey was the oldest theater in Rome and probably the venue where Nero himself had performed most frequently. It had been the focus of his famous Golden Day celebrations in 66 when the sunshades over the audience bore images of Nero in the guise of the sun god driving his chariot, all embroidered in gold.[19] In the case of the *Octavia*, perhaps more than for any other surviving imperial play, its context in the theater in Rome in late 68 appears essential to its interpretation.

The decision to put Nero back on stage in Rome is striking, one might even say shocking. Our (later) ancient sources are virtually unanimous in their criticisms of Nero as a public performer.[20] There seems little doubt that his public performances were indeed an issue raised against him by his critics during his own lifetime, notably by the conspirators who were part of Piso's plot in 65 and by the Gallic rebel Julius Vindex in the edicts he issued criticizing Nero. The status of the actor and of his profession as exercised on a public stage remained essentially liminal and shameful in Roman society. Actors were subject to the stigma of *infamia* as a result of their profession, which thus deprived them of the legal status and rights of ordinary Roman citizens.[21] It seems that Nero's decision, taken over a number of years, to start performing as an actor and singer on a public stage was perceived by the elite as a profound reversal of Roman values and norms of acceptable behavior. It may have been one of the issues that caused tension between Nero and his mother, and in fact it was after her death in 59 that he started to move steadily toward a role as a public performer. The last few years of his life were increasingly devoted to music and to the public stage, culminating in an artistic tour of Greece that took him away from Rome for a decisive period in 66/67 and in his subsequent artistic triumph.[22] Nero's involvement in the theater can be identified as a significant factor preceding his downfall, both in its controversial essence and in the time that it took from his engagement with the politics of the Roman Empire. Nero's acting is also central to the image of him that became so well established in the historical narratives of Tacitus, of Suetonius, and later of Dio.

With this context in mind, any consideration of Nero on stage *after his death* must appear both paradoxical and yet vital to an understanding of his memory in Rome, especially within the political space created by the Roman audience, seated in the theater according to social rank.[23] It seems likely that at least Nero's prominent public portraits and inscriptions were the subject of attack or removal immediately after his suicide in early June 68. Because he had not received a traditional aristocratic funeral with a eulogy from the *rostra* and with an actor wearing a wax mask (*imago*) to represent him, his appearance on stage would have seemed all the more dramatic. Nero had reappeared again in Rome, in the theater, and was speaking again to the people.

In the *Octavia* the actor must surely have worn a mask to represent Nero, but which mask did he wear?[24] Wax ancestor masks were never worn in theatrical contexts, as far as all our ancient evidence indicates.[25] It must have been a mask such as those commonly used in the theater but made to represent Nero, presumably in a way that had at least some easily recognizable features. Nero himself had acted in masks, often wearing a mask of his own face, and sometimes a mask of his wife Poppaea after her death. On this occasion the actor might have opted to wear one of the masks of Nero that had in fact been used in the theater by Nero himself: such a mask would have had the most meaning for an audience that had seen it before, perhaps in a variety of different dramatic contexts. We do not know how many "masks of Nero" the actor-emperor had used. Alternatively, a special mask of "Nero the tyrant" could have been made in order to represent Nero in deliberate contrast to the way in which he had himself appeared on stage. No matter how the mask of Nero in the *Octavia* looked, there would inevitably be a contrast with the way masks of Nero and Poppaea had been used by Nero himself over the previous four years. Nero's use of Poppaea's mask had expressed his intense memories of her: now Nero himself appeared after his death. Meanwhile, the prefect remained anonymous, partly because Tigellinus was still alive and therefore his mask should not appear on stage, especially in a context where he was probably present as a member of the audience.

The decision to bring Nero back on stage, this time to play himself, must have been closely related both to his career as an actor during his lifetime and to the sanctions against his memory. The *Octavia* dramatizes the need to create a negative picture of Nero and to present that picture to the general public in the city. It goes far beyond traditional Roman memory sanctions of erasure and removal, and of negative historiographic narratives that were accessible only to an elite reading public. The play redefines, at least in the case of Nero, how an attack on his memory might be constituted. If armies and provinces had been mobilized in order to remove an actor-emperor from his stage, why then bring him back for an encore performance almost as soon as a successor had been fully installed in the city?

The most logical answer would seem to lie in Nero's continued popular appeal and especially in the associated phenomenon of his popularity as a performer in front of the people of Rome.[26] The *Octavia* should be related to the other evidence we have that Nero's memory was being cultivated in the city, at his grave that was decorated with spring and summer flowers, in the Forum where his portraits were paraded and his edicts and speeches were read aloud, and presumably also in the homes and workplaces of the urban populace. Nero had indeed been and still was popular, as an emperor and as a showman, and his public was missing him. At the same time, the theater continued to provide a political forum where the views of the people were regularly expressed. In this light, the choruses of the *Octavia*, composed of Roman citizens who turn against Nero, take on special significance.[27]

The *Octavia* showed the people of Rome how tyrannical and bloodthirsty Nero had been. At the same time, it reenacted one of the few securely attested episodes when the populace had in fact demonstrated against Nero in public and with some consistency, namely the year 62 when Nero divorced Octavia in order to marry Poppaea, who was then pregnant with his child.[28] Popular pressure in Octavia's favor prompted her removal, first from Rome and then from Italy, and her subsequent death after an accusation of plotting treason. People had taken to the streets and had paraded Octavia's images while attacking those of Poppaea. This play reminds the Roman people of their own opposition to Nero and their original, inherited loyalty to the family of Octavia's father Claudius, of which Nero had not really been a member, as his burial in the tomb of the Domitii was at pains to make clear. The first chorus of Romans represents a central voice in the play, a voice that is as significant as that of Seneca or of Nero himself. Their words recall traditional, republican ideals of the people's voice in politics, especially in opposition to a tyrant.

The message of the play, however, goes beyond a historical commentary on certain events of 62 and on the tragic fate of Octavia, daughter of Claudius. Rather the drama deals also and perhaps even mainly with memory sanctions and the political struggles of 68. Despite tensions between Nero and the inhabitants of Rome in the immediate aftermath of the great fire of 64, fond memories persisted after his death. Hence it was considered a worthwhile project to bring Nero back on stage, as a tyrant and a murderer, and to reenact the people's own opposition to him, with special reference to the political use of images in attacks on status, on portraits, and on memory. The repeated theme of headhunting and the decapitation of political enemies provided an especially vivid way of connecting Nero with previous warlords and their savagery: his first words on stage demand the heads of his relatives Sulla and Plautius.[29] It is a fine piece of dramatic irony, in the context of historical drama, to have Nero call for the head of Sulla.

It is interesting that the fire of 64 does not play a larger role in the drama, and that the playwright thought the situation in 62, with flashbacks to the murder of Agrippina in 59, would be most compelling and damaging for Nero. Meanwhile, the familiar tragic themes of murder within the family were used to suggest the inevitability of Nero's fall and of the end of the Julio-Claudian dynasty, an end now conveniently attributed to Nero himself rather than to any rebellious senators or provincial governors or disloyal Praetorians. The *Octavia* as political rhetoric is designed to have the same effect as the memory sanctions themselves: Nero is to bear the blame for everything, while others around him are to be exonerated or even rehabilitated in various ways.[30]

Agrippina's ghost speaks bitterly of the sanctions Nero has imposed on her memory, sanctions that she describes as widespread and enforced by the death penalty.[31] Yet our other ancient evidence about her disgrace does not support these assertions, and we should be cautious about accepting them at face value. Despite his carefully crafted accusations of treason, Nero continued to react with deep ambivalence to his mother's memory, and her death weighed on him. If she had died in the original shipwreck caused by the collapsible boat, he would probably have accorded her divine honors. As it was, there is no indication that an official decree condemning her memory was ever sent out from Rome; her statues in Rome were removed, but in some haste and a few wry comments. In the end, Nero even seems to have held a series of games in her honor.

The reproaches of Agrippina's ghost should be seen as an attempt to label Nero as one who was especially harsh in his own use of memory sanctions, even in a context that violated basic norms of filial piety. Her words are intended more to tell us about the difficulties involved in dealing with Nero's memory in late 68 than to give us any special insight into the situation of 59. Attempts to discredit Nero were proving ineffective; such attempts had perhaps been ambitious at first, but they were meeting with resistance. Now the people were meant to learn, in the theater (their accustomed political classroom by now?), both that they had participated, over many years, in the opposition to Nero and in political attacks on imperial images, and that such memory sanctions were not really new but were, in fact, exactly what Nero deserved on the basis of his own past behavior. In the play it is the people who take the first initiative in attacking Nero and Poppaea. The *Octavia* presented its audience with a number of overlapping and complementary negative pictures of Nero, both in person and in the mouths of the other main characters.[32] At the same time, it represented sanctions against memory and attacks on images both in terms of traditional popular revolt and as the logical response to the cruelty of a tyrant.

A number of possible conclusions follow from the examination of the *Octavia* as political drama. The position of Galba upon his return to Rome in 68 was not strong. There were no precedents for dealing with the memory of a disgraced emperor, and the people's fondness for Nero was a continuing factor in politics. Memory sanctions themselves could be characterized as cruel and may have been especially associated in people's minds with the last years of Tiberius and with the dramatic fall of Messalina. It is not easy to see why Messalina emerges in such a relatively positive light in the play; perhaps a possible rehabilitation of the mother of Britannicus, Claudius' true heir, was being contemplated.[33] A much more positive picture of Claudius, the good Julio-Claudian, was also in the air but not yet developed in its later Flavian form. A change of ruler was by now expected to involve a recasting of memory, at least in terms of Julio-Claudian family history, but a change of dynasty was completely unprecedented. The first false Nero had already appeared in the guise of a lyre player and had served as a portent of things to come.[34]

Much has been written, both in antiquity and more recently, about Nero's turning Rome into a stage for his own role-playing and about his subversion of the real into a world of illusion created by his own ever more novel and extravagant spectacles.[35] The *Octavia* suggests the degree to which he had *succeeded* in turning the theater into the prime political forum for the interaction of the emperor and his adoring fans. His immediate successor soon also turned to the theater in order to try to control Nero's memory, represented here by his vivid stage presence, while hoping to establish his own rapport with the audience, as they watched a play that recalled the traditions of Greek tragedy and Senecan drama, as well as the more republican tones of a *praetexta*.[36]

Yet Galba failed both in his bid to become ruler of Rome and in his efforts to put his own interpretation of the figure of Nero on stage. His failure can be measured by the fact that he was succeeded by two emperors who hurried to recall Nero's memory. Otho was quick to replace the statues of Nero and of Poppaea in January 69, thus reversing whatever damage had been done in the latter part of 68. His ability to undo the actions of the senate and of Galba suggests that many statues had simply been put in warehouses and in other places out of public view, rather than being destroyed. Vitellius went a step further in having some of Nero's own songs performed again, presumably in a public venue.[37] Thus Nero the performer kept reappearing on various public stages throughout the period of the civil war. The disquiet of later authors with the figure of Nero as a "Phantom of the Opera" makes sense in light of this singular phenomenon.

The argument presented here has interpreted the *Octavia* as a monument to Nero the actor-tyrant in the particular context of the struggle over his memory in 68. Its equivalent, in a Flavian context, can be seen in the building of Rome's first monumental stone amphitheater, later known as the Colosseum.[38] This massive structure, which still embodies the image of Rome perhaps more than any other ancient building, was built over the site of Nero's ornamental lake near the *vestibulum* of the Domus Aurea with its colossal statue of the sun god. Planned by Vespasian, the amphitheater was dedicated by Titus in 80 and was inscribed with the most traditional of Roman texts that recorded its construction from war booty. The performance space seems to have taken up a larger area than Nero's lake, and so it competed with the vast scale of his building program. At the same time it celebrated and monumentalized the old republican and Italic traditions of gladiatorial combats and other sporting events under the aegis of an emperor whose patronage was expressed in terms borrowed from the republican political elite. In this sense it offered a further development of the culture of spectacle, in terms of lavish scale, vast audience, and the novelty of its wide variety of entertainments. It can be seen as a counterbalance, not merely to the architecture and design of the Golden House and its great park, but particularly to the image of Nero on the stage and to the dominant position that the theater had come to occupy in the political and cultural life of Julio-Claudian Rome. Although it took about a decade to build, the design and purpose of the amphitheater can be taken to reflect the intentions of the new Flavian dynasty at the very beginning of its time in power.

Vespasian felt the need to distance himself from Nero, but also from Otho and Vitellius, who had behaved as true successors of Nero.[39] Vitellius was by far the more important target, since he was the political rival whom Vespasian had actually fought in order to win the Empire. Consequently, Vespasian's agent Antonius Primus set about restoring Galba's images as soon as he was near Rome. Like Galba, Vespasian sought to associate himself with the families of Nero's most prominent victims, most notably by marrying his younger son Domitian to Domitia Longina, daughter of Nero's famous general Corbulo. A rehabilitation of Galba, to the extent that he could be recalled in a positive way, can also help to explain the survival of the text of the *Octavia*, as well as to the more general revival of interest in the works of Seneca in the 70s. Yet Galba's reign did not offer much of an image of success to bolster the new Flavian regime, especially in view of Vespasian's active role and stellar career in the last years of Nero. Hence it was essential for Vespasian to distance himself as much as possible from the image and style of Nero. He did this in various positive ways by appealing to the memory of Claudius, whose temple on the Caelian he completed, and by cultivating a deliberately simple life-style, in complete contrast to the court of Nero. The events of 69, however, had in themselves shown that restoring various "memories" could be as important as erasing others.

Neronians after Nero

Both the *Octavia* and the Flavian amphitheater provide specific evidence about the power of Nero's memory in 68–70 and beyond. The attempt to convert Nero into a cautionary figure can be traced through Pliny's *Panegyricus*, which presents a scornful picture of the actor-emperor, to the historical and biographical writings of Pliny's friends Tacitus and Suetonius.[40] Yet there is also evidence that attests the quality and longevity of Nero's popularity at various levels of Roman society, even into the second century. In the western provinces a number of graves were accompanied by mirrors in the form of round boxes, which could also be used as containers for cosmetics (figure 49). The outsides of some mirror-boxes were decorated with coins of Nero,

FIGURE 49. Top and bottom of a mirror box decorated with a coin of Nero,
showing a portrait of Nero and a seated goddess Roma, Cologne. *Rheinisches Bildarchiv,
Köln 83181, 83182, Römisch-Germanisches Museum, Cologne.*

thus associating the emperor with beauty and the personal care of the self.
The coins, all struck at Lugdunum, date from the last two years of Nero's
reign and attest to his continuing popularity in Gaul and the Rhineland. It is
suggestive that people chose to be buried with their portraits of Nero, presumably often many years after his death.[41]

Pliny the Younger himself was well aware of the appeal of Nero's life-style
to some within his own elite circle. One such Neronian character was Ummidia Quadratilla, who died around 107 at a great age.[42] Pliny was friendly
with her and with her family, whose younger members reflected the clean-
cut image first introduced by Vespasian and especially cultivated by Trajan.
Meanwhile, Quadratilla continued to live the way the elites had under Nero,
and much of her life was focused on the theater and on her own troupe of
actors. Her private house was a venue for performances, but she was also a
regular theatergoer and a public patron of drama.

Inscriptions supplement Pliny's vivid picture by recording the fact that Quadratilla built an amphitheater in her hometown of Casinum (presumably under the Flavians), where she was an important local patron who continued a family tradition of euergetism.[43] Quadratilla knew how to pay tribute to Flavian style in architecture without necessarily renouncing her passion for Neronian entertainments. Her life was a life of leisure dominated by games and spectacles, even though she acknowledged that such pursuits were no longer suitable to her grandson and to his prospects for a career in politics and in the law. Meanwhile, there was nothing secret about her way of life, and like Nero she had her own group of fans in the theater who applauded her entrances and imitated her gestures in various flattering ways throughout the performances that she organized and funded. Quadratilla herself was part of the show provided by her actors, and her role as patron of the crowd was essential to her position in society. Neither Pliny nor the inscriptions record the name of her husband; she led the luxurious life of the independently wealthy widow. Both she and her fans probably recalled Nero's shows with nostalgia, but also with continued imitation and reflection of his taste.

The picture of Quadratilla can be used to help elucidate a unique funerary inscription from Rome that records the name of a woman who, with her husband Q. Pomponius Rusticus, is erecting a tomb for one of their freedmen and for future use by members of their household. The woman's name is Neronia Saturnina (figure 50).[44] This name in itself conjures up a variety of images and a devotion to an emperor whose own name has been adopted in place of a family name (*nomen*). The name Neronia, of course, also recalls the new Greek-style festival that Nero had founded and had used as the premier venue for his own first performances in the city, as well as the name he gave to the month of April. It is paired with Saturnina, a descriptive *cognomen* that evokes the new age of the god Saturn, as well as the carnival atmosphere of the traditional winter festival of the Saturnalia and the politics of reversal that are so strongly associated with Nero in the literary sources. Under Nero, life could be construed in terms of a Saturnalia, since the emperor now appeared as an actor, a reversal that might have powerful appeal to humbler citizens. It is possible that Neronia was born in the 60s and received her name from her parents as a token of their feelings for their emperor. In that case, she did not change it when she grew up and married, by now well into the Flavian time. Alternatively, she may have chosen the name for herself, instead of her family name, and the inscription could date to the time of Nero. It may be indicative that the two "Neronians" discussed here were both women, albeit from very different social levels. Most owners of mirror-boxes adorned with Nero's

FIGURE 50. Epitaph of the freedman Q. Pomponius Scirtus, dedicated by
his former owners Q. Pomponius Rusticus and Neronia Saturnina, at a tomb
they built for him, themselves, and descendants of members of their household,
Rome, second half of the first century A.D. *Drawing by Harriet I. Flower,
after Avetta (1985) pl. 58, 5 [209], AE 1988.103.*

portrait may also have been women. As such, they may have felt relatively
freer than elite men to recall the emperor of mime and carnival in their own
ways.

Nero's Inscriptions

As already indicated by the few examples cited, the epigraphic record of
Nero and his doings richly enhances what can be learned from literary and
archaeological sources. Many texts were erased, but many were not.[45] The
picture inevitably remains complex, since we are dealing with repeated attempts to replace or to celebrate Nero, and a situation where communication
within the Empire was perhaps at its most uncertain for any time between
Actium and the murder of Commodus in 192. The specter of violence may
have prompted erasure more quickly than any official messages from Rome.
The declaration of Nero as a *hostis* seems to imply official sanctions, but we
do not know when or by whom such sanctions were first imposed, or who
later endorsed or reversed them. As noted, the initial *hostis* declaration by the
senate does not seem to have had much effect on Galba. Conversely, by early
70 the city had been so devastated by war that formal sanctions against Nero,
who had already had three successors by now, were probably low on the list
of pressing concerns for the new regime. The image of Nero was still there,

THE PRINCIPATE

but the traditional context of sanctions, usually closely associated with the death of the affected person, was no longer present. Much had already been destroyed by the great fire of 64 and the civil wars in 69/70.

A few inscriptions can serve to suggest some of the strategies used to address the continuing issue of Nero's memory. Even within the city itself, the pattern of erasure and survival appears random and localized. Quite a number of inscriptions that feature Nero's name are fragmentary and do not reveal their fate at the time of his death, although none of these show a sign of erasure.[46] It is particularly notable that Nero was not erased from two prominent Claudian contexts, namely from a statue group near the arch at the Via Lata (see figure 45) and from the Claudian family monument in the area of the Ara Pacis (figure 51).[47] Because both monumental texts probably had statue groups associated with them, the honor soon accorded to Claudius may have protected the image of the young Nero as his son in the context of family groups from the early 50s.

Equally it may suggest that the real target was "Nero the emperor" rather than any record of Nero from an earlier time in his life. Indeed evidence that representations of children were systematically removed is lacking.[48] Similarly, the pattern of Nero's surviving portraits suggests a much more effective removal or reworking of his images from the later part of his reign; these later portraits remain very scarce and were evidently superseded by reworked images.[49] By contrast, many more survive from his time as heir and from his immediate accession to power. The famous panel from Aphrodisias is the only representation of Nero in relief, and his portraits were systematically removed from dynastic statue groups, some of which then had the Flavians added to them.

Outside the sphere of official texts, Nero's name can be found in a striking dedication to the emperor and to the god Silvanus from the Via Praenestina, some six kilometers from Rome (figure 52).[50] This simple inscription records the dedication (at his own expense) of a small shrine and a cult image by Fausius, a slave of the imperial household. It shows no sign of mutilation, although it is possible that it was removed from public view. Yet it seems more probable that it was simply not important enough to attract much attention, especially outside the city boundaries. Moreover, only a single cult image is mentioned. If that image represented Silvanus, the hallowed nature of the shrine might have helped to preserve it. Meanwhile, the word *imago*, perhaps inserted as an afterthought in the text, is not a usual Latin term to designate the image of a god.

The text offers a fascinating glimpse of the special reverence felt for Nero

FIGURE 51. Inscriptions from a dynastic monument of the Claudii, Campus Martius, Rome, A.D. 22. Drusus, father of Claudius, and Nero, after his adoption as son of Claudius. This stone dates to A.D. 50–54, after Nero's adoption. *Ministero per i Beni e le Attività Culturali, Soprintendenza Archeologica di Roma, Museo Nazionale Romano,* CIL 6.40424.

within his own household: his name appears first and in bigger letters than that of the god. Silvanus was originally a rustic deity who became very popular, in Rome and throughout the Empire, and whose cult was often personal and mostly associated with the lower levels of society.[51] Nero is not directly labeled with a divine epithet, yet such a status is surely implied and might have emerged more clearly from the appearance of the shrine itself. Silvanus was not a god Nero himself seems to have cultivated, yet it is possible that the image in this case recalled the features of Nero, thus assimilating him to a popular indigenous deity. Other evidence also connects Silvanus with the imperial cult in Rome.

A useful comparison can be made with an altar dedicated to the sun and the moon by Eumolpus, a slave in charge of the furniture in Nero's Domus Aurea, and his daughter Claudia Pallas (figure 53).[52] This unique piece depicts only a bust of the sun god with his radiate crown; the moon goddess remains absent from the iconography, even though she is mentioned in the inscription. The text does not mention Nero and is not dated, yet the features of the sun god bear a striking resemblance to those of the emperor, especially in the hair style. Indeed this iconography, which makes most sense near the end of Nero's reign when construction on the Domus Aurea had made some progress, may reflect the aspect of the colossal statue of Nero that was being designed to stand at the entrance to the Domus Aurea. Thus we can see that

FIGURE 52. Dedication of a small shrine and cult image to
Nero and Silvanus by Fausius, a slave of Nero, Rome, A.D. 54–68.
*Ministero per i Beni e le Attività Culturali, Soprintendenza Archeologica di Roma,
Museo Nazionale Romano*, CIL 6.927 = ILS 236.

within Nero's own household he was indeed cultivated in various ways during his own lifetime, both in words and in images, and that this context was
probably not an official target for removal or erasure.

Similarly, Nero's name was preserved in dating formulae in a variety of
texts put up by ordinary Romans in the city, perhaps because the texts did
not honor him in any direct way. Yet his name could also be erased in such
a context, as is revealed by the ex-voto dedication of an altar by P. Acilius
Cerdo to Jupiter Optimus Maximus and to the genius of the slave trade (Genius Venalicius) on the Aventine in 60.[53] Both sides of the stone bear the
same inscriptions and both sides have been erased, although not in exactly
the same pattern. Acilius may perhaps have been a slave trader who put up
this dedication in a public shrine or market. Nero's name had originally been
given more prominence than that of his fellow consul. This text demonstrates
that the sacred nature of a dedication made to the gods did not in itself prevent the text from being adapted later. Indeed such texts, if prominent, might
be likely candidates for erasure since removing the inscriptions altogether
would offend the gods.

Nero's name is preserved in more than a dozen funerary texts from Rome

FIGURE 53. Altar dedicated to the sun and moon by Eumolpus, a slave of Nero
in charge of the furniture in the Domus Aurea, and his daughter Claudia Pallas,
Rome, A.D. 64–68. *Soprintendenza per i Beni Archeologici di Firenze,
Museo Archeologico di Firenze 86025,* CIL *6.3719 = 31033 =* ILS *1774.*

that commemorate members of his personal German bodyguard, who were to be the last to desert him in early June 68.[54] The men mentioned in the inscriptions all presumably died during Nero's lifetime and were buried in a cemetery set aside for them near their camp in Trastevere. Many of their tombstones, erected by fellow members of their units, are in very good condition. Only one is a Roman citizen. It was typical for them to identify themselves as part of the Batavian nation and the *collegium Germanorum*. It is notable that these units were disbanded shortly after Nero's death and the men returned to Germany, where their tribe was soon to revolt from Rome. Yet neither their ethnic origin nor their loyalty to Nero caused their cemetery to be disturbed or vandalized.

Just as in Rome, both erased and unerased inscriptions of Nero can be found all over the Empire, often in virtually equal numbers and in many seemingly random patterns. Other texts are too fragmentary to be analyzed in any detail. Some of these texts attest cult addressed to Nero in his lifetime, such as a tablet from Chichester and an ex-voto to Nero from Châteauneuf.[55] There is no evidence to demonstrate that such texts were more targeted than others. Particularly notable are the texts of two statue groups from Luna (Italy), neither of which has been damaged. On the other hand, Nero's name has been removed from an important inscription from Ficulea, which recorded the dedication of some local public buildings. And three lines were erased from a statue's base at Bubon in Turkey (figure 54). Similarly, Nero's evident popularity in Greece did not protect his inscriptions there in any special way.[56] At Athens his name has been removed from most texts that have come to light so far. His name had also been put in large bronze letters on the eastern architrave of the Parthenon in 61/62 in a text that seems to have summarized a decree in his honor, with a gilt crown affixed to it. This text was taken down, presumably soon after his death. His name was erased at Sparta from a statue base dedicated by Klaudia Kallistonika. The removal of his name (and that of Statilia Messalina) from his letters and speeches at Akraiphia in Boeotia and on Rhodes is evidence for the desire to maintain the privileges he had extended to the Greeks, especially the "freedom" he granted to them on the occasion of his visit in 67. At the same time, such texts afford important insights into the tone of his words, especially near the end of his life. In this context a roadside text from Knossos (Crete) is especially interesting: it preserves Nero's name intact while the name of the proconsul has been erased.[57]

It may come as no surprise that Nero's name has been removed from a dedication in Lycia in honor of C. Licinius Mucianus, the governor of Syria

FIGURE 54. Dedication of a statue or other object for Nero by C. Licinius Mucianus, later a close ally of Vespasian, Bubon, Turkey, Neronian. Erasure of Nero's name in lines 1–3 and line 7. *Deutsches Archäologisches Institut, Istanbul, SEG 27 (1977) 916.*

who was to propel the Flavians to power in Rome.[58] Nero's name had also become controversial in Germany, where Vitellius' revolt started on 1 January 69 and where the Flavians faced continued unrest. Three prominent examples attest to widespread political changes in the northern parts of the Empire. In Cologne a large and fine dedicatory inscription in Nero's name has survived the chances of civil strife; it originally labeled a statue or building put up in 66 by the fifteenth legion, which was stationed locally at Vetera (Xanten) (figure 55).[59] This text was removed, turned, and used as a cover for a canal, with the result that even the original red paint in the letters has been preserved. Nero's name is written in the newly fashionable style with *Imp(erator)* now used as a *praenomen* in a manner not seen since the early days of Augustus. Nero's descent is traced back to Divus Augustus through the adopted line of the Julio-Claudians that comprised (in an order represented somewhat misleadingly as successive generations) Tiberius, Germanicus, and Divus Claudius. This unbroken genealogy obscures many complexities in actual relationships (especially through women) and conveniently takes no account of the emperor Gaius, who seems virtually replaced by his father Germanicus in what looks like, but is not quite, a list of previous emperors. Nero's titulature stresses his legitimate descent and a new military style of naming; it resonates with the emperor's problems in 66 as he faced senatorial opposition, the revolt of Judea, and criticisms of his increasing focus on his artistic interests.

FIGURE 55. Inscription of Nero put up by P. Sulpicius Scribonius Rufus,
governor of Lower Germany, Cologne, A.D. 66. Removed by 68, if not before,
and turned for reuse as a paving stone. *Rheinisches Bildarchiv, Köln 132567,
Römisch-Germanisches Museum, Cologne,* AE *1969/70 443.*

The plaque was put up by P. Sulpicius Scribonius Rufus, the local governor from 59 to 67. However, Rufus himself had fallen from the emperor's
favor and was summoned to Greece where he, together with his brother, was
forced to commit suicide in 67. His fall is connected in some way to the death
of Corbulo and to the senatorial plot that came to light at Brundisium just
before Nero was about to embark for his tour in Greece. Conceivably, the Sul-
picii were already plotting against Nero at the time when the inscription was
made. It is possible that it was removed from public view before Nero's death
in order to eliminate the governor's name, yet this would seem to dishonor
the emperor himself and might well have been a dangerous move to make in
late 67 or early 68. In addition, the fifteenth legion was one that supported
Vitellius in 69 and was then dissolved after the Flavian victory. Consequently,
this text provides a snapshot of a moment when Nero was being honored by
a governor and a legion, both of whom would be ruined in close proximity to
the emperor's own fall. Clearly the text became "dated" less than three years
after it was put up.

Meanwhile, Sulpicius Rufus' brother, P. Sulpicius Scribonius Proculus, was
serving as governor in nearby Mainz. There Proculus' name is recorded on
the great column put up to Jupiter as a dedication for the safety of Nero and
on behalf of the local population by Q. Iulius Priscus and Q. Iulius Auctus
(figure 56).[60] This extraordinary testimony to local resources and to indigenous artistic talent seems to have dominated the commercial and civic center
of the community. It was erected in response to a crisis in Nero's principate,
probably in 59 in connection with the accusation of treason against Agrip-

FIGURE 56. Inscription from a column dedicated to Jupiter for the safety of Nero
by P. Sulpicius Scribonius Proculus, governor of Upper Germany,
Mainz, Germany, A.D. 59? *Landesmuseum Mainz.*

pina. In other words, it reflects a local reaction to a message sent from Rome
that the emperor had survived a threat. Resting on a double base, the column
is composed of five drums, intricately carved with the images of a wide variety of deities, including both Roman and local gods, and a Genius Neronis. The top bore a bronze statue, probably of Jupiter. The work is signed by
Samus and Severus, sons of Venicarus, who may have been artists especially
brought to Mainz to work on this costly expression of local loyalty to Nero.
Here "Nero" has been completely obliterated, leaving a dedication that looks
as if it honors Claudius.

A similar erasure can be found on an altar now in the parish church at
Rindern not far from Xanten. The altar was also dedicated *pro salute Neronis*

THE PRINCIPATE

FIGURE 57. Dedication of an altar to Mars Camulus for the health and safety of Nero, presently used as an altar in the Catholic parish church of Rindern, Germany, A.D. 54–68. *Verlag Butzon & Bercker, Kevelaer, Josef Fink,* Der Mars Camulus-Stein in der Pfarrkirche zu Rindern. Römisches Denkmal und christlicher Altar *(1970),* pl. 10, CIL 13.8701 = ILS 235.

to Mars Camulus, a Celtic deity assimilated to Mars, by the local community of the Remi (figures 57, 58).[61] Both sides of the altar are decorated with a bay tree, and the back features an oak wreath awarded for the saving of citizen lives. It can be associated with the local temple to the same god. In later times and again now the same altar was reused in the church and a local antiquarian (in the sixteenth century?) went so far as to fill in the erasure with the first name "Tiberius," thus restoring the honor to Claudius without ever recogniz-

FIGURE 58. Detail of inscription to Mars Camulus, parish church of
Rindern, Germany. Erasure of Nero's name, which was replaced with Claudius in
the Renaissance. *Verlag Butzon & Bercker, Kevelaer, Josef Fink,* Der Mars Camulus-Stein
in der Pfarrkirche zu Rindern. Römisches Denkmal und christlicher Altar *(1970),*
pl. 11, CIL 13.8701 = ILS 235.

ing the disgrace of Nero. These inscriptions demonstrate how a renewal of the honors for (Divus) Claudius after Nero's death could help provide a practical solution to the problem of what to do with a variety of Nero's texts that were on prominent local monuments throughout the Empire. A later reader would not necessarily be able to surmise the reason for the original erasure. At the same time a record of the community's loyalty to the Claudian house could be preserved.

Remembering and Forgetting in the Grove of Dea Dia

The focus of the present discussion of the events of 68–70 has been largely on the memory of Nero and on how it was treated by his various successors. Unlike Nero, little was left to commemorate Galba, Otho, or Vitellius.[62] None of them can have had a large number of monuments before he aspired to the Empire, and each was then more concerned with the struggle to stay in power than with other issues. They were recalled in later historiography largely in terms of various cautionary tales colored by Flavian moralizing. Galba fared the best of the three, but that is not saying much. Their coins provide virtually the only independent contemporary source about them and their self-presentation, while portraits are rare. There is, however, one place where the bitterness and depth of the crisis of 69 can be traced more vividly — in the sacred grove dedicated to Dea Dia, which was tended by the Arval brothers.[63]

The Arval brothers were a highly exclusive priesthood, comprised at any one time of twelve members with the reigning emperor as a possible thirteenth. They were co-opted from the ranks of the most elite senators, and their main duties were connected with the cult of the mysterious Dea Dia, apparently an ancient agricultural goddess. Dea Dia's temple was built in a sacred grove by the Tiber, on the road leading to Ostia, some five Roman miles from the city. Only the brothers themselves, and the public servants assigned to the cult, could enter this sacred precinct, and then only in a condition of ritual purity. They did so only on specific occasions, for traditional purposes, and with solemn rituals.

The staff of the goddess included a secretary who kept the minutes of meetings held and of religious duties fulfilled. Under Augustus, who promoted the cult, these records started to be inscribed on stone revetment plaques of Luna marble that were housed either in or perhaps even on the temple inside the grove. The fragments of these Arval records, stretching from 21 B.C. to A.D. 304, provide an unparalleled glimpse into the details of one aspect of Roman state cult. The minutes were solemnly transferred onto stone once a year; the procedure required special rituals to allow the introduction into and the subsequent removal of the engraving tools from the grove. Dea Dia did not normally allow any metal tool or blade to enter her sacred space. Rather than bringing the finished plaques into the grove, the Arval brothers performed the actual act of inscribing within this ritual space, surely a religious duty in its own right. Dated by both the calendar dates recorded next to each item of business and their fairly rapid inscription after the fact, the Arval records are replete with invaluable details about observances in honor of the ruling family, such as birthdays and special anniversaries, and the changing fashions in such rituals over the generations. Several fragments also record sacrifices of thanksgiving, performed by all the official priests in Rome, after a plot had been discovered or when the emperor had escaped some other danger.[64]

There are very few erasures within this record, and all but one of them relate to the events of the troubled year 69. Other records have remained intact, whether for Gaius, Nero, or Domitian. Despite the fact that the Arval brothers included the very same senators who were responsible for passing decrees against the memory of disgraced persons, and who apparently despised each of these emperors, they took no action to modify the stone archive of the goddess. This choice reveals the nature of the sacred grove, the limited access to its texts and even to the tools required to effect an erasure, and the whole issue of whether these texts were ever supposed to be reread and by whom. The Arvals' own search for precedents for ritual problems seems to have addressed itself to the original notes kept by the secretary rather than to the inscribed record on stone inside the sacred grove.

The Arval texts show that memory took on a special quality within the sacred grove of Dea Dia, a quality that transcended categories of "public" or "private" inscriptions in other temples and their precincts. Moreover, the characteristic nature of separate "memory spaces" was presumably also demonstrated by differences observed between the sacred area of the grove itself and the buildings technically outside the sacred precinct but actually right next to it, such as the altars, baths, tetrastyle, circus, and other structures built nearby over the years. The Arvals could meet and dine together in these buildings on the edge of the grove. At least from the Flavian period and perhaps earlier, each emperor was represented by a statue here in the ceremonial dress of an Arval. It is tempting to assume that disgraced emperors would have had their images and texts removed from these contexts, in complete contrast with what was or rather what was not being done inside the grove.

The Arval record for the year 69 is especially telling for the study of memory and disgrace.[65] It is powerful testimony to the importance attached to the rituals of the Arvals that these seem to have continued even during times of extreme uncertainty and while being carried out by a reduced staff. Nor was the inscribing of the record delayed so that the Arval brothers could see what the outcome of various political struggles might be. This fact in itself suggests the ritual nature of the annual act of inscribing the record. Consequently, the record for this year contains the names of all three of the emperors who controlled Rome at one time or another during the year. The adoption of Piso by Galba on 10 January is duly noted, and Piso is called by his new adoptive name of Servius Sulpicius Galba Caesar.

Throughout the text, which is best preserved in the central section, there are repeated, neatly executed, erasures of the name of both the emperor Vitellius and of his brother L. Vitellius. These erasures in this context provide striking confirmation of the chaos in Rome as described by Tacitus. The records of Vitellius' action must have been inscribed before the final Flavian victory became clear (figure 59). Yet Vitellius had not attacked Otho's name, nor does there seem to have been any change in the entries for Galba or Piso in January. Some entries that should name Otho have been attributed to Vitellius in a recasting of the events. The datable fragments end with the record for early June of 69, and so we do not know what was written about the end of the year. The fierce attack on the memory of A. Vitellius the emperor is further revealed by the erasure of his brother's name (L. Vitellius) under the record for the year A.D. 53 (12 October) (figure 60).[66] Whether these erasures were designed to target the emperor (his brother having been erased by mistake) or whether both brothers were subject to the same censure by the Arvals, we can see that after Vitellius' death on 20 December 69 the first (and only attested) thoroughgoing effort was made to erase a person from the Arval records, a project that included a search through the records of previous years.

The crisis of the state represented a crisis for the brotherhood, whose composition seems to have undergone significant change as a result, and whose elaborate cultivation of the *divi* and of the family festivals of the Julio-Claudians was inevitably affected by the advent of a new dynasty. It would be interesting to know whether a blade was brought into the grove on a certain day specifically for the purpose of effecting these erasures in the dossier or whether the changes were made when the first Flavian records were being inscribed. In either case, the result appears to reflect a decision of the brothers, presumably taken at a meeting (were these minutes also recorded on stone?), rather than a direct order from the new dynasty or the initiative of

FIGURE 59. Erasure of the emperor Aulus Vitellius in the Arval Acta, A.D. 69.
From the grove of Dea Dia near Rome, erasure in late 69 or 70. *Ministero
per i Beni e le Attività Culturali, Soprintendenza Archeologica di Roma,
Museo Nazionale Romano*, MNR 205822.

FIGURE 60.
Erasure of the emperor Vitellius'
brother Lucius Vitellius in the
Arval Acta, A.D. 53. From the
grove of Dea Dia near Rome,
erasure in late 69 or 70. *Ministero
per i Beni e le Attività Culturali,
Soprintendenza Archeologica di
Roma, Museo Nazionale Romano,
MNR 386–387.*

the secretaries in the grove. It remains unclear what effect, if any, an erasure on the stone might have on the archival records (*codices*) of the secretary. The erasures of Vitellius are powerful symbols of the politics of 69 and of the meaning of the Arval dossier as a commemorative and validating text for the most elite members of the Roman community.

The only other erasure attested in the fragments we currently have is of the person who was chosen to replace Augustus as an Arval in 14.[67] This individual was not an emperor, and his identity has not so far been securely established. Although the stone has not survived and thus the erasure itself can no longer be studied, it is noted (presumably correctly?) in Accursius' manuscript of the early sixteenth century. It seems probable that Augustus' replacement was also subject to sanctions, probably quite widespread ones, against his memory. The fact that he was later labeled a conspirator made it unacceptable to have his name next to that of Augustus. L. Scribonius Libo Drusus, who was subject to sanctions against his memory in A.D. 16, remains the most attractive candidate, especially since his name was now officially banned from his family. Such an erasure could make good sense in the context of Tiberius' interest in the Arvals and their documents. The Arval calendar, dating to between 36 and 21 B.C., also contains some erasures and editing, although not apparently for an overtly political reason.

The Image of Flavian Rome

The Flavians inherited a city that had been repeatedly ravaged, first by the fire of 64 and then by battles in the streets, culminating in the final intense struggle between the supporters of Vitellius and their own troops. The Capitol with its great temple of Jupiter lay in ruins, and many central parts of the city must have presented scenes of extreme devastation. Flavian Rome was built on these ruins in order to mark a new beginning and to try to cope with the bitter memories of civil war.[68] Vespasian's vision for Rome contained much more than a response to Nero's Rome and to the memory of one emperor or of a single age. Indeed his initial project of faithfully restoring the Capitol and the temple of Jupiter recalled the Republic and its values. Similarly, the most important construction to be dedicated in his own lifetime was the Temple of Peace, a complex designed to address the aftermath of civil strife; it represented the ideal of peace under the patronage of a civically minded emperor and the victories over rebellious provinces, especially Judea and its capital Jerusalem.[69]

It is unclear how many of Nero's buildings remained unscathed to become targets of deliberate political obliteration and reconstruction under the Flavians. Nero's famous arch on the Capitol was probably destroyed in the fire there rather than as a result of a separate dismantling effort.[70] The effort required to take apart a whole arch would have been considerable, and it seems unlikely that such a project would have been undertaken by Galba. The arch may have been attacked in other ways, especially as regards its attic inscription. Yet it remained an important model for later arches even after it had vanished.

Similarly, many of Nero's most significant building projects were incomplete at the time of his death, since they had been undertaken after and as a result of the fire of 64. This is especially and interestingly the case for those projects that were most censured by later writers. The image of Nero's megalomania is often identified closely with the famous colossal statue that was designed to stand in or near the entrance to the Golden House.[71] Various reconstructions of this statue have been made on the basis of later coins, and it remained an important landmark for many centuries. However, its original iconography and meaning have been obscured. It is tempting to imagine it as a statue dedicated to the sun god, an interpretation that would be confirmed by the iconography of Eumolpus' altar. At the same time, whether it had been installed or dedicated by 68 or was not put up until later under Vespasian is unknown. Vespasian's decision to adapt it, or to install it in the first place, suggests that it had always been seen as a statue of a divinity rather than as a secular portrait of Nero. The fact that it seems to have survived the events of 68/69 should raise some doubts: either it did not closely resemble Nero, or it was still in a workshop at the time of his death, rather than being an obvious public representation of the dead emperor in Rome. What was new here was the scale of the image, not necessarily the notion that a god's portrait might recall some features of the ruler. An analogous colossal portrait on canvas in the more private context of the Horti Maiani was destroyed by lightning.

The Domus Aurea itself stood in the middle of Rome and assumed an equally central location in the criticism of Nero voiced by later historians (map 1).[72] Its splendor and innovative design were quite new, but its luxury was increasingly out of place in a time of financial crisis and of growing unrest in the provinces. Ultimately there are two "Golden Houses" for generations living after Nero, the actual one, which is being steadily revealed by further excavation in Rome, and the image of the Golden House created in literature. Although Suetonius' famous description of Nero's new palace does allude to what seem to have been some of the salient features of the complex, his purpose is also highly moralistic. His writing cannot be taken as a reliable

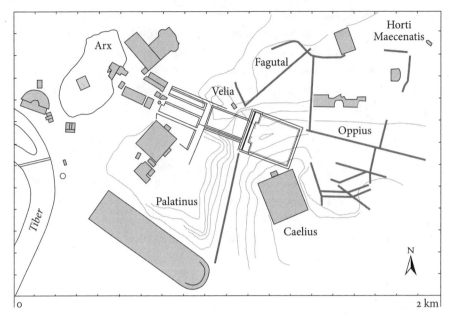

Arx

Fagutal

Horti
Maecenatis

Velia

Oppius

Tiber

Palatinus

Caelius

N

o   2 km

MAP 1. Nero's Domus Aurea. Overview with traces of roads.

guide to how the palace was originally viewed in the mid-60s, more than half a century earlier.

Because both Otho and Vitellius lived in and worked on the completion of the palace,[73] its image as the ultimate example of Nero's folly must date to Flavian times and be seen as part of a concerted policy to deal with Nero's memory in the city. Moreover, the fact that much of the palace remained incomplete, and that even what there was may have been further damaged by the fighting in Rome, made it easier for later ages to put their own construction on what Nero would have built if he had lived. An alternative reading of the Flavian reaction to the Golden House, including especially the Flavian amphitheater, the temple of Divus Claudius, and the Arch of Titus, would be to see these as attempts to erase Nero's projects from memory precisely because they had been popular and successful, or at least potentially so. Nero's building projects after 64, whether they were all strictly to be seen as part of the same palace complex or not, decisively displaced the elites from their traditional houses in the political center of the city, and also from some nearby commercial districts.[74] The clash of many senators with Nero can be related to this, as to other aspects of his behavior after 64. Few ordinary citizens were forcibly removed, and much of the land in the center had belonged to the imperial estates even before the fire.

The evidence does not suggest that Nero took land away from Rome's citizens in order to appropriate it for his private palace. Rather, a more plausible case can be made for the view that Nero took land from the wealthy and powerful in order to create a series of recreational spaces that would have been open to the public. Such a reconstruction certainly fits better with his desire to be a public figure in constant contact with the ordinary people in the city and to share his life with them, at least to some extent and on certain occasions. The boldness of his vision for a rustic-style villa overlooking a pleasure lake in the middle of the city was evidently satirized, even as the palace was being built. The ultimate question about the Domus Aurea, however, concerns not its size and extent, which we simply cannot estimate accurately in the present condition of our knowledge,[75] but its accessibility and the function assigned to its various areas.[76] It seems to have included a formal palace on the Palatine and a rustic villa in a more Hellenistic style on the Oppian. Yet the whole area, including especially several temples and a number of major roads through the city center, cannot have been blocked off and made "private" in the sense of being closed to traffic. It is notable that no detailed exposition of the complex as a public park and civic space has been undertaken so far by modern scholars.

Everything we know about Nero suggests his desire to have Rome as a stage for his special role as the artistic emperor, continually performing for an audience of his adoring fans. His vision also included a life of luxury focused on art, but a life that included sharing many of its features with a wider public, another aspect that was unwelcome to many of the more conservative senators. In this sense, Nero can be seen as a truly "popular" emperor, in that he sought out more direct contacts between himself and the people and thus tried to redefine his role as ruler to the exclusion of the senators and their traditional life-styles and habits. Hence, it seems logical that many would indeed see him as a threat to the elite, whether or not he ever actually talked of abolishing the senate.

Meanwhile, archaeological work continues to reveal further clues about the building undertaken by Nero. The famous palace on the Oppian was not completely finished in the 60s but continued in use; it seems that Titus may have lived there in the 70s.[77] The building was not destroyed until the construction on top of the Baths of Trajan, a complex dedicated in 109. Similarly, Nero's public reception rooms on the Palatine can be traced beneath the massive new palace built by Domitian after the fire of 80.

The recent excavations in the area of the Meta Sudans, next to the Arch of Constantine, have revealed the impressive efforts exerted in this area immediately after the fire.[78] A deep fill level underlies the series of terraces that were built to surround Nero's lake and to afford various views of the hills with their landscapes and buildings. The Domus Aurea, a project on an exceptional scale, had been started in the last years of Nero, with a flurry of activity in the two years between the time of the fire and Nero's departure for Greece in the autumn of 66. To what extent its final design was in place or could be appreciated by mid-68 is likely to remain unclear. Some of this building surely also included items that were not strictly part of the Domus Aurea. That project in itself became a symbol for Nero's last years, but a symbol largely invoked by his critics for their own particular purposes. The Flavian amphitheater bears witness to the perceived need to compete with Nero as a provider of mass entertainments in the center of the city. It is notable that no land seems to have been returned by the Flavians to domestic use, especially for senators. Meanwhile, Nero's extremely popular monumental bath complex on the Campus Martius remained in use and was not renamed until the third century.[79]

Epilogue: Fannius' Dream

The fall of the Julio-Claudians ran parallel with the virtual extinction of the aristocratic families of the old Republic, who had always been seen as the most serious rivals by Augustus himself and by each of his immediate successors. Just as the dynasty destroyed its own family through internal struggles (mainly over the succession), it simultaneously brought down most of what had remained of the old *nobiles*. Their obliteration is symbolized by the ravages of the fire of 64, which destroyed the traditional houses of the established political families with their trophies of war and all their other family mementos, memorials of the power of those families in earlier times and *loci* for the *auctoritas* associated with their family memories.[80] The image of Nero as an arsonist speaks not only to distaste for his person, but also to the devastating sense of loss experienced by the political elite in the aftermath of 64. From now on only the emperor would live on the Palatine and in its surroundings, and that emperor would live in a palace, not in a *domus* that recalled the spirit of the Republic or of Augustus as the leading citizen among his fellow aristocrats. Removing the actor-emperor Nero from his stage could not restore the traditional memory spaces of the republican political families. The new Flavian dynasty could not itself rely on a venerable pedigree and did not value the traditional prestige associated with republican ancestors. The Flavians sought out new senators and other associates from a wide variety of municipal and provincial backgrounds rather than according to republican traditions.[81]

The strong and sustained hatred for Nero felt by senators is perhaps best conjured up for us by a dream of Gaius Fannius, a lawyer and friend of the younger Pliny who died during Trajan's reign. Fannius was perhaps a relative of Thrasea Paetus, one of Nero's most prominent victims. Over many years he was engaged in writing a multivolume work about Nero's victims, which may have started as a family history, and which seems to have been his main undertaking. Early on in the project, he dreamed that Nero came into his room.[82] Fannius saw Nero sit at his desk and read through three papyrus rolls of his historical work, and then get up and leave. Fannius took this to mean that he would only finish three volumes before his own death, and this was indeed what happened. Fannius' dream presents us with a striking image of the psychology of a senator watching Nero read his account, an account designed to rehabilitate and commemorate other prominent men who had died in disgrace under Nero. Nero's ghost appears as a vivid presence: he has the last word even without speaking. By contrast, Fannius experiences a feeling of helplessness and futility in his attempt to salvage the past in the face of Nero. Nero's memory lives, while his victims appear to be no more than incomplete entries in an unfinished history book.

The Shadow of Domitian and
the Limits of Disgrace

▼   ▼   ▼

Condicionem principum miserrimam
aiebat, quibus de coniuratione comperta
non crederetur nisi occisis.
Suetonius, *Domitian* 21

Neque enim satis amarit bonos principes qui
malos satis non oderit. Adice quod imperatoris
nostri non aliud amplius ac diffusius meritum est
quam quod insectari malos principes tutum est.
Pliny, *Panegyricus* 53.2–3

Hoc sub principe, si sapis, caveto verbis,
Roma, prioribus loquaris.
Martial 10.72

The Flavians stand at the center of imperial sanctions against memory, between the contrasting but equally formidable figures of Nero and of their
own Domitian. Both emperors proved hard to exorcise or obliterate. The Flavians were the first to effect a successful change of dynasty and to deal with
the memory of a disgraced emperor whose fall marked the end of his family's
power. In this sense, the Flavians were the first to maintain consistent memory sanctions against a predecessor. Yet only a generation later, their own
family suffered the uniquely fierce sanctions passed against the memory of
Domitian immediately after his murder.[1] The attacks on Domitian's memory
appear both more severe and more sustained than those initiated against any

previous male in a ruling house; indeed, they have obscured many aspects of the policies and spirit of the Flavian age. They extended beyond Domitian himself, a figure who seems to have evoked exceptionally strong feelings of hatred among Rome's political elite, to affect the tradition about his father and his brother, as well as about his own relationship to them. At the same time, the memory of Nero and his demise lasted throughout Flavian times and was still very real in the early part of the second century.[2]

Despite the relatively poor condition of our extant sources for the Flavians in general, and for Domitian in particular, we are much better informed about the nature and extent of the sanctions against Domitian than about those against Nero.[3] Since Tacitus' narrative breaks off after the year 70, we must rely on Suetonius and Dio for information about Domitian. Suetonius' biography of him, the shortest of his imperial lives, is both negative and essentially superficial. In this context it is perhaps a little surprising that he focuses in some detail on the death of Domitian, on the exact chronology of the plot, and on who was involved. He paints a vivid and sordid picture of palace intrigue, with particular emphasis on the grievances of freedmen and on the atmosphere of tension and fear surrounding the tyrannical emperor. Domitian died a pathetic death at the hands of his family's freedmen, who were supported by a faction in the Praetorian Guard. His body was then rapidly cremated by his nurse Phyllis, who mixed his ashes with those of Julia, the daughter of his brother Titus, in the Flavian family mausoleum at the Templum Gentis Flaviae. As a result Domitian disappeared rapidly, leaving the Flavian family cult that he had worked so hard to create essentially intact. His murder is not dramatized by images of senatorial independence or of debates about the restoration of a republic. Rather the principate itself and the pattern of transition from one dynasty to the next seem already to have been well established. As is noted in the *Fasti Ostienses*, Domitian was succeeded on the same day (18 September 96) by M. Cocceius Nerva, who was destined to be the last emperor of purely Italian background, and who was the last to be buried in the Mausoleum of Augustus.

Nerva's Coup and the Disgrace of Domitian

Suetonius and Dio both describe the harsh sanctions that were passed against Domitian's memory in a packed senate meeting.[4] Dio singles out Domitian's portraits in precious metal and his many honorific arches as special targets of the senate. Suetonius speaks in more general terms about public attacks on his portraits and inscriptions, and mentions as well a sweeping senatorial decree targeting his memory. Ample evidence testifies to the effects of this decree, which was surely soon circulated around the Empire. A large number of Domitian's inscriptions were mutilated and many portraits were recarved, while numerous other texts and images were destroyed.[5] Hence Domitian provides the classic example of the disgraced emperor, a murder victim who was immediately replaced by a new dynasty, whose very success guaranteed the durability of the sanctions that had been imposed.

As a result, it is now exceedingly difficult to write a detailed and balanced account of Domitian's reign: the evidence is largely unreliable and intractable.[6] The outlines of the chronology survive and a bare list of achievements on the frontiers and in domestic policy can be drawn up. But the obvious limitations of this unsatisfactory picture have tempted succeeding generations of scholars either to construct sweeping revisionist accounts or to assert the reliability of the received traditions, despite their evident biases and omissions.[7] It is not easy to admit that the tradition has become hopelessly corrupted and confused. What appears most notable here is the apparent success of the memory sanctions that must originally have been designed by, or at least in consultation with, the new *princeps* Nerva. Nerva's sudden emergence as Domitian's successor seems unlikely to have been a result of chance (especially given his age and poor health). Clearly he was involved with the successful conspiracy and was waiting in the palace for news of Domitian's death, poised to seize power himself.[8] If he was to succeed, he would have to deal with the memory of Domitian (and of the Flavians), whose name could be seen on his many buildings all over Rome.

Domitian's disgrace illustrates the essential nature of memory sanctions: they reflect the ambitions and fears of those who implement them, while providing no more than a distorting mirror to view the individual who is the subject of the sanctions. Consequently, it is only logical that successful sanctions can destroy and/or efface the image of the victim for later generations: this was precisely what they were originally designed to do. Such sanctions were at their most powerful when they were officially imposed and in cases where they were followed by a stable new dynasty, in this instance almost a century of Antonine rule. As Pliny and Tacitus demonstrate, the excellent character of the new regime could be viewed as a mirror image of the oppressive past. In this sense the "best" emperor (*optimus princeps*) emerged fully only in contrast with the "worst." The sanctions themselves appear as a cultural artifact, created by the senators and by Nerva to serve their own specific interests at a particular moment of imperial transition. At the same time, the sanctions took into account the tradition of Roman memory sanctions under the principate, in its various Julio-Claudian and Flavian incarnations, as well as the figure of the emperor Domitian himself, a man with an impressive list of achievements to his credit.

The fierceness of these sanctions can be seen, in simple terms, as the logical climax to the evolution of such penalties throughout the first century, as they were extended and refined under successive rulers. Domitian himself had been at odds with the senate during the last years of his life. Tacitus is an especially eloquent witness to the terror and feeling of helplessness that Domitian inspired in senators who feared that his disapproval would result in death and oblivion for individuals, or even for whole families.[9] A very elite section of society was affected by this fear, but that does not make their feelings any less real: their literacy and political influence ensured that their personal interpretations of these experiences would be recorded for posterity.

An illustration of this principle can be found in an inscription from a bridge built by the Roman army at Coptos in Egypt (figure 61).[10] This fascinating text must have been set up next to the bridge in 90/91 and seems to have stayed *in situ* after the death of Domitian. It contains a striking double erasure, displayed in a prominent place where many passersby would have a chance to see it. Domitian's name has been erased from the beginning of the text, leaving a nameless *Imperator Caesar* as the builder of the bridge. The second erasure has removed the first name in the list of local dignitaries. By order of precedence this should be the prefect of Egypt, and close study of the stone has confirmed this hypothesis. The prefect in question was Marcus Mettius Rufus, whose name was also erased in several other texts from Egypt.[11] The symbolism of the text is powerful: Domitian had erased the name of Rufus but later his own name was removed from the same inscription. The attack on Domitian can, therefore, be understood in terms of his own autocracy in the sphere of memory and could consequently be presented as a "just" or "proportional" punishment. Meanwhile, Mettius' fall and even his family background have been obscured; apparently he was not the only one in his family to incur the wrath of Domitian. In the long run, however, the disgrace of Domitian did not serve to restore the memory of many of his victims.

On another level, the sanctions against Domitian may also reflect the long-term difficulties in dealing with the memory of previous disgraced emperors, in this case Gaius and more especially Nero. The sudden death of Domitian and the succession of the elderly senator Nerva surely summoned up the ghost of the senatorial usurper Galba and his succession to Nero in 68. Nerva's success reflects his study of the failures of Galba. Nerva was more generous than Galba and sought to appease a wide range of Romans; he also

FIGURE 61. Inscription from a bridge with erasures of Domitian and of M. Mettius Rufus, Coptos, Egypt, A.D. 90/91. Mettius erased (below) in 90/91–96; Domitian erased (above) in 96 or soon after. *The Trustees of the British Museum,* CIL *3.13580.*

chose more wisely in adopting a successor according to the needs of the Empire. Yet the ghost of Nero may also have haunted the senators who gathered to celebrate the death of Domitian. This time their sanctions were to be more sweeping and were to be enforced with every formality of the law.

The attention given to the attack on the memory of Domitian must reflect the priorities of Nerva, both as a senator and as an emperor. His own career illustrates the force and significance of memory and of its destruction since the age of Nero.[12] Nerva had entered the senate under Nero, around the year 61, and seems to have served as the emperor's quaestor. He emerged, as praetor designate, suddenly and with great prominence and exceptional rewards, in 65 in the aftermath of the Pisonian conspiracy. Despite his close association with Nero and with the crushing of senatorial opposition, he then held the consulship with Vespasian in 71, soon after the establishment of the Flavian regime. Similarly, his second consulship came in 90 as colleague of Domitian. It is striking to see Nerva, who seems to have been a close personal

THE PRINCIPATE

adviser to every emperor he served, advance his own standing as a result of the three most significant crises during his senatorial career: in 65 after the conspiracy of Piso, in 70/71 after the civil war, and in 89/90 in the aftermath of the revolt of Saturninus against Domitian. Nerva's political acumen must have been formidable. Because he was a witness to the disgrace of many and knew how to build a career on the ruin of others, he had no trouble constructing his own image, even at the expense of his previous patron. His actions suggest the usefulness of disgrace to those who survived. By the time Nerva succeeded to imperial power, he must have been one of the most expert among the senators in the matter of memory sanctions and their uses.

Yet his expertise and success under others was not matched by the record of his own reign. Most senators were apparently happy to see the fall of Domitian and the elevation of one of their own number. However, no other group in Roman society seems to have been as enthusiastic. The army in general cherished the memory of Domitian, and the Praetorian Guard was openly hostile to Nerva and to the successful conspirators.[13] The desire of the soldiers in Rome to avenge Domitian and to deify him could not have been more at odds with official policy. Nerva's need to adopt a successor and his choice of Trajan as virtual co-ruler reflect his loss of control over the Praetorians, as well as his fear of potential unrest in the provincial armies.[14] The atmosphere seems to have been especially tense around the anniversary of Domitian's death. The Praetorians forced Nerva to purge those implicated in the murder of Domitian and to make a public speech glorifying the brutal revenge the soldiers had chosen to take. These bloody reprisals were matched by Trajan, who effected his own purge of the guard as soon as he succeeded to power. The continuing unrest of the Praetorians reflects the struggle over the memory of Domitian, a struggle that was continuous and fiercely fought. The need to efface or to compete with the memory of Domitian was very real both for Nerva and for Trajan. Nerva's efforts, however, met with little success and he had to be rescued for posterity by Trajan.

In contrast to the soldiers' position, the attitude of the people of Rome is harder to recover. According to Suetonius, they were indifferent to the news of Domitian's death.[15] However, it is unclear how such indifference might have been measured and what sources Suetonius is using. Dio does not take note of the views of the common people. Domitian had fulfilled many of the expectations traditionally associated with the populace through his provision of lavish games and festivals, his involvement with spectacle especially in the *ludi saeculares* and in the new Capitoline games, as well as through his extensive program of public building. There is no particular evidence for food shortages, and Domitian's foreign victories and military image should have provided very positive publicity at home. Moreover, the evidence furnished by Nerva's coinage suggests that he was especially generous with the Roman *plebs*, both in specific programs and in his need to advertise his efforts in public.[16] Were the *plebs* resistant to Nerva? If they were, then it is hard to disassociate this completely from their feelings about Domitian. Nerva's courting of the *plebs* may reflect a general insecurity about his popularity or perhaps a more specific memory of Galba and his lack of generosity. Yet a perceived need to appease and to win over the *plebs* cannot have been a mere reflection of the politics of a previous generation. It must also have been a response to current norms and expectations that had been shaped by Flavian populism and showmanship, most recently during the reign of Domitian. Our inability to document Domitian's popular standing in 96 stands in marked contrast to the evident popularity of Nero in 68 and the equally well-attested problems of Gaius in 41.

Domitianic Epigraphy: Patterns and Pitfalls

The epigraphic record for Domitian is especially rich and is enhanced every year by new discoveries. More than four hundred texts recording Domitian's name are presently extant, and many more were surely destroyed at the time of his death.[17] About 40 percent of these texts show some sign of deliberate mutilation. Consequently, Domitian's texts offer a superb illustration of the full range of treatments of the written word in the Roman Empire after an officially mandated erasure of memory. The possibility for a thorough study of a significant body of texts has yielded more general conclusions than are possible in most other cases of disgrace. The parts of Domitian's name that were most often targeted for erasure are *Domitianus* and *Germanicus*, the latter being a military honorific that was a particular source of pride for Domitian.[18] More recent texts, from the years immediately before Domitian's death, were more likely to be erased. Funerary or private dedications tended to remain intact, while milestones exhibit a seemingly random pattern. Some texts were reinscribed, but most extant erasures were apparently left standing. Some later texts omitted the mention of Domitian, especially those put up by senators or equestrians.[19] By contrast, individual soldiers from various units continued to recall Domitian, even many years after his death.

While this overall picture is not likely to change as a result of new discoveries, the case of Domitian also illustrates the complexities of memory and forgetting.[20] Even the fiercest of sanctions were not universally applied, and individuals of widely varying social status might defy the senate's decree by preserving or creating their own memorials to the past. Ultimately, as in many other areas of Roman life, there were few formal mechanisms to enforce sanctions against memory, and the topicality of disgrace lay in the political moment. Domitian's life had impinged on the lives of many Romans, and their subsequent biographies in turn involved their individual constructions of Domitian and of his role. Meanwhile, the carefully constructed patterns revealed by scholarly inquiry (based exclusively on evidence that is now extant) cannot reproduce the precise experience of any individual or group of Romans.

Domitian's name surely disappeared from many contexts, in whatever way seemed most convenient locally. A good example comes from the dedicatory text of a clubhouse of athletes at Olympia in Greece, which was opened in A.D. 84.[21] Here the marble slabs bearing the text were simply removed from their setting, turned, and recarved with a decorative frieze. This solution proved both economical and ingenious, since the slabs fitted perfectly into their architectural setting. It is not possible to say how often such a strategy was used.

Erasure was a popular option for dealing with his memory in a variety of situations in which the preservation of the text was desirable. As a member of the imperial family, Domitian had played an important role in Roman politics from the Flavian victory in late 69 to his own assassination in 96, with the result that he had already been widely commemorated for more than a decade before he became emperor. His name was regularly erased on monuments and in statue groups that had been put up to celebrate the Flavian dynasty, especially under Vespasian.[22] Vespasian's two adult sons were a vital part of his promise of a peaceful and secure empire. Meanwhile, Vespasian's age and Titus' lack of male children or grandchildren ensured that Domitian needed to be kept in the public eye, and he minted his own coins even during his father's reign. Just as the Flavians had appealed to Claudius as a virtuous and legal predecessor, so Nerva also had no desire to attack the memory of the Flavian family, most of whose members had been deified.[23] Rather it was necessary for Nerva to isolate Domitian and remove him from what had originally been a coherent and symmetrical family group. A particularly striking example of this isolation can be seen in a text put up by Agricola, the father-in-law of Tacitus, at Verulamium in Britain.[24]

Within the city of Rome, Domitian's name has virtually disappeared: the most obvious exception is the obelisk presently in Domitian's stadium (now the Piazza Navona) on which his name was recorded in Egyptian hieroglyphics (figure 62).[25] Presumably it survived because no one could read the archaic language, although it still recalls the typically Flavian interest in the Egyptian gods, whom they had especially cultivated in the Campus Martius. By contrast, Domitian is a close second to Trajan and Hadrian in the record he has left, by virtue of the inscription of his name on the water and sewer pipes below the city. Yet the erasure of Domitian's name in the record of his *ludi saeculares* of A.D. 88 has remained on display for all to see. The inscription of these special games had been particularly motivated by the stated desire to preserve memory. In this case, a decision was made that the memory of the games, which had marked an epoch in the city's history, needed to survive their organizer. Similarly, Domitian's name was erased from at least some of the series of altars he had erected in 92 as a result of a vow to commemorate the great fire of 64. Such altars were put up in several, and perhaps in all, of the fourteen regions of Rome. Their reference to *Neronianis temporibus* recalled Nero more than twenty years after his death.

In Rome itself, dedications to deities were similarly good candidates for erasure, since they could not easily be removed from their votive settings without risking an insult to the god(s). Most dedicators of humble means presumably could in any case not afford to replace a whole *stele*, which now belonged to the god. Two examples from Rome are particularly notable. The prominent charioteer Thallus made a dedication to the god Silvanus, while he was still a slave of L. Avillius Planta.[26] The gift can be dated to the year 90, since the consuls, Domitian and Nerva, are named. It is understandable that a stone bearing Nerva's name needed to be preserved, especially after he had himself attained the status first of emperor and then of *divus* early in 98. It is equally clear why Domitian's name has been removed, although only the word *Domitianus* has actually been erased. There must have been quite a number of inscriptions where Domitian and Nerva were juxtaposed as consuls: this example can suggest their fate.

Domitian's name has also been erased from the consular date for A.D. 86 on the dedication of Q. Iulius Felix, freedman of Maximus, and his wife Iulia Romana, to Jupiter Optimus Maximus, the divine Sun, and the Guardian Spirit of the Slave Trade (Genius Venalicius) (figure 63).[27] This ex-voto dedication came from the area of the Aventine and seems originally to have consisted of an altar. The text reveals a vivid glimpse of a former slave who has now become a free Roman citizen, who has married a freeborn Roman woman (probably the daughter of a fellow freedman), and who has amassed enough money to dedicate a stone altar to the gods of his choice, an eclectic group whom he has apparently selected himself as his special benefactors.

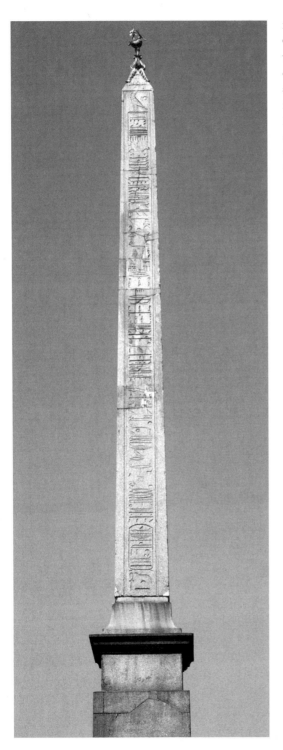

FIGURE 62.
Obelisk of Aswan granite with hieroglyphic text of a hymn to Domitian and the Flavian family in the Piazza Navona, Rome. Pamphili obelisk above Bernini's Fountain of the Four Rivers. *Photo courtesy of Eric R. Varner.*

FIGURE 63. Ex-voto dedication of Q. Iulius Felix, freedman of Q. Julius Maximus, and his wife Iulia Romana to Jupiter Optimus Maximus, the Divine Sun, and the *genius* of the slave trade, Aventine, Rome, A.D. 86. Erasure of Domitian's name in the dating formula. *Musei Capitolini, Rome, archivio fotografico dei Musei Capitolini,* photo Maria Teresa Natale, CIL 6.398 = ILS 3673.

He may well also be the one who decided to conform to the new political climate by erasing Domitian. The mere fact that Domitian had held the consulship seventeen times, more than any previous emperor, must in itself have produced a multitude of texts in which his name appeared as part of a dating formula.[28]

The decision to erase can be documented across the Empire in a variety of settings, including such mundane texts as milestones, boundary markers, and inscriptions on aqueducts.[29] More distinctive examples include the virtually complete edict from Antioch in Pisidia issued by L. Antistius Rusticus concerning the shortages of grain in 92/93.[30] Under this ruling there was to be a forced sale of surplus grain at a fixed price in order to effect a redistribution of food in the local area during a time of shortage. The decree is particularly interesting in showing a provincial governor dealing with a local food shortage. The removal of Domitian's name has led to several large erasures in the opening section recording the career of Antistius, which was written in larger letters than the rest of the text. It is interesting to see such a modification of a text that would by 96 have lost nearly all of its relevance to local conditions. The stone seems to have stayed *in situ* throughout antiquity.

A similarly striking example comes from the Civitas Mactaritana, near Carthage in North Africa (figures 64, 65). This monumental inscription records the erection of a basilica and two warehouses on public land but at private expense by the *collegium* of young men (*iuvenes*), devotees of Mars Augustus.[31] The inscription is followed by a list of sixty-nine individual members of the group, whose names reflect the use of the Latin, Punic, and Numidian languages. Only three members are freedmen; most were born free, but no member is labeled with the nomenclature of a Roman citizen. Domitian's title, in his fourteenth consulship (A.D. 88), was originally recorded as the first line of the text, in letters that were twice the size of the next two lines. The style of the writing used to inscribe the emperor's name also seems to have been closer to official style than the lettering of the rest of the inscription. Since the original was thus characterized by its dedication to Domitian, whose name was by far the most prominent feature, the erasure of the entire first line has produced an equally dramatic negative effect: the actual letters can be reconstructed without too much trouble from their surviving edges. The inscription was found associated with a building that may be the basilica mentioned in the text, a structure that survived to be put to other uses in late antiquity. There is every reason to believe that the text remained on view for many years.

As a counterbalance it is important to take note of the numerous inscrip-

FIGURE 64. Bronze building inscription of the *iuvenes cultures Martis Augusti*, Civitas Mactaritana near Carthage, North Africa, A.D. 88. Erasure of Domitian's name and titles at the top. Karthago, révue d'archéologie méditerranéenne 8 (1957), pl. 29, AE 1959.172.

FIGURE 65. Bronze building inscription of the *iuvenes cultures Martis Augusti*, Civitas Mactaritana near Carthage, North Africa, A.D. 88. Karthago, révue d'archéologie méditerranéenne 8 (1957), fig. 4, AE 1959.172.

tions where Domitian's name was not mutilated. The special case of the records of the Arval brothers has been discussed before. Perhaps the best known example is the Flavian municipal law (*lex Flavia Irnitana*) from Spain with its appended letter of Domitian from 91.[32] Many inscriptions recording grants of citizenship to men who had served in the Roman army or fleet have survived intact, carefully preserved as testimony to the citizen status of the individuals in question, of their right to legal marriages under Roman law, and of the

THE PRINCIPATE

legitimacy of their children (figure 66).[33] The tablets are said to be true copies (*diplomata*) of the decree in question, which would have been inscribed on bronze and put up on the Capitol in Rome. These copies have the names of Roman citizens (usually seven) recorded on the back as witnesses. It was preferable to preserve such records in order to ensure the precious gift of citizenship for the whole family. Any changes made to a certified copy of an official text might make that copy seem less authoritative. Presumably, extra care may also have been taken in cases where the disgrace of the emperor had perhaps led to the mutilation or destruction of the original public decrees in Rome, leaving the individual copies as the only remaining texts. In this context, it is understandable that officials might expect to be presented with a text that was intact, regardless of which emperor was named at the top.

Similarly, the context of a funerary inscription usually preserved the name of even the most notorious figure. An especially illuminating example is provided by the tombstone of Tiberius Claudius Zosimus, who died in Mainz, probably in 89 (soon after the revolt of Saturninus had been crushed?) (figure 67).[34] Zosimus, a former slave, had risen through the ranks of the imperial household to reach the distinguished status of chief food taster to the emperor. When he died in Mainz, he was accorded a fine memorial, presumably arranged by other members of the emperor's entourage with whom he was traveling (and discovered in the area of the university in 1967). On his tombstone Domitian's name can still be read today, marked out in red paint. There was no attempt to deface the name, even though it would have been fully visible on the outside of a prominent tomb in what was the local capital of Roman government and headquarters for several legions. The explanation seems to lie in two factors. The funerary context discouraged mutilation of a monument whose function it was to recall Zosimus, rather than to honor Domitian. Meanwhile, Zosimus was a freedman, probably of the emperor Nero (or perhaps even of Claudius) as is suggested by his name; he did not belong to the class of persons who were themselves ever officially subject to sanctions.

His case gains further interest because there is a second monument in his memory, this one an altar put up by his family in Rome (although it is presently in the Uffizi Gallery in Florence) (figure 68).[35] This altar, erected by his wife Claudia Entole and his daughter Claudia Eustachys, refers to his profession but does not name the emperor whom he was serving at the time of his death. If we had only the monument from Rome, we would surely date his death to a much earlier period. By contrast, some have supposed that this was a later monument with a deliberate omission of the name of the disgraced

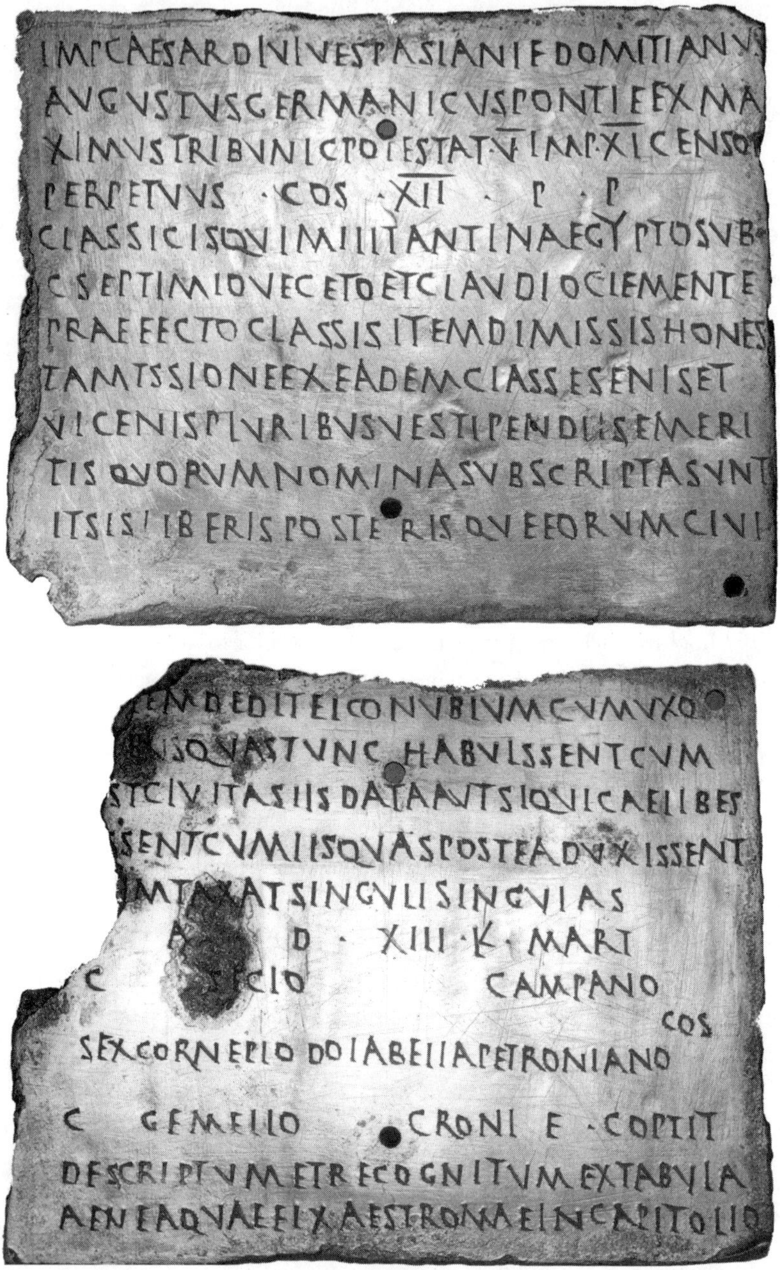

FIGURE 66. Military diploma granting Roman citizenship to Gaius Gemellus, Coptos, Egypt, A.D. 86. Domitian's name and titles are intact. *Musei Vaticani, archivio fotographico XXXI.13.36 & XXXI.13.38, CIL 16.32.*

FIGURE 67. Epitaph of Tiberius Claudius Zosimus, chief taster to
the emperor Domitian, Mainz, Germany, A.D. 89? *Landesmuseum Mainz,
Selzer, Decker and do Paço (1988) no. 130.*

Domitian. In fact, comparison with other epitaphs of the imperial household
suggests that in many cases the individual emperor is not named next to the
job performed in his household. So the difference we see here between the
two memorials for Zosimus can best be explained in terms of the contrast
between the "official" context of a memorial, put up for an imperial freedman
who died while on tour with the emperor in the provinces, and a text commissioned by his family as a mark of its own personal esteem.

A striking example comes from another well-known dossier of public
texts, this time from Ostia, the port city of Rome (figure 69). Within the
community of Ostia a public calendar and historical chronicle of events was
kept on stone, commonly known as the *Fasti Ostienses*.[36] Well known already
to Cicero, the chronicle has survived in fragments that cover the years 49 B.C.
to A.D. 175, albeit with many gaps. Probably the chronicle was originally displayed on a wall, and it included fairly standard types of entries for each year,
such as the consuls in Rome, the local magistrates, and important events both
in Rome and in Ostia, each with a precise date. The procedure seems to have
been to inscribe the entries for several years in batches rather than to add to
the record year by year. As we have them at the moment, these records do
not contain any erasures of names or of events. However, the small fragments

FIGURE 68. Funerary altar of Tiberius Claudius Zosimus,
erected by his wife Claudia Entole and his daughter Claudia Eustachys,
Rome, A.D. 89 or 90? *Soprintendenza Speciale per il Polo Museale Fiorentino,
Uffizi Gallery (Florence)*, CIL 6.9003 = ILS 179b.

FIGURE 69. *Fasti Ostienses* for A.D. 96, recording the death of Domitian and the accession of Nerva on 18 September, Ostia. *Archivio fotografico della Soprintendenza per i Beni Archaeologici di Ostia, Fd.*

preserved for Domitian show that his name was simplified here. Instead of being referred to by his proper title as emperor, he is simply "Domitianus," which does not constitute a complete name for a Roman citizen. This pattern of naming is a clear sign of denigration, recalling the naming pattern of slaves, and it does not recognize the status Domitian had in his lifetime.[37] It also contrasts with the designation of Gaius as C. Caesar. No other inscription designates Domitian with this single name. Such an appellation would certainly have been unacceptable to Domitian himself. Yet, at the same time, it represents a complete reversal of the usual strategy of erasure: as already alluded to, the name Domitianus was in fact statistically the most likely element to be removed, as it was closest to being a specific signifier for the individual person. The same name is used in the unusual notice that records Domitian's murder and the succession of Nerva on the same day.

This evidence seems to indicate that in Ostia the whole record of Domitian's reign, or at least the last years of it, was recarved after his death in order to create a different kind of commemoration than what had originally been envisaged. In this case there was a carefully conceived local reaction to the news of his official disgrace. A decision was made not to erase any part of this venerable chronicle, despite the fact that this choice entailed the cost of buying new marble plaques and the need to reformulate and to reinscribe the official record, which covered as many as fifteen years. The evidence from Ostia suggests the essential nature of the problem posed by the disgrace of Domitian, who had been an active leader over a significant period of time. His name was still needed, at the very least to mark off the years in which he had held eponymous offices. It was hard to disassociate him from the major events of the period without also removing those events from the official record. At the same time, local officials did not hesitate to make their decision to suit the purposes of their own particular traditions of public writing, even as they kept an eye on the changing political climate in Rome.

The evidence from Ostia can serve as a salutary warning that a mere tabulation of erased and unerased inscriptions can be misleading. The *Fasti Ostienses*, although recorded under the years of Domitian's reign, actually reflect a reinscription under a later political climate, rather than a series of examples of Domitian's name that were not erased in 96. There are a number of other examples of Domitian's name recorded in later texts, usually by those who chose to recall him regardless of what had happened. Particularly striking is the series of roof tiles produced from factories owned by Domitian's wife, Domitia Longina, who survived him by at least thirty years with her great personal fortune intact.[38] Each of these tiles, which have been found

in a variety of locations in Rome, is stamped with her name, recorded as
Domitia, wife of Domitian. It was not usual for a Roman woman to continue
to refer to a deceased husband in an inscription, and such a usage is obviously even more anomalous in a case of disgrace. Consequently, the picture
of Domitia, the faithful widow who is still choosing to invoke Domitian's
name even under Hadrian, is at variance with the evidence of the literary
sources that suggest she was implicated in his murder. A comparison can be
made with the widows of the disgraced buried in the tomb of the Licinii on
the Via Salaria.[39] They also seem to have chosen not to remarry but to remain
faithful to the memory of their previous husbands, even after death and disgrace. Equally notable is the restoration under Hadrian of a temple of Jupiter
Optimus Maximus, Juno Regina, Minerva Augusta, and the *genius loci* on
the Quirinal near the Templum Gentis Flaviae by another family of Flavians,
who were clearly recalling Domitian and his dedication to Minerva.[40]

In addition, the inscriptions of a number of soldiers confirm the army's
continuing loyalty to the memory of Domitian, even many years after his
death and in cases of men who never served with any units in the city of
Rome. The most striking example can serve as the best illustration. The monumental tombstone of Tiberius Claudius Maximus from the area of Philippi
in Macedonia was erected after the death of Trajan (and therefore presumably under Hadrian) (figure 70).[41] Maximus, perhaps a descendant of one of
Caesar's veterans who had established a colony at Philippi in 42 B.C., had had
a long and distinguished career in the Roman army. Its climax came with his
spectacular capture of the dying Decebalus, the Dacian chieftain who was
Trajan's main opponent, in a scene immortalized on Trajan's column (figure
71). It was Maximus who brought Decebalus' head to Trajan. Maximus' tomb
also commemorates the moment of capture of a recognizably individualized Decebalus (who is still alive). Trajan himself had displayed Decebalus'
head to his army before sending it to Rome to be thrown on the Gemonian
stairs. Maximus' tomb reflects the glory he had won and his close personal
association with Trajan's lucrative victory in Dacia in 106, as well as with the
emperor's subsequent Parthian campaign.

In this context it is all the more striking to see the bold recording of Domitian's name, just above Trajan's (*divo Troiano*!), as another emperor who decorated Maximus, in another Dacian war (which had ended in 89). Maximus
is at pains to stress the military awards he received throughout his career,
and the reliefs also depict some of them in a large format below the scene of
the capture of Decebalus. His testimony speaks against the typical denigration of Domitian found in Dio, who dismisses Domitian's military awards as

FIGURE 70. Tomb of Tiberius Claudius Maximus, captor of Decebalus, Philippi, Hadrianic. *Museum of Drama*, AE 1969/70.583, *courtesy of Michael P. Speidel.*

FIGURE 71. Scene from the spiral frieze on the column of Trajan:
capture of Decebalus, the Dacian chieftain, Rome, A.D. 113.
DAIR 41.1217, photo Deichmann.

undeserved because he had not conquered Decebalus.[42] Here the actual captor of Decebalus celebrates Domitian's Dacian campaigns and dignifies his former commander with the title *Imperator*. His text presents an alternative, eyewitness account of a series of Roman wars in Dacia and of an unbroken tradition of heroism and achievement. Yet it would not have been difficult for Maximus to omit Domitian while still recording the number and occasion of his own awards; his choice to give this version of his experiences goes beyond a mere concern for his own image and status. It may reflect a time when the memory of Domitian seemed less threatening, and it certainly demonstrates a desire to rectify most public statements recorded in the twenty years after Domitian's death. It may also suggest that Maximus saw Trajan as an imitator of Domitian and a natural successor to him, especially in war, rather than as a figure of complete contrast.[43]

Domitian at Puteoli and Misenum

A picture of Nerva and Trajan as imitators of Domitian who were competing with his formidable record of achievement and self-presentation emerges from an examination of the new road (Via Domitiana) built from Sinuessa to Puteoli and opened in 95.[44] This road along the rocky Campanian coast was a stunning feat of engineering that considerably shortened the journey from Puteoli to Rome by means of a direct link with the Via Appia. It is especially celebrated by Statius (*Silv.* 4.3), who gives us an insight into the splendid festivities that marked the opening of the road. Statius' Domitian is a mature ruler, who appears as a benefactor to the towns of Italy. Whereas Vespasian had stayed away from the area of the Bay of Naples that was so closely associated with the Julio-Claudians and especially with Nero, Titus and Domitian returned there as rulers who favored this traditional vacation spot of the Roman elite. Indeed, Statius portrays Domitian's road as a successful version of an abandoned project of Nero, a canal that would have provided a similar link between Puteoli and Rome. A court poet writing twenty-five years after the Flavians came to power could still portray Domitian's ambitions as the reverse image of Nero.

Statius also gives us an insight into the variety of monuments put up by local communities along the way, as they were vying with each other to celebrate the emperor when he came to open the new road. The monuments to be found along the road included an arch of white Ligurian marble to mark its beginning at Sinuessa, the monumental bridge over the river Volturnus with another arch, the Arco Felice at Monte Grillo, and probably another arch where the road entered the town of Puteoli, which had been expanded and enhanced by numerous buildings during the Flavian time.[45] It can hardly be coincidence that no milestones naming Domitian have survived from this whole area, while many attest to the activities of renewal under Nerva, Trajan, the Severans, and Constantine.[46] Yet a whole series of brand-new milestones must surely have been in place by the year of Domitian's death.

A rare example of a completely erased monumental text from Puteoli, originally dating to the last year of Domitian's life, bears witness to the fierce erasure of Domitian's memory here (figure 72).[47] So far this is the only example of a completely erased text of Domitian. It was acquired for the University of Pennsylvania Museum in Philadelphia in 1909 (soon after its discovery) because the other side bears a fine relief of Roman soldiers of the Praetorian Guard. The erased inscription was only noticed several years later. It is Parian marble from Greece that was probably imported specifically for use in a public monument in a wealthy community. It was first inscribed in 95, in very fine letters, with a singularly eulogistic text in honor of Domitian on the occasion of the opening of his new coastal road. This inscription originally accompanied a statue of Domitian set up by the local community of Puteoli.

However, Domitian was murdered only about a year later, and a decision was made to erase the text while it was still standing *in situ*, as can be seen from the pattern of the erasure marks. Everything was removed, including the name of Puteoli itself (a Flavian colony) and the record of its warm relationship with its former patron and benefactor Domitian. The erasure signals both the willingness of the local people to embrace political change and their fears based on their traditional closeness to the Flavian family, whose side they had been quick to join in the civil conflict after the death of Nero. Soon after, the erasure itself was removed, presumably to the workshop of some local sculptors, where it was recycled for use in another public monument. This new monument seems to have been an arch connected with another new road, this time a restoration of the old road south from Puteoli to Naples, a project started by Nerva but inaugurated by Trajan in 102.

In the life of this stone, then, we can reconstruct three distinct moments over a period of only about seven years. First it was used for a eulogistic text in honor of Domitian, a text that closely mirrored Statius' language in the image of moving Puteoli closer to Rome, here simply called Domitian's city. Presumably this metaphor was current at the time when the road was dedicated. Unfortunately, it is hard to say what Domitian himself would have thought of the inscription. However, the aftermath is clear: the text became distinctly inappropriate in the political climate immediately after his murder.

FIGURE 72. Completely erased inscription originally honoring Domitian,
Puteoli, A.D. 95. *University of Pennsylvania Museum of Archaeology and Anthropology,
MS 4916, NC 35.3325, AE 1973.137.*

Yet the fierce erasure in itself served to commemorate Domitian's fall, and it
was presumably easy to understand while still in its original urban context. It
seems deeply ironic that the stone that subsequently featured a rather idealized portrayal of members of the Praetorian Guard accompanying the new
emperor should on its back have carried a text in honor of Domitian, the

FIGURE 73. Relief of Praetorians from an arch (?) of Trajan at Puteoli, c. A.D. 102.
Reverse of the stone with the erased inscription for Domitian. *University of Pennsylvania Museum of Archaeology and Anthropology, MS 4916, S4-142867.*

emperor so sorely missed by this same elite corps of soldiers (figure 73). At
the same time, the fate of the stone mirrors the experience of the local people:
many who saw Trajan open his new road in 102 must have recalled a very
similar scene enacted with Domitian a few years before.

The magnificent bronze equestrian statue of Domitian at Misenum also

FIGURE 74. Bronze statue of Domitian on horseback reworked as Nerva,
collegium of the Augustales, Misenum, original c. A.D. 95/96, reworked in 97/98.
Soprintendenza per i Beni Archeologici delle provincie di Napoli e Caserta.

seems to date from late in Domitian's reign (figure 74).[48] The face of the statue
was later removed and replaced by a portrait of the emperor Nerva. The statue
was found in the *collegium* (*templum Augusti*) of the Augustales and seems
originally to have been positioned on one of the two pedestals on either side
of the staircase leading to the sanctuary, which was closely associated with
the imperial cult under the Flavians. A marble plaque bearing a dedicatory
inscription to Domitian was fixed to the left-hand pedestal; this plaque was
subsequently turned and reinscribed in honor of Nerva.[49] Only small fragments of the marble bearing the two inscriptions have been recovered. But
reversed impressions of the letters remain in the mortar on the face of the left
pedestal (figure 75). These traces of the first six lines allowed a reconstruction of Domitian's titulature, dating to late 94 or early 95. This inscription

THE PRINCIPATE

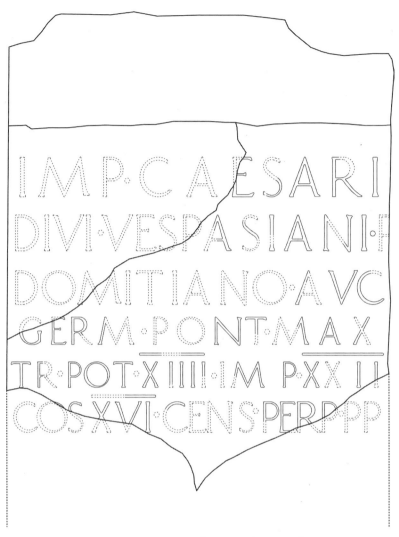

IMP·C AESARI
DIVI·VESPASIANI·F
DOMITIANO·AVG
GERM·PONT·MAX
TR·POT·XIIII·IM P·XX II
COS·XVI·CENS·PER·P·PP

FIGURE 75. Inscription of Domitian from near the
collegium of the Augustales, Misenum, late A.D. 94 or early 95.
Drawing by Leslie Rae Witt, after Camodeca (2000) fig. 3.

was, then, not erased but turned and immediately reused for Nerva. It seems
to show that the high honors for Domitian at Misenum, and probably the
spectacular bronze horse, are a little earlier than the dedication of the road.

When put together, the various pieces of evidence for Domitian's honors
around the Bay of Naples give a vivid picture both of the prominence of his
image in Italy's towns and along its roads, and of the sudden and thorough
attack on his memory that followed under Nerva. Nearly all of Nerva's por-

traits are reworked from earlier portraits of Domitian. At the same time, the local image of the new emperors, Nerva and Trajan, is clearly constructed to compete with and to efface the impression of Domitian in areas of particular public benefaction. It would have required a thorough and very public effort to remove Domitian around the Bay of Naples. Meanwhile, the Puteoli and Misenum texts can help to corroborate the descriptions by Suetonius and Dio of widespread attacks on statues and monuments.

The effect in Rome must have been on an even wider scale. The number of buildings that could be associated with Domitian was large, and many of them — for example, the new palace on the Palatine — went on being used for essentially the same functions.[50] It would have been too costly to destroy these buildings, or even all the arches. Yet Domitian's name was surely removed, and an organized effort went into changing the face of the city and into appropriating his legacy, perhaps most obviously attested by the forum of Nerva with its very Domitianic celebration of Minerva and by the recarving of the Cancelleria reliefs.[51] One may doubt whether such a widespread and sudden change of texts and images had been seen before, and it was not repeated until the Severan period. The fact that civil war was averted on this occasion contributed to the energies available to reshape the public sphere.

Praising Trajan/Blaming Domitian

The continuing struggle over Domitian's memory is illustrated in a different way by Pliny's *Panegyricus*, a greatly expanded version of the speech of thanks he delivered in front of Trajan on the occasion of becoming consul in the autumn of 100.[52] The decision to publish a version of this set-piece eulogy is unusual in a number of ways and particularly so given Pliny's hesitancy in publishing many of his other speeches, even his most successful forensic orations. His letters reveal the effort he put into revising the text, probably not long after its original delivery, and into trying out the new version in public readings to groups of friends. On the one hand, the speech serves, especially among his peers, to commemorate Pliny's own attainment of consular rank; on the other, the emperor remains the addressee and surely also the primary intended reader. It is perhaps surprising to see Pliny, speaking almost exactly four years after Domitian's assassination, spending such a significant time denigrating the memory of Domitian and insisting that Trajan be understood as his exact opposite.

The unusual nature of the *Panegyricus* is further highlighted by Pliny's protests about his own sincerity and about the true and transparent quality of his praises of Trajan. He is at pains to make clear to readers and to listeners how his text is to be understood.[53] His publicly declared concerns conjure up a world of doublespeak and political innuendo in which meanings are always multiple and fear colors every word. This rhetorical stance fits with the theme of the new age of Trajan. Pliny insists that everything has now changed from the previous political climate under Domitian. This change is, of course, in itself a principal reason to praise and to thank Trajan, whose own presence has set such a different tone. In the correspondence of Trajan addressed to Pliny in Bithynia we can catch glimpses of the emperor himself subscribing and trying to live up to the concept of this new age of political freedom and justice.[54] It seems fair to see the main themes of Pliny's address as echoing the official self-representation of Trajan's court.

At the same time, Pliny is not entirely accurate in everything he says. For example, his claim that criticism of a bad emperor was an innovation only permitted under the new political order is misleading.[55] In fact, the whole image of the Flavians was built on their denigration of Nero, and it seems that Domitian continued this theme, perhaps precisely because his own interest in spectacle, in the arts, and in building might recall Nero, whose memory was still vivid for many. It seems that Trajan returned to the frugal image cultivated by Vespasian and embraced by the municipal elites, of whom Pliny was a member. In this context, Pliny needs to appropriate the very practice of denigration as in itself a virtuous custom cultivated by "good emperors." His words reflect the complex history of denigration and memory games that had been practiced throughout the Julio-Claudian and Flavian periods. His equation of freedom of speech with denigration of a previous ruler begs the question of what political speech now consisted of either in the past or in the present.[56] Meanwhile, Pliny himself is compromised, to a greater or lesser extent, since during Domitian's reign he had spoken publicly as a preferred magistrate to many of the same senators, delivering similar speeches of praise and thanks.[57]

The atmosphere in the senate probably did change after the death of Domitian; there is no need to discard completely the testimonies of Pliny and Tacitus about the tensions and terror, especially in the last three years of Domitian's reign. However, that should not distract attention from the position of Pliny himself and from his evident need to make the transition from being a close adviser to Domitian to being equally valued by Nerva and Trajan. His legal and financial expertise, as well as his hard work and reliability, would have been factors in his favor. However, he also needed to demonstrate his loyalty and to disassociate himself completely from his *own* past by criticizing Domitian. Rather than engaging in any self-criticism or political reeducation, as he might have been required to do in a different culture, Pliny could turn his vituperation against Domitian, while conveniently reshaping and obscuring his own career during the 90s.

Characterizing the *Panegyricus* simply as a reflection of imperial propaganda does not seem sufficient, because it also contains Pliny's own agenda — his way of shaping the present climate and of ensuring his own place as an opinion maker rather than a mere mouthpiece of official policy. By its very nature, such a speech posed many of the problems that senators saw as inherent in the principate itself. Instead of thanking the people in a *contio* for election to high office as a result of a vote, the new consul now thanked the emperor for his favor.[58] As year after year was filled with a rotation of suffect consuls, similar speeches must have multiplied, and many themes would have appeared well-worn. Yet it is precisely in this context that Pliny sought to make his mark, both on the day of his speech and in the specially expanded published version. He wanted the ideas presented to be seen as representative of his own views. His speech shows how closely he identified with the disgrace of Domitian and with the tradition of denigration and vituperation.

A collection of inscriptions, many from around Pliny's native Comum, have revealed the details of Pliny's highly distinguished career and have made it one of the best documented in the imperial period.[59] This epigraphical evidence elucidates the aspects of his career that Pliny simply passes over in his letters, even as he gives us an unparalleled insight into his world. His political and legal career was always stellar, starting as the emperor's quaestor in 89 and then rapidly progressing to the praetorship by 93. In an unusual pattern, he held two treasury posts consecutively, starting with the prefecture of the *aerarium militaris* in the last two years of Domitian's life, suggesting that Pliny must have been one of Domitian's close associates, whose career the emperor had fostered from its very beginnings. Subsequently, he managed an apparently seamless transition to become the faithful servant of the new regime and to achieve the consulship at the remarkably early age of thirty-nine. His career was crowned by his special mission to govern Bithynia and Pontus. There is no real reason to think that letters he would have exchanged with Trajan would have been so very different from those he wrote to and received from Domitian.[60]

More striking for the present study is Pliny's role as a witness to Domitianic history and as a participant in it. His career had begun with his quaestorship in 89, the year of Saturninus' revolt. This has been seen as a crucial turning point in Domitian's principate, when the emperor first revealed the extent of his mistrust of the elite through his widespread search for accomplices to the conspiracy, despite the fact that the revolt had been swiftly and effectively crushed by the commanders of the adjacent legions.[61] It was this moment that saw Nerva and Trajan both emerge as mainstays of Domitian's regime. As has been noted before, crises and conspiracies offered signal opportunities for advancement. Nerva's whole career seems to have been built around such moments and Pliny seems to have followed a not entirely dissimilar pattern.

Although his role as quaestor would not have been particularly prominent, Pliny must have served the emperor well in one of his great moments of uncertainty, when loyalty was the main issue of the day. Similarly, Pliny was praetor in 93 at the moment when Domitian seems to have turned against another group of senators, primarily those associated with the so-called Stoic opposition to the principate. In the years following his praetorship, moreover, Pliny's leading position at the military treasury would have put him in an excellent position to observe and even to oversee Domitian's notorious confiscation of senatorial wealth, a policy partly linked to his need to finance the legions whose pay he had increased. Pliny's expertise in the drawing up of wills put him at the center of much of Roman imperial politics, both within elite families and within the political culture of Rome.[62]

Pliny's fame rested on his publications, especially the *Panegyricus* which was to inspire the tradition of eulogies for later emperors, and his letters, the first such publication of carefully crafted opinion pieces, also influential throughout antiquity. Both major publications were novel in format and designed to attract attention. Both were also published soon after the change in government in 96. Despite the fine family tradition established by his uncle and adoptive father, Pliny the Elder, Pliny does not seem to have published much before 96.[63] Other personal circumstances may have played a role, but politics also seems to provide an explanation. Pliny needed to associate himself as quickly as possible with the new political order. Most of the forty-four letters in his first two books seem to have been written under Nerva and in the earliest part of Trajan's reign, and they were probably published before the *Panegyricus*. He also published his speech of mid-97 attacking Publicius Certus. Pliny's aim is to characterize the great political change, as well as to situate himself within it as an influential and stable figure, a man of culture and refinement who is untroubled by political turmoil. Yet this very announcement of a new age of freedom surely appeared somewhat premature during the troubled reign of Nerva.[64]

The Memory World of Pliny's Letters

Pliny's letters range across a broad spectrum of subjects and should really be studied as a whole for the tremendous variety of insights they can afford into the intellectual and cultural world of the author and his friends. Domitian appears regularly in books 1–9, always in a highly unflattering context. In that sense, his memory has certainly not been erased. Meanwhile, Pliny is careful never to refer to the priesthood of Titus that he held at Comum (early in Domitian's reign) or to his post at the military treasury under Domitian. The references to Domitian in the letters Pliny published himself contrast with those in book 10, which did not come out until after his death. Here most of the references to Domitian come in discussions of precedents for legal rulings. In this context Domitian is referred to in a very matter of fact way both by Pliny and by Trajan, as just another previous emperor who may have established a precedent that is still useful.[65] Pliny the lawyer, in search of the right legal precedent, is at odds with Pliny the politician, invested in the symbolic shame of the past.

Pliny's correspondence in itself, therefore, reveals the nature of Domitian's memory. His disgrace is essentially a facade or stage set that has been superimposed on historical fact to obscure what he did. The truth underneath is not forgotten but is hidden from public view. Trajan was a practical man, who had served Domitian loyally, who lived in the palace built by Domitian, and who could appreciate the usefulness of Domitian's legal precedents, whatever may have been said publicly about invalidating Domitian's laws. Yet, in his formal thanks to Trajan for the gift of the *ius trium liberorum*, Pliny adds the superfluous observation that, although he has always wanted to be a father, he would much rather have children under the new regime.[66] Clearly both Pliny and Trajan knew that this was just a figure of speech, a new kind of doublespeak. Its value was symbolic as a token of Pliny's loyalty rather than as a statement of fact or even of sentiment.

Similarly, Pliny evokes the memory of Domitian in a series of letters that are in fact as much concerned with himself as with the dead emperor.[67] The letter about Regulus' fears soon after Domitian's death, and his attempts at a reconciliation with Pliny, is really more about Pliny's calm and poise than about Regulus' situation. Regulus provides Pliny with a favorite subject: he seems to feel the need for a villain to hold up as a cautionary example. As Nerva's dinner conversation revealed, the new emperor himself was not eager to pursue the ghosts of the past but thought more in terms of a new start and a sort of gentleman's amnesty among those who had survived. Yet, Pliny

266   THE PRINCIPATE

returns to the theme of the prosecution of *delatores* in 97. Senators were no doubt keen for a purge, and Pliny wants to be seen as one of them.

Pliny's stance against Domitian is complex and must be partly defined in cultural and intellectual rather than in purely political terms. Hence, he condemns Greek games at length, in the context of their abolition at Vienne in Gaul.[68] His call for the abolition of the similar Capitoline games in Rome is an attack on Domitian's legacy that goes well beyond official policy. Similarly, Pliny dwells in several letters on his closeness to Fannia and Arria, and to their family of imperial martyrs.[69] He tells their stories, including the heroic tales associated with the women, and creates his own memorial to their family history. He places them firmly in a Stoic context, while also appealing to republican precedents. He portrays himself as a close friend of the family, who is called upon to act on its behalf. Some of this is intended to create a new image of his own past. He evokes a heroic image of resistance to the principate with himself as a special mediator and confidante, always the figure of the wise adviser. This image has effectively replaced a more factual narrative of his own doings during these years.

Pliny is a master of the evocative vignette that brings an individual or a whole era to life for his readers. For example, his visit to the philosopher Artemidorus, who is about to be banished from Rome in 93, conjures up that time of uncertainty and risk.[70] Pliny's shared interest in philosophy helps to suggest his association with Artemidorus and with the distinguished circle of Musonius Rufus. All this cleverly avoids any account of what Pliny was doing as praetor that year. Similarly, he uses the figure of the senator Valerius Licinianus, wearing Greek dress in exile in Sicily, to introduce a dramatic version of the execution of the chief Vestal Cornelia by Domitian in 89 or 90. Pliny's story has become a set piece from a tragedy, with the noble and chaste Vestal bravely meeting her death at the hands of the bloodthirsty and godless tyrant Domitian. The death of Corellius Rufus also conjures up a noble senatorial tradition, as the brave and suffering Corellius had told Pliny that it was worth living through years of painful illness in the hope of surviving the brigand (*latro*) Domitian even by a single day.

In other words, Pliny is using a multiplicity of scenes and of voices to create a picture of his times that is closely tied to his own self-representation. His choice of the epistolary format inevitably recalls Cicero, while his tone of criticism of society and of current issues is sometimes closer to the satires of Horace. Pliny is claiming to have been liberated from the evil Domitian, a claim closely tied to his relationship to certain of Domitian's victims. Pliny asserts that he was in danger himself, on a number of occasions. He stresses his closeness to Nerva and to Trajan, as well as to his guardian Verginius Rufus, who emerged in old age as something of a political icon in 97.[71] Pliny is trying to capture the spirit of the new age, even as he struggles with memory and disgrace.

At the same time his own position does depend on that of others in his world. He must define who the resisters were and also who their friends were. On the other side, the *delatores* also need to be clearly delineated, a task that takes on added meaning in light of Pliny's own success as a prosecutor of fellow senators.[72] Pliny, the new man from Comum, the lawyer and bureaucrat in the service of the emperor, reveals his own need for an idealized republican past that he can own as a senator, despite the fact that he does not belong to a noble republican family. He is concerned not only with public memory but also with private memory and its cultivation.

Pliny lived in a time when memorials were being erected and histories were being written, notably by Tacitus.[73] Who will define Pliny's memory and that of his friends if he does not take the initiative? Yet he finds the prospect of writing a narrative history daunting. His first letters seem to be published precisely in the gap in his career in 97, before he was appointed to the Treasury of Saturn by Nerva and Trajan early in 98. It might even seem that the unusual second treasury post could serve as a substitute for the first such appointment, now erased by Domitian's disgrace. That memory itself is an important theme in his works comes as no surprise. His treatment of Domitian (and Nero) must be read in relation to his many other statements about memory and oblivion throughout his correspondence.

The fear of oblivion was very real for a self-made man like Pliny. He speaks of it in relation to Verginius Rufus, a man from a background similar to his own. A visit to Verginius' grave some ten years after his death causes Pliny to deplore its unkept state. This leads him to reflect that each citizen needs to cultivate the memories of great men of the past or else Rome's heritage will be lost. His friend Titinius Capito appears as just such a person, an assiduous cultivator of memory.[74] Under Nerva, Capito secured permission to set up a statue of L. Junius Silanus (presumably a victim of Nero) in the Forum in Rome. He was also well known for displaying the portraits of Brutus, Cassius, and Cato in his home. Cn. Octavius Titinius Capito was an equestrian and was close to Nerva and to Trajan. His cultivation of a republican past is typical of the habits of the Empire's new bureaucrats. Pliny would like to see such memory cultivation move beyond the idiosyncratic or pretentious. It was also Capito who urged Pliny to write history, even as he himself was composing a work on the deaths of famous men.

Pliny himself feels unequal to the task of historical writing but is eager to supply material for others, especially for Tacitus, whose histories he is confident will be famous.[75] He wants to ensure that he and his uncle will appear in these histories. For him the immortality of the historiographic account is closely linked to the undying fame of the historian himself. Pliny's obsession with history and memory seems to be closely connected with his awareness of oblivion as more than a historiographic commonplace and to his clear sense of the rapid passing of time with its changing fashions. He refers to the shame of censorship in the senate and to the abolition of legislation for a previous governor of Bithynia.[76] Inevitably he recalls his own role in an age when the past was being erased and rewritten. Even as he had personally witnessed and taken part in the rewriting of past events, Pliny is eager to leave a positive record of himself that will not be subject to alteration. His desire to be remembered may be further connected with the fact that he never had his own children and that he spent a considerable time helping others with their wills and legacies.

Pliny also comments with great vehemence on the commemoration of the unworthy: his special example is the honors paid to Pallas, a freedman of Antonia who was prominent under Claudius.[77] Pliny ridicules the wealth and praetorian rank granted to Pallas by the senate on the occasion of his retirement from public life in 52. Pliny fears and despises the power of freedmen, but he feels that it is safe to criticize a man who has probably been dead for fifty years, especially at a time when Trajan has removed such men from high office. It is typical of Pliny that he chooses to single out the language of the senate's decree honoring Pallas, as well as the epitaph on his tomb. The senate's decree (posted at the statue of Julius Caesar) and the tomb at Tibur both represent the stuff of memory and the special preserve of the elite. Here Pliny is searching for a reassuring link with the republican past and for some indication that society will reject such anomalies in the long run. Public *memoria* should belong to the senate, and his own hard work to achieve similar rewards appears threatened by the upward mobility of a Pallas. At the same time, the commemoration of Pallas is also a reminder of the power of the emperor and of the slavish role of the senate in confirming that power. It captures the spirit of an earlier Julio-Claudian age, which Pliny objects to enough to give it his own negative form of commemoration.

Pliny's concern with memory and commemoration mirrors not only the spirit of his own times but also his special situation and aspirations as a provincial, as a lawyer, and as a new Roman senator. Partly because the memory of his career had been affected by Domitian's fall, he turned to literature and to other intellectual pursuits to define his own worth and status. The public sphere was fraught with dangers and with the unpredictable rise and fall of emperors. Consequently, a senator also needed to find a space for himself in a more personal sphere, in the cultivation of his *otium*, and in his relationship to his peers and to the past. In this sense, Pliny's letters address many aspects of the question raised by Tacitus about how to live under an emperor, especially a bad one.[78] Both men admire but eschew the heroism of the great martyrs, while condemning the slavishness of many senators. Both wanted to have a hand in shaping and editing the picture of the past that would be handed on to posterity. Meanwhile, freedom of speech under Trajan seems to have been largely defined or at least practiced in terms of the liberty to speak about the past, a freedom to give one's own account of history.

Memory and Transitions of Power in the First Century A.D.: 69/96

Pliny's anxieties reflect those of his generation as they looked back at the events of their own and of the previous generation. Pliny was born in 61 or 62, at the height of Nero's power. He would have been old enough to recall something of the turmoil of the civil wars and would certainly have known many eyewitnesses to it, notably his guardian Verginius Rufus. The members of his family were consistently loyal supporters of the Flavians, as is revealed by his father's decision to build a temple to the Aeternitas of Rome and to the Augusti at Comum, which Pliny was to dedicate himself.[79] He continued this tradition with his own priesthood of Titus in his early twenties. His uncle and adoptive father, the elder Pliny, was especially devoted to Titus, and dedicated his major work on natural history to him. Yet Pliny had experienced the disintegration of his own nuclear family, and the death of his uncle in the eruption of Vesuvius, which he was to describe so vividly. Pliny had seen whole cities wiped from the earth, just as he was to see powerful senators and their families ruined and erased from memory. His close association with the Flavians continued under Domitian, and he survived many turbulent times, emerging wealthy and respected under a new dynasty, the third to hold power by the time he was in his mid-thirties. It is logical that Pliny should see both the past and the future as uncertain territory and should view the power of memory as an unstable but compelling illusion.

The ghosts of Nero and of the battles of 69 haunted the coup of 96, even as Nerva seemed to hope that a shared consulship with the legendary Verginius

Rufus, senatorial hero of 68, would shore up his own wavering popularity. By now the erasure of an emperor was not new. Yet the record of profligacy and distraction from public affairs associated with Gaius and Nero had also created a stereotype for the discredited emperor that Domitian did not fit. He was no dilettante, and even his autocracy was completely different from theirs. Moreover, the ranks of his associates had not been weeded out by war or by proscription. This transition needed to be handled somewhat differently. Nerva, however, was an expert. Domitian had been a formidable enemy, whose memory attracted vigorous attacks. At the same time, the critiques of Nero had necessitated some kind of Flavian continuity. The complex political situation reflected the challenges each surviving senator faced in his own life.

Pliny wrote to Trajan in the summer of 98 or 99 about his plan to build a temple to the imperial cult on his estates at Tifernum, with a design that seems to have been partially modeled on his father's project at Comum in the 70s.[80] Pliny had previously approached Nerva and had obtained permission for his plan. Now he needed both a leave of absence from Rome to arrange for the construction and a further permission to add the statue of Trajan to those of the deceased emperors, a collection that he had inherited and amassed from various sources over the years. Pliny's imperial statue group sums up his own ongoing memory project. As soon as a new emperor succeeded, an adjustment was made both in the imperial cult and in the imagery of the current ruler. Pliny and his family reacted to each event, according to what was deemed most appropriate. In this case Pliny was also positioning himself as a candidate for a future consulship. His collection of imperial images had changed over the years, and we can be sure that it had once included portraits of Domitian. The new ensemble would be designed to place Trajan in his present context, as ruling emperor, as son of the deified Nerva, and as legitimate successor to the deified Flavians, Vespasian and Titus, themselves direct heirs of their patron, the deified Claudius, and ultimately of the divine Augustus, with an image of Tiberius included for good measure. Pliny and his contemporaries had seen continual changes in such statue groups as a result of death and politics; the changes in his own collection reflected his need to survive and his ambition to prosper even in changing times. By the end of the first century, oblivion and disgrace had emerged as the logical opposite of deification for each emperor, or so it might appear.

Hadrian's Legacy

Some forty-two years after the murder of Domitian, Hadrian's death again raised the specter of a disgraced emperor, in the context of a conflict between the senate and Hadrian's designated successor, the man who was to reign from A.D. 138 to 161 under the name of Antoninus Pius. The senators hated Hadrian, for a wide variety of reasons, and wanted to impose a full array of memory sanctions upon him.[81] Such sanctions would have comprised both a political commentary on his reign and a more personal condemnation of Hadrian as a man, as well as of his tastes and priorities. However, the senate was forced to yield before deft but firm pressure put on them by Antoninus. Not only did Hadrian not suffer any erasure (although he was certainly remembered unfavorably by many) but he was even deified. As a result, the decision to turn away from memory sanctions emerges as a characteristic feature of the political culture of the high Empire and the era of the adoptive emperors, which was described as Rome's high point by Edward Gibbon in the eighteenth century. Antoninus broke the habitual pattern of denigration that had become gradually established under the Julio-Claudians and Flavians, who had demanded a reaction to political change through erasure and vilification.

Despite the poor quality of the literary sources for the period, the basic outline of events in the months after Hadrian's death seems well established. Hadrian died at Baiae on 10 July 138, supposedly in the arms of his faithful friend and designated heir Antoninus. Initially his body was buried at Cicero's villa at Puteoli, an arrangement that reveals the impracticality of bringing Hadrian's body back to Rome for an immediate funeral in the accustomed fashion.[82] In other words, the heated nature of the debate over Hadrian's memory does not seem to have come as a surprise to Antoninus. Yet it is all the more striking that the senators discussed wide-ranging punitive sanctions for an emperor who had died a natural death after a reign of more than twenty years, a reign marked by stability, effective administration, ambitious building programs, and flourishing cultural patronage. It is also remarkable that this challenge to Hadrian was in no way directed at his choice of imperial heir, one of their own fellow senators. It seems that all were delighted to acclaim Antoninus, and no surviving evidence suggests that there were other contenders for the leading position in the Empire.

Rather the senate was asserting its own ultimate role in defining memory, even in a system now undoubtedly based on one-man rule, in which the Republic seemed no more than a nostalgic but distant era in Rome's past. The senate was drawing attention to its particular concerns, especially its anger over the deaths of senators whose executions raised the issue of the relationship between the emperor and the senate. Once again, a senate was claiming that as an institution, it would have the final say in defining the memory and legacy of an emperor at the time of his death. If sanctions had indeed been imposed on Hadrian, the result would have been not a new Republic but a different kind of principate, perhaps even one not shaped by monarchical principles. The very idea of erasing Hadrian's memory was huge, both in practical and in political terms. Hadrian had had a profound impact on Rome and on the other cities of the Empire.[83] He had operated on a dynastic principle, upheld by strategic adoptions in the tradition of Nerva and Trajan, if not of Augustus himself. If he were erased, the senate would rewrite history and would present itself as the body that had chosen the next ruler from among its own members. Such a system may have been thought of and debated over the generations, but it had never been put into effect. It represented a challenge to a dynastic system of adoption within a "family" by replacing it with a different kind of "choice," exercised by a much larger group of people.

The senate's proposal of 138 recalled distorted and refracted echoes of senatorial debate almost a century before, at the time of Gaius' murder (although Hadrian may have seemed more like Nero or Domitian than like Caligula). In effect, the senate imagined that it could appropriate Hadrian's choice of successor at the same time as it erased Hadrian himself. This scenario involved a number of ironies, not least of which was the fact that the senators apparently did not have a different candidate of their own to put forward. They wanted to construct a memory of choosing Antoninus that would erase Hadrian and suggest a decisive agency on their part and, therefore, their active role in the mechanism of succession. Not unlike Tacitus, who was surely dead by then, the senators may have been thinking of defining the imperial system through its modes and moments of succession. Moreover, if it was the senators who ultimately defined memory and commemoration, then each emperor should give priority to his relationship with them, as opposed to provincials or soldiers or any other constituency.

It is suggestive that this senatorial solution did not appeal to the senator Antoninus and that he was able to win his peers over to his point of view, without the use of any force or bloodshed. The details of Antoninus' struggle with the senate in 138 over Hadrian's memory are lost, but the final result is evident. Hadrian was deified and thus joined his wife Diva Sabina, who had predeceased him by a year or two. All his legislation and acts as emperor were recognized, although some policies were soon modified, and in 140 he was buried in his new mausoleum, now completed by Antoninus. The splendid new tomb, in its strategic location on the banks of the Tiber overlooking the Campus Martius, marked the final establishment of Hadrian's position after his death.[84] It was his mausoleum that served as the new dynastic "family" tomb of the Roman emperors, so that the Antonines and Severans were buried there. Moreover, Antoninus' characteristic *cognomen* Pius, with its undertones of Augustan and Virgilian virtue, was primarily linked to his cultivation of the memory of his adoptive father Hadrian. Antoninus was named Pius in recognition of his fidelity to Hadrian's memory and his refusal to build his own image on a denigration of his predecessor, as so many earlier Roman rulers had done. The concept of *pietas* suggested correct and dutiful behavior in all relationships, starting with the family and the gods, but also extending to every other social interaction. In this sense the name Pius could recall the circumstances of Antoninus' accession, while also constituting a promise, especially to the senators, of how he would behave as emperor.

The coins minted in Rome in 138 confirm that the struggle over Hadrian's memory was real and that it was not neatly settled at a single senate meeting.[85] Early in the year Antoninus described himself as consul designate (*cos des*), but after Hadrian's death he became simply consul (*cos*), in reference to the office he had held before. In other words, while Hadrian's arrangements were in doubt, and might be overturned, Antoninus called the senate's bluff by saying that his own position as successor would become void as a logical consequence of Hadrian's erasure. In this way, the coins provide an invaluable confirmation of this same debate as sketched in the literary sources. The small number of coins minted throughout the year also shows that uncertainty continued for some time. Antoninus challenged the senators to honor Hadrian's memory if they wanted him as their next emperor. It is a tribute to his character and standing, as well as to his skills as a politician, that his fellow senators accepted his proposal to move forward and to erase their own bitterness in a kind of amnesty rather than to seek a posthumous vengeance against Hadrian. In this way, the man born T. Aurelius Fulvus Boionius Arrius Antoninus (*cos.* 120) had first become T. Aelius Aurelius Antoninus Caesar, on 25 February 138 when he was adopted by Hadrian, and was then to emerge by the beginning of the following year as Imperator Caesar T. Aelius Hadrianus Antoninus Augustus Pius, consul II, *pater patriae*, the new Roman emperor and the father of two (adopted) sons, L. Verus and M. Aurelius.

As a result of the memory crisis of 138, the Antonine monarchy emerged as firmly dynastic, since Antoninus also confirmed Trajan's adoption of

Hadrian. The ruling family traced its origins back to Nerva, and to his adoption of Trajan in 98. Antoninus Pius' pattern was followed by the remaining emperors in his line and was then taken up, after a short hiatus during the civil wars of the 190s, by the Severans, who also claimed to be "Antonines." Pius imposed his own (and Hadrian's) fictional genealogy at the expense of the senate's fictional narrative of independence. He thereby confirmed the position and image of the dynastic emperor in the Roman state, and he managed to do this while giving recognition to the grievances and concerns of the senate. Pius created an image of a world without punitive sanctions, in which Hadrian would not be remembered as another Nero or Domitian. His new politics of memory reflected a novel sense of elite consensus, as the senators recognized Pius as one of their own and were willing to deify Hadrian as a gesture of goodwill toward his successor. It is notable that Pius enjoyed a fine reputation in the surviving ancient sources, meager though they are for his reign. Meanwhile, his rejection of memory sanctions characterized the particular political climate of Antonine Rome and the culture of the high Empire in the mid-second century A.D. Almost a century separated Domitian's disgrace from the fall of Commodus in 192/193 but Commodus was rehabilitated and deified by Septimius Severus in 197.[86]

Conclusion

Roman Memory Spaces

▼   ▼   ▼

> . . . all they want is that the King
> should be lost to memory — like an old
> umbrella in a dusty cupboard.
> Amitav Ghosh, *The Glass Palace*

The Romans, and especially those who wrote history, saw memory (*memoria*) as if it were a discrete space, filled with the monuments, inscriptions, portraits, written accounts, and other testimonies to the life of a Roman citizen (in most cases an elite male). This symbolic space, a powerful and definitive marker of elite status, stretched across the various visual and textual media and between the generations to ensure the survival and continuity of the community and of the particular culture of its political families. Memory in this formal sense also formed a bridge between public and private, between domestic and political. The guardians of memory during the centuries of the Republic were the political families. Nor did they abruptly lose their role once there was one family, headed by one father, who overshadowed all the others in the "imperial" period. Memory sanctions were (re)designed and (re)created by each generation of Romans to preserve its own characteristic memory space as the defining symbol of its political system. The politics of the present was expressed in terms of a narrative of the past, by those who had or claimed the authority to shape and to pass on that narrative.

Memory in Roman culture could be found in three essential media: monument, text, and ritual. In other words, it was visible and legible, but also dramatic and able to be recreated, for example, by actors impersonating ancestors at an aristocratic funeral. The memory world of the past was open and familiar to all citizens; indeed, it was celebrated by the entire community. The literate and educated, however, always had access to the largest number of different versions of the past, especially those attested in documents or in historiographic accounts. The topographical context of each monument, text, and ritual was essential to its meaning and effect. Meanwhile, commemoration expanded from the home into the various parts of the city, and then outward into the Empire. The city of Rome, however, always constituted the ultimate location for memory.

The various components of memory existed in a tension created by the delicate and continually evolving balance between competition and cooperation in Roman political culture. The excellence of the individual, and also of the family he belonged to, suggested and reaffirmed the brilliance of the elected political class as a whole. These were the men who had made Rome great, and during the Republic they did so by working together with others like themselves. At the same time, intergenerational dialogue set up competition with other Roman leaders throughout the history of the city — a notion that is already attested in the third century B.C., even before the war with Hannibal prompted the birth of Roman historical writing. In other words, the ancestors formed a special audience and reference point for contemporary achievement. At the same time, actively cultivated commemoration, in both traditional and innovative media, was addressed to a wide variety of audiences including all levels of Roman society, as well as to a growing circle of foreigners, both those who visited the city and those who never came. The expanding Empire created an increasingly broad Mediterranean context for Roman memory: leading Romans were now recalled in many distant places, even as their exploits abroad were represented and memorialized within the city.

Destruction, modification, and erasure of texts and monuments were part of this dynamic and ongoing cultural memory project. Many assertions of individual achievement and prowess must necessarily have been made at the expense of others, especially contemporaries, whether they were actually rivals or merely associates and colleagues operating at the same time and with similar political aspirations. Comparisons would likewise have arisen with those in the past who had been active in the same spheres of operation, especially in the same provinces or in similar conflicts, often against traditional enemies. Hence the political system of the classic Republic, which emerged in the late fourth century B.C., encouraged not only the regular denigration of opponents and predecessors, but also the desire to eclipse others, both among one's peers and in earlier generations. Within this aristocratic world, erasure targeted and defined memory spaces precisely. It was specifically the texts and monuments of the elite that were affected. Attacks on memory, therefore, acknowledged and even asserted that memory was itself an artifact created in a specific context and for a designated political and cultural purpose. Memory was seen as reified in portraits, or inscriptions, or houses and other physical monuments. Memory was made in certain accepted ways, with the result that it could also be unmade in those same locations. The wording of the legal bans we do know about in detail are very specific as to the media involved and the locations of the affected objects. Such memory was highly symbolic, not literal or universal or abstract.

Fully developed memory sanctions removed the visible displays of the status of the targeted Roman politician both from the home and from the city, with the result that the individual was symbolically removed from the community in many ways like an exile. He forfeited his identity and status as a citizen, while being labeled with a new status: he became an outsider, sometimes explicitly an enemy (*hostis*). In many cases, this process can be better described as the reversal of identity, rather than a simple loss of identity. With this stigma came a disinheritance from the family, which meant social death in terms of Roman society. The family was the basic and essential unit of Roman life: the individual could have no existence as a citizen outside the context of a citizen family. Freedmen also gained their new status as citizens through their connection with the family of their former owner, whose name they took as their citizen name. Only slaves had no family and therefore no legally recognized connections to parents or other relatives, but even they "belonged" to someone, at least in the eyes of the law.

Sanctions, then, also delineated the social relationships within the community. The individual's relationship to his parents and to his extended family group was closely interconnected with the role of that family as a unit in society. Hence, descriptions of early sanctions, whether historical or not, nearly always stress the role of the family, which removes or punishes an errant member but does so for the good of the whole community. This picture of Roman sanctions reaffirms the role of consensus in Roman republican politics, from the earliest times. Within the family, ranks tend to close and the past is remolded. The survival and prosperity of the family unit is more important than the loss of any individual member. It is in the realm of traditional family politics, which was synonymous with republican practices, that we see the paradigm shift introduced by the first sanctions imposed by the senate. It is surely no coincidence that these first punitive sanctions of 121

B.C. were implemented at a time when the first *senatus consultum ultimum* also created a legal emergency that was completely outside the traditional political sphere. At the same time, punitive sanctions can be related to Hellenistic practices, as memory games of various kinds were enacted in the relationships between Hellenistic monarchs and Greek city-states. During the second century B.C., Roman politicians became fully conversant with the political vocabulary of Hellenistic sanctions as they themselves took on the role of participants and powerbrokers in that extensive Greek-speaking world of the eastern Mediterranean.

The profound political crisis that saw the first use of punitive sanctions was exacerbated and entrenched by the harsh rhetoric developed during the Gracchan age. Punitive sanctions had now become a weapon in the internal political struggle against personal rivals, who were characterized as traitors or as those who wanted to seize absolute personal power (*regnum*). The use of such sanctions marks a breakdown in traditional republican politics, a rupture that coincided with the loss of a shared narrative about the immediate past. This divided and divisive past, distorted by the use of violence, the spilling of citizen blood, and the denial of honorable memory to the victims of civil strife, characterized and shaped the developing political rift in Rome after 121 B.C., culminating in the civil wars of Marius, Cinna, and Sulla. The loss of a shared past contributed in significant ways to the loss of a shared future.

The dictator Sulla himself emerges against this background as the inventor of the lawless sanctions he imposed through the proscription of his political enemies. A state of complete civil war led to the annihilation of political opponents and the re-creation of a New Republic, the Republic of Sulla, based on the unparalleled honors accorded its founder, as well as on the simultaneous erasure of his political rivals and their families from public life. Such a solution imposed through force was in complete contrast to the traditional politics of the middle Republic. Consequently, the new world of Sulla was also marked by the emergence of extraordinary honors and privileges accorded to individual military leaders (already foreshadowed in the career of Marius), and by the shadow cast by the image of Sulla himself, a divinely inspired dictator, who tried to erase memory, rewrite history, and recast society to suit his own purposes and goals. Subsequently, repeated outbreaks of civil war and factional struggles between citizens marked the unraveling of Sulla's Republic in the generation after his death.

Some fifty years after Sulla's death, Octavian not only changed his name to Augustus when he "restored" a new republic, but also worked swiftly to modify and to control the divisive and bitter impact of memory sanctions in Roman political culture. The idealized picture of a republic restored by a generous and modest "leading citizen" (*princeps*), who sought and achieved consensus, peace, and the common good, needed to be sharply distinguished from the accumulated rhetoric of punitive sanctions and memory battles. Nevertheless, the very existence of a single leader had an enormous and lasting impact on commemoration and monuments in Rome. Even as the *princeps* now encroached steadily on the traditional memory spaces of the *nobiles*, sanctions became legalized as part of the treason law (*maiestas*). Under Augustus' successor Tiberius, *maiestas* trials became increasingly common and memory sanctions came to be used as the formalized weapon of the *princeps* in asserting his power over potential rivals and in defining his relationship with the senate. Senators in turn themselves used such accusations of treason and the threat of political annihilation in their power struggles with each other. The deep-seated fear of the senators, that they would lose their status and their place in history, helped to make memory sanctions the ultimate tools of intimidation and of revenge in the Roman imperial period. Meanwhile, the *princeps* might even impose such sanctions on his own relatives, as a way to control and eliminate attempts to gain power within the ruling family, and especially to influence the succession. The sanctions of the Julio-Claudian period reveal both the competition between the ruling family and rivals with distinguished republican pedigrees, as well as the increasing violence inside that leading family itself.

Memory sanctions could also be imposed on emperors themselves, whether in a formal, legal manner, or informally and without much fanfare. In this way sanctions marked political transitions, between rival individuals and between rival families. This use was of course completely divorced from the legal penalties imposed in cases of *maiestas*: in a monarchical system of government the emperor could not himself be guilty of treason under the law. Gaius was the last Julian, Nero the last Claudian, and Domitian the last Flavian. These three emperors were subject to increasingly harsh and public memory sanctions, although only those against Domitian were fully enacted in law by the senate. Consequently, the history of the first century A.D. is characterized by a rich variety of sanctions and by complex memory battles over the past, battles that aimed to define the authority of the ruling family and various individuals within it, the position of the emperor, and the very nature of the principate itself.

By contrast, the second century A.D., although marked at its beginning by the long shadow of Domitian's disgrace, developed a different style of politics. It was an age that tried — with considerable success — to distance itself again from the memory wars of the past. The decision taken by Antoninus Pius, and imposed by him on a reluctant senate, not to shame or to erase the memory of Hadrian stands out as a defining moment of that Antonine age and a decisive precedent in its own right. Only civil war and a drastic rupture of continuity saw the reinvention of new and more fierce memory sanctions by L. Septimius Severus, the first of the Severan emperors. For these reasons, the present study stops with the death and honorable commemoration of Hadrian. The new sanctions of the Severan age belong to a very different chapter in Roman history and reflect a changed world, dominated by an African royal house that deployed military power to enforce its picture of the past in a way that was unprecedented in earlier times.

The disgrace of emperors can be read especially clearly in certain symbolic texts that bear witness to points of transition. A particularly good example is provided by the law conferring imperial power on the emperor Vespasian (*lex de imperio Vespasiani*). In it Vespasian, the victor in the recent civil wars, is represented as the legitimate successor to an unbroken series of earlier emperors, but with no mention of Gaius, Nero, Galba, Otho, or Vitellius. The list of previous Roman emperors has been edited, leaving only three emperors for the century before Vespasian, namely Augustus, Tiberius, and Claudius. Vespasian's other predecessors have all been omitted, although their memories had been treated in varied ways at the actual time of their deaths. Similarly, Claudius is mocked by Seneca in the satire entitled *Apocolocyntosis*, which dates soon after Claudius' death and deification. Nero is vilified in the *Octavia*, a play performed on stage in Rome, probably only a few months after the emperor's suicide. Domitian was excoriated in Pliny's praise of Trajan in the *Panegyricus*, delivered before the emperor Trajan and the public in Rome in A.D. 100.

Each of these, whether in the form of an inscribed law, a satirical pamphlet, a political play, or a formal speech, captures a moment when memory was recast through vituperation and erasure. Each needs to be read in the context of its own times: none can offer a definitive reading even of contemporary views, let alone for subsequent ages. Claudius went on to receive a temple, a rehabilitation of his memory, and formal cult under the Flavians, while Nero's memory was cherished by some to the end of the first century and beyond. The study of memory sanctions at pivotal moments of change reminds us that politics always has its own rhetoric, which expresses, above all, the partisan mood of the moment.

The need to stigmatize the powerful memory of an emperor was its own phenomenon, necessarily enacted both in the city and in the Empire. The display of a tyrant figure and of the terror he caused also served as a warning to future rulers, especially once thoughts of restoring a republic receded into the realms of fantasy. Imperial sanctions returned to a Hellenistic pattern, with disgrace being the opposite of divine honors. A ruler was either a success or a complete failure. This political outcome was the result of a long struggle over who was to control and to define that imperial memory space. Was it the emperor or the senate who had the ultimate say? The history of memory sanctions reflects these struggles over the role of the senate in a system of one-man rule. Yet both the emperor and the senate were operating largely outside the family context of memory sanctions typical of the Republic. The republican senate had had only some limited control over the media used to preserve memory. In the imperial period, sanctions mirror the dilemma of senators, who had lost their central position in political discourse to the overpowering presence of Rome's ruler and his new patterns of self-representation, and now sought ownership over at least some aspects of memory.

The paradigms employed reflect the aspirations of each age, as sanctions of various kinds went in and out of fashion. Harsh sanctions, such as those imposed on the memory of the victims of Sulla's proscriptions or on Domitian by Nerva, seem more capable of causing a backlash than necessarily setting a precedent. In this sense sanctions appear two-edged: they could also go on to shape the image of those who had invented or approved them. Indeed, the image of the proverbial "bad" emperor came to consist of a tyrant who attacked the memory of citizens and relatives alike with harsh memory sanctions. Sanctions that had displayed the family's traditional authority over memory were used to enforce the political solutions of a Marius and a Sulla. The power to impose punitive sanctions, which the senate had arrogated to itself at various moments — for example, against Gaius Gracchus or Mark Antony — was turned against it by a series of emperors in the first century A.D. Cicero, who had so often proposed punitive sanctions against his political rivals on the pretext of preserving a republic, himself became the victim of a new proscription. Octavian challenged the senate in its erasure of his former brother-in-law Antony and the family of the Antonii, even as he asserted what would be the *princeps'* ultimate claim to define and control public memory in Rome.

Sanctions also provide paradigms that can set up an intertextuality of memory between different historical turning points. It is striking to see the concept of amnesty, as developed by the Athenians in 403 B.C. after the fall of the Thirty Tyrants, being invoked by Cicero after the Ides of March in 44 B.C. and again by the emperor Claudius in A.D. 41, when another Gaius Julius Caesar had been assassinated. Yet in A.D. 41 the concept of amnesty was not the only idea being discussed. The senate, as it debated what should happen after the death of Gaius, considered the erasure of all the Caesars, along the lines of what had happened to King Philip V and his predecessors in Athens in 200 B.C. In both A.D. 69 and 96 Romans struggled to find a model for the treatment of an emperor who had fallen victim to a coup. Yet, in A.D. 138 the senate tried to rewrite history without either an assassination or a violent change of government. Sanctions were invoked as necessary in dealing with such liminal moments, even as they also fitted in with a general recasting of the past, including the rehabilitation of the previous emperor's victims. A history of memory sanctions, therefore, produces a complex and shifting picture of competing political narratives as it testifies to the continuing desire of each generation to control and categorize the past to suit its own particular needs and purposes.

NOTES

▼   ▼   ▼

Abbreviations

AAntHung	*Acta Antiqua Academiae Scientiarium Hungaricae.*
AE	*L'Année epigraphique.*
ANSMusN	*American Numismatic Society Museum Notes.*
BCH	*Bulletin de correspondence hellénique.*
BM	British Museum.
BMC	British Museum. *Coins of the Roman Empire in the British Museum.* 6 vols. London, 1923–62.
Bruns[7]	C. G. Bruns. *Fontes Iuris Romani Antiqui*[7]. Tübingen, 1909.
CAH[2]	*The Cambridge Ancient History*[2]. 14 vols. Cambridge, 1970–2000.
CIG	*Corpus Inscriptionum Graecarum.* 8 vols. Berlin, 1828–77.
CIL	*Corpus Inscriptionum Latinarum.* Vols. 1– . Berlin, 1893– .
CLE	F. Bücheler. *Carmina Latina epigraphica*[2]. Leipzig, 1930.
FGH	F. Jacoby. *Die Fragmente der griechischen Historiker.* 14 vols. Leiden, 1957–99.
Fornara	C. W. Fornara. *Archaic Times to the End of the Peloponnesian War*[2]. Cambridge, 1983.
IAssos	R. Merkelbach. *Die Inschriften von Assos.* Bonn, 1976.
ICorinth	A. B. West. *Corinth 8.2: The Latin Inscriptions 1896–1926.* Cambridge, Mass., 1931.
IDidyma	A. Rehm. *Didyma 2: Die Inschriften.* Berlin, 1958.
IEphesos	H. Wankel et al. *Die Inschriften von Ephesos.* Vols. 1– . Bonn, 1979– .
IG	*Inscriptiones Graecae.* Vols. 1– . Berlin, 1873– .
IGLSyr	W. H. Waddington. *Inscriptions grecques et latines de la Syrie.* Paris, 1870.
IGR	*Inscriptiones Graecae ad res Romanas pertinentes.* 4 vols. Paris, 1901–27.
IGUR	L. Moretti. *Inscriptiones Graecae urbis Romae.* 5 vols. Rome, 1968–90.
II	*Inscriptiones Italiae.* 13 vols. Rome, 1931– .
IIlion	P. Frisch. *Die Inschriften von Ilion.* Bonn, 1975.
ILindos	C. Blinkenberg and K. F. Kinch. *Lindos, fouilles et recherches, 1902–1914.* Vol. 2. Berlin, 1941.
ILLRP	A. Degrassi. *Inscriptiones Latinae Liberae Rei Publicae.* 2 vols. Florence, 1957–63.
ILS	H. Dessau. *Inscriptiones Latinae Selectae*[2]. 5 vols. Berlin, 1954–55.

IMagn.	T. Ihnken. *Die Inschriften von Magnesia am Sypilos.* Bonn, 1978.
IPriene	F. Hiller von Gaertringen (ed.). *Inschriften von Priene.* Berlin, 1906.
IRT	J. M. Reynolds and J. B. Ward-Perkins. *The Inscriptions of Roman Tripolitania.* Rome, 1950.
ISardis	W. H. Buckler and D. M. Robinson. *Greek and Latin Inscriptions.* Leiden, 1932.
ISE	L. Moretti. *Iscrizioni storiche ellenistiche.* 3 vols. Florence, 1967–76.
ISestos	J. Krauss. *Die Inschriften von Sestos und der thrakischen Chersones.* Bonn, 1980.
IStrat.	M. Ç. Sahin. *Die Inschriften von Stratonikeia.* 2 vols. Bonn, 1981–82.
LTUR	E. M. Steinby. *Lexicon Topographicum Urbis Romae.* 6 vols. Rome, 1993–2000.
ML	R. Meiggs and D. Lewis. *A Selection of Greek Historical Inscriptions to the End of the Fifth Century* B.C. Oxford, 1969.
MNR	Museo Nazionale Romano, Terme di Diocleziano.
MRR	T. R. S. Broughton. *The Magistrates of the Roman Republic* 3. New York, 1951–86.
NP	H. Cancik and H. Schneider. *Brill's New Pauly.* Vol. 1– . Leiden, 2002– .
NSA	*Notizie degli scavi di antichità.*
*OCD*³	S. Hornblower and A. Spawforth. *The Oxford Classical Dictionary³.* Oxford, 1996.
OGIS	W. Dittenberger. *Orientis graeci inscriptiones selectae.* 2 vols. Leipzig, 1903–5.
PIR²	*Prosopographia Imperii Romani saec. I, II, III².* Vols. 1– . Berlin, 1933– .
RE	G. Wissowa. *Paulys Real-encyclopädie der classischen Altertumswissenschaft.* Vols. 1– . Stuttgart, 1894– .
RIB	R. G. Collingwood and R. P. Wright. *The Roman Inscriptions of Britain.* Oxford, 1965-95.
RIC	H. Mattingly et al. *The Roman Imperial Coinage.* 12 vols. London, 1923–81.
RRC	M. Crawford. *Roman Republican Coinage.* 2 vols. Cambridge, 1974.
SCPP	*Senatus Consultum de Cn. Pisone patre (CIL 2² 5 900).*
SEG	*Supplementum epigraphicum graecum.* Vols. 1– . Amsterdam, 1984– .
*SIG*³	W. Dittenberger. *Sylloge inscriptionum graecarum³.* 4 vols. Leipzig, 1915–24.
Tab. Siar.	*Tabula Siarensis.* González, 1984.
TAM	*Tituli Asiae Minoris.* Vols. 1– . Vienna, 1901– .
Tod	M. N. Tod. *A Selection of Greek Historical Inscriptions².* 2 vols. Oxford, 1946–50.

Preface

1 Kienast (1996).
2 Assmann (1995) 366.
3 Meyer (2004) 34–35.

Chapter 1

1 For an overview of memory theory, see Schacter (1995) 1–43 and (2001).

2 For the bias of hindsight, see Schacter (2001) 138–60, esp. 139–49.

3 For a similar conception, see Charlotte Brontë's introduction to her sister Emily's novel *Wuthering Heights* dated 19 September 1850. "This notice has been written, because I felt it a sacred duty to wipe the dust off their gravestones, and leave their dear names free from soil."

4 Agr. 46.4: *nam multos veterum velut ingloriosos et ignobiles oblivio obruet: Agricola posteritati narratus et traditus superstes erit.*

5 See esp. *Il.* 6.144–236 for the speech of Glaukos to Diomedes.

6 Herodotus' *Histories* opens in the following way (in the 1998 translation by Robin Waterfield). "Here are presented the results of the enquiry carried out by Herodotus of Halicarnassus. The purpose is to prevent the traces of human events from being erased by time [*to chrono exitela genetai*], and to preserve the fame of the important and remarkable achievements produced by both Greeks and non-Greeks; among the matters covered is, in particular, the cause of the hostilities between Greeks and non-Greeks."

7 For Drusus' death, see Dio 55.1.

8 For Drusus' funeral, see Livy *Per.* 142, Sen. *Cons ad Marc.* 3.1, Tac. *Ann.* 3.5, Suet. *Claud.* 1.5, Dio 55.2.2 with Flower (1996) 242–43. Drusus was apparently the last person to receive a statue among the parade of Roman heroes in the niches in Augustus' new Forum, something that would also have honored his memory in a special and very public way in Rome.

9 See Sherwin-White (1966) *ad loc.*

10 Hedrick (2000) 242: "The modern totalitarian purge is, in its way, a denial of the reality of history. It is an assertion that the state can control not only the present but the past as well; that the truth of the past is dependent on the representations of the present, and thus exists only at the pleasure of present power. The *damnatio memoriae* was understood by Roman critics like Tacitus as a confirmation of memory, not a destruction of it. . . . The erasure, too, asserts the historicity of what it eradicates, even as it eradicates it. It is through activities such as erasure that authentic, historical documents are created."

11 Pekáry (1985) 136 compares the Romans unfavorably with the Germans: "Ein Blick in die Indices von Dessau, ILS lehrt uns jedoch daß auch hier nicht mit deutscher Gründlichkeit gearbeitet wurde. . . ."

12 Allende (1995) 23.

13 See Ma (1999) 226 on Hellenistic Asia Minor and Antiochus III: "The manipulation of social memory — swiftly cast into monuments, iterated in public and private rituals to mobilize civic subdivisions and human groupings, and proclaimed by inscriptions in visible spots of the city — would ensure the uniformity of remembrance and impose consensus. The creation and perpetuation of an agreed-on version of the recent past could help to reinstate social harmony and *polis* coherence after the potentially divisive adhesion to a new power."

14 P. Stewart (2003) 267–99 offers a very different reading, which conflates and blurs

the distinction between officially sanctioned destruction of images and spontaneous attacks of various kinds by crowds. See esp. 272: "It will be more fruitful here to concentrate on the end product—the violence itself—and to leave aside the question of legal process or organization." Stewart's discussion also deliberately mixes examples from centuries apart, thus obscuring historical developments and the different practices of various periods in Roman history. See 278: "The written sources themselves militate against any attempt to chart a developing history of iconoclasm through the Roman period."

15 For Piso's statues, see esp. Tac. *Ann.* 3.14.4 with Gregory (1994) 96–97.

16 For attacks on Nero, see Suet. *Ner.* 39, 45.2, Dio 61.16.1–3, 62.18.4 with Champlin (2003) 91–92.

17 See *CIL* 6.38417a, presently in the collection of the New York University Classics Department. My thanks to Michael Peachin for bringing this text to my attention and letting me reproduce a photograph of it.

18 See also *ILS* 8284–86 for examples of quarrels mentioned on gravestones and 8290 for an erasure.

19 See Granino Cecere and Magioncalda (2003). My thanks to Rudolf Haensch for this reference.

20 Kundera (1996) 3–4.

Chapter 11

1 Rose (1994) = *AE* 1994.1644.

2 See Meyer (2004) 184–87 for the case of Q. Veranius, governor of Lycia and Pamphylia (A.D. 43–48) who imposed "Roman" standards by curbing erasures and editing in Greek legal texts and documents.

3 For civil conflict in Greek cities, see Lintott (1982), Gehrke (1985), and J. Price (2001).

4 For the Locrian law of 525–500 B.C.? on a bronze plaque, see *ML* 13 lines 12–16 with Connor (1985) T3.

5 For the murder of Hesiod, also at Locri, see Plut. *Mor.* 162b–e with Connor (1985) 83 and T1. For Greek tragedies and the fall of houses, see Connor (1985) 88–89 and Allen (2000) 86–94.

6 For the expulsion of the Cypselids from Corinth, see Nic. Dam. *FGH* 90 F 60 with Connor (1985) T2 and Kurke (1991) 15. For Spartan examples, see Connor (1985) T6–7, Her. 6.72 (Leotychidas c. 476 B.C.), and Thuc. 5.63 (Agis). Cf. Diod. 12.78.5 for an Argive example.

7 For Glaukus the Spartan, see Her. 6.86 with Loraux (2002) 132.

8 For the razing of the house in Greek law and culture, see esp. Connor (1985) for the extant examples from Athens, Sparta, Corinth, Syracuse, and Locri. Further discussion in Parker (1983) 194–95, Kurke (1991) 15–16, and Pomeroy (1997) 85.

9 See Allen (2000) 217 for the argument that destroyed houses were not marked outside Athens. However, lack of evidence may have obscured the picture we now have.

10 For pollution, see Lyc. 1.129, Dem. 18.296 with Connor (1985) 91–93. Parker (1983) 45–47 shows that the corpse of the outlaw was probably not considered polluted.

11 For denial of burial as a legal penalty, see Allen (2000) 216–24, esp. 217: "Their corpses were cast into the utter oblivion and dishonor of forgetfulness."

12 For the Cypselids, see note 5 above. For the Alcmeionids, see Her. 5.71; Thuc. 1.126–27, 2.13; Isocr. 16.26 with J. Davies (1971) 9688; Connor (1985) T4; R. Thomas (1989) 144–54, 272–81; and Pomeroy (1997) 83–84.

13 For the Athenian pits (*barathron* and *orugma*), see Allen (2000) 218–21 and 324–25 with the literary and archaeological evidence.

14 For Timoleon, see Plut. *Tim.* 22 with Connor (1985) T11, Westlake (1952), Talbert (1974), and Westlake in *CAH*² 6 (1994) chap. 13.

15 For self-imposed exile as a norm, see Allen (2000) 200–202.

16 For Athenian law in general, see now Todd (1993).

17 For *atimia* and the development of Athenian tyranny laws, see Ostwald (1955), Hansen (1976), Carawan (1993), and Todd (1993) 142–43. For the case of Andocides, see And. 1.77–85, 95–98 with Furley (1996). For *atimia* at Sparta, see MacDowell (1986) 42–46.

18 For ostracism, see now Forsdyke (2000), who places the practice in the context of the politics of exile and gives bibliography.

19 For the recording of Athenian penalties on *stelai*, see Arist. *Rhet.* 1400a32–36 and Dem. 47.22 with Allen (2000) 202–5. For the Peisistratids, see Thuc. 6.54 with Gomme, Andrewes, and Dover (1970) 324–25 (cf. *SIG*³ 58 = *ML* 43 from Miletus c. 450 B.C.); Hipparchus, son of Charmus (Lyc. *Against Leocrates* 117); Antiphon and Archeptolemus (Craterus at Plut. *Mor.* 833d–834b); Phrynichus (Craterus *FGH* 342 F17); Athenian supporters of King Cleomenes (scholiast to Arist. *Lys.* 273).

20 For the silent consent of the community, see Allen (2000) 197–98, 223. See esp. 203: "The community's networks of social knowledge and social memory were the executioner of reputation not only in the city's public spaces but also across time — some of the force of punishment lay in its guarantee that a wrongdoer would be remembered precisely as a wrongdoer; the city's narrative of his life and not the wrongdoer's would be what persisted in the social memory."

21 For the dedication of Peisistratus in 521 B.C., see *ML* 11, Jeffrey (1990) 78 no. 37 pl. 4, Thuc. 6.54.6. Lavelle ([1993] 76) speaks misleadingly of deliberate effacement, but it may be that the letters were not recolored with red. For the Peisistratids in general, see Stein-Hölkeskamp (1989), de Libero (1996), and Sancisi-Weerdenburg (2000).

22 *Me mnesikakein*: Her. 8.29; Thuc. 4.74, 8.73; Arist. *Lys.* 590; Dem. 18.96, 23.193; Lys. 18.19, 30.9; Ant. 2.1.6; And. 1.81, 95; Xen. *Hell.* 2.4.43; Isocr. 14.14 with Loraux (2002) 149 and Wolpert (2002) 76–84. See Her. 6.21 for the ban on Phrynichus' play about the sack of Miletus as bringing back a distressing memory of sorrow. For *medena medeni mnasicholesai*, see *SEG* 25.447.

23 For *amnestia*, see *SIG*³ 633 of c. 180 B.C.

24 For Athens and the Bottiaians, see *IG* 1³ 76 lines 15–16, 20–21 (422 B.C.). For Athens

and Iulis, see Tod 142 lines 58–62 (362 B.C.) with Te Riele (1967). For Aliphera, see *SEG* 25.447 lines 4–5 (late third century B.C.).

25 For Poseidon and Athena, see Plut. *Mor.* 489 b–c and 741 a–b (Altar of Lethe at the Erechtheium) with Loraux (2002) 41, 153, 171–90. For the west pediment of the Parthenon, see A. Stewart (1990) 151–54 with figs. 354–60 and Lagerlöf (2000) 48–60.

26 See Aes. *Eum.* 382–83 with Loraux (2002) 30–41.

27 For the amnesty of 403 B.C., see *Ath. Pol.* 38.3–40.4, Xen. *Hell.* 2.4.38 and *IG* 2² 10, Tod 100, *SEG* 12.84 (= Harding [1985] no. 3) for the modest rewards for the liberators. For discussion, see Allen (2000) 237–42, Loraux (2002) esp. 145–69 and 245–64, and now esp. Wolpert (2002) 84 (who calls it "a kind of erasure of the past from civic memory"). For the earlier amnesty on Samos, see Thuc. 8.73.6. For the Thirty, see Krentz (1982).

28 Wolpert (2002) 48–71 reviews the main lawcourt speeches and the different points of view that they represent.

29 For the character of fourth-century Athenian democracy, see esp. Ostwald (1986) and Hansen (1991).

30 For the epigraphic habits of various Greek cities, see R. Thomas (1995). For Athens, see Habicht (1997) 71 and Hedrick (1999); for Sparta, see Millender (2001). Allen (2000) 241 notes that the *demos* controlled writing and memory in public spaces.

31 For erasure in Greek inscriptions, see Guarducci (1967) 1.485–86 and Woodhead (1981) 9. Loraux (2002) 15: "Nothing is more official than an erasure." For destruction of whole *stelai*, see *IG* 1³ 236–41 (restorations after the revolution of 411), Tod 98, Woodhead (1948), and *SEG* 14.35, 40 (for the destruction caused by the Thirty Tyrants). For discussion of the Thirty, see esp. Wolpert (2002) 15–24, 37. For the erasure of the Athenian sacrificial calendar, see Ostwald (1986) 479–80, Robertson (1990), and Rhodes (1991).

32 For Euphron of Sicyon, see *IG* 2² 448 = *SIG*³ 310 (Harding [1985] no. 123A) with Habicht (1997) 45–49.

33 For the Delphi charioteer inscription, see Jeffrey (1990) 266, pl. 51.9 (Delphi Mus. 3517). The two texts have been tentatively dated to 478 and 460 B.C. respectively. Seven dedications made by the Deinomenid brothers (Gelon, Hieron, and Polyzelus) are attested at Delphi and Olympia, see Jeffrey (1990) 266–67, 460, 275 nos. 5–9. The great Panhellenic sanctuaries could serve to memorialize previous alliances and former leaders; see Paus. 2.3.14–16.

34 The erasure of a title could also be left standing, as in the multiple erasures of the name of the Athenian general Timotheus in a fourth-century Athenian naval catalog (*IG* 2² 1606). After Timotheus' name, his title as general (*strategos*) has been removed. Timotheus was exiled twice; in 372 he joined Artaxerxes II, and he died soon after being exiled a second time shortly after 357/6.

35 For Pausanias and Spartan attempts to denigrate his memory, see Thuc. 1.128–35, [Dem.] 59.98, *ML* 27 = Fornara 59 (Istanbul), with Hornblower (1991) *ad loc.*, and Allen (2000) 218.

36 For the treaties, see *ML* 63 (Rhegium) and *ML* 64 (Leontini) of 433/2 B.C. *IG* 1³ 21 has the last two lines erased in a treaty about Miletus of 450/49 B.C.

37 For Athens and Neapolis, see *ML* 89 lines 7–8 of 409–7 B.C.

38 For Dionysus Eleuthereus, see *IG* 2² 410 = *SIG*³ 289 (c. 330 B.C.) from the Theater of Dionysus at Athens. The erasure must date to a time when Eleutherai belonged to Boeotia rather than to Athens. Wilhelm (1943–47) notes that a word could be restored over plaster used to smooth over the erasure once an epithet was put back in place.

39 For the Second Athenian Confederacy of 378/77 B.C., see *IG* 2² 43 = *SIG*³ 147 = Tod 123 = Bengston (1975) 257 = Harding (1985) 35 (EM 10 397) with Accame (1941). Tod 123: "the most interesting epigraphic legacy of fourth-century Athens." For discussion, see Cawkwell (1981), Jehne (1994) 24–25 with n. 88, and Rhodes and Osbourne (2003) no. 22.

40 For the anti-tyranny law from Ilion, see *Illion* 25 with commentary and pls. 6–8 and Habicht (1970) 83. On the reuse of erased spaces in Greek inscriptions, see Loraux (2002) 151: "To erase in the Greek sense is to destroy by additional covering: they recoat the surface of a whitewashed official tablet, and once the lines condemned to disappear are covered up, space is available for a new text; similarly, they insert a correction with paint and brush on an inscribed stone, hiding the old letter with a new one."

41 For euergetism and the relationship between Greek cities and Hellenistic kings, see Billows (1995) esp. 70–80, and now Ma (1999) 179–242, esp. 225 for the ruler cult as creating "instant memory."

42 For the Hellenistic ruler cult, see Habicht (1970) esp. 236–42, Billows (1990) esp. 231–36, Cawkwell (1994), Badian (1996), M. A. Flower (1997) 258–62, and Ma (1999) 1–25.

43 The Athenians tried to persuade Demetrius to make war on the Aitolians in 290 B.C. (Athen. *Deipn.* 253b–f with Billows [1995] 75–76).

44 For the Teos inscriptions, see Herrmann (1965) 33–40, 51–85, pl. 1 (*SEG* 41.1003, I and II) and now Ma (1999) nos. 17 and 18 with translation and bibliography. For the letter of M. Valerius Messalla to the Teians in 193 B.C., see Ma (1999) no. 38.

45 For memory in the Teos inscriptions, see line 34 (the goddess *Mneme*) and lines 64–67: ". . . and in order that Queen Laodike should have, in addition to the honors given to her, other honors which not only contain gratitude in the present but also create memory for the rest of time . . ." (tr. Ma [1999]).

46 For Teos' change of politics after 190 B.C., despite their previous loyalty to Antiochus, see Ma (1999) 248–50.

47 For Philip II at Eresus and Ephesus, see Arrian *Anab.* 1.17.10 with Habicht (1970) 14–15, 186. The honors may have been restored by his son Alexander.

48 For the disgrace of Demetrius Poliorketes, see Plut. *Dem.* 30 and 46.1 and *IG* 7 2419 = *SIG*³ 337 (Thebes Museum) with Wilhelm (1943–47) and Habicht (1970) 187–89. For the removal of ruler cults, see Habicht (1970) 185–92.

49 For Philip V and Athens, see Habicht (1982) 142–58 and now Habicht (1997) 194–219. For Philip, see also Badian (1958) 55–95; Gruen (1984) 132–57, 373–402; Walbank (1984) 473–81; and Hammond and Walbank (1988) 317–36.

50 For the "freedom of the Greeks," see Gruen (1984) 132–57 and Billows (1990). For a dossier on kings and tyrants from Eresus in the later fourth century B.C., see Tod 191.

51 Livy 31.44.4–8: *rogationem extemplo tulerunt plebesque sciuit ut Philippi statuae et imagines omnes nominaque earum, item maiorum eius uirile ac muliebre secus omnium tollerentur delerenturque, diesque festi sacra sacerdotes, quae ipsius maiorumque eius honoris causa instituta essent, omnia profanarentur; loca quoque in quibus positum aliquid inscriptumue honoris causa fuisset detestabilia esse, neque in iis quicquam postea poni dedicarique placere eorum quae in loco puro poni dedicarique fas esset; sacerdotes publicos quotienscumque pro populo Atheniensi sociisque, exercitibus et classibus eorum precarentur, totiens detestari atque exsecrari Philippum liberos eius regnumque, terrestres naualesque copias, Macedonum genus omne nomenque. Additum decreto si quis quid postea quod ad notam ignominiamque Philippi pertineret ferret, id omne populum Atheniensem iussurum; si quis contra ignominiam proue honore eius dixisset fecissetue, qui occidisset eum iure caesurum. Postremo inclusum ut omnia quae aduersus Pisistratidas decreta quondam erant eadem in Philippo seruarentur. Athenienses quidem litteris verbisque, quibus solis ualent, bellum aduersum Philippum gerebant.* See also Briscoe (1973) *ad loc.* and [Dio Chrys.] *Or.* 37.41 and Paus. 1.36.5 and 2.9.4. For the ban on Macedonians in Attica, see Livy 41.23.1.

52 For the erasure of the Macedonian tribes at Athens, see *SEG* 14.64 (271/0 B.C.) = *ISE* 18 (photo at pl. 63 in *Hesperia* [1954]). Pritchett (1954) gives a list of demes from the acropolis that was left unfinished at this time. For the new honors for Attalus, see Ferguson (1911) 267 and Habicht (1997).

53 For the association of the Macedonian kings with Harmodius and Aristogeiton, see Habicht (1970) 191 and (1997) 68–69.

54 For an anachronistic equation between the Peisistratids and Philip V, see Lavelle (1993) esp. 76–79, who also sees Athenian sanctions in terms of erasure and oblivion, regardless of the testimony of the *stelai.*

55 The Altar of the Twelve Gods was not overbuilt until the third quarter of the fifth century B.C. (Lavelle [1993] 76). For the Athenian owls as a symbol of democracy, see now Shapiro (1993). For the culture of Peisistratid Athens in general, see Kolb (1977) and Shapiro (1989).

56 For the erasure of the names of the Macedonian kings at Athens, see the lists of Dow (1937) 48–50 and Habicht (1982) 148–49, esp. n. 137. Especially notable examples include *ISE* 25 (236/35), 28 (226/25); Chapoutier (1924); *SIG*³ 466; *IG* 2/32 677 (263/2), 682 (263/2), 780 (250/49). See also Habicht (1970) 189–90 and *SIG*³ 547 from Eleusis that shows erasure beyond what Livy implies. For the statue in the well, see *ISE* 7, Shear (1973) 165–68, pl. 36, and Habicht (1982) 148 n. 137. For the overstriking of bronze coins, see M. Thompson (1981) 354.

57 For the Athenian curses, see Briscoe (1973), commenting on Livy 31.44.

58 For the outbreak of the Second Macedonian War, see *OGIS* 283, Pol. 16.1 and 25.4–6, 26.6–8, Livy 31.2.1 and 15.1–6 with Gruen (1984) 21–22, 392–95, Errington (1989) 255–58, Ma (1999) 79–105. The chronology has now been reconstructed in detail by Warrior (1996), who notes that Livy has obscured the role of the Roman ambassadors in Greece and the East. They were C. Claudius Nero (cos. 207), P. Sempronius Tuditanus (cos. 204), and M. Aemilius Lepidus.

59 For Rome's old grudges against Philip V, see Gruen (1984) 382–98.

60 For Aemilius Paullus and the monument of Perseus at Delphi, see chapter 3.

61 For the inscription from Stratonikeia, see *IStrat.* 9 with Ma (1999) 236, 249 and photo at Roos (1975) pl. 60.3. Cf. also Ma (1999) 252 and no. 22 for the consecration of the city of Xanthos to Leto, Apollo, and Artemis by Antiochus III in 197 B.C. The inscription was completely erased, probably by the Carians, although the text is still legible.

62 See esp. Purcell (1995) 144–48 for Rome's role as a Hellenistic power that could control and impose its own narrative of explanation. For memories of Greece as a Roman province, see Alcock (1993, 2002).

Chapter III

1 The study of memory sanctions was decisively affected by the magisterial study of Vittinghoff (1936), who chose to start his doctoral dissertation with M. Antonius since his subject was the imperial period.

2 See now the detailed treatment in Varner (2004).

3 For Greek influences in Rome, see Ferrary (1988), Gruen (1990, 1992), Vogt-Spira and Rommel (1999), and Purcell (2003).

4 Purcell (1995) 145–46 discusses Rome's power to impose a narrative on others. Cf. Ma (1999) for the discarded and erased texts of Antiochus III (the Great), one of Rome's victims.

5 For the growth of the city of Rome in the Republic, see Kolb (1995) 175–249 and Scheidel (2001). For new ideas about the republican demographic context, see now Rosenstein (2004).

6 For the life-styles of the ancestors, as viewed by their descendants, see Hölkes-kamp (1996), Braun, Haltenhoff, and Mutschler (2000), and Linke and Stemmler (2000).

7 Flower (1998) discusses the role and status of the family in the *Senatus Consultum de Cn. Pisone patre* of A.D. 20.

8 For the origins of Roman historical writing, see Bucher (1987/1995), Verbrugghe (1989), Timpe (1996), Marincola (1999), Walter (2001), and Purcell (2003).

9 For Appius Claudius Caecus, see Linke (2000) and Humm (2005).

10 For early Roman historical writing, see Badian (1966), Cornell (1986), Oakley (1997) 21–110, Forsythe (2000), and now Eigler et al. (2003). For the fragments of the first historians, see Beck and Walter (2001) with its incisive introduction. Saller (1991) sees the early history of Rome as an insoluble problem. See also Wiseman (1996) for a critique of Cornell (1995), which he describes as "systematically opti-mistic" about the extant sources for early Rome.

11 The negative image of the monarchy in republican Rome has been studied in de-tail by P. Martin (1982). Mustakallio (1994) 24–28 links the first use of postmor-tem sanctions with the expulsion of the kings. Cornell (1995) 148 discusses the "almost pathological dislike" of kings during the Republic. For the tradition of violence and its association with sanctions in early Rome, see Lintott (1970) 12–13, 24–29.

12 For an overview of sanctions in early Rome, see the useful charts in Mustakallio

(1994) 90–91 and Vigourt (2001a) 285. For the differences between Livy and Dionysius (for Cassius and Maelius), see Valvo (1975). Dionysius' account of Manlius only survives in small fragments. For the construction of the three traitors, see esp. Chassignet (2001) and Vigourt (2001b).

13 For Maelius in Cincius Alimentus and Piso, see Dion. 12.4.2–5 (F6 Cincius, F 24 Piso in Peter [1914], F8 in Beck and Walter [2001] 142–43) with Forsythe (2000) 3. Cornell (1986) 58–62 argues for the authenticity of a basic historical core in this elaborated tradition.

14 The association of the three with each other as canonical examples is first attested in Cicero (*Dom.* 101; *Phil.* 2.87, 114; *Rep.* 2.49) and not in the republican annalists (Chassignet [2001] 87–88). See Mommsen (1871); Münzer in *RE* for each individual; P. Martin (1982) 354–58; Panitschek (1989) 232–33; P. Martin (1990) 50–52, 67–69; and Vigourt (2001a).

15 See chapters 4 and 5 for the later Republic.

16 For the effect of the Gracchi, Sulla, and Catiline on the history of early Rome, see Lintott (1970) 22; Valvo (1983); Gutberlet (1985); Nippel (1988) 81–87; Oakley (1997) 86–88, 481–82; and Chassignet (2001). Oakley (1997) 482: "In a society so conscious of precedent, it was inevitable that the stories of Cassius, Maelius, and Manlius should be cited in the context of these accusations and refashioned in annalistic accounts so as to reflect more modern politics."

17 For social and economic problems in early Rome, see P. Martin (1990) 55–62 (with responses by Harris and Raaflaub at 87–88) and Cornell (1995) 265–71. Cornell (1995) 150 sees *adfectatio regni* as a charge that described elite mavericks who were helping the poor.

18 See Lovisi (1999) esp. 26–28, 54–56, 176–77, 223 who sees traditions about the three canonical traitors as hopelessly corrupt.

19 For Sp. Cassius, see Cic. *Rep.* 2.60 (= Fabius Pictor) Livy 2.41; Dion. 8.68–80, esp. 78–79; Val. Max. 5.8.2, 6.3.2 and 16; Diod. 11.37.7; Dio 5.19; Flor. 1.17.25. Cassius appears in the *fasti* as consul in 502, 493, 486 but all known later Cassii are plebeians. For discussion, see Gabba (1964, 1966); Ogilvie (1965) 337–45; Lintott (1970) 18–22; Wiseman (1979a) 74–75; Drummond (1989) 175, 183–84, 206–7; Cornell (1989b) 264–81; de Cazenove (1989); Panitschek (1989) 234–37; P. Martin (1990) 49–72; Cantarella (1991) 148–49; Mustakallio (1994) 30–38; Cornell (1995) 253–55, 263, 271; Liou-Gille (1996) 170–78. Ogilvie (1965) 339 sees "no foundation in fact or legend."

20 For the temple of Tellus, see Ogilvie (1965) 345, Lintott (1970) 20, Ziolkowski (1992) 155–62, and Coarelli in *LTUR* 1999.

21 For Cassius' inscription on a statue (*ex Cassia familia*), see Livy 2.41.10, Dion. 8.79, Val. Max. 5.8.2, Pliny *NH* 34.15 with Coarelli in *LTUR* 1993 for the temple of Ceres, Liber, and Libera. For the statue of Cassius himself in front of the temple of Tellus, see Pliny *NH* 34.30 with Sehlmeyer (1999) 79–81 who interprets the notice as a misrepresentation of an ancient cult image. It is hard to see how Cassius' statue could have survived the Gallic sack.

22 For Sp. Maelius, see Cic. *Dom.* 101, *Div.* 2.17.39; Varro *LL* 5.157; Livy 4.13–16; Dion. 12.2–4; Diod. 12.37.1; Val. Max. 6.3.1c; Quint. 3.7.20; *vir ill.* 17. Maelius is not men-

tioned in the consular or triumphal *fasti*. Ogilvie (1965) 550–57 sees the killing of Maelius, designated as a *homo sacer* by Ahala, as the core of the story, which was then elaborated to reflect events in the time of the Gracchi and the Ides of March (esp. in Dion.). Lintott (1970) 13–18 notes that the *cognomen* Ahala is already attested for the consul of 478. Garnsey (1988) 171: "The authentic core of this multi-layered fabrication defies identification." For further discussion, see esp. Valvo (1975), Garnsey (1988) 167–77, Panitschek (1989) 237–41, Salerno (1990) 84–87, Mustakallio (1994) 39–47, Cornell (1995) 268, and Liou-Gille (1996) 178–85. For the *Aequimelium*, see Pisani Sartorio in *LTUR* 1993. On the Minucii, see Wiseman (1998a).

23 For M. Manlius Capitolinus, see Claud. Quadrig. F7–8 (Peter [1914]), Cic. *Dom.* 101, Livy 6.11–20, Dion. 14.4, Diod. 15.35.3, Val. Max. 6.3.1a, Quint. 3.7.20, Gell. 17.21.24–25 (Varro and Nepos), Plut. *Cam.* 36.1–9, App. *Ital.* 9, Dio (Zon.) 7.26, *vir ill.* 24.5–7. For discussion, see Lintott (1970) 22–24; Wiseman (1979b) who blames Antias for the confusions in Livy; Cantarella (1991) 206–7; Jaeger (1993) and (1997) 57–93; Mustakallio (1994) 48–58; Kraus (1994) 146–219; Cornell (1995) 317, 330–31; Liou-Gille (1996) 186–93; and Oakley (1997) 476–92 who discusses Manlius cast as Catiline. Cornell (1989) 331: "The surviving accounts of this obscure event are unreliable and highly elaborated rhetorical narratives." For the Gallic sack, see now von Ungern-Sternberg (2000).

24 For the *cognomen* Capitolinus as used by various patrician families (Manlii, Quinctii, Maelii, ?Tarpeii), see Livy 6.20.13 (cf. 5.31.2) with Horsfall (1981) and Kraus (1994) *ad loc.* Valvo (1984) connects the obsolescence of the name with the rebuilding of the Capitol as a sacred area after the Gallic sack. In other words, there is no compelling reason to see this change of name in terms of a punishment.

25 For Manlius' house and the temple of Juno Moneta, see Giannelli (1980/1981) and in *LTUR* 1995, Ziolkowski (1992) 71–73 and (1993), Purcell (1993), Oakley (1997) 566–67, and now Meadows and Williams (2001). The earliest extant version of the sack in Ennius (*Ann.* 7.227–28 with Skutsch [1985] *ad loc.*) has the Gauls capture the Capitol with no Manlius in sight. For the house of Titus Tatius, see Plut. *Rom.* 20.5, Solin. 1.21.

26 For the ban on *praenomina*, see Livy 6.20.14 (Manlius) and Suet. *Tib.* 1–2 (Claudii) with Tac. *Ann.* 3.17.8 (Piso).

27 For the impact of Manlius' disgrace, see Cornell (1989) 324–25, but 332: "This romance was spun out of a very few authentic facts." Jaeger (1997) 87: "Like all acts of *damnatio memoriae*, this one calls attention to the fact of obliteration." Vigourt (2001a) 282–83 suggests that Dio (7.26) has assimilated Manlius' fall to the harsh sanctions imposed on Geta, which Dio himself had witnessed. Cic. *Sul.* 27 suggests that in 62 B.C. the Manlii Torquati were displaying an ancestor mask of Capitolinus without any hesitation.

28 For the destruction of the house in early Rome, see Ogilvie (1965) 345, Mustakallio (1994) 10, and Bodel (1997) 6–9. See Coarelli in *LTUR* 1995 for a discussion of the house of Publicola on the Velia, whose site is occupied by the basilica of Constantine. For the land of the Tarquins consecrated to Mars as the *Campus Martius*, see Livy 2.5 and Plut. *Publ.* 8. For Vitruvius Vaccus, see Cic. *Dom.* 101 and Livy

8.19–21 with P. Martin (1990) 65–66, 68, Mustakallio (1994) 59–64, and Papi in *LTUR* 1995.

29 For the razing of houses in Greece, see Connor (1985) and chapter 2.

30 Mustakallio (1994) figure 2 illustrates a topography of disgrace in Rome. For discussion, see Nippel (1988) 81 who argues that the topography in itself serves to confirm the authenticity of early memory sanctions. Vigourt (2001a) 279: "Le lien existant entre l'emplacement d'une maison et un monument est un lien 'psychologique': à un moment donné ou peut-être en une lente élaboration, les Romains ont été amenés à considerer que la maison de Cassius avait été là où se voyait désormais le parvis du Temple de la Terre, que celle de Manlius avait été là où s'élevait le temple de Junon Moneta; c'était perpétuer leur souvenir."

31 For the *nobiles*, see Gelzer (1912/1975), Hölkeskamp (1987) and (1993).

32 See now Hölkeskamp (2004).

33 For sumptuary legislation, see Clemente (1981), Baltrusch (1989) 127–31, and Wyetzner (2002).

34 For the censors and the oversight of morals, see Livy 4.8, 39.42.6, 42.10.4, 45.15.8; Festus 290L. For discussion, see Schmähling (1938), Suolahti (1963) 47–52, Nicolet (1976) 71–121, Astin (1988) 32, and Baltrusch (1989) 5–30.

35 For erasure from the censors' list and the *nota*, see now Meyer (2004) 93.

36 For defeated generals, see Rosenstein (1990).

37 For memory and politics, see Flower (1996), Walter (2002), and Flaig (2003) esp. 69–98.

38 For the concept of *nobilitas*, see Flower (1996) 60–70 and Goldmann (2002) with very full bibliography.

39 For the monuments and material culture of the *nobiles*, see Hölscher (1978), (1980), and (2001); Lahusen (1989); and esp. Hölkeskamp (2001) with full bibliography.

40 For the *imagines* of the Roman officeholders, see Flaig (1995) and (2003) 49–68 and Flower (1996) and (2006).

41 For ancestors on Roman coins, see Zehnacker (1973) 477–627, 969–1081 and Flower (1996) 79–88, 333–38. For family and memory, see Mustakallio (1994) 77–81.

42 For the distortion of history in family traditions, see esp. Cic. *Brut.* 62 and Livy 8.40.3–5 (cf. 22.31.8–11) with Flower (1996) 145–50.

43 Zevi (*LTUR* 1999) estimates that the tomb of the Scipios probably contained about thirty-five adults, over four to five generations, of whom we have eleven attested by inscriptions in the tomb itself, and about twenty in other sources, although some family members (such as Scipio Africanus) were not buried in the family grave. These totals include only two known women.

44 For the sarcophagus of L. Cornelius Scipio Barbatus, see *CIL* 6.8.3.284 (= 31587 with full bibliography and stemma) = *ILS* 1 = *ILLRP* 309 with Degrassi (1965) no. 132, Wachter (1987) 301–42, Flower (1996) 170–77, and Zevi *LTUR* (1999) for the tomb.

45 For P. Scipio, *flamen Dialis*, see *CIL* 6.8.3.1288 = 37039 p. 3134 = *CLE* 8 = *ILS* 4 = *ILLRP* 311 with Degrassi (1965) no. 134, Moir (1986) and (1988), Tatum (1988), Flower (1996) 167–68, and Chioffi in *CIL* 6.8.3. Kruschwitz (1999) argues against the addition of the line at the top but without any alternate explanation or any detailed discussion of the physical aspects of the inscription.

46 See *RE* 331 (Münzer) for the augur of 180 B.C. (Livy 40.42.13). For his bad health, see Cic. *Brut.* 77, *Cat.* 35, *Off.* 1.121.

47 Livy 38.55.9–12.

48 For the disgrace of Africanus, see Livy 38.50–60 with Gruen (1995).

49 For Lucius Scipio being deprived of his ring, see Livy 41.27.2, Val. Max. 3.5.1 with Suolahti (1963) 48 and Flower (1996) 87–88.

50 For the family traditions of the patrician Claudii, see Wiseman (1979a) and (1994a), Vasaly (1987), Kavanagh (1990), and Tatum (1999) 32–33.

51 For memories of Marcellus, see Flower (2000) and (2003).

52 For Livy and Marcellus' death, see Caltabiano (1975), Carawan (1984–85), and Flower (2003) 48–51.

53 For other examples of booty, see esp. Q. Fabius Maximus at Tarentum: Pol 9.10; Cic. *Rep.* 5.10; Livy 25.40.1–2, 26.21.7–8, 27.16.8; Plut. *Marc.* 21, *Fab.* 19, 22 with Gros (1979); Ferrary (1988) 573–78, 581–82; Fabbrini (2001). For another ambush, see Tiberius Sempronius Gracchus (*RE* 51, cos. 215, 213) Polyb. 8.35, Sall. *Jug.* 42.1, Livy 25.15.10–17, Dio 44.30.4 with Pelling (1989) and Swain (1990).

54 For magistrates and games, see Nicolet (1976) 456–505 and F. Bernstein (1998). Writing was subject to fewer formal restrictions since it tended in any case to be limited to the elite.

55 For Kineas in the Roman senate, see Plut. *Pyrrh.* 19 with Purcell (1995) 145 on Romans as Hellenistic kings. See Hölscher (1990) for the archaeological evidence. For Africanus' life-style see Polyb. 31.26 with Schwarte (2000).

56 For L. Aemilius Paullus (*RE* 114) at Delphi, see *CIL* 1.622 = *ILS* 8884 = *ILLRP* 323 with Polyb. 30.10, Livy 25.27.6, Plut. *Aem.* 28.4, and Alcock (1993) 196–98 on annexing monuments. Other texts were also inscribed later on the monument. The riderless horse refers to the famous start to the battle. For discussion, see Kähler (1965); de Maria (1988) figs. 1–3, 34, 39–40; D. Kleiner (1992) 26–27, pl. 5; Holliday (2002) 91–96. Budde (1973) 801–2 notes the novel design and attributes it to the Athenian artist Metrodoros, who is attested as working for Paullus. For Paullus' life, see now Flaig (2000).

57 For the destruction of Corinth and Carthage, see Ridley (1986), Piccaluga (1988), Kallett-Marx (1995) 84–94, and esp. Purcell (1995). Aemilianus compared Carthage to Troy (cf. Polyb. 38.1 and 19–22, App. *Pun.* 132). Purcell (1995) 138: "His famous vision of the transience of power is a clear bid to put Rome on the map of historical culture." For the symbolism of Hellenistic city destruction, see Connor (1985) 97–99.

58 For the patrician Manlii, see Baltrusch (1989) 7–8.

59 Cic. *Sull.* 27.

60 For D. Junius Silanus in 140 B.C., see Cic. *Fin.* 1.7.24, Livy *Per.* 54, *Oxy. Per.* 54, Val. Max. 5.8.3, Sen. *Contr.* 2.3.18, Plut. *Mar.* 12.2 with Rosenstein (1990) no. 43 (cf. No. 44), Flower (1996) 218, and Bodel (1999b) 260: "He earned a reputation not only for severity but also for a perverse obstinacy." Silanus' son was consul in 109 B.C., his grandsons may be the consul of 62 B.C. and the praetor of 77 B.C.

61 Perhaps Silanus was buried by a freedman of his father Torquatus. Alternatively, he may have been buried by his adoptive family the Junii, or by one of their freed-

men. It would be interesting to know if the plebeian Junii were less severe in their treatment of his memory than the patrician Manlii.

62 The *quaestio de rebus repetundis*, established in 149 B.C. by a *lex Calpurnia* (L. Calpurnius Piso Frugi, *RE* 96, the historian and consul of 133 B.C.), was the first permanent criminal jury court in Rome. It was overseen by a praetor and had a senatorial jury. Its purpose was to control the behavior of provincial governors. See Cic. *Brut.* 106, *Verr.* 2.3.195, 2.4.56, *Off.* 2.75; Schol. Bob. 96S; Val. Max. 6.9.10; Tac. *Ann.* 15.20.

Chapter IV

1 See Cic. *De Rep.* 1.19.31, Vell. Pat. 2.3.3, Plut. *TGracch.* 20, App. *BC* 1.2, 1.17 with Syme (1939) 16, Ungern-Sternberg von Pürkel (1970) 1, Badian (1972) 677, Bernstein (1978) 228, Binot (2001) 202, Linderski (2002) 339, Christ (2002) 45–46. Sources for the period from 133 to 70 B.C. can be found in Greenidge and Clay (1960), full references are in *MRR*.

2 For *patria potestas*, see Voci (1980), Saller (1987, 1994), Cantarella (1991) 129–57.

3 The pairing is suggested by Plutarch's arrangement of their biographies. Burckhardt (1988) 40 decides to treat them together in order to bring out the reaction of the *nobiles* more clearly. Nippel (1988) 71–78 puts the Gracchi with Saturninus, and therefore argues (79–87) that the legal issues stayed essentially the same.

4 For the events of 121 B.C., see Cicero *In Cat.* 1.2.4, 4.5.10; *Phil.* 8.4.14; Sall. *Jug.* 16.2, 31.7, 42.1; Livy *Per.* 61; Diod. 34.28a; Vell. Pat. 2.6.4–7, 2.7; Pliny *NH* 33.3.48; Plut. *CGracch.* 13–18; App. *BC* 1.25–26; *vir ill.* 65; Oros. 5.12. The most useful discussions include Ungern-Sternberg von Pürkel (1970) 55–67; Stockton (1979) 176–205; Burckhardt (1988) 135–41; Nippel (1988) 71–79, 84; and Lintott (1994) 77–86.

5 The price on heads was highly unusual at the time: Cic. *De Or.* 2.67.269, Diod. 34.29, Val. Max. 9.4.3, Vell. Pat. 2.6.5, Pliny *NH* 33.48, Plut. *CGracch.* 17, App. *BC* 1.26, *vir ill.* 65.6, Flor. 2.3, Oros. 5.12.9. See also Ungern-Sternberg von Pürkel (1970) 66 and Stockton (1979) 197.

6 Plut. *TGracch.* 19 with Linderski (2002) 353.

7 For Scaevola (*RE* 17 Kübler) in 133 B.C., see esp. Ungern-Sternberg von Pürkel (1970) 4 and Badian (1972) 711. Astin (1967) 228 attributes the senate's policies after Tiberius' death to Scaevola, but doubts that Cicero is right in claiming that Scaevola approved Nasica's actions after the fact (*Dom.* 91, *Planc.* 88). Note App. *BC* 1.16, who wonders why a dictator was not appointed. The answer must surely be that there was a perfectly competent consul in charge and that he had expressed his considered opinion based on the law.

8 Cic. *Cat.* 1.1.3: *P. Scipio pontifex maximus Ti. Gracchum mediocriter labefactantem statum rei publicae privatus interfecit . . .* (Publius Scipio, the chief priest but not a magistrate in office, killed Tiberius Gracchus, who was causing some disturbance in the state of the commonwealth). See also Livy *Per.* 58 (*auctore P. Cornelio Nasica* [on the authority of Publius Cornelius Nasica]), Val. Max. 3.2.17, and App. *BC* 1.16. For Nasica, see now Binot (2001), who notes (198–99) that the fathers of Nasica

and Tiberius had already been political opponents, although they were married to the two daughters of Scipio Africanus.

9 For the corpses thrown into the river, see Val. Max. 1.4.2 (Nepos), 4.7.1, 6.3.1d; Vell. Pat. 2.6.7; Plut. *TGracch.* 20.3 (cf. *CGracch.* 3.3); Livy *Per.* 58; App. *BC* 1.16; Oros. 5.9; *vir ill.* 64.8 with Astin (1967) 227; Badian (1972) 727; and Lea Beness (2000) 1–2.

10 Plut. *TGracch.* 20.4 claims that Tiberius' body was denied to a brother (*adelphos*) who made the request on behalf of the family on the evening of the same day. Astin (1967) 227 is mistaken that this was Gaius, who was in Spain at the time. Stockton (1979) 87 simply assumes that Plutarch has made a mistake. Yet, is this another brother of Tiberius, who must, therefore, have been older than Gaius, who was the youngest sibling? Or is it a cousin? Note that there had already been disturbances earlier in that year at the funeral of one of Tiberius' followers (Plut. *TGracch.* 13.4–5).

11 Tiberius' death has been interpreted in many different ways. Astin's argument ([1967] 218–24) that the death was an accident in a riot that nobody could later admit to, has been followed by Bernstein (1978) 224–25 and Stockton (1979) 75–77. By contrast Ungern-Sternberg von Pürkel (1970) 16–19, followed by Meier (1979) 50, see Nasica as leading an *evocatio*, albeit an illegal one. Nippel (1988) 71–75, 80 thinks Nasica had no real plan but had an *evocatio* in mind. Lintott (1994) 72 interprets the declaration of war in a Greek context of tyrant slaying but calls it "private violence" (84). Binot (2001) 193–94 claims that Nasica did not intend to kill Tiberius, but did plan a violent confrontation.

12 For the consul Piso in Sicily, see Livy, *Per.* 58; Val. Max. 2.7.9, 4.3.10; Front. *Strat.* 4.1.26; and esp. Oros. 5.9.6. *CIL* 10.8063 is a slingshot from the siege of Henna inscribed with the consul's name. Piso captured Morgantina, crucifying any fugitive slaves he caught, and then started the Roman siege of Henna, the headquarters of the rebels.

13 For the trials of the followers of Tiberius in 133–32, see Cic. *Amic.* 37, Sall. *Jug.* 31.7, Val. Max. 4.7.1, Vel. Pat. 2.7.3–4, Plut. *TGracch.* 20 with Nippel (1988) 82. Spaeth (1996) 77 and Lea Beness (2000) discuss the meaning of the snakes in the ritual execution of P. Villius.

14 For the so-called Bacchanalian conspiracy, see Paillier (1986) and Gruen (1990).

15 For Nasica's embassy to Pergamum in 132 B.C., see Cic. *Rep.* 1.3.6, Val. Max. 5.3.2e, Plut. *TGracch.* 21 and *ILS* 8886 = *ILLRP* 333. Astin (1967) 230 points out that Nasica's death was itself seen as an omen. Nasica was succeeded as *pontifex maximus* by P. Licinius Crassus Dives Mucianus (*RE* 72 Münzer), brother of Scaevola and an ally of Tiberius, most probably after Crassus had already been elected consul for 131. He himself went to Asia to fight the revolt of Aristonicus and was killed there. Crassus was succeeded as *pontifex maximus* by his brother Scaevola. For Nasica's statues, see Sehlmeyer (*LTUR* 1999).

16 For discussion of the prodigies both before and after Tiberius' death, see Nippel (1988) 81–82 and Rawson (1974) 151–53. For consultation of the Sybilline Books during the Republic (before the books were destroyed by a fire in 83 B.C.), see

Orlin (1997) 76–96, 203–7. See also Val. Max. 1.4.2, 5.3.2; Oros. 5.9; Florus 2.2, 3.14; Obseq. 27a (86); *vir ill.* 64.8.

17 Scipio Aemilianus apparently quoted a version of Athena's words about Orestes killing Aegisthus (*Od.* 1.47), suggesting that he may have supported Nasica's actions. See Cic. *De Orat.* 2.106, *Mil.* 8; Diod. 34/35.7.3 (Poseidonius); Val. Max. 6.2.3; Vell. Pat. 2.4.4; and Plut. *TGracch.* 21.7, who especially stresses how much this remark cost Aemilianus in political terms. For discussion, see Astin (1967) 226, 234 and Nippel (1988) 83.

18 For the ancient cult of Ceres at Henna, see Le Bonniec (1958) 283–86, 339–41 with Spaeth (1990) 194–95 and (1996) 74–79. Bradley (1989) 57 argues that Eunous would have presented the Syrian goddess as another form of Demeter, in order to appeal to the population of Henna. The slave revolt in Sicily is mainly attested in the fragments of Diodorus 34/35, probably relying on Poseidonius. Eunous, a Syrian slave from Apamea, was a prophet, diviner, fire-breather, and devotee of the Syrian goddess. He called himself King Antiochus and his followers were known as the "Syrians." He also seems to have provided some inspiration for Aristonicus and his rebel slaves around Pergamum. See Greenidge and Clay (1960) 284 for a bronze coin of "King Antiochus" with an ear of wheat on it. See Brennan (1993) and Shaw (2001) 12–13, 79–106 for sources, discussion, and bibliography.

19 The chronology of the slave revolt in Sicily is unclear. *MRR* 483 n. 1 dates its beginning as early as 139 B.C. It was brought to an end by the consul P. Rupilius (*RE* 5 Münzer) in 132 B.C., who then reorganized the province, with a commission of ten senators, as if it was a new conquest (Diod. 34.2.20–23; Livy *Per.* 59; Val. Max. 2.7.3, 6.9.8, 9.12.ext.1; Oros. 5.9.7). The crisis point seems to have come in the years 133 and 132, accompanied by much loss of life. Eunous was captured when his capital, Henna, was taken by siege, and he died in prison at Morgantina. Rupilius may have celebrated a triumph, but he died not long after his return to Rome (before Aemilianus in 129). Spaeth (1990) is therefore mistaken that the Roman mission to Sicily took place in 133. Rather, it cannot have happened, or perhaps even been planned, before news reached Rome that Rupilius had recaptured Henna and its sanctuary of Ceres from the rebels in 132 B.C.

20 Cicero (*Verr.* 2.4.112) describes the traditional statue of Ceres at Henna as holding a goddess of Victory in her hand.

21 For Tiberius' remarks, see App. *BC* 1.9. Badian (1972) 679, 684–85, 689 and Kolb (1995) 227–39 discuss the probable impact of the slave revolt on the grain supply arriving in Rome.

22 Le Bonniec (1958) 367–70 discusses the general appeasement of Ceres for Eunous' sacrilege, as well as keeping the Roman plebs and the Sicilians happy, without exploring the direct connection with Tiberius' death that is suggested in the sources. Spaeth (1990) 193–95 links Ceres' anger to the fact that Tiberius' goods had not been consecrated to the goddess because of the power of his family.

23 For defeats and the gods, see Rosenstein (1990) 54–91.

24 For the work of the Gracchan land commission, see Val. Max. 7.2.6, Plut. *TGracch.* 21 with Gargola (1995) 147–74, esp. 159–62, and Lintott (1994) 73–77. Most of the work seems to have been done by 129 B.C., which also suggests that there was no

delay in putting the commission into operation after the death of Tiberius. Reelection to the office of tribune of the plebs was discussed in 131 B.C.: Cic. *Am.* 96, *De Orat.* 2.170; Livy *Per.* 59.

25 For the *consecratio* of Tiberius, see Badian (1971) 3–5 and (1972) 723–26; Spaeth (1990); and esp. now Linderski (2002). For the concept of the *homo sacer*, see Festus 424L; Livy 2.8.2, 3.55.7; Dion. 6.89.3; Pliny *NH* 18.3.13 with Ogilvie (1965) 343; Spaeth (1996) 69–73; and now esp. Lovisi (1999) 11–64.

26 Nasica had received the *cognomen* Serapio (seller of pigs or, more probably, slave of a pig seller) from the tribune C. Curatius during his consulship of 138 B.C. (Livy *Per.* 55, Val. Max. 9.14.3, Pliny *NH* 7.120.54, 21.7.10). The name, therefore, already advertised Nasica's clash with a tribune, five years before the events in 133. See Binot (2001) and Linderski (2002) 348. The aedile Lucretius was called Vispillo or Vespillo after the undertaker (slave) who disposed of the bodies of those who could not afford a funeral (Lea Beness [2000] 1). It is typical of Roman political culture that the family kept the name and passed it from one generation to the next without any apparent embarrassment.

27 For Ceres at Rome, see Le Bonniec (1958) and Spaeth (1996).

28 For Tiberius and his unconstitutional methods, see Astin (1967) 215–16, Badian (1972), Bernstein (1978) 198–225, Stockton (1979) 40–74, Lintott (1994) 62–77, and Bleicken (1999) 61–64, 189–99.

29 For early republican "tyrants" in Rome, see chapter 3.

30 For the memory sanctions imposed in 121 B.C., see especially the discussion of Nippel (1988) 85–87. Published speeches by both brothers survived and continued to circulate. For the bodies being unburied, see Val. Max. 1.4.2, 6.3.1d; Sen. *Marc.* 16.3. For the bodies in the river, see Vell. Pat. 2.6.7, Plut. *CGracch.* 17.7, App. *BC* 1.16, *vir ill.* 64.8, Flor. 2.3. Oros. 5.12.9 is the only source to suggest that Gaius' headless body was sent to his mother Cornelia at Misenum. For the ban on mourning by wives, and presumably other women in the family, see Plut. *CGracch.* 17.5. For confiscation of property, see Plut. *CGracch.* 17.5, App. *BC* 1.26, Oros. 5.12.9, Dig. 24.3.66. For the destruction of houses, see Cic. *Dom.* 102, Val. Max. 6.3.1c with Ungern-Sternberg von Pürkel (1970) 67. For the deaths of children, see Vell. Pat. 2.6.2, App. *BC* 1.26, and Oros. 5.12.9. For the annulling of Gaius' laws, see App. *BC* 1.27 with Meister (1974) and Christ (2002) 50–51. However, as Lintott (1994) 85 notes: "[The senate] could not erase what Gaius had done."

31 For Licinia's dowry, which seems to have been saved by (her uncle) Scaevola, see Plut. *CGracch.* 17.6, Dio 43.50.2, 47.14, *Dig.* 24.3.66 with Münzer (*RE* 180) and Stockton (1979) 198.

32 For Flaccus' house, see *LTUR* 1995 (Papi) with Cic. *Dom.* 38. The empty space was known as the *area Flacciana* (Val. Max. 6.3.1c). For Catulus' house, see Coarelli (*LTUR* 1995) with Cerrutti (1997) 422–24. *Contra* Berg (1997) 127 who argues that Flaccus' house was not destroyed but left in ruins.

33 For destruction of houses in early Rome, see chapter 3.

34 For Gaius Gracchus' house, see Eck (*LTUR* 1995) and Guilhembet (*LTUR* 1999) for the house on the Palatine that he presumes Gaius had inherited from his father Tiberius Gracchus (cos. 177 B.C.). Plutarch *CGracch.* 12.1 dates his move to near

the Forum after his return from Carthage, near the end of his life. The move was designed to stress his solidarity with the poor. See Purcell (*LTUR* 1995) 328 for possible locations Gaius may have moved to.

35 Plut. *CGracch.* 17.6, Oros. 5.12.9.

36 Plut. *CGracch.* 17.6. But see *Dig.* 24.3.66: *ea sententia Publii Mucii est: nam is in Licinnia Gracchi uxore statuit quod res dotales in ea seditione, qua Gracchus occisus erat perissent, ait, quia Gracchi culpa ea seditio facta esset, Licinniae praestari oportere* (This is the opinion of Publius Mucius. For he made the following ruling in the case of Licin(n)ia the wife of Gracchus with regard to the dowry goods that had been destroyed in the sedition, in which Gracchus was killed, because Gracchus was responsible for causing that sedition, restitution must be made to Licin(n)ia.). See App. *BC* 1.26 for attacks by the *demos* on the houses of Gracchus and Fulvius.

37 For Cornelia after 121 B.C., see Plut. *CGracch.* 19. For Sempronia after 121 B.C., see Rawson (1974) 163, Dettenhofer (1992) 775–76, and Flower (2002b) 176–77.

38 For the *lustrum* of the city, see App. *BC* 1.26 and Aug. *CD* 3.25–26 with Nippel (1988) 85. For the temple of Concord, and the neighboring basilica Opimia (Cic. *Sest* 140), built by L. Opimius before his disgrace and exile, see Ferroni (*LTUR* 1993) with full references. See Purcell (*LTUR* 1995) 325 for the location of these buildings at one end of, but technically outside, the Forum. Excavations have revealed no trace of the earlier temple attributed to Camillus and associated with the end of the Conflict of the Orders. Opimius' temple was built on a monumental scale and was completely new, including the massive podium. Opimius seems to have been the first to use travertine in a public building. The temple's birthday was 22 July, possibly a date significant in the fall of Gaius Gracchus. When the future emperor Tiberius restored the temple in A.D. 10, he changed its name to *Concordia Augusta* and its festival day to 16 January (the day the name Augustus had been adopted in 27 B.C.).

39 For temple building in the Republic, see Ziolkowski (1992) 193–234, 258–61, 307–10; Aberson (1994); and Orlin (1997) 18–33. Orlin discusses the situations in which temples were vowed, four-fifths of which were related to external military threats. The remaining fifth were responses to plagues, droughts, portents, or mutinies. He does not discuss either Camillus' or Opimius' temple to Concord. Had Opimius made a vow to the goddess, which might have assimilated Gaius to a foreign enemy?

40 See Plut. *CGracch.* 17.8–9 and Aug. *CD* 3.25.

41 For the posthumous honors paid to the Gracchi, see Plut. *CGracch.* 18.3. Classen (1963) 324, followed by Sehlmeyer (1999) 185–87, describes these as ordinary grave offerings. But see Alföldi (1971) 134–35 and (1973) 24, and Simon and Pina Polo (2000) 155–56, who think these honors were in the *vici*. Weinstock (1971) 295 argues that the honors for Marius Gratidianus in the *vici* are evidence for an ancient tradition, largely lost to us. Rawson (1974) 152–53, 163 dates the cult to 100 B.C. and associates it with Saturninus. Wiseman (1998b) and Lea Beness and Hillard (2001) are surely mistaken that there was a play (*fabula praetexta*) about the death of Gaius that was performed in Rome during the Republic.

42 For the fifteen extant Gracchan boundary stones, see now Campbell (2000) 452–53, with 468–71 for how boundary marking was done by the Romans during the Republic.

43 For plebeian culture, see Laurence (1994), Horsfall (2003), Flaig (2003) 13–31, and Morstein-Marx (2004) 119–59.

44 Simon and Pina Polo (2000) 154 interpret the cult of the Gracchi as a reaction to Opimius' temple of Concord.

45 For Opimius (*RE* 4 Münzer) after 121 B.C., see Cic. *De Orat.* 2.25.106, 2.30.132, *Part. Orat.* 30.104, *Brut.* 127–28, *Planc.* 70, *Sest.* 140 (conviction in 109); Livy *Per.* 61 (acquittal in 120) with Lintott (1994) 84–85, 89. Vell. Pat. 2.7.3 stresses the memory of his savagery (cf. Plut. *CGracch.* 18.2). He lived for many years in exile at Dyrrhachion. For discussion, see also Ungern-Sternberg von Pürkel (1970) 68–71, Bauman (1970) 50, Stockton (1979) 200, and Burckhardt (1988) 121–22.

46 For Saturninus (*RE* 29 Klebs) and his death in 100, see esp. Badian (1984), Lintott (1994) 95–103, and Cavaggioni (1998) 137–71. Burckhardt (1988) 141–49 stresses the real threat Saturninus and Glaucia posed to the state.

47 For Saturninus and his gangs, see Lintott (1994) 103: "It is important to recognize that their use of violence was a reasoned reaction to the defeat of the Gracchi by force." See also Kolb (1995) 239–43 for violence in Rome from the time of the Gracchi to Sulla. For the formation of the first triumvirate, see now Wiseman (1994a) 358–67.

48 For Saturninus and the memory of the Gracchi, see esp. *Ad Her.* 4.67: *Noli, Saturnine, nimium populi frequentia fretus esse: inulti iacent Gracchi* (Saturninus, do not trust too much to the crowd of ordinary people: the Gracchi lie unavenged). See also Cic. *Sest.* 101, Val. Max. 9.7.2, Oros. 5.17.3 with Badian (1972) 730–31 and (1984) 118, and Christ (2002) 51. For Equitius (*RE* 3 Münzer), see Nippel (1988) 58 and Cavaggioni (1998). For Sempronia at the *contio* in 101, see *II* 13.3 no. 16; Val. Max. 3.8.6, 9.7.1–2, 9.15.1; *vir ill.* 73.4; Flor. 2.4; Oros. 5.17 with Flower (2002b) 176–77.

49 For the statue of Tiberius Sempronius Gracchus (cos. 177 B.C.) in the Forum, see Plut. *CGracch.* 14.4–5 with Sehlmeyer (1999) 150–51, who dates the statue to the 170s B.C.

50 For the statue of Cornelia, mother of the Gracchi, see Coarelli (1978) dating it to 100 B.C., Chioffi (*LTUR* 1999) dating it to the Augustan period, and Flower (2002b) dating the statue to around 111 B.C.

51 For the portico of Q. Lutatius Catulus (cos. 102) on the Palatine, see Berg (1997) 127 and Papi (*LTUR* 1999), with Cic. *Dom.* 102 and Val. Max. 6.3.1c. For Clodius' subsequent erasure of Catulus' name, see Cic. *Dom.* 137.

52 For the sanctions imposed in 100 B.C., see Ungern-Sternberg von Pürkel (1970) 71–74 with Badian (1984) 130–33. For the confiscation of property, see Oros. 5.17.8–10. For Saturninus' legislation, see Cic. *Balb.* 48, *Leg.* 2.44 with Cavaggioni (1998) 168–71. For Saturninus' house, see Val. Max. 6.3.1c with Palombi (*LTUR* 1995). For Saturninus' head as a trophy, see *vir ill.* 73.

53 For the ban on Saturninus' portrait, see Cic. *Rab. Perd.* 24–25 and Val. Max. 8.1 damn. 3. For discussion, see Mommsen (1899/1955) 990; Vittinghoff (1936) 14, 17; and Rollin (1979) 157, 170–72.

54 For the trials of Sextus Titius (*RE* 23 Münzer) and Decianus, see Gruen (1968) 189–90 and Bauman (1970) 48–54. Badian (1984) 140 calls Titius and Decianus the last open supporters of Saturninus. Gregory (1994) 90 is clearly mistaken that Titius was keeping an *imago* mask of Saturninus in his house, since Saturninus was not entitled to such a mask in any case and Titius was most probably not his relative.

55 For Titius' career and agrarian legislation, see Cic. *De Orat.* 2.11.48, *Leg.* 2.14, 2.31; Val. Max. 8.1 damn. 3; Obseq. 46 with Burckhardt (1988) 150.

56 *MRR ad loc.* shows that neither the Gracchi nor Saturninus had held any curule office that would have granted them a mask after death.

57 For the politics of portraiture in the later second century B.C., see Rollin (1979) 151–63; Sehlmeyer (1999) 166–67, 196–97; and Simon and Pina Polo (2000).

58 For glass paste signets handed to political adherents, see Vollenweider (1955) and Flower (1996) 86–88.

59 For the *lex Appuleia de maiestate* of 103 B.C., see Cic. *De Or.* 2.25.107 with Bauman (1970) 1–15, 16–33, esp. 34–58. Bauman imagines that Saturninus' original law addressed both internal concerns over the abuse of magisterial power and failures of Roman generals on the battlefield against the Cimbri and Teutones. There is very little direct evidence.

Chapter v

1 For the debate over Sulla, see Diehl (1988) 211–25 for ancient authors and Christ (2002) 167–94 for Sulla's *Nachleben*. For modern scholarship, see Badian (1964) and (1970), Hantos (1988), Brennan (1992), and Hölkeskamp (2000). For Sulla's image, see Ramage (1991), Behr (1993), Barden Dowling (2000), Mackay (2000), and Thein (2002).

2 For the *hostis* declarations of 88 B.C., see Ungern-Sternberg von Pürkel (1970) 74–75, Nippel (1988) 91, Seager (1994) 171, and Christ (2002) 81.

3 For Marius' career, see Van Ooteghem (1964), Carney (1970), Evans (1994), and Lintott (1994) 86–103.

4 For Sallust and the *nobiles*, see Syme (1964) 16–28, 125–27. For Sallust and Sulla, see Rawson (1987) and Barden Dowling (2000) 313–16.

5 For the declaration of Sulla as a *hostis*, see Plut. *Sul.* 22; *Comp. Lys. and Sul.* 5; App. *BC* 1.73, 77, 81; *Mithr.* 51; Eutrop. 5.7.3. For discussion, see Ungern-Sternberg von Pürkel (1970) 78, Nippel (1988) 92, Behr (1993) 171–79, Seager (1994) 179, Thein (2002) 94–95, and Christ (2002) 90–92, 100–101. For Sulla's house, see Papi (*LTUR* 1995 under P. Cornelius Sulla, cos. 66 B.C.). For the destruction of the Bocchus monument, see Hölscher (1980) 369.

6 Q. Lutatius Catulus (cos. 102, *RE* 7 Münzer) was related, through his mother's second marriage, to the Julii Caesares. Sulla praised Catulus in his memoirs, as did Cicero at *Brut.* 132–34. For Catulus' temple of Fortuna Huiusce Diei (Largo Argentina temple B), see Gros (*LTUR* 1995) and Hinard (1987). For an older temple on the Palatine, see Coarelli (*LTUR* 1995). For the *vicus huiusce diei*, see Coarelli (*LTUR* 1999). It is interesting to note that Catulus managed to obtain most of the

booty after Vercellae (Plut. *Mar.* 27.6, Eutrop. 5.2.2), although he triumphed jointly with Marius. For the funeral of Popilia (probably in 102 B.C.), see Cic. *De Orat.* 2.44 with Flower (1996) 122. For Catulus' memoirs, see Cic. *Brut.* 132–33, Fronto *Ad Ver.* 2.1.17 with Peter (1914) 191–94.

7   For libations poured to Marius after Vercellae (30 July 101 B.C.) as third founder of Rome, see Val. Max. 8.15.7, Plut. *Mar.* 27.9 with Classen (1963) 327–29, Simon and Pina Polo (2000), and Thein (2002) 14–15. Marius triumphed in 104 B.C. over Jugurtha (Sall. *Jug.* 114, Livy *Per.* 67, Plut. *Mar.* 12), and in 101 B.C. over the Celts (Plut. *Mar.* 27, Livy *Per.* 68, *ILS* 59). For Marius' trophies, see Sehlmeyer (1999) 192–93 and Reusser (*LTUR* 1999). For Marius' temple of Honos and Virtus, see Palombi (*LTUR* 1996). Vitruv. 3.2.5–6 suggests that it resembled the porticus of Metellus, Marius' former commander and rival. Marius also built a house near the Forum, perhaps next to his temple (Plut. *Mar.* 32.1). There seems to be confusion in the sources about Marius' building activities, which are imagined to have been on the Sacra Via near the later site of the Arch of Titus or the temple of Venus and Rome.

8   For Marius entering the senate in triumphal dress, see *ILS* 59 with Livy *Per.* 67, Pliny *NH* 33.12, Plut. *Mar.* 12.

9   The quarrel between Marius and Sulla has been variously dated by scholars. Behr (1993) 120 dates it to 91 B.C., Christ (2002) 68 to immediately after the Cimbrian war in 101 B.C., although with some earlier tensions, Thein (2002) 16 to the period after the death of Saturninus in 100 B.C.

10 For Sulla's ring, see Val. Max. 8.14.4, Pliny *NH* 37.8, Plut. *Sul.* 3.9, *Mar.* 10.8. For the Bocchus monument, see the *denarius* of Faustus Sulla from 56 B.C. depicted in figure 13 (*RRC* 426/1) with Plut. *Sul.* 6.1 and *Mar.* 32.4. This may have been the first statue group in Rome to show a historical scene in motion. For discussion, see Behr (1993) 114–21; Sehlmeyer (1999) 194–96 and (*LTUR* 1999); Mackay (2000) 162–68; Christ (2002) 65, 74; and Thein (2002) 16, 20. Note also the painting of Sulla with his grass crown (*corona graminea*) that was later to be found at Cicero's villa at Tusculum (Pliny *NH* 22.12; cf. 22.7).

11 For Marius and Metellus, see Cic. *Off.* 3.20.79, Sall. *Jug.* 64–65, Vell. Pat. 2.11, Plut. *Mar.* 8–9, Dio fr. 89.3.

12 For the rebuilding of the Bocchus monument after Sulla's return from the East, see Ramage (1991) 111–13, and esp. Hölscher (1980), who identifies the S. Omobono base as being from the restored monument of Bocchus (rejected by Thein [2002] 374–77).

13 For a detailed discussion of proscriptions, see Hinard (1985), who was able to identify only about seventy-five of what were probably thousands of victims. For memory sanctions and proscriptions, see Hinard (1985) 49–51, 81, 134 (with Dio fr. 109.16). For discussions since Hinard, see esp. Nippel (1988) 92–93; Seager (1994) 197–99; Christ (2002) 113–21; Thein (2002) 63–70, 115–35; and Lovano (2002) 55–59.

14 See Hinard (1985) 13: "Mais surtout la proscription est une mesure qui frappe des individus et des familles notamment en abolissant leur souvenir: ceux dont nous avons encore le nom ne sont pas les plus représentatives de l'ensemble."

15 For the sons of the proscribed, see Cic. *Att.* 2.1.3, Sall. *Hist.* 1.55.6M, Livy *Per.* 89, Vell. Pat. 2.28.4, Dion. 8.80, Plut. *Sul.* 31 with Diehl (1988) 179–81. Vedaldi Iasbez (1981) offers a prosopography of affected individuals, whom she identifies as adherents of Cinna.

16 For head-hunting under Sulla, see Val. Max. 3.1.2b, Sen. *Prov.* 3.7, *Clem.* 1.12.1, Lucan 2.160, Plut. *Cat. Min.* 3.2–4, App. *BC* 1.71, *Mithr.* 51, scholiast to Lucan 2.160. The best overall discussion is Hinard (1984), esp. 301. See also Flower (1996) 220 and Christ (2002) 115–16. The price on offer was two talents for killing any of the proscribed. This high price also suggests the elite status of the targeted victims, as well as the careful planning of the events. See App. *BC.* 71 and 73 for the Marians exposing the heads of praetors and consuls for the first time, starting in 87 B.C. See also Jervis (2001).

17 For the ten thousand Cornelii in Rome, see *ILLRP* 353 = *ILS* 871 with App. *BC* 1.100 and 104. For discussion, see Seager (1994) 203, Coarelli (*LTUR* 1996, Lacus Fundani) 167–18, Lintott (1999) 77–83, Thein (2002) 183, and Christ (2002) 134.

18 It is notable that there are no entries at all for statues of Marius under *statua* in *LTUR* 1999: Sulla would probably be gratified. For Marius and Sulla, see Varner (2004) 18. For the scattering of Marius' ashes, see Cic. *Leg.* 2.56, Val. Max. 9.2.1, Lucan 1.583–84 with Hinard (1985) 80–81.

19 For Sulla's building program in general, see Ramage (1991) 113–15 and Behr (1993) 124–35. For the Forum, see Purcell (*LTUR* 1995) 331. For the *curia* and *comitium*, see Coarelli (*LTUR* 1993). It is hard to imagine that Sulla did not put his own name on his new senate house, although there is no specific entry for *curia Cornelia* in *LTUR*. For the *Tabularium*, see Mura Sommella (*LTUR* 1999).

20 For Sulla's gilded equestrian statue at the *rostra*, see Cic. *Phil.* 9.13, App. *BC* 1.97–98 with *ILLRP* 351 = *ILS* 827. For discussion, see Behr (1993) 121–23, Sehlmeyer (1999) 204–9, Coarelli and Papi (*LTUR* 1999), Thein (2002) 191–94, and Christ (2002) 120. The statue is depicted on a Sullan coin (80 B.C., *RRC* 381; see figure 15). For other coins of Sulla, see esp. *RRC* 359 and 367 with Luce (1968), Zehnacker (1973) 573, Lahusen (1989), and Ramage (1991) 102–6. See *RRC* 434.1 for a coin of Q. Pompeius Rufus showing a portrait of Sulla (54 B.C. according to Crawford in *RRC*, 59 B.C. according to Lahusen [1989] 41, 45).

21 For Sulla's three trophies, see *RRC* 426/3 for Faustus' *denarius* with Venus and the three trophies. Dio 42.18.3 with Hölscher (1980) 366 and Mackay (2000) 206–10.

22 For the death of Marius Gratidianus, see *Comm. Pet.* 3.10, Sall. *Hist.* 1.44M, Livy *Per.* 88, Val. Max. 9.2.1, Lucan 2.173–92, Flor. 2.9.26, Oros. 5.21.7, Ascon. 84C, and Aug. *CD* 28. The most notorious description is probably Sen. *De Ira* 3.18.1–2. See Hinard (1984) and (1985) 377–80 for the meaning of these ritualized killings as the reverse of the aristocratic funeral, esp. (1982) 303–7 for the death of Gratidianus. Thein (2002) 127: "The sacrality of Gratidianus' execution was a symbolic negation of his semi-divine status as popular saviour and hero." The tomb of the Lutati Catuli was on the Janiculum.

23 For the honors offered to Marius Gratidianus in the neighborhoods (*vici*) of Rome, see Cic. *Off.* 3.80, Pliny *NH* 33.132, 34.27. For discussion, see Taylor (1931) 49; Classen (1963) 326–27; Alföldi (1971) 135; Flambard (1981) 162; Fraschetti (1994) 259–60;

Sehlmeyer (1999) 199–201 and (*LTUR* 1999); Simon and Pina Polo (2000); Gradel (2002) 51; and Lott (2004) 49–50, 59, 171. For Gratidianus' coinage reform, see esp. Crawford (1968), Lo Cascio (1979), and Brennan (2000) 2.460. *CIL* 6.1297 = *ILS* 872 = *ILLRP* 352 attests to honors for Sulla in the *Vicus Laci Fundani* (cf. *ILLRP* 350 dedicated by *collegia* on Delos in 87). It may be that the neighborhoods not only removed their honors for Gratidianus when Sulla arrived, but honored Sulla in his place. Ramage (1991) 110 posits honors for Sulla in all the *vici*. However, these honors need not have been exactly the same as those for Gratidianus. Sulla's *genius* may also have been associated with the *genius publicus*, as Caesar's was (for the feast day on 9 October).

24 For Catiline's role in the death of Gratidianus, see esp. *Comm. Pet.* 3.10; Sall. *Hist.* 1.44–45; Plut. *Sul.* 32; Ascon. 84C, 87C; schol. Bern. to Lucan 2.173. Gelzer (*RE* 23) accepted that Catiline was married to Gratidianus' sister (Gratidia), which would also have connected him to Cicero. Marshall (1985) argues that it was not Catiline, but Catulus' son (cos. 78, *RE* 8 Münzer) who killed Gratidianus, although the ancient evidence is very slight.

25 For the clearing of unauthorized statues in 158 B.C., see Pliny *NH* 34.30 with Flower (1996) 70 and Sehlmeyer (1999) 152–54.

26 The temple of Jupiter Optimus Maximus burned down on 6 July 83. For the new temple, which was dedicated in 69 B.C., see De Angeli (*LTUR* 1996); Thein (2002) 218–23, 225–27, 232–35; and Christ (2002) 107. Sulla's one regret was that he knew he would not live to dedicate it (Pliny *NH* 7.138, Tac. *Hist.* 3.72.3). For the temple on coins, see *RRC* 385/1 of 78 B.C. and *RRC* 487.1–2 of 43 B.C.

27 For Sulla's victory games, see Cic. *Verr.* 1.10.31, Val. Max. 2.8.7, Vell. Pat. 2.27.6 with Behr (1993) 136–43, Christ (2002) 120–21, and Thein (2002) 24, 136–42.

28 For Sulla's memoirs, see Peter (1914) 195–204 and now Chassignet (2004). Nearly all the fragments are from Plutarch. There may have been both a Greek and a Latin version. For discussion, see Ramage (1991) 95–102, Lewis (1991), Behr (1993) 9–21, Christ (2002) 135, Thein (2002) 359–63, and esp. Scholz (2003).

29 Memories of L. Cornelius Cinna (*RE* 106 Münzer) were always fraught with difficulty. Cic. *Quinct.* 70: *Cinnanum tempus . . . cuius omnino rei memoriam omnem toli funditus et deleri arbitror oportere* (The time of Cinna . . . the whole memory of which period I think should be completely rooted out and destroyed). For discussion, see Badian (1964), Frier (1971), Meier (1980) 229–37, Diehl (1988) 132–41, Seager (1994) 173–85, Christ (2002) 99–103, and Lovano (2002), esp. 141–59 for an appendix of sources.

30 For Julius Caesar and Sulla, see Gelzer (1968) 263, 272, 279, 282 and Christ (2002) 152 with Cic. *Att.* 9.7C.1. For possible influences of Cinna on Caesar, see Gelzer (1968) 20, 279.

31 For Sulla's funeral, see Cic. *Leg.* 2.22.57; Livy *Per.* 90; Plut. *Sul.* 38; App. *BC* 1.105–6; Licinian. 32F with Wesch-Klein (1993) 11, 92; Flower (1996) 123–24; Thein (2002) 313–35; Christ (2002) 137. For Sulla's tomb, which survived to be restored by Caracalla (Dio 77.13), see La Rocca (*LTUR* 1999).

32 For the last generation of the Roman Republic, see Gruen (1974).

33 Cicero gave two speeches during Sulla's lifetime (*Pro Rosc. Amer.* and *Pro Quinct.*)

that are still extant (see discussion in Butler [2002] 4–23). The most detailed discussion of Cicero's evolving attitude to Sulla is Diehl (1988). Note also Barden Dowling (2000) 306–13; Thein (2002) 31, 62, 70–72, 256–312; and Christ (2002) 157. ·

34 For Cicero's politics in 63 B.C., see Rawson (1975) 60–88 and Stockton (1971) 84–109. For the role of Cicero's divisive rhetoric, see esp. Burckhardt (1988) 129–34.

35 For Catiline and Sulla, see esp. Syme (1964) 123–24. For Marius' eagle as used by Catiline, see Cic. *Cat.* 2.13 and Sall. *BC* 59.3. See Christ (2002) 67 for the importance of the silver eagles introduced by Marius in the late second century.

36 For Cicero and L. Sergius Catilina (*RE* 23 Gelzer), see Yavetz (1963), Ungern-Sternberg von Pürkel (1970) 86–129 (and in the *Neue Pauly*), Nippel (1988) 94–107, Wiseman (1994a) 346–60, and Heider (2000). For Catiline and the problem of debts, see Giovannini (1995). Tatum (1999) 61 notes that Clodius sided with Cicero against Catiline in 63 B.C. See Habinek (1998) 70–72 for the rhetoric of bandits applied by Cicero to both Catiline and Clodius.

37 For the treatment of the Catilinarians, see Ungern-Sternberg von Pürkel (1970) 102–11, Meier (1979), Drummond (1995), and von Ungern-Sternberg (1997). For the suggestion that the *nones* of December should be regarded as the new birthday of Rome, see Cic. *Flacc.* 102, *De Cons. Suo* FPL fr. 17M with Gotter (1996) 248–49.

38 For Cicero as a tyrant figure, see Cic. *Att.* 1.16.10, *Cat.* 1.30, 2.14, 4.11, *Pis.* 14, *Sull.* 22, *Dom.* 75, 94; Plut. *Cic.* 23.4.

39 For Lepidus' revolt in 78–77 B.C., see esp. Cic. *Off.* 1.76, *Cat.* 3.24; Sall. *Hist.* 1.65–69, 77M; Livy *Per.* 90; Val. Max. 2.8.7; App. *BC* 107 with Burckhardt (1988) 152–53 and Christ (2002) 141–42.

40 For the trial of C. Rabirius (*RE* 5 von der Mühll) in 63 B.C., see Cic. *Rab. Perd.*, Suet. *Jul.* 12, Dio 37.26–28 with Ungern-Sternberg von Pürkel (1970) 81–85, Gruen (1974) 277–79, and Nippel (1988) 105. Lintott (1994) 103 notes the continuing popularity of Saturninus and Glaucia even some thirty-seven years after their deaths.

41 For the "First Catilinarian" conspiracy, see Cic. *Mur.* 81, *Sull.* 11, 67, *Cat.* 1.15, Sall. *Cat.* 18.5; Livy *Per.* 101; Suet. *Jul.* 9; Ascon. 92C with Seager (1964); Syme (1964) 88–102; Sumner (1965); Wiseman (1994a) 342–43; and Fraschetti (1994) 220.

42 For Catiline as a *hostis*, see Sall. *Cat.* 36. On Cicero's first speech against Catiline, see Konstan (1993), Batstone (1994), and Butler (2002) 85–102.

43 For Cicero after his return from exile, see esp. Rawson (1975) 122–45. Binot (2001) 201–2 discusses how Cicero creates an image of Scipio Nasica as an *exemplum* for his own purposes.

44 For the flowers on Catiline's grave when M. Antonius Hybrida was convicted, see Cic. *Flacc.* 95; cf. *Pis.* 16. Antonius had sent Catiline's head to Cicero in Rome (Dio 37.40.2). For Catiline's grave, see Papi (*LTUR* 1999). For discussion, see Classen (1963) 324 and Gruen (1974) 287–89.

45 For the quarrel between Cicero and Clodius, see Nippel (1988) 108–28, Laurence (1994), Wiseman (1994b), and Tatum (1999) 151–65, who stresses the escalation in violence in the 50s. Tatum (1999) 158: "Clodius' law rendered Cicero an outlaw. Furthermore, it initiated a sequence of public actions that assimilated Cicero to the most infamous of the state's enemies." In other words, Cicero faced a situation

not entirely unlike the one Sulla lived with while he was in the East in the 80s. Although Cicero was soon recalled, his execution of the Catilinarians was never legally justified. Rather, he had simply received a (political) pardon.

46 For the destruction of houses, see Bodel (1997). For Cicero's house, see Papi (*LTUR* 1993) and Guilhembet (*LTUR* 1999). See Tatum (1999) 157–65, 186–220 with Nippel (1988) 116–23 and Berg (1997) 122–35. In 58 B.C. Clodius also shattered the *fasces* of the consul Gabinius and tried to dedicate Gabinius' property to Ceres. In turn, the tribune L. Ninnius threatened to consecrate Clodius' property to Ceres, see Tatum (1999) 170–71.

47 The relation of the published version of Cicero's *Pro Milone* to what was said on the day in court remains unclear. For discussion, see Nippel (1988) 128–42, 147 and Schuller (1997). For the new era, starting on 18 January 52 B.C. (the date of Clodius' murder), see Cic. *Mil.* 98. However, the senate condemned the violence and assassination as being *contra rem publicam* (against the public interest). For the memory of Clodius, see Tatum (1999) 241–42. Dolabella proposed a statue of Clodius in 47 B.C. (*Att.* 11.23.3), and Caesar refused to recall Milo from exile.

48 For the aftermath of the Ides of March, see Rawson (1994b) and Gotter (1996) 149–55, 254 who stresses the active role played by Cicero in furthering conflict, partly by means of *hostis* declaration.

49 For Brutus after the Ides of March, see Ortmann (1988), Nippel (1988) 144–47, and Gotter (1996) 207–32. It is notable that Brutus was consistently resistant to Cicero's policy of treating Antony as a *hostis*. See Cic. *Ad Brut.* 7.3, 11.2, 23.3, 23.10. For Brutus and his context, see MacMullen (1966) 1–18, Gotter (2000), Welwei (2001), and Walter (2002) 335–39.

50 For Cicero's death in the second proscription, see Plut. *Cic.* 47–49, *Brut.* 27; App. *BC* 4.8–11; Dio 47.8 with Hinard (1985) 239, 244, 319, 322–26 and Gotter (1996) 193–94. Dio 47.11 attests a statue and inscription of Popillius Laenas, who killed Cicero, portrayed with the orator's head next to him. Diehl (1988) 166 notes that Cicero's death came as the fulfillment of the constant fear he had lived with, that the proscriptions he had seen in his youth would return to Rome. For the sale at public auction of Cicero's house (to L. Marcius Censorinus, cos. 39 B.C.), see Vell. Pat. 2.14.3. However, Augustus is remembered as being favorable to Cicero's memory. For Cicero's son Marcus, see Plut. *Cic.* 49.3–4.

51 It is notable that the young Caesar refused to divorce Cornelia, despite the grave dangers involved and the fact that she had surely lost all her father's property and her dowry. A divorce would, of course, have immediately made him ineligible for the office of *flamen Dialis*, from which Sulla wanted to remove him. Caesar and Cornelia were surely married by the rite of *confarreatio*, as required for a *flamen Dialis*. A divorce from Cornelia, therefore, carried with it significant ritual and religious implications (Gell. 10.25.23, Plut. *QRom.* 50), and would have left Cornelia without immediate family or money. See Gelzer (1968) 21 and Beard, North, and Price (1998) 1.131.

52 For Caesar's first prosecutions, see Plut. *Cat. Min.* 17; Suet. *Jul.* 11; Dio 37.10.2; Ascon. 91C with Gelzer (1968) 22, 38, 42, 44; Nippel (1988) 105–6; and Jehne (2001) 20. Note, however, Caesar's leniency toward Catiline (Dio 37.10.3, Ascon. 90/91C).

53 For Julia's funeral, see Plut. *Caes.* 5 with Flower (1996) 124.

54 For Cornelia's funeral, see Plut. *Caes.* 5. Plutarch does not stress a political message at this funeral, but rather the pathos evoked by Caesar over his personal loss and the novelty of a grand funeral for a younger woman. Did Caesar speak of the painful past and of the times of Cinna? Did he speak of how he had risked his life in order to stay married to Cornelia, who later became the mother of his daughter Julia?

55 For Caesar and the amnesty for the followers of Lepidus, see Gelzer (1968) 29 and Lovano (2002) 27. Cinna's son (*RE* 107 Münzer) returned under the *lex Plautia* in 73 B.C. and married the daughter of Pompey. Caesar himself had hurried back to Rome when he heard of Sulla's death and Lepidus' revolt (Suet. *Jul.* 3).

56 For the restoration of Marius' trophies in 65 B.C., see Vell. 2.43.4, Plut. *Caes.* 6.1–2, Suet. *Jul.* 11. Reusser (*LTUR* 1999) wrongly assumes that Sulla's removal of these monuments was illegal and that Caesar was, therefore, not breaking the law. In the senate debate that followed, Catulus was the most strident denouncer of Caesar (Plut. *Caes.* 6.4). Sehlmeyer (1999) 217–18 notes the coincidence with the great games Caesar celebrated in memory of his father (*RE* 130 Münzer), who had been dead for twenty years (Pliny *NH* 33.53).

57 For Caesar in 64 B.C., see Gelzer (1968) 42.

58 Q. Lutatius Catulus (cos. 78, *RE* 8 Münzer) had arranged the public funeral for Sulla, the first funeral at public expense in Rome. For his completion of the Tabularium, see *ILS* 35, 35a. He rededicated the temple of Jupiter Optimus Maximus on the Capitol, now with a gilded roof, in 69 B.C. (Cic. *Verr.* 4.69, *Cn. Pomp.* 51; cf. Gell. 2.10.2 [Varro]). He gave magnificent games at the time, the first to feature large sunshades to protect the crowds (Val. Max. 2.4.6, Pliny *NH* 19.6). For Caesar's accusations in 62 B.C., see Cic. *Att.* 2.24.3, Suet. *Jul.* 15, Dio 37.44.1. For the senate's vote in 46 B.C., see Dio 43.14.6. In fact, Catulus' name stayed on the front of the temple, in shiny letters, until it burned down in the fire of A.D. 69 (Val. Max. 6.9.5, Tac. *Hist.* 3.72). Catulus' descendant, the emperor Galba, referred to him as Catulus Capitolinus (Suet. *Gal.* 2.3–4, Plut. *Gal.* 3.1, Tac. *Hist.* 1.15). It is notable that Caesar seemed lenient to Catiline but implacable in his hatred for Catulus; Cicero's attitude was the exact reverse.

59 For Caesar and the rights of the proscribed, see Vell. Pat. 2.43.4, Suet. *Jul.* 11, Plut. *Cat. Min.* 17.4–5, Dio 43.50.5 with Jehne (2001) 88 and Thein (2002) 74.

60 For Caesar's *commentarii*, see Rüpke (1992) and Wiseman (1998c).

61 For Pompey's statue at the *rostra* and its restoration by Caesar after his return to Rome, see Sehlmeyer (1999) 209–11, 231–34, and Papi (*LTUR* 1999).

62 For Pompey's statue marked with Caesar's blood, see Sehlmeyer (1999) 219–21 and Papi (*LTUR* 1999). This statue was also one that had been restored by Caesar (Plut. *Caes.* 57.4, Suet. *Jul.* 75). After Caesar's murder, the *curia Pompeii* (Coarelli *LTUR* 1993) where he died was closed by Octavian, even as the Ides was declared a day of ill omen (Suet. *Jul.* 88), and the room was eventually turned into a latrine (Dio 47.19.1). Later Augustus moved the statue to a new position on an arch (Suet. *Aug.* 31), partly as a sign of healing. Brutus' head had been sent by Antony to Rome but was lost at sea (Suet. *Aug.* 13.1). It was said that Tiberius Gracchus had fallen

at the feet of the statues of the old Roman kings on the Capitol. See App. *BC* 1.16 with Stockton (1979) 77 and Nippel (1988) 81. Moltesen (2003) 81–84 identifies the famous head of Pompey from the tomb of the Licinii (now in Copenhagen) as a marble copy of the bronze portrait from the theater of Pompey. Plut. *Brut.* 17.1 has Cassius address the statue.

63 For divine honors for Caesar during his lifetime, see Jehne (1987) 216–25, who argues that the honors had been voted but were not all in effect yet at the time of the Ides. For example, Antony had been named as Caesar's *flamen* but had not been inaugurated.

64 For a detailed discussion of Caesar's position, see Jehne (1987) 191–371. For Caesar as the first Roman to have his statues all over the city, see Sehlmeyer (1999) 225–38.

65 For events immediately after the Ides, see Syme (1939), Yavetz (1979) 186–214, and esp. Gotter (1996). Gotter (1996) 21–29 details events between 15 March and mid-April when the Liberators left Rome. Dolabella had suggested that the Ides be the new birthday of Rome and Tib. Claudius Nero (father of the emperor Tiberius) that the Liberators be rewarded as tyrant slayers (Plut. *Brut.* 19.1, App. *BC* 2.122, 127).

66 For Julius Caesar's funeral on 20 March 44 B.C., see Plut. *Ant.* 14.6–8, *Brut.* 20.2–4, *Cic.* 42.4, Suet. *Jul.* 84, App. *BC* 2.143–48, Dio 44.35–50. For discussion, see Fraschetti (1994) 54–67, Flower (1996) 116–17, and Gotter (1996) 27, 267. Nippel (1988) 146 argues that this grand funeral staged by Antony eliminated any possibility of formal sanctions against Caesar's memory.

67 For Amatius and his cult of Caesar, see Cic. *Phil.* 1.5, 2.107; *Att.* 14.6.1, 14.8.1; Livy *Per.* 116 (Chamates); Val. Max. 9.15.1; Suet. *Jul.* 85; App. *BC* 3.2–4, 3.16, 3.36; Dio 44.51 with Nippel (1988) 146–49; Fraschetti (1994) 68–72; and Gotter (1996) 28–29, 40–44. Antony was very unpopular for this execution. Meanwhile, some of Caesar's statues were being taken away to be destroyed or reworked. People who had heard of this attacked the sculptors' workshops, and this disturbance was also put down by Antony (*Att.* 14.15, 14.16.2; App. *BC* 3.3; Dio 44.51.2). For Octavian's celebration of the *ludi* in commemoration of Caesar's victories, see Gotter (1996) 64.

68 For *hostis* declarations used as political weapons after the Ides, see Gotter (1996) for a detailed reconstruction of the shifting alliances.

69 For Caesar's deification as Divus Iulius in 42 B.C., see Suet. *Jul.* 88; Dio 47.18–19.3 with Syme (1939) 54–55, 202, 250, 301, 318, 471; Nippel (1988) 149; and Fraschetti (1994) 73–78.

70 For the memory of the Liberators, see Clarke (1981), Rawson (1991), and Gotter (2000) 329. Plut. *Brut.* 53.3–4 notes the return of Brutus' ashes to Rome, to be handed over to his mother, Servilia. On the advice of his grandmother Livia, the emperor Claudius simply left out the triumviral period in his Roman history (Suet. *Claud.* 41).

71 For the funeral of Junia in A.D. 22, see Tac. *Ann.* 3.76 with Flower (1996) 253.

72 For portraits of the Liberators in the imperial period, see Dio 53.23.4 (L. Sestius cos. 23 B.C. had statues of Brutus, under whom he had served as *proquaestor*),

Pliny *Ep.* 1.17 (Titinius Capito had them *domi ubi potest*), Tac. *Ann.* 16.7.3 (C. Cassius Longinus' portrait of his relative Cassius was labeled *duci partium*).

73 For the trial and death of Cremutius Cordus in A.D. 25, see Tac. *Ann.* 4.34–35 (App. *BC* 4.114) with Rawson (1991) 488–89.

74 For the Liberators cited in A.D. 41, see Sentius Saturninus' speech after the murder of Caligula (Jos. *AJ* 19.184).

75 Coarelli (1969) argued for Scipio Nasica. See also Pulte (*LTUR* 1999) who points out that Sulla had freed both Athens and Rome from "tyranny." For Sulla in Athens, see Habicht (1997) esp. 305–14 and Christ (2002) 84–88, 96. Habicht (1976) 135–42 notes that Athens struck coins in 84/83 that featured Harmodius and Aristogeiton as an allusion to Sulla's victory.

76 See Loraux (2002) 261 for the practice of disarming the present through the distant past.

77 Note, for example, Linderski 1987/1995 for M. Aurelius Cotta (cos. 74), a missing Ponticus.

78 See Flower (1996) 122–26 for the evolution of the aristocratic funeral to include women, starting in 102 B.C.

Chapter VI

1 For the *domus Augusta*, see esp. *Tab. Siar.* 1.9–11 with González (1984) 64; *SCPP* lines 123–65 with Eck, Caballos, and Fernández (1996) 236, 254; Corbier (1994, 1995); Dettenhofer (2000) 16; and Cogitore (2002) 163–64. The *domus divina* is first attested in A.D. 33 by *AE* 1978.295 and *AE* 1988.552 (cf. Phaedr. 5.7.35).

2 For the senate's sanctions against Antony (*RE* 30, Will in *NP*) in 30 B.C., see Strabo 14.685, Plut. *Cic.* 49.6, *Ant.* 86.9, Dio 51.19.3. Suet. *Aug.* 17.2 has Antony declared a *hostis*, while Dio 50.21.1 refers this term only to his followers. For the sanctions against his *praenomen*, see Solin (1995) 190–94. Freed slaves retained the name Marcus (Val. Max. *De Praen.*).

3 For the erasure of the Antonii, see *ILLRP* 342 for Antony's grandfather at Corinth, as well as the evidence from the *Fasti Capitolini* and *Colotiani*. For portraits of Antony and Cleopatra, see Varner (2004) 18–20.

4 For Octavian's partial rehabilitation of Antony, see Tac. *Ann.* 3.18.1 with the *Fasti Capitolini* (Antony is restored under 47 and 37, his grandfather under 99 and 97) with Steinby (1987), Simpson (1993), Rich (1998), and Nedergaard (2001). The *Fasti Colotiani* from near the Aqua Virgo (*II* 13.1.18) also show reinscriptions. There was never any erasure in the Augustan triumphal *fasti* of 19/18 B.C. However, Antony's birthday remained a *dies vitiosus*. Hänlein-Schäfer (1985) 20 discusses Augustus' mausoleum as a response to Antony's tomb in Alexandria.

5 The *Res Gestae* (esp. 1–3) do not name Augustus' political opponents such as Brutus, Cassius, Sextus Pompeius, Antony, Lepidus, or any of the "conspirators." Tac. *Ann.* 1.10 seems to name them deliberately as a reversal of Augustus' own rhetoric. For the triumviral period, see Bleicken (1990), Gotter (1996), Pelling (1996), Bleicken (1999) 87–296, and J. H. C. Williams (2001). For the clash between Octa-

vian and Antony, see now also Dettenhofer (2000) 43–59. For the role of women, see Fisher (1999).

6 For Octavia, see *PIR*² 66, Fischer in *NP*, and especially the detailed analysis in Fischer (1999) 67–138. Her popularity is attested by Plutarch (*Ant.* 57.1–2 at Athens), who depicts her as an independent player in the unfolding events. For her honors, see Dio 49.38.1 with Flory (1993), Rose (1997) 8, Bartman (1999) 62, Fischer (1999) 101–2, Dettenhofer (2000) 41, and Flower (2002b). For Antony's house (which had belonged to Pompey) see Plut. *Ant.* 54 and 57.3 with Papi and Rodriguez Almeida in *LTUR* 1995. For the divorce, see Livy *Per.* 132, Dio 50.3.2 with Dixon (1992) 142, Pelling (1996) 51. For Octavia on Antony's coins, see Fischer (1999) 171–215 with pls. V–VII.

7 After the execution of M. Antonius Antyllus, Antony's surviving children were Iullus Antonius by Fulvia, the two Antonias by Octavia, and his three children by Cleopatra (see Suet. *Aug.* 17). Alexander Helios did appear in the triumph (Dio 51.21.8). See esp. Fischer (1999) 109–15 and Dettenhofer (2000) 147–48. Bleicken (1999) has all three of Cleopatra's children by Antony raised by Octavia. Pelling (1996) 64 has both of Cleopatra's sons by Antony die very shortly. For the erasure of Cleopatra's heir and co-ruler Ptolemy XV Caesarion, see Weill Goudchaux (2001) esp. 139 for the reliefs from the temple of Hathor at Dendera and the entrance to the temple at Edfu. His text has been erased from a basalt statue from Karnak (Walker and Higgs [2001] no. 171, Ashton [2001] no. 33, Egyptian Museum, Cairo 13/3/15/3). His granite portrait was recovered from the harbor at Alexandria (Walker and Higgs [2001] no. 172, Greco-Roman Museum, Alexandria, 1015).

8 For Cleopatra's statue in the temple of Venus Genetrix (still there in the third century A.D.), see App. *BC* 2.102 and Dio 51.22.3 with Flory (1993) 295–96, Meadows (2001) 25, Alfano (2001) 277, Weill Goudchaux (2001) 134, Walker (2001), Ashton (2001). A statue of her as Isis could also be found on the acropolis at Athens (Dio 50.15.2). For recent discussions of Cleopatra, see esp. Clauss (1995) and Rice (1999).

9 For the erasure of Antony's name, see Vittinghoff (1936) 20–21 and Kajava (1995) 201. The obelisk inscribed by Cornelius Gallus was perhaps originally intended to honor Antony; see Alföldy (1990) 66–67, 95; cf. 45–47, 51. Other inscriptions: letter to the *koinon* of Asia (Sherk [1969] no. 57; cf. Sherk [1984] no. 85), Letter to Aphrodisias (Sherk [1969] no. 28 with Robert [1966] 408–11), archive of triumviral texts from Aphrodisias (Reynolds [1982] nos. 6, 7, 8, 10, 12), dedication to the new Dionysus at Athens (*IG* II/III² 1043 with Dio 48.39.2 with Marasco [1992] and Fischer [1999]), statue base from Alexandria (Walker and Higgs [2001] no. 213 with Fraser [1957] and Plut. *Ant.* 71.4 for his drinking club), the later epitaph of a legate (*CIL* 6.1364 = *ILS* 943).

10 See Plut. *Ant.* 60 with Blanck (1969) 15.

11 For the asylum decree from Sardis, see Herrmann (1989, 1995) with pl. 1.2.

12 For Iullus Antonius, see *PIR*² 800 and chapter 7. Rohr Vio (2000) argues for continuing Antonian factions throughout Augustus' reign, especially among his relatives.

13 For the two Antonias, see *PIR*² 884 and 885, Raepsaet-Charlier (1987) no. 73 for Antonia Minor with Kokkinos (1992). *CIL* 6.40331 (Alföldy [1992b] 35–38) is a dedication from the Forum of Augustus from around 2 B.C.; *CIL* 6.5536 = *ILS* 5220 records the basilica of the two Antonias (Lega in *LTUR* 1993).

14 For Gaius' restoration of Antony, see Sen. *Ad Polyb.* 35.1, Suet. *G.* 23.1, Dio 59.20 with Herz (1978) 1159–60. For Claudius' similar policy, see Sen. *Ad Polyb.* 16.1, Suet. *Claud.* 11.3 with Levick (1990) 46, 90. Antony's birthday (14 January) fell on the same day as the birthday of the elder Drusus, the father of Claudius and grandfather of Gaius; see *Fasti Maff.*, *Fasti Opp.*, *Fasti Praen.*, and *Fasti Ver.* For the Actium holiday, see *Fasti Amit.*, *Fasti Ant. Min.*, *Fasti Vall.* with Hölscher (1985), Gurval (1995), and Rüpke (1995a). For the Actium monument, see Murray and Petsas (1989) and Schäfer (1993). For Germanicus' memories of both Augustus and Antony at the site of Actium, see Tac. *Ann.* 2.53.

15 For Augustus' building policy in Rome, see Suet. *Aug.* 29.4–5 with Gros (1976) and Favro (1996). For monuments of senators in the imperial period, see Alföldy (2001a).

16 For the *Porticus ad Nationes* (Largo Argentina), see Coarelli (1981) for topography; Kajanto, Nyberg, and Steinby (1982) for inscriptions; Alföldy (1991); and Coarelli in *LTUR* 1999.

17 For the inscriptions of L. Aelius Lamia, see *CIL* 6.41034–41041 with Eck (1984a) 204, 212 and (1984b) 146; Mattei (1986) 157–59ff.; Alföldy (1992b) 113–23. For the text of Ap. Claudius Pulcher from the same area, see *CIL* 6.41046.

18 For M. Licinius Crassus Frugi, see *CIL* 6.41052 = *IGUR* 64.

19 For Rufus, see *CIL* 6.41054, 41055 (MNR no. 107.873) = *IGUR* 71 (see 40421 for the palimpsest) with Eck (1984a, 1984b), who dates it to the very late Republic.

20 For senatorial self-representation under Augustus, see Eck (1984a, 1984b), with a list of senatorial dedications, and Alföldy (1992b), and his entries in the new volumes of *CIL* 6.8.2 and 6.8.3. Alföldy (1991) gives a general overview of the impact of the new principate on inscribed texts. C. Vibius Postumus (*PIR*² 392, suff. cos. A.D. 5) seems to be the last Roman outside the imperial family to receive divine or heroic honors after death; see *IG* 12.6.1 no. 365 (of around A.D. 15) from Samos, written over an erasure.

21 For L. Munatius Plancus (*PIR*² 728, Eder in *NP*), see Fellmann (1957) with Coarelli (1982) 354–59, Walser (1957), Syme (1986) 369, Pelling (1996) esp. 51–52, Watkins (1997), and Morello (1997). For his epitaph at Gaeta, see *CIL* 10.6087 = *ILS* 886 (cf. Virg. *Aen.* 7.1–4 for the burial of Aeneas' nurse Caieta on the same spot). *AE* 1995.278 may be another inscription of Plancus from the same area (Coarelli [1982] 354–59). *CIL* 6.1316 = *ILS* 41 is his dedication of the temple of Saturn in the Roman forum. For Munatius' painting of Victory on the Capitol, see Pliny *NH* 35.36.108.

22 For Augst (perhaps originally Colonia Munatia Triumphalis in 44 B.C.), see Laur-Belart (1959), Isaac (1971), Wells (1972), Watkins (1997) 62. For Lyons (Colonia Copia Munatia Felix in late 43 B.C., afterward Colonia Copia Claudia Augusta Lugdunum), see Dio 46.50.4–6 with Watkins (1997) 89–90. Isaac (1971) posits rapid abandonment by the first settlers (veterans of Caesar's ninth legion) due to the civil war, followed by resettlement soon after 16 B.C.

23 M. Licinius Crassus: *PIR*² 186, Groag in *RE* 58, Dettenhofer (2000) 69–72 and esp. the incisive discussion of Tarpin (2003).

24 Dessau's point ([1906] 144) is still valid: Augustus could not let his former enemy enter Rome as the new Romulus.

25 Groag *RE* 58 offers a dramatic and compelling reconstruction with Crassus as Octavian's powerful enemy who receives the consulship and Macedonia as the prize for his change of allegiance, but who then threatens to upstage Augustus immediately after his triple triumph. Cf. Liou-Gille (1998) 44–47. Tarpin (2003) 275: "un oubli précoce et volontaire."

26 For Crassus' triumph, see *II* 13.1 86–87 and 571 with Dio 51.25.2.

27 We may suspect that Crassus was still young in 27, since he had not held the praetorship. For *stemma*, see *PIR*² L opp. p. 40 and Syme (1979) 496–509. Groag *RE* 58 estimates that Crassus was born c. 67 and his son c. 47 (too early?). See Eck (1993a) and (1996b) 78–79 for an estimate that a young man from an established family might expect to hold the consulship at about age thirty-two to thirty-three. Cf. Tarpin (2003) 276–78.

28 Livy *Per.* 134, 135; Dio 51.23.2–27; Zon. 10.32; Florus 2.26.

29 Dio 51.26.5: τὰ σημεῖα ἃ τοῦ Ἀντωνίου τοῦ Γαΐου οἱ Βαστάρναι πρὸς τῇ τῶν Ἰστριανῶν πόλει ἀφῄρηντο (. . . the standards of Gaius Antonius which the Bastarnae brought to the city of the Istrians). Cf. Dio 38.10.

30 *AE* 1928.44 (Thespiae), *ILS* 8810 = *IG* III² 4118 (Athens). Note Mócsy (1966) and Wilkes (1969) 550 on the suppression of Crassus' achievements in the Balkans, which may have included victories over the Dacians, Caesar's intended enemies, immediately after Actium.

31 At *RG* 29 Augustus refers to various standards he recaptured in Spain and Gaul (the successes of his generals in 25?), from the Dalmatians (Octavian's Illyrian campaigns of 35/34), and from the Parthians (the diplomatic settlement of 19).

32 Armor not dedicated at a temple would usually be taken to the general's house and kept there after the triumph. See Polyb. 6.39.10; Livy 10.7.9, 23.23.6; Prop. 1.16.1–4; Pliny *NH* 35.7 with Rawson (1990) and Flower (1996) 41. See also Flower (1998) for an exceptional breastplate with a Latin inscription recording the fact that it was taken as booty at Falerii Veteres in 241 B.C.

33 *Fast. Capit.* with Schumacher (1985), who is particularly clear here, but see also Cassolà (1970) 7 and Rampelberg (1978) 201–4. *Contra* Rich (1996) 104, who follows Giovannini (1983) 31–56 in arguing that promagistrates did not really have *auspicium.*

34 Rich (1996) argues that Crassus never tried to make a dedication but also that Augustus had nothing to gain politically in this matter.

35 Livy 4.20.5–6: *Omnes ante me auctores secutus, A. Cornelium Cossum tribunum militum secunda spolia Iovis Feretri templo intulisse exposui; ceterum, praeterquam quod ea rite opima spolia habentur, quae dux duci detraxit, nec ducem novimus nisi cuius auspicio bellum geritur, titulus ipse spoliis inscriptus illos meque arguit consulem ea Cossum cepisse* (I have followed all the writers who came before me when I stated that Aulus Cornelius Cossus dedicated the second *spolia opima* in the temple of Jupiter Feretrius as a military tribune. Nevertheless, apart from the

fact that [only] those spoils are duly considered *opima* which a leader took from a leader, and we have never known a leader who did not wage war under his own auspices, the label itself written on the spoils refutes both me and them [the earlier writers] in its demonstration that Cossus took them as consul).

36 For the *pontifices*, see conveniently Beard (1990) 34–48 and note 82 above. Liou-Gille (1998) 51 writes of the dedications of Cossus and Marcellus: "Il était inévitable que l'on consultât les pontifes sur ce qu'il fallait faire en des circonstances si exceptionnelles: cela était de leur ressort et nous avons maint exemple de consultations analogues." Augustus was a member of all the main priestly colleges (*RG* 7.3), although not *pontifex maximus* until 12 B.C.

37 C. Cornelius Gallus: *PIR*[2] 1369, Stroh in *NP*, Courtney in *OCD*[3] with bibliographies. For the fragments, see Anderson, Parsons, and Nisbet (1979). For a possible portrait, see Walker and Higgs (2001) no. 307. For Cornelius Gallus as the last of the late republican *praefecti fabrum*, see Welch (1995) 143–44.

38 For Gallus' bad behavior and disgrace, see Ovid *Am.* 3.9.61, *Trist.* 2.445–46, Suet. *Aug.* 66.2, Suet. *Gramm.* 16, Dio 53.23.5–6. For the issue of self-advertisement, see Eck (1984b) 131. For the issue of the *renuntiatio amicitiae*, see now the *SCPP* lines 28–29 with Eck, Caballos, and Fernández (1996) 155–57. There is no evidence that Gallus' poems were destroyed (Speyer [1981] 59). Servius on Verg. *Ecl.* 10.1 claims that the praise of Gallus in the poem was replaced at the request of Augustus himself.

39 For Gallus' arraignment and suicide, see Suet. *Aug.* 66.2–3, Dio 53.23.6–24.1, Serv. *Ecl.* 10.1, Amm. Marc. 17.4.5 with Syme (1939) 309–10. Daly and Reiter (1979) see Octavian handling Gallus more deftly than Crassus. See now also Raaflaub and Samons (1990) 423–25 and Dettenhofer (2000) 93–95. According to Rohr Vio (2000) 76–96, 147–69, Augustus was forced to sacrifice Gallus to the senators after his refusal of the *spolia opima* to Crassus. See also Cogitore (2002) 141–45.

40 For the Philae inscription on a rose-colored granite *stele*, dated to 17 April 29, see *CIL* 3.14147 = *IGR* I/II 1293 = *OGIS* II 654 = *ILS* 8995, Bernand (1969) vol. 2. no. 128 with pls. 94–97, Mazzarino (1982), Sherk (1984) no. 93. A new reading of the Latin text is provided by Alföldy (1990) 96–100.

41 *CIL* 6.882; cf. 31191 = *CIL* 6.8.2 p. 4302 = *ILS* 115 = A. Gordon (1983) 35 with Pliny *NH* 16.76.201. See Fishwick (1987/1995) 62–72; Alföldy (1990), who gives a full reassessment with new photographs; D'Onofrio (1992) 99–184; and Welch (1995) 133. Alföldy (1991) discusses the inscription on the obelisk in the context of Augustan epigraphy.

42 The obelisk was moved to its present position in front of St. Peter's at the Vatican in 1586. The inscription is now high off the ground and can only really be seen with binoculars. When it was originally in Egypt it was surely near to ground level.

43 See *AE* 1964.255 with Magi (1963) 50–56.

44 The place mentioned may be the one later called Forum Augusti in Alexandria. So Fraser (1972) 1.30 and 2.96 n. 218 and Alföldy (1990) 55–67.

45 *CIL* 6.40304 of 27 or 26.

46 For some definitions of "opposition," see Raaflaub (1987) 17–18, 23–25 and Flaig (1992).

47 For very different views about the opposition to Augustus, see Raaflaub (1987), Raaflaub and Samons (1990), Dettenhofer (2000) esp. 13–27, and Cogitore (2002) 47–62. Badian (1982) has clarified the chronology of Augustus' developing constitutional position, independent of his opponents.

48 For resistance to social and moral reforms, see Raaflaub and Samons (1990) 433–35 and Dettenhofer (2000) 128–44, 148–50.

49 Tacitus (*Ann.* 1.2) speaks of *nullo adversante,* but specifically in a context of extensive previous bloodshed. Raaflaub and Samons (1990) 432 note that most plots, outside family struggles over the succession, can be dated to the first twelve to fifteen years. They treat the conspirators individually, notably M. Aemilius Lepidus, Caepio and Murena, M. Egnatius Rufus, and Cn. Cornelius Cinna Magnus. Rohr Vio (2000) stresses Augustus' manipulation of the image of conspiracies for his own purposes. Cogitore (2002) explores the legitimacy and strength of the regime as it faced conspiracies and challenges throughout the Julio-Claudian period.

50 Rohr Vio (2000) 353–55 argues that Augustus never used formal sanctions.

51 For Augustus' use of images, see Hofter et al. (1988), Zanker (1988), and Galinsky (1996).

52 For Pompey, see Raaflaub and Samons (1990) 446 and Flower (1996) 245, 258. For Brutus and Cassius, see MacMullen (1966) 1–18 and 18–28, Rawson (1991), and Flower (1996) 88–89. For the Forum of Augustus and its temple of Mars Ultor, see Zanker (1968), Bonnefond (1987), Galinsky (1996), and Flower (1996) 224–36. Cogitore (2002) 89 emphasizes the Pompeian connections of many early conspirators.

53 For silences and the powerful, see Dio 53.19.1–6 and Dettenhofer (2000) 26–27.

54 For Ovid in exile, see the varying reconstructions by Syme (1978) esp. 214–29 and Green (1982), who gives a detailed analysis of all Ovid's own references in his exile poetry. See now also Knox (2001).

55 For *maiestas* and Tiberius, see Chilton (1955), Koestermann (1955), Allison and Cloud (1962), Bauman (1974), Levick (1976b) 180–200 and (1979).

56 For memory sanctions under Tiberius, see Vittinghoff (1936) 64 and Levick (1976b) esp. 187–88 with 282 nn. 50–51. There were three principal legal cases (Vel. Pat. 2.130.3) that involved official memory sanctions: M. Scribonius Libo Drusus in 16 (*Ann.* 2.32, *Fasti Amit.* for 13 September); Cn. Calpurnius Piso in 20 (*Ann.* 3.10–18 and *SCPP*); C. Silius in 24 (*Ann.* 4.20). For the trial of Silius, see Shotter (1967); Hennig (1975) 47–51, 65–67; and Flaig (1993). Memory sanctions were also applied to people who had never been convicted (or even tried), such as Sejanus, Asinius Gallus, and (to a lesser extent) Agrippina. See also *Ann.* 4.42 for erasure of Merula from the senate record for not swearing to the *acta* of Augustus.

57 For Tiberius and the law, see Suet. *Tib.* 61.206 with Vittinghoff (1936) 29 and Levick (1976b) 89 and 188.

58 For the funeral of Junia in 22, see Tac. *Ann.* 3.76 with Flower (1996) 253.

59 For the *SCPP* (*CIL* 2.5.900) and the trial of Piso (Tac. *Ann.* 3.7–19), see Eck, Caballos, and Ferández (1996), Caballos, Eck, and Fernández (1996), Woodman and Martin (1996), Griffin (1997), Richardson (1997), Flower (1998), Potter (1998), Potter and Damon (1999), Damon (1999a and b), Potter (1999), Bodel (1999a), Suer-

baum (1999), Lebek (1999), Champlin (1999), Talbert (1999), Eck (2000), Severy (2000). For the political crisis of 19/20, see Tac. *Ann.* 2.72.2–3, 82–84, 3.2.3, 3.4.1, 3.6.1–3; Suet. *Tib.* 52, *Cal.* 6.2 with Versnel (1980); Lebek (1990); Eck (1995); Griffin (1997); and Flower (1998) 176.

60 For the question of the murder charge, see esp. Flower (1997), *contra* Yacobson (1998) who believes a murder trial was necessary to appease public opinion.

61 For Piso's house, see *SCPP* lines 105–8 and Tac. *Ann.* 3.9.3 with Eck, Caballos, and Fernández (1996) 207–11, Flower (1998) 169–70, Bodel (1999a) 58–60, and Eck in *LTUR* 1995. For houses as monuments in general, see Bodel (1997). For Piso's *praenomen*, see *SCPP* lines 99–100 with Eck, Caballos, and Fernández (1996) 215 and Flower (1998) 164–65, 172–73. For naming patterns, name changes, and disgrace, see esp. Solin (1995).

62 For additional penalties that were rejected by Tiberius, see Tac. *Ann.* 3.18.3 with Woodman and Martin (1996) *ad loc.* and Flower (1998) 171–72.

63 For the publishing of the *SCPP*, see lines 166–72 with Eck, Caballos, and Fernández (1996) 254–72, 279–87 and Eck (1993a).

64 For mourning, see *SCPP* lines 73–75 with Eck, Caballos, and Fernández (1996) 192–94 and Flower (1998) 158–60. See Tac. *Ann.* 6.10 and Suet. *Tib.* 61 for such a ban as typical of the Tiberian period. For portraits of Piso, see *SCPP* lines 75–76 with Eck, Caballos, and Fernández (1996) 194–95, Tac. *Ann.* 3.14.6. For portraits, politics, and disgrace, see Rollin (1979) 151–74, Gregory (1994), and Varner (2004). For Piso's *imago*, see *SCPP* lines 76–82 with Eck, Caballos, and Fernández (1996) 195–97, Flower (1996) 23–31 and (1998) 161. For funerary penalties in general, see *CIL* 6.6894b = 31194b, Fraschetti (1994) 96–129, Bodel (1999a) 45–51.

65 For Piso's estate in Illyricum, see *SCPP* lines 85–90 with Eck, Caballos, and Fernández (1996) 202–7 and Flower (1998) 163–69. For the whole property clause, see *SCPP* lines 84–105 and Eck, Caballos, and Fernández (1996) 211–22.

66 For the erasure of Piso, see *SCPP* lines 82–84 with Eck, Caballos, and Fernández (1996) 197–202, Flower (1998) 162–63, Bodel (1999a) 51–58 with a map. For erasure in general, see Vittinghoff (1936) 18–41 and Kajava (1995).

67 For the quarrel between Germanicus and Piso, see *SCPP* lines 27–29 (cf. Tac. *Ann.* 3.14 and Suet. *Tib.* 52.3) with Eck, Caballos, and Fernández (1996) 154–57.

68 For the votive games of 7 B.C., see *CIL* 6.385 = *ILS* 95 (Dio 55.8). For another example from Rome, see *CIL* 6.7461 (now in the Vatican) where Piso's name remains but the name of the honorand has been erased.

69 For the erasure in the Arval record under A.D. 14, see Scheid (1998) no. 2, line 21, figure 2 (now lost), with Syme (1986) 369 n. 12, Scheid (1990a) 59 n. 36 and 187. The person who has been erased here replaced Augustus as an Arval. Piso seems too old: M. Scribonius Libo Drusus would be a preferable candidate.

70 For the altar from Spain of A.D. 9/10, see *CIL* 2.2703 and Syme (1939) 371: "It was an envious or malicious *Ignotus* who in 20 ordained the obliteration."

71 For Statilia's statue base at Samos, see Herrmann (1960) no. 30 = *IG* 12.6.1.364.

72 For Piso's text at Leptis, see *IRT* 520 = *AE* 1948.9 with di Vita-Évrard (1990) 315–31 (cf. *IRT* 625). For other unerased texts of Piso, see *RG* 16.2, *CIL* 10.924 = *ILS* 6381, *CIL* 6.7461, 1.747, 5.8112.83, 9.5308.

73 Piso is the villain throughout the *SCPP* and Tacitus; see Eck, Caballos, and Fernández (1996) 289–303 for an overview, with Bodel (1999a) 44–45. For issues of political theory behind the rhetoric of the *SCPP*, see Potter (1999).

74 The chronological discrepancy between the *SCPP* and Tacitus has been the subject of much debate: Eck, Caballos, and Fernández (1996) 109–21, Griffin (1997), Talbert (1999), and Flower (1999) 110–15 (with a summary of various previous views).

75 For Agrippina's (*PIR²* 463, Raepsaet-Charlier [1987] 812, Kienast in *NP*) exile and death, see Tac. *Ann.* 5.3–5, 6.23–25; Suet. *Tib.* 52.3,53–54, 64; *Gaius* 7; Dio 58.22.4–5. For discussions, see Hennig (1975) 86–100; Barrett (1996) 33–34 and (1989) 19, 21–24, 29, 32; Wood (1999) 183–84, 203–17.

76 For her disgrace, see Tac. *Ann.* 6.25.2. For Sejanus and Agrippina, see Barrett (1996) 17–32. For the date of her fall, see Barrett (2002) 335–36. See also Wood (1988) and Varner (2004) 90–91.

77 For private (portable) images of Agrippina, see Tac. *Ann.* 5.4.2 and 4 with Wood (1999) 207–8. Agrippina had apparently referred to herself as the true *imago* of Augustus (*Ann.* 4.52).

78 For Agrippina in the East (during her own lifetime), see Samos (Herrmann [1960] no. 14 = *IG* 12.6.1 no. 394? and *IG* 12.6.1 no. 401), Thespiae 16–13 B.C. (*AE* 1928.49 = Rose [1997] no. 82), Andriaca (*IGR* 3.716 = Rose [1997] no. 101), Lindos? (*ILindos* 2.414). Cf. also Aesernia? A.D. 18/19 (*CIL* 9.2635). For discussion, see Hahn (1994) 130–50, 337–41 and Milkocki (1995) 36–38, 176–78. For the posthumous honors for Germanicus, see Tac. *Ann.* 2.83. Agrippina's name has been twice restored in the *Tab. Siar.* (*AE* 1991.200) of A.D. 19, at lines 7 and 20, both among those consulted about the honors and as part of the statue group on the arch at the Circus Flaminius. This statue group is reflected in a slightly later one in the forum at Leptis (Rose [1997] no. 125 pl. 224, with Trillmich [1988]). For the *SCPP* of 20, see lines 137–39 with Eck, Caballos, and Fernández (1996) 242–44.

79 For Gaius' restoration of Agrippina's memory in 37, see Suet. *Gaius* 15.1–2 with Trillmich (1978), Wood (1988), Barrett (1989) 60–62, and Kragelund (1998) 154–55. For portraits of Agrippina, see Wood (1988); Boschung (1993) 61–62; Rose (1997) 32, nos. 50 and 64, pls. 133, 141, 142; and Wood (1999) 203–10. A full catalog can now be found in Tansini (1995).

80 Dio 59.37.

81 For Agrippina's burial in the Mausoleum of Augustus, see Suet. *Tib.* 54.2, *Gaius* 15.2, Dio 58.22.5, 59.3.5. For the epitaph, see *CIL* 6.40372 = *ILS* 180 (Capit. Mus. no. 2094) with *CIL* 6.40374 and Panciera (1994) 136–42. For the *carpentum* coins, see Trillmich (1978) 10–17, 33–48 pls. 1–5, esp. 2 (cf. 99–142 for extensive local issues), Tansini (1995) 22–24, Wood (1999) 208–9 figure 80. For the celebration of her birthday in the Arval records for 39, see Scheid (1998) no. 13 fgh lines 9–16.

82 For Gaius' popularity at the beginning of his reign, see Philo *Leg.* 8–13, Suet. *Tib.* 75, *Gaius* 13–14.1 with Barrett (1989) 40, 50–60. For the temple of Augustus, see Torelli s.v. *divi Augusti, templum novum* in *LTUR* 1995. For the annulling of Tiberius' will, see Suet. *Cal.* 14; for reactions to his death, *Tib.* 75. The many nega-

tive traditions about Tiberius on Capri to be found in Suetonius may have been encouraged by Gaius.

83 For Agrippina under Claudius, see Rose (1997) 42–45 and no. 94 and Wood (1999) esp. 216–17. For her portrait from Tenos, see Rose (1997) 158 no. 94.

84 Aphrodisias: *AE* 1980.874 = Reynolds (1980) 80 pl. 8 = *SEG* 30.1250. Messenia: *IG* 5.1.1394 = *CIG* 1.1301 (now lost) with Tansini (1995) 19–21. For glass phalerae from Aventicum, see Rose (1997) pl. 25. For other inscriptions of Agrippina from the time of Gaius: Thera (*ILS* 8790b = *IG* 12.3 Suppl. 1393 = Rose [1997] no. 97), Mytilene (*IG* 12.2.212 = *ILS* 8788, 208?, 210, 12. suppl. 690), Spain (*CIL* 2².5.4), Ephesos (*IEphesos* 256 = Rose [1997] no. 117), Velleia (*CIL* 11.1167 = *ILS* 179 = Rose [1997] no. 50), Rusellae (Rose [1997] no. 45), Ruscino (Gayraud [1980] no. 4 = Rose [1997] no. 57), Aventicum (Rose [1997] no. 64). For unsure additional texts, see *IGR* 1.621, *IMagn.* 158, *CIG* 2960.

85 For the golden shield portraits from Gabii, see *CIL* 14.2794 = Rose (1997) no. 13.

86 For Agrippina in Tacitus, see esp. *Ann.* 1 and 2. For Germanicus as a romantic and old-fashioned figure, see Pelling (1993). O'Gorman (2000) 47, 69–77, 91–95 juxtaposes Agrippina with Sejanus.

87 For Asinius Gallus, see *PIR*² 1229 (Groag) with Eck in *NP*, Raepsaet-Charlier (1987) pl. VII, and Cogitore (2002) 202–5. For Asinius in the senate, see Tac. *Ann.* 1.8, 76, 77, 2.32, 33, 35, 36, 3.11, 4.20, 30, 71, with analysis in Shotter (1971) and Bosworth (1977). For his marriage to Vipsania, see *Ann.* 1.12, Dio 57.2.7, 58.3.1. See also *AE* 1997.862 with Rodriguez Colmenero (1997) for the well-preserved *Tabula Lougeiorum*, although the authenticity of this text is still hotly disputed.

88 For Asinius Gallus' confinement and suicide, see Tac. *Ann.* 6.23, Suet. *Tib.* 61.4, Dio 57.2.7, 58.3, 58.23.6 with Levick (1976b) 172–73, 198, 206–7 and Barrett (1989) 26. Shotter (1971) argues for official sanctions.

89 Asinius Gallus' sons: C. Asinius Pollio (cos. 23, in Asia prob. 38/39, *PIR*² 1242); Ser. Asinius Gallus (cos. suff. 38, *PIR*² 1225); M. Asinius Agrippa (cos. 25, *PIR*² 1223); Asinius Gallus (*PIR*² 1228); Asinius Saloninus (betrothed to a daughter of Germanicus; Tac. *Ann.* 3.75.1); Cn. Asinius (*PIR*² 1221). For the family, see Alföldy (1992a) 125–43 with a description of the tomb and epitaph of Vipsania Agrippina (*CIL* 6.40321). Celer and Gallus conspired against Claudius (Sen. *Apoc.* 13.5; Dio 60.27.5).

90 For the boundary stones from the Tiber, see *CIL* 6.31541 (= 1235), 40860, 40861 (with A. Gordon [1958] no. 20 and no. 53, MNR nos. 737, 832). Of a total of twenty-two extant boundary markers, all but one have Asinius Gallus' name restored in an erasure.

91 For the votive games of 8 B.C., see *CIL* 6.36789 = *ILS* 8894 (marble plaque, MNR no. 15034) = A. Gordon (1958) no. 21 pl. 14a. See also *CIL* 6.458 for an unerased New Year's dedication of 8 B.C. from near the Arch of Septimius Severus.

92 For the *ludi saeculares* of 17 B.C., see *CIL* 6.32323 = *ILS* 5050, lines 107, 151, 168 (the last one erased) with Pighi (1965) 107–19.

93 For the *Fasti* of the *vicomagistri* (Luna marble plaque found at the Via Marmorata in 1928), see *II* 13.1 no. 20 and *II* 13.2 no. 12, with A. Gordon (1958) no. 32 pl. 19 (MNR no. 121558) and Rüpke (1995a) 58–63 and (1998). C. Asinius Pollio (*PIR*²

1241) was erased about seventy years after his consulate of 40 B.C. The freestanding marble stele may have come from the clubhouse of the local *vicus* and was found with a series of altars and other related material.

94 Laude Pompeia: *CIL* 5.6359 = *ILS* 165.

95 Artemis at Ephesus: *CIL* 3.7118 = Hicks (1886–90) 522–24 = *ILS* 97 of the first half of 5 B.C.

96 Geneva: *CIL* 12.2623 = Walser (1980) no. 23. For dating formulae from Italy, see *CIL* 5.4201 = *ILS* 4902 (Brixia) and *CIL* 11.844 (Mutina).

97 Teate Marrucinorum: *CIL* 9.3018 = *ILS* 5761.

98 Augustus' letter to the Cnidians: Sherk (1969) no. 67, line 11 = *SIG*³ 780 = *IGR* 4.1031 = *IG* 12.3.174. Compare *IG* 3.583 for a dedication of the Demos in Attica for Gallus or for his son.

99 Suet. *Cal.* 16.1 with Speyer (1981) 65.

100 For the emperor Gaius (*PIR*² 217, Eder in *NP*), see Balsdon (1934), Nony (1986), Barrett (1989) esp. 244–54 on the sources, Ferrill (1991), Yavetz (1996), Wiedemann (1996a) 221–29, Wardle (1998), Beacham (1999) 165–86, and now esp. Winterling (2003). For Suetonius, see Wallace-Hadrill (1983) and Hurley (1993).

101 See now the detailed reading in Winterling (2003). His Gaius is closer to Tiberius, and more sinister.

102 For an attempt to reconstruct the lost sources (Cluvius Rufus, Fabius Rusticus, Pliny the Elder, and others) of Josephus and the later historians, see Wiseman (1991) xii–xiv, 111–18. For Josephus, see Timpe (1960), Rajak (1983), Wiseman (1991), and Wandrey in *NP*.

103 For the murder of Gaius, see Jos. *AJ* 19.1–273 with Wiseman (1991), Suet. *Gaius* 56–59 with Hurley (1993), Suet. *Claud.* 10–11 with Hurley (2001), Dio 59.29–30. See also Barrett (1989) 154–71, Levick (1990) 29–39, Wiedemann (1996a) 230–32, Beacham (1999) 181–86, and Winterling (2003) 163–74. See Cogitore (2002) 63–78 for a reading that stresses religious elements.

104 Winterling (2003) 164–65.

105 Barrett (1996) 73 argues that the senate had declared Claudius a *hostis* at first. For Claudius' accession, see also Timpe (1962) 77–93.

106 For the revolt of A.D. 42 (Vinicianus, Q. Pomponius Secundus, Arruntius Scribonianus), see Tac. *Ann.* 16.34.3; Suet. *Claud.* 13.2; Dio 60.15.1–6 and 16.6–7 with Swan (1970); Levick (1990) 58–60; Flaig (1992) 224–28 and (1993); Voisin (1998) 183. For the erasure of Pomponius, suff. cos. 41, see Tac. *Ann.* 13.43.2 and *CIL* 6.2015. For L. Arruntius Camillus Scribonianus as legate of Gaius, see *ILS* 5950. For the younger Scribonianus, see Tac. *Ann.* 12.52.1 and Pliny *Ep.* 3.16.7–9 with Cogitore (2002) 243–49.

107 *Contra* Winterling (2003) 153, who thinks Gaius remained popular with ordinary people in Rome to the end of his life.

108 For the memory of Cassius Chaerea, see Jos. *AJ* 19.272 with Wiseman (1991) *ad loc.* on the *Parentalia* and Dio 59.30.1a. See also Barrett (1996) 80 and Beacham (1999) 186.

109 For Gaius' ghost, see Philo *Leg.* 358 and Suet. *Gaius* 59: *satis constat, prius quam id fieret, hortorum custodes umbris inquietatos; in ea quoque domo, in qua occuberit,*

nullam noctem sine aliquo terrore transactam, donec ipsa domus incendio consumpta sit (It is well established that before that happened [the reburial] the staff at the gardens were troubled by ghosts. In addition, in the house in which he died no night passed without some terror, until that house was burned to the ground in a fire). For other Roman ghosts, see Ovid *Fast.* 2.555–56, Suet. *Aug.* 6, Pliny *Ep.* 7.27.11. For the Horti Lamiani, see Cima and La Rocca (1986), Häuber (1991), and Cima di Puolo in *LTUR* 1996.

110 For Gaius' reburial, see Suet. *Gaius* 59 with Hurley (1993) *ad loc.* Cf. also Suet. *Ner.* 50 and *Dom.* 17.3 for Nero and Domitian. Permission for such a move would probably have been required from the *pontifices*, as in the case of M. Ulpius Phaedimus (*CIL* 6.1884 = Walser [1984] no. 13 = *ILS* 1791). Normally such moves were not allowed (*Dig.* 11.7.39).

111 For the topography of the Palatine and the place of Gaius' death, see Wiseman (1987), (1991) 105–10, Krause in *LTUR* 1995 *domus Tiberiana*, Royo (1999) 275–88. The whole area burned in A.D. 80 (Suet. *Tit.* 8.3).

112 For Polla's dedication from Spoletium, see *CIL* 11.4778.

113 For the removal of Gaius' statues, see Levick (1990) 88–89, Dio 59.26.3, 59.30.1C, 60.4.5–6. (Cf. Jos. *AJ* 19.185.) For his portraiture, see Boschung (1989) and (1993) 67–68 and Rose (1997) 66 no. 16.

114 For the recarving of Gaius' portraits, see Jucker (1981, 1982); Ramage (1983); Pekáry (1985) 38, 137; Boschung (1989); D. Kleiner (1992) 126–27; Rose (1997) 37–38; and Varner (2004) 21–45, 225–36 (thirty-eight examples). The treatment of Gaius provided the impetus and model for the fashion of recarving in the first century A.D.

115 For portraits of Gaius in a small format, see Varner (2000) 102–7 nos. 6–9 with full bibliography and (2004) 40. Boschung (1989) 103 notes the number of small format portraits of Gaius (seven in bronze and one in marble). For examples that have been mutilated before being discarded, see Boschung (1989) no. 19 and no. 30 with Jucker (1982) 112–13.

116 For Sentius' ring, see Jos. *AJ* 19.185 with Wiseman (1991) *ad loc.*

117 For Gaius' own interest in portraits, see Philo *Leg.* 135, Blanck (1969) 16, and Boschung (1989).

118 For the debate in the senate after Gaius' death, see Suet. *Gaius* 60: *et senatus in asserenda libertate adeo consensit, ut consules primo non in curiam, quia Iulia uocabatur, sed in Capitolium conuocarent, quidam uero sententiae loco abolendam Caesarum memoriam ac diruenda templa censuerint* (In making their claim to political freedom, the senate was so much in agreement that the consuls would call their meeting not in the senate house, because it was called the Julian curia, but on the Capitol. They thought this the right place to propose the abolishing of the memory of the Caesars and the destruction of their temples). (with Swan [1970] and Hurley [1993] *ad loc.*). Did the senate declare Claudius a *hostis* (Sen. *Apoc.* 6.1; Jos. *BJ* 2.205 with Barrett [1996] 173)? Josephus' version (*AJ* 19.158–200) depends on a source very sympathetic to the republicanism of the senate, which met on the Capitol for the first time since the construction of the Curia Julia in 29 B.C. Whether or not this account is idealized and romanticized, it represents what senatorial sources

chose to record, perhaps partly with a view to obscuring the power struggles of
A.D. 41 and the ultimate role of the Praetorians. See also Suet. *Claud.* 11.1 and Dio
60.3.5 for Claudius' amnesty. Swan (1970) stresses the seriousness of the proposal
to restore the Republic, both in 41 at the time of Gaius' death and in 42 with the
revolt of Scribonianus against Claudius.

119 The temples of the Caesars should include primarily the temples of Divus Iulius,
Clementia Caesaris, and the two for Divus Augustus. It is much less clear whether
Venus Genetrix or Mars Ultor or even Agrippa's Pantheon could have become
targets in the same way without incurring religious faults. Presumably there would
also have been a move to suppress or at least to modify the cult of the *lares Augusti*
in the local neighborhoods. For the temples built under Augustus, see Gros (1976)
and Hänlein-Schäfer (1985).

120 For Gaius' own use of destruction and erasure, see Suet. *Gaius* 34–35 for the destruction of republican statues on the Campus Martius and the suppression of
individual status symbols of some prominent families; Suet. *Gaius* 20 for the
erasures of the names of losers in athletic competitions; Suet. *Gaius* 23 for the
memory of Agrippa and Livia; Suet. *Gaius* 23.1, 26.3, Dio 59.20.1 for the ban on the
Actian games. See also Claudius, who expunged the names of some jurors (Suet.
Claud. 15) and erased names from the list of the censors (Suet. *Claud.* 16).

121 For erasures of Gaius from bases in honor of Drusilla, see Milan (*CIL* 5.5722 = *ILS*
194); Samos (*IG* 12.6.1 no. 411); Cos (Maiuri [1925] no. 467); Caere (*CIL* 11.3598 =
Rose [1997] no. 5) with Wood (1995). For the one erasure of Drusilla herself at Halasarnae, see (*IGR* 4.1098). See also Epidaurus (*IG* 4.600). At Velleia Drusilla's whole
text seems to have been recarved to remove Gaius (*CIL* 11.1168 = Rose [1997] 50).

122 For erasures at Pompeii, see *CIL* 10.901 and 904 = *ILS* 6396 and 6397. In the same
series, *CIL* 10.902 remains unerased. Barrett (1989) 178 sees the erasures as local
and spontaneous.

123 Alexandria: *IGR* 1.1086 (unerased) and 1.1087 (erased); Cyzicus: *SIG*³ 798 (unerased) and 799 (erased); Samos *IGR* 4.981; Attica *IG* II/III² 2292; Bologna *CIL*
11.720 = *ILS* 5674. For the lead ingot from Corsica, see Maréchal (1987/1989) = *AE*
1992.913.

124 *CIL* 8.1478 = Khanoussi and Maurin (2000) no. 24. It is the only extant example of
a monument in honor of Gaius in Africa. Khanoussi (1997) discusses the archaeological and topographical context.

125 For fragmentary texts of Gaius, which are inconclusive with regard to the erasure
of his name, see Lycia (*AE* 1995.1551); Sardis (*AE* 1995.1459 and 1460); Cos (*AE*
1994.1642); Messenia (*IG* 5.1394); Lusitania (*CIL* 2.4639); Pompeii (*CIL* 10.796);
Lugdunum (*AE* 1980.5a); Ephesus (*AE* 1990.908 with a possible erasure of Lepidus); milestones from Switzerland (*CIL* 12.2331 = Walser [1980] no. 272; *AE* 1985.659
= *CIL* 12.5524).

126 For Gaius' temple at Miletus, see *IDidyma* 148 with Robert (1949) and Clauss
(1999) 88–94, 331, 509. Cf. Segre (1944–45/1952) on Kalymna.

127 Thera: *IG* 12.3 suppl. 1392 and 1393 = *ILS* 8790 a and b.

128 Syene (Assuan) (*CIL* 3.14147 = *ILS* 8899, 28 April 39); Vienne (*CIL* 12.1848 and 1849

= *ILS* 189); Mytilene (*IG* 12.2.172b = *ILS* 8789, 209, 210); Mentesa Bastitanorum (*CIL* 2.5.4 = 2.3379); Narcissus' dedication from near lago Maggiore (*CIL* 5.6641 = *ILS* 191). For the oaths of allegiance, see Assos (*IAssos* 26 = Bruns[7] no. 102, *SIG*[3] 797, *IGR* 4.251); Sentinum (*CIL* 11.5998a); Lusitania (*CIL* 2.172 = *ILS* 190); Akraiphia (*IG* 7.2711 = *ILS* 8792); and Cyzikus *SIG*[3] 798 and 799.

129 For imperial statue groups under Gaius, see esp. Rose (1997), who lists 18: Aesis (1), Caere (5), Luna (20), Ocriculum (25), Paestum (26), Rusellae (45), Velia (49), Vellia (50), Ruscino (57), Augusta Emerita (60), Aventicum (64), Corinth (69), Gortyn (85), Mytilene (90), Thera (95), Aphrodisias (104), Ephesus (117), Leptis (125).

130 For examples of Gaius recut to Claudius, see, for example, Rose (1997) no. 25 pl. 92 (Ocriculum), no. 45 (Rusellae), and no. 50 pls. 132, 135, 136 (Velleia), and Varner (2000) no. 17 in the Vatican. See also Varner (2000) no. 19 for Gaius recut as Augustus from Pietrabbondante (now in the Getty Museum). See now Varner (2004) 25–30 (Gaius recut to Claudius) and 30–33 (Gaius recut to Augustus).

131 For the surviving portraits of Gaius in various media, see Boschung's catalog (1989) 105–24. For the portraits that have been recut or mutilated, see Varner (2004) 225–36.

132 Gaius appears in the texts he put up at the Mausoleum of Augustus (*CIL* 6.40372–74). See *CIL* 6.892 = *ILS* 172 = A. Gordon (1958) no. 80 with Panciera (1994) xxiv for the epitaph of Tiberius Gemellus, who is not designated as the adopted son of Gaius in this context. Gaius certainly appeared on many other inscriptions from Rome: see the fragments *CIL* 6.811 of 38 and *CIL* 6.31281 = 40355. We may assume that Gaius was honored at the Meta Sudans, at the restored theater of Pompey (Suet. *Gaius* 21.1, *Claud.* 21.3, Dio 60.6.8 with Gros in *LTUR* 1999), and especially in the dedicatory text of the new temple of Divus Augustus dedicated by Gaius on his birthday in 37 (Suet. *Gaius* 21, Dio 59.7.1, *RIC* 1[2] 111 no. 36, *LTUR* 1995). See Hänlein-Schäfer (1985) 120–28, who traces the temple's development as *Aedes Caesarum*.

133 For Gaius' coins, see *RIC* 1[2] 102–13 pls. 13–15 (106–7 argues for a largely symbolic attack on the coins rather than a thorough recall) and *BMC* 1.146–63 with Trillmich (1978) and Boschung (1989) pls. A–E. For the recalling of his *aes* coinage in 43, see Dio 60.22.3, Stat. *Silv.* 4.9.23 with Coleman (1988) 230, Barrett (1989) 178–79, Levick (1990) 88–89, and Varner (2000) 108–11. For examples of erasures and overstrikes, see BM 45 and 140, Varner (2000) nos. 11 and 12.

134 For the *Fasti Ostienses* for 37 and 38, see Vidman (1982) and Bargagli and Grosso (1997) pl. C. There is no notice to mark the succession of Gaius, who is simply referred to as C. Caesar, and very little about his particular program. Gaius also appears in the *Fasti Ant. Min. II* 13.2.26 as consul for 39 and 40 and in the *Fasti Vall. II* 13.1.30, where his birthday has been added to an earlier calendar.

135 For the Arval records, see Scheid (1998) nos. 11–16. The records for 38 are particularly well preserved. For erasure in the Arval records, see chapter 8.

136 For the *Aqua Virgo*, see *CIL* 6.1252 = *ILS* 205 (25 January 45/46) with Suet. *Gaius* 21 and Rodríguez Almeida in *LTUR* 1993.

137 For the edict of Claudius (15 March 46), see *CIL* 5.5050 = *ILS* 206. By contrast

Claudius pointedly does not name the disgraced Valerius Asiaticus in his famous speech about admitting Gauls to the senate.

138 See also Jos. *AJ* 19.284–85 for Claudius referring to Gaius' madness.

Chapter VII

1 For Vestal Virgins, see Beard (1980, 1995), Scheid (1992) 381–84, and Beard, North, and Price (1998) 1.51–54, 189–91, 194.

2 Allen (2000) 208 discusses how Greek cities expelled men but consumed women.

3 For women in 186 B.C., see Livy 39.18.6, Val. Max. 6.3.7 with Cantarella (1991) 146–47.

4 Appuleia Varilla: Tac. *Ann.* 2.50.3.

5 For the funeral of Popilia, mother of Q. Lutatius Catulus, cos. 102 B.C., see Cic. *De Or.* 2.11.44 and for the funeral of Cornelia, wife of Caesar, see Plut. *Caes.* 5, both with Flower (1996) 122–25. For statues of republican women and their images on coins, see Flower (2002b). For statues of Hellenistic and Roman women in the East, see Pliny *NH* 34.31 and van Bremen (1996).

6 For Fulvia, see Delia (1991), Fischer (1999), and Virlouvet (2001).

7 For naming patterns of Roman women, see Kajava (1994).

8 Honors for Livia and Octavia in 35 B.C.: Dio 49.38.1 with Purcell (1986), Flory (1993), Rose (1997) 8 (eighteen attestations of Livia in forty Augustan statue groups), Bartman (1999) 62, and Barrett (2002) 31–32. For Julio-Claudian women more generally, see esp. Corbier (1994). Frei-Stolba (1998) discusses juridical aspects. For inscriptions naming Livia, see now the collection in Barrett ([2002] 265–93) who lists more than two hundred items.

9 For Augustan moral legislation and married women, see Treggiari (1991) 275–90, 294–98, 507–10. Dettenhofer (2000) 128–44 stresses the intention of social control and the intrusion into *patria potestas*. For Munatia Plancina (Raepsaet-Charlier [1987] no. 562), see Tac. *Ann.* 3.15.1, *SCPP* 109–20 with Eck, Caballos, and Fernández (1996) 222–28.

10 Julia, daughter of Augustus: *PIR*² 634; Raepsaet-Charlier (1987) no. 421; Syme (1939) 427, (1978) 192–98, and (1984); Levick (1972, 1975); Raaflaub and Samons (1990) 428–30; Bauman (1992) 108–19; Dettenhofer (2000) 176–80. Barrett (2002) 39–42, 47–51 takes at face value the ancient sources' claim that Julia's promiscuity, revealed in 2 B.C., "shattered the serenity of the *domus Augusta*" (50). Rohr Vio (2000) 208–50 sees an Antonian faction putting active pressure on Augustus in the period from 10 to 2 B.C. Cogitore (2002) 165–72 sees political opposition on the part of Julia but no conspiracy.

11 Fagan (2002) 577: "Thus the political dimensions of adultery by imperial women lay in the act of adultery itself, and in some cases there is no need to go hunting for plots and schemes."

12 Iullus Antonius (cos. 10 B.C.): *PIR*² 800; *CIL* 6.30974 = *ILS* 92; *AE* 1911.89; *CIL* 6.12010 (34051); Vel. Pat. 2.100.4–5; Sen. *Brev.* 4.6; Tac. *Ann.* 1.10, 3.18 and 24, 4.44; Dio 55.10.15. See Hor. *Od.* 4.2 with Speyer (1981) 59 for his epic poem *Diomeideia* in twelve books, now lost. His son L. Antonius: *PIR*² 802, Tac. *Ann.* 4.44.

13 Julia's exile: Vel. Pat. 100.3–5; Sen. *Ben.* 6.32; *Clem.* 1.9.6; Pliny *NH* 7.149; Tac. *Ann.* 1.52–53; Suet. *Aug.* 19.1, 63–64, 101.3; *Tib.* 7.2–3, 11.4; Dio 55.12–16, 57.18. Linderski (1988) 199: ". . . the death of Julia Tiberius preferred to keep veiled in obscurity." See Bauman (1974) 13–14, 173–75 for a different reconstruction, which has both Julias tried under the *maiestas* law. For a Julian party, see now Barrett (2002) 59–60. Barrett ([2002] 71–72) refers rather euphemistically to Julia's death of "weakness and malnutrition." Syme (1958) 423 was not sure that Tiberius caused Julia's death ("that cannot be substantiated"). Woodman (1995) argues that Livia (and Sallustius Crispus) was responsible for the order to kill Agrippa Postumus, not Tiberius.

14 For Julia's portraits (probably at least two types), see Boschung (1993) 48–50; D. Kleiner (1992) 78; Hahn (1994) 106–11, 334–36; Mikocki (1995) 30–32, 170–71; Winkes (1995); Rose (1997) 21 and 61 (nos. 32, 52, 70, 76, 82, 87, 91, 92, 95, 112, 122); Wood (1999) 29–74; and Varner (2004) 86–88, who argues that most portraits would have been warehoused or destroyed. It remains unclear whether Julia has been recarved on the Ara Pacis.

15 Julia's inscriptions: Eresos, before 27 B.C. (*IG* 12.2.537 = *IGR* 4.9 = *ILS* 127). As wife of Agrippa (mostly 16–13 B.C.): Halasarnae, Kos (*IGR* 4.1095), Mytilene and Plakados, Lesbos (*IG* 12.2.204 = *IGR* 4.64, *IG* 12.2.482 = *IGR* 4.114), Sestos, Thrace (*ISestos* 8 = *IGR* 1.821 = Rose [1997] no. 122), Cyzicus? (*AE* 1983.910), Andros (*IG* 12.5.740), Thasos (*IG* 8.381 = *ILS* 8784 = Rose [1997] no. 95), Megara (*IG* 7.65 = Rose [1997] no. 76), Sardis? (*ISardis* 7.1.197), Delos (*SIG*³ 777), Delphi (*SIG*³ 779 = Rose [1997] 70), Assos (*IAssos* 16–17), Priene (*IPriene* 225), Ceramos (*BCH* 1880, 517), Thespiae (*AE* 1928.50 = Rose [1997] no. 82), Paros? (*SEG* 26.958 = Rose [1997] no. 92), Aphrodisias? (*AE* 1980.877), Samos? (*IG* 12.6.1, 392), Euromos (*AE* 1993.1521 with Habicht [1996]).

16 Inscriptions put up after the death of Agrippa in 12 B.C.: Noricum (*AE* 1954.241), Lindos (*ILindos* 2.385c = Rose [1997] no. 87), Palaepaphos, written over the erasure of a Hellenistic text (*IGR* 3.940 = Rose [1997] no. 91, Ephesos (*IEphesos* 3006 = *ILS* 8897 = Rose [1997] no. 112), Egypt (*IGR* 1.1109).

17 When he went to Rhodes, Tiberius' own busts and statues had been thrown down at Nemausus (Suet. *Tib.* 13).

18 Julia's freedmen at Rhegium: *AE* 1975.289 from the reign of Claudius, with Linderski (1988). See also Buonocore (1989) 62–64 nos. 15 (Scribonia) and 16 (Julia and Livia [Diva Augusta]).

19 For Tiberius' *ovatio* in 9 B.C., see Dio 55.2.4. Barrett (2002) 51 stresses Livia's possible help for Julia.

20 See Palmer (1974) 137–41 for Julia and the cult of Pudicitia Patricia that may have been restored by her. For a possible thaw, see Linderski (1988) 199–200. For her continued popularity, see Suet. *Aug.* 65.3 and Dio 55.13.1.

21 Julia, granddaughter of Augustus: *PIR*² 635; Raepsaet-Charlier (1987) 813; Tac. *Ann.* 3.24, 4.71; Suet. *Aug.* 19.1, 65.2–5, 72.3, 101.3; *Schol. Juv.* 6.157 with Levick (1976a); Syme (1978) 206–20 and (1986) 115–27; Green (1982); Raaflaub and Samons (1990) 428–30; Bauman (1992) 119–24; Dettenhofer (2000) 195–98; and Varner (2004) 89–90. Barrett (2002) 60: "As confusing as the affair of Julia the Elder might have been, the details of the crisis that swept up her daughter are even more baffling."

Rohr Vio (2000) 250–80 stresses the parallels with her mother Julia. For the destruction of her villa, see Suet. *Aug.* 72.3; for her exclusion from the Mausoleum of Augustus, see Suet. *Aug.* 101.3; for the exposure of her child, see Suet. *Aug.* 65.4. At the same time, Claudius gave up his engagement with her daughter (Tac. *Ann.* 3.24, Suet. *Claud.* 26.1).

22 *ILS* 8784 with Dunant and Pouilloux (1958) 62–64. The inscription for the elder Julia seems earlier and the lettering is recorded as being different from that for the younger Julia and Livia. The loss of the stone makes this unusual text hard to discuss.

23 L. Aemilius Paullus (cos. A.D. 1): *PIR*² 391 with Scheid (1975b) 89–93, Syme (1986) 115–27, *CIL* 6.36841 = *ILS* 9337 and *IG* 3.590 (now lost). His name is erased in the epitaph of a freedman at *CIL* 6.4499. Neither Julia nor Paullus is discussed in Boschung (1993), Hahn (1994), or Rose (1997). Syme (1984) 935: "The bare name of Paullus has all but vanished from the pages of history." Cogitore (2002) 172–75 focuses on L. Aemilius Paullus and Rubellius Plautus.

24 See Knox (2001) esp. 175–81, who argues that Ovid's exile should not be connected with Julia's disgrace. Luisi (2000) contends that Ovid was involved in a political movement that focused on the memory of Antony.

25 Livi(ll)a: *PIR*² L 303, Raepsaet-Charlier (1987) 239 with Syme (1986) 93–94, 169–71, 309. Her freedmen's tombs: *ILS* 1751, 1752, 1828, 1843, 1844, 8052; *CIL* 6.5226, 15502, 19747, 38304.

26 The epitaph of Vipsania Agrippina: *CIL* 6.40321 with Alföldy (1992a).

27 *SCPP* 142–46 with Eck, Caballos, and Fernández (1996) 235–38: . . . *et Liviae sororis Germ(anici) Caesar(is) de qua optume et avia sua et | socer idemq(ue) patruos, princeps noster, iudicaret, quorum iudicis, etiam si non contin- | gere{n}t domum eorum, merito gloriari posset, nedum tam coniunctis necessitu- | dinibus inligata femina: quarum aeq(ue) et dolorᶠeᵓm fidelissumum et in dolore | moderatione<m> senatum probare* . . . (and of Livia, sister of Germanicus Caesar, of whom both her grandmother and her father-in-law [who is] at the same time her father's brother, our *princeps*, had a most favorable opinion, people whose opinions, even if she did not belong to their house, she would be able deservedly to take pride in, and much more so as a woman bound by such close personal ties; the senate commended both the most loyal grief of these women [Agrippina, Antonia, Livia] and their moderation in grief. . .).

28 L. Aelius Seianus: *PIR*² 225, Eck in *NP*, *LTUR* 1995 *Fortuna Seiani, aedes* with Absil (1997) no. 5 who gives a full bibliography and Cogitore (2002) 212–28.

29 Livi(ll)a in Tacitus has been analyzed by Sinclair (1990) (*Ann.* 2.43.6, 2.84.1–2, 3.34.6, 4.3–4, 4.10–12, 4.39–40, 6.2.1). His parallel with Lucretia, especially in Livy 1, can be amplified by considering further echoes of the wicked Tullia in the same book of Livy. Fagan (2002) takes Tacitus completely at face value on Livi(ll)a, even as he offers a critical analysis of Messalina's fall.

30 Suetonius (*Tib.*) does not connect Livi(ll)a's fall with Sejanus.

31 For the disgrace of Sejanus, see Juv. *Sat.* 10.54–113; Suet. *Tib.* 65–67; Dio 58.12.4–6 (contrast with Vel. Pat. 2.127–28); *ILS* 157, 158, 159, 6044 = *CIL* 6.10213, 6.40347?, 10.898; *AE* 1953.88 and 89 with Syme (1958) 401–5, 752–54; Hennig (1975) 139–56;

Levick (1976b) 186–87, 202; Herz (1978) 1157–58; and Varner (2004) 92–93. For Sejanus' children, see Tac. *Ann.* 5.9, Dio 58.11.5, *Fasti Ostienses* for 31. Tiberius apparently published an autobiography blaming Sejanus for the ruin of Germanicus' family (Suet. *Tib.* 61.1).

32 See Yavetz (1998) for Sejanus and the plebs.

33 *CIL* 10.898 from Puteoli has Sejanus' name erased as consul for 31 and replaced with an extended version of Tiberius' titles.

34 Dio on the death of Livi(ll)a: 58.11.6–7 and 24.5; cf. *Oct.* 932–51, Pliny *NH* 29.20, Suet. *Tib.* 62 with Vittinghoff (1936) 31, 51, 164 and Levick (1976b) 200.

35 For the Mausoleum of Augustus, see Panciera (1994) 82 and 156 no. XXV, and Alföldy in *CIL* 8.6.2.

36 For Livi(ll)a in art, see Megow (1987) 293–301, D18–32; Boschung (1993) 63–64; Hahn (1994) 126–29, 337; Mikocki (1995) 34–36, 174–76; Flory (1996); Rose (1997) 24–30, 72, 238 n. 44 (nos. 35, 37, 65, 125); Wood (1999) 180–84, 190–202; and Varner (2004) 93–95, who accepts the thirteen cameos listed in Megow.

37 Dedication of Philon, son of Apollonios, for Antonia, perhaps to mark Germanicus' visit to Ilion in A.D. 18: *Illion* 88 = *ILS* 8787 = *IGR* 4.206 with Trillmich (1978) 3.

38 Dedication to the imperial family in the forum at Leptis Magna, A.D. 23–31: Levi della Vida (1935), Aurigemma (1940), Levi della Vida and Amadasi Guzzo (1987) no. 22, Trillmich (1988), Rose (1997) no. 125.

39 For the arch of Germanicus in the Circus Flaminius, voted in A.D. 19: *Tab. Siar.* 1.1–21, de Maria (1988) no. 65, Rose (1997) no. 37. For the arch of Drusus, voted in A.D. 23: *Fasti Ostienses* for 30 (Bargagli and Grosso [1997] 24 lines 9–10), *CIL* 6.912 = 31200, Tac. *Ann.* 2.83.2 and 4.9.2 with de Maria (1988) no. 66. For a dedication from Brixia to Livi(ll)a as mother of twins, see *CIL* 5.4311 = *ILS* 170 with Cogitore (1992) 835.

40 For Norbanus' statue group, probably erected in A.D. 15, see *Tab. Siar.* 1.1–21 with Flory (1996) and Rose (1997) no. 35.

41 For Ovid and the *domus Augusta*, see Flory (1996) for a narrow definition, and Millar (1993), followed by Eck, Caballos, and Fernández (1996) 238, for the broader view adopted here. See now Corbier (2001) and Barrett (2002) 317. The earliest literary reference is Ovid *Pont.* 2.2.74 (around A.D. 14). Norbanus' statue group of 15 conveyed much the same idea.

42 Decree from the Sebasteion at Messenia: *SEG* 41.328 = *AE* 1993.1414, with Themelis (1990). For the Kaisereia festival at Gytheum in A.D. 14–19, see *SEG* 11.922–23 = Rose (1997) no. 74.

43 For Sejanus' betrothed, see Dio (Zonaras) 58.3.9 and 7.5 with Hennig (1975) 98 (cf. 57.22.2 on the problem of the name); Tac. *Ann.* 5.6, 6.8; Suet. *Tib.* 65.1. For Julia, daughter of Livi(ll)a and Drusus, see *PIR*² 636, Tac. *Ann.* 6.27.1 with Sumner (1965) 144–45.

44 Livi(ll)a and the *Fasti Ostienses*: *Fasti Ostienses* for 31–32, Bellemore (1995), tentatively accepted by Eck in *NP*. For Sejanus' family, see Sumner (1965) and Syme (1986) 300–312. Sumner (1965) 145 suggests that Apicata's family name could be Gavia: "The possibility that Antonia was in some sense allied with Seianus will have to be borne in mind in any attempt to understand the rise and fall of the

Volsinian." For Antonia's letter to Tiberius, see Josephus *AJ* 18.181, 250. For Apicata, see also *CIL* 6.12126.

45 Valeria Messalina: *PIR²* 161, *RE* 403, Raepsaet-Charlier (1987) no. 774, Eder in *NP* with Levick (1990) 55–67, Rose (1997) 41. Titus Saunders (1994) shows that Messalina never officially received the title Augusta. Fagan (2002) gives a detailed discussion but is unsure of the effects of memory sanctions on our picture of Messalina. He concludes (579): "Messalina had crossed a line in the sand and there was already a long and sorry tradition of punishing analogous behaviour among princesses."

46 Adoption of Nero: dated to 25 February 50 in the Arval record (Scheid [1998] no. 27); cf. Tac. *Ann.* 12.25.1, Suet. *Claud.* 27.2, *Ner.* 7.1, Dio 60.32.2.

47 For Messalina in Tacitus, see, Tac. *Ann.* 11.26–38 with Joshel (1997) for bibliography. *Versa ex eo civitas et cuncta feminae oboediebant, non per lasciviam, ut Messalinae, rebus Romanis inludenti. Adductum et quasi virile servitium: palam severitas ac saepius superbia; nihil domi inpudicum, nisi dominationi expediret. Cupido auri immensa obtentum habebat, quasi subsidum regno pararetur (Ann.* 12.7: From that time onwards the political situation changed and everyone gave their allegiance to a woman, and not one who toyed with Rome for her own sensual enjoyment, as Messalina had. Rather this was a strict and almost masculine domination. In public there was severity and often arrogance. In private there was no adultery, unless it served to increase political power. She had an immense desire for acquiring money, as if it would furnish the support of her reign). See O'Gorman (2000) 115–21, esp. 121: "The memory of Messalina is preserved in the narrative, as is the memory of her obliteration."

48 Fagan (2002) esp. 570–71 argues for accepting Tacitus on the grounds that he is a careful historian (*Ann.* 11.27.1–2) without taking into account his biases toward adulterous women, especially Julio-Claudians.

49 Levick (1990) 56: "Messalina should not be seen as an adolescent nymphomaniac: in the main she used sex as a means of compromising and controlling politicians."

50 For Claudius' accession, see most conveniently Levick (1990) 29–39, 41–46.

51 Messalina's family connections: Ehrhardt (1978), Syme (1986) 155–67, Corbier (1994), Questa (1995).

52 Marriage of Messalina and Silius in A.D. 48: Jos. *AJ* 20.8.1 (149–50), *BJ* 2.12.8; Tac. *Ann.* 11.26–38; Suet. *Claud.* 26–27, 29.3, 36, Dio 60.31.1–5 with Griffin (1984) 29; Levick (1990) 64–67; Eck (1993b) 24; and Barrett (1996) 91–94. Much is made of the fact that Messalina died in the gardens of Lucullus, which she had acquired after the judicial murder of Valerius Asiaticus (Tac. *Ann.* 11.37, Dio 60.31.5). Fagan (2002) 573 with n. 32 gives a convenient summary of the many modern theories about who was conspiring against whom in 48.

53 For the sanctions against her memory, see Tac. *Ann.* 11.38: *iuvit oblivionem eius senatus censendo nomen et effigies privatis ac publicis locis demovendas* (The senate promoted her oblivion by decreeing that her name and image should be removed from private and public places). Cf. Suet. *Claud.* 39 with Fagan (2002) 572–73. Of thirty Claudian statue groups in Rose (1997), Messalina is attested in three (nos. 108, 126, 128), Agrippina in eleven. According to Dio 60.12.4–5 senators

had "voluntarily" celebrated Messalina's birthday, although she had not received the title Augusta. For Messalina's portraits and coins, see Wood (1992); Boschung (1993) 71–73; Hahn (1994) 175–78, 345–47; Mikocki (1995) 44–45; Varner (2004) 95–97, 257–58. Cat. 4.3 = figure 101 a–d is the only example of a recarved portrait of an empress, in this case Messalina redone as Agrippina.

54 Messalina's freedmen: *CIL* 6.8952 = *ILS* 1781, *ILS* 1664, *CIL* 6.5537. Note especially *CIL* 6.28132 which is her dedication to a freedman. From the *monumentum Marcellae* (some could have belonged to Messalina's father): *CIL* 6.4426, 4459, 4468, 4474, 4548, 4662, 4664, 4665, 4666, 4667, 4668, 4671, 4698, 4700, 4704, 4705, 4706.

55 Postumus' dedication (*PIR*^{2} 483), A.D. 47/48: *CIL* 6.918 (31202, and further comments by Alföldy *ad loc.* in *CIL* 6.8.2) = *ILS* 210 = A. Gordon (1958) no. 94, Pal. dei Conservatori, Museo Nuovo, inv. no. 6944, cat. no. 2161. Further *pro salute* texts of Claudius: from the Palatine (A.D. 46) *CIL* 6.3751 = 31282 = 36894 (with Alföldy in *CIL* 6.8.2); from the area of the basilica Julia/temple of Divus Augustus? (A.D. 46) *CIL* 6.917 = 40413; from Narbonne (A.D. 43) *CIL* 12.4334; from Roselle (A.D. 45) *AE* 1980.457; from Lugdunum (Bérard, Cogitore, and Tarpin [1998]), probably also in connection with the British campaign. Tac. *Ann.* 4.12.6 for Postumius as prefect of Egypt.

56 Verona gate text (A.D. 44): *AE* 1992.739b with Cavalieri Manasse (1992) (cf. *CIL* 5.3326 = *ILS* 204). The local white-stone plaque, found in 1988 reused in a medieval tower, shows signs of long exposure to the elements. Leptis base, apparently discovered virtually *in situ*: *IRT* 340 = *AE* 1948.16 = Rose (1997) no. 126, Aurigemma (1940) figure 19 (printed upside down). Arnae statue base: *TAM* 2^3 760 = Rose (1997) no. 108.

57 *Monumentum Claudianum*: *CIL* 6.40420–30 with de Caprariis (1993).

58 For the spectacle and imagery of the British triumph, see now Richard (1998). For the arch on the Via Lata, see *CIL* 6.920–23 with 40416 = *ILS* 216, de Maria (1988) no. 69, *LTUR* 1993 (Rodríguez Almeida), Rose (1997) 263 n. 5, no. 42. Messalina may have been the first woman to use a *carpentum* in a triumph.

59 Dedication of the *aenatores, tubicines, liticines, cornicines romani* near the Meta Sudans in A.D. 42 (discovered in 1992–93): *CIL* 6.40307 with Morizio (1996). See Panella (1996) 40–46 for the archaeological context.

60 A fire swept through this area under Claudius, who restored the nearby temple with his own money between 51 and 54 (Panciera [1996]). The shrine may also have been affected by the same fire(s).

61 For the image of Messalina in literary sources, see *Apoc.* 11; *Oct.* 10–17, 102; Juv. *Sat.* 6.115–32, 10.324–45 with Questa (1995). Joshel (1997) offers a feminist critique. For the medical imagery, see Gourevitch and Raepsaet-Charlier (1991) 10–12 and Fagan (2002) 571 ("amoral nymphomaniac").

62 Iulia Agrippina: *PIR*^{2} 641, Raepsaet-Charlier (1987) no. 426, Eck in *NP*. Two recent biographies are by Eck (1993b) and Barrett (1996).

63 Agrippina's freedmen: *CIL* 6.8720, 20384, 37591 (in Rome). See *SEG* 31.1405 of A.D. 50–54 from Jericho for the tomb of Theodotos (also known as Nath(an)el), who may have been employed to manage her property locally.

64 For Agrippina's coup, see Tac. *Ann.* 14.3–8, 9.2–5, 10–12; cf. 15.67.3, Suet. *Ner.* 34.3,

Dio 61.13–14, 16.1 with Griffin (1984) 75–76, 98, Eck (1993b) 72–76, and Barrett (1996) 181–95, 244–46. The chronology is elucidated by the Arval records for A.D. 59 under 5 April and 23 June; see Scheid (1998) no. 28. For the sanctions against her memory, see Tac. *Ann.* 14.12 and Dio 62.16.2a with Eck (1993b) 88 n. 196 and Barrett (1996) 190. For Nero's reaction to the murder, see Champlin (2003) 90–103.

65 Agrippina's powers are best summarized by Eck (1993b) 40–43, 46–64; cf. 65–71 for limits gradually imposed on her under Nero. See Barrett (1996) 152–53 for Nero as the first emperor to use his mother's name in his filiation in Latin texts. For the title Augusta, see Flory (1998) and Barrett (2002) 322–25. For Agrippina and Nero, see Champlin (2003) 84–90.

66 Spartiaticus' inscription: *AE* 1927.2 = *ICorinth* 8.2.68 = *IG* 4.1469 = *SIG³* 790 with Taylor and West (1926). The statue base of Acrocorinthian limestone is very worn, but there is no erasure of Agrippina's name here. The wording of the Latin suggests that it is a translation of a Greek original.

67 For Agrippina in art and on coins, see Boschung (1993) 73–74; Eck (1993b) 38; Hahn (1994) 186–97, 348–54; Mikocki (1995) 177–83; Barrett (1996) 196–229 (a list of sources); Rose (1997) 69–70; Wood (1999) 255–70, 289–95 (coins), 295–304 (portraits), 305–14 (glyptic images). For the Cologne cameo, see Eck (1993b) figure 6. For an inscribed gem of Agrippina, see *CIG* 7061. For the Aphrodisias reliefs, see Rose (1997) no. 105 with pls. 204 and 207. Barrett (1996) 216: "There must at one time have been numerous sculpted portraits of Agrippina throughout the empire, the great majority of which would have disappeared soon after her death." See now Varner (2004) 97–99.

68 Texts from the Asclepeium at Epidaurus: *IG* 4.603–4 with 623 for a base originally used for a statue of Thearidas of Megalopolis, brother of Polybius, in 182 B.C., which was probably removed either by Sulla or by some pirates. Subsequently, the same base was reinscribed, first for Agrippina (an erasure is below her name) and then for Statilia Messalina, wife of Nero. *AE* 1980.855 has Agrippina's name erased, also on a base that had been used for a Hellenistic text before. For the *aureus* of Claudius, see Eck (1993b) figure 23 (cf. figure 11), *BMC* 1.174 no. 72, RGM-Köln N 12361. Agrippina's (other) inscriptions: Mytilene, Lesbos (*IG* 12.2.176b = *ILS* 8789, 208?, 211), Lugdunum (*AE* 1980.638), Nemi (*ILS* 220), Ilion (*Illion* 90), Cos (*SIG³* 804, *IG* 4.1104, Patton and Hicks [1891] no. 119, Maiuri [1925] 468, 471), Paros (*IG* 12.5.275), Ruscino (Gayraud [1980] no. 12), Sardis? (*AE* 1995.1460 with Nero erased), Delphi (*SIG³* 809), Aizanoi (*IGR* 4.560), Lusitania (*AE* 1990.483), Avellino (*AE* 1997.397, a *flaminica* of Agrippina), Portugal (*CIL* 2.963), Ephesos (*SEG* 1978.885, *AE* 1930.85, *AE* 1990.905), Arval records (Scheid [1998] nos. 27 and 28), uncertain texts: *CIG* 3858 and *CIL* 9.6362. Agrippina may also have been represented in two recently discovered statue groups at Narona (Marin 2001) and Eretria (Schmid 2001).

69 *Oct.* 310–76, 593–617 (cf. 44–45, 93–96, 125–29, 150–67, 634, 952). For Agrippina's ghost, see also Tac. *Ann.* 14.10 and Suet. *Ner.* 34.3. For divine honors in case of accidental death, see Tac. *Ann.* 14.3.3.

70 For Agrippina at the Via Lata Arch of Claudius in A.D. 51, see *CIL* 6.921a, 31204 = *ILS* 222, A. Gordon (1958) pl. 45a (squeeze), Mus. Capit. cat. no. 419. Barrett (1991)

elucidates the archaeological context. For Agrippina at the Monumentum Claudianum (A.D. 50–54), see *CIL* 6.40426 with de Caprariis (1993).

71 For the dedication of the musicians near the Meta Sudans in A.D. 55/56, see *CIL*
6.40307 = *AE* 1996.246a–d with Morizio (1996).

72 *CIL* 10.1574 of A.D. 56 from Puteoli; cf. *CIL* 10.1418 from Herculaneum with Cogitore (1992) 824, 837.

73 For Agrippina's possible "rehabilitation," see *CIL* 6.40452 (Agrippina appears with
Flavia Domitilla under Vespasian) and 6.36911 (under Trajan), 15676, 24164, 33737.
Alföldy has argued forcefully for a rehabilitation in *CIL* 6.8.2. For her (controversial) posthumous portraits, see Wood (1988) 424–25 figs. 15–16. *Contra* Eck (1993b)
76 with n. 176, who argues that her negative image was so strong that no woman
played much of a role in Roman politics for the next 150 years. Kragelund (1998)
167 discusses a possible rehabilitation of Agrippina by Galba.

74 For the newly reassembled basanite statue of Agrippina from the Caelian, see Belli
Pasqua (1995) 74 no. 12 and 82–84 no. 26, Wood (1999) 299 (evidence for a diadem or wreath now lost), and Bertoletti, Cima, and Talamo (1999) II.44 opposite
25, 29. For the temple of Divus Claudius on the Caelian, see Suet. *Vesp.* 9.1 with
LTUR 1993 *Claudius divus, templum* (Buzzetti) and Turcan (1998). Varner (2004)
99 argues that this statue was deliberately smashed in order to attack Agrippina's
memory. Yet the temple of Claudius was not built until after her death.

75 For Tacitus, see Syme (1986) 168–87 for women in the *Annales*, Ehrhardt (1978) 71,
Kaplan (1979), Barrett (1996) 209–11, Späth (2000), and O'Gorman (2000) 122–43
for the younger Agrippina. For Agrippina's memoirs as a source, see Pliny *NH*
7 pref. and Tac. *Ann.* 4.53.3, 13.14.3 with Wood (1988) and (1999) 257. See Fagan
(2002) 570 on Messalina in Agrippina's memoirs. Note the moralizing tone in Barrett (2002) 115, who comments that both Julias and both Agrippinas "suffered the
dire consequences of their willfulness."

Chapter VIII

1 For the growth of the imperial cult, see Herz (1978) 1164–66 for Nero, Clauss
(1999) 98–111 for Nero, and now esp. Gradel (2002). Rüpke (1995a) 424: "Vom Fest
für Nero blieb auch unter Vespasian noch die Erinnerung an den fetten Schweine-
braten und den Wein, der marmorne Kalender mit den Neronischen Daten bleib
dagegen einfach nur peinlich, sei es durch die Einträge oder die deutlich sicht-
baren Rasuren."

2 For usurpers, especially in the first century A.D., see Timpe (1962) 106–21, Flaig
(1992), and now Cogitore (2002). See Pabst (1997) for the question of how to become a Roman emperor, esp. 203–9.

3 For Galba's imperial titles and self-presentation, see Flaig (1992) 230–32 and Wiedemann (1996b) 258 and 263.

4 For Nero declared a *hostis* by the senate, see Suet. *Ner.* 49.2 with Bradley (1978)
ad loc.; Dio 63.27.2b. For the meaning of *hostis*, see Hellegouarc'h (1963) 188–89.
F. Kleiner (1985) 94–95 calls this a "*de facto damnatio memoriae*" very similar to

that of Caligula. For Galba declared a *hostis*, see Plut. *Gal.* 5.3–5. For Otho as a *hostis*, see Dio 65.1.1. For Nero's death, see Champlin (2003) 1–9, 49–51.

5 For Nero and the Praetorians, see esp. Tac. *Hist.* 1.5. Plut. *Gal.* 14.5 has the Praetorians who kill Nymphidius Sabinus describe themselves as avengers of Nero. For discussion, see Griffin (1984) 182, 185; Flaig (1992) 241, 275–81; Malitz (1999) 103–13; Beacham (1999) 249–54. See Absil (1997) 141 no. 15 for C. Nymphidius Sabinus and 139–40 no. 14 for Ofonius Tigellinus, with bibliographies.

6 For Nero's funeral, see Suet. *Ner.* 50: *Funeratus est impensa ducentorum milium, stragulis albis auro intextis, quibus usus Kal. Ian. fuerat* (His funeral was celebrated at a cost of 200,000 sesterces and he was buried in the white robes embroidered with gold that he had worn for the Kalends of January [the New Year's celebration]). Bradley (1978) *ad loc.* feels that the expenses involved suggest that Nero perhaps received a funeral at public expense despite being a *hostis* and what he interprets as a formal imposition of memory sanctions. See Kragelund (1998) esp. 165–66 for Galba's rehabilitation of Nero's victims, juxtaposed with Nero's own funeral, in a pattern reminiscent of Gaius' burials in Augustus' Mausoleum in 37. See *CIL* 6.34916 with Champlin (2003) 29 for the tomb of Nero's nurse Claudia Ecloge, apparently at the site of his suicide.

7 See Champlin (2003) 29–31 for no actual "*damnatio memoriae*" imposed on Nero.

8 For Nero's tomb and its cultivation, see Suet. *Ner.* 50 and 57.1: *et tamen non defuerunt qui per longum tempus uernis aestiuisque floribus tumulum eius ornarent ac modo imagines praetextatas in rostris proferrent, modo edicta quasi uiuentis et breui magno inimicorum malo reuersuri* (And for a long time some people decorated his tomb with spring and summer flowers. Sometimes they carried images of him in a purple-bordered toga to the *rostra* and sometimes they read his edicts as if he was alive and would soon reverse the great wrong done by his personal enemies). Bradley (1978) *ad loc.* See also Beacham (1999) 253–54 and Malitz (1999) 112. See Suet. *Ner.* 41.1 with Griffin (1984) 22 and Corbier (1994) 269–72 for Nero identifying with the Domitii throughout his life. In this context, it is notable that Suetonius' biography of Nero opens with a rather hostile account of the family history of the Domitii Ahenobarbi, thus affording a suitable setting for his critical portrait of Nero. Vindex had already used the name Ahenobarbus for Nero in 68 (Suet. *Ner.* 41.1, Dio 63.22). In *PIR*² Nero is also classified as a Domitius (D 129) and the treatment of his reign is sparing. For Otho's tomb at Brixium, see Plut. *Otho* 18. For popular feeling, see Tac. *Hist.* 1.4 with Champlin (2003) 28–30. Wallace-Hadrill (1983) 113 claims that Suetonius has distorted popular mourning for Nero.

9 For the events of the long year 69, see Brunt (1959), Wellesley (1975), Greenhalgh (1975), Sancery (1983), Levick (1985), Flaig (1992), Wiedemann (1996b) 256–82, Levick (1999) 43–64.

10 For Otho and Nero, see Tac. *Hist.* 1.13, 16, 26, 30, 2.78; Suet. *Otho* 7.1; Plut. *Otho* 3, 5.2 with Murison (1993) 75–80; Wiedemann (1996b) 268; and Carrée (1999). The reappointment of Flavius Sabinus as urban prefect was also said to have been a gesture toward the memory of Nero. For Otho and Sporus, Nero's "widow," see Champlin (2003) 146–47.

11 For Vitellius and Nero, see Tac. *Hist.* 1.50, 74, 2.95.1; Suet. *Vit.* 11.2; Eutrop. 7.18 with Griffin (1984) 186; Kragelund (1998) 171; Levick (1999) 63. Flaig (1992) 342–44 can make little sense of this; see 343: "Die Code-Funktion dieses Aktes ist schwer zu bestimmen." Carrée (1999) 180–81 sees references to Nero at the end of Vitellius' term when he is already in trouble. For the *inferiae* for Vindex, see Plut. *Gal.* 27.2.

12 For the Flavians and Nero, see Griffin (1984) 207; Christ (1995) 239–46; Levick (1999) 65–78, esp. 71–73; Ripoll (1999); Kragelund (2000) 512–15. Royo (1984) 194: "L' image de Néron est au centre des luttes politiques qui entourent sa succession." Darwall-Smith (1996) 74 discusses how Vespasian adopted Nero's euergetism. For Nero and the historians, see esp. Jos. *AJ* 20.154–57. For Vespasian at the court of Nero, see B. Jones (1992) 10–12. Darwall-Smith (1996) 253 discusses the role of Helvidius in prompting Vespasian's obliteration of Nero. P. Davies (2000a) 41 points out that scholars are often too simplistic about Flavian propaganda against Nero.

13 For an introduction to the extensive bibliography on the *Octavia*, see Kragelund (1982, 1988, 1998, 2000, 2002), Royo (1984), G. Williams (1994), Schubert (1998) 254–89, Manuwald (2001) 259–339, Flower (2002a), J. Smith (2003), and the detailed commentary by Ferri (2003).

14 See Ferri (2003) 31–54, 70–75, 408–10 for the *Octavia* and the works of Seneca. Ferri (2003) 70: "When Nero repeats the thundering *sententiae* of Seneca's mythological tyrants, the point is probably made that all those fictional characters were aliases of Nero, as if the tyrant had taken off their masks at last."

15 For a Galban date, see Barnes (1982) followed by Kragelund (1988) and Wiseman (2001). Manuwald (2001) 337–39 leaves the question more open. Schubert (1998) 288–89 argues for a date under Domitian, Fagan (2002) 569 and Champlin (2003) 104 for soon after the death of Nero, J. Smith (2003) 427–30 for a date under Vespasian. The fact that Galba was booed by the audience at an Atellan farce (Suet. *Gal.* 13.1) may be an argument for rather than against a performance under that emperor. Ferri (2003) 5–30 argues in detail for a date in the 90s under Domitian. Ferri believes that the playwright used Flavian written sources, such as the histories of Pliny the Elder, Cluvius Rufus, and Fabius. He sees the play as closely based on such a lost historiographic text, and not as a drama that was ever performed (54–69).

16 See J. Smith (2003) for the staging, esp. 393 where he calls the *Octavia* "the textual relic of a stage production that was meant for an imperial Roman audience."

17 For Octavia's reburial as the context, see Kragelund (1998).

18 For the *ludi plebei* of 68, see Wiseman (2001).

19 For the Golden Day of 66, see Tac. *Ann.* 16.23–24, Suet. *Ner.* 13, Dio 62.1–7 with Griffin (1984), Bergmann (1998) esp. 181–85, Champlin (1998) 337–38, Beacham (1999) 243–44.

20 For Nero the actor, see Tac. *Ann.* 15.67 (Subrius Flavus in 65), Suet. *Ner.* 41 (Vindex' edicts), Juv. *Sat.* 8.198–99, Dio Chrys. *Dis.* 71.5–9, Plut. *De Adul. et Amic.* 56F, Dio 62.9–10. Pliny *Ep.* 5.3 does not wish to have Nero as a precedent for his own habit of reciting his poetry in front of an audience. Woodman (1993) 121: "The perception of Nero as an actor could eclipse all other aspects of the emperor." For further discussion, see Griffin (1984) 160–63, Bartsch (1994), and Beacham (1999) 209,

who locates Nero in a Hellenistic tradition of aristocratic performers. See Champlin (2003) 53–83, 92–111 for Nero as a performer both on stage and in sports.

21 For actors in Roman society, see Ducos (1990), Leppin (1992), Edwards (1993) chap. 3 and (1997).

22 For Nero's performances, see Schmidt (1990) with a list of sources at 157–60, Morford (1985), Malissard (1990), Woodman (1993), Bartsch (1994) 36–62, Edwards (1994), Beacham (1999) 197–254.

23 For the segregated seating and the theater as a political space, see Nicolet (1980) 361–73; André (1990); Rawson (1991); Flaig (1992) 53, 223; Bartsch (1994) 30–31, 63–82; Bernstein (1998) 193–95, 245.

24 For Nero's masks, see Suet. *Ner.* 21.3; Dio 63.9.5, 63.10.2 with Bartsch (1994) 46; Edwards (1994) 91; Slater (1996); Beacham (1999) 239–42. The confusion of the young recruit suggests a mask that was realistic, at least in some respects. Nero's entrance in the *Octavia* is carefully prepared for, not least by line 436: . . . *trucique vultu* (. . . with a savage expression). Champlin (2003) 96 suggests that masks of Nero's face already deliberately identified him with his theatrical roles during his own lifetime, especially with Oedipus and Orestes.

25 J. Smith (2003) 401 seems to go too far in describing Nero's court in the *Octavia* as "a cabinet of living *imagines*." But clearly decisions needed to be made about the masks for all these historical characters.

26 For Nero's popularity on stage, see Pliny *Pan.* 46.4; Tac. *Ann.* 16.4.3–5, *Hist.* 1.4.3; Suet. *Ner.* 10.2, 21.1; Suet. *Vit.* 4 with Bartsch (1994) 29 and Malitz (1999) 65. Beacham (1999) 209: "Nero's activity therefore represented not just an indulgence of personal inclination but also a degree of political calculation." For Nero's theatricality, see Champlin (2003) 236–37.

27 For the chorus in the *Octavia*, see esp. Manuwald (2001) 292–96, 323–32, who has both choruses representing Roman citizens. Schubert (1998) 265, 276, 278 has the second chorus as composed of Praetorians. Kragelund (2002) compares the voice of the people (chorus) with Galba's use of the slogan *libertas*. J. Smith (2003) esp. 419–21 sees two choruses, one for and one against Poppaea. Ferri (2003) 205–6, 388 sees one chorus.

28 For Octavia and the popular protests of 62, see Tac. *Ann.* 14.59–60, Suet. *Ner.* 35.2, Dio 62.13.4 with Bauman (1974) 188–90 and Griffin (1984) 99, 112. For Octavia, daughter of Claudius and Messalina, see *PIR*² 1110, Strauss in *NP* with *CIL* 4.4788 and *IG* 12.6.1.414 from Samos. According to Boschung (1993) 75–76, no portraits can be securely identified.

29 For head-hunting in the *Octavia*, see *Oct.* 437–38. Nero is effectively juxtaposed with the image of Sulla, an earlier notorious headhunter. Head-hunting apparently emerged again in Roman politics in 69. See Dio 63.23.2 (Vindex); Tac. *Hist.* 1.49; Plut. *Gal.* 27–28 (Galba, Piso, Vinius with Kragelund [1998] 170); Dio 64.21.1 (Vitellius). For Nero and head-hunting in Tacitus, see *Ann.* 14.58 (Sulla's head), 14.59 (Plautus' head), 14.64 (Poppaea and Octavia's head).

30 J. Smith (2003) 425 notes how Nero's suicide became synchronized with the anniversary of Octavia's death (Suet. *Ner.* 57.1).

31 For Agrippina's ghost and the sanctions against her memory, see *Oct.* 593–645, esp.

609–13. Agrippina is haunted by the memory (*memoria*) of her own death. For discussion, see Tschiedel (1995). For reactions to her death in Rome, see esp. Dio 62.16.

32 Schubert (1998) 254–89 explores complementary and contrasting pictures of Nero offered by various characters in the context of Nero's image in Latin poetry. Manuwald (2001) 306–7 points out that there are no explicit references to Nero as a singer or an actor in the play itself.

33 For Messalina, see *Oct.* 10–18, 257–72. Octavia recalls her mother, who is never actually named in the play, perhaps in deference to the sanctions against her memory. Messalina herself "forgot" her marriage in her madness. The image of the fury's torch links her marriage with Poppaea's.

34 For the three false Neros (in 68–69, c. 80, and 88–89), see Tac. *Hist.* 1.8, 2.8.1–9; Dio 64.9.3; Zon. 11.15 with Brunt (1959) 532; Gallivan (1973); Syme (1980b) 88; B. Jones (1983); Griffin (1984) 214–15; Tuplin (1989); Varner (2004) 81, 85; and Champlin (2003) 10–12. Dio of Prusa (*Or.* 21.9–10) says that Nero was widely believed to be alive under Domitian.

35 For Nero's world of illusion, see Bartsch (1994) 61 and Beacham (1999). For Tacitus' reaction to Rome's evolving culture of spectacle, see Aubrion (1990).

36 J. Smith (2003) 395–97 discusses parallels with Senecan tragedy.

37 For Nero's songs under Vitellius, see Suet. *Vit.* 11.2. Suetonius found manuscript copies of some of Nero's own poems while he was doing his research in the imperial archives.

38 For the Flavian amphitheater, see Rea in *LTUR* 1993 with *CIL* 6.40454a and Alföldy (1995). Darwall-Smith (1996) 76–90, 89: "Perhaps it was the ultimate exorcism of the spectre of Nero." P. Davies (2000a) 42 sees it as an attempt to outdo the Domus Aurea. See also Gunderson (2003).

39 For Nero in poetry, see Schubert (1998) 412–38 (in his lifetime) and 439–46 (after 68). For Galba, see esp. Jucker (1975), Zimmermann (1995), and now also Ripoll (1999). Carrée (1999) 181 sees the variety of reactions to Nero as expressions of complex social tensions. See Tac. *Hist.* 2.55 for the celebration of Galba's memory at the death of Otho; *Hist.* 3.7 for Antonius Primus setting up Galba's statues in the Italian towns; *Hist.* 3.85.1 for Vitellius being tormented by the memory of Galba; *Hist.* 4.40.1 for Domitian's formal restoration of Galba. However, it was decided not to erect a memorial at the *lacus Curtius* at the place where Galba was killed (Suet. *Gal.* 23). It is unclear whether there had ever been formal sanctions against his memory, which seems to have been something of an issue of contention between some senators and Vespasian. Galba is named as emperor in *CIL* 10.8038 and in the Domitianic *lex Flavia Irnitana*.

40 Pliny *Pan.* 46.4: *idem ergo populus ille, aliquando scaenici imperatoris spectator et plausor, nunc in pantomimis quoque aversatur et damnat effeminatas artes et indecora saeculo studia* (And so that same populace, which once watched and applauded an actor-emperor, now turns away in disgust from pantomimes and condemns effeminate professions and interests unbecoming to our age). See also Tac. *Ann.* 15.59.2 where the conspirators of 65 refer to Nero as *ille scaenicus* (that stage performer). For Nero's posthumous image, see now Champlin (2003) 12–35.

41 See Dahmen (1998) for a complete catalog and discussion.

42 For Ummidia Quadratilla, see *PIR*² 606, *RE* 3, Raepsaet-Charlier (1987) no. 829 with *stemma* 25, Pliny *Ep.* 7.24 of A.D. 107 with Sherwin-White (1966) and Syme (1968).

43 For Ummidia's inscriptions, see *CIL* 6.28526, 15.7576, 10.5183 = *ILS* 5628 (amphitheater at Casinum with Fora (1991) 203–15, 10.5304; *NSA* 1929 29–30 (Ummidia C. f. Quadratilla Asconia Secunda); *AE* 1985.189 and 255; *AE* 1992.244 (= 1946.174) with Fora (1992) on the restoration of the theater. For slaves and freedmen of Quadratilla, see *CIL* 10.1946 and *AE* 1985.189. Sick (1999) puts Quadratilla's mimes in context and argues that she could have made a handsome profit from their performances.

44 For Neronia Saturnina, see *AE* 1988.103 with Avetta et al. (1985) no. 234 pl. 58.5. Champlin (1998) 340, 343 and (2003) 148–77, esp. 150–60 discusses Nero as *princeps Saturnalicius* and his reign as a perpetual Saturnalia. April was renamed *Neroneus* in the aftermath of the Pisonian conspiracy of 65 (Tac. *Ann.* 15.74.1; Suet. *Ner.* 55); perhaps Neronia was born in an April (65–67) or at the time of one of the Neronia games (60 or 64/65)? Champlin (2003) 151: "By freeing saturnalian behavior from its strict seasonal confines, by redefining it, by introducing it deliberately into other parts of Roman life, Nero not only amused himself, he drew empire and people, ruler and ruled, closer together. Saturnalian behavior made him popular."

45 Paillier and Sablayrolles (1994) 14 have about 12 percent of Nero's texts erased in *CIL* and *AE*: the civil war distracted from the need to remove Nero. For some examples of Nero's erased inscriptions, see *CIL* 10.1574 = *ILS* 226 (Puteoli); *CIL* 10.5204 = *ILS* 5365 (Casini); *ILS* 2491 (Mainz); *CIL* 5.2035 = *ILS* 5622 (Castel Lavazzo); *ILS* 8901 (Cnossos); *ILS* 5682 (Thracian Chersonese); *CIL* 11.395 = *ILS* 2648 (Arimini); *CIL* 3.14387 = *ILS* 9199 (Heliopolis, Syria); *AE* 1996.1466 (Ephesus); *AE* 1995.1505 (Sardis); *CIL* 2.963 (Mora, Portugal); *CIL* 9.4968 = *ILS* 5543 (Curae Sabinorum); *AE* 1990.905 (Samos); *AE* 1995.1505 (Aizanoi). For examples of unerased inscriptions of Nero, see *CIL* 17.29, 44, 45, 48, 49, 50 (milestones); *CIL* 10.932 = *ILS* 224 (Pompeii); *CIL* 2.4719 = *ILS* 225 (Corduba); *CIL* 2.4734 = *ILS* 227 (Gades); *CIL* 12.5471 = *ILS* 228 (Forum Iulii); *CIL* 2.183 = *ILS* 5640 (Olispone); *CIL* 3.6741 = *ILS* 232 (Armenia); *CIL* 13.3491 = *ILS* 8709 (ingot); *CIL* 10.5182 = *ILS* 972 (Montecassino); *AE* 1994.1557 (Larissa, Macedonia); *ILS* 1987 (Vindobona); *CIL* 8.8837 = *ILS* 6103 (Hippo Regius); *CIL* 2.2958 = *ILS* 6104 (Pamplona); *ILS* 8848 (Iconium); *AE* 1996.1466 (Ephesos); *SEG* 16.748 (Amisus); *IGR* 4.330 (Pergamum); *IGR* 4.560 (Aezanis); *AE* 1995.1633 (Apollonia-Susa); *AE* 1990.993 (Cilicia); *CIL* 6.1185 and *ILS* 5145 (Pompeii).

46 Fragmentary inscriptions from Rome: *CIL* 6.845 (= A. Gordon [1958] no. 105 pl. 45c), 926, 1984 = *ILS* 5025, 31288, 31289, 36912, 40418, 41073, 41075?, 41077. For Poppaea, see *CIL* 6.40419.

47 For the Via Lata arch, see *CIL* 921 = 31203 = *ILS* 222. For the Claudian family monument, see *CIL* 6.40424 with de Caprariis (1993) no. 5.

48 Bergmann and Zanker (1981) suggest that portraits of the young Nero may often have been too small to recarve.

49 For Nero's portraiture, see Hiesinger (1975); Jucker (1981) 295–311; Bergmann and

Zanker (1981); Pekáry (1985); D. Kleiner (1992) 135–39; Boschung (1993) 76–77; Rose (1997) 46–50, 71–72 (add *AE* 1993.1413 = *SEG* 41.353 from Messenia); Croisille (1999); and Varner (2004) 46–83. For Nero's coins, see *RIC* 1² 133–87. Darwall-Smith (1996) 40 stresses Nero's coins with buildings on them. For Poppaea in imperial statue groups, see Rose (1997) nos. 21, 22, 98, 109.

50 For Nero and Silvanus, see *CIL* 6.927 = *ILS* 236 = A. Gordon (1958) no. 121 pl. 52a = MNR no. 39801 from Tor de Schiavi.

51 For the cult of Silvanus, see Palmer (1978); Dorcey (1992) esp. 51, 88–89, 103–4, 154–78 (for the corpus of more than eleven hundred inscriptions of Silvanus); and Clauss (1994). *CIL* 6.644 records a *Silvanus Flaviorum*.

52 For Eumolpus' dedication from the sanctuary of solar divinities in Trastevere, see *CIL* 6.3719 = 31033 = *ILS* 1774 (Florence Archaeological Museum 86025) with Bergmann (1993) 9 and (1998) 194–201; Champlin (1998) 336; Clauss (1999); R. Smith (2000) 539. Eumolpus' daughter Claudia Pallas seems to be free, perhaps because her mother was a freedwoman. It is unclear whether any buildings were still referred to as the Domus Aurea under the Flavians.

53 For dating formulae from Rome with Nero's name in them, see *CIL* 6.268 = A. Gordon (1958) no. 106 (dedication to Minerva by some fullers on the Esquiline); *CIL* 6.7303 = *ILS* 7863 = A. Gordon (1958) no. 108 (epitaph of baby Spendusa from Via Appia); A. Gordon (1958) no. 113 (dedication to Hercules by C. Calvenus Callipus, a freedman). For P. Acilius Cerdo's inscription from the Aventine, see *CIL* 6.396 = 30753 = *ILS* 3671 = A. Gordon (1958) no. 114 pl. 49b (MNR no. 69).

54 For Nero's German bodyguards, see Bellen (1981) for a catalogue and discussion.

55 *RIB* 1² 92 from Chichester; *AE* 1993.1149 and 1150? from Châteauneuf; *CIL* 11.6955 = *ILS* 8902 = Rose (1997) 21 from Luna; *CIL* 1.1331 = *ILS* 233 = *AE* 1992.577 = Rose (1997) 22 from Luna; *AE* 1994.360 = 1964.115 from Ficulea with di Stefano Manzella (1994) A figure 1; *SEG* 27.916 = *AE* 1981.791 = Rose (1997) 109 from Bubon with Jones (1977–78) no. 5 pl. 76.1, see figure 54 (cf. no. 13 for Poppaea).

56 For Nero in Greece: Athens: *IG* 2² 1990 (erasure), 3182 (erasure), 3278 (erasure), 3279 (erasure), 3280 (no erasure), 1989 (erasure); Benjamin and Raubitschek (1959) p. 82 no. 12 (erased); *AE* 1994.1617 (erased). Elsewhere in the Greece: *ILindos* 433; *SEG* 16.748 (Amisus); *IGR* 4.330 (Pergamum); *IG* 7.2713 = *SIG*³ 814 = *ILS* 8794 (Akraiphia, Boeotia); *SIG*³ 804 (Cos); *IGR* 4.560 (Aezanis); *SIG*³ 810 = *ILS* 8793 (Rhodes); *SIG*³ 808; *IG* 3.158 and 1085.

57 *AE* 1996.1660 with Chaniotis and Preuss (1990) 200–201 no. 17.

58 For Mucianus in Lycia, see *ILS* 8816 = *OGIS* 558.

59 For Nero in Cologne, see *AE* 1969–70.443 with Galsterer (1975) no. 178 pl. 38; Schumacher (1988) 87; Walser (1993) no. 4.

60 For the Jupiter column at Mainz, see *CIL* 13.11806 and 11806b = *ILS* 9235 (Landesmuseum S 137 and S 157), Bauchhenß (1984), Selzer, Decker and do Paço (1988) 90–91 with full illustrations and bibliography.

61 *CIL* 13.8701 = *ILS* 235 = Schumacher (1988) 51 with Fink (1970).

62 See Tac. *Hist.* 2.62 with Levick (1999) 65: "Against the luridly painted failings of Vitellius, Vespasian's was a persona that he put on, grew into, and had to live with and, when practicable, up to." For Galba's surviving inscriptions, see esp. *CIL* 6.471

= *ILS* 238; *ILS* 1988; *CIL* 6.8680 = *ILS* 239 = A. Gordon (1958) 129; *IRT* 537. For Vitellius, see *CIL* 6.929 = *ILS* 242; *CIL* 10.8016 = *ILS* 243.

63 For the Arvals, their grove, and their records, see Scheid (1975b), Syme (1980b), Beard (1985, 1991, 1998), Broise and Scheid (1993), Scheid (1993). For the calendar, see Rüpke (1995a) 45–48, 178–81. Scheid (1998) has republished the inscriptions (Gaius nos. 11–16, Nero nos. 24–39, Domitian nos. 52–60, Commodus nos. 94–96; there are no Severan fragments before 213).

64 For conspiracies in the Arval records, see Scheid (1990) 394–403 with table 12 and Scheid (1998) nos. 13, 28, 30, 55, 94, 95. Those implicated in these various plots are never named by the Arvals.

65 For the record of 69, see Scheid (1998) no. 40 with erasures both of A. Vitellius the emperor (lines I 1–7, 82, 85; II 6, 16) and of his brother L. Vitellius (lines I 1–7, 40, 54, 58, 63, 68, 77); cf. Beard (1985) 126 for the date. In 69 each successive emperor in Rome succeeded his predecessor as an Arval. By March Galba is named as a private citizen (I 1–7, 55). On 14 March Vitellius' name has been substituted for what should originally have been Otho, but he has subsequently been erased. L. Maecius Postumus has been inserted here in place of Otho's brother. Vitellius' *dies imperii* was not celebrated until 1 May. Beard (1998) 99 sees the emperor as "the perfect implied reader of every priestly archive."

66 For the record of 53, see Scheid (1998) no. 20, line 19, who has restored A. Vitellius in this erasure.

67 For the record of 14, see Scheid (1998) no. 2. Scheid (1990) 187–88 questions whether this is really a deliberate erasure.

68 For Flavian Rome, see esp. Darwall-Smith (1996) and Levick (1999) 126–29. For the survival of Nero's buildings, see P. Davies (2000a) esp. 35–37. For the temple of Jupiter Optimus Maximus, see *LTUR* 1996 (de Angeli) and Darwall-Smith (1996) 41–47. For the Temple of Peace, see *LTUR* 1999 (Coarelli) and Darwall-Smith (1996) 55–68, 73. For the temple of Claudius, see *LTUR* 1993 (Buzzetti), Darwall-Smith (1996) 48–55, and Turcan (1998) 161–67. For Rome under Domitian, see esp. Frederick (2003) and Packer (2003).

69 See now Noreña (2003) on the Temple of Peace and its message in context.

70 For the Arch of Nero dedicated in 62, see F. Kleiner (1985) (94–95 on the ultimate fate of the arch), de Maria (1988) no. 70, *LTUR* 1993 (Kleiner).

71 For the colossus of Nero, see Pliny *NH* 34.45–46; Mart. *Ep.* 2; Suet. *Ner.* 31; *Vesp.* 18 with Blanck (1969) 16–18; Pekáry (1985) 81; Bergmann (1993) 4–17 with a reconstruction as a type 4 portrait of Nero; *LTUR* 1993 (Lega); Bergmann (1998) 189–201. Dio 66.15.1 claims that the statue was dedicated by Vespasian in 75 (so also R. Smith [2000] 537). For the painting in the Horti Maiani, see Pliny *NH* 35.51. See Champlin (2003) 129–32 for the statue in context, 112–44 for Nero and Apollo/Sol.

72 For the Domus Aurea, see Tac. *Ann.* 15.42; Mart. *Ep.* 2; Suet. *Ner.* 31, 39. The bibliography is vast, and relevant entries in *LTUR* 1993–99 can be found under the following 9 headings: *Domus Aurea, Vestibulum, Area dello Stagnum, Porticus Triplices Miliariae, Palazzo sul Esquilino, Complesso del Palatino, Domus Transitoria, Domus Tiberiana, Aedes Fortunae Seiani*. Otherwise, the following are espe-

cially notable: Morford (1968); Hemsoll (1990); Bergmann (1993) 18–30 and (1998) 189–201; Elsner (1994); Ball (1994); Moormann (1995, 1998); Darwall-Smith (1996) 36–40, 70–72; Champlin (1998); Ripoll (1999) 147; Royo (1999) 209–301; Champlin (2003) 178–209, esp. 200–209. For various maps, see *LTUR* (1995) figs. 18, 20, 26; Bergmann (1998) figure 5; Beacham (1999) figure 27; Champlin (2003) 204. For the Baths of Titus, see *LTUR* 1993 (Caruso) and Darwall-Smith (1996) 90–94.

73 For Otho and Vitellius in the Domus Aurea, see Suet. *Otho* 7; *Vit.* 11.2; Dio Chrys. 47.15; Dio 64.4 with Morford (1968) 165 and P. Davies (2000a).

74 For the land occupied by the Domus Aurea, Morford (1968) 159–62 is still the fundamental discussion.

75 The size of the Domus Aurea has been much disputed. A vast size of around two hundred acres is advocated by Hemsoll (1990) 11, Moormann (1998), Beacham (1999) 224–29. By contrast Warden only sees the complex as half that size. Elsner (1994) 122–24 argues that it was only outrageous after, and as a result of, Nero's fall. Champlin (1998) 334, 339 sees the Domus as only really consisting of the Oppian wing and the lake below it. See Medri (1996) for recent archaeological evidence.

76 For the accessibility of the Domus Aurea, see Griffin (1984) 138–41; Hemsoll (1990) 16; Darwall-Smith (1996) 37–38; Champlin (1998) 335, 343 and (2003) 205–6; P. Davies (2000a) 41.

77 For the Oppian palace, see *LTUR* 1995 (Fabbrini), Ball (1994), Moormann (1995), Darwall-Smith (1996) 70–71. For the wall paintings, see Peters and Meyboom (1982).

78 For the Neronian levels excavated near the Meta Sudans, see *CIL* 6.40307 with Panella (1996) 68–69 on the topographical history; Medri (1996) on the Domus Aurea with figs. 154, 156, 162, 167; Morizio (1996) on the epigraphical evidence; and Peña (2000) 555–58.

79 For the Baths of Nero, see Mart. *Ep.* 7.34, *LTUR* 1993 (Ghini) with figure 39, and P. Davies (2000a).

80 For the fire of 64 and the houses of the *nobiles*, see Suet. *Ner.* 38.2 with Flower (1996) 41, 259, 280. For the fire, see Champlin (2003).

81 See now Mellor (2003) on the new aristocracy of Flavian Rome.

82 See Pliny *Ep.* 5.5.5–6: *Gaius quidem Fannius, quod accidit, multo ante praesensit. Visus est sibi per nocturnam quietem iacere in lectulo suo compositus in habitum studentis, habere ante se scrinium (ita solebat); mox imaginatus est uenisse Neronem, in toro resedisse, prompsisse primum librum quem de sceleribus eius ediderat, eumque ad extremum reuoluisse; idem in secundo ac tertio fecisse, tunc abisse. Expauit et sic interpretatus est, tamquam idem sibi futurus esset scribendi finis, qui fuisset illi legendi: et fuit idem* (For Gaius Fannius anticipated what happened long before. He dreamed that he was lying on his little bed that was set up in his study and that he had his desk in front of him (as was his custom). Soon he saw that Nero had entered, sat down on the couch, unrolled the first book scroll that he had written about that emperor's evil deeds, and read through it to the end. He did the same with the second and the third scroll, then Nero departed. Fannius was filled with fear and came to the following conclusion; that his writing would

have the same end as Nero's reading, and that came to pass). See Sherwin-White (1966) *ad loc.* For the opposition of Stoics under Nero, see Griffin (1984) 171–77. In *Ep.* 3.7 about the death of Silius Italicus (around the year 100), Pliny remarks that Nero's death still seems like a recent event. For later historiography on Nero, see Champlin (2003) 36–52.

Chapter IX

1 For the sanctions against Domitian, see Paillier and Sablayrolles (1994) 15: "Domitien, le premier à subir au sens plein du terme cette atteinte à la mémoire, fut aussi probablement celui qui la subit de la façon la plus accomplie." See also Sablayrolles (1994) and Flower (2001a) 642–44. For Domitian's portraits, see now Varner (2004) 111–35, 260–69. Three were mutilated, twenty-eight extant examples were recarved, especially as Nerva (82 percent of his portraits once represented Domitian), but also as Trajan, Titus, Augustus, and other emperors from late antiquity. However, a significant number of Domitian's portraits had themselves been recarved from ones of Nero and could not be reworked again.

2 For the memory of Nero in the second century, see chapter 8.

3 For the Flavians, see Bengtson (1979), Griffin (2000a) 1–83, and Levick (1999) for Vespasian. For Domitian, see Syme (1983a) and Jones (1992) with *PIR*² 259 and Eck in *NP*. For literature, see Coleman (1986) and (1990/2000), and Boyle and Dominik (2003), especially the wide-ranging introduction by Boyle. For Domitian's coins, see Carradice (1983, 1993, and 1998). For Suetonius' biography, see Paillier and Sablayrolles (1994) 35–40, Sablayrolles (1994) 136–37, and Lambrecht (1995).

4 For Domitian's murder and the sanctions against him, see Suet. *Dom.* 17 and 23, Dio 68.1. See now Grainger (2003) 1–27 for a rather speculative reconstruction of the conspiracy and 45–51 for immediate reactions. For the Templum Gentis Flaviae, see Coarelli in *LTUR* 1995 and Darwall-Smith (1996) 159–65. Saller (1990/2000), 17: "The senatorial hostility toward Domitian is obvious, but it is not obvious that the modern historian has the kind of alternative evidence needed to penetrate the hostility in order to tell a more accurate story of Domitian's attitudes and policies."

5 For Domitian's portraiture, see Daltrop, Hausmann, and Wegner (1966), Jucker (1981), Bergmann and Zanker (1981), Pekáry (1985), D. Kleiner (1992) 176–77, Varner (2004).

6 For the difficulties in assessing Domitian, see esp. Saller (1980, 1990/2000) with Giovannini (1987) 219. Griffin (2000b) 96: "Contemporary sycophancy was almost immediately overwhelmed by posthumous invective."

7 For various revisionist treatments, see Syme (1930, 1983a), Pleket (1961), Waters (1964, 1969), Levick (1982), and Jones (1992). Paillier and Sablayrolles (1994) 42–45 make a case for the need of further revisions. Sablayrolles (1994) 135 sees the Domitianic age as a climax of prosperity obscured by autocracy and *damnatio memoriae*. By contrast Southern (1997) accepts nearly all the negative anecdotes at face value. See also Wiseman (1996) and Wilson (2003).

8 For Nerva, see Garzetti (1950), Syme (1958) 1–18, Garzetti (1974), Cizek (1983) 100–

121, Goodman (1989), Griffin (2000b) 84–96, Eck (2002a and b), and Grainger (2003) 52–65. For portraits, see D. Kleiner (1992) 199–201 and Varner (2004) 115–22 (fourteen items, 82 percent recarved).

9 For Tacitus on Domitian, see *Agr.* 45 and *Hist.* 4.52.2 with von Fritz (1957) and Paillier and Sablayrolles (1994) 30–35. *Agr.* 42.4 also comments on the undue admiration for Domitian's martyrs.

10 For the Coptos bridge text (A.D. 90/91) in the British Museum, see *CIL* 3.13580 and Flower (2000) 66 with figure 10. Different parts of the stone display very different styles of erasure. The D of Domitianus is partly visible, as is the G of Germanicus. The stone was broken in half across the prefect's name (at the end of antiquity) making it harder to read. The following restoration may be tentatively suggested: M METTIVS RVFVS PRAEF AEGYPTI.

11 For M. Mettius Rufus, see *PIR*² 572 with Eck (1980), who argues for an eastern origin as opposed to a Gallic one and gives a hypothetical stemma. Of eleven inscriptions, four are erased, all from Egypt (see esp. *IGR* 1.1183 = *OGIS* 2.674 also from Coptos). Mettius is mentioned in twenty-one papyri. His brother is probably Mettius Modestus (*PIR*² 565), who was also disgraced under Domitian.

12 For Nerva's career, see *PIR*² 1227 and Eck in *NP*. Darwall-Smith (1996) offers the opposing point of view at 253: "There was little, if any, opposition to the succession of Nerva, and even after a serious threat to his position in 97, he was still able to leave the empire to a chosen and acceptable successor." See also Grainger (2003) 28–44, table 3 on xiv, and esp. 30: "The appearance as emperor of this man, who had helped save the ghastly emperor Nero and had now connived at the murder of the unpleasant but efficient Domitian, his apparent friend, must have stunk in at least some senatorial nostrils."

13 For Domitian and the Praetorians, see Durry (1938), Syme (1983a) 141–42, Absil (1997), and Flower (2001a) 635–40, 642–44. For the Praetorians in general, see Le Bohec (1998), Rankov (1994), and Stäcker (2003). Grainger (2003) 19, 40–41, 94–95, 110–12 sees the Praetorians as no more than the puppets of their new commander, Casperius Aelianus.

14 See now the detailed reconstruction of Trajan's adoption in Eck (2002 a and b).

15 For Domitian and the *plebs*, see Yavetz (1986) and B. Jones (1992). Flaig (1992) 449–50 sees Domitian as very popular in Rome in 89 but argues that this had changed by the time of his death in 96. For other reactions, see Philostrat. *Soph.* 1.7.2 (Dio of Prusa in Moesia), Plut. *Mor.* 828a (Plutarch in Greece), Philos. *Apoll.* 8.26/27, Dio 67.18.1–2 (Apollonius of Tyana at Ephesus).

16 For the coinage of Nerva, see *RIC* 2 220–33, *BMC* 3.xxxii–li, 1–30, pls. 1–8 with Shotter (1983) and now esp. Brennan (1990/2000). Paillier and Sablayrolles (1994) 19 see Nerva's coinage as systematically anti-Domitianic.

17 For Domitianic epigraphy, see A. Martin (1987). New texts appear regularly every year. See also Newlands (2002) 8–17 on Domitian and the monuments.

18 Plut. *Num.* 19 notes that September and October were briefly known as Germanicus and Domitianus under Domitian.

19 For omissions of Domitian in the careers of senators, see, for example, C. Velius Rufus (*ILS* 9200, Baalbek), T. Cominius Severus (*ILS* 9193, Sirmium), Q. Glitius

Atilius Agricola (*CIL* 5 6974, 6977 = *ILS* 1021a, Taurini), L. Roscius Aelianus Mae-
cius Celer (*CIL* 14.3612 = *ILS* 1025, Tibur), L. Iulius Marinus Caecilius Simplex
(*CIL* 9.4965 = *ILS* 1026, Pisa), S. Attius Suburanus Aemilianus (*AE* 1939.60 = *IGL-
Syr* 2785, Baalbek).

20 Grainger's discussion ([2003] xxii map 5, 49–51) exemplifies the dangers of merely
measuring erasures statistically, without even considering the many texts that
were destroyed.

21 For the clubhouse of the guild of athletes at Olympia, see *AE* 1995.1406.

22 For erasures of Domitian's name in inscriptions put up before his reign, see *CIL*
6.932 = *ILS* 246 (Rome, 72); *CIL* 2.2477 = *ILS* 254 (Portugal, 79); *AE* 1991.1666a–b
(= 1987.1023 = Kallala [1997] no. 3) (Thougga, N. Africa, under Vespasian).

23 See Palmer (1993) for the continuation of a healing cult of Vespasian and Titus, as
well as the celebration of their birthdays, well after 96.

24 For Agricola's inscription from Verulamium, see *AE* 1957.169 of 79. Cf. *AE* 1974.653
for an unerased mention of Domitian in a text put up by Trajan's father in Syria.

25 For the Pamphili obelisk in the Piazza Navona, see Grenier (1987), Darwall-Smith
(1996) esp. 146–47, and Newlands (2002) 11–13. For the *ludi saeculares*, see Pighi
(1965) 40–42. For Domitian and the pipes under the city, see Paillier and Sablayrolles (1994) 15 and Sablayrolles (1994) 113. For the *ara incendii Neronis*, see *CIL*
6.826 = 30837b = *ILS* 4914, 1266, and Mart. 7.62 with Rodríguez Almeida in *LTUR*
1993.

26 For Thallus' dedication, see *CIL* 6.621 = *ILS* 3532 (see also *CIL* 6.10048 line 14 and
Mart. 4.67.5). For unerased dedications, see esp. *CIL* 10.444 = *ILS* 3546 for a dedi-
cation to Silvanus for Domitian's safety and *ILS* 3453 for an ex-voto dedication to
Hercules Saxsanus and the Flavians by a soldier.

27 For the dedication of Q. Iulius Felix, see *CIL* 6.398 = *ILS* 3673 = A. Gordon (1958)
no. 147 of 1–12 January 86 = Almar (1990) no. 119 = Gregori and Mattei (1999) no.
122. For a comparative example, see *CIL* 2².5.291 for a dedication to Venus Victrix
of A.D. 83 from Baetica.

28 Augustus was consul thirteen times, but no other Julio-Claudian held the office
more than five times. Vespasian died des. ten, Titus des. nine. Trajan was consul
six times, Hadrian only three.

29 For milestones, see *CIL* 3.312 = *ILS* 268 and French (1981) nos. 2 and 3. For boundaries, see *CIL* 2.2349 = *ILS* 5973, 2².7.871, and *IRT* 854 = Thomasson (1996) leg. 3
Aug. Numidia no. 12. For aqueducts, see *CIL* 10.7227 = *ILS* 5753, *CIL* 2².7.220. For a
canal, see *ILS* 9369 = *OGIS* 673.

30 For L. Antistius Rusticus' edict of 92/93, see Ramsay (1924), Sherk (1988) no. 107,
and Wiemer (1997) = *AE* 1997.1482 with Syme (1983a).

31 For the association of *iuvenes* near Carthage in A.D. 88, see *AE* 1959.172 (= Charles-
Picard [1957] 77–95) with Jaczynowsky (1978) 104–5 no. 213, Lepelley (1981) 291–92,
and Ginestet (1991) 263–64 no. 232. For other African examples, see *IRT* 346, 347,
348, 349, 349a, with Thomasson (1996) proconsuls nos. 49, 51, 54, 55.

32 González (1984).

33 For *diplomata* as historical sources, see Roxan (1978, 1985) with Eck and Wolff
(1986). Particularly interesting Domitianic examples include C. Gemellus from the

fleet in Alexandria (*CIL* 16.32 = A. Gordon [1983] no. 51, see figure 66 a&b) and Mucapor, a Thracian horseman at Mainz (*CIL* 16.36). For the marriages of Roman soldiers, see now Phang (2001).

34 For Tib. Claudius Zosimus in Mainz, see Selzer, Decker, and do Paço (1988) no. 130 with pl. 59 (color) with Walser (1989). For Roman emperors in Mainz, see Schumacher (1982). For other tasters, see *CIL* 6.9005 = *ILS* 1795 (Augustus), *CIL* 10.6324 = *ILS* 1734 (Nero), *CIL* 11.3612 = *ILS* 1567 (Domitian), and *CIL* 6.9004 = *ILS* 1797. *CIL* 6.1884 of A.D. 130 records the moving of the body of Trajan's taster to Rome some years after he died with Trajan at the front.

35 For Zosimus at Rome, see *CIL* 6.9003 = *ILS* 1796 (Uffizi 940) = Mansuelli (1958) no. 218 = Boschung (1987) no. 89. Schumacher (1976) did not realize that this is a funerary altar. For possibly related inscriptions, see *AE* 1979.55 and 1985.199. For slaves of the imperial household and their names, see Chantraine (1967).

36 For Domitian and the *Fasti Ostienses*, see Zevi (1979), Vidman (1982), Bargagli and Grosso (1997) pl. F.

37 For slaves with Latin names in Rome, see now Solin (1996) vol. 1.

38 For Domitia's roof tiles, see *CIL* 15.548, 549, 550, 551, 552, 553, 554–58, mostly dating to 123, but some as late as 126 (*Domitiae Domitiani* or *ex fic(linis) Domitiae Domitiani Sulpic(ianis)*). Grainger (2003) 131 n. 60 is unconvincing in suggesting that Domitia might not have known about the inscriptions on what he calls her "bricks." For Domitia Longina herself, see *PIR*² 181, Raepsaet-Charlier (1987) no. 327, and Eck in *NP* with Vinson (1989) and Griffin (2000a) 69. For other inscriptions, see esp. *CIL* 10.1422 = *ILS* 271 from the theater at Herculaneum and *CIL* 14.2795 = *ILS* 272 recording her temple at Gabii in 140. See Levick (2002) for an imaginative reconstruction of Domitia's point of view.

39 See now Kragelund (2003).

40 *CIL* 6.401 of A.D. 139.

41 For the tomb of Tib. Claudius Maximus, see *AE* 1969–70.583 = Speidel (1970) with Mihailov (1974); Molisani (1982); Strobel (1984) 77, 216; and Schumacher (1988) no. 187. The relevant scenes on Trajan's column are nos. 145–47. Dio 68.14.3 mentions Decebalus' head at Trajan's triumph. For comparative mentions of Domitian by soldiers, see L. Magius Dubius of the *leg. I Flavia Minervia pia fidelis Domitiana* from Bonn (*CIL* 13.8071) and M. Carantius Macrinus from Geneva (*CIL* 12.2602 = *ILS* 2118). For Decebalus, see now Bruun (2004).

42 For Domitian's Dacian awards, see Dio 67.7.2–4.

43 Grainger (2003) 65: "Throughout his reign Nerva's army was fighting Domitian's war."

44 For the Via Domitiana, see Dio 67.14.1; *CIL* 10 p. 58 no. 6; Stat. *Silv.* 4.3 (with Coleman [1988] *ad loc.* and Newlands [2002] 284–325, 18–27 on Statius' poetry of praise for Domitian); D'Arms (1970) 103 and (1974) 113; Ostrow (1977) 36–38; Fredericksen (1984) 18, 336; P. M. Rogers (1984) 68–69; Cébeillac Gervasoni (1993) 23; Gialanella (1993) 91–95 with color photos; Laurence (1999) 47, 65, 90–91; and Flower (2001a) 632–35.

45 For the monuments along the Via Domitiana, see Stat. *Silv.* 4.3, Mart. 8.65, Dio 67.14 with Ostrow (1977) 36–38, Fredericksen (1984) 18, Coleman (1988) 127–28,

de Maria (1988) no. 105 for the Arco Felice, Gialanella (1993) 95 for traces of the foundation of an arch at Puteoli.

46 For the milestones from the Via Antiniana, see *CIL* 10.6926–28 of 102.

47 For the Puteoli relief in Philadelphia, see *AE* 1973.137 now republished in Flower (2001a). For other Domitianic texts from Puteoli, see *CIL* 10.1631 = *ILS* 6322 and *CIL* 10.1632. For examples of Domitianic texts with erasures that were then broken into pieces, see Galsterer (1975) no. 179 pl. 37 and Bingen et al. (1992) 11–13.

48 For the bronze equestrian statue of Domitian from Misenum, see Adamo Muscettola (1987) esp. 63–65 and Bergemann (1990) P31.

49 For the Misenum text, see Camodeca (2000) who suggests that it was dedicated at the same time as the Templum Gentis Flaviae on the Quirinal in Rome. For the shrine of the Augustales, see de Franciscis (1991). *AE* 1993.476 is an earlier text for Domitian as Caesar from 80/81 that was reused for Vespasian.

50 For Domitian as a builder in Rome, see B. Jones (1992) 79–98, Darwall-Smith (1996) 101–252, and Frederick (2003). Further bibliography and discussion for each building can be found in *LTUR*. For the arches, see de Maria (1988) nos. 75, 76, 77. For the *equus Domitiani*, see Stat. 1.1. (with Newlands [2002] 46–73) and Giuliani in *LTUR* 1995: the base seems to have survived 96 and may have been reused for another statue. For the palace on the Palatine, see Royo (1999). For other survivals, see P. Davies (2000a) 31–35 and Boatwright (1990/2000). For a possible destruction of the temple of Jupiter Conservator on the Capitol, see Arata (1997). Sablayrolles (1994) 114 describes the basic opposition between Domitian's grand Rome and the erasure imposed upon it by the memory sanctions.

51 For the Forum Transitorium, see J. Anderson (1984) 119–39, Meneghini (1991), D'Ambra (1993), and Bauer and Marselli in *LTUR* 1995. For the Cancelleria reliefs, see D. Kleiner (1992) 199–201, Varner (2004) 119–20, and Paillier and Sablayrolles (1994) 18–19. Grainger (2003) 55 also notes Domitian's planning or perhaps his work (as revealed by brick stamps) on the forum of Trajan and the Baths of Trajan (begun by Titus).

52 For the *Panegyricus* of Pliny, see Durry (1938), Giovannini (1987), Fedeli (1989), Ramage (1989) 642–46, Paillier and Sablayrolles (1994) 25–30, and Strobel (2003). *Pan.* 34–42 claims that Domitian encouraged the *delatores* (see Giovannini [1987] 221). For Pliny's revisions, see *Ep.* 3.18. For continuities between Domitian and Trajan, see Griffin (2000b) 106–8 and Levick (1999) 83. Méthy's (2000) detailed analysis of the eulogistic elements of the speech in comparison with motifs on coins does not discuss the negative aspects. For Frontinus *De Aquis* (published in 98 or 100) as a comparable text praising the new regime in terms of a completely new start after a time of neglect, see Peachin (2004) 3–4, 48–50, 111, 113–27.

53 For doublespeak in the *Pan.*, see Bartsch (1994) 148–87, Paillier and Sablayrolles (1994) 26–27, and Méthy (2000).

54 For Trajan on his own times, see esp. *Ep.* 10.97.2 commenting on anonymous accusations: *nam et pessimi exempli nec nostri saeculi est* (for [such accusations] set a bad example and are not in harmony with the spirit of our age). On Trajan, see González (1993), Bennett (1997), and esp. Seelentag (2004). For parallels between the letters and panegyric, see Hoffer (1999) 5–10.

55 For *Pan.* 53, see the epigraph of this chapter. Giovannini (1987) 232 assumes that Trajan required Pliny to condemn Domitian.

56 See O'Gorman (2000) 178, speaking of Tacitus: "Nerva and Trajan, then, make the writing of history possible, but the nature of that writing is determined by the reign of Domitian."

57 See now Strobel (2003) for a stern assessment of Pliny as a collaborator with a Domitian who is represented as another Stalin (cf. Ludolph [1997] 44–49).

58 For the opening *contio* of a new magistrate during the Republic, see Cic. *Fin.* 2.74 and Suet. *Tib.* 32.1 with Flower (1996) 18–19, 154–56 and Morstein-Marx (2004) 10. Cic. *Leg. Agr.* 2 is an example of such a speech.

59 For Pliny's career, see esp. Syme (1958) 75–85, Sherwin-White (1966) 72–82, Corbier (1974) 131–43 no. 32, Giovannini (1987) with *PIR²* 490 and Krause in *NP*. Soverini (1989) 522–33 discusses the date of Pliny's praetorship and suggests a short retirement late under Domitian. For the inscriptions, see *CIL* 5.5262 = *ILS* 2927 (with Eck [1997b] 98–99 and [2001], and Alföldy [1999]), 5263, 5264, 5279, 5667, *CIL* 6.1152 = 9.5272 (with Alföldy in *CIL* 6.8.3), *AE* 1972.212, *AE* 1983.443. Pliny's consulship appears in the *Fasti Ostienses* under Sept. 100 (Fl). For a different chronology of Pliny's offices, which allows him a period in retirement at the end of Domitian and therefore moves his first treasury post under Nerva, see Birley (2000c) 5–17. Birley's reconstruction justifies what Pliny says in his letters about danger at the end of Domitian's reign.

60 See Soverini (1989) for a nuanced analysis of Pliny's relationship with both Domitian and Trajan.

61 For the Revolt of Saturninus in 89, see Suet. *Dom.* 10.5 with Syme (1978), Flaig (1992) 417–50, Griffin (2000a) 65–67. For the erasure of Saturninus, see Suet. *Dom.* 7.3 with Syme (1978). Nerva was *consul ordinarius* with Domitian at the beginning of 90. Trajan, who helped put down the revolt, was *consul ordinarius* in 91 (Flaig [1992] 447).

62 For Domitian's confiscations, see Giovannini (1987) 236–39, who sees Pliny as heavily involved, and Rutledge (2001) 129–35 for the *delatores*. For the fiscal crisis and army pay, see P. M. Rogers (1984) and Griffin (2000a). For Pliny and wills, see Giovannini (1987) 221–30 with Champlin (1991) for Roman wills in general. Pliny *Pan.* 90.5 calls Domitian the despoiler and executioner of the best men.

63 For Pliny's publications and their chronology, see Aubrion (1989) esp. 311–14, Conte (1994), and Fantham (1996) 200–221. It is hard to document much published before 96. For the chronology of the letters, see Aubrion (1989) 318–19. Recent studies of the letters and of Pliny's self-presentation in them include Ludolph (1997), Radicke (1997), Riggsby (1998), Hoffer (1999), Beutel (2000), Henderson (2002), Castagna and Lefèvre (2003), and a special edition of *Arethusa* 36.2 (2003) edited by R. Morello and R. K. Gibson.

64 On the new freedom of speech, see Hoffer (1999) 161–76.

65 For Domitianic precedents cited in *Ep.* 10, see 58–60 (Flavius Archippus), 65–66 (foundlings), 72–73 (freeborn rights for former slaves). For Pliny in Bithynia and Pontus, see Levick (1979), Talbert (1980), and Millar (2000).

66 For the *ius trium liberorum*, see *Ep.* 10.2.

Notes to Pages 263–66

67 For Regulus' fears after Domitian's death, see *Ep.* 1.5. For other mentions of Regulus, see 1.20, 2.11, 2.20, 4.2, 4.7, 6.2 with Rutledge (2001) 192–98 no. 9. For Nerva's
dinner conversation, see 4.22 with Sherwin-White (1966) *ad loc.* and *ILS* 274 (Nerva's *libertas*). For other *delatores* in 97, see esp. 9.13 on Pliny's attack on Publicius
Certus. Pliny published his speech *De Helvidi Ultione.* Hoffer (1999) 55–91 analyzes
the figure of Regulus in detail.

68 For Greek games, see *Ep.* 4.22 and Caldelli (1993).

69 For Arria and Fannia, see 3.16 and 7.19 with Sherwin-White (1966) (Arria = *PIR*²
1113 = Raepsaet-Charlier [1987] no. 96; Arria = *PIR*² 1114 = Raepsaet-Charlier
[1987] no. 159; Fannia = *PIR*² 118 = Raepsaet-Charlier [1987] 259 with *stemma* 31).
For further discussion, see Syme (1958–63) 92, 535, 559 and (1985); B. Jones (1973,
1992). For the Stoic opposition to Vespasian and the Flavians in general, see Levick
(1999) 79–94.

70 For Artemidorus, see 3.11. For Pliny and Nerva in 93/94, see 7.33. See Tac. *Agr.*
45 for the trials of late 93, with Syme (1983b), Giovannini (1987) 233, and Griffin
(2000a) 66–68. Pliny claims that he was in danger toward the end of Domitian's
reign and that he did not hold office (*Ep.* 1.5, 3.11, 7.14, 7.27, 7.33, 4.24 with *Pan.* 90.5
and 95.3–5). Sherwin-White (1966) 304 dates this claim to after 100 rather than before. Cf. 426: "Pliny's persistent but improbable claim to have been under a cloud
in 95–96 may well cover the feeling that he had not been a loyal friend in 93." For
Valerius Licinianus, see 4.11 with Juv. 4.5, Stat. *Silv.* 1.1.36, Tac. *Hist.* 1.2, Suet. *Dom.*
8.4, Dio 67.3, and Griffin (2000a) 80. It is notable that Nerva did not recall him.
Sherwin-White (1966) 282: "The whole letter is a remarkable example of special
pleading." For Corellius Rufus (*PIR*² 1294), see 1.12 written under Nerva.

71 For Verginius Rufus (*PIR*² 84), see *Ep.* 2.1, 6.10, and 9.19 with Dio 68.2.4 on the
fame of his epitaph. Pliny first hopes that Verginius will become even more famous
after death but is then disappointed. Vindex has faded out in this version of events
(cf. Tac. *Hist.* 1.52, Suet. *Ner.* 47.1, Dio 63.25.2–3).

72 For the chronology of Pliny's extortions trials, see Sherwin-White (1966) 56–62
with *Ep.* 3.4, 10.8, 4.9, 5.20, 6.5, 6.13, 7.6, 7.10, 9.13.

73 According to *Ep.* 8.12 it looks as if Tacitus is the only historian writing about the
Flavians around 105–7. The *Agricola* seems to have been published around 98, the
Germania also soon after Domitian's death, and the *Dialogus* around 101–2 or a bit
later. The *Histories* were written under Trajan, before Tacitus became proconsul of
Asia in 112, and the *Annals* afterward, perhaps mostly under Hadrian.

74 For Cn. Octavius Titinius Capito (*PIR*² 62, Eck in *NP*), see 1.17 and 5.8 where he is
urging Pliny to write history. His career is referred to in *CIL* 6.798 = *ILS* 1448 and
AE 1934.154 (with Eck [1996b]), both of which texts omit any mention of Domitian. See also Pflaum (1960–61) 60 and Griffin (2000b) 106–7.

75 Pliny provides material for Tacitus' *Histories* at 6.16 and 6.20 (the death of the elder
Pliny and the eruption of Vesuvius) and 7.33 (Pliny and Nerva in 93/94).

76 For the censorship of Marius Priscus, see 2.11. For the invalidation of the *acta* of
Julius Bassus in Bithynia, see 10.56–57 with 4.9.

77 The honors for Pallas are described at 7.29 and 8.6. A useful comparison can be
made with the case of Epaphroditus, who was rewarded with extraordinary hon-

ors in 65 (Tac. *Ann.* 15.55.1) but was eventually executed by Domitian (Suet. *Ner.* 49.3 and *Dom.* 14.4). His honors are recorded in *ILS* 9505; see Eck (1976) and Syme (1983a) 135.

78 Tacitus also sees a new age of hope dawning at *Agr.* 3.1 and 44.5.

79 For the temple at Comum, see *AE* 1983.443 = Alföldy (1983) and (1999). For Pliny's priesthood of Titus, see *CIL* 5.5667 line 10 (*fl(amen) divi T(iti) Aug*). For the elder Pliny and Titus, see the preface to the *NH*, esp. 36–37. For the eruption of Vesuvius, see *Ep.* 6.16 and 20.

80 For the temple at Tifernum, see *Ep.* 10.8.

81 For the debate over Hadrian's memory, see Hüttl (1936/1975) 47–56, Garzetti (1974) 439–41, Chantraine (1988) 75–76, and Birley (1997) 279–300 and (2000a) 151. For S. Price ([1987] 93), Pius' victory showed that the emperor was now in charge.

82 For Hadrian at Puteoli, see *SHA Hadr.* 25.6–7, 27.3; *SHA Marc.* 6.1; Artemid. 1.26 with *CIL* 10.515; *IG* 14.737, 830; *CIG* 1.1068, 3.3208; *IGR* 1.442. Hadrian was celebrated with quinquennial games (later renamed Eusebeia in honor of Pius) and a temple at Puteoli.

83 For Hadrian as an emperor, see esp. Boatwright (1987, 2000) with Birley (1997) and Mortensen (2004) with a summary of earlier views.

84 For Hadrian's mausoleum (Castel Sant'Angelo), see Boatwright (1987) 161–81 and P. Davies (2000b) 34–40, 95–96, 106–9, 158–63, 189–90.

85 For the coins of A.D. 138, see Hüttl (1936/1975) 50–52 and Mattingly (1940) esp. xlviii–xlix.

86 See Varner (2004) 136 for the fact that no portraits of Commodus were recut at the time of his disgrace.

BIBLIOGRAPHY

▾   ▾   ▾

Aberson, M. 1994. *Temples votifs et butin de guerre dans la Rome républicaine.* Rome.

Absil, M. 1997. *Les préfets du prétoire d'Auguste à Commode.* Paris.

Accame, S. 1941. *La lega ateniense del IV secolo a. C.* Rome.

Adamo Muscettola, S. 1987. "Una statua per due imperatori. L'eredità difficile di Domiziano." In *Domiziano/Nerva. La statua equestre da Miseno. Una proposta di ricomposizione,* 39–66. Naples.

Alcock, S. E. 1993. *Graecia Capta: The Landscapes of Roman Greece.* Cambridge.

———. 2002. *Archaeologies of the Greek Past: Landscape, Monuments and Memories.* Cambridge.

Alexiou, M. 1974. *The Ritual Lament in the Greek Tradition.* Cambridge.

Alfano, C. 2001. "Egyptian Influences in Italy." In S. Walker and P. Higgs (eds.), *Cleopatra of Egypt,* 276–91. London.

Alföldi, A. 1971. *Der Vater des Vaterlandes im römischen Denken.* Darmstadt.

———. 1973. *Die zwei Lorbeerbäume des Augustus.* Bonn.

Alföldy, G. 1969. *Fasti Hispanienses.* Wiesbaden.

———. 1983. "Ein Tempel des Herrscherkultes in Comum." *Athenaeum* 61:362–73.

———. 1990. *Der Obelisk auf dem Petersplatz in Rom. Ein historisches Monument der Antike.* Heidelberg.

———. 1991. "Augustus und die Inschriften: Tradition und Innovation." *Gymnasium* 98:289–324.

———. 1992a. "Il monumento vaticano di Vipsania Agrippina e degli Asinii." In *Studi sull'epigrafia augustea e tiberiana,* 125–43. Rome.

———. 1992b. *Studi sull'epigrafia augustea e tiberiana di Roma.* Rome.

———. 1995. "Eine Bauinschrift aus dem Colosseum." *ZPE* 109:195–226.

———. 1999. "Die Inschriften des jüngeren Plinius und seine Mission in Pontus et Bithynia." *AAntHung* 39:21–44.

———. 2001a. "Zur Präsenz hispanischer Senatoren in Rom: Ehren- und Grabmonumente aus der Hohen Kaiserzeit." In C. Castillo, F. Javier Navarro, and R. Martínez (eds.), *Da Augusto a Trajano. Un siglo en la historia de Hispania,* 69–91. Pamplona.

———. 2001b. "*Pietas immobilis erga principem* und ihr Lohn: Öffentliche Ehrenmonumente von Senatoren in Rom während der Frühen und Hohen Kaiserzeit." In G. Alföldy and S. Panciera (eds.), *Inschriftliche Denkmähler als Medien der Selbstdarstellung in der römischen Welt,* 11–46. Stuttgart.

Allen, D. 2000. *The World of Prometheus: The Politics of Punishing in Democratic Athens*. Princeton.

Allende, I. 1995. *Paula*. New York.

Allison, J. E., and J. D. Cloud. 1962. "*Lex maiestatis*." *Latomus* 21:711–31.

Almar, K. P. 1990. *Inscriptiones Latinae: eine illustrierte Einführung in die lateinische Epigraphik*. Odense.

Altmann, W. 1905. *Die römischen Grabaltäre der Kaiserzeit*. Berlin.

Anderson, J. C. 1984. *The Historical Topography of the Imperial Fora*. Brussels.

Anderson, R. D., P. J. Parsons, and R. G. M. Nisbet. 1979. "Elegiacs by Gallus from Qasr Ibrîm." *JRS* 69:125–55.

André, J. M. 1990. "Die Zuschauerschaft als sozialpolitischer Mikrokosmos zur Zeit des Hochprinzipats." In J. Blänsdorf (ed.), *Theater und Gesellschaft im Imperium Romanum*, 165–73. Tübingen.

Andrewes, A. 1956. *The Greek Tyrants*. London.

Arata, F. P. 1997. "Un 'sacellum' d'età imperiale all'interno del Museo Capitolino: una proposta di identificazione." *BCAR* 98:129–62.

Arce, J. 1988. *Funus Imperatorum: los funerales de los emperadores romanos*. Madrid.

Arjava, A. 1998. "Paternal Power in Late Antiquity." *JRS* 88:147–65.

Ashton, S.-A. 2001. "Identifying the Egyptian-Style Ptolemaic Queens." In S. Walker and P. Higgs (eds.), *Cleopatra of Egypt*, 148–55. London.

Assmann, J. 1995. "Ancient Egyptian Antijudaism: A Case of Distorted Memory." In D. Schacter (ed.), *Memory Distortion. How Minds, Brains and Societies Reconstruct the Past*, 365–76. Cambridge, Mass.

Astin, A. E. 1967. *Scipio Aemilianus*. Oxford.

———. 1988. "*Regimen morum*." *JRS* 78:14–34.

Aubrion, E. 1989. "La 'correspondance' de Pline le Jeune: problèmes et orientations acutelles de la recherche." *ANRW* 33.1:302–74. Berlin and New York.

———. 1990. "L'historien Tacite face à l'évolution des jeux et des autres spectacles." In J. Blänsdorf (ed.), *Theater und Gesellschaft im Imperium Romanum*, 197-211. Tübingen.

Aurigemma, S. 1940. "Sculture del Foro Vecchio di Leptis Magna raffiguranti la Dea Roma e principi della casa dei Giulio Claudi." *Africa Italiana* 8:1–94.

Avetta, L. 1985. *Roma: Via imperiale*. Rome.

Badian, E. 1958. *Foreign Clientelae*. Oxford.

———. 1964. "Waiting for Sulla." In *Studies in Greek and Roman History*, 206–34. Oxford.

———. 1966. "The Early Historians." In T. A. Dorey (ed.), *Latin Historians*, 1–38. London.

———. 1970. *Lucius Sulla: The Deadly Reformer*. Seventh Todd Memorial Lecture. Sydney.

———. 1971. "Three Fragments." In *Pro Munere Grates: Studies Presented to H. L. Gorin*, 1–6. Praetoria.

———. 1972. "Tiberius Gracchus and the Beginning of the Roman Revolution." *ANRW* 1:668–731. Berlin and New York.

———. 1982. "'Crisis Theoris' and the Beginning of the Principate." In G. Wirth (ed.), *Romanitas-Christianitas: Untersuchungen zur Geschichte und Literatur der römischen Kaiserzeit, Johannes Straub zum 70. Geburtstag gewidmet*, 18–41. Berlin and New York.

———. 1984. "The Death of Saturninus. Studies in Chronology and Prosopography." *Chiron* 14:101–47.

———. 1990/2000. "Introduction." In *The Year 96: Did It Make a Difference? AJAH* 15.1:1–3.

———. 1990. "The Consuls, 179–49 BC." *Chiron* 20:371–413.

———. 1996. "Alexander the Great between two Thrones and Heaven." In A. M. Small (ed.), *Subject and Ruler: The Cult of the Ruling Power in Classical Antiquity*, 11–26. Ann Arbor, Mich.

Baldwin, B. 1995. "Roman Emperors in the Elder Pliny." *Scholia* 4:56–78.

Ball, L. F. 1994. "A Reappraisal of Nero's *Domus Aurea*." *JRA Suppl. 11 Roman Papers*, 183–254.

Balsdon, J. P. V. D. 1934. *The Emperor Gaius*. Oxford.

Baltrusch, E. 1989. *Regimen morum. Die Reglementierung des Privatlebens der Senatoren und Ritter in der römischen Republik und frühen Kaiserzeit*. Munich.

Barbieri, G. 1982–83. "La collezione epigrafica Iaia." *BCAR* 88:105–89.

Barden Dowling, M. 2000. "The Clemency of Sulla." *Historia* 49:303–40.

Bargagli, B., and C. Grosso. 1997. *I Fasti Ostienses: documento della storia di Ostia*. Rome.

Barnes, T. 1982. "The Date of the *Octavia*." *MH* 39:215–17.

Barrett, A. A. 1989. *Caligula: The Corruption of Power*. London.

———. 1991. "Claudius' British Victory Arch in Rome." *Britannia* 22:1–19.

———. 1996. *Agrippina: Sex, Power and Politics in the Early Empire*. New Haven.

———. 2002. *Livia: First Lady of Imperial Rome*. New Haven.

Bartman, E. 1999. *Portraits of Livia: Imaging the Imperial Woman in Augustan Rome*. Cambridge.

Bartsch, S. 1994. *Actors in the Audience: Theatricality and Doublespeak from Nero to Hadrian*. Cambridge, Mass.

Batstone, W. W. 1994. "Cicero's Construction of Consular Ethos in the First Catilinarian." *TAPA* 124:211–66.

Bauchhenß, G. 1984. *Die grosse Iuppitersäule aus Mainz*. Mainz.

Bauman, R. 1970. *The Crimen Maiestatis in the Roman Republic and Augustan Principate*. Johannesburg.

———. 1974. *Impietas in Principem: A Study of Treason against the Roman Emperor with Special Reference to the First Century A D*. Munich.

———. 1992. *Women and Politics in Ancient Rome*. London.

Beacham, R. C. 1999. *Spectacle Entertainments of Early Imperial Rome*. New Haven.

Beard, M. 1980. "The Sexual Status of Vestal Virgins." *JRS* 70:12–27.

———. 1985. "Writing and Ritual. A Study of Diversity and Expansion in the Arval Acta." *PBSR* 53:114–62.

——— (ed.). 1990. *Pagan Priests: Religion and Power in the Ancient World*. Ithaca, N.Y.

———. 1991. "Writing and Religion: Ancient Literacy and the Function of the Written Word in Roman Religion." In *Literacy in the Roman World*, 35–58. Ann Arbor, Mich.

———. 1995. "Re-reading (Vestal) Virginity." In R. Hawley and B. Levick (eds.), *Women in Antiquity: New Assessments*, 21–43. London.

———. 1998. "Documenting Roman Religion." In *La mémoire perdue. Recherches sur l'administration romaine*, 75–101. Rome.

Beard, M., J. North, and S. Price. 1998. *Religions of Rome*. Vols. 1 and 2. Cambridge.

Beck, H., and U. Walter. 2001. *Die frühen römischen Historiker* 1. Darmstadt.

———. 2004. *Die frühen römischen Historiker* 2. Darmstadt.

Behr, H. 1993. *Die Selbstdarstellung Sullas. Ein aristokratischer Politiker zwischen persönlichem Führungsanspruch und Standessolidarität*. Frankfurt.

Bellemore, J. 1995. "The Wife of Sejanus." *ZPE* 109:255–66.

Bellen, H. 1981. *Die germanische Leibwache der römischen Kaiser des julio-claudischen Hauses*. Mainz and Wiesbaden.

Belli Pasqua, R. 1995. *Sculture di età romana in "basalto."* Rome.

Bengston, H. 1975. *Die Staatsverträge des Altertums. 2. Die Verträge der griechisch-römischen Welt von 700 bis 338 v. Chr.*² Munich.

———. 1979. *Die Flavier. Geschichte eines römischen Kaiserhauses*. Munich.

Benjamin, A., and A. E. Raubitschek. 1959. "*Arae Augusti.*" *Hesperia* 28:65–85.

Bennett, J. 1997. *Trajan, optimus princeps: A Life and Times*. Bloomington, Ind.

Bérard, F., I. Cogitore, and M. Tarpin. 1998. "Une nouvelle inscription claudienne à Lyon." In *Claude de Lyon: empereur romain*, 373–89. Paris.

Berg, B. 1997. "Cicero's Palatine House and Clodius' Shrine of Liberty. Alternative Emblems of the Republic in Cicero's *de domo sua*." In C. Deroux (ed.), *Studies in Latin Literature and Roman History* 8:122–43. Brussels.

Bergemann, J. 1990. *Römische Reiterstatuen: Ehrendenkmäler im öffentlichen Bereich*. Mainz.

Bergmann, M. 1993. *Der Koloß Neros, die Domus Aurea und der Mentalitätswandel im Rom der frühen Kaiserzeit*. Mainz.

———. 1998. *Die Strahlen der Herrscher. Theomorphes Herrscherbild und politische Symbolik im Hellenismus und in der römischen Kaiserzeit*. Mainz.

Bergmann, M., and P. Zanker. 1981. "'Damnatio Memoriae' Umgearbeitete Nero- und Domitiansporträts. Zur Ikonographie der flavischen Kaiser und des Nerva." *JdI* 96:317–412.

Bernand, E. 1969. *Les inscriptions grecques et latines de Philae 2: haut et bas empire*. Paris.

Bernstein, A. H. 1978. *Tiberius Sempronius Gracchus: Tradition and Apostasy*. Ithaca, N.Y.

Bernstein, F. H. 1998. *Ludi Publici: Untersuchungen zur Entstehung und Entwicklung der öffentlichen Spiele im Republikanischen Rom*. Stuttgart.

Bertoletti, M., M. Cima, and E. Talamo (eds.). 1999. *Sculptures of Ancient Rome: The Collections of the Capitoline Museums at the Montemartini Power Plant*. Rome.

Berve, H. 1967. *Die Tyrannis bei den Griechen*. Vols. 1 and 2. Munich.

Beutel, F. 2000. *Vergangenheit als Politik: neue Aspekte im Werk des jüngeren Plinius*. Frankfurt.

Billows, R. 1990. *Antigonos the One-eyed and the Creation of the Hellenistic State*. Berkeley.

———. 1995. *Kings and Colonists: Aspects of Macedonian Imperialism.* Leiden.

Bingen, J., A. Bülow-Jacobsen, W. E. H. Cockle, H. Cuvigny, L. Rubinstein, and W. van Rengen. 1992. *Mons Claudianus. Ostraca Graeca et Latina* 1. Cairo.

Binot, C. 2001. "Le rôle de Scipion Nasica Serapio dans la crise gracquienne, une relecture." *Pallas* 57:185–203.

Birley, A. R. 1987. *Marcus Aurelius.* London.

———. 1997. *Hadrian: The Restless Emperor.* London.

———. 2000a. "Hadrian to the Antonines." In *The Cambridge Ancient History* 11²: *The High Empire, A.D. 70–192,* 132–94. Cambridge.

———. 2000b. "The Life and Death of Cornelius Tacitus." *Historia* 49:230–47.

———. 2000c. *Onomasticon to the Younger Pliny.* Munich and Leipzig.

Blanck, H. 1969. *Wiederverwendung alter Statuen als Ehrendenkmäler bei Griechen und Römern.* Rome.

Bleicken, J. 1962. *Senatsgericht und Kaisersgericht.* Göttingen.

———. 1990. *Zwischen Republik und Prinzipat. Zum Charakter des Zweiten Triumvirats.* Göttingen.

———. 1999. *Augustus: eine Biographie.* Berlin.

Blinkenberg, C. 1941. *Lindos. Fouilles de l'acropole 1902–1914. Inscriptions* 2. Berlin and Copenhagen.

Blümner, H. 1911. *Die römischen Privataltertümer³.* Munich.

Boatwright, M. T. 1987. *Hadrian and the City of Rome.* Princeton.

———. 1990/2000. "Public Architecture in Rome and the Year 96." *AJAH* 15.1:67–90.

———. 2000. *Hadrian and the Cities of the Roman Empire.* Princeton.

Bodel, J. 1997. "Monumental Villas and Villa Monuments." *JRA* 10:1–35.

———. 1999a. "Punishing Piso." *AJP* 120:43–63.

———. 1999b. "Death on Display: Looking at Roman Funerals." In B. Bergmann and C. Kondoleon (eds.), *The Art of Ancient Spectacle,* 259–81. New Haven.

Bonnefond, M. 1987. "Transferts de fonctions et mutation idéologique: le Capitole et le Forum d'Auguste." In *L'urbs. Espace urbain et histoire (Ier siècle av. J.-C.–IIIe siècle ap. J.-C.),* 251–78. Rome.

Born, H., and K. Stemmler. 1996. *Damnatio Memoriae: das Berliner Nero-Porträt.* Berlin.

Boschung, D. 1986. "Überlegungen zum Liciniergrab." *JdI* 101:257–287.

———. 1987. *Antike Grabaltäre aus den Nekropolen Roms.* Bern.

———. 1989. *Die Bildnisse des Caligula.* Berlin.

———. 1993. "Die Bildnistypen der iulisch-claudischen Kaiserfamilie: ein kritischer Forschungsbericht." *JRA* 6:39–79.

Bosworth, A. B. 1977. "Tacitus and Asinius Gallus." *AJAH* 2:173–92.

Boyle, A. J., and W. J. Dominik (eds.). 2003. *Flavian Rome: Culture, Image, Text.* Leiden.

Bradley, K. R. 1978. *Suetonius' Life of Nero: An Historical Commentary.* Brussels.

———. 1989. *Slavery and Rebellion in the Roman World, 140–70 B.C.* Bloomington, Ind.

Braun, M., A. Haltenhoff, and F.-H. Mutschler (eds.). 2000. *Moribus antiquis res stat Romana: römische Werte und römische Literatur im 3. und 2. Jh. v. Chr.* Munich.

Brecht, C. H. 1938. *Perduellio, eine Studie zu ihrer begrifflichen Abgrenzung im römischen Strafrecht bis zum Ausgang der Republik*. Munich.

Brennan, T. C. 1990/2000. "*Principes* and Plebs: Nerva's Reign as a Turning-Point?" *AJAH* 15.1:40–66.

———. 1992. "Sulla's Career in the Nineties: Some Reconsiderations." *Chiron* 22:102–58.

———. 1993. "The Commanders in the First Sicilian Slave War." *RFIC* 121:153–84.

———. 1995. "Notes on Praetors in Spain in the Mid-Second Century BC." *Emerita* 63:47–76.

———. 2000. *The Praetorship in the Roman Republic*. Vols. 1 and 2. Oxford.

Briscoe, J. 1973. *A Commentary on Livy 31–33*. Oxford.

Broise, H., and J. Scheid. 1993. "Étude d'un cas: le *lucus* deae Diae à Rome." In *Les bois sacrées*, 143–57. Naples.

Brunt, P. A. 1959. "The Revolt of Vindex and the Fall of Nero." *Latomus* 18:531–59.

———. 1977. "*Lex de imperio Vespasiani*." *JRS* 67:95–116.

———. 1984. "Did Emperors Ever Suspend the Law of 'maiestas?'" In V. Giuffrè (ed.), *Sodalitas. Scritti in onore di Antonio Guanno*, 469–80. Naples.

———. 1988. *The Fall of the Roman Republic and Related Essays*. Oxford.

Bruun, C. 2004. "The Legend of Decebalus." In L. de Ligt, E. A. Hemelrijk, and H. W. Singor (eds.), *Roman Rule and Civic Life: Local and Regional Perspectives*, 153–75. Amsterdam.

Bucher, G. 1987/1995. "The *Annales Maximi* in the Light of Roman Methods of Keeping Records." *AJAH* 12:2–61.

Budde, L. 1973. "Das römische Historienrelief." *ANRW* 1.1.4:800–804. Berlin and New York.

Buonocore, M. 1989. "Rhegium Iulium — Regio III." *Supplementa Italica* 5:29–84.

Burckhardt, L. A. 1988. *Politische Strategien der Optimaten in der späten römischen Republik*. Stuttgart.

Butler, S. 2002. *The Hand of Cicero*. London.

Caballos, A., W. Eck, and F. Fernández. 1996. *El Senadoconsulto de Gneo Pisón Padre*. Seville.

Cagiano de Azevedo, M. 1939. "Una dedica abrasa e i rilievi puteolani dei musei di Filadelphia e Berlino." *BCAR* Suppl. 10:45–56.

Calboli, G. 1998. "Le 'Senatus Consultum de Cn. Pisone patre', quelques considérations linguistiques." In B. Bureau and C. Nicolas (eds.), *Moussyllanea. Mélanges de linguistique et de littératures anciennes offerts à Claude Moussy*, 117–130. Bibliothèque d'Études Classiques, 15. Association Vita Latina. Louvain and Paris.

Caldelli, M. L. 1993. *L'agon capitolinus. Storia e protagonisti dall'istituzione domizianea al IV secolo*. Rome.

Caltabiano, M. 1975. "La morte del console Marcello nella tradizione storiografica." *CISA* 3:65–81.

Camodeca, G. 2000. "Domiziano e il collegio degli Augustales di Miseno." In G. Paci (ed.), *Epigraphai. Miscellenea epigrafica in onore di Lidio Gasperini* 1:171–87. Rome.

Campbell, B. 2000. *The Writings of the Roman Land Surveyors: Introduction, Text, Translation and Commentary. JRS* monograph 9. London.

Cancik, H. 1990. "Grösse und Kolossalität als religiöse und aethetische Kategorien: Versuch einer Begriffsbestimmung am Beispiel von Statius *Silv.* 1.1. *Ecus maximus Domitiani imp.*" *Visible Religion* 7:51–68.

Cantarella, E. 1991. *I supplizi capitali in Grecia e a Roma. Origini e funzioni della pena di morte nell'antichità.* Milan.

Carawan, E. M. 1984–85. "The Tragic History of Marcellus and Livy's Characterization." *CJ* 80:131–41.

———. 1993. "Tyranny and Outlawry: Ath. Pol. 16.10." In R. M. Rosen and J. Farrell (eds.), *Nomodeiktes: Greek Studies in Honor of Martin Ostwald*, 305–19. Ann Arbor, Mich.

Carney, T. F. 1970. *A Biography of C. Marius.* Chicago.

Carradice, I. A. 1983. *Coinage and Finances in the Reign of Domitian, A.D. 81–96.* Oxford.

———. 1993. "Coin Types and Roman History: The Example of Domitian." In M. Price, A. Burnett, and R. Bland (eds.), *Essays in Honour of R. Carson and K. Jenkins*, 161–75. London.

———. 1998. "Towards a New Introduction to the Flavian Coinage." In M. Austin, J. Harries, and C. Smith (eds.), *Modus Operandi: Essays in Honour of G. Rickman*, 93–117. London.

Carrée, R. 1999. "Otho et Vitellius, deux nouveaux Nérons?" In J.-M. Croisille, R. Martin, and Y. Perrin (eds.), *Neronia V. Néron: histoire et légende*, 152–81. Brussels.

Carroll, K. K. 1982. *The Parthenon Inscription (IG 2² 3277), A.D. 61/62.* Durham, N.C.

Carter, J. M. 1977. "A New Fragment of Octavian's Inscription at Nicopolis." *ZPE* 24:227–30.

Cassolà, F. 1970. "Livio, il tempio di Giove Feretrio e la inaccessibilità dei santuari in Roma." *RSI* 81:5–31.

Castagna, L., and E. Lefèvre (eds.). 2003. *Plinius der Jüngere und seine Zeit.* Munich.

Cavaggioni, F. 1998. *L. Apuleio Saturnino, tribunus plebis seditiosus.* Venice.

Cavalieri Manasse, G. 1992. "L'imperatore Claudio a Verona." *Epigraphica* 54:9–41.

Cawkwell, G. L. 1981. "Notes on the Failure of the Second Athenian Confederacy." *JHS* 101:40–55.

———. 1994. "The Deification of Alexander the Great: A Note." In I. Worthington (ed.), *Ventures into Greek History*, 293–306. Oxford.

Cébeillac Gervasoni, M. 1993. "La colonia romana di Puteoli: storia politica e istituzionale." In F. Zevi (ed.), *Puteoli*, 17–30. Naples.

Cerutti, S. M. 1997. "The Location of the Houses of Cicero and Clodius and the Porticus Catuli on the Palatine Hill in Rome." *AJP* 118:417–26.

Champlin, E. 1991. *Final Judgments: Duty and Emotion in Roman Wills, 200 BC–AD 250.* Berkeley.

———. 1998. "God and Man in the Golden House." In M. Cima and E. La Rocca (eds.), *Horti Romani. Atti del convegno internazionale*, 333–44. BCAR Suppl. 6. Rome.

———. 1999. "The First (1996) Edition of the *Senatus Consultum de Cn. Pisone Patre*: A Review." *AJP* 120.1:117-22.

———. 2003. *Nero*. Cambridge, Mass.

Chaniotis, A., and G. Preuss. 1990. "Neue Fragmente des Preisedikts von Diokletian und lateinische Inschriften aus Kreta." *ZPE* 80:189–202.

Chantraine, H. 1967. *Freigelassene und Sklaven im Dienst der römischen Kaiser. Studien zu ihrer Nomenklatur*. Wiesbaden.

———. 1988. "Der tote Herrscher in der Politik der römischen Kaiserzeit." *GWU* 39:67–80.

Chapoutier, F. 1924. "Note sur un décret inédit de Rhamnonte." *BCH* 48:264–75.

Charles-Picard, G. 1959. "*Civitas Mactaritana*." *Karthago* 8:77–95.

Chassignet, M. 2001. "La 'construction' des aspirants à la tyrannie: Sp. Cassius, Sp. Maelius et Manlius Capitolinus." In M. Coudry and T. Späth (eds.), *L'invention des grands hommes de la Rome antique = Die Konstruktion der grossen Männer Altroms*, 83–96. Actes du colloque du Collegium Beatus Rhenanus, Augst, 16–18 septembre 1999. Paris.

———. 2004. *L'annalistique romaine 3: l'annalistique récente, l'autobiographie politique*. Paris.

Chilton, C. W. 1955. "The Roman Law of Treason under the Early Principate." *JRS* 45:73–81.

Christ, K. 1995. *Geschichte der römischen Kaiserzeit von Augustus bis zu Konstantin*[3]. Munich.

———. 2000. *Krise und Untergang der römischen Republik*[4]. Darmstadt.

———. 2002. *Sulla. Eine römische Karriere*. Munich.

Christol, M. 1991. "Remarques sur une inscription de Thugga: le pagus de la colonie de Carthage au 1er siècle ap. J.-C." In *Epigrafia. Actes du colloque international d'épigraphie latine en mémoire d'Atilio Degrassi*, 607–28. Rome.

Cima, M., and E. La Rocca. 1986. *Le tranquille dimore degli dei. La residenza imperiale degli horti Lamiani*. Venice.

Cizek, E. 1983. *L'époque de Trajan. Circonstances politiques et problèmes idéologiques*. Paris and Bucharest.

Clarke, M. L. 1981. *The Noblest Roman: Marcus Brutus and His Reputation*. London.

Classen, A. J. 1963. "Gottmenschentum in der römischen Republik." *Gymnasium* 70:313–38.

Clauss, M. 1994. "Die Anhängerschaft des Silvanus-Kultes." *Klio* 76:381–87.

———. 1995. *Kleopatra*. Munich.

———. 1999. *Kaiser und Gott. Herrscherkult im römischen Reich*. Stuttgart.

Clemente, G. 1981. "Le leggi sul lusso e la società romana tra III e II secolo a.C." In A. Giardina and A. Schiavone (eds.), *Società romana e produzione schiavistica 3. Modelli etici, diritto e trasformazioni sociali*, 1–14. Bari.

Coarelli, F. 1969. "Le tyrannoctone du Capitole et la mort de Tiberius Gracchus." *MEFRA* 81:137–60.

———. 1978. "La statue de Cornélie, mère des Gracques et la crise politique à Rome au temps de Saturninus." In R. Villiers (ed.), *Le dernier siècle de la république romaine et l'époque augusteenne*, 13-28. Strasbourg.

———. 1981. "Le iscrizioni." In I. Kajanto, U. Nyberg, and M. Steinby, *L'area sacra di Largo Argentina* 1: *Topografia e storia, le iscrizioni, i bolli laterizi*, 25–28. Rome.

———. 1982. *Lazio*. Rome.

Cogitore, I. 1992. "Séries de dédicaces italiennes à la dynastie julio-claudienne." *MEFRA* 104:817–70.

———. 2002. *La légitimité dynastique d'Auguste à Néron à l'épreuve des conspirations.* Rome.

Coleman, K. M. 1986. "The Emperor Domitian and Literature." *ANRW* 2.32.5:3087–3115. Berlin and New York.

———. 1988. *Statius Silvae IV*. Oxford.

———. 1990/2000. "Latin Literature after A.D. 96: Change or Continuity?" *AJAH* 15:19–39.

Connor, W. R. 1985. "The Razing of the House in Greek Society." *TAPA* 115:79–102.

———. 1987. "Tribes, Festivals and Processions: Civic Ceremonial and Political Manipulation in Archaic Greece." *JHS* 107:40–50.

Conte, G. B. 1994. *Latin Literature: A History*. Baltimore.

Corbier, M. 1974. *L'aerarium Saturni et l'aerarium militare: administration et prosopographie sénatoriale*. Rome.

———. 1987. "L'écriture dans l'espace public romain." In *L'urbs. Espace urbain et histoire (Ier siècle av. J.-C.–IIIe siècle ap. J.-C.)*, 27–60. Rome.

———. 1990. "Les comportements familiaux de l'aristocratie romaine (IIe siècle av. J.-C.–IIIe siècle ap. J.-C.)." In J. Andreau and H. Bruhns (eds.), *Parenté et stratégies familiales dans l'antiquité romaine*, 225–49. Rome.

———. 1994. "La maison des Césars." In P. Bonté (ed.), *Épouser au plus proche. Inceste, prohibitions et stratégies matrimoniales autour de la Méditerranée*, 243–91. Paris.

———. 1995. "Male Power and Legitimacy through Women: The *domus Augusta* under the Julio-Claudians." In R. Hawley and B. M. Levick (eds.), *Women in Antiquity: New Assessments*, 178–93. London.

———. 2001. "*Maiestas domus Augustae*." In A. Bertinelli and A. Donati (eds.), *Varia Epigraphica. Atti del Colloquio Internazionale di Epigrafia*, 155–99. Faenza.

Cornell, T. J. 1981. "Some Observations on the '*Crimen Incesti*.'" In *Le délit religieux dans la cité antique*, 27–37. Rome.

———. 1986. "The Value of the Literary Tradition concerning Archaic Rome." In K. A. Raaflaub (ed.), *Social Struggles in Archaic Rome: New Perspectives on the Conflict of the Orders*, 52–76. Berkeley.

———. 1989. "Rome and Latium to 390 B.C." In *The Cambridge Ancient History*² 7.2: *The Rise of Rome to 220 B.C.*, 243-308. Cambridge.

———. 1995. *The Beginnings of Rome: Italy and Rome from the Bronze Age to the Punic Wars (c. 1000–264 B.C.)*. London.

Crawford, M. 1968. "The Edict of M. Marius Gratidianus." *PCPS* 14:1–4.

Cristes, J. 2002. "*Sed bono vinci satius est (Iug. 42,3)*. Sallust über die Auseinandersetzung der Nobilität mit den Gracchen." *Gymnasium* 109:287–310.

Croisille, J.-M. 1999. "Néron dans la statuaire: le problème des identifications et des faux." In J.-M. Croisille, R. Martin, and Y. Perrin (eds.), *Neronia V. Néron: histoire et légende*, 397–406 Brussels.

Crook, J. A. 1973. "Intestacy in Roman Society." *PCPS* 19:38–44.

———. 1986. "Women in Roman Succession." In B. Rawson (ed.), *The Family in Ancient Rome: New Perspectives*, 58–82. Ithaca, N.Y.

D'Ambra, E. 1993. *Private Lives, Imperial Virtues: The Frieze of the Forum Transitorium in Rome*. Princeton.

D'Arms, J. H. 1970. *Romans on the Bay of Naples: A Social and Cultural Study of the Villas and Their Owners from 150 B.C. to A.D. 400*. Cambridge, Mass.

———. 1974. "Puteoli in the Second Century of the Roman Empire: A Social and Economic Study." *JRS* 64:104–24.

D'Onofrio, C. 1992. *Gli obelischi di Roma: storia e urbanistica di una città dall'età antica al XX secolo³*. Rome.

Dahmen, K. 1998. "Ein Loblied auf den schönen Kaiser. Zur möglichen Deutung der mit Nero Münzen verzierten römischen Dosenspiegel." *AA* 319–45.

Daltrop, G., U. Hausmann, and M. Wegner (eds.). 1966. *Die Flavier. Das römische Herrscherbildnis* 2.1. Berlin.

Daly, L. J., with W. W. J. Reiter. 1979. "The Gallus Affair and Augustus' *lex Iulia maiestatis*. A Study in Historical Chronology and Causality." In C. Deroux (ed.), *Studies in Latin Literature and Roman History* 1:289–311. Brussels.

Damon, C. 1999a. "*Relatio* vs. *Oratio*: Tacitus *Ann.* 3.12 and the *Senatus Consultum de Cn. Pisone Patre*." *CQ* 49:336–38.

———. 1999b. "The Trial of Cn. Piso in Tacitus' *Annals* and the *Senatus Consultum de Cn. Pisone Patre*: New Light on Narrative Technique." *AJP* 120:143–62.

Damon, C., and S. Takács. 1999. "Introduction." *AJP* 120:1–12.

Darwall-Smith, R. H. 1996. *Emperors and Architecture: A Study of Flavian Rome*. Brussels.

Daube, D. 1965. "The Preponderance of Intestacy at Rome." *Tulane Law Review* 39:253–62.

David, J.-M. 1984. "Du Comitium à la Roche Tarpéienne . . . ; sur certains rituels d'exécution capitale sous la République, les règnes d'Auguste et de Tibère." In *Du châtiment dans la cité. Supplices corporels et peine de mort dans le monde antique*, 131–75. Rome.

Davies, J. K. 1971. *Athenian Propertied Families, 600–300 B.C.* Oxford.

Davies, P. J. E. 2000a. "'What worse than Nero, what better than his baths?' '*Damnatio memoriae*' and Roman Architecture." In E. R. Varner (ed.), *From Caligula to Constantine: Tyranny and Transformation in Roman Portraiture*, 27–44. Atlanta.

———. 2000b. *Death and the Emperor: Roman Imperial Funerary Monuments from Augustus to Marcus Aurelius*. Cambridge.

de Caprariis, F. 1993. "Un monumento dinastico tiberiano nel Campo Marzio settentrionale." *BCAR* 95:93–114.

de Cazanove, O. 1989. "Spurius Cassius, Cérès et Tellus." *REL* 67:93–116.

de Franciscis, A. 1991. *Il sacello degli Augustales a Miseno*. Naples.

de Libero, L. 1996. "Die sogennante 'zweite Tyrannis' des Peisistratos." *Hermes* 122:114–16.

de Maria, S. 1988. *Gli archi onorari di Roma e dell'Italia romana*. Rome.

Degrassi, A. 1947. *Inscriptiones Italiae* 13.1. Rome.

———. 1963. *Inscriptiones Italiae* 13.2. Rome.

———. 1965. *Inscriptiones latinae liberae rei publicae. Imagines.* Berlin.

Delia, D. 1991. "Fulvia Reconsidered." In S. B. Pomeroy (ed.), *Women's History and Ancient History*, 197–217. Chapel Hill, N.C.

Desbat, A. 1998. "*Colonia Copia Claudia Augusta Lugdunum*: Lyon à l'époque claudienne." In Y. Burnand, Y. Le Bohec, and J.-P. Martin (eds.), *Claude de Lyon: empereur romain*, 407–31. Paris.

Dessau, H. 1906. "Livius und Augustus." *Hermes* 41:142–51.

Dettenhofer, M. 1992. "Zur politischen Rolle der Aristokratinnen zwischen Republik und Prinzipat." *Latomus* 51:775-95.

———. 2000. *Herrschaft und Widerstand im augusteischen Principat. Die Konkurrenz zwischen respublica und domus Augusta.* Stuttgart.

di Stefano Manzella, I. 1994. "*Accensi velati consulibus apparentes ad sacra*: proposta per la soluzione di un problema di battuto." *ZPE* 101:261–79.

di Vita-Évrard, G. 1990. "*IRT* 520, le proconsulat de Cn. Calpurnius Piso et l'insertion de Lepcis Magna dans la provincia Africa." In *L'Afrique dans l'occident romain* (Ier s. av. J.-C.–IVe s. ap. J.-C.), 315–31. Rome.

Diehl, H. 1988. *Sulla und seine Zeit im Urteil Ciceros.* Hildesheim.

Dixon, S. 1985. "Polybius on Roman Women and Property." *AJP* 106:147–70.

———. 1992. *The Roman Family.* Baltimore.

Dorcey, P. F. 1992. *The Cult of Silvanus: A Study in Roman Folk Religion.* Leiden.

Dow, S. 1937. *Prytaneis: A Study of the Inscriptions Honoring the Athenian Councilors. Hesperia* Suppl. 1. Princeton.

Drummond, A. 1989. "Rome in the Fifth Century II: The Citizen Community." In *The Cambridge Ancient History*[2] 7.2: *The Rise of Rome to 220 B.C.*, 172-242. Cambridge.

———. 1995. *Law, Politics and Power: Sallust and the Execution of the Catilinarian Conspirators.* Stuttgart.

Ducos, M. 1990. "La condition des acteurs à Rome: données juridiques et sociales." In J. Blänsdorf (ed.), *Theater und Gesellschaft im Imperium Romanum*, 19–33. Tübingen.

Dunant, C., and J. Pouilloux. 1958. *Recherches sur l'histoire et les cultes de Thasos. De 196 av. J.-C. jusqu'à la fin de l'Antiquité.* Paris.

Durry, M. 1938. *Les cohortes prétoriennes.* Paris.

Eck, W. 1976. "Neros Freigelassener Epaphroditus und die Aufdeckung der Pisonischen Verschwörung." *Historia* 25:381–84.

———. 1980. "Epigraphische Untersuchungen zu Konsulen und Senatoren des 1.–3. Jhdts. n. Chr." *ZPE* 37:31–68.

———. 1984a. "*CIL* VI 1508 (Moretti *IGUR* 71) und die Gestaltung senatorischer Ehrenmonumente." *Chiron* 14:201–17.

———. 1984b. "Senatorial Self-Representation: Developments in the Augustan Period." In F. Millar and E. Segal (eds.), *Caesar Augustus, Seven Aspects*, 129–67. Oxford.

———. 1990. "Cn. Calpurnius Piso, cos. ord. 7 v. Chr. und die *lex portorii provinciae Asiae*." *EA* 15:139–45.

———. 1993a. "Das s. c. de Cn. Pisone patre und seine Publikation in der Baetica."
Cahiers Glotz 4:189–208.

———. 1993b. *Agrippina, die Stadtgründerin Kölns. Eine Frau in der*
frühkaiserzeitlichen Politik. Cologne.

———. 1995. "Plebs und Princeps nach dem Tod des Germanicus." In I. Malkin and
Z. W. Rubinsohn (eds.), *Leaders and Masses in the Roman World: Studies in Honor*
of Zvi Yavetz, 1–10. Leiden.

———. 1996a. "Mord im Kaiserhaus? Ein politischer Prozeß im Rom des Jahres 20 n.
Chr." *Jahrbuch des Historischen Kollegs, München*: 99–132.

———. 1996b. *Tra epigrafia, prosopografia e archeologia.* Rome.

———. 1997a. "Die Täuschung der Öffentlichkeit. Der Prozeß gegen Cnaeus
Calpurnius Piso im Jahre 20 n. Chr." In U. Manthe and J. von Ungern-Sternberg
(eds.), *Große Prozesse der römischen Antike*, 128–45. Munich.

———. 1997b. "Rome and the Outside World: Senatorial Families and the World They
Lived In." In B. Rawson and P. Weaver (eds.), *The Roman Family in Italy: Status,*
Sentiment, Space, 73–99. Oxford.

———. 2000. "Die Täuschung der Öffentlichkeit — oder: die 'Unparteilichkeit' des
Historikers Tacitus." *AA* 46:190–206.

———. 2001. "Die große Pliniusinschrift aus Comum: Funktion und Monument."
In A. Bertinelli and A. Donati (eds.), *Varia Epigraphica. Atti del Colloquio*
Internazionale di Epigrafia, 225–35. Faenza.

———. 2002a. "Traian — der Weg zum Kaisertum." In A. Nünnerich-Asmus (ed.),
Traian. Ein Kaiser der Superlative am Beginn einer Umbruchzeit?, 7–20, 174. Mainz.

———. 2002b. "An Emperor Is Made: Senatorial Politics and Trajan's Adoption by
Nerva in 97." In G. Clark and T. Rajak (eds.), *Philosophy and Power in the Graeco-*
Roman World: Essays in Honour of Miriam Griffin, 211–26. Oxford.

Eck, W., A. Caballos, and F. Fernández. 1996. *Das senatus consultum de Cn. Pisone*
patre. Munich.

———. 1997. "*Il senatus consultum de Cn. Pisone patre.*" In J. Arce, S. Ensoli, and
E. La Rocca (eds.), *Hispania Romana: da terra di conquista a provincia dell'impero*,
215–21. Milan.

Eck, W., and H. Wolff. 1986. *Heer und Integrationspolitik: die römischen*
Militärdiplome als historische Quelle. Cologne.

Edwards, C. 1993. *The Politics of Immorality in Ancient Rome.* Cambridge.

———. 1994. "Beware of Imitations: Theatre and Subversion of Imperial Identity."
In J. Elsner and J. Masters (eds.), *Reflections of Nero: Culture, History, and*
Representation, 83–97. London.

———. 1997. "Unspeakable Professions: Public Performance and Prostitution in
Ancient Rome." In J. P. Hallett and M. B. Skinner (ed.), *Roman Sexualities*, 66–95.
Princeton.

Ehrhardt, C. 1978. "Messalina and the Succession to Claudius." *Antichthon* 12:51–77.

Eigler, U., U. Gotter, N. Luraghi, and U. Walter. 2003. *Formen römischer*
Geschichtsschreibung von den Anfängen bis Livius: Gattungen--Autoren--Kontexte.
Darmstadt.

Elsner, J. 1994. "Constructing Decadence: The Representation of Nero as Imperial

Builder." In J. Elsner and J. Masters (eds.), *Reflections of Nero: Culture, History, and Representation*, 112–27. London.

Engelmann, H., and D. Knibbe. 1989. "Das Zollgesetz der Provinz Asia. Eine neue Inschrift aus Ephesos." *EA* 14.

Erdkamp, P. 2000. "Feeding Rome or Feeding Mars? A Long-Term Approach to C. Gracchus' *lex frumentaria*." *AncSoc* 30:53–70.

Ermann, J. 2002. "Das *senatus consultum de Cn. Pisone patre* und die Funktion des *consilium* im römischen Strafprozeß." *ZRG* 119:380–88.

Errington, R. M. 1989. "Rome against Philip and Antiochus." In *The Cambridge Ancient History* 8²: *Rome and the Mediterranean to 133 B.C.*, 244–89. Cambridge.

Evans, R. J. 1994. *Gaius Marius: A Political Biography*. Pretoria.

Fabbrini, F. 2001. "La ricerca di opere d'arte nel 3 e 2 secolo a. C. come momento per uno definizione di 'classicità.'" In F. Fabbrini (ed.), *Maecenas. Il collezionismo nel mondo romano dall'età degli Scipioni a Cicerone*, 13–46. Arezzo.

Fagan, G. 2002. "Messalina's Folly." *CQ* 52:566–79.

Fantham, E. 1996. *Roman Literary Culture: From Cicero to Apuleius*. Baltimore.

Favro, D. G. 1996. *The Urban Image of Augustan Rome*. Cambridge.

Fedeli, P. 1989. "Il 'Panegirico' di Plinio nella critica moderna." *ANRW* 33.1:387–514. Berlin and New York.

Fell, M. 1992. Optimus Princeps? *Anspruch und Wirklichkeit der imperialen Programmatik Kaiser Traians*. Munich.

Fellmann, R. 1957. *Das Grab des Lucius Munatius Plancus bei Gaëta*. Basel.

Ferguson, W. S. 1911. *Hellenistic Athens: An Historical Essay*. London.

Ferrary, J.-L. 1988. *Philhellénisme et impérialisme: aspects idéologiques de la conquête romaine du monde hellénistique, de la seconde guerre de Macédoine à la guerre contre Mithridate*. Rome.

Ferri, R. 2003. *Octavia: A Play Attributed to Seneca*. Cambridge.

Ferrill, A. 1991. *Caligula: Emperor of Rome*. London.

Ferrua, A. "Iscrizioni pagani nelle catacombe di Roma. Via Nomentana." *Epigraphica* 24:106–39.

Fink, J. 1970. *Der Mars-Camulus Stein in der Pfarrkirche zu Rindern. Römisches Denkmal und christlicher Altar*. Kevelaer.

Fischer, R. A. 1999. *Fulvia und Octavia. Die beiden Frauen des Marcus Antonius in den politischen Kämpfen der Umbruchszeit zwischen Republik und Principat*. Berlin.

Fishwick, D. 1987/1995. "The Caesareum at Alexandria Again." *AJAH* 12:62–72.

Flaig, E. 1992. *Den Kaiser herausfordern. Die Usurpation im römischen Reich*. Frankfurt.

———. 1993. "Loyalität ist keine Gefälligkeit. Zum Majestätsprozeß gegen C. Silius 24 n. Chr." *Klio* 75:289–305.

———. 1995. "Die Pompa Funebris. Adlige Konkurrenz und annalistische Erinnerung in der Römischen Republik." In O. G. Oexle (ed.), *Memoria als Kultur*, 115–48. Göttingen.

———. 2000. "Kulturgeschichte ohne historische Anthropologie." *IJCT* 7.2:226–44.

———. 2003. *Ritualisierte Politik. Zeichen, Gesten und Herrschaft im Alten Rom*. Göttingen.

Flambard, J.-M. 1981. "Collegia compitalicia: phénomène associatif, cadres territoriaux et cadres civiques dans le monde romain à l'époque républicaine." *Ktema* 6:143–66.

Flory, M. B. 1984. "*Sic exempla parantur*: Livia's Shrine to Concordia and the Porticus Liviae." *Historia* 33:309–30.

———. 1993. "Livia and the History of Public Honorific Statues for Women in Rome." *TAPA* 123:287–308.

———. 1996. "Dynastic Ideology, the *domus Augusta*, and Imperial Women: A Lost Statuary Group in the Circus Flaminius." *TAPA* 126:287–306.

———. 1998. "The Meaning of Augusta in the Julio-Claudian Period." *AJAH* 13.2:113–38.

Flower, H. I. 1996. *Ancestor Masks and Aristocratic Power in Roman Culture*. Oxford.

———. 1997. Review of W. Eck, A. Caballos, and F. Fernández, *Das senatus consultum de Cn. Pisone patre* (1996). *BMCR* 8.8:705–12.

———. 1998. "Rethinking '*Damnatio memoriae*': The Case of Cn. Calpurnius Piso pater in AD 20." *CA* 17:155–86.

———. 1999. "Piso in Chicago: Commentary on the *APA* Seminar on the *S. C. de Cn. Pisone patre*." *AJP* 120:99–115.

———. 2000. "The Tradition of the *Spolia Opima*: Marcus Claudius Marcellus and Augustus." *CA* 19.1:34–64.

———. 2001a. "A Tale of Two Monuments: Domitian, Trajan, and Some Praetorians at Puteoli (*AE* 1973, 137)." *AJA* 105.4:625–48.

———. 2001b. "Damnatio Memoriae and Epigraphy." In E. R. Varner (ed.), *From Caligula to Constantine: Tyranny and Transformation in Roman Portraiture*, 58–69. Atlanta.

———. 2002a. "Roman Historical Drama and Nero on Stage. A Commentary on P. Kragelund, 'Historical Drama in Ancient Rome: Republican Flourishing and Imperial Decline.'" *SO* 77:68–72.

———. 2002b. "Were Women Ever 'Ancestors' in Republican Rome?" In J. Munk Højte (ed.), *Images of Ancestors*, 157–82. Aarhus Studies in Mediterranean Antiquity 5. Aarhus, Denmark.

———. 2003. "Memories of Marcellus: History and Memory in Roman Republican Culture." In U. Eigler, U. Gotter, N. Luraghi, and U. Walter (eds.), *Formen römischer Geschichtsschreibung von den Anfängen bis Livius: Gattungen — Autoren — Kontexte*, 39–52. Darmstadt.

———. 2006. "Die Ahnen kommen wieder: der Leichenzug." In K.-J. Hölkeskamp and E. Stein-Hölkeskamp (eds.), *Genius Loci: Erinnerungsorte der Antike, Band II Rom*. Munich.

Flower, M. A. 1997. *Theopompus of Chios: History and Rhetoric in the Fourth Century B.C.* Paperback edition with postscript. Oxford.

Fora, M. 1991. "Testimonianze epigrafiche sugli anfiteatri del Latium Adiectum: i casi di Vellitrae, Circeii e Casinum." *MGR* 16:191–215.

———. 1992. "Ummidia Quadratilla ed il restauro del teatro di Cassino (per una nuova lettura di *AE* 1946.174.)." *ZPE* 94:269–73.

Forsdyke, S. 2000. "Exile, Ostracism and the Athenian Democracy." *CA* 19.2:232–63.

Forsythe, G. 2000. "Roman Historians of the Second Century B.C." In C. Bruun (ed.), *The Roman Middle Republic: Politics, Religion, and Historiography, c. 400–133 B.C.*, 1–11. Rome.

Fraschetti, A. 1984. "La sepoltura delle vestali e la città." In *Du châtiment dans la cité*, 97–128. Rome.

———. 1994. *Rome et le prince*. Paris.

Fraser, P. M. 1957. "Mark Antony in Alexandria—a Note." *JRS* 47:71–73.

———. 1972. *Ptolemaic Alexandria* 1. Oxford.

Frederick, D. 2003. "Architecture and Surveillance in Flavian Rome." In A. J. Boyle and W. J. Dominik (eds.), *Flavian Rome: Culture, Image, Text*, 199–227. Leiden.

Fredericksen, M. 1984. *Campania*. London.

Freidel, H. 1937. *Der Tyrannenmord in Gesetzgebung und Volksmeinung der Griechen*. Würzburg.

Frei-Stolba, R. 1998. "Recherches sur la position juridique et sociale de Livie, l'epouse d'Auguste." *Études de letters* 1:65–89.

French, D. H. 1981. "Milestones of Pontus, Galatia, Phrygia and Lycia." *ZPE* 43:149–74.

Frier, B. W. 1971. "Sulla's Propaganda: The Collapse of the Cinnan Republic." *AJP* 92:585–604.

Furley, W. D. 1996. *Andokides and the Herms: A Study of Crisis in Fifth Century Athenian Religion*. BICS Suppl. 65. London.

Gabba, E. 1964. "Studi su Dionigi d'Alicarnasso." *Athenaeum* 42:29–41.

———. 1966. "Dionigi D'Alicarnasso sul processo di Spurio Cassio." In *La storia del diritto nel quadro delle scienze storiche*, 143–53. Florence.

Gagarin, M. 1981a. *Drakon and Early Athenian Homicide Law*. New Haven.

———. 1981b. "The Thesmothetai and the Earliest Athenian Tyranny Law." *TAPA* 111:71–77.

———. 1986. *Early Greek Law*. Berkeley.

Gagé, J. 1976. *La chute des Tarquins et les débuts de la république romaine*. Paris.

Galinsky, K. 1996. *Augustan Culture: An Interpretive Introduction*. Princeton.

Gallivan, P. A. 1973. "The False Neros: A Re-examination." *Historia* 22:364–65.

Galsterer, H. 1975. *Die römischen Steininschriften aus Köln*. Cologne.

Gardner, J. F. 1987. *Women in Roman Law and Society*. London.

Gargola, D. 1995. *Lands, Laws, and Gods: Magistrates and Ceremony in the Regulation of Public Lands in Republican Rome*. Chapel Hill, N.C.

Garnsey, P. 1988. *Famine and Food Supply in the Graeco-Roman World: Responses to Risk and Crisis*. Cambridge.

Garthwaite, J. 1993. "The Panegyricus of Domitian in Martial Book 9." *Ramus* 22:78–102.

Garzetti, A. 1950. *Nerva*. Rome.

———. 1974. *From Tiberius to the Antonines: A History of the Roman Empire, A.D. 14–192*. London.

Gayraud, M. 1980. "Les inscriptions de Ruscino." In G. Barruol (ed.), *Ruscino* 1:67–98. Paris.

Gazda, E. K., and A. E. Haeckl. 1996. *Images of Empire: Flavian Fragments in Rome and Ann Arbor Rejoined*. Ann Arbor, Mich., and Rome.

Gehrke, J. 1985. *Stasis. Untersuchungen zu den inneren Kriegen in den griechischen Staaten des 5. und 4. Jhdt. v. Chr.* Munich.

Gelzer, M. 1912/1975. *The Roman Nobility.* Oxford.

———. 1968. *Caesar: Politician and Statesman.* Cambridge, Mass.

Gialanella, C. 1993. "La topografia di Puteoli." In F. Zevi (ed.), *Puteoli*, 73–98. Naples.

Giannelli, G. 1980/1981. "Il tempio di Giunone Moneta e la casa di Marco Manlio Capitolino." *BCAR* 87:7–36.

Ginestet, P. 1991. *Les organisations de la jeunesse dans l'Occident romain.* Brussels.

Giovannini, A. 1983. *Consulare imperium.* Basel.

———. 1987. "Pline et les délateurs de Domitien." In *Opposition et résistances à l'empire d'Auguste à Trajan*, 219–48. Geneva.

———. 1995. "Catilina et le problème des dettes." In I. Malkin and Z. W. Rubinsohn (eds.), *Leaders and Masses in the Roman World: Studies in Honor of Zvi Yavetz*, 15–32. Leiden.

Goldmann, F. 2002. "*Nobilitas* als Status und Gruppe — Überlegungen zum Nobilitätsbegriff der römischen Republik." In J. Spielvogel (ed.), *Res publica reperta. Zur Verfassung und Gesellschaft der römischen Republik und des frühen Prinzipats (Festschrift Jochen Bleicken)*, 45–66. Stuttgart.

Gomme A. W., A. Andrewes, and K. J. Dover. 1970. *A Historical Commentary on Thucydides IV.* Oxford.

González, J. 1984. "*Tabula Siarensis, Fortunales Siarenses et Municipia Ciuium Romanorum.*" *ZPE* 55:55–100.

——— (ed.). 1993. *Imp. Caes. Nerva Traianus Aug.* Seville.

Goodman, M. 1989. "Nerva, the Fiscus Judaicus and Jewish Identity." *JRS* 79:40–44.

Gordon, A. E. 1958. *Album of Dated Latin Inscriptions.* Berkeley.

———. 1983. *Illustrated Introduction to Latin Epigraphy.* Berkeley.

Gordon, G., J. Reynolds, M. Beard, and C. Roueché. 1997. "Roman Inscriptions 1991–5." *JRS* 87:203–40.

Gotter, U. 1996. *Der Diktator ist Tot! Politik in Rom zwischen den Iden des März und der Begründung des Zweiten Triumvirats.* Stuttgart.

———. 2000. "Marcus Iunius Brutus — oder: die Nemesis des Namens." In K.-J. Hölkeskamp and E. Stein-Hölkeskamp (eds.), *Von Romulus zu Augustus. Große Gestalten der römischen Republik*, 328–39. Munich.

Gourevitch, D., and M.-T. Raepsaet-Charlier. 2001. *La femme dans la Rome antique.* Paris.

Gradel, I. 2002. *Emperor Worship and Roman Religion.* Oxford.

Grainger, J. D. 2003. *Nerva and the Roman Succession Crisis of A.D. 96–99.* London.

Granino Cecere, M. G., and A. Magioncalda. 2003. "L'ara di C. Vibullius Fidus e i procuratori della Syria." *MEFRA* 115:615–38.

Green, P. 1982. "*Carmen et error: prophasis* and *aitia* in the Matter of Ovid's Exile." *CA* 1:202–20.

———. 1990. *Alexander to Actium: The Historical Evolution of the Hellenistic Age.* Berkeley.

Greenhalgh, P. A. L. 1975. *The Year of the Four Emperors.* London.

Greenidge, A. H. J., and A. M. Clay. 1960. *Sources for Roman History, 133–70 B.C.*² Oxford.

Gregori, G. L., and M. Mattei. 1999. *I Musei Capitolini*. Rome.

Gregory, A. P. 1994. "'Powerful Images': Responses to Portraits and the Political Use of Images in Rome." *JRA* 7:80–99.

Grenier, J.-C. 1987. "Les inscriptions hiéroglyphiques de l'obélisque Pamphili: un témoinage méconnu sur l'avènement de Domitien." *MEFRA* 99.2:939–61.

Griffin, M. T. 1984. *Nero: The End of a Dynasty*. New Haven.

———. 1997. "The Senate's Story." *JRS* 87:249–63.

———. 1999. "Pliny and Tacitus." *SCI* 18:139–58.

———. 2000a. "The Flavians." In *The Cambridge Ancient History* 11²: *The High Empire, A.D. 70–192*, 1–83. Cambridge.

———. 2000b. "Nerva to Hadrian." In *The Cambridge Ancient History* 11²: *The High Empire, A.D. 70–192*, 84–131. Cambridge.

Gros, P. 1976. *Aurea templa: recherches sur l'architecture religieuse de Rome à l'époque d'Auguste*. Rome.

———. 1979. "Les statues de Syracuse et les 'dieux' de Tarente." *REL* 57:85–114.

Gruen, E. S. 1968. *Roman Politics and the Criminal Courts, 149–78 BC*. Cambridge, Mass.

———. 1974. *The Last Generation of the Roman Republic*. Berkeley.

———. 1984. *The Hellenistic World and the Coming of Rome*. Vols. 1 and 2. Berkeley.

———. 1990. *Studies in Greek Culture and Roman Policy*. Leiden.

———. 1992. *Culture and National Identity in Republican Rome*. London.

———. 1995. "The 'Fall' of the Scipios." In I. Malkin and Z. W. Rubinsohn (eds.), *Leaders and Masses in the Roman World: Studies in Honor of Zvi Yavetz*, 59–90. Leiden.

Guadagno, G. 1978. "Supplemento epigrafico ercolanese." *Cronache ercolanesi* 8:132–55.

Guarducci, M. 1967. *Epigrafia Greca* 1. Rome.

Gunderson, E. 2003. "The Flavian Amphitheatre: All the World as Stage." In A. J. Boyle and W. J. Dominik (eds.), *Flavian Rome: Culture, Image, Text*, 637–58. Leiden.

Gurval, R. 1995. *Actium and Augustus: The Politics and Emotions of Civil War*. Ann Arbor, Mich.

Gutberlet, D. 1985. *Die erste Dekade des Livius als Quelle zur gracchischen und sullanischen Zeit*. Hildesheim.

Habicht, C. 1970. *Gottmenschentum und griechische Städte*². Munich.

———. 1976. "Zur Geschichte Athens in der Zeit Mithridates VI." *Chiron* 6:127–42.

———. 1982. *Studien zur Geschichte Athens in hellenistischer Zeit*. Göttingen.

———. 1990. "Athens and the Attalids in the Second Century B.C." *Hesperia* 59:561–77.

———. 1995. *Athen. Die Geschichte der Stadt in hellenistischer Zeit*. Munich.

———. 1996. "Julia Kalliteknos." *MH* 53:156–59.

———. 1997. *Athens from Alexander to Antony*. Cambridge, Mass.

———. 1998. "Titus Flavius Metrobius: Peridonike aus Iasos." In P. Kneissel and V. Losemann (eds.), *Imperium Romanum. Studien zu Geschichte und Rezeption. Festschrift K. Christ*, 311–16. Stuttgart.

Habinek, T. N. 1998. *The Politics of Latin Literature: Writing, Identity, and Empire in Ancient Rome*. Princeton.

Hahn, U. 1994. *Die Frauen des Römischen Kaiserhauses und ihre Ehrungen im griechischen Osten anhand epigraphischer und numismatischer Zeugnisse von Livia bis Sabina*. Saarbrücken.

Hammond, N. G. L., and F. Walbank, 1988. *A History of Macedonia* 3. Oxford.

Hänlein-Schäfer, H. 1985. *Veneratio Augusti: eine Studie zu den Tempeln des ersten römischen Kaisers*. Rome.

Hansen, M. H. 1976. *Apagoge, endeixis and ephegesis against kakourgoi, atimoi and pheugontes: A Study in the Athenian Administration of Justice in the Fourth Century* B.C. Odense.

———. 1991. *The Athenian Democracy in the Age of Demosthenes: Structure, Principles, and Ideology*. Oxford.

Hantos, T. 1988. *Res publica constituta. Die Verfassung des Diktators Sulla*. Stuttgart.

Harding, P. 1985. *From the End of the Peloponnesian War to the Battle of Issus*. Cambridge.

Harris, W. V. 1986. "The Roman Father's Power of Life and Death." In R. S. Bagnall and W. V. Harris (eds.), *Studies in Roman Law in Memory of A. Arthur Schiller*, 81–95. Leiden.

Häuber, C. 1991. "Horti Romani. Die Horti Maecenatis und die Horti Lamiani auf dem Esquilin. Geschichte, Topographie, Statuenfunde." Diss. Munich.

Hedrick, C. 1999. "Democracy and the Athenian Epigraphic Habit." *Hesperia* 68:387–439.

———. 2000. *History and Silence: Purge and Rehabilitation of Memory in Late Antiquity*. Austin, Texas.

Heider, U. 2000. "Lucius Sergius Catilina — ein Verbrecher aus verlohrener Ehre?" In K.-J. Hölkeskamp and E. Stein-Hölkeskamp (eds.), *Von Romulus zu Augustus. Große Gestalten der römischen Republik*, 268–78. Munich.

Hellegouarc'h, J. 1963. *Le vocabulaire latin des relations et des parties politiques sous la République*. Paris.

Hemsoll, D. 1990. "The Architecture of Nero's Golden House." In M. Henig (ed.), *Architecture and Architectural Sculpture in the Roman Empire*, 10–38. Oxford.

Henderson, J. 2002. *Pliny's Statue: The Letters, Self-Portraiture and Classical Art*. Exeter.

Hennig, D. 1975. *L. Aelius Seianus. Untersuchungen zur Regierung des Tiberius*. Munich.

Herrmann, P. 1960. "Die Inschriften römischer Zeit aus dem Heraion von Samos." *MDAI(A)* 75:68–183.

———. 1965. "Antiochos der Grosse und Teos." *Anatolia* 9:22–160.

———. 1989. "Rom und die Asylie griechischer Heiligtümer: eine Urkunde des Diktators Caesar aus Sardeis." *Chiron* 19:127–58.

———. 1995. "Sardeis zur Zeit der iulisch-claudischen Kaiser." In E. Schwertheim (ed.), *Forschungen in Lydien*, 21–36. Bonn.

Hershkowitz, D. 1995. "Pliny the Poet." *G & R* 42:168–81.

Herz, P. 1978. "Kaiserfeste der Prinzipatszeit." *ANRW* 2.16.2:1135–1200. Berlin and New York.

Hesberg, H. von, and S. Panciera. 1994. *Das Mausoleum des Augustus: der Bau und seine Inschriften*. Munich.

Hicks, E. L. 1886–90. *Priene, Iasos and Ephesos* 3. In C. T. Newton (ed.), *The Collection of Ancient Greek Inscriptions in the British Museum*. Oxford.

Hiesinger, U. 1975. "The Portraits of Nero." *AJA* 79:113–24.

Hinard, F. 1984. "La male mort. Exécutions et statut du corps au moment de la première proscription." In *Actes du colloque "Du Châtiment dans la cite,"* 295–311. Rome.

———. 1985. *Les proscriptions de la Rome républicaine*. Paris.

———. 1987. "Sur une autre forme de l'opposition entre *virtus* et *fortuna*." *Kentron* 3:17–20.

———. 2003. "Entre république et principat. Pouvoir et urbanité." In *Laurea internationalis. Festschrift für Jochen Bleicken*, 331–58. Wiesbaden.

Hoffer, S. E. 1999. *The Anxieties of Pliny the Younger*. Atlanta.

Hofmann-Löbl, I. 1996. *Die Calpurnii. Politisches Wirken und familiäre Kontinuität*. Frankfurt.

Hofter, M., et al. 1988. *Kaiser Augustus und die verlohrene Republik*. Mainz.

Hölkeskamp, K.-J. 1987. *Die Entstehung der Nobilität. Studien zur sozialen und politischen Geschichte der Römischen Republik im 4. Jhdt. v. Chr*. Stuttgart.

———. 1993. "Conquest, Competition and Consensus: Roman Expansion in Italy and the Rise of the *Nobilitas*." *Historia* 42:12-39.

———. 1996. "*Exempla* und *mos maiorum*: Überlegungen zum kollektiven Gedächtnis der Nobilität." In H.-J. Gehrke and A. Möller (eds.), *Vergangenheit und Lebenswelt. Soziale Kommunikation, Traditionsbildung und historisches Bewußtsein*, 301-338. Tübingen.

———. 2000. "Lucius Cornelius Sulla — Revolutionär und restaurativer Reformer." In K.-J. Hölkeskamp and E. Stein-Hölkeskamp (eds.), *Von Romulus zu Augustus. Große Gestalten der römischen Republik*, 199–218. Munich.

———. 2001. "Capitol, Comitium und Forum. Öffentliche Räume, sakrale Topographie und Erinnerungslandschaften der römischen Republik." In S. Faller (ed.), *Studien zu antiken Identitäten*, 97–132. Würzburg.

———. 2004. *Rekonstruktionen einer Republik. Die politische Kultur des antiken Rom und die Forschung der letzten Jahrzehnte*. Munich.

Holliday, P. J. 2002. *The Origins of Roman Historical Commemoration in the Visual Arts*. Cambridge.

Hölscher, T. 1978. "Die Anfänge römischer Repräsentationskunst." *MDAI(R)* 85:315-57.

———. 1980. "Römische Siegesdenkmähler der späten Republik." In H. A. Cahn and E. Simon (eds.), *Tainia, R. Hampe zum 70. Geburtstag*, 351–71. Mainz.

———. 1985. "Denkmäler der Schlacht von Actium: Propaganda und Resonanz." *Klio* 67:81–102.

———. 1990. "Römische Nobiles und Hellenistische Herrscher." In *Akten des XIII. Internationalen Kongresses für Klassische Archäologie Berlin 1988*, 73–84. Mainz.

———. 2001. "Die Alten vor Augen. Politische Denkmäler und öffentliches Gedächtnis im republikanischen Rom." In G. Melville (ed.), *Institutionalität und*

Symbolisierung. Verstetigung kultureller Ordnungsmuster in Vergangenheit und Gegenwart, 183–211. Cologne.

Hornblower, S. 1991. *A Commentary on Thucydides*. Oxford.

Horsfall, N. M. 1981. "From History to Legend. M. Manlius and the Geese." *CJ* 76:298–311.

———. 2003. *The Culture of the Roman Plebs*. London.

Humm, M. 2005. *Appius Claudius Caecus. La République accomplie*. Rome.

Hurlet, F. 1993a. "La lex de imperio Vespasiani et la légitimité augustéenne." *Latomus* 52:261–80.

———. 1993b. *La dictature de Sylla. Monarchie ou magistrature républicaine*. Rome.

———. 1997. *Les collègues du prince sous Auguste et Tibere: de la légalité républicaine à la légitimité dynastique*. Rome.

Hurley, D. W. 1993. *An Historical and Historiographical Commentary on Suetonius' Life of Caligula*. Atlanta.

———. 2001. *Suetonius, Divus Claudius*. Cambridge.

Hüttl, W. 1936/1975. *Antoninus Pius* 1. Prague and New York.

Isaac, B. M. 1971. *"Colonia Munatia Triumphalis* and *legio nona triumphalis?" Talanta* 3:11–43.

Jaczynowska, M. 1978. *Les associations de la jeunesse romaine sous le Haut-Empire.* Warsaw.

Jaeger, M. K. 1993. *"Custodia fidelis memoriae*: Livy's Story of M. Manlius Capitolinus." *Latomus* 52:350–63.

———. 1997. *Livy's Written Rome*. Ann Arbor, Mich.

Jeffrey, L. H. 1990. *The Local Scripts of Archaic Greece²*. Revised with a supplement by A. W. Johnston. Oxford.

Jehne, M. 1987. *Der Staat des Dictators Caesar*. Cologne.

———. 1994. *Koine Eirene. Untersuchungen zu den Befriedungs- und Stabilisierungsbemühungen in der griechischen Poliswelt des 4. Jhdts. v. Chr.* Stuttgart.

———. 2001. *Caesar*. Munich.

Jeppesen, K. K. 1993. "Grand Camée de France. Sejanus Reconsidered and Confirmed." *MDAI(R)* 100:141–75.

Jervis, A. E. 2001. "Talking Heads: The Iconography of Mutilation in the Roman Republic." Ph.D. diss., Stanford.

Jones, B. W. 1973. "Domitian's Attitude to the Senate." *AJP* 94:79–91.

———. 1983. "Vettulenus Civica Cerialis and the 'False Nero' of A.D. 88." *Athenaeum* 61:516–21.

———. 1992. *The Emperor Domitian*. London.

Jones, C. P. 1968. "A New Commentary on the Letters of Pliny." *Phoenix* 22:111–42.

———. 1977/1978. "Some New Inscriptions from Bubon." *MDAI(I)* 27–28:288–96.

———. 2000. "Nero Speaking." *HSCP* 100:453–62.

Joshel, S. R. 1997. "Female Desire and the Discourse of Empire: Tacitus' Messalina." In J. P. Hallett and M. B. Skinner (eds.), *Roman Sexualities*, 221–54. Princeton.

Jucker, H. 1975. "Die Glasphalerae mit dem Porträt des Nero Iulius Caesar." *SchwMbll* 25:50–60.

———. 1981. "Julische-claudische Kaiser-und Prinzenporträts als 'Palimpseste.'" *JdI* 96:236–316.

———. 1982. "Die Bildnisstrafen gegen den toten Caligula." In B. von Freytag gen. Löringhoff, D. Mannsperger, and F. Prayon (eds.), *Praestant Interna. Festschrift für Ulrich Hausman*, 110–18. Tübingen.

Kähler, H. 1965. *Der Fries vom Reiterdenkmal des Aemilius Paullus in Delphi*. Berlin.

Kajanto, I., U. Nyberg, and E. M. Steinby. 1982. *L'area sacra di Largo Argentina: le iscrizioni*. Rome.

Kajava, M. 1994. *Roman Female Praenomina: Studies in the Nomenclature of Roman Women*. Rome.

———. 1995. "Some Remarks on the Erasure of Inscriptions in the Roman World (with Special Reference to the Case of Cn. Piso, cos. 7 BC)." In H. Solin, O. Salomies, and U.-M. Liertz (eds.), *Acta Colloquii Epigraphici Latini*, 201–10. Helsinki.

Kallala, N. 1997. "Nouveaux témoinages épigraphiques sur la vie religieuse à Thugga à l'époque romaine." In M. Khanoussi and L. Maurin (eds.), *Dougga (Thugga). Études épigraphiques*, 141–74. Paris.

Kallett-Marx, R. M. 1995. *Hegemony to Empire: The Development of the Roman Imperium in the East from 148 to 62 B.C.* Berkeley.

Kaplan, M. 1979. "*Agrippina semper atrox*: A Study in Tacitus' Characterization of Women." In C. Deroux (ed.), *Studies in Latin Literature and Roman History*, 410–17. Brussels.

Kavanagh, B. J. 1990. "The Admission of the Claudian Family to Rome." *AHB* 4.6:129–32.

Keil, J. 1930. "Vorläufiger Bericht über die Ausgrabungen in Ephesos." *Jahrheft des österreichischen archäologischen Instituts in Wien* 26: Beiblatt, 50–57.

Keppie, L. 1991. *Understanding Roman Inscriptions*. London.

Khanoussi, M. 1997. "Thugga. Épigraphie et constructions publiques." In M. Khanoussi and L. Maurin (eds.), *Dougga (Thugga). Études épigraphiques*, 117–25. Paris.

Khanoussi, M., and L. Maurin (eds.). 2000. *Dougga. Fragments d'histoire. Choix d'inscriptions latines*. Bordeaux and Tunis.

Kienast, D. 1996. *Römische Kaisertabelle. Grundzüge einer römischen Kaiserchronologie²*. Darmstadt.

Kierdorf, W. 1969. "Die Einleitung des Piso-Prozesses, Tac. *Ann.* 3.10." *Hermes* 97:246–51.

———. 1980. *Laudatio funebris: Interpretationen und Untersuchungen zur Entwicklung der römischen Leichenrede*. Meisenheim am Glan.

Kirchner, J. 1948. *Imagines inscriptionum atticarum. Ein Bildatlas epigraphischer Denkmähler Attikas²*. Berlin.

Kleiner, D. E. E. 1992. *Roman Sculpture*. New Haven.

Kleiner, F. S. 1985. *The Arch of Nero in Rome: A Study of the Roman Honorary Arch before and under Nero*. Rome.

———. 1990. "An Extraordinary Posthumous Honor for Livia." *Athenaeum* 78:508–14.

Knibbe, D., H. Engelmann, and B. Iplikçioglu. 1989. "Neue Inschriften aus Ephesos XI." *Jahresheft des österreichischen archäeologischen Instituts, Wien* 59:163–238.

Knox, P. 2001. "Il poeta e il 'secondo' principe: Ovidio e la politice all'epoca di Tiberio." *Maecenas* 1:151–81.

Koestermann, E. 1955. "Die Majestätsprozesse unter Tiberius." *Historia* 4:72–106.

———. 1958. "Die Mission des Germanicus im Orient." *Historia* 7:331–75.

Kokkinos, N. 1992. *Antonia Augusta: Portrait of a Great Roman Lady.* London.

Kolb, F. 1977. "Die Bau-, Religions- und Kulturpolitik der Peisistratiden." *JDAI* 92:99–138.

———. 1995. *Rom: die Geschichte der Stadt in der Antike.* Munich.

Konstan, D. 1993. "Rhetoric and the Crisis of Legitimacy in Cicero's Catilinarian Orations." In T. Poulakos (ed.), *Rethinking the History of Rhetoric*, 11–30. Boulder.

Kragelund, P. 1982. *Prophecy, Populism and Propaganda in the Octavia.* Copenhagen.

———. 1987. "Vatinius, Nero and Curiatius Maternus." *CQ* 37:197–202.

———. 1988. "The Prefect's Dilemma and the Date of the Octavia." *CQ* 38:492–508.

———. 1998. "Galba's *pietas*, Nero's Victims and the Mausoleum of Augustus." *Historia* 47:152–73.

———. 2000. "Nero's *luxuria* in Tacitus and in the *Octavia*." *CQ* 50:494–515.

———. 2002. "Historical Drama in Ancient Rome: Republican Flourishing and Imperial Decline?" *SO* 77:5–51.

———. 2003. "Shadows of a Great Name. An Aristocratic Family under the Early Empire." In P. Kragelund, M. Moltesen, and J. Stubbe Østergaard, *The Licinian Tomb: Fact or Fiction?*, 19–45. Copenhagen.

Kraus, C. S. 1994. *Livy: Ab urbe condita VI.* Cambridge.

Krenz, P. 1982. *The Thirty at Athens.* Ithaca, N.Y.

Kruschwitz, P. 1998. "Die Datierung der Scipionenelogien *CLE* 6 und 7." *ZPE* 122:273–85.

———. 1999. "CLE 8, Zeile 1 — ein späterer Zusatz?" *ZPE* 124:261.

Kuhoff, W. 1993. "Zur Titulatur der römischen Kaiserinnen während der Prinzipatszeit." *Klio* 75:244–56.

Kundera, Milan. 1996. *The Book of Laughter and Forgetting.* Translated by A. Asher. New York.

Kunst, C., and U. Riemer (eds.). 2000. *Grenzen der Macht: zur Rolle der römischen Kaiserfrauen.* Stuttgart.

Kurke, L. 1991. *The Traffic in Praise: Pindar and the Poetics of Social Economy.* Ithaca, N.Y.

Lagerlöf, M. R. 2000. *The Sculptures of the Parthenon: Aesthetics and Interpretation.* New Haven.

Lahusen, G. 1983. *Untersuchungen zur Ehrenstatue in Rom.* Rome.

———. 1984. *Schriftquellen zum römischen Bildnis* 1. Bremen.

———. 1989. *Die Bildnismünzen der römischen Republik.* Munich.

Lambrecht, U. 1995. "Suetons Domitian-Vita." *Gymnasium* 102:508–36.

Lasfargues, J., and M. LeGlay. 1980. "Découverte d'un sanctuaire municipal du culte impériale à Lyon." *CRAI* 394–414.

Latte, K. 1960. *Römische Religionsgeschichte.* Munich.

Laur-Belart, R. 1959. *Über die Colonia Raurica und den Ursprung von Basel*. Basel.

Laurence, R. 1994. "Rumour and Communication in Roman Politics." *G & R* 41:62–74.

———. 1999. *The Roads of Roman Italy: Mobility and Cultural Change*. London and New York.

Lavelle, B. M. 1993. *The Sorrow and the Pity: A Prolegomenon to a History of Athens under the Peisistratids, c. 560–510 BC*. Historia Einzelschrift 80. Stuttgart.

Le Bohec, Y. 1998. *L'armée romaine sous le haut-empire*[2]. Paris.

Le Bonniec, H. 1958. *Le culte de Cérès à Rome*. Paris.

Lea Beness, J. 2000. "The Punishment of the Gracchani and the Execution of C. Villius in 133/132." *Antichthon* 34:1–17.

Lea Beness, J., and T. W. Hillard. 2001. "The Theatricality of the Deaths of C. Gracchus and Friends." *CQ* 51.1:135–40.

Lebek, W. D. 1990. "Welttrauer um Germanicus: das neugefundene Originaldokument und die Darstellung des Tacitus." *A & A* 36:93–102.

———. 1999. "Das *Senatus Consultum de Cn. Pisone Patre* und Tacitus." *ZPE* 128:183–211.

Lepelley, C. 1981. *Les cités de l'Afrique romaine au Bas-Empire*. 2. Paris.

Leppin, H. 1992. *Histrionen. Untersuchungen zur sozialen Stellung von Bühnenkünstlern im Westen des römischen Reiches zur Zeit der Republik und des Prinzipats*. Bonn.

Levi, M. A. 1990. "Sul patriziato romano." *PP* 45:431–42.

Levi della Vida, G. 1935. "Due iscrizioni imperiali neopuniche di Leptis Magna." *Africa Italiana* 6:1–29.

Levi della Vida, G., and M. G. Amadasi Guzzo. 1987. *Iscrizioni puniche della Tripolitana (1927–1967)*. Rome.

Levick, B. M. 1972. "Tiberius' Retirement to Rhodes in 6 B.C." *Latomus* 31:779–813.

———. 1975. "Julians and Claudians." *G & R* 29–38.

———. 1976a. "The Fall of Julia the Younger." *Latomus* 35:301–39.

———. 1976b. *Tiberius the Politician*. London.

———. 1979. "*Poena Legis Maiestatis*." *Historia* 28:358–79.

———. 1982. "Domitian and the Provinces." *Latomus* 41:50–73.

———. 1985. "L. Verginius Rufus and the Four Emperors." *RhM* 127:318–46.

———. 1990. *Claudius*. London.

———. 1999. *Vespasian*. London.

———. 2002. "Corbulo's Daughter." *G & R* 49.2:199–211.

Lewis, R. G. 1991. "Sulla's Autobiography: Scope and Economy." *Athenaeum* 79:509–19.

Linderski, J. 1987/1995. "A Missing Ponticus." *AJAH* 12.2:148–66.

———. 1988. "Julia in Rhegium." *ZPE* 72:181–200.

———. 1996. "Q. Scipio Imperator." In J. Linderski (ed.), *Imperium sine fine: T. Robert S. Broughton and the Roman Republic*, 156–61. Historia Einzelschrift 105. Stuttgart.

———. 2002. "The Pontiff and the Tribune: The Death of Tiberius Gracchus." *Athenaeum* 90.2:339–66.

Linke, B. 2000. "*Religio* und *res publica*. Religiöser Glaube und gesellschaftliches Handeln im republikanischen Rom." In B. Linke and M. Stemmler (eds.), *Mos maiorum: Untersuchungen zu den Formen der Identitätsstiftung und Stabilisierung in der Römischen Republik,* 269–98. Stuttgart.

Linke, B., and M. Stemmler (eds.). 2000. *Mos maiorum: Untersuchungen zu den Formen der Identitätsstiftung und Stabilisierung in der Römischen Republik.* Stuttgart.

Lintott, A. 1970. "The Tradition of Violence in the Annals of Early Rome." *Historia* 19:12–29.

———. 1982. *Civil Strife and Revolution in the Classical City, 750–330 B.C.* Baltimore.

———. 1994. "Political History, 146–95 B.C." In *The Cambridge Ancient History* 9²: *The Last Age of the Roman Republic, 146–43 B.C.,* 40–103. Cambridge.

———. 1999. *The Constitution of the Roman Republic.* Oxford.

Liou-Gille, B. 1996. "La sanction des *leges sacratae* et l'*adfectatio regni*: Spurius Cassius, Spurius Maelius et Manlius Capitolinus." *PP* 51:161–97.

———. 1998. *Une lecture "religieuse" de Tite-Live I: cultes, rites, croyances de la Rome archaïque.* Paris.

Lo Cascio, E. 1979. "Carbone, Druso e Gratidiano: le gestione della res nummaria a Roma tra la lex Papiria e la lex Cornelia." *Athenaeum* 57:215–38.

Loraux, N. 2002. *The Divided City: On Memory and Forgetting in Ancient Athens.* New York.

Lott, J. Bert. 2004. *The Neighborhoods of Augustan Rome.* Cambridge.

Lovano, M. 2002. *The Age of Cinna: Crucible of the Late Republic.* Stuttgart.

Lovisi, C. 1999. *Contribution à l'étude de la peine de mort sous la république romaine (509–149 av. J.-C.).* Paris.

Luce, T. J. 1968. "Political Propaganda on Roman Republican Coins, c. 92–82 B.C." *AJA* 72:25–39.

Ludolph, M. 1997. *Epistolographie und Selbstdarstellung. Untersuchungen zu den 'Paradebriefen' Plinius des Jüngeren.* Tübingen.

Luisi, A. 1991. "Domiziano tra mito e realtà." In M. Sordi (ed.), *L'immagine dell'uomo politico: vita pubblica e morale nell'antichità,* 227–33. Milan.

———. 1993–94. "Auctoritas e potestas di Domiziano pontifice massimo." *Invigilata lucernio* 15–16:159–78. Bari.

———. 2000. "Ovidio e la corrente filo-antoniana di opposizione al regime." In M. Sordi (ed.), *L'opposizione nel mondo antico,* 181–93. Milan.

Luraghi, N. 1994. *Tirannidi archaiche in Sicilia e magna Grecia da Panezio di Leontini alla caduta dei Dinomenidi.* Florence.

Ma, J. 1999. *Antiochos III and the Cities of Western Asia Minor.* Oxford.

MacDowell, D. M. 1986. *Spartan Law.* Edinburgh.

Mackay, C. S. 2000. "Sulla and the Monuments: Studies in His Public Persona." *Historia* 49.2:161–210.

MacMullen, R. 1966. *Enemies of the Roman Order: Treason, Unrest, and Alienation in the Empire.* Cambridge, Mass.

———. 1982. "The Epigraphic Habit in the Roman Empire." *AJP* 103:233–46.

Magi, F. 1945. *I rilievi Flavi del Palazzo della Cancelleria.* Rome.

———. 1963. "Le iscrizioni recentemente scoperte sull'obelisco Vaticano." *StudRom* 11:50–56.

Maiuri, A. 1925. *Nuova silloge epigrafica di Rodi e Cos.* Florence.

Malissard, A. 1990. "Tacite et le théâtre ou la mort en scène." In J. Blänsdorf (ed.), *Theater und Gesellschaft im Imperium Romanum,* 213–22. Tübingen.

Malitz, J. 1999. *Nero.* Munich.

Mansuelli, G. 1958. *Galleria degli Uffizi. Le sculture.* Rome.

Manuwald, G. 2001. *Fabulae praetextae. Spuren einer literarischen Gattung der Römer.* Munich.

Marasco, G. 1992. "Marco Antonio 'nuovo Dioniso' e il *De sua ebrietate.*" *Latomus* 51:538–48.

Maréchal, J.-F. 1987/1989. "Note sur un lingot de plomb inscrit d'époque romaine retrouvé en Corse." *BSAF:* 258–66.

Marin, E. 2001. "The Temple of the Imperial Cult (*Augusteum*) at Narona and Its Statues: Interim Report." *JRA* 14:81–112.

Marincola, J. 1999. "Genre, Convention, and Innovation in Greco-Roman Historiography." In C. S. Kraus (ed.), *The Limits of Historiography: Genre and Narrative in Ancient Historical Texts,* 281–324. Leiden.

Marshall, B. 1985. "Catilina and the Execution of M. Marius Gratidianus." *CQ* 35:124–33.

Martin, A. 1987. *La titulature épigraphique de Domitien.* Frankfurt.

Martin, D. B. 1996. "The Construction of the Ancient Family: Methodological Considerations." *JRS* 86:40–60.

Martin, P. M. 1982. *L'idée de royauté à Rome 1: de la Rome royale au consensus républicain.* Clérmont-Ferrand.

———. 1990. "Des tentatives de tyrannies à Rome aux Ve–IVe siècles?" In W. Eder (ed.), *Staat und Staatlichkeit in der frühen römischen Republik,* 49–72. Stuttgart.

———. 1994. *L'idée de royauté à Rome 2: haine de la royauté et séductions monarchiques (du IVe siècle av. J.-C. au principat augustéen).* Clérmont-Ferrand.

Mattei, M. 1986. "Testimonianze epigrafiche e attestazioni letterarie relative all'area degli Horti Lamiani." In M. Cima and E. La Rocca (eds.), *Le tranquille dimore degli dei: la residenza imperiale degli Horti Lamiani,* 153–64. Venice.

Mattingly, H. 1940. *Coins of the Roman Empire in the British Museum 4. Antoninus Pius to Commodus.* London.

Mattingly, H., and E. A. Sydenham. 1923. *The Roman Imperial Coinage.* Vol. 1. London.

Mazzarino, S. 1982. "L'iscrizione latina nella trilingue di Philae e i carmi di Gallus scoperti a Qasr Ibrîm." *RM* 125:312–37.

McGlew, J. F. 1993. *Tyranny and Political Culture in Ancient Greece.* Ithaca, N.Y.

Meadows, A. 2001. "Sins of the Fathers: The Inheritance of Cleopatra, Last Queen of Egypt." In S. Walker and P. Higgs (eds.), *Cleopatra of Egypt: From History to Myth,* 14–31. London.

Meadows, A., and J. Williams. 2001. "Moneta and the Monuments: Coinage and Politics in Republican Rome." *JRS* 91:27–49.

Medri, C. 1996. "Suetonius *Nero* 31.1: elementi e proposte per la riconstruzione del progetto della Domus Aurea." In C. Penella (ed.), *Meta Sudans,* 165–96. Rome.

Megow, W.-R. 1987. *Kameen von Augustus bis Alexander Severus.* Berlin.

Meier, C. 1979. "Der Ernstfall im alten Rom." In R. Altmann (ed.), *Der Ernstfall*, 40–73. Berlin.

———. 1980. *Res publica amissa. Eine Studie zu Verfassung und Geschichte der späten römischen Republik²*. Wiesbaden.

Meiggs, R., and D. Lewis. 1969. *A Selection of Greek Historical Inscriptions to the End of the Fifth Century B.C.* Oxford.

Meister, K. 1974. "Die Aufhebung der gracchischen Agrarreform." *Historia* 23:86–97.

Mellor, R. 2003. "The New Aristocracy of Power." In A. J. Boyle and W. J. Dominik (eds.), *Flavian Rome: Culture, Image, Text*, 69–101. Leiden.

Meneghini, R. 1991. *Il Foro di Nerva*. Rome.

Merkelbach, R. 1978. "Ephesische parerga 21. Ein Zeugnis für Ti. Claudius Balbillus aus Smyrna." *ZPE* 31:186–87.

Méthy, N. 2000. "Éloge rhétorique et propagande politique sous le haut-empire: l'example du Panégyrique de Trajan." *MEFRA* 112:365–411.

Meyer, E. A. 2004. *Legitimacy and Law in the Roman World: Tabulae in Roman Belief and Practice*. Cambridge.

Migliorati, G. 2000. "Il *Brutus* di Accio e l'opposizione ai Gracchi." In M. Sordi (ed.), *L'opposizione nel mondo antico*, 155–80. Milan.

Mihailov, G. 1974. "À propos de la stèle du Captor Decebali à Philippes." In *Mélanges hélleniques offerts à G. Daux*, 279–87. Paris.

Mikocki, T. 1995. *Sub specie deae. Les impératrices et princesses romaines assimilées à des déesses*. Rome.

Millar, F. 1993. "Ovid and the *domus Augusta*: Rome Seen from Tomoi." *JRS* 83:1–17.

———. 2000. "Trajan: Government by Correspondence." In J. González (ed.), *Trajano emperador de Roma*, 363–88. Rome.

Millender, E. G. 2001. "Spartan Literacy Revisited." *CA* 20.1:121–64.

Miltner, F. 1960. "Vorläufiger Bericht über die Ausgrabungen in Ephesos." *Jahreshefte des österreichischen archäologischen Instituts in Wien* 45: Beiblatt, 1–75.

Mócsy, A. 1966. "Der vertuschte Dakerkrieg des M. Licinius Crassus." *Historia* 15:511–14.

Moir, K. M. 1986. "The Epitaph of Publius Scipio." *CQ* 36:258–59.

———. 1988. "The Epitaph of Publius Scipio: A Reply." *CQ* 38:264–66.

Molisani, G. 1982. "D. Terentius Scaurianus, *consularis exercitus provinciae novae*." *Atti del colloquio internazionale AIEGL su epigrafia e ordine senatorio. Tituli* 4:499–505. Rome.

Moltesen, M. 2003. "The Portraits." In P. Kragelund, M. Moltesen, and J. Stubbe Østergaard (eds.), *The Licinian Tomb: Fact or Fiction?*, 81–100. Copenhagen.

Mommsen, T. 1871. "Sp. Cassius, M. Manlius, Sp. Maelius, die drei Demagogen des 3. und 4. Jahrhunderts der römischen Republik." *Hermes* 5:228–80.

———. 1888/1963. *Römisches Staatsrecht³*. Leipzig and Basel.

———. 1899/1955. *Römisches Strafrecht*. Leipzig and Graz.

Moormann, E. M. 1995. "A Ruin for Nero on the Oppian Hill." *JRA* 8:403–5.

———. 1998. "Vivere come un'uomo: l'uso dello spazio della Domus Aurea." In M. Cima and E. La Rocca (eds.), *Horti Romani. Atti del convegno internazionale*, 345–61. *BCAR* Suppl. 6. Rome.

Morello, A. 1997. *Lucio Munazio Planco. Raffinato interprete di un'epoca incoerente.* Venafro.

Morello, R., and R. K. Gibson (eds.). 2003. "Re-imagining Pliny the Younger." *Arethusa* 36.2.

Moretti, L. 1967. *Iscrizioni storiche ellenistiche* 1. Florence.

Morford, M. P. O. 1968. "The Distortion of the Domus Aurea Tradition." *Eranos* 66:158–79.

———. 1985. "Nero's Patronage and Participation in Literature and the Arts." *ANRW* 2.32.3:2003–31. Berlin and New York.

———. 1992. "*Iubes esse liberos*: Pliny's *Pangyricus* and Liberty." *AJP* 113:575–93.

Morizio, V. 1996. "Le dediche ad Augusto e ai Giulio-Claudi." In C. Panella (ed.), *Meta Sudans 1. Un area sacra in Palatio e la valle del Colosseo prima e dopo Nerone,* 201–16. Rome.

Morley, N. 2001. "The Transformation of Italy, 225–28 B.C." *JRS* 91:50–62.

Morris, I. 1987. *Burial and Ancient Society: The Rise of the Greek City State.* Cambridge.

Morrmann, E. M. 1995. "A Ruin for Nero on the Oppian Hill." *JRA* 8:403–5.

Morstein-Marx, R. 2004. *Mass Oratory and Political Power in the Late Roman Republic.* Cambridge.

Mortensen, S. 2004. *Hadrian. Eine Deutungsgeschichte.* Bonn.

Mowat, R. 1901. "Martelage et abrasion des monnaies sous l'empire romaine." *RN*:443–71.

Murison, C. L. 1993. *Galba, Otho and Vitellius: Careers and Controversies.* Hildesheim.

Murray, W. M., and P. M. Petsas. 1989. *Octavian's Campsite Memorial for the Actian War.* Philadelphia.

Mustakallio, K. 1994. *Death and Disgrace: Capital Penalties with post mortem Sanctions in Early Roman Historiography.* Helsinki.

Nedergaard, E. 2001. "Facts and Fiction about the *Fasti Capitolini*." *ARID* 27:107–27.

Newlands, C. E. 2002. *Statius' Silvae and the Poetics of Empire.* Cambridge.

Nicolet, C. 1976. *Le métier de citoyen dans la Rome républicaine.* Paris.

———. 1980. *The World of the Citizen in Republican Rome.* London.

Nippel, W. 1988. *Aufruhr und "Polizei" in der römischen Republik.* Stuttgart.

Nony, D. 1986. *Caligula.* Paris.

Noreña, C. 2003. "Medium and Message in Vespasian's Templum Pacis." *MAAR* 48:25–43.

Nylander, C. 1980. "Earless in Nineveh: Who Mutilated 'Sargon's' Head?" *AJA* 84:329–33.

O'Gorman, E. 2000. *Irony and Misreading in the Annals of Tacitus.* Cambridge.

Oakley, S. P. 1997. *A Commentary on Livy Books VI–X.* Oxford.

Ogilvie, R. M. 1965. *A Commentary on Livy 1–5.* Oxford.

Orlin, E. M. 1997. *Temples, Religion, and Politics in the Roman Republic.* Leiden.

Ortmann, U. 1988. *Cicero, Brutus und Octavian. Republikaner und Caesarianer. Ihr gegenseitiges Verhältnis im Krisenjahr 44/43 v. Chr.* Bonn.

Orwell, G. 1949/1981. *Nineteen Eighty-four.* New York.

Ostrow, S. E. 1977. *Problems in the Topography of Roman Puteoli*. Ph.D. diss., University of Michigan.

Ostwald, M. 1955. "The Athenian Legislation against Tyranny and Subversion." *TAPA* 86:103–28.

———. 1986. *From Popular Sovereignty to the Sovereignty of Law: Law, Society and Politics in Fifth Century Athens*. Berkeley.

Pabst, A. 1997. *Comitia Imperii. Ideelle Grundlagen des römischen Kaisertums*. Darmstadt.

Packer, J. E. 2003. "Plurima et Amplissima Opera: Parsing Flavian Rome." In A. J. Boyle and W. J. Dominik (eds.), *Flavian Rome: Culture, Image, Text*, 167–98. Leiden.

Paillier, J.-M. 1986. *Bacchanalia. La repression de 186 av. J.-C. à Rome et en Italie: vestiges, images, tradition*. Rome.

Paillier, J.-M., and R. Sablayrolles. 1994. "Damnatio memoriae: une vraie perpétuité." *Pallas* 40:11–55.

Paladini, M. L. 1996. "Il processo pisoniano nella Roma di Tiberio." In M. Sordi (ed.), *Processi e politica nel mondo antico*, 219–36. Contributi dell'Istituto di storia antica 22. Scienze storiche 62. Milan.

Palmer, R. E. A. 1974. "Roman Shrines of Female Chastity from the Caste Struggle to the Papacy of Innocent I." *RSA* 4:113–59.

———. 1978. "Silvanus, Sylvester, and the Chair of Peter." *PAPS* 122:222-47.

———. 1993. "Paean and Paeanists of Serapis and the Flavian Emperors." In R. M. Rosen and J. Farrell (eds.), *Nomodeiktes: Greek Studies in Honor of M. Ostwald*, 355–65. Ann Arbor, Mich.

Panciera, S. 1994. "Il corredo epigrafico del Mausoleo di Augusto." In H. von Hesberg and S. Panciera, *Das Mausoleum des Augustus: der Bau und seine Inschriften*, 66-175. Munich.

———. 1996. "L'iscrizione di Claudio." In C. Panella (ed.), *Meta Sudans 1. Un area sacra in Palatio e la valle del Colosseo prima e dopo Nerone*, 133–37. Rome.

Panella, C. 1987. "L'organizzazione degli spazi sulle pendici settentrionali del colle oppio tra Augusto e i Severi." In *L'urbs. Espace urbain et histoire (Ier siècle av. J.-C.–IIIe siècle ap. J.-C.)*, 611–51. Rome.

——— (ed.). 1996. *Meta Sudans 1. Un area sacra in Palatio e la valle del Colosseo prima e dopo Nerone*. Rome.

Pani, M. 1987. "La missione di Germanico in Oriente: politica estera e politica interna." In G. Bonamente and M. P. Segoloni (eds.), *Germanico. La persona, la personalità, il personaggio nel bimillenario della nascita*, 1–23. Rome.

Panitschek, P. 1989. "Sp. Cassius, Sp. Maelius, M. Manlius als *exempla maiorum*." *Philologus* 133: 231–45.

Parker, R. 1983. *Miasma: Pollution and Purification in Early Greek Religion*. Oxford.

Patton, C. W. R., and E. L. Hicks. 1891. *Inscriptions of Cos*. Oxford.

Peachin, M. 2004. *Frontinus and the Curae of the Curator Aquarum*. Stuttgart.

Peek, W. 1972. *Neue Inschriften aus Epidauros*. Berlin.

Pekáry, T. 1985. *Das römische Kaiserbildnis in Staat, Kult und Gesellschaft, dargestellt anhand der Schriftquellen. Das römische Herrscherbild* 3.5. Berlin.

Pelling, C. B. R. 1988. *Plutarch: Antony*. Cambridge.

———. 1989. "Plutarch: Roman Heroes and Greek Culture." In M. Griffin and J. Barnes (eds.), *Philosophia Togata: Essays on Philosophy and Roman Society*, 199–232. Oxford.

———. 1993. "Tacitus and Germanicus." In T. J. Luce and A. J. Woodman (eds.), *Tacitus and the Tacitean Tradition*, 59-85. Princeton.

———. 1996. "The Triumviral Period." In *The Cambridge Ancient History* 10²: *The Augustan Empire, 43 B.C.–A.D. 69*, 1–69. Cambridge.

Peña, J. T. 2000. "Two Tales of the City: Final Reports from the Caelian 'Caput Africae' and the Meta Sudans." *JRA* 13:549–58.

Peter, H. 1914. *Historicorum Romanorum Reliquiae²*. Leipzig.

Peters, W. J. T., and P. G. P. Meyboom. 1982. "The Roots of Provincial Roman Painting: Results of Current Research in Nero's Domus Aurea." In J. Liversidge (ed.), *Roman Provincial Wall Painting of the Western Empire*, 33–74. Oxford.

Pflaum, H.-G. 1960-61. *Les carrières procuratoriennes équestres sous le Haut-Empire romain*. Paris.

Phang, S. E. 2001. *The Marriage of Roman Soldiers (13 B.C.–A.D. 235): Law and Family in the Imperial Army*. Leiden.

Piccaluga, G. 1988. "Chi ha sparso il sale sulle rovine di Cartagine?" *Cultura e scuola* 105:153–65.

Pighi, I. B. 1965. *De ludis saecularibus populi Romani Quiritium. Libri sex*. Amsterdam.

Pleket, H. W. 1961. "Domitian, the Senate, and the Provinces." *Mnemosyne* 14:297–315.

Polleichtner, W. 2003. "Das 'Senatus Consultum de Cn. Pisone patre' und Tacitus' Bericht vom Prozess gegen Piso. Zur Frage der Datierung des Prozesses gegen Piso." *Philologus* 147.2:289–306.

Pollini, J. 1984. "Damnatio Memoriae in Stone: Two Portraits of Nero Recut to Vespasian in American Museums." *AJA* 88:547–55.

Pomeroy, S. B. 1997. *Families in Classical and Hellenistic Greece: Representations and Realities*. Oxford.

Potter, D. S. 1999. "Political Theory in the *Senatus Consultum de Cn. Pisone patre*." *AJP* 120:65–88.

Price, J. J. 2001. *Thucydides and Internal War*. Cambridge.

Price, S. R. F. 1987. "From Noble Funerals to Divine Cult: The Consecration of the Roman Emperors." In D. Cannadine and S. Price (eds.), *Rituals of Royalty: Power and Ceremonial in Traditional Societies*, 56–105. Cambridge.

Pritchett, W. K. 1954. "An Unfinished Inscription *IG* 2² 2362." *TAPA* 85:159–67.

Purcell, N. 1986. "Livia and the Womanhood of Rome." *PCPhS* 32:78–105.

———. 1993. "Atrium Libertatis." *PBSR* 61:125-55.

———. 1995. "On the Sacking of Carthage and Corinth." In D. Innes, H. Hine, and C. Pelling (eds.), *Ethics and Rhetoric: Classical Essays for Donald Russell on His 75th Birthday*, 133–48. Oxford.

———. 2003. "Becoming Historical: The Roman Case." In D. Braund and C. Gill (eds.), *Myth, History, and Culture in Republican Rome: Studies in Honour of T. P. Wiseman*, 12-40. Exeter.

Questa, C. 1995. "Messalina *meretrix augusta*." In R. Raffaeli (ed.), *Vicende e figure femminili in Grecia e a Roma,* 399–423. Ancona.

Raaflaub, K. A. 1987. "Grundzüge, Ziele und Ideen der Opposition gegen die Kaiser im 1. Jhd. n. Chr. Versuch einer Standortbestimmung." In A. Giovannini (ed.), *Opposition et résistances à l'empire d'Auguste à Trajan,* 1–55. Geneva.

Raaflaub, K. A., and L. J. Samons II. 1990. "Opposition to Augustus." In K. A. Raaflaub and M. Toher (eds.), *Between Republic and Empire: Interpretations of Augustus and His Principate,* 417–54. Berkeley.

Radicke, J. 1997. "Die Selbstdarstellung des Plinius in seinen Briefen." *Hermes* 125:447–69.

Raepsaet-Charlier, M. T. 1987. *Prosopographie des femmes de l'ordre sénatorial (Ier–IIe siècles).* Vols. 1 and 2. Louvain.

Rajak, T. 1983. *Josephus: The Historian and His Society.* London.

Ramage, E. S. 1983. "Denigration of a Predecessor under Claudius, Galba, and Vespasian." *Historia* 32:202–6.

———. 1989. "Juvenal and the Establishment: Denigration of a Predecessor in the 'Satires.'" *ANRW* 33.1:640–707. Berlin and New York.

———. 1991. "Sulla's Propaganda." *Klio* 73:93–121.

Rampelberg, R. H. 1978. "Les dépouilles opimes à Rome, des débuts de la République à Octave." *RHDFE* 56:191–214.

Ramsay, W. M. 1924. "Studies in the Roman Province of Galatia." *JRS* 14:172–205.

Rankov, B. 1994. *Guardians of the Roman Empire.* Oxford.

Rawson, E. 1974. "Religion and Politics in the Late Second Century B.C. at Rome." *Phoenix* 28:193–212. Reprinted in *Roman Society and Culture* (Oxford, 1991), 149–68.

———. 1975. *Cicero.* London.

———. 1987. "Sallust on the Eighties." *CQ* 37:163–80.

———. 1990. "The Antiquarian Tradition: Spoils and Representations of Foreign Armor." In W. Eder (ed.), *Staat und Staatlichkeit in der frühen römischen Republik,* 158–73. Stuttgart.

———. 1991. "Cassius and Brutus: The Memory of the Liberators." In *Roman Culture and Society,* 488–507. Oxford.

———. 1994a. "Caesar: Civil War and Dictatorship." In *The Cambridge Ancient History* 9²: *The Last Age of the Roman Republic, 146–43 B.C.,* 424–67. Cambridge.

———. 1994b. "The Aftermath of the Ides." In *The Cambridge Ancient History* 9²: *The Last Age of the Roman Republic, 146–43 B.C.,* 468–90. Cambridge.

Reynolds, J. M. 1980. "The Origins and Beginning of Imperial Cult at Aphrodisias." *PCPS* 26:70–84.

———. 1982. *Aphrodisias and Rome.* London.

Rhodes, P. J. 1991. "The Athenian Code of Laws, 410–399 B.C." *JHS* 101:87–100.

Rhodes, P. J., and R. Osbourne. 2003. *Greek Historical Inscriptions: 404–323 B.C.* Oxford.

Rice, E. E. 1999. *Cleopatra.* Stroud, Glos.

Rich, J. 1996. "Augustus and the *spolia opima*." *Chiron* 26:85–127.

———. 1998. "Augustus's Parthian Honours, the Temple of Mars Ultor and the Arch in the Forum Romanum." *PBSR* 66:71–128.

Richard, F. 1998. "Les images du triomphe de Claude sur la Bretagne." In Y. Burnand, Y. Le Bohec, and J.-P. Martin (eds.), *Claude de Lyon: empereur romain*, 355–71. Paris.

Richardson, J. S. 1997. "The Senate, the Courts, and the *SC de Cn. Pisone patre*," *CQ* 47:510–18.

Ridley, R. T. 1986. "To Be Taken with a Pinch of Salt: The Destruction of Carthage." *CP* 81.1:140–46.

Riggsby, A. M. 1998. "Bellocissimus Princeps." In A. Nünnerich-Asmus (ed.), *Traian. Ein Kaiser der Superlative am Beginn einer Umbruchzeit?* 22–40, 174. Mainz.

Rihll, T. 1989. "Lawgivers and Tyrants (Solon fr. 9–11 West)." *CQ* 39:277–86.

Ripoll, F. 1999. "Aspects et fonction de Néron dans la propagande impériale flavienne." In J.-M. Croisille, R. Martin, and Y. Perrin (eds.), *Neronia V. Néron: histoire et légende*, 137–51. Brussels.

Robert, L. 1949. "Le culte de Caligula à Milet et la province d'Asie." *Hellenica* 7:206–38.

———. 1960. "Recherches épigraphiques V: inscriptions de Lesbos." *REA* 62:285–300.

———. 1966. "Inscriptions D'Aphrodisias." *L'Antiquité classique* 35:377–432.

Robertson, N. 1990. "The Laws of Athens, 410–399 B.C.: The Evidence for Review and Publication." *JHS* 100:43–75.

Rodriguez Colmenero, A. 1997. "La nueva 'tabula hospitalitatis' de la 'civitas Lougeiorum.'" *ZPE* 117:213–26.

Rogers, P. A. 1979. "The Stigma of Politics: Imperial Conspirators and Their Descendants in the Early Empire." Ph.D. diss., University of Washington.

Rogers, P. M. 1984. "Domitian and the Finances of the State." *Historia* 33:60–78.

Rohr Vio, F. 2000. *Le voci del dissenso. Ottaviano Augusto e i suoi oppositori.* Padua.

Rollin, J. P. 1979. *Untersuchungen zu Rechtsfragen römischer Bildnisse.* Bonn.

Roos, P. 1975. "Alte und neue Inschriftenfunde aus Zentralkarien." *MDAI(I)* 25:335–41.

Rose, C. B. 1994. "The Post-Bronze Age Excavations at Troia." *Studia Troica* 4:75–104.

———. 1997. *Dynastic Commemoration and Imperial Portraiture in the Julio-Claudian Period.* Cambridge.

Rosenstein, N. S. 1990. *Imperatores Victi: Military Defeat and Aristocratic Competition in the Middle and Late Republic.* Berkeley.

———. 2004. *Rome at War: Farms, Families, and Death in the Middle Republic.* Chapel Hill, N.C.

Roxan, M. 1978. *Roman Military Diplomas, 1954–1977.* London.

———. 1985. *Roman Military Diplomas, 1978–1984.* London.

Royo, M. 1984. "L'*Octavie* entre Néron et les premiers Antonins." *REL* 61:189–200.

———. 1987. "Le quartier républicain du Palatin, nouvelles hypothèses de localisation." *REL* 65:89–114.

———. 1999. *Domus imperatoriae: topographie, formation et imaginaire des palais impériaux du Palatin (IIe siècle av. J.-C.–Ier siècle ap. J.-C.).* Rome.

Rudich, V. 1993. *Political Dissidence under Nero: The Price of Dissimulation.* London.

Rüpke, J. 1992. "'You shall not kill': Hierarchies of Norm in Ancient Rome." *Numen* 39:58–79.

———. 1995a. *Kalender und Öffentlichkeit: die Geschichte der Repräsentation und religiösen Qualifikation von Zeit in Rom*. Berlin.

———. 1995b. "*Fasti*: Quellen oder Produkte römischer Geschichtsschreibung?" *Klio* 77:184–202.

———. 1998. "Les archives des petits collèges. Le cas des Vicomagistri." In *La mémoire perdue. Recherches sur l'administration romaine*, 27–44. Rome.

Rutledge, S. H. 2001. *Imperial Inquisitions: Prosecutors and Informants from Tiberius to Domitian*. London.

Sablayrolles, R. 1994. "Domitien, 'Auguste ridicule.'" *Pallas* 40:113–44.

Salerno, F. 1990. *Dalla consecratio alla publicatio bonorum: forme giuridiche e uso publico dalle origini a Cesare*. Naples.

Saller, R. P. 1980. "Anecdotes as Historical Evidence for the Principate." *G & R* 27:69–83.

———. 1987. "*Patria potestas* and the Stereotype of the Roman Family." *Continuity and Change* 1:7–22.

———. 1990/2000. "Domitian and His Successors: Methodological Traps in Assessing Emperors." *AJAH* 15.1:4–18.

———. 1991. "Progress in Early Roman Historiography." *JRS* 81:157–63.

———. 1994. *Patriarchy, Property and Death in the Roman Family*. Cambridge.

Sancery, J. 1983. *Galba ou l'armée face au pouvoir*. Paris.

Sancisi-Weerdenburg, H. 2000. *Peisistratos and the Tyranny*. Gieben.

Schacter, D. L. 1995. *Memory Distortion: How Minds, Brains and Societies Reconstruct the Past*. Cambridge, Mass.

———. 2001. *The Seven Sins of Memory: How the Mind Forgets and Remembers*. Boston.

Schäfer, T. 1993. "Zur Datierung des Siegesdenkmals von Actium." *MDAI(A)* 108:239–48.

Scheid, J. 1975a. "Scribonia Caesaris et les Julio-Claudiens, problèmes de vocabulaire et de parenté." *MEFRA* 87:349–75.

———. 1975b. *Les Frères Arvales: recrutement et origine sociale sous les empereurs Julio-Claudiens*. Paris.

———. 1984. "La mort du tyran." *Du châtiment dans la cité. Supplices corporels et peine de mort dans le monde antique*, 177–93. Rome.

———. 1990. *Romulus et ses frères. Le collège des frères arvales, modèle du culte public dans la Rome des empereurs*. Rome.

———. 1992. "The Religious Roles of Roman Women." In P. Schmitt-Pantel (ed.), *A History of Women: From Ancient Goddess to Christian Saints*, 377–408. Cambridge, Mass.

———. 1993. "Lucus, nemus . . . Qu'est-ce qu'un bois sacré?" In H. Broise and J. Scheid (eds.), *Les bois sacrées*, 13–20. Naples.

———. 1998. *Recherches archéologiques à la Magliana. Commentarii fratrum Arvalium qui supersunt. Les copies épigraphiques des protocoles annuels de la conférie arvale (21 av.–304 ap. J.-C.)*. Rome.

Scheidel, W. 2001. "Progress and Problems in Roman Demography." In *Debating Roman Demography*, 1-81. Leiden.

Schmähling, E. 1938. *Die Sittenaufsicht der Censoren. Ein Beitrag zur Sittengeschichte der römischen Republik.* Stuttgart.

Schmid, S. G. 2001. "Worshipping the Emperor(s): A New Temple of the Imperial Cult at Eretria and the Ancient Destruction of Its Statues." *JRA* 14:113–42.

Schmidt, P. L. 1990. "Nero und das Theater." In J. Blänsdorf (ed.), *Theater und Gesellschaft im Imperium Romanum*, 149–63. Tübingen.

Scholz, P. 2003. "Sullas commentarii — eine literarische Rechtfertigung. Zu Wesen und Funktion der autobiographischen Schriften in der späten römischen Republik." In U. Eigler, U. Gotter, N. Luraghi, and U. Walter (eds.), *Formen römischer Geschichtsschreibung von den Anfängen bis Livius. Gattungen — Autoren — Kontexte*, 172–95. Darmstadt.

Schubert, C. 1998. *Studien zum Nerobild in der lateinischen Dichtung der Antike.* Stuttgart and Leipzig.

Schuller, W. 1997. "Der Mordprozess gegen Titus Annius Milo im Jahre 52 v. Chr. oder Gewalt von oben." In U. Manthe and J. von Ungern-Sternberg (eds.), *Grosse Prozesse der römischen Antike*, 115–27. Munich.

Schumacher, L. 1976. "Der Grabstein des T. Claudius Zosimus aus Mainz. Bemerkungen zu den kaiserlichen *praegustatores* und zum römischen Sepulkralrecht." *Epigraphische Studien* 11:131–41.

———. 1982. *Römische Kaiser in Mainz im Zeitalter des Principats (27 v. Chr.–284 n. Chr.).* Bochum.

———. 1985. "Die imperatorischen Akklamationen der Triumvirn und die *auspicia* des Augustus." *Historia* 34:191–222.

———. 1988. *Römische Inschriften.* Stuttgart.

Schwarte, K.-H. 2000. "Publius Cornelius Scipio Africanus der Ältere — Eroberer zwischen West und Ost." In K.-J. Hölkeskamp and E. Stein-Hölkeskamp (eds.), *Von Romulus zu Augustus. Große Gestalten der römischen Republik*, 106–19. Munich.

Seager, R. 1964. "The First Catilinarian Conspiracy." *Historia* 13:338–47.

———. 1994. "Sulla." In *The Cambridge Ancient History* 9²: *The Last Age of the Roman Republic, 146–43 B.C.*, 165–207. Cambridge.

Seelentag, G. 2004. *Taten und Tugenden Traians. Herrschaftsdarstellung im Prinzipat.* Stuttgart.

Segre, M. 1944–45/1952. "Tituli Calymnii." *ASAtene*: 22–23.

Sehlmeyer, M. 1999. *Stadtrömische Ehrenstatuen der republikanischen Zeit. Historizität und Kontext von Symbolen nobilitären Standesbewußtseins.* Stuttgart.

Selzer, W., K.-V. Decker, and A. do Paço, 1988. *Römische Steindenkmäler: Mainz in Römischer Zeit: Katalog zur Sammlung in der Steinhalle.* Mainz.

Severy, B. 2000. "Family and State in the Early Imperial Monarchy: The *SC de Pisone patre*, *Tabula Siarensis*, and *Tabula Hebana*." *CP* 95:318–37.

Shapiro, H. A. 1989. *Art and Cult under the Tyrants in Athens.* Mainz.

———. 1993. "From Athena's Owl to the Owl of Athens." In R. M. Rosen and J. Farrell (eds.), *Nomodeiktes: Greek Studies in Honor of Martin Ostwald*, 123–24. Ann Arbor, Mich.

Shaw, B. D. 2001. *Spartacus and the Roman Slave Wars: A Brief History with Documents.* Boston.

Shear, T. L., Jr. 1973. "The Athenian Agora: Excavations of 1971." *Hesperia* 42:121–79.

Sherk, R. K. 1969. *Roman Documents from the Greek East: Senatus consulta and epistulae to the Age of Augustus.* Baltimore.

———. 1984. *Rome and the Greek East to the Death of Augustus.* Cambridge.

———. 1988. *The Roman Empire: Augustus to Hadrian.* Cambridge.

Sherwin-White, A. N. 1966. *The Letters of Pliny: A Historical and Social Commentary.* Oxford.

Shipley, G. 2000. *The Greek World after Alexander, 323–30 B.C.* London.

Shotter, D. C. A. 1967. "The Trial of Gaius Silius (A.D. 24)." *Latomus* 26:712–16.

———. 1968. "Tacitus, Tiberius and Germanicus." *Historia* 17:194–214.

———. 1971. "Tiberius and Asinius Gallus." *Historia* 20:443–57.

———. 1974. "Cn. Calpurnius Piso, Legate of Syria." *Historia* 23:229–45.

———. 1983. "The Principate of Nerva. Some Observations on the Coin Evidence." *Historia* 32:215–26.

Sick, D. H. 1999. "Ummidia Quadratilla: Cagey Businesswoman or Lazy Pantomime Watcher?" *CA* 18.2:330–48.

Simon, F. M., and F. Pina Polo. 2000. "Mario Gratidiano, los compita y la religiosidad popular a fines de la republica." *Klio* 82:154–70.

Simpson, C. J. 1993. "The Original Site of the *Fasti Capitolini.*" *Historia* 42:61–81.

Sinclair, P. 1990. "Tacitus' Presentation of Livia Julia, Wife of Tiberius' Son Drusus." *AJP* 111:238–56.

Skutsch, O. 1985. *The Annals of Q. Ennius.* Oxford.

Slater, N. 1996. "Nero's Masks." *CW* 90:33–40.

Small, J. P. 1995. "Recent Advances in the Understanding of Memory." *Helios* 22:156–58.

Smith, J. A. 2003. "Flavian Drama: Looking Back with Octavia." In A. J. Boyle and W. J. Dominik (eds.), *Flavian Rome: Culture, Image, Text,* 391–430. Leiden.

Smith, R. R. R. 2000. "Nero and the Sun-God: Divine Accessories and Political Symbols in Roman Imperial Images." *JRA* 13:532–42.

Solin, H. 1986. "Obbligo o libertà? Sull'onomastica dell'aristocrazia romana." *ORom* 3:70–73.

———. 1989. "Namenwechsel und besondere Vornamen römischer Senatoren. Betrachtungen zur kaiserlichen Namenpolitik." *Philologus* 133:252–59.

———. 1995. "Namensgebung und Politik. Zum Namenswechsel und zu besonderen Vornamen römischer Senatoren." *Tyche* 10:185–210.

———. 1996. *Die stadtrömischen Sklavennamen: ein Namenbuch.* Stuttgart.

Southern, P. 1997. *Domitian, Tragic Tyrant.* London.

Soverini, P. 1989. "Imperio e imperatori nell'opera di Plinio il Giovane: aspetti e problemi del rapporto con Domiziano e Traiano." *ANRW* 33.1:515–54. Berlin and New York.

Spaeth, B. 1990. "The Goddess Ceres and the Death of Tiberius Gracchus." *Historia* 39:182–95.

———. 1996. *The Roman Goddess Ceres.* Austin, Texas.

Späth, T. 2000. "Agrippina minor: Frauenbild als Diskurskonzept." In C. Kunst and U. Riemer (eds.), *Grenzen der Macht. Zur Rolle der römischen Kaiserfrauen,* 115–33. Stuttgart.

Speidel, M. P. 1970. "The Captor of Decebalus. A New Inscription from Philippi." *JRS* 60:142–53.

Spetsieri-Cherenni, A. 1995. "The Library of Hadrian at Athens. Recent Finds." *Ostraka* 4:137–47.

Speyer, W. 1981. *Büchervernichtung und Zensur des Geistes bei Heiden, Juden und Christen.* Stuttgart.

Stäcker, J. 2003. *Princeps und miles. Studien zum Bindungs- und Nahverhältnis von Kaiser und Soldat im 1. und 2. Jahrhundert n. Chr.* Hildesheim.

Steinby, E. M. 1987. "Il lato orientale del Foro Romano. Proposte di lettura." *Arctos* 21:139–84.

Stein-Hölkeskamp, E. 1989. *Adelskultur und Polisgesellschaft.* Stuttgart.

Stewart, A. 1990. *Greek Sculpture: An Exploration.* Vols. 1 and 2. New Haven.

Stewart, P. 2003. *Statues in Roman Society: Representation and Response.* Oxford.

Stockton, D. 1971. *Cicero: A Political Biography.* Oxford.

———. 1979. *The Gracchi.* Oxford.

Strobel, K. 1984. *Untersuchungen zu den Dakierkriegen Trajans.* Bonn.

———. 1989. *Die Donaukriege Domitians.* Bonn.

———. 2003. "Plinius und Domitian: der willige Helfer eines Unrechtssytems? Zur Problematik historischen Aussagen in den Werken des jüngeren Plinius." In L. Castagna and E. Lefèvre (eds.), *Plinius der Jüngere und seine Zeit*, 303–16. Munich and Leipzig.

Stylow, A., and S. Corzo Pérez. 1999. "Eine neue Kopie des *senatus consultum de Cn. Pisone patre.*" *Chiron* 29:23–28.

Suerbaum, W. 1999. "Schwierigkeiten bei der Lektüre des *SC de Cn. Pisone patre* durch die Zeitgenossen um 20 n. Chr, durch Tacitus und durch heutige Leser." *ZPE* 128:213–34.

Sumner, G. V. 1965. "The Family Connections of L. Aelius Seianus." *Phoenix* 19:134–45.

Suolahti, J. 1963. *The Roman Censors: A Study on Social Structure.* Helsinki.

Swain, S. C. R. 1990. "Hellenic Culture and the Roman Heroes of Plutarch." *JHS* 100:126–45.

Swan, M. 1970. "Josephus *AJ* 19.251–52: Opposition to Gaius and Claudius." *AJP* 91:149–64.

Syme, R. 1930. "The Imperial Finances under Domitian, Nerva and Trajan." *JRS* 20:55–70.

———. 1939. *The Roman Revolution.* Oxford.

———. 1958–63. *Tacitus.* 2 vols. Oxford.

———. 1960. "Piso Frugi and Crassus Frugi." *JRS* 50:12–20. Reprinted in *Roman Papers* 2 (Oxford, 1979), 496–509.

———. 1964. *Sallust.* Berkeley.

———. 1968. "The Ummidii." *Historia* 17:72–105.

———. 1970. *Ten Studies in Tacitus.* Oxford.

———. 1971. *Emperors and Biography: Studies in the Historia Augusta.* Oxford.

———. 1978. *History in Ovid.* Oxford.

———. 1979. "Livy and Augustus." In *Roman Papers* 1:400–454. Oxford.

———. 1980a. "The Sons of Piso the Pontifex." *AJP* 101:333–41. Reprinted in *Roman Papers* 3 (Oxford, 1984), 1226–35.

———. 1980b. *Some Arval Brethren*. Oxford.

———. 1983a. "Domitian: The Last Years." *Chiron* 13:121–46.

———. 1983b. "Eight Consuls from Patavium." *PBSR* 51:102–24.

———. 1984. "The Crisis of 2 B.C." In *Roman Papers* 3:912–36. Oxford.

———. 1985. "Correspondents of Pliny." *Historia* 34:324–59.

———. 1986. *The Augustan Aristocracy*. Oxford.

Talbert, R. J. A. 1974. *Timoleon and the Revival of Greek Sicily, 344–317 B.C.* Cambridge.

———. 1980. "Pliny the Younger as Governor of Bithynia and Pontus." In C. Deroux (ed.), *Studies in Latin Literature and Roman History* 2, 412–35. Latomus 168. Brussels.

———. 1999. "Tacitus and the *S. C. de Cn. Pisone patre*." *AJP* 120:89–97.

Tanner, J. 2000. "Portraits, Power, and Patronage in the Late Roman Republic." *JRS* 90:18–50.

Tansini, R. 1995. *I ritratti di Agrippina Maggiore*. Rome.

Tarpin, M. 2003. "M. Licinius Crassus Imperator et les dépouilles opimes de la République." *Rev Phil* 77.2:275–311.

Tatum, W. J. 1988. "The Epitaph of Publius Scipio Reconsidered." *CQ* 82:253–58.

———. 1999. *The Patrician Tribune: P. Clodius Pulcher*. Chapel Hill, N.C.

Taylor, L. R. 1931. *The Divinity of the Roman Emperor*. Middletown, Conn.

Taylor, L. R., and A. B. West. 1926. "The Euryclids in Latin Inscriptions from Corinth." *AJA* 30:389–400.

Te Riele, G.-J.-M.-J. 1967. "Le grand apaisement de Rogoziò." In *Acta of the V Epigraphic Congress*, 89–91. Rome.

Thein, A. G. 2002. "Sulla's Public Image and the Politics of Civic Renewal." Ph.D. diss., University of Pennsylvania.

Themelis, P. 1990. "Anaskaphe Messenes." *Praktika tes en Athenais Archaiologikes Hetaireias* 145:56–103.

Thomas, R. 1989. *Oral Tradition and Written Record in Classical Athens*. Cambridge.

———. 1995. "Written in Stone? Liberty, Equality, Orality and the Codification of Law." *BICS* 40:59–74.

Thomas, Y. 1984. "Vitae necisque potestas. Le père, la cité, la mort." In *Du châtiment dans la cité. Supplices corporels et peine de mort dans le monde antique*, 499–548. Rome.

Thomasson, B. E. 1996. *Fasti Africani. Senatorische und ritterliche Amtsträger in den römischen Provinzen Nordafrikas von Augustus bis Diokletian*. Stockholm.

Thompson, L. 1984. "*Domitianus Dominus*: A Gloss on Statius *Silv.* 1.6.84." *AJP* 105:469–75.

Thompson, M. 1981. "The Cavalla Hoard (IGCH 450)." *ANSMusN* 26:33-49.

Timpe, D. 1960. "Römische Geschichte bei Flavius Josephus." *Historia* 9:474–502.

———. 1962. *Untersuchungen zur Kontinuität des frühen Prinzipats*. Wiesbaden.

———. 1996. "Memoria und Geschichtsschreibung bei den Römern." In H.-J. Gehrke and A. Möller (eds.), *Vergangenheit und Lebenswelt. Soziale Kommunikation, Traditionsbildung und historisches Bewußtsein*, 277–99. Tübingen.

Titus Saunders, R. 1994. "Messalina as Augusta." *PP* 49:356–63.

Todd, S. C. 1993. *The Shape of Athenian Law*. Oxford.

Toynbee, J. M. C. 1971. *Death and Burial in the Roman World*. Ithaca, N.Y.

Treggiari, S. 1979. "Sentiment and Property: Some Roman Attitudes." In A. Parel and T. Flanagan (eds.), *Theories of Property: Aristotle to the Present*, 53–85. Waterloo, Ontario.

———. 1991. *Roman Marriage: Iusti Coniuges from the Time of Cicero to the Time of Ulpian*. Oxford.

Trillmich, W. 1978. *Familienpropaganda der Kaiser Caligula und Claudius. Agrippina Maior und Antonia Augusta auf Münzen*. Berlin.

———. 1988. "Der Germanicus-Bogen in Rom und das Monument für Germanicus und Drusus in Leptis Magna. Archäologisches zur *Tab. Siar.* 1.9–21." In J. González and J. Arce (eds.), *Estudios sobre la Tabula Siarensis*, 51–60. Madrid.

Tschiedel, H. J. 1995. "Agrippina — Ultrix Erinys: zur Bedeutung ihres Auftretens in der *Praetexta Octavia*." *ZAnt* 45:403–14.

Tuplin, C. 1989. "The False Neros of the First Century." In C. Deroux (ed.), *Studies in Latin Literature and History* 5, 364–404. Brussels.

Turcan, R. 1998. *Rome et ses dieux*. Paris.

Ungern-Sternberg von Pürkel, J. Baron. 1970. *Untersuchungen zum spätrepublikanischen Notstandsrecht: senatus consultum ultimum und hostis-Erklärung*. Munich.

Valvo, A. 1975. "Le vicende del 44–43 a. c. nella tradizione di Livio e di Dionigi su Spurio Melio." *CISA* 3:157–83.

———. 1983. *La sedizione di Manlio Capitolino in Tito Livio*. Milan.

———. 1984. "Il 'cognomen Capitolinus' in età repubblicana e il sorgere dell'area sacra sull'arce e il Campidoglio." In M. Sordi (ed.), *I santuari e la guerra nel mondo classico*, 92–106. Milan.

Van Bremen, R. 1996. *The Limits of Participation: Women and Civic Life in the Greek East in the Hellenistic and Roman Periods*. Amsterdam.

Van Ooteghem, J. 1964. *Caius Marius*. Brussels.

Van Sickle, J. 1987. "The Elogia of the Cornelii Scipiones and the Origin of Epigram at Rome." *AJP* 108:45–47.

Varner, E. R. 2000. "Tyranny and the Transformation of the Roman Visual Landscape." In E. R. Varner (ed.), *From Caligula to Constantine: Tyranny and Transformation in Roman Portraiture*, 9–26. Atlanta.

———. 2004. *Mutilation and Transformation: Damnatio Memoriae and Roman Imperial Portraiture*. Leiden.

Vasaly, A. 1987. "Personality and Power. Livy's Depiction of the Appii Claudii in the First Pentad." *TAPA* 117:203–26.

Vedaldi Iasbez, V. 1981. "I figli dei proscritti sillani." *Labeo* 27:163–213.

Verbrugghe, G. P. 1989. "On the Meaning of *Annales*, on the Meaning of Annalist." *Philologus* 133:192–230.

Versnel, H. S. 1980. "Destruction, Devotio and Despair in a Situation of Anomy: The Mourning for Germanicus in Triple Perspective." In *Perennitas: studi in onore di Angelo Brelich*, 541–618. Rome.

Vidman, L. 1982. *Fasti Ostienses: edendos, illustrandos, restituendos.* Prague.

Vigourt, A. 2001a. "L'intention criminelle et son châtiment: les condamnations des aspirants à la tyrannie." In M. Coudry and T. Späth (eds.), *L'invention des grands hommes de la Rome antique = Die Konstruktion der grossen Männer Altroms,* 271–87. Actes du colloque du Collegium Beatus Rhenanus, Augst, 16–18 septembre 1999. Paris.

———. 2001b. "Les 'adfectores regni' et les normes sociales." In M. Coudry and T. Späth (eds.), *L'invention des grands hommes de la Rome antique = Die Konstruktion der grossen Männer Altroms,* 333–40. Actes du colloque du Collegium Beatus Rhenanus, Augst, 16–18 septembre 1999. Paris.

Vinson, M. P. 1989. "Domitia Longina, Julia Titi, and the Literary Tradition." *Historia* 38:431–50.

Virlouvet, C. 2001. "Fulvia, the Woman of Passion." In A. Fraschetti (ed.), *Roman Women,* 66–81. Chicago.

Vittinghoff, F. 1936. *Der Staatsfeind in der römischen Kaiserzeit; Untersuchungen zur damnatio memoriae.* Berlin.

Voci, P. 1980. "Storia della *patria potestas* da Augusto a Diocleziano." *Ivra* 31:37–100.

Vogel-Weidemann, U. 1982. *Die Stadthalter von Africa und Asia in den Jahren 14–68 n. Chr. Eine Untersuchung zum Verhältnis Princeps und Senat.* Bonn.

Vogt-Spira, G., and B. Rommel. 1999. *Rezeption und Identität. Die kulturelle Auseinandersetzung Roms mit Griechenland als europäisches Paradigma.* Stuttgart.

Voisin, J.-L. 1998. "Visages de la mort volontaire à l'époque de Claude." In Y. Burnand, Y. Le Bohec, and J.-P. Martin (eds.), *Claude de Lyon,* 181–89. Paris.

Vollenweider, M. L. 1955. "Verwendung und Bedeutung der Porträtgemmen für das politische Leben der römischen Republik." *MH* 12:96–111.

von Fritz, K. 1957. "Tacitus, Agricola, Domitian, and the Problem of the Principate." *CP* 52:73-97.

von Ungern-Sternberg, J. 1997. "Das Verfahren gegen die Catalinarier oder: der vermiedene Prozeß." In U. Manthe and J. von Ungern-Sternberg (eds.), *Große Prozesse der römischen Antike,* 85–99. Munich.

———. 2000. "Eine Katastrophe wird verarbeitet: die Gallier in Rom." In C. F. H. Bruun (ed.), *The Roman Middle Republic: Politics, Religion, and Historiography, c. 400–133 B.C.,* 207–22. Rome.

Wachter, R. 1987. *Altlateinische Inschriften: sprachliche und epigraphische Untersuchungen zu den Dokumenten bis etwa 150 v. Chr.* Bern.

Walbank, F. 1984. "Macedonia and Greece." In *The Cambridge Ancient History*² 7.1: *The Hellenistic World,* 221-56. Cambridge.

Walker, S., and P. Higgs (eds.). 2001. *Cleopatra of Egypt.* London.

Wallace-Hadrill, A. 1981. "Galba's *Aequitas.*" *NC* 21:20–39.

———. 1983. *Suetonius: The Scholar and His Caesars.* London.

Walser, G. 1957. *Der Briefwechsel des L. Munatius Plancus mit Cicero.* Basel.

———. 1980. *Römische Inschriften der Schweiz.* Vols. 1 and 2. Bern.

———. 1984. *Summus Poeninus. Beiträge zur Geschichte des Grossen St. Bernhard-Passes in römischer Zeit.* Wiesbaden.

———. 1989. "Kaiser Domitian in Mainz." *Chiron* 19:449–56.

———. 1993. *Römische Inschriftkunst: römische Inschriften für den akademischen Unterricht und als Einführung in die lateinische Epigraphik*². Stuttgart.

Walter, U. 2001. "Die Botschaft des Mediums. Überlegungen zum Sinnpotential von Historiographie im Kontext der römischen Geschichtskultur zur Zeit der Republik." In G. Melville (ed.), *Institutionalität und Symbolisierung. Verstetigungen kultureller Ordnungsmuster in Vergangenheit und Gegenwart*, 214–79. Cologne.

———. 2002. "Geschichte als Lebensmacht im republikanischen Rom." *GWU* 53:326–39.

———. 2004. *Memoria und res publica. Zur Geschichtskultur im republikanischen Rom*. Frankfurt am Main.

Wardle, D. 1998. *Memorable Deeds and Sayings by Valerius Maximus*. Oxford.

Warrior, V. M. 1996. *The Initiation of the Second Macedonian War*. Stuttgart.

Waters, K. H. 1964. "The Character of Domitian." *Phoenix* 18:49–77.

———. 1969. "*Traianus Domitiani continuator*." *AJP* 90:385–405.

Watkins, T. H. 1997. *L. Munatius Plancus: Serving and Surviving in the Roman Revolution*. Atlanta.

Watson, A. 1971. *The Law of Succession in the Later Roman Republic*. Oxford.

———. 1975. *Rome of the XII Tables: Persons and Property*. Princeton.

———. 1979. "The Death of Horatia." *CQ* 29:436–47.

Weill Goudchaux, G. 2001. "Cleopatra's Subtle Religious Strategy." In S. Walker and P. Higgs (eds.), *Cleopatra of Egypt*, 128–41. London.

Weinstock, S. 1971. *Divus Julius*. Oxford.

Welch, K. E. 1995. "The Office of *Praefectus Fabrum* in the Late Republic." *Chiron* 25:131–45.

Wellesley, K. 1975. *The Long Year, A.D. 69*. London.

Wells, C. M. 1972. *The German Policy of Augustus: An Examination of the Archaeological Evidence*. Oxford.

Welwei, K.-W. 2001. "Lucius Iunius Brutus." *Gymnasium* 108:123–35.

Wesch-Klein, G. 1993. Funus publicum. *Eine Studie zur öffentlichen Beisetzung und Gewährung von Ehrengräbern in Rom und den Westprovinzen*. Stuttgart.

Westlake, H. D. 1952. *Timoleon and His Relations with Tyrants*. Manchester.

Wiedemann, T. E. J. 1996a. "From Tiberius to Nero." In *The Cambridge Ancient History* 10²: *The Augustan Empire, 43 B.C.–A.D. 69*, 198–255. Cambridge.

———. 1996b. "From Nero to Vespasian." In *The Cambridge Ancient History* 10²: *The Augustan Empire, 43 B.C.–A.D. 69*, 256–82. Cambridge.

Wiemer, H.-U. 1997. "Das Edikt des L. Antistius Rusticus: eine Preisregulierung als Anwart auf eine überregionale Versorgungskrise?" *AS* 47:195–215.

Wilhelm, A. 1943–47. "Dionysios Eleuthereus." *WS* 61–62:162–66.

Wilkes, J. J. 1969. *Dalmatia*. London.

Williams, G. 1994. "Nero, Seneca and Stoicism in the *Octavia*." In J. Elsner and J. Masters (eds.), *Reflections of Nero: Culture, History, and Representation*, 178–95. London.

Williams, J. H. C. 2001. "'Spoiling the Egyptians': Octavian and Cleopatra." In S. Walker and P. Higgs (eds.), *Cleopatra of Egypt*, 190–99. London.

Wilson, M. 2003. "After the Silence: Tacitus, Suetonius, and Juvenal." In A. J. Boyle
    and W. J. Dominik (eds.), *Flavian Rome: Culture, Image, Text*, 523–42. Leiden.
Winkes, R. 1995. *Livia, Octavia, Iulia: Porträts und Darstellungen*. Louvain.
Winterling, A. 2003. *Caligula: eine Biographie*. Munich.
Wiseman, T. P. 1966. "Domitian and the Dynamics of Terror in Classical Rome."
    History Today 46:19–24.
———. 1979a. "Topography and Rhetoric: The Trial of Manlius." *Historia* 28:32–50.
———. 1979b. *Clio's Cosmetics: Three Studies in Greco-Roman Literature*. Leicester.
———. 1987. "Conspicui postes tectaque digna deo: The Public Image of Aristocratic
    and Imperial Houses in the Late Republic." In *L'urbs: espace urbain et histoire (Ier
    siècle av. J.-C.–IIIe siècle ap. J.C.)*, 393–413. Rome.
———. 1991. *The Death of an Emperor*. Exeter.
———. 1994a. "The Senate and the *Populares*, 69–60 B.C." In *The Cambridge Ancient
    History* 9²: *The Last Age of the Roman Republic, 146–43 B.C.*, 327–67. Cambridge.
———. 1994b. "Caesar, Pompey, and Rome, 59–50 B.C." In *The Cambridge Ancient
    History* 9²: *The Last Age of the Roman Republic, 146–43 B.C.*, 368–423. Cambridge.
———. 1996. "What Do We Know about Early Rome?" *JRA* 9:310–15.
———. 1998a. "The Minucii and Their Monument." In *Roman Drama and Roman
    History*, 90–105. Exeter.
———. 1998b. "The Theatricality of the Death of Gaius Gracchus." In *Roman Drama
    and Roman History*, 52–59. Exeter.
———. 1998c. "The Publication of the *De Bello Gallico*." In K. Welch and A. Powell
    (eds.), *Julius Caesar as Artful Reporter: The War Commentaries as Political
    Instruments*, 1–9. London.
———. 2001. "The Principal Thing." Classical Association Presidential Address.
    Sherborne.
Wolpert, A. 2002. *Remembering Defeat: Civil War and Civic Memory in Ancient
    Athens*. Baltimore.
Wood, S. 1988. "*Memoriae Agrippinae*: Agrippina the Elder in Julio-Claudian Art and
    Propaganda." *AJA* 92:409–26.
———. 1992. "Messalina, Wife of Claudius: Propaganda Successes and Failures of His
    Reign." *JRA* 5:219–34.
———. 1995. "Diva Drusilla Panthea and the Sisters of Caligula." *AJA* 99:457–82.
———. 1999. *Imperial Women: A Study in Public Images, 40 B.C.–A.D. 68*. Leiden.
Woodhead, A. G. 1948. "Greek Inscriptions." *Hesperia* 17:54–60.
———. 1981. *The Study of Greek Inscriptions*². Cambridge.
Woodman, A. J. 1993. "Amateur Dramatics at the Court of Nero (Tac. Ann. 15.48–74)."
    In T. J. Luce and A. J. Woodman (eds.), *Tacitus and the Tacitean Tradition*, 104–28.
    Princeton.
———. 1995. "A Death in the First Act: Tacitus *Ann.* 1.6." *Papers of the Leeds
    International Latin Seminar* 8:257–73.
Woodman, A. J., and R. H. Martin. 1996. *The Annals of Tacitus Book 3*. Cambridge.
Wyetzner, P. 2002. "Sulla's Law on Prices and the Roman Definition of Luxury." In
    J.-J. Aubert and B. Sirks (eds.), *Speculum Iuris: Roman Law as a Reflection of Social
    and Economic Life in Antiquity*, 15–33. Ann Arbor, Mich.

Yacobson, A. 1998. "The Princess of Inscriptions: *Senatus Consultum de Cn. Pisone Patre* and the Early Years of Tiberius' Reign." *SCI* 17:206–24.

Yavetz, Z. 1963. "The Failure of Catiline's Conspiracy." *Historia* 12:485–99.

———. 1979. *Caesar in der öffentlichen Meinung.* Düsseldorf.

———. 1986. "The Urban Plebs: Flavians, Nerva, Trajan." In A. Giovannini (ed.), *Opposition et résistances à l'empire d'Auguste à Trajan*, 135–86. Geneva.

———. 1996. "Caligula, Imperial Madness and Modern Historiography." *Klio* 78:105–29.

———. 1998. "Seianus and the Plebs." *Chiron* 28:187–91.

Zanker, P. 1968. *Forum Augustum: das Bildprogramm.* Tübingen.

———. 1987. "Drei Stadtbilder aus dem augusteischen Rom." In *L'urbs. Espace urbain et histoire (Ier siècle av. J.-C.–IIIe siècle ap. J.-C.)*, 475–89. Rome.

———. 1988. *The Power of Images in the Age of Augustus.* Ann Arbor, Mich.

Zecchini, G. 1999. "Regime e opposizioni nel 20 d.C.: dal S.C. 'de Cn. Pisone patre' a Tacito." In M. Sordi (ed.), *Fazioni e congiure nel mondo antico*, 309–35. Contributi dell'Istituto di storia antica 25. Scienze storiche 68. Milan.

Zedler, G. 1885. "De memoriae damnatione quae dicitur." Diss. Leipzig.

Zehnacker, H. 1973. *Moneta: recherches sur l'organisation et l'art des émissions monétaires de la République romaine (289–31 av. J.-C.).* Rome.

———. 1987. "Tensions et contradictions dans l'empire au 1er siècle. Les témoinages numismatiques." In A. Giovannini (ed.), *Opposition et résistances à l'empire d'Auguste à Trajan*, 321–57. Geneva.

Zevi, F. 1979. "Un frammento dei Fasti Ostienses e i consolati dei primi anni di Traiano." *PP* 34:179–201.

——— (ed.). 1993. *Puteoli.* Naples.

Zimmermann, M. 1995. "Die *restitutio honorum* Galbas." *Historia* 44:56–82.

Ziolkowski, A. 1992. *The Temples of Mid-Republican Rome and Their Historical and Topographical Context.* Rome.

———. 1993. "Between Geese and the *Auguraculum*: The Origin of the Cult of Juno on the Arx." *CP* 88:206–19.

INDEX

▼ ▼ ▼

Names are by *nomen* (family name) except for emperors
(and their relatives) and writers.

Apicata, wife of Sejanus, 171, 181, 328
(n. 44)
Apollonis, wife of Attalus of Pergamum,
33
Appian and his writings, 78, 109, 302
(nn. 36, 38)
Appuleia Varilla, 161, 325 (n. 4)
Appuleius Decianus, Gaius (tr. pl.
98 B.C.), 83
Appuleius Saturninus, Lucius (tr. pl. 103,
100 B.C.), 81–85, 89, 100, 106, 303
(nn. 46–48)
Archeptolemus, 22, 289 (n. 19)
Arch of Germanicus (Circus Flaminius),
178
Aristoteles, 28–30, 291 (n. 39)
Arvals and their *acta*, 136, 158, 192, 223–
28, figs. 59–60, 318 (n. 69), 324 (n. 135),
331 (n. 64), 339 (nn. 63–67)
Asinius Gallus, Gaius (cos. 8 B.C.), 138,
143–48, figs. 26–28, 320 (nn. 87–93),
321 (nn. 94–98)
Asinius Pollio, Gaius (cos. 40 B.C.), 109,
125, 146, 320 (n. 93)
Athenian tribes, renaming of, 35, fig. 6,
292 (n. 52)
Attalus of Pergamum, 33, 35, 40, 292
(n. 52)
Augusta Raurica, 123–24, 314 (n. 22)
Augustus (Octavian), 4, 8, 59, 94, 103–4,
108, 115–32, 154, 159, 188, 198, 218,
223, 228, 271, 279–81, 312 (nn. 4–5),
314 (n. 15); opposition to, 130–32, 316
(n. 46), 317 (nn. 47–50, 52)

Bacchanalian scandal of 186 B.C., 71–76,
160–61, 299 (n. 14), 325 (n. 3)
Baring, Maurice, 2
Bocchus of Mauretania, 89
Boundary stones, Gracchan, 80, 303
(n. 42)
Britannicus, son of Claudius, 182, 187,
207
Brontë, Charlotte and Emily, 287 (n. 3)

Calpurnius Piso Frugi Licinianus, Lucius
(Servius Sulpicius Galba Caesar), heir
of Galba, 225
Calpurnius Piso Frugi, Lucius (cos.
133 B.C.), and his writings, 46, 71, 294
(n. 13), 299 (n. 12)
Calpurnius Piso pater, Cnaeus (cos.
7 B.C.), 9–10, 132–38, figs. 22–23, 317
(n. 59), 318 (nn. 60–72), 319 (nn. 73–
74); and his sons and grandsons,
136, 288 (n. 15); and his inscriptions,
136–38
Cassius, Gaius, 103, 107–8, 109, 123,
130–31, 133, 311 (n. 72), 312 (n. 5)
Cassius, Spurius (485 B.C.), 45, 47–48,
294 (nn. 19–21)
Cassius Chaerea, 149–50, 321 (n. 108)
Cassius Longinus, Gaius, 109, 312 (n. 72)
Cassius Severus, 148
Censors and their duties, 52, 60–61, 296
(nn. 34–35)
Ceres at Henna in Sicily, 71–76, 300
(nn. 18, 20, 22)
Cincius Alimentus, Lucius, and his
history, 46, 48, 294 (n. 13)
Claudia, Quinta, 161
Claudia Antonia, daughter of Claudius,
121
Claudii, 49, 297 (n. 50)
Claudius, 4–5, 17–18, 24, 121, 149, 154,
158–59, 169, 207, 209, 218, 223, 281,
271; and his wives, 182–96, 324–25
(nn. 137–38), 321 (n. 105), 322 (n. 118),
323 (n. 120)
Claudius Caecus, Appius, 43, 45, 293
(n. 9)
Claudius Marcellus, Marcus (cos. 222,
215, 214, 210, 208 B.C.), 59–60, 89, 124,
297 (nn. 51–52)
Claudius Marcellus, Marcus, nephew of
Augustus, 59, 118
Claudius Maximus, Tiberius, 253–56,
figs. 70–71, 344 (n. 41)
Claudius Nero, Gaius (cos. 207 B.C.), 40,
292 (n. 58)

Claudius Zosimus, Tiberius, 247–49, figs. 67–68, 344 (nn. 34–35)

Cleisthenes, 21

Clementis, Vladimir, 13

Cleopatra VII, 118–19, 123, 313 (nn. 7–8)

Cleopatra Selene, daughter of Cleopatra VII and Antony, 118, 313 (n. 7)

Clodius, Publius (tr. pl. 58 B.C.), 99, 102–4, 107, 308 (n. 45), 309 (nn. 46–47)

Colossus of Nero, fig. 53, 229, 339 (n. 71)

Commodus, 212, 275, 348 (n. 86)

Consecratio, 74–75, 301 (n. 25)

Corinth and Carthage, destruction of, 62–63, 297 (n. 57)

Cornelia, daughter of Africanus and mother of the Gracchi, 77–78, 301 (n. 30), 302 (n. 37)

Cornelia, daughter of Cinna and wife of Julius Caesar, 97, 104, 105, 111, 161, 309 (n. 51), 310 (n. 54), 325 (n. 5)

Cornelii (ten thousand freedmen of Sulla), 92–93, 306 (n. 17)

Cornelius Cinna, Lucius (cos. 87, 86, 85, 84 B.C.), 87, 90, 93, 97, 99, 105, 279, 307 (n. 29)

Cornelius Cinna, Lucius (the son), 105, 310 (n. 55)

Cornelius Cinna Magnus, Cnaeus, 130, 317 (n. 49)

Cornelius Dolabella, Lucius, 104, 107

Cornelius Gallus, Gaius (poet and first prefect of Egypt), 125–29, figs. 19–21, 316 (nn. 37–44)

Cornelius Merula, Lucius, 97

Cornelius Scipio, Lucius (pr. 174 B.C.), 58, 297 (n. 49)

Cornelius Scipio, Publius (*flamen Dialis*), 57, fig. 10, 296 (n. 45)

Cornelius Scipio Aemilianus, Publius, 57, 63, 72, 75

Cornelius Scipio Africanus, Publius, 57–58, 296 (n. 43), 297 (n. 48)

Cornelius Scipio Asiagenus, Lucius, 57–58

Cornelius Scipio Barbatus, Lucius, 56, fig. 9, 60, 296 (n. 44)

Cornelius Scipio Nasica Serapio, Publius (*pontifex maximus*), 70–76, 82, 88, 100, 102, 104, 109, 298 (n. 8), 299 (n. 15), 301 (n. 26)

Cornelius Sulla, Faustus, 89, 305 (n. 10)

Cornelius Sulla Felix, Lucius (dictator), 18, 46, 85, 86–98, figs. 13–15, 102, 104–6, 109, 116, 279, 282, 304 (n. 1); signet ring of, 89–90, 93–94, 122, 305 (n. 10); and the Forum, 93–94, 96, 306 (n. 19); and his Victory Games, 96, 307 (n. 27); and his memoirs, 96–97, 307 (n. 28); and his funeral at public expense, 97, 307 (n. 31)

Cremutius Cordus, Aulus, 109, 148, 312 (n. 73)

"Cultural repression," xix–xx

Cypselids, 19–20, 288 (n. 6)

Damnatio memoriae, xix

Death penalty, 21–22, 160–61

Decebalus, 253–56, figs. 70–71, 344 (n. 41)

Delphi, 19, 26–27, 41, 61–62

Demetrius Poliorketes, 33, 38, 291 (n. 48)

Denial of burial, 20–23, 70, 289 (n. 11), 299 (nn. 9–10)

Destruction of inscriptions/*stelai*, 22–23, 26

Dio, Cassius, and his writings, 116, 124, 125, 130, 149, 169, 174, 180, 188, 192, 235, 239, 253, 262, 328 (n. 34)

Dionysius of Halicarnassus and his writings, 45

Diplomata, 246–47, fig. 66, 343 (n. 33)

Divine honors: for Gracchi (posthumous), 79–81, 88, 94, 302 (n. 41); for C. Marius, 88–89, 94, 305 (n. 7); for Marius Gratidianus, 94–95; for Julius Caesar, 107–8, 311 (nn. 63, 67, 69)

Domitia Lepida, mother of Messalina, 183

Generals, treatment after defeat, 52–53, 296 (n. 36)

German bodyguard, of Nero, 199, 217, 338 (n. 54)

Germanicus, 132–40, 142, 150, 156, 169, 171, 176–78, 187–88, 196, 218, 318 (nn. 60, 67), 320 (n. 86), 328 (nn. 38–40)

Ghosts: of Drusus the Elder, 3–5; of Gaius, 150, 321 (n. 109); of Messalina, 188; of Agrippina the Younger, 192, 206–7, 331 (n. 69), 335 (n. 31); of Nero, 233, 340 (n. 82)

Glaukus the Spartan, 19, 288 (n. 7)

Gottwald, Klement, 13

Hadrian, xxi, 253, 272–75, 281, 283, 348 (nn. 81–83); mausoleum of, 274, 348 (n. 84)

Hannibal, 40, 58–60

Headhunting, 69, 92, 94, 206, 298 (n. 5), 303 (n. 52), 306 (n. 16), 335 (n. 29)

Herodotus, 3, 287 (n. 6)

Hesiod, murder of, 19, 288 (n. 5)

Hindsight, bias of, 2, 287 (n. 2)

Hipparchus, son of Charmus, 22, 289 (n. 19)

Historiography, birth of at Rome, 44–45, 53, 60, 277, 293 (nn. 8, 10)

Hostis, declaration of citizen as, 69, 86–87, 90–98, 99–100, 117, 199–200, 212, 278, 304 (nn. 2, 5), 308 (n. 42), 309 (nn. 48–49), 311 (n. 68), 312 (n. 2), 321 (n. 105), 332 (n. 4); not applied to women, 161

House, destruction of: Greek, 18–20, 21, 288 (nn. 8–9), 296 (n. 29); Manlius Capitolinus', 49–50, 295 (nn. 25, 28); Fulvius Flaccus', 76–77, 83, 301 (nn. 32–33); Saturninus', 83, 303 (n. 52); Sulla's, 87, 304 (n. 5); Cicero's, 102–3, 309 (n. 46); Piso's, 134, 318 (n. 61); Agrippina the Younger's, 189; Julia the Younger's, 189, 327 (n. 21)

Imago (wax ancestor mask), 53–56, 64, 84, 88, 92, 104–5, 108, 110, 135, 138, 204, 277, 335 (n. 25)

Jason of Pherae, 30, 291 (n. 39)

Josephus and his writings, 109, 149, 152, 174, 321 (n. 102), 322 (n. 118), 328 (n. 44)

Jugurtha of Numidia, 87, 89, 122

Julia, wife of Marius, 104, 310 (n. 53)

Julia, daughter of Julius Caesar, 111

Julia, daughter of Augustus, 118, 138, 143, 163–67, figs. 35–37, 168, 170, 325 (n. 10), 326 (nn. 13–20)

Julia, granddaughter of Augustus, 167–69, 189, 326 (n. 21), 327 (nn. 22–24)

Julius Agricola, Cnaeus, 241, 287 (n. 4), 343 (n. 24)

Julius Caesar, Gaius, 93, 97, 100, 103–11, 119, 123, 130, 149, 159, 307 (n. 30), 309 (nn. 51–52), 310 (nn. 53–62), 311 (nn. 63–69)

Julius Callistus, Gaius, 149

Julius Postumus, Gaius, 185, 330 (n. 55)

Julius Spartiaticus, Gaius (procurator Caesaris et Augustae Agrippinae), 190, 331 (n. 66)

Julius Vindex, Gaius, 203, 334 (n. 11)

Junia, sister of Marcus Brutus, 108–9, 133, 311 (n. 71), 317 (n. 58)

Junius Brutus, Marcus, 103, 107–9, 123, 130–31, 133, 309 (n. 49), 311 (nn. 70, 72), 312 (n. 5)

Junius Silanus, Decimus (pr. 141 B.C.), 64–66, 297 (nn. 60–61)

Junius Silanus, Decimus (lover of Julia), 168–69

Juvenal, 188, 330 (n. 61)

Kineas, 61, 297 (n. 55)

Kingship, Hellenistic at Rome, 121, 148

Kundera, Milan, 13

Labienus, Titus (c. 100–45 B.C.), 83, 106

Labienus, Titus (Augustan), 148

Index

110–11, 282, 298 (n. 4), 301 (nn. 30, 34), 302 (nn. 35–41)

Sempronius Gracchus, Gaius (lover of Julia), 164

Sempronius Gracchus, Tiberius, 67, 69–76, 87, 107, 109, 298 (n. 1), 299 (nn. 9–16), 300 (n. 21), 301 (n. 28), 302 (n. 41)

Sempronius Tuditanus, Publius (cos. 204 B.C.), 40, 292 (n. 58)

Senatus Consultum de Cn. Pisone patre, 133–38, fig. 22, 170, 202, 293 (n. 7), 317 (n. 59), 318 (nn. 61–67), 319 (nn. 73–74), 327 (n. 27)

Senatus Consultum Ultimum, 46, 69, 81, 278–79, 298 (n. 4), 303 (n. 46)

Seneca and his writings, 130, 188, 190, 202, 206, 208, 281, 334 (n. 14)

Sentius Saturninus, Cnaeus (cos. A.D. 41), 152, 312 (n. 74), 322 (n. 116)

Septimius Severus, Lucius, xxi, 275, 281

Sergius Catilina, Lucius, 46, 94–95, 99–102, 307 (n. 24), 308 (nn. 35–38, 44)

Sertorius, Quintus, 98

Servilii, 48

Servilius Glaucia, Gaius, 81

Silius, Gaius, 183–84, 329 (n. 52)

Slave revolt, first in Sicily, 73, 300 (nn. 18–19)

Solon, 21, 25

Spolia opima, 123–24, 315 (nn. 24, 33–35), 316 (n. 36)

Stasis, 18, 87

Statilia, wife of Lucius Piso, 136, 318 (n. 71)

Statilia Messalina, wife of Nero, 192, 201, 217

Statius and his poetry, 256, 344 (n. 44)

Statues: of Harmodius and Aristogeiton, 38, 109, 312 (n. 75); of Cornelia, mother of the Gracchi, 82, 161, 303 (n. 50); of Tiberius Semponius Gracchus (cos. 177 B.C.), 82, 303 (n. 49); of Pompey, 107, 310 (nn. 61–62)

— equestrian (bronze): of Demetrius, 38; of Lucius Aemilius Paullus, 62, 297 (n. 56); of Sulla, 93–94, fig. 15, 106, 306 (n. 20); of Domitian/Nerva, 259–61, figs. 74–75, 345 (nn. 48–49)

Suetonius and his writings, 152, 169, 180, 188, 209, 229, 235, 239, 262, 333 (n. 8)

Sulpicius, Publius (tr. pl. 88 B.C.), 86–87

Sulpicius Scribonius Proculus, Publius, 219–20, fig. 56, 338 (n. 59)

Sulpicius Scribonius Rufus, Publius, 219–20, fig. 55, 338 (n. 60)

Sybilline books, 72–73, 299 (n. 16)

Tacitus and his writings, 3–5, 109, 138, 142–43, 149, 163, 171–72, 180, 182, 184, 188, 194–96, 209, 236, 263, 269, 320 (n. 86), 327 (n. 29), 329 (nn. 47–48), 332 (n. 75), 342 (n. 9), 346 (n. 56), 347 (nn. 73, 75), 348 (n. 78)

Tarquins, 8

Temples: of Apollo Medicus, 94; of Concord, 78–79, 80–81, 302 (nn. 38–39); of Divus Augustus, 140, 154, 157, 319 (n. 82), 323 (n. 119), 324 (n. 132); of Divus Claudius, 194, 209, 332 (n. 74); of Fortuna Huiusce Diei, 88, 304 (n. 6); of Honos and Virtus (Marius'), 89, 93, 305 (n. 7); of Juno Moneta on Capitol, 48–49, 295 (n. 25); of Mars Ultor, 131; of Tellus, 47, 294 (n. 20)

Terentius Varro Murena, Aulus, 130, 317 (n. 49)

Tiberius, 4, 126, 132–49, 156–57, 159, 161, 169–70, 172, 174–75, 181, 207, 228, 250–51, 271, 317 (nn. 55–57), 318 (n. 62), 319 (n. 82); and his wife, Julia, 163–64, 166, 326 (nn. 13, 17, 19)

Timoleon, 21, 289 (n. 14)

Timotheus, 290 (n. 34)

Titius, Sextus (tr. pl. 99 B.C.), 81–85, 304 (nn. 54–55)

Titus, 208, 210, 241, 256, 270–71, 348 (n. 79)

Tomb of the Scipios, 56–58, 296 (n. 43)